ISBN 978-1-330-94233-8
PIBN 10124351

1 MONTH OF
FREE
READING

at

www.ForgottenBooks.com

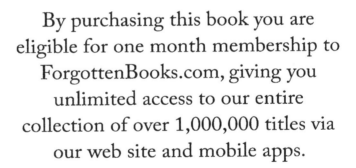

By purchasing this book you are
eligible for one month membership to
ForgottenBooks.com, giving you
unlimited access to our entire
collection of over 1,000,000 titles via
our web site and mobile apps.

To claim your free month visit:
www.forgottenbooks.com/free124351

THE

LIFE

OF

JAMES THE SECOND

KING OF ENGLAND, &c.

COLLECTED OUT OF MEMOIRS WRIT OF HIS OWN HAND.

TOGETHER WITH

THE KING'S ADVICE TO HIS SON,

AND

HIS MAJESTY'S WILL.

PUBLISHED FROM THE ORIGINAL STUART MANUSCRIPTS
IN CARLTON-HOUSE,

BY THE REV. J. S. CLARKE, LL.B. F.R.S.

HISTORIOGRAPHER TO THE KING, CHAPLAIN OF THE HOUSEHOLD,
AND LIBRARIAN TO THE PRINCE REGENT.

———

IN TWO VOLUMES.

VOL. II.

LONDON:

PRINTED FOR LONGMAN, HURST, REES, ORME, AND BROWN, PATERNOSTER-ROW;
FOR PAYNE AND FOSS, AND BUDD AND CALKEN, PALL-MALL.

1816.

CONTENTS

OF

VOLUME THE SECOND.

―――

TOME III. OF THE MS.

1685.

viii

1687.

1688.

a 2

*** Prior to this, and as appears, on the very day he left
London for Salisbury, the King had signed his Will, which
is inserted at page 643.

*** *Colly Cibber* in his Apology, (3d Ed. 1750. p. 57.) as referred to in a Note at page 227, says, " That the Princess
ANNE, fearing the King her Father's resentment might fall
upon her, for her Consort's Revolt, had withdrawn herself
in the night from London, and was then within half a day's
journey of Nottingham; on which very morning we were
suddenly alarmed with the news, that two thousand of the
King's dragoons were in close pursuit to bring her back
prisoner to London. But this Alarm it seems was all stratagem, and was but a part of that general Terror which was
thrown into many other places about the Kingdom, at the
same time, with design to animate and unite the People in
their common defence; it being then given out, that the
Irish were every where at our heels, to cut off all the Protestants within the reach of their fury."

*** Tindal, the Translator of Rapin, in continuing the English
History from The Revolution, has prefixed to his account
of The Reign of KING WILLIAM, *The Rise and Progress of
the Several Parties at the time of the Revolution, in a short
Review of the Reign of James I. Charles I. Charles II. and
James II.* And in one of the Notes (Vol. XVI. p. 88.
Ed. 1744.) he has inserted a long Letter from one of the
Gentlemen who came to JAMES THE SECOND, when he was
detained at Feversham.

TOME IV. OF THE MS.

1689—1701.

⁂ Amongst the Collection of English History which the
Prince Regent has made in his Library at Carlton House, is
a Scarce Tract giving *An Account of the Affairs of Scotland,
relating to the Revolution in* 1688: *As sent to the late King
James II. when in France. By the Right Honourable the
Earl of B.* (Balcarres) *Never before printed. London,
Printed for J. Baker, at the Black Boy in Pater-Noster-Row,*
1714.

The names of persons mentioned, which had only the
initials printed, are in this Copy filled up by a pen, and
some MS. notes have been added. " All I intend," says the
writer to JAMES, " is to give you a short View of your
Affairs in Scotland since the beginning of the Revolution,
that your Majesty may know, when you attempt the recovery of your just Rights, whom you may rely on: for all
these that has kept firm to their Duty, after so long and
severe a Trial, you may safely depend on; and these that
appeared at first against you, and now pretend to be in your
Interest, having missed what they expected by this Revolution, you may be persuaded nothing will ever make them
throughly so, but a sufficient force."

*** Mr. Home, in his History of the Rebellion of 1745, says, " To the Victory which the Highlanders gained at the Battle of Killiecrankie, General M'Kay, who commanded the King's Army, ascribes that confidence which the Highlanders had in themselves, as equal or superior to regular Troops."

1690.

SECOND CAMPAIGN IN IRELAND.

d 2

Page

1691.

1692.

The War being thus ended both in Scotland and Ireland,
JAMES fixes himself at St. Germains, and regulates his
family and mode of living according to his Pension of six
hundred thousand livres a year from the French Court —

*** TINDAL, in his Reign of King WILLIAM, (Vol. 17. p. 268.) observes, " Monsieur du Larey in his *Histoire sous Louis XIV.* says, ' That when the Fog was dissipated, Monsieur *Tourville* was surprised to find it was the whole English and Dutch United Fleet which he was going to engage, whereas before he imagined it was only part of it. But however, considering that an hasty retreat would bring his Fleet in to such a confusion as might prove more hazardous than a Battle, he continued his Orders for the Engagement." TINDAL adds, (p. 277.) " On Monday the 23d of May, he (the English Admiral) sent in Mr. *Rooke*, then Vice Admiral of the Blue, with a Squadron, fire ships, and the Boats of the Fleet..... The Boats burnt six of them that night, and about eight *the next morning*, the other seven were set on fire, together with several Transport Ships, and some small Vessels with ammunition. .... Thus at *La Hogue* and *Cherbourg* were burnt two Ships of 104 guns each, one of 90, two of 80, four of 76, four of 60, and two of 56 guns.... According to a relation which we find in *Kennet*, the French lost Five great Ships in the Fight ; in the whole 21 of their biggest Ships were destroyed, besides the two Frigates and other small Vessels. On our side not one Ship was lost, but the Fire-

1696.

⁕ On the 29th of August the Duke of Savoy had made a separate Peace with France.

1697.

⁕ The Conferences of the Plenipotentiaries, (who according to JAMES's Secretary were sent away in March to *Ryswick, a House* belonging to the Prince of Orange,) were opened on the 10th of February, at a Palace belonging to King WILLIAM, situated between the Hague and Delft, close to the Village of Ryswick. They were again renewed, after the death of the King of Sweden, who had been received as Mediator, on the 29th of April O. S. The Treaty was finally signed on the 20th of September between France, England, Spain, and Holland; and ratified by King William at Loo. The English Plenipotentiaries were the Earl of Pembroke, Lord Villiers (afterwards created Earl of Jersey), and Sir Joseph Williamson. With whom were associated on the part of France, Harlay, Crecy, and Cailleres.

1701.

CONTENTS OF THE APPENDIX.

ERRATA IN THIS VOLUME.

Page 221. (Note, l. 2.) *For* " representing" *read* " represented."
Page 231. (Note, l. 3.) *For* " Jame" *read* " James."
Page 310. (Side note, l. 4.) *For* " now" *read* " not."
Page 371. (Note, l. 7.) *For* " exemply" *read* " exemplify."

THE LIFE

OF

H.R.H. JAMES DUKE OF YORK,

KING OF GREAT BRITAIN,

COMPILED

BY HIS ROYAL HIGHNESS'S PRIVATE SECRETARY

OUT OF MEMOIRS WRITTEN BY THAT PRINCE.

From an Engraving found amongst the Stuart M.S.S.

GENEALOGIE ROYALLE DE — DE LA MAISON — LA GRANDE BRETAGNE.

The Diamantid branch under Jacques II. records what would have been, & filled up, the blot wth his tumults magnifico.

Editor.

From this Title & Queen of Sicily it appears that this Tree was Graved during the short period after the Peace of Utrecht, when Sicily was the Royal Title of the House of Sovoy.

Editor.

JAMES THE SECOND,

KING OF GREAT BRITAIN,

COLLECTED OUT OF MEMOIRES WRITT IN HIS OWN HAND.

TOM. III.

1685.

ASSOON as the breath was out of the King's body, the Duke (whom hence forward we must call by the name of KING JAMES THE SECOND) to avoid the importunity of complements which were then crowding in upon him, retired immediately into his closet; haveing more inclination to satisfy his grief and anguish at the late sorrowfull object, than please himself with the thoughts of a Crown so unexpectedly fallen

upon his head, which with all its glettering charms was not
able to asswage that sencible affliction he suffer'd, in parteing
with a Brother he loved and honour'd so much; haveing
therefore for some time giuen full scope to his tears, necessity
and order (thō much against his inclination) obliged him to
appear, and receiue at last the complements and congratulations
of those, who waited with impatience to make them.

It was on this occasion that the world stood astonished to
see the Metamorphoses in a manner of a whole Kingdom;
this Prince, who so little a while before had been persecuted,
banished, and by the wishes of the people as well as the violent
endeavours of the Parliament on the point of being disinherited;
that had suffer'd all the affronts which the malice of his bitterest
enemies, or the rigours of the penal Laws was capable of puting
upon him, whom the meanest wretches of the Nation could
treat with impunity with the title of rogue and traitor, to see
(I say) this same Prince wellcom'd to the Throne with such
uniuersal acclamations of joy, such unexpressible testimonys
of duty and affection from all ranks of people, was what
history has no example of, and may be a lesson to posterity,
that no temporiseing or straigned complyance in a Prince,
will ever gain so much upon the World, as a steddy aherence
to the rules of vertue, and a rigorous observance of those
maxims of honour and justice, which scarce ever fails, sooner
or later, to force both obedience and loue from the generality
of mankind.

The Celerity with which all things necessary were prepar'd
for proclaming him King according to custom, and the
testimonys of loue and duty with which it was performed in all
the three Kingdoms, was soon repayd by the hast his Majesty
made, to quiet peoples minds and aprehentions both in reference
to Religion, Liberty, and their imployments; for the next
morning at his first apearance in Council, he confirmed all the

members of it (that were there present). in their stations, and order'd a proclamation to be published for continuing all other persons in their respectiue imployments thorough the Nation, til his pleasure were further known, and then made them a short Speech which gaue unspeakable satisfication to all " persons, but especially to those who by the malicious " insinuations of his enemies were in some doubt what might " become of their liberties and religion : Since it has pleased " Almighty God (says he) to place me in this Station, and that now I am to succed so good and gracious a King, as well as so kind a Brother, I think fit to declare, that I will endeavour to follow his example, and more especially in that of his great clemency and tenderness to his people. I have been reported to be a man for arbitrary power, though that is not the only story which has been made of me ; I shall make it my endeavour to preserue the government in Church and State as it is by Law established, I know the principles of the Church of England are for Monarchy, and that the Members of it, haue shewn themselves good and Loyall Subjects, and therefore I shall always take care to defend and support it. I know likewise that the Laws of England are sufficient to make the King as great a Monarch as I can wish, and therefore as I will never depart from the just rights and prerogatiues of the Crown, so I never will invade any man's property. I haue often ventured my life in defence of the Nation, and will go as far as any man in preserving it in its just rights and priuiledges.

Never was greater joy express'd within the walls of the Council Chamber, than on this occasion, they were astonished to find themselves deliver'd of their apprehensions so unexpectedly; several therefore begg'd leaue they might take copies of this benigne and gracious declaration, to the end others might partake of their satisfaction, but to this his Majesty answer'd, That truly what he had said, was from the abundance of his

T O M.
III.
1685.

KING JAM.
LOOS SHEETS
pag. 1.

heart, without much premeditation, and that he had it not in writing at all; upon which M' Finch replyd, That what his Majesty had been pleas'd to say, made so deep an impression upon him, that he believed he could repeat the very words, and that in case his Majesty would pleas to permit him, would write them downe, which the King agreeing too, he went to the Clarke's seat and did it accordingly ; which being shewn to the King he aproued of it, and it was immediately published to the unspeakable Satisfaction of the Nation.

No one can wonder that M. Finch should word the Speech as strong as he could in fauour of the Established religion, nor that the King in such a hurry should pass it over without reflection ; for thō his Majesty intended to promis both security to their religion and protection to their persons, he was afterwards conuinced it had been better express'd by assureing them, he never would endeavour to alter the established religion, rather than that he would endeavour to preserue it, and that he would rather support and defend the professors of it, rather than the religion itself ; they could not expect he should make a conscience of supporting, what in his conscience he thought erroneous, his engageing not to molest the professors of it, nor to depriue them or their Successors of any spiritual dignity, revenue, or employment, but to suffer the Ecclesiastical affaires to go on in the track they were in, was all they could wish or desire from a Prince of a different perswasion : but haueing once aproued that way of expressing it, which M'Finch had made choise of, he thought it necessary not to vary from it in the declarations or speeches he made afterwards, not doubting but the world would understand it in the meaning he intended, and which alone was agreable to the circumstances he was in ; nor could the Kingdom expect more from the most benigne and mercyful Prince upon earth, than that the only revenge he would take for so many former indignities and

afronts, should be, to assure them that the sole use he would
make of the power which was now put into his hands, should
be, to defend and protect them in the peaceable enjoyment of
their Laws, liberties, and Religion it self, from which houre
those Lords and the rest of the Nation might have counted
themselues the happyest people upon earth, had they been as
faithfull in the obseruance of their duty to him, as he was kind
and sincere in his expressions and intentions to them : Tis true
afterwards *it was* pretended, he kept not up to this engagement,
but had they deviated no further from the duty and allegiance
which both nature and repeated oathes obliged them too,
than he * *did from his word*, they had stil remain'd as happy a
people, as they realy were during the short time of his reign
in England ; for never Prince was better qualifyd to make them
such, or Study'd, or endeavour'd it, more than he.

This candid declaration of his Majestys, was not the less
agreeable to the people, in that it came wholy from himself,
and was not the fruite of previous councel and advice, for it
had never enter'd into his heart or imagination, that he should
out liue the late King ; for thō he was three years and about
four months younger, yet he always looked upon him as of
a much stronger constitution, and consequently never had
the least fancy he should come to the Crown, til the moment
he was Seized with that fit, betwixt which and his death the
great hurry of attending him gaue little leasure for consulting,
what should be done after his decease.

Assoon as his Majesty had dispatch'd what was necessary to
be done in Council, he was impatient to assist at his devotions
on so extraordinary an occasion, so went immediately to Mass
with the Queen in the little Chappel in S^t. James's, where

T O M.
III.
1685.

KING JAM.
LOOS SHEETS
pag. I. 2.

---

* The words in Italics were afterwards interlined by the Son of King James.
the second. EDITOR.

according to his free and generous temper he caus'd the doors to be left open, that all the world might see his present grandure was as uncapable of influenceing him in matters relateing to his duty to God, as his past suffrings had been; and that as he was resolued not to invade other men's Religion, so neither would he conceal his own : it must not therefore be pass'd over as one of the least actions of his life, he was no stranger to the temper of the people, how odious a sight it was to most persons there, how dangerous to suggest new fears and apprehentions to those who were too succeptible of such sort of jealousies; but as plain and open dealing is for the most part the best policy, his Majesty found the effects of it on this occasion, for many who were Shocked with it at first, upon reflection commended his courage and candor, and were the more induced to rely upon the promise he then had made in favour of their religion, when they saw he would not dissemble in reference to his own.

One of the first things which required his Majesty's attention was the funeral obsequies of the late King, which could not be perform'd with so great sollemnity as some persons expected, because his late Majesty dying in, and his present Majesty professing a different religion from that of his people, it had been a difficult matter to reconcile the greater cerimonys, which must haue been preformed according to the rites of the Church of England, with the obligation of not communicateing with it in spiritual things; to avoid therefore either disputes on one hand or scandal on the other, it was thought more prudent to doe it in a more private manner, thō at the Same time there was no circomstance of State and pomp omitted, which possebly could be allow'd of: for (besides, that while the body lay in state the illuminations and mourning was very solemn) all the privy Council, all the houshould, and all the Lords about Town attended at the Funeral, so that no essential point of cerimony was omitted, and what was retrench'd rendered it the more agreeable to Christian humilitié, from which Princes themselves are not exempt, and of which his Majesty as much as his dignity would allow of, was always a strict and rigorous observer.

It is not to be express'd with what Zeal and earnestness all partes of England congratuled his Accession to the Throne; Scotland likewise endeavour'd to distinguish it self on this occasion, and none more expressiue of their duty and affection than the Bishops of that Kingdom; Ireland loaded the Duke of Ormonde with most loyall addresses too, who haveing deliver'd up the sword to the Archbishop of Armagh and Earle of Grenade in qualitie of Lords Justices, came in person, notwithstanding his age and infirmities, to make his own compliments; forreign Princes contended in like manner who should do it first and with greatest splendor, Prince Circlas of Tilly who came from the Marques of Grana Governor of the Spanish Netherlands, got the start as being nearest, after him came the Mareschall de Lorge from his Most Christian Majesty, and Monsr. D'Estamps from the Duke of Orleans, Monsr. Ebrenchel from Denmark, the States of Holland and other Princes were not behind hand in their congratulations; so that no testimony was wanting either at home or abroad to publish the universal joy, that so long and undeserued a suffring was crown'd at last with the peacefull possession of the Throne of his ancestors.

Things being thus settled at least to the Seeming " KJng Jam. Loos sheets p. 1. Satisfaction of all parties, the King immediately fell to work " to put the Government upon such a foot as would most " conduce (he thought) to the publick good, as the repairing " the Navy, the improuement of trade, the paying by degrees " the debts of the Crown, and by it to endeavour the recovering " the credit of the Exchequer which had been so shaken in "

" the Earle of Shaftsbury's time, and to take care that the Ciuil " and Military lists as well as the Houshould might be punctually paid; and when he came to the regulation of his family, and disposition of the great offices of the Crown, his Majesty was too just to forget those in his prosperitie, who had served him with most fidelitie dureing his troubles, but took care however to temper his Kindness so to his friends, as not to exasperate such as had been his enemies, and was so far from retaining any rancor or spleen for past disservices, that several of those too, had their share in this distribution (thō very undeservedly in respect of some) as apeared afterwards: No one haveing served his Majesty with more fidelitie and affection than the Earle of Rochester, he made him Lord High Treasurer of England, and his Brother the Earle of Clarendon Lord Privie Seal, My Lord Halifax President of the Council, the Lord Godolplin Lord Chamberlin to the Queen, the Earles of Sunderland and Middleton were continued Secretaries of State, and indeed he continued the generalitie of imployments throughout the three Kingdoms, in the same hands they were in at the late King's death: for there had been so great an union betwixt them, both in opinion and inclination, that it reconcil'd his present Majesty to any one his Brother had thought fit to trust; thō his generosity and good nature in that, carry'd him beyond the rules of prudence, otherwise he would never haue put such confidence in My Lord Sunderland and Godolphin, who had once so treacherously betrayd him, and were by this means made capable of doing it more efectually a second time.

The King
Shews the late
King's papers
to the Arch-
bishop of
Canterbury.

Some few days after the late King's death, his Majesty looking into the papers he had left behind him found two relateing to Controversie, one in the strong box, the other in the Closet, both writ in his own hand, they were short but sollid, and shew'd, that thō his Conversion was not perfected til a few

houres before his death, his conviction was of a longer date:
The King thought fit to shew them one day to the Archbishop
of Cantorburie in his Closet, no body being by, who seem'd "
much surprised at the Sight of them, and pawsed almost half "
a quarter of an houre before he said any thing; at last tould "
the King, He did not think his late Majesty had understood "
controversie so well, but that he thought they might be "
answer'd: If so, sayd the King, I pray let it be done "
gentleman like and sollidly, and then it may haue the efect "
you so much desire of bringing me back to your Church; "
to which the Archbishop replyd, It would perhaps be "
counted a disrespect in him to contradict the late King, "
but his Majesty reassured him in that point, by telling him "
the change it might produce in himself (if answer'd efectually) "
was of that consequence as to out ballance any other "
consideration, and therefore desired he might see a reply "
either from him or any other of his perswasion; but thō he, "
My Lord Dartemouth, and others, were several times "
reminded of this matter and earnestly press'd to it, never any "
formal reply was produced during the four years of his "
Majesty's reign in England. It is true there was something of
an answer published by an unknown hand, but the drift of it
was rather to proue that the papers were not the late King's
(which was a libel in reality upon the present) than any reply
to the arguments of it, and it is probable the Arch Bishop
dispair'd of answering it so effectually as to bring back his
Majesty to their Communion, whereas the publishing a reply
would have own'd and publish'd the papers too; and he had
reason to aprehend, that the authority and arguments of their
dying Prince would influence more persons to that Religion,
than his answer would perswade to relinquish it.

After this testimony of candor and open dealing, his Majesty
gaue the Arch Bishop an other, how little he was inclin'd to

T O M.
III.

1685.
KINGJAM.Mᵗ.
ToM:9. p.203.

The King
and Queen
Crown'd the
23ᵈ of April.

T O M.
III.
1685.

innovate in any thing, by receiving the Crown from his hands; for thō he had reason to scruple the communicateing in those prayers, preaching, and Cerimonys, which were perform'd according to the rites of the Church of England, yet his Majesty was so desirous to comply as far as any shew of reason or plausible excuse could warrant him, that he readily yielded to it, so on the 23ᵈ of April the King and Queen were crown'd accordingly, with all the splendor and magnificence which is usual on such sollemn occasions, and with full as much publick joy and testimonys of affections as had been ever seen in former times.

A Parliament
call'd in
Scotland.

Assoon as these formality, Cerimonys, and compliments were over, the King made hast to meet his people by their representatiues in Parliament, he issued out the writts immediately after the Coronation, and thō he had no reason to question the duty full behaviour of his English Subjects, yet to distinguish the confidence he had in the Scotch Nobility and Gentry, who had stuck so close to him in his adversitie, he order'd that Parliament to meet first, acquainting them in

The King's
letter, dat.
28. March.

his letter, That the experience he ever had of their fidelitie and singular forwardness to concur in all good and wholsom laws in the Reign of his Brother, occasioned his ordering them to assemble in the begining of his, to give them an oportunity not only of shewing their duty, but of being an example to others in a cheerful complyance to what he requested of them; that what he had to offer had full as great a tendency to the maintenance of their own priuiledges and properties, as to his safety or augmentation of his power, which if he resolued to maintain in its due luster and prerogatiue, it was principally to enable him the better to protect their Religion and Laws, together with their rights and properties, against all fanatical murtherers and assasines, who had heretofore brought them to such difficulties, that nothing but his Brother's steddy resolution

and those he was pleas'd to imploy, could haue extricated them
out of, and that as those unhumain wretches had left nothing
unatempted to disturb the peace, so he hoped they would be
wanting in nothing for his and their own security against
them ; it was once, he sayd, his intention to haue propos'd this
to them in person, but it not being practicable at present, he
had sent the Duke of Queensbury fully instructed in what he
conceiued would conduce to his seruice and their prosperitie ;
not doubting of their ready and dutyfull complyance therein.

- The Duke of Queensbury therefore to second this, assur'd
them the King could not giue a liuelyer testimony of his
confidence in their Loyal dispositions, than by this early
adviseing with them, to the end they might giue the leading to
his other dominions, and he giue them a demonstration that
he intended to follow the example of his Brother's peacefull
reign ; that he gaue them assurances of his Princely resolution
of protecting the government both in Church and State, that
he would defend their rights and properties according to the
established Laws of the Kingdom, that they should not be
injured by any arbitrary oppression of Soldiers or others, that
he would grant his condescention in the business of excise
and militia as far as could be justly expected; and that on the
other side his Majesty hop'd they would assert the rights and
prerogatiues of the Crown, and establish the revenue as
amply upon him, and his Lawfull Successors, as it had
been enjoyed by his Brother, and that effectual means might
be fallen upon, to extirpate the desperate fanatical partie that
had brought the Kingdom to the brink of destruction.

After him the Earle of Perth, then Lord Chancelour (who
had already by his extraordinary zeal for the King's Seruice
prepared peoples minds to a concurrance with his inclinations,
and wrought them to that good temper they appear'd in, at
the begining of his Reign) put them in mind of the great

benefit they had receiu'd from his Majestys presence when Duke of York, that he had wrought an union amongst them, which was almost dispaired of before, and therefore desired them to destroy that brood of vilanous men who were continually working to a contrary end, and mentain'd principles autherising the perpetration of things not fit to be named amongst those who had ever heard of government much less of Religion; he enlarged likewise upon his Majesty's excellent qualifications, which ought, he Sayd, to be more particularly admired in a crown'd head, his personal knowlidg, either as to peace or war, and his experience both in Armes and Courts, his exact temperance, honesty, sobriety, dilligence and courage, his haveing been an example of Loyalty to all his Subjects whilst he was one himself, and now an example to all Kings, of loue, clemency, and care towards his people.

The Scots Nobility and Gentry looking upon themselves to haue giuen a King to England in the person of his Majesty, by zealously contributing to his support when England contended so vehemently to depriue him of his right, were no ways degenerated from their former duty and affection towards him; the great esteem and value they had contracted for his person, gaue a new vigor and life to their settled loyalty to him as their King; which made the Parliament answer to the full, both in words and actions, the King's expectations of them: first therefore in their adress they tell him, that his gracious and kind remembrance of their former seruices to the late King his Brother of ever glorious memory, should rather rais in them an ardent desire of exceeding what they had formerly done, than to look upon themselues as deserueing that esteem he was pleas'd to express, that the death of that excellent Monarck was lamented by them to all the degrees of grief which was consistant with the joy for the Succession of his Sacred Majesty, who had not only continued but secur'd the happiness, which his Brother's wisdom, justice, and clemencie had procured them; that being the first Parliament that met by his authority, he might be confident they would offer such Laws as might best secure his person, the Royal family and government, and that they would endeavour to rais his honour and dignity to the utmost extent of their power, nor would leaue any thing undon which could be thought proper, either for extirpation of fanatisme, or detecting and punishing the late conspirators.

T O M.
III.
1685.

  Accordingly with more than usual concord and expedition, they pass'd a Bill for ratifying and confirming all former Acts in favour of the established Religion, they annex'd the excise of forreign and inland commodities to the Crown of Scotland for ever; and for the better discovering and prosecuting the fanical partie, they ordain'd that all such persons as being cited in cases of treason, field or house conuenticles, or any Church irregularities should refuse to giue testimony, should be punishable as guilty of those crimes respectiuely, in which they refus'd to be witnesses.

  The King's earnestness to haue the field conuenticles suppress'd, was not from any spirit of persecution (thō those wretches deserued no quarter) but from an aprehension of new troubles, which for publick quiet as much as his own security he was desirous to prevent, nor did his caution proue unseasonable, but was an argument of his prudent foresight: he knew the Earle of Argile's turbulent disposition and envenom'd malice against him, would prompt him to some violent attempt now at his comeing to the Crown; and that those Seditious spirits would be always ready to join him; accordingly many days did not pass ere it apear'd the King was not mistaken in his conjecture, and had good cause to use those precautions which proued of no small benefit to him afterwards.

  The Court therefore had all reason in the world to be satisfyd with the Scotch proceeding, which besides the good efect it

The Parliament meets in England the 24th of May.

had in that Kingdom, would be an example and spur to the rest
of his Majestys Subjects, and rais a wholsom emulation in the
English Parliament, which met likewise on the 24ᵗʰ of May,
to whom after they had chosen Sʳ John Trevor their Speaker,
the King made them the following Speech.

After it had pleased Almighty God to take to his mercy
the late King my dearest Brother, and to bring me to the
peaceable possession of the Throne of my Ancestors, I immediately resolued to call a Parliament, as the best means to settle
every thing upon those foundations as might make my reign
both easy and happy to you, towards which, I am disposed to
contribute all that is fit for me to doe; what I sayd to my
privy Councel at my first comeing there, I am desirous to
renew to you, wherein I freely declared my opinion concerning
the principles of the Church of England, whose Members haue
shewn themselves so eminently Loyal, in the worst of times, in
defence of my Father and support of my Brother of blessed
memory, that I will always take care to support and defend it,
I will make it my endeavour to preserue this government both
in Church and State, as it is by law established; and as I will
never depart from the just rights and prerogatiues of the Crown,
so I will never invade any man's propertie, and you may be sure
that haueing hitherto venter'd my life in defence of this realm, I
shall still go as far as any man in preserueing it in all its just
rights and liberties; and haueing given you this assurance of
the care I will haue of your religion and property, which I
haue chosen to doe in the same words I used at my first comeing
to the Crown, the better to evidence to you, that I spoke them
not by chance and consequently that you may more firmly
rely upon a promis so firmly made, I cannot doubt that I shall
fail of sutable returns from you, with all immaginable duty
and kindness on your part, and particularly what relates to the
settling my Revenue, and continuing it during my life as it was

in the time of the King my Brother, I might use many
arguments to enforce this demand, from the benefit of trade,
the support of the Navy, the necessity of the Crown, and the
well being of the government it self, which I must not suffer to
be precarious, but I am confident your own consideration of
what is just and reasonable, will suggest whatever may be
enlarged upon this occasion : there is one popular argument
which I foresee may be used against what I ask of you, from
the inclinations men haue to frequent Parliaments, which some
men think would be the best secured by feeding me from time
to time with such proportions as they shall think convenient ;
and this argument (it being the first time I speak to you from
the Throne) I will answer once for all, That this would be a
very improper method to take with me, and that the best way
to engage me to meet you often is always to use me well. I
expect you will comply with me in what I haue desired, and
that you will doe it speedily, that this may be a short Session
and that we may soon meet again to all our satisfactions.

I must acquaint you that I haue had news this morning
from Scotland, that Argile is landed in the West Highlands,
with the men he brought with him from Holland, and that
there were two Declarations published, one in the name of
those in arms there, the other in his own ; it will be too long
for me to report the substance of them, it is sufficient to tell
you I am charged with usurpation and Tyranny, the shorter
of them I have directed to be forthwith communicated to you.
I will take the best care I can that this declaration of their
treason and rebellion may meet with the reward it deserves,
and I doe not doubt but that you all will be the more zealous
to Support the government, and give me my Revenue as I have
desired it, without delay.

This Speech gaue so much Satisfaction, that there was all
imaginable apearance of a perfect harmony and concord

betwixt the King and them, they immediately return'd him
their humble thanks for his Speech; the Lords in an adress
promis'd to stand by him with their lives and fortunes for
suppressing Argile, and the rest of those Rebells; the
Commons were not behind hand in the like assurances, and
then without any previous complaints, or representation of
grievances, fell immediately upon Settling the Reuenue.

The King had continued to collect the Customs ever since
his Brother's death, thō granted only for the late King's life,
the inconvenience of an interruption he knew would be too
well understood by the judicious Members of Parliament, *or the
generalitie of y* people **, to blame his conduct therein; on the
contrary he had thanks given him for it in a most dutyfull
adress from the Middle Temple, in order to obviate that old
dispute which in the begining of King Charles the first his
reign, had been one of the main origins of the ensuing
troubles; they thank'd him therefore amongst other things for
his preservation of the Customes, the intermission whereof
would not only (sayd they) have disabled him to mentain the
Navy in defence of the Realm, but by takeing away the
ballance of trade, haue ruin'd thousands of his Subjects, that
payd customes in the life of the late King, and by an excessiue
importation and exportation custome free, had render'd that
branch of the Revenue improfitable for some years to come, in
spight of all the care and loyalty of succeeding Parliaments,
that the same had been continually receiu'd by his Royal
predecessors for some hundreds of years, and never question'd
in any Parliament, excepting that in which were sown the seeds
of rebellion against the glorious Martir his Royal Father; that
it was a receiu'd maxim of the Common Law, that *Thesaurus*

---

* Interlined as before by the Son of James the second. EDITOR.

Regis est vinculum pacis et bellorum nervi, and that such was the happy constitution of this Monarchy, that his Majestys high prerogatiue was the greatest security of the libertie and propertie of the Subjects, so that whoever would impair the revenue of the Crown, must by this fundamental maxim (as binding as Magna charta it self) be esteem'd an enemy to the peace and wellfare of the Kingdom.

TOM. III.

1685.

This adress comeing from so learned a body of Lawiers, sayd to be pen'd by Sr Bartlemy Shore, and presented by Sr Humphrey Mackworth, carryd great authority with it, however the King made no mention of this clame by vertue of his prerogatiue, nor did the Parliament find fault with him for collecting it as he had done, So there was no manner of contest one way or other about it; but that, and the rest of the Reuenue, which the late King dyd possess'd of, was settled likewise upon his present Majesty for his life too, wherein they were so expeditous that on the 18th of June he pass'd the Bill, and then made them an other Speech as follows.

TheParliament Settles the Revenue.

MY LORDS AND GENTLEMEN:

I thank you very heartely for the Bill you haue presented me this day, and I assure you the readiness and cheerfullness which has attended the dispatch of it, is as acceptable to me as the Bill it Self; after so happy a begining you may beliue I will not call upon you unecessarily for an extraordinary Supply, but when I tell you that the Stores of the Navy and Ordinance are extreamly exhausted, that the anticipations upon several branches of the Reuenue are great and burthensom, that the debts of the King my Brother to his servants and family are such as deserue compassion, that the Rebellion in Scotland, without puting more weight upon it than it realy deserues, must needs put me to a considerable expence extraordinary, I am sure such considerations will moue you to giue me an aid to prouide for these things, wherein the eas and

The King's second Speech to the Parliament, 18 June.

T O M.
III.
1685.

hapiness of the government are so much concern'd ; but aboue
all I must recommend to you the care of the Navy, the
strenght and glory of the Nation, that you will put it in such
a condition as may make us be respected and considerable
abroad : I cannot express my concern on this occasion more
sutable to my own thoughts of it, than by assureing you I haue
a true English heart, as jealous of the honour of the Nation as
you can be, I pleas myself with the hopes that (by God's
blessing and your assistance) I may carry the reputation of it
yet higher in the world than ever it has been in the time of any
of my Ancestors ; and as I will not call upon you for supplys
but when they are of publick use and advantage, so I promis
you that what you giue me on such occasions, shall be managed
with good husbandry, and I will take care it shall be imploy'd
to the use for which I ask it.

TheParliament grants an augmentation. They were no less pleas'd with this than the former Speech,
so that neither Argile's descent terrifyd them, nor so early a
demand of Supplys shocked them ; but they seem'd so sencibly
touch'd at some expressions, particularly that of his haveing an
English heart, that they waited not the usual formes of thanking
him for it, but by their very jestures and countenance while
he was actually speaking, gaue him so much the more vnfain'd
testimony of their satisfaction, as that manner of shewing it
was less capable of being counterfeit or unsincere ; and in
this good humour, without the least grumbling or hesitation,
went immediately upon augmentations, and granted him
certain new impositions upon wines and vinegars, Sugar,
tobacco, French and east India linnen, and several other
French and Idian commodities ; they revoked the Act which
prohibited the importation of French wines, vinegar, brandy;
linnen &c, so that his Revenue with these aditions amounted to
aboue two millions yeearly, besides what he had before as
Duke of York, which (with his good management) would

haue made him and his people easy, had that good harmony continued to the end with which they so wisely began; but the unruly temper of some and the misguided judgment of other's would not suffer the Nation to be long sencible of those blessings of peace, plenty, and security, without taxes, opression, or any real grieuance, till they had led the people away by spacious dilusions of words, precious in their due signification, but abused to the worst of things, and by perswadihg them their Religion, Laws, and liues were in danger, beguil'd them at last into a real slavery, by those very methods which were pretended to be the only means of avoiding it.

As the Scots had led the way to the English Parliament in their dutifull comportment to the King, so now they take example from the English generositie, and settled two hundred sixty thousand pound a year upon his Majesty, and that for his life too; nor did Argile's landing in the middle of these transactions (thō Some were startled at it) put any check upon their zeal, òr hinder a happy conclusion of that Sessions to the common Satisfaction both of King and people.

That Lord had thè Covenant so rooted in his heart, that he had never been throroughly reconcil'd to the established government, and if he comported himself peacefully during the late King's reign, it was because he had taken the Covenant at his first comeing into Scotland; which fanatical disposition being embitter'd by the hardsheps he conceiu'd had been put upon him in his late tryal and condemnation for equivocateing about the Test, together with his present uneasy circomstances of exile and outlawry, made him think any hazard preferrable to the condition he was in, especially since the King's Religion gaue him so much hopes he should find great numbers no less dissatisfyd than himself.

Haveing therefore concerted maters with the Duke of

Monmouth, he set sail from Vlye in Holland upon the 2^d of May, and apear'd before Orkney the 5th, where sending his Secretary and Chirurgeon on shore, they were both seized by the inhabitants of the Island and sent up to the priuy Council of Edinburgh; which disincouraging his landing there, he made for the West of Scotland and went a shore at Dunstafnage in Lorn, an old ruinous Castle, where he placed a garison and then went further into the Country, publishing a Declaration in the name of the Protestant Noblemen, Gentlemen, Burgesses, &c, of the Kingdom of Scotland, with the concurrance of the true faithfull pastors, and of Severall gentlemen of the English Nation join'd with them in the same cause: This Declaration sett forth the happy success of the war against King Charles the 1st, the goodness of that cause, and the loyalty of the Covenanters, it blamed the Parliament for abolishing the laws made during the war, and turning out the Nonconformist Ministers, it accused the Government for executing men against law, annoying the Churches, changing God's ordinances into those of men, conniveing at Papists, and keeping up standing forces; it renounced the King's supremicy, declared against the warrs with Holland, and the forfeiters of the Lord Argile, the torture of Spence and Castares (the discoverers of the late Conspiracy) against the inquirys made into the insurrection at Bothwell bridg, it declared also against the King's enthronement as incapacetated by the Bill of Exclusion, and so call'd him only James Duke of York, as also against the Parliament of England as illegally elected; and lastely declared, that they threw of all bonds of Subjection and tooke up armes against the Same James Duke of York and all his accomplices, their unnatural and wicked enemys, with intent to restore the Protestant Religion and extirpate Popery, to satify those of their partie; renouncing to all treaty or agreement with the said James Duke of York, promising indemnity to

all such, as would join with them against a persecuting Tyrant
and an Apostate partie.

Besides this general Declaration, Argile put out an other in
his own name, as their leader ; affirming he had no private
ends for himself, but only those in the general Declaration,
that he clam'd nothing but his own particular rights, and
promissed upon the recovery of his estate to pay his own and
father's debts, that he had undergon three years and a halfs
banishment for an unjust Sentence in the late King's reign, to
whom he was always loyal, but that the Duke of York haueing
invaded the Religion and liberties of the Kingdom, he thought
it not only just but his duty to repress his Tyrany and
Vsurpation.

It was no small advantage to the King that he had to doe
with such fiery patriots, and plain spoken enemys, who slighting
those colourable pretences of abuses, grievances, and palliateing
contrivances, to draw men insencibly into the wickedest
attempts, declare at first blow, against the very foundations of
the government both in Church and State ; which was an
argument to unite the Kingdom as readily against them, and
made the Parliament in Scotland denounce him forthwith a
Traitor, declareing they would mentain and assert the Royal
prerogatiue, and order'd all the Subjects of the Kingdom to
take the Oath of Allegiance again.

By this time he was got as far into the Country as a place
called Completown, from whence he sent a general summons
for all to come in to him within the division of Cowel, and
particular letters to Severall gentlemen, threatening some with
military executition if they apéar'd not, others he engaged
by promisses, and when he had got together about Six hundred
foot and a hundred hors, he marched from Completown and
Kintire; at Tarbal he met three hundred Ilia men, being
attended all this while with three Shipps, one of thirty, an other

of twelve, and the therd of Six gunns, with some twenty small
boats; upon which embarKing his men he came to the Town
of Rothsay in the Island of Bute, from thence he sail'd to
Cowel one of the divisions of Argileshire, and would haue
brought his Shipps into Loughfine, but being informed that the
KING's FISHER, and the FALCON two of his Majestys Frigats,
were comeing up to Locke-rowan, he drew his Shipps under a
small fort adjoining to the Castle of Elingrel, which he fortifyd
in the best manner he could, leaveing there his gunns, armes,
and amunition, with a hundred and fifty men for its defence;
but upon the first apearance of the Frigats the garison fled;
abandoning their Shipps, boats, amunition, and armes;
amounting at least to fiue thousand, togather with fiue hundred
barrils of powder, with ball and othet stores proportionable.

The King's forces were in motion some time before this; and
the Marques of Athol at the head of three hundred of his
Majestys foot, meeting with a partie of Argile's men which had
been sent out to make inroads into the Country, thō they were
400 foot and 80 horse, yet he charg'd and defeated them, which
put a Stop to their progress for some time, and gaue the Earle
of Dunbarton who was Commander in Chief, leasure to advance
towards the Rebells, who now were grown to the number of
near three thousand men, and haueing pass'd the riuer Levil
obliged the Earle of Dunbarton to march towards Sterling to
meet them, who accordingly came up with them in the parish
of Killern, but finding them too well posted, and the night
comeing on, he thought it not advisable to attack them till
break of day next morning; but Argile foreseeing the danger,
marched off silently in the night, and swiming the river Clide
with his hors, he found boats to transport his foot, and arriued
at Kenfrew with the greatest part of his forces, thō a pannick
fear had already seized them, and caused a great desertion
during the night.

This put My Lord Dunbarton upon a necessity of marching
to Glasgow, from whence he follow'd the enemy with all the
expedition immaginable, at the head of his horse and dragoons,
leaveing the foot to follow as fast as they could : Argile upon
notice of this, thought to haue shunn'd him by a shorter cut,
and so haue got to Glasgow himself, but by the mistake of his
guide was lead into a boggy ground, where being forced to
abandon his horse and bagage, the foot devided into several
parties, which the Earle of Dunbarton haveing notice of,
devided his forces too, in order to pursue them ; My Lord
Ross at the head of some horse and dragoons came up with a
partie of the Rebells commanded by Sr John Cockram, who
posting himself in a strong inclosure made some resistance,
where the Captain of the Dragoons was kill'd, My Lord Ross
wounded, Sr Adam Blair shot in the neck, and Sr William
Wallace of Cregie in the side ; but the Dragoons alighting off
their horses, forced them at last, and thō Sr John Cockram and
his Son broke their way thorough, they were taken soon after,
and sent prisoners to Edinburg togather with Rumbald, one
who had been a furious stickler in the Rye house Conspiracy,
and had now joined himself with the Scotch invaders.

Argile himself upon the first seperation of his troops, had
fled back towards Clide, and being met by two servants of
Grenock an officer in the King's Army, they not knowing
him call'd to him to surrender, but he standing upon his
defence, receiud a hurt; upon which he abandon'd his hors
and run into the water up to the neck, the nois of this bussle
brought out a Country fellow, who run into the water after
him ; Argile would haue fired his pistol at him, but it mis-
serueing, the man gaue him a blow on the head which stunn'd
him so, that he fell down in the water, and at the same time
cryd out, Unfortunate Argile ; upon which been seized
(*June* 17) he was brought prisoner to Edinburg ; where

Argile Taken.

haveing been already outlaw'd for treason in the late King's reign, there was no need of renewing the process but to wait the King's order for his execution.

The Earle of Perth who was then Chancelor of Scotland, treated him with as much civility and respect, as his circomstances could possebly allow of, respiting his execution for some time at his request, thō he persisted obstinate in his rebellious principles and denyd the King's authority to the last; and when he was press'd with the example of haueing own'd the late King, he sayd, It was because he had taken the Covenant, and that his present Majesty never had done it; all power it seems in his acceptation was subordinate to that, so upon the last of June he was beheaded, which put an absolute end to that insurrection.

But an other, which had been concerted with it and design'd to be carryd on by the Duke of Monmouth was not so easily quell'd; he took his first flight from the cost of Holland too, (a Country which was ever liberal to the King in presents of that nature) and on the 11th of June landed at Lime in Dorsetshire with about a hundred and fifty persons only. The King was concern'd at the news, thō not surprised, for besides the information he had of it from Mr Skelton his Minister there, the Prince of Orange himself, thō he had countenanced the Duke of Monmouth underhand, and had promised to send some supply of armes &c, after him, instead of that, offer'd his seruice to the King, not out of good will to him, but to keep the sweet morsel for himself, proffering to come in person and bring a body of troops along with him to his Majestys assistance, if he pleas'd to permit it; but the King chose rather to trust to the force he had, than to one who (as apear'd by the sequel) and was then sufficiently suspected, had as impatient a thirst after the Crown of England as he that now invaded it.

That ambitious Prince, exempt from the tyranny of honour and conscience, thought nothing unpermited which he fancyd would open his way to the attempt, and made so little account of dissembling where his intrest requir'd it, that his best actions .(as this offer of assistance to his Vncle and Father in law must needs be counted) was not without the brand of deceit and treachery; he consider'd the King who was the present possessor, and the Duke of Monmouth the then pretender, as the only obstacle to his aims, and therefore he had been formerly tould by Fagel the Pentioner of Holland that his business was to play one against the other, and that whichever got the better. would equally advantage his pretentions; if the Duke of Monmouth succeeded, he saw it would be easy for him, that was a Protestant as well as he, and in the right of his wife the next heire, to shoue him out of the Saddle, if on the .contrary the Duke of Monmouth was worsted, he got rid of a dangerous rival, and was sure all his partie would then have recours to him, which proued accordingly, and was his main support, when his turn came to try for it. This made him underhand doe what he could to inflame this young man's fury and ambition, and send him out like a victime to the slaughter, playing a sure game himself, who soever fortune gaue the advantage to at present.

The King being thus necessitated to depend upon his own forces, began to encrease his troops upon the first rumour of the attempt, which, thō he could not doe time enough, to draw any great service from this augmentation at present, yet his Majesty had still so dangerous an enemy behind, that it had been madness not to make use of this occasion to forearme himself against him; and therefore nothing could be more unreasonable than the peoples and the ensuing Parliaments jealousie on that account, and their imputing to a design against their libertie, what was necessary for his Majestys

T O M.
III.

1685.

KING JAM:
LOOS SHEETS
pag. 3.

preservation, and their own security against a lurking and hidden enemy, much more to be aprehended, than him who threaten'd them at present.

" His Majesty had been long before advertised, in the life " of the late King, by one Monpoulan a companion of their " drinking bouts, of the strict correspondence and friendship " betwixt the Prince of Orange and that Duke, when he was " first in Holland; upon which his late Majesty sayd, It seem'd " strange to him how those two should apear so good friends, " and agree so well together, that aim'd both to usurp the Crown, " but his Majesty did not then see into the Prince of Orange's " views in that matter, which apear'd so plainly afterwards; it " behoued the King therefore when he heard how the Prince " of Orange countenanc'd both the Duke of Monmouth and " Argile's preperations at Amsterdam, to encrease his troops " then on foot, there being no time to raise new ones, and even " that could not be done time enough; for the Duke of " Monmouth had such mighty encouragement from the " Fanatick and Republican partie, and several others who call'd " themselves Church of England men, thō in reality they had " neither religion nor principles of honour, some officers of " desperate fortunes, with other turbulent men, that he " venter'd away with the few people he had about him; not " takeing time to make a suitable preparation for such an " attempt, and by consequence hindred his Majesty from " doing it likewise; so that upon notice of his being landed, " the King was forced to content himself with sending downe " My Lord Feversham in hast, with the greatest part of the " horse guards, and granadiers on horsback to secure Bristol, " with orders to the Duke of Beaufort to endeavour the like, " haueing notice that the Duke of Monmouth's first attempt " would be upon that important place; he sent at the Same " time and recall'd his three Scotch regiments that were in

Holland, which the Prince of Orange dimiss'd away with all "
expedition, and offer'd himself and more troops (as was "
sayd) but the King found he could not even trust his own "
Subjects that came from thence, much less Strangers; for "
being advertised by some Officers of those three Regiments, "
and by their seditious discourses in their quarters, that many "
not only of the Souldiers but of the Officers too, were So well "
affected to the Duke of Monmouth that he durst not send "
them downe to the West, but rather trust to the few Troops "
he had there already, than run the risque by sending a "
seeming reinforcement to his own Army to send a real one "
to his enemy. "

 While the Duke of Monmouth was getting his armes and "
amunition ashore, together with some three or four small "
pieces of cannon (which he drew out of the Ships more for "
the name than any use they could be to him) he found nobody "
almost came to join him, which dishearten'd him mightely "
at first, insomuch that he was once in a mind to return; "
but flattering himself with the multitude of engagements both "
from men of great estates and great quality, and even from "
Officers in the standing Army, and being pushed on by "
some violent men about him, he venter'd to march into the "
Country with designe to make himself master of Bristol, and "
then published his Declaration. In this Declaration he begins "
with commending the English government, then taxes the
Duke of York (for so he term'd the King) with a design of
subverting it, by turning the limited Monarchy into an absolute
Tyranny; he charges him with all the ills he could think of, as
the burning of London, the murther of Sᵗ Edmon bury
Godfrey, the suborning witnesses, the taking away innocent
mens lives, the cutting my Lord Essex's throate, and that the
blackest crimes was to be expected from him if necessary to
ruin the Religion and liberties of the people; that in opposition

to the latter he had collected the Customes, and a part of the Excise, thō the grant of them expired at the late King's death, that haveing fill'd the benches with such as were a scandal to the Bar, there was no hopes of redress but by force; which therefore (he sayd) he had recours too, for no private ends of his own, but to vindicate the Religion, Laws, and rights of the people, and to preserue the Kingdom from bondage and Idolatrie; and therefore declares war against him, the said Duke of York, as a murtherer, an assasin of Inocent men, a traitor to the Nation, and Tyrant to the people, he threatens the utmost severity to his abettors, unless they repent and quit his partie, and in that case the very Papists themselues were to find mercy, he solemnly protests his aims are not personal, but to bring things to such a temperament and ballance, as future rulers may be inabled to doe good, and prevented from doing any harme, that the penal Laws against Protestant dissenters may be repeal'd and Parliaments annually assembled, that Judges may be *quamdiu se bene gesserint*, and at the nomination of the Parliament, to the end that no such unjustices may hereafter be commited by the Bench, as the unrighteous judgement against Sr Thomas Armstrong, Col: Algernoon Sidney, and the Lord Russel. He confirmes the old Charters, rescinds the corporation and militia Acts, leaues the Sherifs to be elected by the freehoulders, and frees all from prison or opression for the Protestant Plot, he declares he will pursue the Duke of York as his mortal and bloody Enemy in order to bring him to due punishment, for the horrid paricide upon the late King his Brother, and then waveing his own title for the present, leaves it to the peoples wisdom to make such future settlements as shall seem best to them; and lastly, approveing the Earle of Argile's proceeding, recommends his cause to the Lord of Hosts, to decide betwixt him and his Enemy in the day of battle.

Thus did this poor abandon'd wretch, load himself with the guilt of endeavouring to confirme the blackest Calumnys, with the most horrid and blasphemous imprecations ; but they who had made a propertie of him hithertoo, plaid him now as their last stake against the King and government, and as an ultimate efort for a Common wealth: but this bitter and false Invective made so little impression upon the sober part of the Nation, that it was hard to say, whether the Parliament which was then setting, or the King himself was more sencibly touched at these abominable Falshoods, and hellish Aspertions he cast upon him ; the King issued out a Proclamation to declare him a Traitor, and the Parliament immediately upon the first notice assured his Majesty in an adress, they would stand by him with their liues and fortunes against the Duke of Monmouth and all his adherents, and against all Rebells and Traitors, and Enemys whatsoever of his government ; and were so zealous in this matter, that within three days after the first notice, they had got an Act ready for attainting him, which on the 16th of the same month had the Royal assent.

T O M. III.

1685. The Parliament atteints the Duke of Monmouth.

In the mean time the Duke of Monmouth advanced to Bridgwater and from thence to Taunton, his numbers increasing hugely notwithstanding the late Proclamation against dispersing his Declaration, and notwithstanding the vigilance of the Dukes of Albemarle and Somerset who were sent down upon the first notice, as well as the Duke of Beaufort, to raise and command the Militia of those Countys, whereof they were Ld Lieftenants ; not so much with intent to oppose him, as to hinder the Country from flocking in to him, for the King could have little confidence in the Militia of those parts, who were fram'd (to be sure) of the same mould and temper with their Neibours who so readily had join'd the Invader, notwithstanding his enterpris was discountenanced by all ranks of people in the government, and even the Parliament it self.

This great concours of people did so puff the Duke of Monmouth up, that he suffer'd himself not only to be proclamed King, but declar'd the Parliament a Seditious assembly and set a price upon the King's head ; this unpolitick step would haue ruin'd him in the end, had he been more successfull in the begining (for besides that My Lord Argile who heard it before he suffer'd, complain'd of him for breach of promis, and a solemn engagement to set up for a Commonwealth) the Prince of Orange (to whom (as it was said) the Duke of Monmouth had promiss'd to let him take the Crown, when once he had dispossess'd the King of it) would never have pardon'd that infidelity : but he had too many different intrests to satisfy, and such diversity of Councells to reconcile, that so weak a man could never have disintangled himself from all those tenter hooks that stuck in his way ; which sooner or later was sure to stop his career, and make him of necessitie sink and perish under the burden.

The few Troops his Majesty could assemble on so short a warning exceeded not the number of two thousand Foot and fiue hundred Horse, the command where of he had given to the Earle of Feversham ; who marching with all immaginable expedition came to Somerset, and from thence to Weston, and finding the Enemy so far advanced haulted there, quartering his hors in the Village, and encamping his foot in a pretty advantagious post, haveing a ditch in his front betwixt him and a specious plain called Sedgmore, and within some three miles of Bridgwater where the Enemy now lay, and were encreas'd to near six thousand men ; which being more than the Duke of Monmouth could well arme, and much more than he had mony and provisions to keep long together, his business was, assoon as possible, to push the matter to a decision : so on the 6th of July (haveing drawn out his forces the night before) he marched early with so much sylence and secresy, that tho

My Lord Feversham had notice of his motion, and had sent out parties to gain intelligence, yet they came up to him before he was aware, and indeed before it was light enough to attack him, or pass the ditch without confusion.

This gaue My Lord Feversham time to put himself in a condition to receiue the Enemy, who, assoon as it was light enough, came upon him in good order ; the Duke of Monmouth at the head of his foot began the charge, which he mentain'd well enough for some time (by firing only cross the ditch which still remained betwixt them) and had his horse done their part as well, it might haue render'd the Success more doubtfull : but they were so well receiud at their first fire by Coll: Oglethorp and My Lord of Oxford's Regiment, that they immediately gaue way, and by this time the King's Cañon being brought up and the Horse flanking the foot, they were soon disorder'd too, and entirely broke, leaving three small pieces of Cannon, their bagage, and a good many dead upon the place.

The Duke of Monmouth at first fled with some fifty horse, but not being able to keep them long together, was forced to take a Country man's coat, in which disguise he, and My Lord Gray skulked till next morning in the inclosures near Ringwood ; but that Lord being then discover'd and seized, it occasion'd a more diligent search, in which the Duke of Monmouth likewise was found, under the hollow of a bank trembling with could and aprehention ; My Lord Lumley who then was zealous in the King's seruice took charge of him and My Lord Gray, guarding them very strictly up to Town.

Thō the Duke of Monmouth wanted not personal courage in the day of battle, yet his heart fail'd him, when in cold blood he was forced to look death in the face ; that familiarity which men contract with danger, while they haue so many companions of it in the feild, is not always the same when they are to out braue it alone upon a Scaffold ; of which he had now so liuely

T O M.
III.

1685.

a representation, that there was nothing he would not haue done to saue his life, and haveing so oft experienced the Royal mercy for his former crimes, he dispar'd not of it now, so writ the following letter to the King.

S R

Your Majesty may think it is the misfortune I now ly under makes me make this aplication to you, but I do assure your Majesty, it is the remorse I now haue in me, of the wrong I haue done you in severall things, and now in taking up arms against you ; for my taking up arms it never was in my thoughts since the King dy'd : The Prince and Princess of Orange will be witness for me of the assurance I gaue them, that I would never stir against you ; but my misfortune was such, as to meet with some horrid people, that made me belieue things of your Majesty, and gaue me so many false arguments, that I was fully led away to belieue that it was a shame and sin before God not to doe it; but, S^r, I will not trouble your Majesty at present with many things I could say for my self, that I am sure would moue your compassion, the chief end of this letter being only to beg of you, that I may haue the happiness as to speak to your Majesty, *for I haue that to say to you, S^r,* that I hope may giue you a long and happy reign, I am sure, S^r, when you hear me, you will be convinced of the Zeal I haue for your preservation, and how heartely I repent of what I haue done ; I can say no more to your Majesty now, being this letter must be seen by those that keep me, therefore, S^r, I shall make an end in begging of y^r Maty to belieue so well of me, that I would rather die a thousand deaths than excuse any thing I haue done, if I did not realy think my self in the wrong the most that ever man was, and had not from the bottom of my heart an abhorrence of those that put me upon it, and for the action it self. I hope, S^r, God Almighty will stricke your heart with mercy, and compassion for me, as he has done mine with an abhorrence of what I haue done: wherefore, S^r, I hope I may liue to shew you how Zealous I shall ever be for your seruice ; and could I say but * *one word* in this letter, you would be convinced of it, but it is of that consequence that I dare not doe it, therefore, S^r, I doe beg of you once more to let me speak to you, for then you will be convinced how much I shall ever be your Majestys most humble and dutyful

    MONMOUTH.

---

* Mr FOX, in his History of the early part of the Reign of JAMES THE SECOND, has introduced this Letter, and observes (page 269) " With respect to the mysterious part of the letter, where he speaks of *one word*, which would be of such infinite importance, it is difficult, if not rather utterly impossible, to explain it by any rational conjecture. Mr Macpherson's favourite hypothesis, that the PRINCE OF ORANGE had been a party to the late attempt, and that Monmouth's intention, when he wrote the letter, was to disclose this important fact to the King, is totally destroyed by those expressions, in which the unfortunate prisoner tells his Majesty he had assured the Prince and Princess of Orange that he would never stir against him . . . . The intriguing character of the Secretary of State, the Earl of Sunderland, whose duplicity in many instances cannot be doubted, and the mystery in which almost every thing relating to him is involved, might lead us to suspect that the expressions point at some discovery in which that nobleman was concerned ; and that Monmouth had it in his power to be of important service to James, by revealing to him the treachery of his Minister. Such a conjecture might be strengthened by an anecdote (*Macpherson's State Papers*, I. 146:) that has had some currency, and to the truth of which in part, KING JAMES'S MEMOIRS, if the extracts from them can be relied on, bear testimony." —

The Reader will find this Anecdote detailed in the following page, and at greater length than Macpherson had done. Mr Fox then continues :

" It is to be remarked that in Sheldon's conversation, as alluded to by KING JAMES, the PRINCE OF ORANGE's name is not even mentioned, either as connected with Monmouth or with Sunderland. But on the other hand, the difficulties that stand in the way of our interpreting Monmouth's Letter as alluding to Sunderland, or of supposing that the writer of it had any well-founded accusation against that Minister, are insurmountable. . . . . . A third, and perhaps the most plausible, interpretation of the words in question is, that they point to a discovery of

He was not satisfyd with this letter, but the King haveing sent Mr Ralph Sheldon to meet him upon the road and accompany him up to Town, he reiterated his petition to him, upon a particular instance which he fancyd the King would be more than ordinarily moued with ; the Duke of Monmouth haveing asked Mr Sheldon, who were the persons in greatest credit with the King, he named My Lord Sunderland in the first place, at which the Duke of Monmouth knocking his breast in a mighty surprize, sayd, Why then, as I hope for Salvation, he promised to meet me, and desired Mr Sheldon to acquaint his Majesty with it, and that he would informe him of all his accomplices, whereof he perceiud, (he Sayd) there were some in whom his Majesty put the greatest trust : when Mr Sheldon return'd and was giveing the King an account of what he had learn'd, My Lord Sunderland (uneasy perhapes under the aprehentions he might reasonably be in) pretending business, was admitted into the Closet, at which Mr Sheldon makeing a stop, desir'd to speak to his Majesty in private, but

---

Monmouth's friends in England, when, in the dejected state of his mind, at the time of writing, unmanned as he was by misfortune, he might sincerely promise what the return of better thoughts forbade him to perform. This account, however, though free from the great absurdities belonging to the two others, is by no means satisfactory. The phrase, *one word*, seems to relate rather to some single person, or some single fact, and can hardly apply to any list of associates that might be intended to be sacrificed. . . . . . Perhaps, after all, the Letter has been canvassed with too much nicety, and the words of it weighed more scrupulously, than, proper allowance being made for the situation and state of mind of the writer, they ought to have been." . . . .

Mr Fox adds, (page 278) " There is also mention of a third letter written by him to the King, which being intrusted to a perfidious officer of the name of Scott, never reached its destination (*Dalrymple's Memoirs*, I. 127.) but for this there is no foundation." — A detailed account of the proceedings respecting the Duke of Monmouth, is given by Ralph in his Review of the Reigns of Charles II. and James II. (*Vol: I. p.* 873—886.) EDITOR.

the King tould him, He might say any thing before that Lord, which put Mr Sheldon to Some perplexity what to do; but not dareing to conceal what he imagin'd concern'd his Majesty so near, sayd, He was commission'd by the Duke of Monmouth to assure his Majesty, that My Lord Sunderland * *himself was of intelligence with him, at which my Ld Sunderland* seem'd extreamly struck, so that the King could not but obserue it; but soon recouering himself, sayd with a fain'd laughter, If that be all he can discover to saue his life, it will do him little good; at least it did that Lord no harme, for whether he had got permission from the King to do something of that kind, under pretence of discoverys (thō in reality to secure himself, and under the notion of serving his Majesty more efectually, preserve his own stake whoever won the game) or what other fetch he had to bring himself off, does not apear, but it is certain he found means to wipe off the suspicion and keep up his credit with the King, thō tis probable had the Duke of Monmouth succeeded, he had then made as great a merit of betraying his Master to him, as he did afterwards to the Prince of Orange; for when that unfortunate Duke was discoursing at sea, with those he had most confidence in, of what measures he should take at his landing, Ferguson advised him not to be too hasty in giveing imployments, but reserue them for baits, to bring great men over to him; he sayd, He would follow his councel, and assur'd him, he had promis'd none, but only My Lord Sunderland, that, which he was now in possession of.

There were so many persons ready to second the Duke of Monmouth's request, and amongst the rest Queen Dowager herself, that the King suffring his good nature to overpower

---

* These words in Italics are interlined, and in the hand writing of the Son of James the Second, generally known by the name of the Chevalier St George. EDITOR.

his judgment, at last consented to see him ; which certainly he should not haue done unless he had been disposed to pardon him, but perhaps he was not so entirely cured of that suspicion Mr Sheldon has (*had*) rais'd of his fauorit, as not to be willing to hear something more of the matter, and for the same reason it is strange that My Lord Sunderland did not oppose it ; unless (as it was sayd afterwards) he underhand assur'd the Duke of Monmouth of his pardon if he confess'd nothing, and then, when he had made him destroy his own credit by contradicting himself, took care to haue him dispatched assoon as possible afterwards. When therefore the Duke of Monmouth was brought before the King, he fell upon his knees, crawling upon them to embrace those of his Majesty, and forgeting the character of a Hero, which he had so long pretended too, behaued himself with the greatest meanness and abjection immaginable, omitting no humiliation or pretence of sorrow and repentance to moue the King to compassion and mercy ; but there apearing no great matters of discovery, there was no advantage drawn to either side by this unseasonable * interview ; for thō the King was inclined enough of his own nature to spare him, he was soon made sencible, how cruel a compassion it would be, to expose the publick peace to so great a hazard, and the liues of thousands for that of one man's, who had deserued so little to liue ; that considering how great numbers had join'd him, even after he was attainted by Parliament, and how the people were intoxicated with an Idea of his personal merit and pretended zeal for the Protestant Religion, no one could answer for the consequence if he were at libertie again ; that those fabulous inventions of the late King's being maried to

---

* A more detailed account of this interview, which Mr Fox has cited as authentick, is given by Bishop Burnet. III. 432. EDITOR.

his Mother, thō rediculous in themselves, and disowned by the
King, however had imposed upon many ; and lastly, that his
own little faith or honour in keeping former promisses and
engagements, render'd it the most hazardous and unpolitick
thing in the world to leaue the factious partie such a handle
to shake the foundation of the Throne, whenever they pleas'd
to doe it ; this made the King giue him no encouragement or
hopes of mercy. However the aprehention the Duke had of
dying, made him leaue nothing unatempted which he fancyd
might ward him from the fatal blow ; he thought his intimateing
a certain inclination to become a Catholick, might work with
the King more than any thing, he had indeed been educated
in that religion in his youth, which made his Majesty think he
might probably be willing to dy in it too, but he found by
those he sent to him for that end, that his concern was more
to saue his life, than his soul ; and when he perceiu'd there
was no hopes of the former, he resolued to venter the latter in
the Religion he then profess'd ; which thō he call'd it that
of the Church of England, yet when the Divines of that
Communion who came to assist him, press'd the doctrine of
nonresistance, he never would own he held it ; and then by
declaring the Lady Hariote Wentworth his wife in the sight of
God, thō at the same time he recommended the Children he
had by the Dutchess of Monmouth to the King's mercy, gaue
the world as od an Idea of his Religion, as it did of his
discretion and judgment : for when it was known for certain ”
that he was to dye, the Dutchess of Monmouth asked leaue ”
to see him in the Tower, which was readily grāted her, and ”
comeing into the outward room while yᵉ Bishops were ”
exhorting him to prepare for that terrible passage, of which ”
he had thought little during his life, one of them tould him, ”
the Dutchess of Monmouth was there and desired to see ”

T O M.
III.

1685,

KING JAM.
LOOS SHEETS
pag: 12.

TOM.
III.
1685.

"him ; but in stead of calling her in, he* disowned her, and
"sayd, That indeed according to Law she was his Wife, but
"was not so in the sight of God : The Bishops stood amazed
"at this, which they thought but a scurvy disposition for
"death, however they press'd him to own his fault, and ask
"God's pardon and the King's, without which they could not
"giue him absolution, nor take the Communion with him ;
"but they never could bring him to own, that what he had
"done was any such great crime, he call'd it an † Invasion,
"and that was all they could bring him too, which obliged
"them to leaue him as they found him ; So that this man
whom the people run so blindly after, as the only prop of their
Religion, proued to be of none at all himself, not haveing in
that extremity the usuall assistance of a Divine of any
perswasion whatever ; but with this miserable preparation went
to the Scaffold on Tower hill, where his head was cut off, on
the 16th of July (the 15th). He made no speech at his death,
but gave a paper to the Sherif, wherein he own'd the late

---

* On perusing this passage in the Original Manuscript, my friend Mr Walter
Scott made the following remark,

Although it is unquestionably true, that the Duke of Monmouth persisted in
maintaining that Lady Harriet Wentworth was his Wife in the sight of heaven,
yet the Secretary is mistaken in averring, that he refused to see the unfortunate
Duchess before his execution.   There is a particular account of their last
Interview in the Appendix to Mr Rose's Remarks on the reign of James II.
which I copied for that work from the Original Narrative in possession of the
Duke of Buccleuch.   The meeting passed with decency, but without tokens of
affection.   There is a tradition that upon the morning after the execution, the
King breakfasted with the Duchess of Monmouth, and presented her with a
remission of the forfeiture of blood incurred by the Duke's treason, in so far as
it affected the titles and estates of the Buccleuch family.   W. S.

† See Mr. Fox's History, Page 284.   Editor.

King had tould him, he was never marryed to his * Mother,   T O M.
and that the title of King had been forced upon him, contrary   III.
to his judgment, so hoped his Majesty would not let his   1685.
Children suffer on that account.

Thus did this poor unfortunate man cross and contradict
himself in his actions as well as his words, sometimes
pretending his guilt was a greater torment than a thousand
deaths, when he hoped to avoid death by it, but when that
was certain, he had a mind to reassume the Hero again, and
would scarce owne any fault; so that his behaviour after he ”   King Jam:
was seized answered in no kind the expectation the world ”   loose sheets
had of him, especially considering how high he had carryd ”   pag: 10.
his pretentions, and what an undaunted character he aspired ”
too both at home and abroad; if his head and heart had ”
been answerable to his meen, and personal outside, he had ”
certainly great opertunitys of pursuing his aims by the ”
turbulancy of the times, and unsettled temper of the people, ”
whom My Lord Shaftsbury by his great dexterity in raising
factions and discontent, had so enflamed against the then Duke
of York, that no attempt seem'd impracticable against him;
and finding this yong Duke of a rash, unsteady, and
ambitious mind, hooked him in to serue his malicious purposes,
covering his baits so artificially that he wrested him from the
Kings bosom, and duty to him, by flattering his youthfull

---

* Granger informs us, that " the pretended Secret History of Charles 2ᵈ, and
Lucy Walters, was published, under borrowed names, in THE PERPLEXED PRINCE,
written in the manner of a Novel, and dedicated to William Lord Russel. The
King is there said to have been certainly married to her. This book, which is but
a mean performance, has had a great influence on the populace." — A copy of this
book is in the possession of Walter Scott Esq. Two Letters from the Princess of
Orange to her Brother Charles 2ᵈ, in May and June 1655, in which the Mother of
the Duke of Monmouth is singularly noticed, are to be found in the first Volume of
Thurloe's State Papers, (page 665.) EDITOR.

T O M.
III.

1685.

KING JAM.
LOOSE SHEETS
pag: 10.

pride not only with the ostentation of defending his countrys liberties and Religion, but of gaining the crown it self; and by imaginary suspicions inflaming him into an irreconcilable hatred * to the Duke of York, made him throw aside all measures of respect for his then Royal Highness; thõ there was so little foundation for such a conduct, that till the Duke of Monmouth made himself uncapable of his friendship, he never had a faster friend than the Duke, nor was there scarce any honour or benefit confer'd upon him, but what was obtain'd of his then Majesty, by his Royal Highness' intercession. But " Shaftsbury's sly insinuations overpower'd his weak judgment, " especially when Oates's pretended Plot came so opertunly " to his assistance; and in reality had the Duke of Monmouth " made such use of those favorable occasions as a bould and " judicious person might haue done, he had a fair chance for " the Crown, or at least not to have dy'd unpitied, which by " his poor and dejected cariage after the Battle, he lost all " pretence too; nay he fell so low as to put confidence in a " fortune teller, who it seems had assur'd him that if he out " liued St Swithin's day, he should be a great man: he " therefore writ most pressingly to my Ld Arrundel of Wardour, " My Lord Tyrconnel, and others, to beg a repriue for a few " days; but the King being advised against it, his head was

---

* It appears from the *Memoirs of Sheffield Duke of Buckingham*, that the intimacy between the Duke of York and his nephew, was dissolved, owing to a little inconstancy of one of their Mistresses in favour of Sheffield himself: this " unlucky discovery" as his Lordship terms it, excited the resentment of the Duke of Monmouth, who endeavoured in revenge to obstruct Sheffield's military promotion; while that Nobleman on the other hand takes no small credit for his own ingenuity, by involving the Duke of York in his own private quarrel. This Court Intrigue was the original cause of such a division between these two near relatives, as put the crown of the one into peril, and brought the other finally to the scaffold." (*Vol.* 2. *p.* 32. 2^d *Ed.* 1729.) EDITOR.

cut off, as it happen'd, on that very day it self, perhaps as a "
punishment for giveing credit to so vain a prediction; for thō
Almighty God permits such devinations to fall out some times
according as they are foretould, yet never to the benefit or
advantage of those that belieue them.

Assoon as this flame was quenched and the Throne resettled,
to the seeming satisfaction at least of the people, his Majesty
made hast to giue his subjects of the three Kingdoms, all
immaginable testimonys of his zeal for the publick good, and
to establish peace, plenty, security, and a florishing trade
amongst them; and his greatest enemys will owne, that no
King of England was ever better qualifyd for it, took more
pains to compass it, or did more efectually performe it: His
subjects of Scotland, who had experienced how much steddiness
his former cariage had added to their councels, and vigor to
their resolutions, were charm'd to see him (now that he was
their King) pursue the same methods, he advised when he was
his Brother's Commissioner; so the moderate and judicious
people were so far from aprehending danger to their libertie or
religion, that they assur'd his Majesty that no one could be an
enemie to him, but must be so to their Country and themselves;
nor that it was possible for any considerable numbers amongst
them to be perswaded by malicious impostors, that they had
reason to fear arbitrary government under him, because they
refused to submit to it under them, who endeavor'd to bring
upon the people those very miseries, which their pretended zeal
perswaded them to shun. Ireland was no less sencible of this
blessing, the Protestants seem'd well satisfyd with their security,
and the Catholicks with their libertie; but the people of
England soon began to abate of that fervor with which they
set out at first; and the necessary acts of justice after such an
insurrection, by the mismanagement of such as were imployd
in yᵉ execution of them, or the false insinuations of such as

were sorrie it had miscaryed, was the first argument of souring peoples minds against the King, and laid the first foundation of those discontents which cost him so dear afterwards; for thō to reward Vertue and punish Vice, be the essential dutys of a Prince, yet it is almost impossible to fill either of those obligations, without disgusting infinitely more than one satisfys, or even those that draw their security and advantage from it.

Assoon therefore as the Parliament was prorogued (which the late troubles had forced the King to keep longer togather than their usual time of sitting) to satisfy one of these obligations, his Majesty; confer'd the honour of the Garter upon the Duke of Norfolk, the Earles of Peterborough, and Rochester; the two later in their different Stations had served the King with much affection, and fidelity, and the former thō he could not pretend to it for any particular merite, yet the King, who was always judicious in the distribution of his favours, thought it not reasonable that the first Duke of England should want the badge of the first or chiefest honour in the Kingdom; My Lord Feversham was lickewise soon after admited into their number as a recompence for the late victory, and thō few people allow'd him any great share in the merite, but rather blam'd his conduct or want of vigilance on that occasion, yet the King thought it a proper time to make a gratefull return to the Mareshall de Turenne's former friendship, in the person of his Nephew, who chiefly owed the kindness the King had for him to that great Generall's recommendation.

These favours thō they might rais envy, however they gaue no plausible handle to complaints; but when the King went about to performe the other branch of his duty; and punish some heads of the late rebellion, it encreased in effect that froward and discontented humour he hoped to repress by it: A proclamation had been issued out, against Coll: Danvers, John Trenchard, George Speak, Francis Charleton, and John

Wildman Esq: &c, who were suspected to be deep in it; but T O M.
they absconding, My Lord Stamford, Delamere, and Brandon, III.
were all seized and carryd to the Tower, a Commission of 1685.
Oyer and Terminer was lickewise granted out to the Lord Chief
Justice Jeffreys to go down into the West and make such
further enquirys and inflict such further punishments, as the
example of former reigns and the Security of the present seem'd
to require; but his imprudent zeal, or as some say'd averice,
carrying him beyond the terms of moderation and mercy,
which was always most agreable to the King's temper, so he
drew undeservedly a great obliquy upon his Majestys clemency,
not only in the number but the manner too of several executions,
and in shewing mercy to so few, particularly an old gentlewoman
one Mrs Alice* Lisle, who was condemn'd and executed (*Septr:* 2)
only for harbouring one Hicks and Neltrop, both ill men
enough indeed, and the latter in a proclamation, but as she
pretended was ignorant of it, and therefore perhaps might
suffer for a common act of hospitality : but there could not
be a greater proof that this severity was contrary to the King's
intentions, than the different treatment one Major Holmes
found from the King on one hand, and from My Lord Chief
Justice on the other ; this gentleman had been engaged with
Monmouth, and had lost his son and an arme in the battle,
was taken prisoner, and brought up to Town ; the King being
desirous to see him, he behaved himself in such a manner as
gain'd an esteem from every body ; his cariage was free from
dejection yet full of respect, he own'd his fault and had recours
to his Majestys mercy, but tould him that considering his
losses, and his age, the favour he asked would be more
advantageous to his Majestys reputation to grant, than bene-

---

* This Lady's Husband, who was one of the Regicide Judges, had been
assassinated at Vevay. EDITOR.

ficial to him to receive: the King who loved courage even in an enemie, could not refrain countenanceing of him, discours'd freely with him, and no one was more frequently in the King's antichamber, til it was thought fitt to send him down into the West as one who could best informe the Lord Chief Justice, who were most criminal and who most deserved mercy; and that he might doe some service ere he receiv'd his pardon, which was differ'd (only for that reason) til after his return; but instead of that, the first news the King heard of him was, that he had been hanged with the rest. This his Majesty was very much surprized at, and made him question the Chief Justice at his return; but he palliated that and his other severities, with the pretence of necessary Justice, which the King haveing made him Judg of, knew not how to contradict, especially since he had the precaution not only to send four other Judges as his assistants along with him, but Mr Polexfen lickwise, in quality of his Sollicitor, who being a known favourer of the Presbiterian partie, he hoped would moderate the Chief Justices's heat; so that after all this care, and foresight, his Majesty had reason to acquiess to what had been done, thō it was a great disservice to him in the bottom, but My Lord Chief Justice makeing it pass for an excess of Zeal, hinder'd not his Majesty from confering the title of a Barron upon him as a reward of his former merite; and soon after made him Lord Chancelor, (Sept^r: 28.) as thinking no one better qualifyd to execute that high office than himself; but certainly his Ma^{ty} had acted more prudently, had he refrain'd from heaping such distinguishing favours upon a person, who had by an imprudent Zeal (at best) drawn such an odium both upon his Master and himself.

But it is hard to giue the same colour to Coll: Kerk's severitys on the same occasion; who being apointed to attend upon the Commission with a body of Troops, caused many to be hang'd more out of a bloody disposition and to satisfy his·brutal passions, than the loue of justice or his Master's service ; nay it is not improbable but even then he had in his view, the drawing an odium by it upon the King himself, being no one did it more afterwards, when he could with impunity shew the true bent of his inclinations ; and if the King gaue him no marks of resentment for his unhumain barbaritie, it was partely by ignorance of what had past, and the mildness of his nature, which always inclin'd him to overlook the miscarages even of his enemys, much less those he took to be his friends, amongst whom he had the misfortune to reckon this gentleman, who so ill deserved that honour and Character : so that thō this was made one of the popular topicks to decry his Majestys government, tis certain, the King was hugely injur'd in it, his inclinations were no ways bloody, but ever bent to mercy ; and after all, he pardon'd thousands on this occasion, who had forfeited both life and estate, and his desire to make that sort of people easy, was none of the least motives for his granting liberty of conscience afterwards which cost him so dear in the end.

The punishments which were perform'd in London under the Kings own eye, were much more moderate ; and indeed greater regard was had therein to the treasons committed against the late King his Brother than against himself, as Neltrop and Ayloff two notorious rebells who only now falling into the hands of justice, thō attainted and outlawed for the Rye house plot, were executed upon it ; for which conspiracy Cornish was also tryd and condemned, who thō he had been a furious stickler in those times, and that no one doubted his guilt, yet when his Majesty heard that one of the witnesses against him, did not so positively reach to what is criminal in the case, he was troubled that the least formality in the Law should seem to have been infringed, for his security ; and therefore declar'd he was sorrie he had suffer'd, and order'd his quarters to be taken down and given to his relations to be decently buried.

As to those, whose crimes were purely against himself, he was not so hasty in punishing, so differ'd it, till after the next Sessions of Parliament; and thō it was necessary for publick example to try severall men of distinction who had been tampering in the late rebellion, yet it serued more to manifest his clemency than punish their guilt, for My Lord Brandon Gerrard thō tryd and found guilty, yet was soon after pardon'd; M'. Hampden pleaded guilty, and thō Sentence of death pass'd upon him, had the same mercy shewn him; My Lord Delamere indeed, by an errour in time of one Saxton who was evidence against him, was acquited, and Saxton himself prosecuted and found guilty of perjury afterwards, My Lord Stamford was pardon'd without ever being tryd; there could not therefore be a greater argument than this, how contrary those harsh and bloody proceedings in the West, were, to his Majestys compasionate nature; it not being usual with Princes to pardon the great Traitors and punish the less. So that notwithstanding the false suggestions of his enemies, those who were most so, found not only justice but mercy at his hands, thō neither could prevail upon the generality of them to be either gratefull or just to him in return ; for most of those who had experienced such transcendent marks of his bounty, were ready to swim with the tyde when once it turn'd against him, and cry *crucifige* as furiously as the rest.

While the King's mercy was so signally extended to his enemies, those who deserved better of him felt the effects of his impartial justice; for it haveing been thought necessary before the King's Accession to the Crown, that some marks of infamy should be put upon Oates and Dangerfield who had been the execrable instruments of so many murthers, they had

T O M.
III.
1685.

both been indicted for perjury and found guilty by innumerable evidences ; one of their punishments was to be whipt
to Tyburn, which when Dangerfield had undergon and was
returning in a coach, one M͏ͬ. Francis asking him in derision,
how his back did, he made a very abusiue reply, upon which
the gentleman in a passion thrusting at him with his cane,
unfortunately hurt his eye, ·on which he dy'd some days after;
this proveing a capital crime, the gentleman was tryd and
condemned for it, and though he was one that deserved well
of his Majesty, yet he could not be prevail'd upon to grant his
pardon, but suffer'd him to be hang'd on the same gallows
that Dangerfield had been whipt too.

After this mercifull chastisement of the Rebells (at least
where his Majesty had the inspection himself) he thought it
necessary to calm people's aprehention by granting a general
pardon (with some exceptions)·which was dated the 10ᵗʰ of
March, being desirous that his enemys might as easily forget
their fears as he did their injurys.

The King had prorogued the Parliament from the 4ᵗʰ of August The Parlia-
ment meets
to the 9ᵗʰ of November, which being little more than three months again the 9ᵗʰ
of Nouembͬ.
recess, shew'd his inclination to meet them frequently, and to
doe nothing of moment without their advice: One of the chief
points wherein he desir'd their concurrance, was the encreas he
had thought necessary to make in the guards, or standing
forces; he had found by the late rebellion; there was no
depending on the militia; and the few troops he had were too
inconsiderable to oppose an invader, being but barely sufficient
for the defence of his person, which for that reason was left so
naked on this occasion, that had the designe been put in
execution, which was wisely enough layd by the Duke of
Monmouth's partie, the King might haue fallen into their
hands notwithstanding his Victory at Sedgemore; for M͏ͬ. ” KɪɴɢJᴀᴍ:M͏ͬˢ.
Tᴏᴍ:9.pag.207.
Hook inform'd his Majesty afterwards, that he himself was ”

" sent from Bridgwater to London to forward the riseing,
" which Danvers, Manley, and Payton had undertook to make
" in the Citie; which had they done, the number of the
" disafected persons were so great, and the guards which he
" could possebly spare to keep with him so few, there was no
" probability of his haveing been able to resist such a force,
" when headed by men who made no scruple of the most horrid
" crimes to compass their ends; for Danvers had proposed to
" have his Majesty shot as he came to Somerset-house, or
" stabed in Whitehall, but M^r. Hook opposeing that, sayd,
" they being in an open war, so base an action was against its
" rules, and that if they did not desist from any such thought,
" he would discover them all; which probably was their chief
motiue for laying it aside: upon these considerations therefore
the King had augmented his guards to twelve or fourteen
thousand men, who were aboue half as many before, not
doubting but the House would enter into the reasons of it, and
not only aproue what had been done, but grant him an
additional supply for their future maintenance; and therefore
at the opening of the Sessions (*Nov:* 9th:) he spoke to them to
this effect.

The King's
Speech.

My Lords and Gentlemen : After the storm that seem'd
to be comeing upon us when we parted last, I am glad to meet
you all again in so great peace and quietness. God Almighty
be prais'd, by whose blessing that rebellion was suppressed;
but when I reflect what an inconsiderable number of men
began it, and how long they carryd it on without opposition, I
hope every body will be convinced that the militia which has
hithertoo been so much depended on, is not sufficient for such
occasions, and that there is nothing but a good force of well
disciplined troops in constant pay, that can defend us from
such as either at home or abroad are disposed to disturb us;
and in truth my concern for the peace and quiet of my

Subjects, as well as for the safety of the Government, made me think it necessary to encreas their number to the proportion I haue done; it is what I owed as well to the honour, as the Security of the Nation, whose reputation was so infinitely exposed to all our Neibours, by haveing laine open to this late wretched attempt, that it is not to be repair'd but by keeping such a body of men on foot, that none may haue a thought of finding us again so miserably unprovided; it is for the support of this great charge which is now more than double to what it was, that I ask your assistance in giveing me a supply answerable to the expences, it brings along with it; and I cannot doubt, but what I haue begun so much to the honour and defence of the government, will be continued by you with all the chearfullness and readiness that is requisite, for a work of so great an importance; let no man take exceptions that there are some Officers in the Army not qualifyd according to the late Tests for their imployments, these gentlemen I must tell you are most of them well known to me, and haveing formerly serued me on several occasions, and always proued the loyalty of their principles by their practices, I think them now fit to be imployed under me, and will deal plainely with you, that after haveing had the benefit of their seruices in such a time of need and danger, I will neither expose them to disgrace, nor myself to the want of them, if there should be an other rebellion to make them necessary to me.

I am afraid some men may be So wicked as to hope and expect, that a difference may happen betwixt you and me on this occasion; but when you consider what advantages hath risen to us in a few months, by the good understanding we haue hithertoo had, what wonderfull efects it has already produced, in the change of the whole scene of affairs abroad, so much more to the honour of the Nation and the figure it ought to make in the world, and that nothing can hinder a

T O M.
III.

1685.

further progress in this way to all our satisfactions but fears
and jealousies amongst ourselves, I will not aprehend that such
a misfortune can befall us as a division or a couldness betwixt
you and us, nor that any thing can shake you in your
steddiness and Loyalty to me, who by God's blessing will
ever make you returns of kindness and protection, with a
resolution to venter even my own life in the defence of the
true intrest of this Kingdom.

The Parliament alarm'd at the King's Speech, and debates upon it.

Both Houses seem'd much surprised at this Speech; the
augmentation of forces, and the imploying of Papists, were not
only new things, but what great endeavours and many Laws
had been made to prevent, both Lords and Commons hesi-
tated a little whether they should return his Majesty thanks
for it as usual: it suffer'd indeed no long debate in the House
of Lords, thō the King's ill willers sayd, it was procured rather
by a jest of My Lord Halifax's than any intention of the Peers;
for that Lord sayd, They had good reason to thank the King
for his Speech, which shew'd so plainly what he would be at;
but it was not so easily carryd amongst the Commons, for
when the Earle of Middleton one of the Secretaries of State
moued, not only that thanks might be given, but that they
would take into consideration how to answer the ends of the
Speech; it occasion'd a debate which was referr'd to a committee of the whole House, where My Lord Middleton renew'd
his motion, and was seconded by My Lord Preston, Lord
Renlagh and others; who Sayd, They had lately had an
unfortunate proof how little the militia was to be depended on,
and therefore must in reason agree to his Majestys increasing
his forces to what they were, that France was formidable, and
that Holland had augmented theirs, and that therefore
England ought to doe the like in proportion, to preserve the
peace both at home and abroad; that the harmony which
hithertoo had been betwixt the King and Parliament, had

contributed very much to those ends, that the news of it, and Monmouth's defeat had made the French King recall his Troops that were marching towards Germany, and put up the difference with the Spaniards about Hay and Founterabia; they Sayd, a Soldier was a trade, and must as other trads be learn'd, and that there could not be a greater proof of the insufficiency of the militia, than that the Duke of Monmouth thõ he landed only with 83 men and 300₶ in mony, should in spight of the militia and in spight of all the other forces the King was able to spare, be able to bring it so far as he did ; that if the French had landed then or at the business of Chatham, what would haue become of England? that an additional force was therefore necessáry, and moued.that a supply might be granted to support it.

Others sayd, in opposition to this, That the revenue the King had already, was sufficient for all occasions; that the militia did considerable Seruice in the late rebebellion, and that his Majesty at his first entrance on the Throne tould them, he had been misrepresented, but that he would preserue the Government in Church and State as now established, and mentain the people in all their just rights and priviledges ; that overjoyd at this, they ran in hastely to him, and gaue him four millions at once (reckoning what was added to the former revenue for life was worth) that the present income was near two millions, that the charge of the Government (admiting the Army kept up) could not amount to more than thirteen hundred thousand pounds per annum ; but that when the debate was formerly about the Bill of Exclusion, the main argument for it, was that in case of Popish Successor, there would be a Popish Army, which they said they were in a fair way too ; for that in order to it the Test Act was already broke :.which the late King when he pass'd it, assur'd them, would be an impregnable bulwork against Popery ; but that they began to find the contrary, and that it was very afflicting to see, so early a breach of their liberties, and so great a difference betwixt this Speech, and those made before, which argued a dangerous change of Councel and seem'd to stricke at their all ; they wonder'd how any man durst venter to take an imployment, not being qualifyd for it, and therefore moued, the question might be put, That a standing Army was destructiue to the Country.

It was Sayd in answer to this, That the Standing forces were now not aboue 14 or 15000 men, and were half as many before, that such an adition was but a necessary reinforcement to the militia for the general safety, and that the charge would not be great, being Sixty thousand pound per annum would mentain them : but others thought this a reflection on the militia, and thō many were for a supply, yet they dreaded a standing army, and pretended it was needless; the late rebellion, they sayd, had contributed to their future peace, that those engaged in it had sung their penitential Psalme, that their punishment was rejoiced at by all good persons, that the militia was not to be rejected but new moddel'd, that they would rather pay double to them from whom they fear'd nothing, than half as much to those of whom they must ever be affraid ; that the former force had preserved the peace and had been sufficient to do it, in the late King's time, and therefore might be presumed to be so still ; that all the security of the Nation, was in the shipping, and that if there had been the least frigat in the Channel, it would haue disapointed the enterprize ; that mentaining an army was mentaining so many idle persons to Lord it over the rest of the Subjects, that the King had declar'd no Soldiers should quarter in priuate houses, however they did, that they should pay for what they tooke, but that they payd nothing for almost all they tooke, so that if those men proued good and kind it must proceed from pure generosity ; in fine, that the imploying of Officers who take not the Test was a dispensing with all the Laws at once; and lastly, that it was treason to be reconcil'd to the Church of Rome, the Pope (by law) being declared an enemie to the Kingdom : they concluded therefore, that the granting a supply as moued for, would be a kind of establishing an Army by Act of Parliament, whereas there was (they Sayd) no Country in the world, that had a Law for setting up an Army, and when once that Sort of people had got the power in their hands, the reste of the Kingdom must liue at curtesie.

On the other hand it was again represented, that the late long Parliament always agreed, that some force was necessary, and that it did not belong to them to fix the number, that the King was best judge of that, a great Soldier, and a great Prince; that there was a bitter spirit in the three last Parliaments not yet well allayd, and therefore an additional force seem'd absolutely necessary for the King and Kingdom's Security: At (last) the question was put, If a Supply should be given to his Majesty? and it was carryd in the affirmatiue, but at the same time resolved, to bring in a Bill to make the militia more usefull. They were unwilling to quarell with the King, yet their hearts were against an Army, and therefore the next day instead of either going on with the Supply, or proceeding to a further consideration of his Majestys Speech, it was resolued to present him an adress against imploying Popish Officers; some indeed opposed it as thinking the King would not grant it, and if so, might probably make things worse, others thought the request of that House would weigh mightely with him, and a third partie were for compensating such Catholicks as had been usefull to the King; but at last it was carryd to present the address as follows.

We your Majestys Most Loyal and faithfull Subjects the Commons in Parliament assembled, do in the first place (as in duty bound) return your Majesty our most humble and hearty thanks, for your great care and conduct in suppressing the late Rebellion, which threatned the overthrow of this government both in Church and State, to the extirpation of our Religion as by Law established, which is most dear unto us, and which your Majesty has been pleased to give us repeated assurances you will always defend and mentain, which with all gratefull hearts we will ever acknowlidge.

We further craue leave to acquaint your Majesty, that we haue with all duty and readiness taken into our consideration your Majestys gracious Speech to us; and as to that part of it relateing to the Officers in the Army not qualifyd for their imployments, according to an Act of Parliament made in the 25ᵗʰ year of the Reign of your Royal Brother, intitled an Act for preventing dangers which may happen from Popish recusants, we do out of our bounden duty humbly represent to your Majesty, that those Officers cannot by Law be capable of their imployments, and that the incapacities they bring upon themselves that way, can no way be taken off but by Act of Parliament; therefore out of the great reverence and duty we owe to your Majesty, who haue been graciously pleased to take notice of their Seruices to your Majesty, we are prepareing a Bill to pass both Houses to indemnify them from the penaltys they haue now incurred; and because the continuing them in their employments may be taken to be a dispensing with that Law, without an Act of Parliament, the consequence of which is of the greatest concern to the rights of your Majestys Subjects, and to all the Laws made for the security of their Religion; we the Knights, Citizens, and Burgesses of your Majestys House of Commons, do most humbly beseech your Majesty, that you would be most graciously pleas'd, to giue your directions therein, that no apprehentions or jealousies may remain in the hearts of your Majestys most Loyal Subjects.

After this Address was read, it was moued to desire the Lords' concurrence; but they haveing thanked the King already for

his Speech, it was belieu'd they would not now pick quarrells
with it, *and therefore the Court partie pressed for* * *it* as a means
to quash the Address it self, and it was carryd against them
only by four voices: so when that was determin'd, they went
at last upon the Supply, some thinking two hundred thousand
pound sufficient, other were for twelve; in which debate much
was sayd against a standing force, as that they were disorderly,
and excessiue burthensom to the people; and being (they sayd)
that Mᵣ Blathwait had tould the House, what strict rules had
been prescribed them by the King, it was fear'd, since they
were not complyd with, that the King himself could not govern
them, and then what a condition would the Kingdom be in?
that they owed a duty to posterity, and to leaue them free in
their liberties and properties, that now there was peace and no
army needed, that if a Rebellion should happen, all would run
in to suppress it; and if needfull to assist Allies, the House
would giue an aid when wanted on that Score; others answered,
that those forces were necessary to prevent insurrections, that
it would be too late to rais an army when others were up, that
there was a malignant partie in the Nation, and that were
the forces disbanded they would see a riseing in a few days,
for that Rebells never repent; and that as for what related to
their Neibours, an Island might be atacked (they sayd)
notwithstanding a fleet, and that in such a case new troops
were not soon got togather, nor so usefull as old ones, and yet
more subject to commit disorders than those who haue been
longer in discipline: But notwithstanding all that could be
alledged, the apprehention of a standing force was so terrifying,
that they could not bear the thoughts of its continuance, at least,
for any time; they immagin'd in two or three years the Militia
might be new moddel'd, and made more useful, so after many

---

* Interlined by the Son of James the second. EDITOR.

questions and arguments they voted a Supply of seaven hundred thousand pound, which was conceiued would pay the Army for that time, and went upon ways and means to rais it; but before they came to a conclusion in that matter, Mr Speaker acquainted them with the King's answer to their address, which was to this efect.

The King's
reply to the
address.

MY LORDS AND GENTLEMEN : I did not expect such an address from the House of Commons ; for haueing so lately recommended to your consideration the great advantages a good understanding between us had produced, in a very short time, and giuen you warning of fears and jealousies amongst our Selves, I had reason to hope, that the reputation which God has bless'd me with in the world, would haue seal'd and confirm'd a good confidence in you of me, and of all that I say to you ; but however you proceed on your part, I will be steddy in all the promises I haue made to you, and be just to my word in this, and all my other Speeches.

When the Speaker had ended, the House remain'd in a profound silence for some time, at last it was moued, That a day should be appointed to consider . of it ; upon which Mr Cook stood up and sayd, I hope we are all English men and not to be frighted out of our. duty with a few hard words ; at which exception was taken, and after some debate he was sent to the Tower for his undecent speech : others however were not deter'd by it, from saying, they hoped for a more Satisfactory answer; but it bein urged, that their acquiescence to it when it was read, apear'd to be a sort of silent approbation, and that they ought to look upon it accordingly, it was put to the vote, and carryd, That his Majesty's answer was satisfactory.

The Parliament
prorogued
which met
no more.

The House thereupon adjurn'd to the 19th, when they came to a resolution to lay four pound a Tun upon French wine for nine years and a half, which they reckon'd would raise three hundred thousand pound per annum ; but his Majesty it seems being dissatisfyd with their proceedings in the main, sent for them up to the House of Lords, wher the Chancellor tould them he *was commanded by his Majesty to let them know* [*] it was his pleasure for many weighty reasons that the Parliament should be prorogued to the 10th of February ; but they met not then, nor ever after during his Majestys reign.

The world which has been very free in censuring the King's conduct, in the most material actions of his reign, fail'd not to do it in reference to his keeping up a so much greater standing force, than ever England had been acquainted with; it is indeed hard to say, whether his Majesty did more prudently in jarring with at first, and breaking at last, this Parliament, which, thō avers to the thing, had so much complesance however, as to grant a fund for mentaining the Army three yars ; before which had expired, tis probable they might haue enter'd into his reasons, and perhaps haue yielded afterwards to what shock'd them so much at first ; But as to the necessity of the thing it Self, those who then knew the true situation of his affairs, and now all the world that are witnesses of what has happened since, must owne the King had all the reason in the world to insist upon it.

At first Sight indeed no one wonder'd that a people jealous of their Religion and libertie, should be allarm'd to see a Prince of a different perswasion, mentain a Standing army in time of peace ; but the argument seem'd stronger, when by those of the other partie it was return'd upon themselves, for how much more reason, sayd they, had he to aprehend danger from a people, who had used his Royal Father so ill, because they only suspected him to be inclin'd to that Religion, of

---

[*] Interlined with the same hand writing as before. EDITOR.

T O M.
III.

1685.

which he had declar'd himself a member? he saw a factious partie
both in the People and Parliament, labouring to possess the
Nation with apprehentions not only of the Popish Religion, but
Popish Violence too; that two rebellious armys had already
been brought into the field upon that pretence, and he had
great ground to expect a therd would not be long behind them;
whereas on the other hand, what probability was there of his
being able to establish Popery with a Protestant army, did he
design it; or with a handfull of his own people subjugate a
nation, which the power of Rome, when it govern'd the world,
was never able to make an absolute conquest of; had the King
(sayd they) aprehended his factious Subjects only, he might
perhaps haue venter'd himself upon the fidelitie of his Loyal ones,
but he saw a more dangerous cloud still hanging ouer his head
than that he had lately dispers'd, the Prince of Orange's conduct
had rais'd a suspicion of an antient date, the late King made
no mistery of declaring that he look'd upon him as one, that
waited only for a fit opertunity to usurpe the Crown; his
Majesty saw how the troops had been poison'd that came from
Holland, how he had underhand assisted the Duke of

KING JAM.
LOOSE SHEETS
pag. 12.

" Monmouth, and yet no man seem'd more delighted at his
" ruin, for Monsr Bentinck whom that Prince had sent upon
" this occasion to the King with many professions of kindness
" and proffers of service, was in a grievous agony when he
" understood the King was resolued to see the Duke as soon
" as he was made a prisoner; and thō after enquiry, he found
" he had sayd nothing of what he aprehended in relation to his
" master, yet he was never at quiet, til his head was struck off;
" and this was so manifest to all that had any insight into
" affairs, that My Lord Dartmouth when he return'd from the
" execution, and had given the King an account of what had
" passd; tould him, that he had got ridd of one enemy, but
" but had stil remaining a much more considerable and

dangerous one behind, to wit the Prince of Orange: Those " T O M. III. 1685.
therefore who were favorable to the King's inclinations, and
knew that the Prince of Orange was not an enemy to be
slighted, saw plainly that nothing but an Army could fence the
King from that and other dangers ; which not being contrary
to any express Law, nor as he managed it, any burthen to the
people, he merited (they Sayd) rather the thanks, than the ill
will of his Subjects for mentaining at his own expence, a force
so necessary not only for his own security but for the Publick " Ibid. pag. 18.
tranquility at home, and the Nation's credit abroad, which "
in a short time was become the envy of its neibours, who "
began to be jealous of the flourishing condition his "
Majestys just government had brought it too; in which "
they might haue long continued, had not the groundless "
aprehentions of the Church of England, blown up by the "
Prince of Orange's emissaries, and the blackest calumnies "
of angry and implacable men, made the most zealous "
members of that Church quite forget their so much preached "
up doctrine of passiue obedience to their Lawfull Prince, and "
justify his Majesty to the world, by a wofull example, how
necessary it was for him to seek a more sollid security than the
empty promisses of the House of Commons, and those pompous
expressions of Loyalty, which he was not now to learn, how
little they were to be depended on in times of troubles and
publick discontent.

The Parliament now being up gaue his Majesty more leasure Regulations in Ireland.
to attend to his other affairs, and particularly what related
to Ireland. My Lord Clarendon had been nominated to go
Deputy thither, and thō the King had no reason to mistrust his
fidelity and affection to his person, yet it was mixed with such
a zeal against his Religion, that his Majesty was under a
necessity of useing an other hand to make some reformes in his
Army there ; and to mitigate a little the cruel oppression the

Catholicks had so long groan'd under in that Kingdom, he
thought it no injury to others, that the Roman Catholicks, who
had tasted so deeply of his suffrings, should now in his
prosperity haue a share at least of his protection; especially in
that Kingdom, where there had been in the worst of times a
sort of Succession in the ministry of Bishops, Parish Priets &c,
and whose numbers had made the Government (thō it kept a
heavy hand upon them in other things) always think a sort of
tolleration some ways necessary; besides his Majesty had
reason to place a greater confidence in their fidelity and
adherence to him, as haueing the greatest interest in his support,
in case his enemys should again disturb the tranquility of his
reign.

This made him think it necessary to giue a Commission of
Lt General to Coll: Richard Talbot, a gentleman of an antient
family in that Country, a man of good abilities and clear
courage, and one, who for many yars had a true attach to
his Majestys Person and intrest; to him therefore the King
gaue a power to regulate the troops, to place and displace
whom he pleas'd, which he executed very much to the King's
satisfaction and advantage, thō not so to the Lord Leiftenant's;
who besides that he look'd upon it as a diminution of his own
authority, was vexed to see so many Catholicks put into the
Army, but the King had reason (as he sayd himself in his letter
on that occasion to the Lords Justices) to believe that Monmouth's
rebellion had spread its contagion into that Country, that it
had infected many and deluded more: tis certain the Protestants
in Ireland being much inclined to Presbitery, even of the
Cromwelian stamp, were but too succeptible of such impressions,
and by consequence the Army stood in need of being purged
from that dross, wherein no other method was used than what
had been formerly giuen in too and aproued of, by the Duke
of Ormonde himself, thō not perform'd by him before he

came away, which was only to turn out all such, or the Sons of such, as had serued in the Parliament or Cromwelian Army, no one could wonder the King should think those persons not the fittest to be trusted with the deffence of his Government who had the guilt of his Father's blood upon them; however they were so tenderly dealt with, that most of them were bought off, and the Militia armes (which were generally in their possession too) were only taken from them to be put into the magazines; which my Lord Primat himself enter'd so far into the reason of, as to exhort them to it by an elegant speech he made for that purpose, telling them, They could not do more prudently, than to deliuer up their armes to be placed in his Majestys Stores, where they would be in greater readiness for the militia and their own defence, than dispersed about as they then were; which they performing accordingly, and their example being followed in most other places, added no little to the peace and tranquility of the Kingdom..

But these proceedings were no ways liked by My Lord Clarendon, he would not suspect those persons Coll: Talbot thought fit to turn out, thō the sequel shew'd of what disposition they were, when once they had liberty to act according to their own inclinations: but the King conceiud what had been done to be both just and necessary, and therefore found it would be impossible to reconcile two such oposite aims and tempers; so when Coll: Talbot return'd to England to giue his Majesty an account of what he had done, he confer'd upon him the honour of Earle of Tyrconnell, and began to think of sending him his Deputy in My Lord Clarendon's room; there was some opposition made to it even by Several Catholicks themselves, as thinking him of too violent a disposition and too disagreeable to the English of that Kingdom, but the intrest he made with My Lord Sunderland, and the King's antient friendship for him overpower'd that argument, so it was resolu'd on at last:

My Lord
Clarendon
dissatisfyd
with those
regulations.

however out of respect to My Lord Clarendon, whom the King was loath to disoblige, he continued him in his station till the begining of the year 1687.

My Lord Sunderland, who now press'd to haue My Lord Clarendon recall'd, was in great measure the occasion of his being sent, he had a politick fetch in it, and now rejoiced to see it take place so effectually ; that Lord (whos ultimate end in all his contrivances was his own personal pleasure or advantage) upon the King's Accession to the Throne, had good reason to doubt his credit would quite extinguish, or be hugely eclipsed at least by the two Brothers Clarendon and Rochester, whose adherence to the King in his former troubles, (when he so treacherously abandon'd him) had gain'd them great advantages over others as to the King's favour,. and particularly as to him ; who to add to his former disservices was actually contriveing with the Dutchess of Portsmouth, when the late King dyd, how to send the Duke into banishment again : this the King was not ignorant of, however would not use a person too harshly, whom the late King his Brother had favour'd and trusted so much ; so by way of an honorable dismission, his Majesty design'd to haue sent him either abroade on some forreign Embassy, or his Deputy into Ireland, either of which (thō more honorable and advantagious than he could expect) yet My Lord Sunderland foresaw would be his ruin in the end ; for the weak intrest he then had at Court, he knew would soon be blasted and fade away, if he were not personally present to cultiuate it ; still trusting to his dexterity that he could make it budd out again and bear as pleasant fruite as ever, were he but permited to exercise his skill upon the place.

He bethought himself therefore of this stratagem, not only to reconcile those two Lords to him, (who were embitter'd against him) and then by their intrest regain his own ; but to rais it to the pitch he aim'd at, by their ruin in the end, thō now he

hoped to make them his chief instruments towards his own
establishment. He came therefore to My Lord Rochester
immediately after the King's Accession to the Throne, and
tould him, That thō it had been his misfortune to differ with
him formerly, it was rather occasion'd by the infelicity of the
times, that shoued them as it were assunder, than his inclination
or sentiments which always run in conformety with his, that
no man had a greater esteem of his person, or opinion of his
abilities, and as a testimony of his sincerity, he had some
intrest, he sayd, with powerfull people which he was resolued
to imploy, and hoped it would proue efectual enough to make
him Lord Treasurer, and his Brother Lord Lieftenant of
Ireland; by which contrivance he did not only flatter their
ambition, but their modestie too; who were charm'd to think
two such glittering imployments should be confer'd upon them,
without their Seeking or Sollicitation.

By this means My Lord Sunderland made a merite to those
two Lords, of what, tis probable by priuate information he
knew, the King had resolued on of himself; for one of the first "
things his Majesty thought of after his comeing to the Crown, "
was to make My Ld Rochester Lord High Treasurer, which " King Jam:
was then in Commissioners hands, haueing a very great " LOOSE SHEETS. pag. 7.
kindness for him upon many accounts, but especially for his "
faithfull seruice during his banishment in Flanders and "
Scotland; for thō he was a zealous Protestant and had press'd ·"
his Majesty when Duke of York to return to that faith both "
by word and writing, yet his cariage had still been respectfull; "
My Lord Clarendon indeed had giuen the King more reason "
to be dissatisfyd on that Subject, with his behaviour at the "
late Dutchess of York's death, but nothing of that (the King "
sayd) was to be remember'd: So My Lord Sunderland "
found it an easy matter to performe his engagement, which was
purely oweing to the King's bounty and gratitude, and not to

his Sollicitation, however he gain'd what he aim'd at by it ; he made those two Lords forget their former enmity and become intercessors to the King that he might keep the seal. But this being only half his project, the next thing was to ruin those to whom he owed this seruice, and so step into their place and favour, when he found them no longer usefull to him *to support him in * his.*

He was no Stranger to their temper in matters of Religion, and by consequence that it would always be in his power when once he was in credit himself, to put the King upon measures, *he was † sure* they would never concur in ; which soon took efect, in reference to My Lord Clarendon (as has been sayd) and if My Lord Rochester's disgrace was differ'd something longer, it was because he had a longer necessity of his credit for his own support.

1686.
The Scotch
Parliam^t meets
again 29th Apr:

By this time the first fervour began to cool in Scotland likewise as well as it did els were ; the Parliament had been assembled again, according to their adjournment on the 29th of April, at the opening of which the King's letter was read as follows :

My Lords and Gentlemen ; The great testimonys we had of your Loyaltie and affection to our Royal person and government, at your last Sessions (in which you not only made an humble offer of your duty in ample manner, and shew'd your abhorrence of the Rebellion there rais'd against us, and your readiness on that, and on all other occasions to stand by us with your liues and fortunes) but wisely considering how much the forces, which former Parliaments had given us supplys to

---

* Interlined by the Son of James the second. Editor.
† Interlined by the same writer. Editor.

mentain, supported by your assistance and blessed by God, were instrumental in ending that unatural rebellion; you gaue us the occasion by augmenting your supplies, to add to our forces, and by consequence to your own security, for all which, as we haue return'd you our hearty and Royal thanks, and consider'd you as examples to our other Subjects of Loyalty, duty, and affection to us, (as you haue been in our former difficultys) so it stirred up in us, an ardent desire of makeing such returns unto you, as might every way make you find the advantage of your faithfullness and duty to us.

It is for this end that we haue again desired to meet you in this Session; we haue consider'd your intrest as much as our distance from you could bring into our prospect, and those things which we thought proper for it, whether in relation to trade and commerce, or easing some things uneasy to you, amongst yourselves, we haue fully instructed our Commissioner (with your advice and consent) to conclude, so as may be most for the general good, of that our antient Kingdom.

We haue made the opening of a free trade with England our principall care, and are proceeding in it with all immaginable aplication and hope in a short time to make considerable advances in it; we haue consider'd the troubles that many are put dayly too, by prosecutions before our Judges, or the hazard they lie under for their accession to the late rebellions: and to shew the world (even our greatest enemies themselues) that Mercy is our inclination, and Severity (when necessary) is by their wickedness extorted from us, we haue sent down to be pass'd in your presence, our full and ample indemnity, for all crimes committed against our royal person and authority; and while we shew these acts of mercy to the enemies of our person, Crown, and royal dignity, we cannot be unmindfull of our other inocent Subjects, those of the Roman Catholick religion, who haue with the hazard of their liues and fortunes, been always assistant to the Crown in the worst of Rebellions and usurpations, though they lay under discouragements hardely to be named; them we do heartely recommend to your care, to the end that as they haue giuen good experience of their true Loyaltie and peacfull behaviour, so by your assistance they may haue the protection of our Laws and security under our royal government which others of our Subjects haue, not suffring them to ly under obligations, which their religion cannot admit of; by doing where of you will giue a. demonstration of the duty and affection you haue for us, and do us most acceptable Seruice.

This loue we expect you will shew to your breethren; as you see we are an indulgent Father to you all; for these therefore and such other matters as we conceiue for our Seruice, and the universall good of the Nation, we haue sent our Right trusty and Right entirely beloued Cousin and Councellor Alexander Earle of Murray, Secretary of State for that our antien Kingdom, our Commissioner to you, believing that none will be more acceptable than one so immediately employd and trusted about our person, of whose long and faithfull Seruices we haue full experience in every one of the severall imployments he has been in, and of whose Loyalty and affection to our person we are fully convinced; to him we desire you to giue entire credit as one fully instructed and trusted by us, from whose experience and faithfull endeavours, with your loyalty, loue, and duty to us, we haue good reason to expect a happy conclusion to this Session, and you may assure your Selues in generall, and every one of you in particular, *that we shall haue both the generall concern of the Nation and yours in our * particular regard,* which we shall express by our royal favour upon all

---

* Interlined as before mentioned. EDITOR.

sutable occasions; so not only expecting your complyance with us, but that by the manner of it you will shew the world your readiness to meet our inclinations, we bid you heartily farewell : given, &c, 12ᵗʰ of April * 1686.

In conformety to this, the Earle of Murray represented to them how sollicitous his Majesty was, that all persons in their different Stations might reap the benefit of his Royal care and protection, how sencible he was of their dutifull and Loyal comportement; in recompence whereof he was contriveing how to open a free trade betwixt them and England, and was ready to pass any Bill for the publick benefit of the Nation, as the prohibition of importeing Irish Cattle, the Settleing an open mint, to oblige the Soldiers to an exact discipline in their quarters; or what els they thought beneficial to them; that he desir'd no more mony, being abundantly Satisfyd with what they had already giuen, and particularly with the alacrity with which it had been giuen, that he was ready to pass an Act of oblivion with some few necessary exceptions, and therefore doubted not (he Sayd) after such Royal favours, but they would send him back with the good tideings of their continued loyalty and readiness to shew themselves the best of Subjects to the best and most heroic Prince in the world.

The Commissioner was not willing, or thought it not necessary to speak planer, but to be sure his intention was to moue them to what the King desir'd in reference to Catholicks, he doubted not but when it was duly consider'd they would think themselues the happyest people in the world to liue under the government of a Prince, who instead of being a burthen, made it his study how to oblige and enrich them, and desir'd no

The favour the King disir'd for his Catholicks subjects in Scotland, was not well relished there.

---

* The date in the margin, of 1685 is still continued in the MS. and as far as Page 71, which is evidently an error. EDITOR.

K 2

other return for such favours, but that they would permit a
handfull of Catholicks to liue peacably and unmolested amongst
them.

Some indeed pursuant heruntoo proposed an Act in favour
of Catholicks, but the Committee apointed to inspect the penal
Statutes, and report their opinion what was fit to be done,
drew up a Bill, whereby the Papists were to be permited a
quiet enjoyment of their Religion in private, but were not for
repealing the penal Laws; this, thō a seeming contradiction,
however the King would haue been content with, but it met
with so warme an opposition that his Majesty soon perceiu'd
it would not be granted, and therefore resolued to prorogue the
Parliament, since he saw them so reasty in the matter; Thō
many were of opinion the thing might haue been carryed, had
the Commissioner been a man of abillities Sutable to the
undertakeing, and managed the humours and inclination of
his Country men with more dexterity and foresight; but he was
in reality (thō an honest and well meaning man) both weak
and easily imposed upon, and no ways qualifyd for the direction
of such an affair, and in so nice and critical a conjuncture,
otherwise that harsh temper in the Parliament might haue been
sweeten'd and molifyd in the end; for the moderate partie
owned that Those persons who opposed this Bill, had a more
than ordinary propention to persecute their brethren, since they
prefer'd the pleasure of that, before all the eas, plenty, and
protection which the most indulgent, affectionate, and industrious Prince could procure them: his Majesty was ashtonished
that considering the former good disposition of the Scotch
Nobility and Gentry, they should demur to so modest a
request; he gaue them therefore little further trouble, nor was
any thing of moment done that Session, but the aproveing
certain grants the King had made of some Lands in that
Kingdom to the Earle of Melfort and some others, wherein his

Majesty had the fortune to disgust the greatest part of the
Nobilitie and Gentry, by placeing his trust and favours upon
persons no ways esteem'd or beloued by the people.

And now that it became manifest, that no indulgence in
present, or mitigation of former rigours, in reference to
Catholicks, would go down with the King's Protestant Subjects,
and that the Parliament of England was avers to the augmentation of his forces, and especially to the imploying of
Catholicks in them, both which he conceiu'd necessary for the
publick peace and his own security, he thought it to no purpos
to assemble them again; and thō it had a harsh apearance to
the English Constitution to see no prospect of a speedy
Parliament, yet if the common motiues of calling them in
former reigns, had been well consider'd, which was generally
for no other end but to squees money from the people; some
persons thought they had little cause to complain, especially
since the standing force (if it was a novelty) at least was no
charge; the King by his good husbandry found means to pay
them himself, which was done duly and upon as high a foot
as any troops in Europe, which secur'd the Country from
that oppression they haue felt sufficiently since; and if any
disorders of that nature happen'd, it was not out of necessity
on the Soldiers part, or want of due care in the King to repress
them, but either out of a licentious spirit which is hard to
conquer entirely in men of that profession, or els it was
designedly done by some Officers, to render the King odious
to the people, in concurrence with those great men, who
imployd all their credit their eminent Stations gaue them, to
forward the designs of that ambitious Prince, whose dark
contrivances forced the King upon those measures which his
emisaries decrying, turn'd to his Majestys ruin thō conceiued
to be so necessary for his support.

It is certain that infection began already to spread it self amongst all ranks of people, the great honours and beneficial places of those who owed all they had to the King, hinder'd it not from gaining admittance amongst the Ministers and Courtiers; many Officers of the Army (tho a generation of men that pretend to carry honour and gratitude to a higher pitch than the rest of the world) took the King's great pay, and serued an other Master; nay the Church of England Clergie, notwithstanding their so much preached up doctrine of non resistance and passiue obedience, began early to spread jealousies amongst the people, and instead of suffring with patience, they complain'd before they felt any smart, and thought immaginary dangers a good pretence to encourage a real Sedition; they had preached prerogatiue and the Sovereign power to the hyest pitch while it was favorable to them, but when they aprehended the least danger from it, they cryd out assoon as the shoo pinched, tho it was of their own puting on.

The King endeavour'd to put a stop to this growing evil by punishing some notorious offenders, particularly one Samuel Johnson a Clergieman, for publishing a most Seditious libel, which he call'd an adress to the Soldiers and Sea men, wherein amongst other invectiues, he tells them, how much he is ashtonished they should yoke themselues with Idolaters and bloody Papists, who fight for the Mass book and to burn the Bible; that Since the destruction of the Protestant Religion was certainly intended, he exhorts them (in effect) rather to rebel than suffer it; this being proued upon him he was found

guilty, and being degraded by the Bishops of Durham, Rochester, and Peterbourough, he stood in the Pilory, was fin'd, and suffer'd other punishments Sutable to his crime. Prance about the Same time underwent the like treatment for his perjuries in Oates's Plot; which he confess'd haveing pleaded guilty upon the information.

This geñal cabal against the army made the King think an army more necessary, for'if they durst fly thus in the face of authority, and treat their Sovereign as an Idolater, and infidel, while he had such a Support, what would they not haue done had he laine at their mercy?' He took therefore great pains to view and discipline it; and to that end formed a Sort of camp all that Summer on Hounsloe heath, and by the great attention he had to their cloathing, armeing, and discipline, render'd it a very compleat body of men, which thō not very numerous (as not exceeding 13, or 14 thousand) had the reputation however of being the best payd, the best equip'd, and the most sightly troops of any in Europe, and thō they gaue some ombrage at home, they rais'd the King and Kingdom's credit to a great degree abroad.

This was what the King spent the greatest part of the Summer in, till he took a small Progress to the West, where he was receiu'd with great testimonys of duty and respect, especially at Winchester; for thō those who had most obligation to serue him, were then endeavouring to Sow the Seeds of rebellion in the Kingdom, yet hithertoo the generality of the people (in that point wiser than their leaders) were sencible and gratefull for the easy Government and secure protection of their Prince, who guessing at the inward disposition of the whole, by the outward professions of some, he fancyd he might make a further step in favour of Religion; which must be own'd lay nearest his heart, and was his main study how to promote, without breach of the Law, or his engagement at his first accession to the throne, which notwithstanding the clamours of angry and discontented men he never positively went against; and if in Some cases he seem'd not to keep so strictly to the letter of his promis as many persons fancy'd he ought, he was justify'd on one hand by the opinion and aprobation of the Judges, whose fault it

T O M.
III.

1686.
The K: takes a pleasure in modeling his army.

was, if they misguided him; and on the other, by the Sly insinuations of flattering and disembling Councellors, who by favouring what they Saw him inclin'd too, had gain'd a mighty credit with him, which they made use of, to the bassest purposes men could be capable of.

The Earle of Sunderland to whom that character chiefly belong'd, did not only express a greater zeal than others in advanceing the projects relateing to Religion, but by pretending to be a condidate of it himself proued, inefect, the ruin both of it, and the King too, in the end; it may be wonder'd, what should prompt a man that seem'd to be at the top of his expectation, to cut the ground away from under his own feet, and destroy the Government wherein he had the greatest share of authority and advantage; for which reason, I dare not say, it was his primary intention, but when he found the King in a dangerous situation (which he had the chief hand in leading him too) he thrust him forward towards the precipice, to gain an intrest with him he saw was about to supplant him: Besides, his extravagant expences made him seek forreign pensions; for which service was expected, and it was not to be wonder'd at, if he ruin'd one master since he serued so many, for besides the Prince of Orange, he had a pension from the King of France as his most Christian Majesty acquainted the King after the Reuolution, and tould him, he always thought it was by his aprobation, which to be sure the King would never haue suffer'd, had he known it; he was therefore of the most mercinary temper in the world, and with the greatest professions of fidelity and friendship, ment nothing but himself; was always forward to court the prevailing partie, and as ready to abandon it whenever the wind turn'd, and was so fearfull of being too late at every chang, that his caution run before the danger, and therefore never fail'd to make an intrest with him from whom it was aprehended: It was for this

reason he courted the Duke of York in the late reign when he
thought him in a prosperous way, and as treacherously
abandon'd him when he fancy'd him like to be overpower'd;
then again he moued heaven and earth to recouer his favour
at his return from Scotland, and most especially at his
accession to the Throne, and yet kept a correspondence with
the Duke of Monmouth who was then the dangerous Riual;
and when the Prince of Orange's turn came to try for it, his
settled principle led him into the same method, which his
Ladys constant correspondence with the Princess of Orange,
and his Vncle Henry Sidney's residence there, gaue him a
favourable occasion of doing; all therefore that can be
presum'd to extenuate his guilt, is by supposeing, that since the
secure enjoyment of his imployment and pleasures, was the
ultimate end of his actions, it was indifferent to him whether he
ow'd them to his natural Sovereign, or an other, and thō
perhaps he might not wish success to the invader, preferable
to the Prince he Served; yet by endeavouring to secure himself,
at all hazards, in the possession of his imployments, he of
necessity concur'd to the ruin of him, he so undeservedly ow'd
them too; but his own justification which he publishéd after
the Reuolution will scarce allow us to put so favorable a
construction upon his intentions, he pretends indeed he
opposed those councells that were displeasing to the publick, and
when he could not hinder them, owns he should have quitted;
but instead of that, he quitted his Religion (or pretended to do
it) to secure a predominant credit, which, he Says, he made
use of to the publick good; and it soon appear'd by the high
encomiums he giues of the Prince of Orange's undertakeing,
that the publick good he aimed at, and for which he made that
change, was that Prince's success; which he contribited to by
his conduct all along, but most particularly at last by
disswading the King from accepting the offers made by France,

T O M.
III.
1686.

which infallibly had disapointed that Prince's attempt; nor is it probable that the Prince of Orange, who was never too lavish of his favours to English men, would haue made a person of so infamous a character his prime minister behind the courtin, had he not by some extraordinary secret Seruice, merited a preference before So many others who had Signelized their zeal, So highly in his cause.

The King establishes a Secret Council by My Lord Sunderland's advice.

But to return from this digression, which seem'd necessary to shew, from what fountain the King's misfortunes chiefly sprung; this cunning Statesman when he found his credit prety well established, the first step he made, to gain the King wholy to himself, and exclud not only My Lord Rochester, but any others whose intrest or abilitys might giue the least jealousie;

KING JAM.
LOOSE SHEETS
pag. 17.

" he perswaded the King to apoint some of the most " considerable Catholicks to meet at certain times either at his " office, or at Mr Chivins's, to consult of matters relateing to " Religion, and he pretending to be much inclin'd too and " at the last professing himself a Catholick, was not only " admitted but soon had the chief direction of this Secrect " juncto; it was a sort of Committee from the Cabinet Council " it self, whither by degrees he drew all business and by consequence made himself Vmpire of the whole transactions relateing to the government; he took care that those who were admited into it, should be too weak heads to controwle him, and yet fit instruments by their credit with the King, to work his ends by: for such was the diffidence his Majesty had of his own judgment, that he oft times follow'd the Councells of much weaker men, that he might not seem opiniatre in his own, or out of a condiscention to those he thought his friends, and that they realy design'd his good. Indeed my Lord Arundell of Wardour before he was superanuated, might have deserued a place in that assembly (but it matters not which way a disability comes) but as for

the rest, which was Father Petre, the Marques of Powis, the
Lord Bellasis, and Dover, and some time after My Lord
Castlemain; it is no disparagement to them, to say, they were
very unequally match'd, with one of the most cunning,
dissembling, and designing statesmen of his time.

One of the first resolutions of this Council was to send "
My Lord Castlemain on a Solemn Embassy to Rome, the "
King was perswaded it was sutable to his dignity to be "
represented in that Court by a *Titulado*, as they term'd it; "
and he haveing been a sufferer and tryd for his life, in Oates "
his Plot, was supposed a proper person for that imployment, "
and to moue his Holyness in favour of what the King was "
perswaded too, rather than he thought fit to Commision him: "
for his Majesty knew well enough, that this piece of ostentation
would signify little there, as to any sollid good, and would
create great jealousies and suspicions at home, besides he had
already sent thither Mr Caryll a gentleman of greater abilitys
as well as estate, and one much more capable of executeing
such a Commission, and which he had accordingly perform'd
with great fidelitie, privacy, and success, which made it of
little expence to the King, and no dissatisfaction to the people;
his business, besides the common compliment of advertising
his Holyness of his Majestys Accession to the Throne, was to
desire D^{tr} Leiburn, then resideing in that Court, might be
made Bishop *in partibus* for England, and to Sollicite a
Cardinal's Cap for Prince Regnaldo D'Esté, the Queen's
Vncle: the former demand was readily granted, but the
other the Pope demurred too; for besides the common maxim
of that Court, never (if possible they can avoid it) to make
Princes Cardinals, a Prince of that family was still less
agreable than any other, by reason of the antient pretentions
of that house to the Dukedome of Ferarey; and that once a

Mr Caryll
first, and
afterwards
My Lord
Castlemain,
was sent to
Rome.
KING JAM:
LOOSE SHEETS
pag. 17.

Cardinal of that name, had caused great disturbance at Rome;
but what weighed most with him, was an aprehention of his
sideing with the French faction, to which his Holyness had a
mighty adversion: but Mr Caryll finding wher the shoo
pinched, made a conditional proposal, not doubting but it
would be aproued of by the King his master, Whether upon
the Prince D'Estés engagement, not to concern himself with any
intrest but that of England, the Pope would agree to it; which
his Holyness (being desirous to oblige the King, and overlooking
other difficultys) promised he would; but before this matter was
settled, the other Embassy was resolued on, from which every
thing was expected and almost nothing obtain'd.

The King
perswaded to
make Father
Petre a Privy
Councellor,
and to demand
a Cardinall's
cap for him.
KING JAM:
LOOSE SHEETS
pag: 15.

The chief occasion of this unseasonable negociation, wherein
the King's intrest with his people was so little managed, was
the obtaining certain spiritual honours for Father Petre, over
" whom My Lord Sunderland had got such an ascendant,
" and by him so great a power with the King, that he was
" now in a manner, become sole minister: he saw the King
had a personal kindness for that Father, which he endeavour'd
to highten by the huge commendation he gaue of his abilities;
his Majesty was charm'd, to find a Person he afected so much,
extoll'd at that rate by one he knew to be no ill judg of
capacitys, while Father Petre himself, (who was indeed a
plausible but a weak man, and had only the art by an abundance
of words to put a Gloss upon a weak and shallow judgment)
was the more easily dazled with the dust which this cunning
Statesman cast in his eyes, so he took him for an unfain'd
friend, and did him all the good offices he could in return;
whereas, this artefull dissembler, did but dress him up, like a
victime for the sacrifice, which gain'd him the King, without
loosing the people; for he not only supported his credit with his
Majesty, by it, but screen'd himself from the Kingdom's hatred

too ; he knew that Father's Caracter would draw the odium of
all displeasing Councells upon himself, and so, be both an
instrument, and a cloke to all his dark designs.

T O M.
III.
1686.
KING JAM:
LOOSE SHEETS
pag: 15.

Hence it came that the King, contrary to his own judgment ”
and the Queen's advice made Father Petre a Privy ”
Councellor (thō he was not sworn till some time after) for ”
assoon as the Queen heard what was design'd, she ernestly ”
beg'd of the King not to do it, that it would giue great Scandal ”
not only to Protestants, but to thinking Catholicks and even ”
to the Societie it self, as being against their rule ; notwith- ”
standing which the King was so bewitched (to use his ”
Majestys own words) by My Lord Sunderland, and Father ”
Petre, as to let himself be prevail'd upon to doe so undiscreet ”
a thing. ”

This however was not the only bait, this cunning Lord had
cast in Father Petre's way, he proposed that his Majesty should
ask a Cardinal's cap for him, as was said before, and that to be
sure was the main drift of this pompous Embassy to Rome ; ”
which had been the result also of a former consultation soon ”
after his Majestys Accession to the Throne, betwixt this Lord, ”
Father Petre, Mr Germin, and My Lord Tyrconnel, where ”
it was agreed that Father Petre should be a Cardinal, Lord ”
Sunderland Lord Treasurer, Lord Tyrconnel Lord Lieftenant ”
of Ireland (who engaged to procure My Lord Sunderland ”
fiue thousand pounds per annum out of that Kingdom, or ”
fifty thousands pounds in mony) and that Mr Henry ”
Germin should be made a Lord, and Captain of the Hors ”
Guards ; the last was soon executed, which made My Lord ”
Tyrconnel expostulate with My Lord Sunderland, the delay ”
of his part of that contriuance, and threaten'd to acquaint ”
his Maty with the whole design, if not speedily comply'd ”
with : tis probable this Message had its intended efect, being ”
My Lord Tyrconnel was sent soon after in that Quality into

KING JAM:Mem
To:9. Pag.387.

T O M.
III.

1686.

My Lord
Castlemain
sent out on his
Embassie in
September,
1686.

King Jam.
Loose Sheets
pag. 18.

Ireland, it was but fitting therefore to think of Father Petre in the next place; but Mʳ Caryll who was then at Rome, they knew to be a man of too much judgment to giue blindly into all their measures, they aprehended his arguments might influence the King against so indiscreet a thing, the first step was therefore to recal him, and send (as was sayd) My Lord Castlemain in his stead; who thō he was a fitter instrument for their purpose, he was much less fit for the imployment, for being of a hot and violent temper, and meeting with a *Pope no less fixed and positiue in his determinations, they jarr'd in almost every point they went upon; The Ambassador thought his apeareing there from one of the most powerfull Princes of Europe, and a Convert too, should haue mett with no denyalls of any kind, but the Pope haueing a mighty aversion to the French intrest (which the King, thō in a private business only, to oblige an old friend the Mareschal d'Humiers, had imprudently concern'd himself in) and no ways afecting the Order of the Jesuits, which this Embassie principally related too, in the person of Father Petre; created in conclusion, such heats and misunderstandings, that My Lord Castlemain thinking himself injur'd, writ his reasons and caus'd them to be published; which gaue so great offence to that Court, that he receiud a flat denyal as to Father Petre, and thō the Prince D'Esté was made a Cardinal, the Pope declared it was not at " the Ambassador's request: the only thing he succeeded in,

---

* Welwood in his Memoirs, (page 185.) says, that "Lord Castlemain had severall audiences of the Pope, but to little purpose, for whenever he began to talk of business, the Pope was seasonably attacked with a Fit of Coughing, which broke off the Ambassador's discourse for that time, and obliged him to retire. These Audiences and Fits of Coughing continued from time to time, while Castlemain continued at Rome; and were the subject of diversion to all but a particular Faction at that Court." EDITOR.

was a permission for the King, to name three Vicar generals " **T O M.**
more, Viz: Dr Giffard, Dr Smith, and Father Elice, a " **III.**
Benedictin Monk, who the King caused soon after to be " 1686.
consecrated accordingly; immagining that character would "
be less disgustfull to his Protestant Subjects then to take the "
titles of Bishoppricks in England, thō the contrary had been "
constantly practised in Ireland. *For which reason** it was
wished by many, that the Bishops had been made Ordinarys
(thō not of any particular Bishoprick) yet of some part of
England, as in reality their districts were divided; whereby
they had been less dependant on the Court of Rome, and more
agreeable to the humour as well as the antient Laws of the
Kingdom.

But it was impossible for the King to doe the least thing in SomeCatholick
favour of Religion, which did not giue disgust, notwithstanding Chappells set up.
all his precautions not to break in upon his engagement; and
that the liberties he permited to Catholicks should no ways
interfere with the possessions, priviledges, and immunities of
the Church of England; however the Kingdom was so generally
prepossess'd that the King's intentions were otherwise, that
nothing apear'd indifferent to them in that matter, they "
grumbled at his takeing the Chappel of St James' into his " KING JAM.
own hands, which then lay useless, thō to avoid all reasonable " LOOSE SHEETS. pag. 18.
cause of complaint he took care to leaue the Chappel of "
Whitehall to the Protestants, and built one there from the "
ground for his own use; he settled 14 Benedictin Monks in "
that of St James', and gaue leaue to the Jesuits to build one "
in the Savoy, and Settled a Colledg there for the education "
of Children, in which they had so good Success that in a "
little time there was at least two hundred Catholick Scollars, "

* Inserted by the Son of James the second, instead of ye word *But.*

T O M.
III.
1686.

" and about as many Protestants who were no ways constrain'd
" in their Religion or required to assist at Mass, or any of their
" publick devotions ; the Recolet Franciscan Fryers built a
" Chappel in Lincolnsinn fields, and some Carmes settled in
" the Citie ; in the Country likewise several Catholick Chappels
were erected, but all upon new foundations, keeping rigorously
to his Majestys engagement not to seize upon any thing, which
the Church of England could lay the least clame or pretence
too.

The 12 Judges
opinion about
dispensing
power.

But all this caution could not cure the jealousies and
aprehentions people were in, for though the King took care
not to trespass upon *what belong'd* * *to* others, he suffer'd
or rather encouraged an imprudent zeal in erecting more
Chappels, than there were faithfull sufficient to fill, or
Priests to be found well qualifyd to officiate in ; which did
but unnecessarily expose the holy misteries to the mockery
and dirision of the people; as did likewise the suffring Monks
and Fryers to appear in their habits, which irritated and
allarmed them without any essential good, or advantage to
Religion. This made every step of that nature be conceiu'd as
an incroachment, if not upon Religion, at least upon the Laws,
of which kind none stuck more with them than the admiting
Catholicks into the Army, which was conceiud to be an absolute
breach of the Test Act ; by which all persons, besides takeing
the oathes, were obliged, under the penalty of forfeiting fiue
hundred pounds, to receiue the Sacrament, according to the
rites of the Church of England, within Six months after their
admission into any imployment civil or military ; but the King
imagined to himself that Act was not binding upon him, and

King Jam:
loose papers
pag. 2.

" one great inducement not to boggle at dispenseing with it,
" was his calling to mind that in the late King's time, after his

---

* Interlin'd as before. EDITOR.

return from Scotland, and that he began to be much imployd "
in his business, Mr Herbert then Chief Justice of Chester "
tould him, That if he desired to reenter into his former "
imployment, he could make it apear, it was in the King's "
power to dispense with the Test Act; upon which, my Lord "
Chief Justice Jeffreys was discours'd with on the point, who "
agreed it might be done, only differ'd in some Law terms no "
ways material, which happening before his Majestys Accession
to the Throne, could not be presumed to come from partiality or
intrest; however he was resolved to sift that point to the
bottom, on which so much depended, and for that end
convened the twelve Judges in the Exchequer chamber, whom
he took to be at all times, and especially in the recess of
Parliament, the undoubted interpreters of the sense and
purport of their acts; to them therefore it was proposed,
whether the King might dispense with any man's taking the
Oaths and Test, before he was admitted to hould any office or
place of trust in the Kingdom; who after a solem debate
agreed unanimously (all but one) That the King was an
independent Prince, that the Laws of the Kingdom was the
King's Laws, that the Kings of England might dispense with
all Laws that regarded penaltys and punishment, as oft as
necessity required, and were themselves judges, of the necessity
when such dispensations were expedient; and lastly, that the
Kings of England could not renounce the prerogatiues annexed
to the Crowne:

This cleere decision in the King's favour, (whatever cavils or
exceptions might be mayd to it by learned men in the Law)
his Majesty took to be a full Vindication of his proceedings, he
had no other rule to go by, nor no other oracle to apply to for
exposition of difficult and intricate points; however to set
things if possible in a cleerer light, and that no pretence might
be taken of its being surreptitiously obtain'd, the matter was

judicially tryd in S' Edward Hale's case, against whom an
action was brought on the Stat. of the 25ᵗʰ Car. 2: c: 2. for the
penalty of fiue hundred pound, on account of his executing
the office of a Coll: of Foot without taking the Communion,
Oaths, and test; to which the Defendant pleaded, he had a
dispensation under the broad Seal, to act *non obstante* the
Statute: to this the Plaintiue demurr'd, and in conclusion,
judgment was given for the Defendant, that his plea was good.

My Lord Chief Justice Herbert before whome this Cause was
brought, besides his eminent learning and known integrity
sufficient to free him without other proof from the censure of
partiality however for his further vindication when he found
the world alarm'd at it, published his reasons with some of the
many citations and examples he might haue brought from the
Law books; which put the matter so far beyond dispute, that
all the erudition of his adversarys, or malice of his detractors
could never furnish them with the least colour of a reply; tis
true he separates the case which had been brought before him,
from the declaration for liberty of conscience, because he tys
himself up to his own personal defence; but the authoritys he
brings, are as aplicable to one as the other; and because this
rais'd so great a clamour against the King, and was urged as
a main argument for the *peoples* * defection afterwards, it is
necessary for his Majestys vindication to shew, how unjustly
he was aspers'd and traduced on this account, by citeing some
of the reasons he went upon; by which it will appear, that the
actions of the best and most cautious Princes, are Seldom so
well warented as this appear'd to be.

My Lord Cook says, It was ever held an unquestion'd
axiom in the Law, that evills that are only such because they
are prohibited, may be dispensed with by the King; *for in as*

---

* Interlined as before. EDITOR.

much (says the book) *as an Act of Parliament which generally* T O M.
prohibits any thing upon a penalty, which is popular, or only giuen III.
to the King, may be inconvenient to divers particular persons, in 1686.
respect of persons, time, and place, for this reason the Law gives a
power to the King to dispence with particular persons: it is
certain, there is no Law whatever but what may be dispens'd
with, by the Law giver, God himself dispens'd with his own
Law when he commanded Abraham to Sacrifice his Son, but
as for human Laws, since they may be too wide or too narrow,
and that it is impossible to foresee all inconveniences, nothing
can be more reasonable, than that a power should be vested in
the Prince to dispence with certain Laws, which relate only to
Government and prohibit things which are not *mala in Se.*

This power is no where more fully determin'd and establish'd
than in the year book of Henry the 7th, *There is a diversity* fol. 11. and 12.
(says it) *betwixt malum prohibitum and malum in se ; as the Statute*
forbids any man to coin mony, if he does he shall be hanged, this
is malum prohibitum, for before the Statute, coining of mony was
lawfull, but now it is not So, and therefore the King may dispense
with it, but cannot giue a man leaue to kill an other, because it is
malum in se, and yet the King may pardon that too, which shews
the difference betwixt pardons and dispensations, the former
only remits the penalty due to the fault, the other giues a right
and power to doe what is otherways prohibited; from whence
it follow'd, that since it was lawfull for any man before the
Statute, to bear an office without takeing the Test, &c,
therefore the King's dispensation made it Lawfull for Sʳ. Ed:
Hales to bear one since.

The case of Sheriffs, which was also resolued by all the Sta: 23. H:C.
Judges in Henry the 7th time, is still if possible a stronger cap: 8.
proof of the legality of what the King did; The Statute
disables the partie to take, and the King to grant it, enacts
that no man shall be Sheriff aboue a year, that all letters

T O M.
III.
_____
1686.

patents in that case made for life or years shall be void, that no *non obstante* shall make it good, and that whowever acts by colour of such letters patents, shall forfeit two hundred pound, that he shall ever after be disabled from being Sheriff, and lastly that every pardon for such offence shall be void. Here is a *non obstante* obviated, a penalty granted, the person dis-abled, and the very pardon annul'd, *yet notwithstanding all this, it was* * *determined* by all the Judges of England, that the King's dispensation with that Statute was good ; and a grant made to the Earle of Northumberland to be Sheriff during life, was accounted valid by vertue thereof, and was ever cited as a judged case by Fitz Harbert, Plowden &c.

Fitz: Tit:
Grants 33.
Plowd: Com-
mentarys
pa: 502.
Cook 12
Report
pag: 18.

But My Lord Cook whose authority cannot be suspected as too favorable to the prerogatiue, sets this matter in a more perspicuous light, *No Act* (says he) *can bind the King from any prerogatiue which is sole and inseparable to his person, but that he might dispence with it, by a non obstante ; as for example a Sovereign power to command any of his Subjects to Serue him for the publick Weal, and this is soly and inseperably annexed to his person, and this royal power cannot be restrain'd by any Act of Parliament neither in Thesi nor Hipothesi, but that the King by his royal prerogatiue might dispence with it ; for upon the commandement of the King and obedience of the Subject does his government con-sist, as it is provided by the Statute of the 23ᵈ of H: the 6 cap: 8: that all patents made, or to be made of any office of as Sheriff, &c, for terme of years or life in fee simple or intail, are void and of no effect &c: yet the King by his royal Sovereign power of Commanding may command any man, by his Patent (for such causes as he in his wisdome does think fit, meet, and profitable for himself and the Common weal, and of which he himself is Soly Judg) to serue him and the weal publick as Sherif of such a County for years or for*

---

* Interlined as before mentioned. Editor.

life &c, and so it was resolved by all the Judges of England in the T O M.
Exchequer chamber 2 H: 7: The same is sayd as to a Welsh- III.
man's being Justice &c: in Wales notwithstanding it is pro- 1686.
hibited by the Act; the like was resolued also by all the Sec: 4 H: 4. Ca: 31.
Judges of England in Calvin's case; the Act of Parliament the 7 Report pag. 14.
8: R: 2: 2: which orders that no man shall be judg of Assise in
his own Country, and that of the 10ᵗʰ: E: 3: 3: that whoever
has a pardon for felony shall find Surities for his good
behaviour or the pardon shall be void, haue been constantly
dispensed with accordingly as occasion required.

Those therefore who stood up in the King's defence, urged,
That besides the general reasons for dispensations with penal
Laws, this particular one, of hindring the King from makeing
use of his Subjects Service, *ought more particularly to * be*
insisted on, as confirm'd by constant practice of all times;
and that it was not possible to shew any disparity betwixt these
cases and the King's makeing use of his Catholick Subjects in
the manner he thought fit to do it; if therefore the King (*sayd
they †*) was led into an errour in point of Law, it was all the
Judges in England that led him into it, and if they err'd, it
was the solem consultations and resolutions of their predecessors
and the reports of the most eminent men of that profession,
that made them er, and if such reports and resolutions be not
Law, what ground had Judges to stand upon? But what (they
Sayd) put the matter beyond all reply, was the clear concession
of the Commons of England in the very point in question; in
Hen: the 5ᵗʰˢ time, the Commons prayd that the Statute for Rot: Par: 1: H: 5. pag: 15.
voiding Aliens out of the Kingdom might be executed, to which
the King agreed, Saveing his prerogatiue that he might dispence
with whom he pleased, and upon this the Commons answer'd,

---

* Inserted by the same writer, instead of, *was most earnestly.* EDITOR.

† Interlined as before. EDITOR.

T O M.
III.
1686.

that their intent was no other nor ever should be, by the Grace of God, and yet, as My lord Chief Justice Herbert obseru'd, there was more danger of inconvenience from Aliens in those days, than from Roman Catholicks now ; the Same was done in reference to the Statute of Provisors. But they alledged, that the clearest concession, and that in a time when the Parliament assumed the greatest authority, was in the 3ᵈ year of King Charles the first, in the debate betwixt the two Houses about the petition of right, where Mʳ. Glanvil a learned man, of himself, but on that occasion speaking the sence of the whole House of Commons, in a business debated (as he Sayd) with the greatest gravity and Solemnity, with the greatest concurrance of opinions and unanimity that ever was; then comeing to the point, deliuers the sence of the Commons in these words, *There is a trust inseperably reposed in the person of the Kings of England, but that trust is regulated by law; for example, when Statutes are made to prohibite things not mala in Se, but only mala quia prohibita, under certain forfeitures and penalties to acrue to the King and to the informers, that shall sue for the breach of them, the Commons must and ever will acknowlidg, the Regal and Sovereign prerogatiue in the King, touching such Statutes that it is in his Majestys absolute and undoubted power to grant dispensations to particular persons, with the clause of non obstante, to doe as they might haue done before those Statutes, wherein his Majesty conferring grace and favour on some, doth not doe wrong to others: but there is a difference between those Statutes, and the Laws and Statutes whereon the petition is grounded; by those Statutes the Subjects haue no intrest in the penaltys, until by sute or information commenced, he become entitled to the particular forfeitures, whereas the Laws and Statutes mentioned in our petition, are of an other nature ; there shall yᵉ Lordshipps find us to rely upon the good old Statute càll'd Magna Charta, which declareth and confirmeth the antient Common Laws of the Liberties of England &c: .... Laws not inflicting penalties upon*

Rushw:
Collec:
1. part.
23 May.
1628.

10

offenders in malis prohibitis, but Laws declaratiue or positiue confirming, ipso facto, an inherent right and intrest of liberty and freedom in the Subjects of his Realm, as their birth rights, and inheritances descendable to their heirs and posterity; Statutes incorporated into the body of the Common Law, over which (with reverence be it spoaken) there is not trust in the King's Sovereign power or prerogatiue Royal to enable him to dispense with it &c:

This instance besides the proof of the point in question was urged in answer to that clamerous objection, that if the King could dispence with one Law he might with an other, and so with all; for he distinguishes in the first place, Laws that concerne government, from Laws that concerne propertie; 2dly those Laws that either prohibite things *mala in se*, or that giue and confirme a right to each particular Subject: it is true, in some of those Statutes, which the King may dispence with, there is a penalty to the informer, but he has no right to it till after conviction, which a dispensation prevents, as Granvil himself obserues; but, Sayd they, should the King dispence with them all, what a miserable condition would the Nation be in? To which it was answer'd, that nothing was more unreasonable than from the possible abuse of a thing, to draw an argument against the thing it Self; that no one doubted but the King could pardon a Robbery and Murther, but should he pardon all Robbers and Murtherers, one had better liue with Canebals than in England, that the King could create a Peer, but should he make every man in the Kingdom a Peer, he would destroy the legislatiue power, so that there was a high trust reposed in the King, which it was reasonable to beleiue he never would make an unreasonable use of, for that ther was no one point of his Prerogatiue, but might be abused to the ruin of the people in case the King was so minded; in fine, since all agreed that the King might dispence with Laws that prohibite things that are not evil in themselues, they Saw no reason, (they Sayd) how he could be restrain'd by any act of Parliament, either from makeing use of his Subjects; or be depriued of any Royal prerogatiue annexed to his person. These and many other arguments were insisted upon to vindicate the King from haveing acted either arbitrarly, or rashly, and to stop the clamours of prepossess'd and angry men, who pretended that this Test Act was the only Bulworke against Popery, and the sole preservation of Religion, which being dearer to them than their liues and liberties, was as sacred as Magna Charta itself; but others answer'd that these were only big words to strik terrour and inflame the giddy multitude, for if this Law (*sayd * they*) was the only support of the Protestant Religion, *how did it subsist before in former * Reigns?* when Catholicks were both more numerous, and nearer the time of the first Reforme, and that yet they were not wholy restrain'd from publick imployments, not even the Council it self; hence they infer'd that those scatterers of fears and jealousies amongst the people, had more hopes of Success from the temper of the Nation, than any reason or sollid ground of suspicion, there being no probabilitie of a Kingdom's being enslaued by a few Catholicks, thō in imployment; or by a Prince of whom his Subjects entertain'd an inveterate aprehention, even before his Accession to the Throne? or that a handfull of Papists could endanger the Religion and propertie, which millions of Protestants were the keepers of.

The resolution of the Judges about the Ecclesiastical commission which the King Set up.

Thus each partie reason'd in this matter rather in private and amongst themselves, than in publick *or bare faced **, the discontented Partie haveing yet So much defference for the King as not openly to decry his conduct, thō they soon lost that respect, being heated with other disputs, which the King

---

* Inserted by the same Writer for a word that has been blotted out. EDITOR.

had the misfortune to giue rise too soon after; wherein by his too great attention to what might in rigour be warrented by the law, he lost sight of the danger, which the pressing points disagreable to the people is ever sure to bring upon a Prince, *whether they be justifyable or* * *no :* ther was an other question therfore of great moment moued at that time, and which his Majesty thought fit to consult the Judges in likewise, in relation to an Ecclesiastical Commission; it seem'd incongruous to him, that professing a different Religion himself, he should exercise in person that Jurisdiction over the Church of England, which the Law vests in the Sovereign, his Majesty found by them that the power of conferring it upon Commissioners had been inacted in Queen Elizabeth's time, that it was grounded upon the Law which establishes the King's supremacy, and had been practised in former reigns; that thō it was seemingly put down in the 17th of King Charles the first, by forbiding Ecclesiastical Judges to fine, imprison, or tender the oath *ex officio*, yet in the 13th of King Charles the Second it was declared, That nothing therein contain'd should take away the ordinary power, but that they might proceed to exercise, &c, all Ecclesiastical jurisdiction, censures, and coercions apertaining to the Same, according to the King's Ecclesiastical Laws; nay My Lord Cook and all the Judges in his time declared, the King might haue done it by the antient Laws of the Land; and that in the Saveing express'd in those very Acts, which seem'd to annul that power, Vicar Generalls are mention'd amongst other Ecclesiastical Jurisdictions, and by consequence the King's extraordinary power therein was reserued : this made his Majesty think it beyond dispute that his Commission was legal, especially So long as the Commissioners kept within the

* Interlined by the Son of James the 2^d. Editor.

T O M.
III.
1686.

bounds of Ecclesiastical censures, and neither fin'd, imprison'd, nor tender'd oathes *ex officio ;* he thought therefore he could not doe a more gracious act, than to convey that power into the hands of such persons as to be sure would not be byaced against a Religion they themselves profess'd, especially haveing the Arch Bishop of Canterbury at their head, to whom he join'd the Lord Chancellor Jeffreys, the Earle of Rochester Lord High Treasurer, the Earle of Sunderland President of the Council and Secretary of State, the Bishopps of Duresme, and

Rochester, and Sʳ Ed. Herbert chief Justice of the Common pleas ; to these persons he granted (during pleasure) the power of exerciseing all manner of Ecclesiastical Jurisdiction, preheminence, &c, to correct and amend all abuses, which were under the connusance of Ecclesiastical Laws, with power for them, or any three of them (My Lord Chancellor being one) to enquire into all abuses, &c, and to punish by censure of the Church ; to call any Ecclesiastical persons before them, of what degree soever ; to enquire into, and punish their mis-demainors by suspention, or depriveing them of spiritual promotion according to the said Laws ; to punish adultery, or whoever shall be refractory to their orders or authority, to award cost of sute, to inspect and correct, if needful, the Statutes or rules of any Colledges, Scooles, Collegiate Church, &c, or make new ones if wanted, to order their temporals for the best, and to execute that Commission notwithstanding any apeal, &c.

But the Arch Bishop of Canterbury refuseing to act, the Bishop of Chester was put in his room ; it is hard to say what reason he had to shun the exerciseing that jurisdiction which his Majesty was willing to put into his hands, to avoid all danger of its being abused, but when men are angry with their Prince (as he then began to be) they study more how to express their own discontents, than how to appeas them in others, and an occasion soon offer'd itself of doeing it to a great degree.

It was not long after the opening of this Commission, that Dr Sharp Rector of St Giles was complain'd of, for useing reflecting expressions on the King, and his government; upon which his Majesty order'd the * Bishop of London to suspend him: The Bishop replyd in a letter to My Lord Sunderland, he was ready to obey his Majesty in any thing he could with a safe conscience, but that it was contrary to the rules of Law and justice, for him who was judge in the case, to condemn any man before he had knowledg of the fault, and what he could say in his own justification; and sent the D^{r} himself to Windsor (where the Court then was) *with the † letter*; this excuse thō plausible was not taken to be sincere in the bottom, for it was † *easely* immagin'd that the Bishop either knew what he had sayd, or might haue examin'd the matter as juridically as he had pleas'd? and so haue either punished the Offence, or haue justifyd the thing; but the latter he durst not doe, and was not willing, by the former to put a check upon that libertie which now began to be taken of makeing reflections of the like nature; which therefore the King thought behoued him so much the more, to put a stop to if possible, in order to which the matter was brought before the Ecclesiastical Commissioners: who summoneing the Bishop himself, to shew why he disobeyd the King's orders, his answer was, That (as he had been inform'd) he could not doe it by law; the Chancellor sayd, He wonder'd his Lordship knew not the Law better himself in those cases, however if he had any thing to bring in his own vindication, they were ready to hear him; upon

T O M.
III.

1686.
The Bishop
of London
Suspended
ab officio.

The King writ
to the Bishop
of London
June 14:

Aug: 4: 1686.

---

* Henry Compton, youngest son of Spencer, Earl of Northampton, called The Protestant Bishop. EDITOR.

† Interlined as before. EDITOR.

which the Bishop desir'd a coppie of the Commission,
but that looking like a design to quarrel with it, the
Chancellor tould him it could not be allow'd of, and that
it would be too great a wast of time should every one require
it; that he wonder'd in a thing, which concern'd him so much,
he should now be to seek, being the Commission it self was so
publick and that he might so easily haue it; but that if his
Lordship were not ready, they would allow him more time
which was twice done accordingly: at last, after some debate
concerning the Commission, the Bishopp's Councel was heard,
who argued, That there was no such thing in their Laws as
suspention without citation, forme of proceeding, judgment,
and degree; that the order should haue been to Sylence the
D^{tr}, which the Bishop in effect had obeyd, by sending his
Majestys letter to him and adviseing him not to preach, which
advice the D^{tr} had follow'd; but the Commissioners upon full
consideration of that, and all that was urg'd in his favour,
were no ways satisfyd with the plea, they saw plain enough,
that whatever formes were requisit, it was in the Bishopp's
power to haue pursued them, had he been sincere and hearty
in the matter, and that therefore they could put no other
construction upon it, but that either he question'd the King's
authority in Commanding, or had disobeyd what he had
power to command; so Sentence was pass'd upon him, and
he suspended from the function and execution of his Episcopal

office, but not from his benifice or revenue: This was thought
a very harsh proceeding, thō the suspention *ab officio* too, was
taken off soon after; but the King's moderation herein stop'd
not the murmuring of disaffected people, which made him think
it more needfull by some such punishment (if this might be So
call'd) to prevent the infection from spreading, being tould,
that if he tamely suffer'd himself, his actions, and intentions, to
be censur'd and traduced from the Pulpit, the Throne must
soon giue way to it; and since an inspection into their

conduct was necessary, he could not place (as he immagined) the execution of that Office in more disinteress'd hands, than *those of * the* Bishopps of the Church of England, and Chief Officers of the Crown ; and that it was the Archbishop of Canterbury's own fault that he was not of the number himself; and that if after all, there was any hardship in the Sentence, the learned in the Cannon Law ought to (*have*) answer'd for it, and not he who refer'd the matter to them.

This froward disposition of the Clergie and people, which began now to take up a great deal of his Majestys time and exercise his patience so much, hinder'd not however his attention to what ever he conceiud beneficial to the Kingdom, or encouraging to trade; which had he not been obstructed in, nothing could have been immagin'd of that nature, which his Majestys knowledg in the true intrest of the Nation, his prodigious application to business, and his most affectionate care of the good and welfare of the people, would not haue enabled him to haue brought about; for this end he not only concluded a certain peace or good correspondence with the French, in reference to America, but a newtrality there, even in case of a breach in Europe : what gaue occasion to this, was the difficulty of fixing the bounderys betwixt Canada and Hudson's bay, and other territorys of the Crowns of England and France in that part of the world ; the Count d'Auaux was sent from France on purpose to Settle this matter, and the King thought it prudent to prevent by this negociation a falling out about a thing which it was not possible to decide, and to make the union more perfect, they agreed that a peace, unity, and good correspondence, should be obserued betwixt the fortes, Colinies, &c, of both Nations, that they should not

T O M. III.
_____
1686.

A newtrality agreed with the French in America. Nov: 6. 1686.

---

* Interlined as before. EDITOR.

attack or molest each other, nor assist the Indians, with which either of them were in war, nor fish or trade on each others coasts or roads, but that if by stress of wether, they should be driven into each others portes, to be kindly used and furnished with what they should want at reasonable rates; that the King of Great Britan's Subjects inhabiteing the Island of St Christopher might fetch Salt from the Salt pans there, and the French take water in the river of the great road, provided each did it only in the day time, that the Commanders of privateers of both Nations, should giue security at the takeing out their Commissions, not to doe any act contrary to the Treaty, that neither should protect or assist Pirates of any Nation, that all disputes betwixt the Subjects of both Kings should be determined by the Governours of each jurisdiction, where they happen'd, and that in case of a breach between the two Crowns in Europe, there should still remain a firme peace and and neutralitie between their Subjects in America, and that the treaty of Breda and St Christopher should still stand good as formerly.

168$\frac{5}{6}$.
The E. of
Tyrconnell
sent Lord
Deputy to
Ireland in
Feb: 168$\frac{5}{6}$.

BUT the King's Sollicitude for the publick good of his people, was obstructed and hinder'd by the pevish and discontented humour of those he had more reason to expect assistance from: My Lord Clarendon, who was one of the number, was by this time become as uneasy in himself, as he had been to others all along, which put a necessity upon the King of sending My Lord Tyrconnell to * succeed him; he

---

* See the State Letters of Henry Earl of Clarendon (Vol. 2. P. 151.) printed at the Clarendon Press, Oxford, 1763. In a former Letter (Page 142) to the Lord Treasurer, Lord Clarendon thus expressed himself, " Though I have been enough prepared to expect the worst, yet, I confess, I cannot but be

arriued in that Kingdom in February, and assoon as the Earle
of Clarendon heard it, he assembled the Councel at the
Archbishopp of Dublin's house, and there surrender'd the
sword to him, commending in his Speech, the duty and
Loyalty of the people in general, thō he lamented much the
fewds and animositys amongst them ; he used many arguments
to establish the reputation of the Protestants of that Country,
affirming they were of the Church of England's principles,
and not at all fanatically inclined, and had been as early as
any of the King's Subjects in returning in their duty, after
the late rebellion ; enlargeing much in their commendation,
but pretended not thereby (as he Sayd) to derogate from
the Loyalty and merite of the Roman Catholicks, who he
own'd had serued the King and suffer'd so much for him
both at home and abroad : The Earle of Tyrconnell was not
wanting on the other hand, to say what was necessary to calm
the minds of people, and was carefull all along to render
impartiall justice to all parties without regard to Religion ; for
thō his own inclination as well as the King's direction, led him
to shew some encouragement to the Catholicks, who had
labour'd under so long an opression, he was cautious however
neither to disgust or injure others, and therefore by a
proclamation he endeavour'd to stifle a malicious report of
some insendiarys, as if the King design'd to break in upon the

extremely troubled at what you tell me: God's will be done. It is a great comfort,
you are not removed for any fault, and that the King cannot so much as pretend
to be dissatisfied with you. For myself, I shall not be half so much troubled when
my own doom comes, as I am for this upon you : and, as poor as I am, I hope,
God will give both you and me the grace to beg, rather than that we should falter
in the Religion wherein we have been bred ; and for his steady adhering to which
my Father was ruined, which can never be forgotten by me : I am so full at
present, that I cannot say more.   God Almighty preserve the King." — The
same Volume contains the Diary of the same Earl, from 1687 to 1690.   EDITOR.

Laws and constitution of the government; assureing them,
It was far from his Majestys intentions to invade any man's
right, and that he for his part should, pursuant to his orders,
govern according to Law; that he would protect them in their
respectiue properties, and priviledges, and secure all persons,
thō of different perswasions, in the free exercise of their
Religion, provided they remain'd in a dutifull comportement to
the government, and unbyaced allegiance to the King. He
took great care to prevent any irregularitys being commited
by the Soldiers in their quarters or els where, made many
orders for the obseruation of good discipline in the Army, and
good manners amongst all ranks of people, obliged the Soldiers
to be assistant to the civil Majestrates, in secureing Tories,
Robbers, &c, and gaue So much content by his impartial
cariage (that the contrary haveing been expected) he rais'd a
greater esteem of his conduct; and there apear'd a perfect
concord and unity for a considerable time in that Kingdom,
till those fiery spirits and emisarys of the Prince of Orange
began to breathe their infection there, as they had done already
with So much success in other places.

The Rom:
Catholicks
made free of
Corporations
in Ireland.

At his first entrance upon his imployment he had acquainted
the Council with the King's desire, that the Roman Catholicks
might be admited into the freedom of Corporations in that
Kingdom, but being sencible how ill the people would relish
any favour he should ask for Catholicks, he did what he could
to convince them of the advantage it would be to their
temporal concerns, and no damage to their Religion; which he
constantly assur'd them, he would in no manner intrench
upon; whereas this union he desired would unite their
affections, and be a mighty encouragement to trade. This
matter being first proposed to the Citie of Dublin, the Lord
Major call'd a general assembly, who objected that it was
against the Laws of their Corporation, and that they might

forfeit their Charter if they did it : My Lord Leiftenant finding
them avers, thought fit not to press them any further, till he
had tryd the Succeeding Major, who readyly consented to it,
and then the example was follow'd by other Corporations all
ouer the Kingdom.

But the E: of Tyrconnel finding the Citie of Dublin had
made so early an objection on account of their Charter, he
thought it necessary to call it in, togather with others, to avoid
future arguments from that head ; not with intent to take from
them any essential priviledges, but only such niceties as he
conceived were a real obstruction to their true intrest : he
acquainted therefore the Major and Aldermen of Dublin,
with his Majestys desire in that particular, assureing them the
King's intent, in reality, was to augment their priviledges ; but
they began to grow so suspicious of the contrary, that no
reason nor argument could convince them to doe by fair
means, what it would always be in the Sovereign's power to
force them too when he pleased, for they could not be
ignorant that it was morally impossible any Corporation could
be so cautious in all his actings, as not to giue some one blot
which a Sharpe witted Lawier would not fail to hit ; dureing
therefore the several reasonings upon this matter, the Citie
of Dublin sent their Recorder S' Richard Rivers to petition
the King in their behalf, but his Majesty being resolved to
leaue it to the Law, refused to hear him ; and accordingly the
cause comeing to a tryal, judgment was giuen against them,
and the Charter forfeited into the King's hands ; the same
being done in all other Corporations either by volentary
resignation, or a short tryal more for forme than with design
to avoid it, it cost no great trouble except at Londonderry
(a stubborn people as they appear'd to be afterwards) who
stood an obstinate sute, but were forced at last to undergo the
same fate with the rest.

T O M.
III.

1687.

The Charters
call'd in,
in Ireland.

My Lord Tyrconnel to shew the King's intentions were sincere, and that he had nothing so much in view herein, as the publick good and advancement of trade, he made several regulations which were very beneficial to the people, and even stretch'd his power in their favour beyond its due limits, by ventring to repeal the duty layd ·upon Iron, which he knew would bring spanish coin into the Nation; but when that was known in England and found to be contrary to an Act of Parliament there, orders was given to revoke it: however his zeal for the good and welfare of the Country apear'd no less, and whatever their jealousies might be in reference to Religion, it is certain that Kingdom was never in a more flourishing way, than dureing the time he govern'd it.

This dissatisfaction of My Lord Clarendon's was sure to be follow'd by that of his Brother, they had been ever much united in their sentiments, as well as advancement, and fortuned to be so in their disgrace too; thō this proceeded more from a stratagem of his great rival the E: of Sunderland than any dissatisfaction of the King's, or any perhaps of ill will at first in the Treasurer, however he managed it so in the Sequel, as to highten the publick disgust against the King, as much as any thing that had hithertoo happen'd.

The E: of Sunderland, as was sayd before, haveing made use of My Lord Rochester's credit (which he gains by a wheedle) to establish his own; he now (according to certain rules of court gratitude) made it his business to ruin his benefactor, that by possessing the King's favour soly to himself, he might with more security driue on those darke and hidden practices, which the King discover'd not till it was too late to obviate them: It is true he had other sharers still in the King's favour and esteem, but he had the dexterity to make those such usefull instruments to his purposes, that he had no reason either to be envious or jealous of their credit. My

Lord Rochester of all the favorites was the only dangerous spy upon his Councels, whose zeal for the Protestant Religion on one hand, and the King's true intrest on the other, he knew would twart all those measures by which he had cunningly projected to rais his own credit with his Majesty, by puting him upon methods, which visibly lead him to his ruin at last: for in all disputes and difficultys, which had any tendency to Religion, he fail'd not to espouse the opinion which was most favorable in apearance to Catholicks, and by consequence to the King's inclination; and would frequently by his creatures put the King underhand upon measures of that kind, and when his Majesty advised with him about them, would not only aproue, but aplaud the King in his great wisdome for the prudent contrivance of what he himself was the first forger, and few Princes are sufficiently upon their guard, not to to be caught by such artefull flaterers: But My Lord Rochester's aims run directly counter to this, he saw the danger and inconvenience of the King's straining points of Law, and therefore as well for the King's security, as for the advantage of the established Church (of which he was a zealous Member) he opposed all methods which were lyable to the least cavil or objection on that Score. As for other Councellors, My Lord Sunderland had rid himself of the danger of being twarted by them, by hooking all business into that Secret Committee at Mr Chivens's; so that not only the Privy Council was unacquainted with all transactions, till it was resolued they should be made publick, but the Cabinet Council itself was as much a stranger to them as the other, few matters of moment being treated of there, but the reading forreign letters; and even least by that, they might get too much light into affairs, the King was prevail'd with to giue private instructions to his Envoys abroad, never to write any thing but Common news or publick transactions to the Earle of Middleton, the other Secretary of

State; and for matters of consequence to mention them to none
but himself, My Lord Sunderland, or Father Petre: thus he
kept the Veil upon other people's eyes, My Lord Rochester
was the only person whose high imployment and former credit
made capable of giveing him the least jealousie, or opposition,
which made his ruin so necessary to My Lord Sunderland's
establishment, and for which reason it had been all along the
first article in his scheme: The manner he now took to execute
it, was to perswade the King that My Lord Rochester had
great dispositions to change his Religion, and when once that
was done, he might be more freely consulted with; the King
who had a personal kindness for him, wished it extreamly,
and therefore more readily gaue into the belief of it, so upon
occasions press'd him on the point, and as naturally one falls
from proposalls to arguments, and from arguments to heats, it
happen'd accordingly with them; the King finding his inclinations quite otherwise, grew hot and dissatisfyd, and he
perceiveing what was aim'd at grew angry too, and presently
began to immagin he should be forced off the stage, upon
which he resolved with himself to manage his exit so, as to
gain credit with the Church of England partie, and that if he
must loose his intrest at Court, to establish it * *at least* with the
people; so a conference of Devines haveing been proposed,
he foresaw that would be the properest occasion to gain this
point of popularitie, and make the world believe, that he was
turn'd out of his imployment, because he would not turn from
his religion: he readily therefore accepted the offer, and the
Doctors appointed for this conference met accordingly; but
before any point was thorowly handled, or so much almost as
enter'd upon, he rose up abruptly and sayd, He was more
confirm'd in his opinion than before, upon which the assembly

---

*. Interlined as before. EDITOR.

broke up; which shew'd he had taken his resolution before TOM.
hand, and chose this method, not with intent to be better III.
inform'd in his faith, but to make the world believe it was for 1687.
that he suffer'd: so that thō, by his long service to the King
he had merited extreamly well of him, nor dose there apear
any reason to suspect his fidelity or zeal while he remain'd in
it, yet his exit is not to ,be excused from spight and animosity;
since to establish his own credit with the people, he contriv'd
to draw so great an odium upon the King, as to haue it thought,
that no man must expect or possess long any imployment at
Court, that either was not actually, or at least inclined·to
profess the same Religion with the Prince, and indeed the
King's recalling his Commission of Lord High Treasurer at
thʻat time, gaue some colour to the conjecture; whereas the
main motiue for the King's doing that, besides the present
heats and disgust, was his opinion that it was much " King Jam:M⁰ⁿ
properer to haue the treasury manag'd by * Commissioners " To:9. pag.214.
than as it was, and from that time took a resolution accord- "
ingly never to trust it in the hands of a Single person again; "
and thō My lord Rochester seem'd to forget his duty on this
occasion, to the King, yet his Majesty forgot not the obligation
he had to him for his former services; he settled therefore

---

* When the White Staff was taken from Lord Rochester, the Commissioners
appointed for executing his late office of Lord Treasurer were John Lord Bellasis, Sidney Lord Godolphin, (another circumstance says Ralph, which our
Historian of his Own Times has thought proper to forget,) Henry Lord Dover,
Sir John Ernley Chancellor of the Exchequer, and Sir Stephen Fox. — Ralph
after noticing this Event, cites a curious Letter (Vol: 1. p. 941.) from a Jesuit at
Liege, dated Febr: 2. 1686-7, to a brother of his at Friburgh. This Letter is
also quoted by Rapin, and Bishop Burnet, who says, that Dykvelt gave the King
a Copy of it, " He promised to him, he would read it; and he would soon see,
whether it was an imposture framed to make them (the Jesuits) more odious, or not.
But he never spoke of it to him afterwards. This Dykvelt thought, was a confessing
that the letter was no forgery." (Vol 2. p. 421. 8ᵛᵒ; Ed:) EDITOR.

4000^{lt} per an: upon him for his life, and 1200^{lt} per an: land of inheritance, which made his exit rather a profitable exchange, than a dishonorable dismission; however he seem'd then to haue a longing after an other intrest, so beg'd leaue to go to the Spaw in Germany under pretence of health, but with design undoubtedly to See the Prince of Orange in his way; but the King aware of that, gaue him free leaue to go to the Spaw provided he went not into Holland: This answer of the King's gravell'd him extreamly, for had he not gon at all, after this, it would haue apear'd too manifestly what was his primary intention; so he durst not but go, thō he durst not disobey the King in the other point, and therefore when the Prince of Orange heard where he was, and found he had not pass'd by him, took it for a slight; which lost his credit in both places, and was probably the occasion of his being so little *regarded** by that Prince when he had got the reines into his hands.

The King resolves upon granting a liberty of Conscience.

This defection of those his Majesty had hithertoo put the greatest confidence in, and the sullen disposition of the Church of England partie in general, made him think it necessary to reconcile another, and yet he hoped to do it in such a manner, as not to disgust quite the Church men neither; but by assurances of protection to them, prevent their repineing at the indulgence he purposed to grant to others, and so to settle he hoped his government upon such a foundation, as might unite his people to him by inclination as well as duty; he found that all the endeavours of the four last reignes to reduce the Kingdom to an exact conformity in Religion, had proued unsuccessfull, that on the contrary it had bred animositys and made parties, depopulated the Country and been a great hindrance to trade; he doubted not but liberty of conscience

---

* Inserted by the Son of James 2^d, instead of the word *trusted*. EDITOR.

would haue a contrary efect, he consider'd how much it would
conduce to preserue peace amongst the people, and to take
away that handle, which factious spirites had all along made
use of, to foment those civil broils the Nation had so lately
groan'd under; for it is so natural for sufferers in Religion to
seek redress, that discontented persons count upon them as sure
instruments of their malicious purposes, a man who perhaps
upon his own intrest cannot rais twenty men, shall be formidable
to a government, by haveing thousands at his command
who ly under a pressure of conscience; but besides these
advantages, and the eas it was so natural for him to giue his
Subjects of his own perswasion, it always was his settled
opinion, that men's consciences ought not to be forced : Upon
these considerations, therefore, the King had been resolved
ever since the begining of this year, to grant by proclamation
an indulgence, or libertie of * conscience; being fully convinced
both by the judgment in S^r. Ed: Hales case, and the opinion
of all the Judges except M^r. Baron Street, that he might by
vertue of his prerogatiue do it; he perceiu'd the Parliament
had shewn a great aversness to any such councells, and he
thought it needless to run the hazard of a refusall, by asking
their consent to what he was advised he had full power to doe
of himself; not, but that he intended to get them if possible
to confirme it afterwards ; but he knew very well, that to desire
their help for doing that, which he was assured he had authority
to do without them, was in efect to divest himself of that
prerogatiue, and then stand to their pleasure whether they

---

* Published April 4th: This had been preceded by some remarks on the subject
which appeared in the Gazette, March 21. See Ralph's History, (*Vol.* 1. *P.* 945.)
who observes, that there is in Lord Somers Tracts, an Almanac for this year,
call'd the Catholic Almanac, printed by Hills, the King's Printer, *for the use of
His Majesty's Household and Chapel.* EDITOR.

would permit him the exercise of it or no ; as it fared oft times with former Kings, who to take the odium of harsh actions from themselves call'd for a Parliamentary aid when noways needfull, which they were sure ever after to clame as a priviledge and insist upon as not faisable without them.

It is certain that the first apearance of such a dispensation wherein the Religion and Laws seem equally concern'd, alarm'd a people jealous of both, and which they conceiued to be so twisted togather with their civil rights and liberties, that whatever struck at one must necessary wound the rest ; they knew not where it might stop when once a breach was made ; it being insinuated that the dispensing with one Law, layd all the rest at mercy, they could not therefore conceive, but the allowing the King such a power was a delivering up all mens liues, liberties, and properties to his Majesties pleasure : but the King on the other hand, both himself in person, when occasion offer'd, and by his friends more universally through the Kingdom, endeavour'd to shew, how unreasonably they suspected his justice and moderation in this affair, assureing them that if they would but weigh the reasons as well as authoritys on which that opinion was grounded, it would appeas their aprehention, and prevent in great measure their dissatisfaction upon the point, for they were tould (as was sayd before) that this power was restrain'd to such Laws only as prohibited things not evil in themselves, 2dly to such as vest no propertie in the subject, and therdly that the King's intent was chiefly to haue a libertie of makeing use of his Subjects as he thought good, which My Lord Cooke sayd was a power so inseperably annexed to his Royal person, that no Act of Parliament could restrain it ; whereby all the danger (they sayd) was reduced to this, Whether the King were likely to make an unreasonable use of this power, which was so limited, that there was scarce room to do it if he would : but if there

were, it was a harsh censure upon his Majestys conduct to
fancy, he would extend it farther than in prudence he conceiu'd
it for the general good of the Nation, and that if they thought
it too great a hazard that any trust should be put in the Prince,
they might as well blame Providence for ordering matters so,
as that men should be under a necessity of trusting almost all
sortes of people they haue to deal with in the world, that
Lawiers, Phisitians, Seruants, Traidsmen, &c, had it in their
power to ruin or distroy us if they pleas'd, and yet there was
no liveing without them; it was urged therefore on the King's
behalf, that if a Prince must haue no power allow'd him, nor
no trust put in him, but such, as it is not possible for him to
abuse, he must haue none at all; and that if Laws were so
sacred that they must in no manner be infringed, what was the
meaning of a Court of Chancery? that the fate of each man's
estate which comes to be tryd there, lys in the breast of a
Chancellor, who had no power but what he deriued from the
Commission of his Prince, and that it could not be immagined
but the Prince himself might be trusted as well as those, that
acted by his authority? that he was trusted with the power of
makeing peace or war, with life and death, which weere
greater trusts than the dispensing with a few penal Laws,
which besides the prudential motiues his Majesty had to lay
them aside as the great advantage it would be to trade, as well
as an eas to his dissenting subjects, besides the opinion of the
Judges, and the solemn judgment given in the case, they had
too great an opposition to the Law of God to be counted
irrefragable; that no one ever doubted but the precept of
Honour thy Father and Mother, exacted an obediance to
Temporal Princes as well as to natural parents; that no law
therefore made by men could annull this obedience to the King,
nor prohibite under a temporal mulct, or punishment, a subject
from serveing his Lawfull Prince (when call'd), who is obliged

to it under the penalty of an eternal one ; that there was no doubt but the general axiom of the Law, That no Act of Parliament can restrain the King from commanding his Subjects to serue him, had its origin from thence, for as My Lord Cooke explain'd it, The essence of Government consists upon the commandement of the King, and obedience of the Subjects, and cites the Statute of the 23ᵈ of Hen. the 6ᵗʰ that provides accordingly.

There being therefore so many reasons that seem'd to convince the King of the power of what he might do, it is not to be wonder'd if he made not so due an attention as otherwise he might, upon what was prudent to be done.; for besides the confidence it was natural for him to haue in the subjects of his own Religion, he was convinced by the example of several forreign Countrys (where trade florished most) that nothing could be more benificial to it than libertie of conscience, that it was the Support of Holland, and that the want of it in England, had not only crampt its trade, but had furnished the seeds of Several rebellions, which had no other origin than one Religion's Lording it over the rest; and he hoped the people would haue so much confidence in him, as not to immagin he would make an unreasonable use of his power or trust, which the Law vested in the Kings of England, being well assured that never any of his Ancestors, had a greater affection for his Country, and zeal for the peoples good, besides the repeated promises that he would in no wise prejudice their liberties or Religion : so that if the King used certain methods for obtaining their aprobation, which were not so agreeable (and as some thought so justifyable) it is very suspicious to whose councels it was oweing. My Lord Sunderland (as he afterwards declared) did nothing (thō never so seemingly oposite) but with a view of serveing the ends of those, who were most zealous for the establissed Church, he saw likewise that libertie of

Conscience was so reasonable a thing that no impartial man
could suspect, it would be ruinous or distructiue to any Religion,
that pretended to be built upon a rock, and by consequence
could not in reason be afraid of being shaken or baffled by the
members of any other perswasion ; that it would be scandalous
to express a fear of shewing its face against an adversary, and
never think herself secure but while screen'd under the severity
of penal Statutes ; it is probable therefore that what he could
not obstruct by reason and argument, he endeavour'd to spoil
by encourageing such methods of bringing it about (especially
when the King attempted the getting it confirm'd by Act of
Parliament) as was sure to crush it in the end ; and so by
humouring and improveing the King's inclination, to forward
this matter, by disgustfull methods in the eye of the people,
and ruinous to himself, it proued abortiue in the end ; which,
had more prudent and pleasing ways been chozen, could not
possibly haue fail'd of Success.

The resolution being taken, it was thought proper to begin
with Scotland ; they had sufficiently acknowledg'd his Majestys
power, in the preamble to the late Act for settling the excise
upon the King, wherein they declared their abhorrance of all
principles and positions, which were contrary or dirogatory to
the King's sacred, supreme, Sovereign, and *absolute power* and
authority, and in an other Act they ordain'd that all Subjects
should sweare to defend, assert, and mentain the King's *absolute
power*, &c : The King therefore immagin'd, that if he exceeded
the bounderys of his legal power, in this, it was the Parliament
it self that lead him astray ; for that what he did could never
be sayd to go beyond an absolute power, which they had both
allow'd him, and sworne to mentain. He writ therefore to the
council at Edinburgh, that he thought fit to giue an additional
eas to tender consciences, and convince the world of his
moderation in Religion ; that it should not hinder his particular

T O M.
III.

1687.

Libertie of
Conscience
published in
Scotland,bear-
ing date the 18.
February 1687.

T O M.
III.
——
1687.

care of the Clergie, and that thō he design'd to giue some eas to such, whose principles he could best trust, that he could noways allow of those enimies of Christianity, as well as of humain Society, the field Conventiclars, and therefore recommends to them the prosecuteing that sort of people with the utmost rigour of the Laws; he doubted not (he sayd) but his proclamation would apear as just and reasonable to them, as it did to him, and that they would assert and defend his royal prerogatiue, which he was resolued to mentain in that splendor and steadyness as was necessary for his own safety, the support of his friends, and terrour of his enemies; that he did not encroach upon any peoples consciences, and was resolved not to suffer others to do, what he would not do himself: he order'd therefore his proclamation to be published, and a due obedience to be had to it, which if any refused, he desired to be informed that he might convince them of his being in ernest.

Pursuant hereunto the Proclamation was published bearing date the * 18 of February 168⅞, which contain'd in substance, That he being resolued to unite the hearts and affections of his Subjects to God in Religion, to him in loyalty, and to their neighbours in Christian loue and charity, he had therefore thought fit by his Sovereign authority, prorogatiue Royal, and absolute power, which all his Subjects were to obey without reserue, to giue and grant his Royal toleration to the several professors of the Christian religion after named; first he allows and tolerates the moderate Presbiterians to meet in their priuate houses only, but that the feild Conventiclars be prosecuted according to the utmost Severities of the Laws; he tolerates in like manner yᵉ Quakers to meet and exercise in their form in any places apointed for their worship, and then says, that

---

* The Experiment of the Declaration, according to *Sir J. Dalrymple*, was first tried in Scotland, Feb: 12. (*Memoirs, Vol:* 1. *p.* 166.) EDITOR.

considering the severe Laws made against Roman Catholicks T O M.
(therein call'd Papists) in the minority of our Royal Grand III.
father, without his consent, and contrary to the duty of good 1687.
Subjects, by his Regents and other enemies to their Lawfull
Sovereign, our Royal Grand mother Queen Mary of blessed
and pious memory, wherein under the pretence of Religion
they cloked the worst of treasons, factions, and usurpations,
and made these Laws not as against the enemies of God but
their own, which laws haue still been continued, of course
without design of executeing them *ad terrorem* only, upon
supposition that the Papists (relying on an external power) were
incapable of duty and true allegience to their natural Sovereigns;
we of our certain knowledge and long experience knowing,
that the Catholicks as it is their principles to be good Christians,
so it is to be dutifull Subjects, and that they haue likewise on
all occasions shewn themselves good and faithfull Subjects to
us and our Royal predecessors, do therefore with the advice
and Consent of our privy Council, by our Sovereign authority,
prerogatiue Royal, and absolute power, suspend, stop, and
disable all Laws or Acts of Parliament made or exercised
against any of our Roman Catholick Subjects in any time past,
to all intents and purposes, makeing void all prohibitions
therein mentioned, pains, or penaltis therein ordain'd to be
inflicted; so that in all things they shall be as free as any of
our Protestant Subjects, not only for the exercise of their
Religion, but for enjoyment of offices &c.: and whereas the
obedience of our Subjects is due to us by their allegiance, and
our Soveraignty, and that no Law, difference in Religion, or
other impediment what so ever, can exempt the Subjects from
their natiue obligations to the Crown, and considering that some
Oathes are capable of being wrested by men of sinistrous
intentions, we therefore cass, annull, and discharge all Oaths
whatsoever, by which any of our Subjects are incapacitated

from houlding places or offices in our Sayd Kingdom &c: instead of which the following Oath was injoin'd : I, A: B, do acknowlidg, testify, and declare, that King James the 7th &c: is rightfull King and supreame governor of this Realm and over all persons therein, and that it is unlawfull for Subjects. upon any pretence whatever, to rise in armes against him or any commission'd by him, and that I will never resist his power and authority, or ever oppose his authority, or his person, as I shall answer to God, but to the utmost of my power assist, defend, and mentain him, his heirs and Lawfull Successors, in the exercise of their absolute power against all deadly &c: and least the Bishopps and Regular Clergie should take exceptions, or umbrage at what he here thought fit to do, his Majesty sollemly declar'd he would mentain them in all their respectiue functions, rights, and properties whatsoever.

Considering that nothing had been done in the late Parliament in Scotland in fauour of Catholicks, thō the King so earnestly recommended it to them, it was more extraordinary that the Council return'd now so respectfull an answer as they did, by assureing his Majesty that the proclamation was printed and published, that they would assert his prerogatiue with the hazard of their liues, and were willing that such as comported themselves Loyally and peacably, whatsoever their profession might be, might liue in ease and Security, and conceiued that such as were imployd by his Majesty, were sufficiently secured by his authority and Commission ; and lastly thank'd his Majesty, for promising with his Royal word to mentain the Church and Religion as by Law established, depending upon that promise as the best and greatest Security they could haue.

But for all this seeming submission and complyance, the people of Scotland were not a * little dissatisfyd with this

---

* Interlined as before. EDITOR.

Declaration, their mouths were stop'd from finding fault with an absolute power they had already voted, yet they did not expect his Majesty would haue extended it so far as to disable the Laws, which they construed to be a disanulling of them, and an efecting of that by his own authoritie, which he had so lately asked, and been refused the assistance of a Parliament to doe : and therefore this Declaration, as it was worded, was blamed by all moderate men of both Kingdoms, and created a greater jealousie of his Majesty's aiming at arbitrary government, than any thing that happen'd during his reign.

But this discontent not appearing so soon, and the Scots on ye contrary seeming so well satisfyd * with his Majestys orders, gaue hopes of the like reception in England ; accordingly the 18th of March, the King declar'd in Council, that he had resolved to issue a Declaration for a general Libertie of Conscience to all persons of what perswasion soever ; which he was moued to do, he Sayd, by haveing obserued, that thō an uniformitie in Religious worship had been endeavour'd to be established within this Kingdom in the successiue reigns of four of his predecessors, assisted by their respectiue Parliaments, yet it had proued all together ineffectual, that the restraint upon the consciences of Dissenters in order thereunto, had been very prejuditial to the Nation, as was sadly experienced by the horrid rebellion in the time of his Majestys Father, that the many penal Laws made against Dissenters, had rather encreas'd than lessen'd the numbers of them ; and that nothing could conduce more to the peace and quiet of the Kingdom, the encreas of the numbers, as well as the trade of his Subjects, than an entire Libertie of Conscience; it haveing always been his opinion (as most sutable to the principles of Christianity)

T O M. III.
1687.

The King resolves to grant liberty of Conscience in England.

---

* Inserted by the same person instead of some words which he had blotted out, beginning with, *his ready obedience however which, &c.* EDITOR.

that no man should be persecuted for conscience sake, which
he thought was not to be forced, and that it would never be the
intrest of a * King of England to endeavour to do it: directing
at the same time the Attorney and Sollicitor General, not to
suffer any process to issue out in his name against any Dissenters
whatever.

These reasons appear'd so † prudent and equitable that there
was not the least objection made against them, so it was published accordingly ; and in the preamble his Majesty declared,
that thō he could not but heartely wish that all his Subjects
were members of the same Religion he profess'd himself, yet
it being his opinion that Consciences ought not to be contrain'd,
he doubt'd not, but the Houses of Parliament would concur
with him therein, and in the mean time thought fit to publish
his Declaration of Libertie of Conscience, much to the same
tenor with that for Scotland: In the first place, he promisses
to mentain the Bishopps and Clergie of the Church, as by
Law established, in the quiet and full possession of their rights
and free exercise of their Religion, then he suspends the
execution of all penal laws against Nonconformists, exempts
all persons whatsoever from takeing the Oaths of Allegiance,
Supremacy, or the Several Tests mention'd in the Acts of the

The Decla-
ration for
Libertie of
Conscience
published in
England April
the 4: 1687.

---

* The Author of the Critical History of England, in his History of The Stuarts,
(Page 721) subjoins Sir E. Coke's reflection on this conduct of King James;
an authority to which the Writer of this Life, so often refers: " Sure no Power
ever acted so in extremes, yet his Actions so diametrically opposite to his Profession ; — pleading for Liberty of Conscience, to the breaking down the Laws which
before he had so often profess'd to maintain, and for such a sort of men whom but
a little before he had slaughter'd, banish'd, and imprison'd, as if he had design'd
to extirpate the whole race of them : If to reconcile these to Truth or Reality be
not as great a Miracle as is in any of the Popish Legends, I'll believe them all, and
be reconcil'd to the Catholick Church how inconsistent soever the terms be."
EDITOR.

† Inserted by the Son of James the second, instead of the word just. EDITOR.

10

25th and 30th of King Charles the Second, and pardons all crimes for non conformity ; and in conclusion assures all his loveing·Subjects he will mentain them in their possessions, and rights, as well in Church as Abbey lands and other properties whatsoever.

The King had good reason to be Satisfyd with what he had done, if words had been security for men's intentions, or others as sincere in what they Sayd, as he was, in what he Sayd and did; all Sort of Nonconformists were so transported with the freedom and Security they enjoyd by this indulgence, that it is not possible to carry expressions of Loyalty, beyond what most of the Adresses on this occasion were fill'd with ; for thō the Roman Catholicks had lain chiefly under the lash of the penal Laws, yet other Dissenters had tasted now and then of their rigour, which made them fond at first of this indulgence ; thō when the tyde turn'd, the generallity of them run in as treacherously with it as the rest, and flew as furiously in the face of their Benefactor, as those of the Church of England who thought themselves so much injur'd by it.

It was those therefore of the establish'd Religion that first took umbrage at this declaration, they pretended still to aprehend that some design against their Church, lurked in the bottom of all this : no assurance the King could giue, was capable of apeasing their doubts and jealousies, besides they had been in possession of the penal Laws so long, and had kept thereby the professors of all other Religions in so awefull a Subjection, that it went to their hearts to part with a power which because it was agreeable to nature and self loue, they thought necessary for their preseruation too ; when the Church of England was under oppression and had felt the heavy hand of perseçution in the late rebellion, it then express'd great condescention to tender consciences, and was inclined enough even to reconcile the different Church governments, but this

kind disposition was soon forgot when it was in full power
again, thō it seem'd to be no great commendation to a Church
to be only meek when humbled, and only mercifull when she
can do no hurte; and therefore the King imagin'd, that since
the Church of England and his Catholick Subjects had once
suffer'd togather under a prevailing partie, when the Lithurgie
was as obnoxious as the Mass book, and that they fought
togather in the same just cause, they would not be so difficult
to unite in affection and intrest, thō they could not in faith :
but the contrary soon appear'd, and the jealousies which the
Churchmen conceiud upon this occasion, made them debase
their function in most places, and turn sowers of division,
instead of teachers of peace and unity; like Micannicks in a
trade, who are afraid of nothing so much as Interlopers, which
gaue great scandal in the main, and made indifferent persons
immagin their ernest contest about Religion, was in reality
more for temporal possessions than the faith which was once
deliver'd to the Saints : This the King endeavour'd to make
them sencible of, and that nothing could be more incongrous
than that a Church which does not pretend to be infallible,
should oblige people under the pain of great punishments,
premunire, and even death itself, to believe as she does; that
thō they did not allways press a rigorous execution of these
laws, yet they delighted to see Dissenters, and especially the
Catholicks, in a continual tremble at the Iron rod which they
took care should allways threaten them; so sweet it seems was
dominion and Superiority, that the very thought of others
becomeing sharers (thō not of their revenue) only of their
freedom, made them forget by degrees their so much preached
up doctrine of obedience to their Prince, that there was no
contrivance which spight and dissatisfaction was capable of
inventing, which they did not put in practice to cast all
immaginable obstacles in his Majestys way, and by industriously

opposeing whatever he aim'd at, thõ never so reasonable in T O M.
it self, they fomented continually new grounds of dissention, III.
till they had made an absolute breach betwixt him and his 1687.
People.

The King indeed dissembled not his inclination to favour
Catholicks, no more than he had done the being one himself,
but still was cautious to keep within the limites of his power
according as it was circomscribed by the proper Judges of it,
whose skill and sincerity he had no reason to suspect, and was
most especially carefull to keep clear of all invasion as to
what belonged to others; the Catholicks themselves concur'd
likewise with the King's intentions, by useing this benifit which
the tolleration gaue them with prudence and moderation, " KING JAM.
they did assure his Majesty they would not fail to behaue " Mᵐˢ To: 9. p. 209.
themselves to God as became good Christians, to the King "
as Loyal Subjects, and to their neighbors as true Englishmen " Ibid. p. 210.
ought to doe, and his Majesty took care to haue the principal "
persons of that perswasion adverticed, to shew their sense of "
being freed from the heavy hand of persecution and breathing "
the free air again, by their more fervent aplication to the "
seruice of God, and not by giveing either Scandal or offence "
to their fellow Subjects, or by seeming too much exalted by "
the liberty they now enjoy'd, or haveing a King of their "
own perswasion; to behaue themselves with a brotherly loue "
and meeknes even towards those who had been the most "
severe to them heretofore, it being the duty of all good "
Christians so to doe, and necessary to justify in the face of "
the world, that they are govern'd by the spirit of meekness "
and charity, and that they abhor that of persecution, which "
their enemies charge them with; and this he hoped would be "
a rule to persons in all ranks and Stations both in Court, "
Country, and the Army, and that the more elevated their "

T O M.
III.

1687.
The Pope's
Nuncio had
admittance
and a publick
audience
July y° 23ᵈ
1687.

condition was, the more earnestly he required a suitable "
obseruance of this doctrine.   "

One would haue thought the King's sincerity in telling so
plainly what he would doe, should haue made his word be
taken for what he promised he would not doe, and haue
reassured the Church of England, he had no further aims than
a bare libertie of conscience ; but jealousie is a sort of incurable
distemper, no precautions or protestations could satisfy them,
every thing that favour'd Catholick religion was new and
odious, the few Chappells which were set up in the Town
or Country, thō the rule prescribed by the proclamation
was strictly obserued, and they used with caution and
moderation, yet it was a sight they could not bear; amongst
which that of a Pope's Nuncio was of the first rank : it was
his Majestys misfortune to think it would render people less
avers to suffer the exercise of Catholick religion amongst them,
by familiarizing the Nation not only with the Ceremonys of
the Church of Rome, but of the Court of Rome too ; this made
his Majesty, besides the solem services which he had in his
own Chappell, permit the Monks in Sᵗ James's to wear their
habits, and admit of a Nuncio from the Pope according to
the formes practised in the most Catholick Countrys : One
Senior Ferdinando D'Adda had resided in a private capacity in
England for some time, but being now declared Nuncio, he was
soon after consecrated Arch Bishop of Amasia in his Majestys
Chappell, who was pleas'd to apoint him a publick audience,
and solemn entry at Windsor. The King consider'd his
Holyness as a great and powerfull temporall Prince, as well as
the Spirituall head of the Church, and being in amitie with him,
he Saw no reason why a Minister from thence might not be
admitted into England, as well as from other States and
Kingdoms; that Ambassadors being sent to the Prince, not

the people, it was no breach of the laws, which could *not be* TOM.
thought * *to* restrain the King from exerciseing that point of III.
his prerogatiue, in what manner he judged fitting, nor from 1687.
treating with, and by consequence receiueing a Minister from
that or any other State in the world; the Ambassadors of
Infidells, and Indian Princes had been a Subject of curiosity,
not of displeasure to the people, and why that should be denyd
to a Christian Prince and Bisshop, his Majesty saw no reason
for it: but the more he endeavour'd by this free and open
dealing to convince them he was a hater of duplicity, the more
they suspected it, and that this outward shew of Religion
would introduce the reality in the end. There is no doubt to
be made, but when his Majesty perceived it would produce a
quite contrary effect to what was aim'd at, it had been more
prudent to haue waued that outward ostentation at least, and
spar'd the people that displeasure, in a thing no ways essential
to religion; besides it was the King's misfortune herein, to
haue † others chuse for him, as ill, as generally he chose for
himself, and as certainly this person was for such a function;
for, being but a young man, who had appear'd at Court for
some time in a secular capacity, he was very improper to draw

---

* Interlined as before. EDITOR.

† *Dr W. Smith*, a great Advocate of James the second, in his History of England
from the Earliest Accounts to the Revolution, printed in 1771. (Vol 2. p. 342.)
thus comments on this Nuncios being sent to England. "The Pope knew
KING JAMES's opinion, as to the Regalia, to be the same with that of the French
King's, and therefore looked upon him, if not the greatest enemy he had, yet as
a dreadful second; therefore he tried all ways to work KING JAMES into his
confederacy against France, for the re-establishment of his Supremacy there.
To this end Count D'Adda was sent over his Nuncio to KING JAMES, but with
this instruction, that if he found the King immoveable, then to promote his
desposition all he could, to bring about the Revolution which had been long
before concerted at Rome. This Count D'Adda himself owned." EDITOR.

that reverence and respect which is due to such a character ; especially from a people of a different Religion, and who being so apt to turn the most Sacred things into ridicule, would hardly be perswaded, that by a man's entring into orders, gravitie, experience, learning, and all other qualifications fit for a Bisshop, would be confer'd in an instant as in the Appostles time ; unless it was thought that his appearing a profess'd Imperialist in his inclinations and discours, would make him go better down with the people ; but that to be sure ought not to haue recommended him to the King : It is not therefore to be wonder'd, that this proued one of the first stumbling blocks, and ought to haue convinced the King, that he must not immagin that either his own engagement to protect them, or their former assurances of being passiuely (at least) obedient to him, would calme their aprehentions, or Secure the peace and quiet of his government.

The Duke of Somerset being Lord of the Bedchamber in waiting, the King apointed him according to custome, to receiue the Nuncio and bring him to his audience ;. but he makeing some difficulty desired time to consider, after which and some * consultations with his friends; he positiuely denyd

* The Duke of Somerset's conduct on that occasion is thus introduced by Burnet, " All commerce with the See of Rome being declared High Treason by Law, this was believed to fall within the Statute. It was so apprehended by Queen Mary. Cardinal Pool was obliged to stay in Flanders till all those Laws were repealed. But the King would not stay for that. The Duke of Somerset, being the Lord of the Bed-chamber then in waiting, had advised with his Lawyers : and they told him, he could not safely do the part that was expected of him in the audience. So he told the King, *that he could not serve him upon that occasion ; for he was assured it was against the Law.* The King asked him, *If he did not know that he was above the Law.* The other answered, *That, whatever the King might be, he himself was not above the law.* The King expressed a high displeasure, and turned him out of all employments." (*Vol.* 2. *8vo. Ed. P.* 427.)

The Author of the History of the Stuarts, already mention'd, notices an

it : the least the King thought he could doe to punish such a
disobedience, was to discharge him from his imployment which
it seems he was not disposed to execute, and thō the Duke of
Grafton did it (which shew'd his scruple was ill grounded)
however it gaue his Majesty just cause to suspect what sort of
complyance he must hope for the future, when in a thing
purely cerimonial he found a person of that distinction chuse
rather to loose so honorable a station, than performe the common
duty of his place, because it had a seeming opposition to the
established Religion.

But now that peoples minds began to souren against the
government, there hapen'd an accident which encreas'd that distemper to a great degree. It was far from his Majestys seeking,
but his authority being once ingaged, he was under a necessity
of going through with it; and it So fell out that what was
realy design'd only as a punishment for a disobedience, was
interpreted afterwards as a design to depriue the established
Church, of what the King had promis'd to mentain them in the
possession of, and to force Popery in upon them in spight of
all opposition ; a thing as impossible in it self, as it was far
from his Majestys thoughts or intentions.

The Presidentship of Magdelen Colledge in Oxford becomeing
vacant by the death of Dᵗʳ Clarke, the King thought fit by his
mandate dated the 11ᵗʰ of April 1687, to order their electing
one Mʳ Farmer; but the fellows haveing exceptions against
him, as not qualifyd according to the Statutes of the Colledge,
nor indeed of a moral life, they beg'd leaue in a formal petition,

T O M. III. 1687.

The dispute aboutMagdelen Colledge began 11 April 1687. Vide Printed relation of proceedings of Magd.Colledge published by the fellows themselves for their own vindication.

Anecdote somewhat similar to this (page 712.) " One day the King gave the Duke
of Norfolk the Sword of State to carry before him to Chapel, and he stood at the
door ; upon which the King said to him, *My Lord, your Father would have gone
further.* To which the Duke answer'd, *Your Majesty's Father was the better Man,
and he would not have gone so far.*" EDITOR.

that the King would pleas either to leaue them to a free election,
*or recommend such a person as might be more seruiciable to his
Majesty and to that his Colledge.* The King, thō not well
satisfyd with this demur, however was pleas'd to waue his
former recommendation, upon what was urg'd against him;
and by a fresh mandate order'd them to elect the Bisshop of
Oxford; but the fellows without waiting his Majesty's pleasure
(thō they had beg'd it in their petition) proceed to an election,
chuse * Dr Hough, and then made hast to get the Bisshop of
Winton, their visitor in ordinary, to confirme him accordingly;
The King was hugely incensed at this proceeding, for to say
nothing to their questioning his power of dispenseing with the
Statutes of a Colledge, and a positiue desobedience to his mandate, there could not, he thought, be a greater insult offer'd
him, than in a suppliant manner to desire him to recommend an
other, and, before it was possible to haue an answer, to elect one
themselves, and then plead that election in bar of his Majestys
mandate ; for they made no other objection against the Bisshop

---

* An interesting Life of the President was published in 1812 by Mr. Wilmot, in
which are some curious original Letters. · Dr Hough died Bishop of Worcester
1743. On the face of ye Sarcophagus in his Monument by Roubiliac in that
cathedral, is a Bas-Relief representing the President before the High Commission
Court held in the hall of Magdalen College Oxford, on Friday, Oct^r: 21, 1687,
before Cartwright Bishop of Chester, Wright Chief Justice of the Kings Bench,
and Jenner one of the Barons of the Exchequer. It was on that occasion the President thus delivered this protest, the words in Italics appear over the Bas-relief.
" Having adjourned till the afternoon, the President came again into the Court,
and having desired to speak a few words, they all took off their hats, and gave him
leave; whereupon he said, *My Lords,* you were pleased this morning to deprive me
of my place of President of this College: *I* do *hereby protest against all your
Proceedings,* and against all that you have done, or hereafter shall do, in prejudice
of me and my right, as illegal, unjust, and null; *and* therefore I *appeal to my
Sovereign Lord the King, in his Courts of Justice.*" D^r. Hough's Character is finely
drawn by Lord Lyttleton, in his Persian Letters, (*Vol.* 1. 309.) when writing to
Mirza. (*Life, page* 40, *and* 112.)

of Oxon, (*whom the King* * *recommended*) but that the place was
full; and their only excuse for makeing it so, was that their
time assigned by the Statutes would haue elapsed, and that
they were bound under an Oath to the obseruance of them :
But it was urged against that, that they knew very well that
the King's mandate implyd an inhibition, that it was no new
thing, and by consequence could not oblige them to deal so
unmanerly with their Prince, nor did they themselues conceiue
in the bottom, they were under any such ty of conscience;
otherwise some of the most violent and factious Members
amongst them, such as D^{tr} Fairfax the Vice President, D^{tr}
Pudsey, and D^{tr} Smith, would not haue moued (as they did) to
haue a Second adress presented to his Majesty and the Election
suspended till the efect of that was known ; but men who haue
ill designes are allways in hast, and the true meaning of this
mighty precipitation was not scruple of conscience, but to
elude his Majestys power of .nominateing, and to make use of
that occasion to get that prerogatiue .to themselves, which had
ever before been an inherent right to the Crown.

While this affair was in agitation, the King made,a progress
into the Northwest partes of England, after haveing conducted
the Queen to the Bath, and in his return took Oxford in his
way : so on the 4th of September he summon'd the fellows of
Magdalen Colledge to attend him, hopeing by his :presence
and perswasion, to mollify their Stubborn Spirites, and bring
them to a more dutifull temper ; he tould them, That hithertoo
they had not used him like a gentleman, but hoped upon
more mature consideration, they would repair their former
undutifullness with their present obedience in electing the
Bisshop of Oxon ; that it was a duty he expected from true

TOM.
III.
1687.

Ibid. pag.1.

The King's
Western
progress, Aug:
16th 1687.

---

* Interlined as before mentioned. EDITOR.

Members of the Church of England, and as he was willing to forget what was passed, he hoped they were no less disposed by a ready complyance to blot out the memory of it likewise. His Majesty deliver'd this to them with some thing more warmth than ordinary, however it made no impression, and since they persisted in their stubborn resolution, the King thought fit to leaue them to the Ecclesiastical Commissioners; who issuing out a citation brought the matter before themselves, and after haveing heard their plea and consulted the learned in both laws, they judged this pretended election null, and renewed the mandate for chuseing the Bisshop of Oxon; but the Fellows disobeying that again, the Bisshop of Chester, the Lord Chief Justice Wright, and Baron Jenner, were deputed to make a visitation, who used all immaginable arguments to perswade a complyance, but they still persevereing in their obstinacy, the Commissioners after heareing all parties, installed the Bisshop of Oxon by his Proxi, and then press'd the Fellows to submit to him now that he was in; thō they would not elect him themselves; which at first they seem'd inclinable too, and

Ibid: pag. 26. sign'd a submission accordingly to the said Bisshop of Oxon, with this restriction, viz. As far as was lawfull and agreeable to the Statutes of the Colledge: Thō this salvo was harsh, however the Commissioners for peace sake were contented to admit it, and had the Fellows abided by it, the dispute had ended there, and they remain'd in the quiet possession of their Fellowships; but as if they were sorry they had shewn any disposition to a healing and complyant temper, they came next day to explain their meaning with a downeright equivocation; that by the word Submission they meant not to render any future obedience to

Ibid: pag: 29. the said Bisshop of Oxon, but only that they did not oppose or resist his installment. This shew'd there was no compounding matters with these angry people, who sought not justice, but a ground of complaint, by puting a necessity upon the

Commissioners of punishing their disobedience, thõeven thatwas not hastely. done; for they went first to London to giue a full account to his Majesty how far they had proceeded, and found that his patience was yet proof against all these provocations, for he order'd them once more to tender a forme of submission as favorably worded as possible, promising to forgiue what was pass'd upon their signing it, but they rejected all offers of accommodation; so that no other way remain'd but to quit their. Fellowships, *which all did excepting two, and therefore were not in * reality* turn'd out by the Commissioners, but by themselves, by refuseing obedience to their then President.

Nothing therefore can be more evident, than that the King was hugely injured in this famous dispute which raised him so many enemys, and so much envy afterwards; it was far from his intention to dispossess the Church of England of this Colledge, on the contrary all immaginable endeavours were used, to perswade a complyance, and then not a man had suffer'd; and all their pretence of conscience had been avoided also, had they waited an answer to their own request in their petition, which the most considerable Doctors made no scruple of; besides it was rediculous to dispute the King's power in dispensing with the local Statutes of a Colledge, which had been so frequently practised in former reigns, after it had been decided in his Majestys favour that he might dispense with certain standing Laws of the Land; had they not therefore forgot the oath of Allegience amongst those they insisted so much upon, they would not have been so refractory to a Lawfull command of their Prince, or so nice in admiting the King's dispensation with their rules, which they were easy enough in dispenseing with themselves, for their own eas and

---

* Interlined by the Son of James the second. EDITOR.

convenience; otherwise (as the Commissioners tould them) so much scandal would not have been given by the breach of that, which enjoins their being serued only by men.

There is no doubt but the King had done more prudently, had he not carryd the thing so far; but few Princes are of a temper to receiue a baffle patiently in a thing they heartely espouse, or suffer their authority to be render'd precarious, when they conceiue it to be back'd with Law and reason; as all the Civilians as well as Judges asured his Majesty it was, and that the least failure of a Colledge in any point, forfeited its grant, and layd it open to his Majestys disposal; so that if their usage apear'd harsh, it was not his Majestys primary intention, it was they who willfully (not to say maliciously to raise envy) drew it upon themselves: nor was it, by consequence, the King (as was clamerously sayd afterwards) that turn'd his Subjects out of their freehould, to make room for Roman Catholicks, on the contrary all immaginable industry and arguments were used, to make them stay; but refuseing to own their Superiour they could not possess their Fellowships, which had so immediate a dependance upon him, so the whole argument turn'd upon this single point, whether they had power peremptorily to disobey yᵉ King's mandate or no; if not, then the Bisshop of Oxon was duly elected, and the Fellows justly seclueded for not submitting to him, and their pretence of being bound to the contrary by their Oath, was groundless not to say seditious, for they could not swear to disobey the King's Lawfull authority, and the Kings of England were never denyd that of sending their Mandates when they thought fitting; and by consequence those Oaths or obligations only concern'd them, when they were left to elect of themselves, which shews it was a confederacy to be stubborn only to draw an odium upon their Prince.

Not long after this the Bisshop of Oxon dying, and the King conceiveing this Colledge to be forfeited into his hands, and by consequence at his disposall, made the Catholick Bisshop Gifford President of it, and fill'd up most of ye Fellowships with Catholicks, because few Protestants would accept them; but not many months after, the nois of the Prince of Orange's Invasion encourageing severall Bisshops to petition the King to restore it, he readily yielded to their request, when he found how grievously they resented what he had done; but they attributeing that complyance to fear, not good will, took no care to make him reparation for the troubles they had brought upon him by their resentment, and notwithstanding their mighty scrupulosity in matters of Oathes when their intrest was engaged, made no difficulty (most of them at least) to renounce their uncontested obligation of fidelity, to reveng a supposed invasion of their right, which the King had yeilded up again so soon, and which at best was but a disputable case.

It was unfortunate enough to the King's affairs, that some thing of the like nature happen'd about the same time, at Cambridge too; which help'd to rais this envy and jealousies, *still higher** and to set the Church of England partie entirely in opposition to his intrest: the King had immagined it would be a means to familiarise those of different Religions, and make them liue in greater peace and unity together, pursuant to the intent of liberty of conscience (which his Majesty observed produced that effect in forreign Countrys) in case some few Catholicks, were incorporated into the Vniuersitys; and one Father Alban Francis a Benedictin Monk liveing then at Cambridge, the King thought fit to order the Vniuersity

T O M.
III.

1687.

The dispute aboutadmiting F^r Francis to be Master of Artes in Cambridge.

---

* Interlined as before mentioned. `Editor.`

to admit him to the degree of Master of Artes, without requiring the Oathes, from which he granted him a dispensation, with a *non obstante* to any Laws or Statutes to the contrary: The Vice Chancellor haveing communicated this to the Senate, they agreed to petition the King to revoke his Mandate, writ to the Duke of Albemarle their Chancellour to that efect, who advised them only to send up their petition, but they rather chose. to depute two of their body D^{tr} Smault and Mr Norris to represent the illegality of admiting any one unless he took the Oathes. This delay occasion'd a second Mandate, which was answer'd by an other deputation of Mr Braddoc, and Mr Stanhop, who were tould by My Lord Sunderland at their arrival, that the King had seen the Vice Chancellour's letter, which gaue no satisfaction, but on the contrary was much offended at the proceeding of the Vniuersitie, and accordingly, the Vice Chancellor himself D^{tr} Peachel, was summon'd to apear before the Ecclesiastical Commissioners, whereupon he and several others came up accordingly: At their first apearance before the Commissioners (who were then, the Lord Chancellor, the Bisshops of Duresm, and Rochester, the Earls of Sunderland, Mulgraue, and Huntington, and Lord Chief Justice Harbert) the Vice Chancellor required time to answer; the Commissioners tould him it was strang, he should then have his reasons to seek, for what he had already done, and so positiuely persisted in, however a week was allow'd him ; at the end of which, he gave in writeing several quotations of Statutes, which order'd the Oathes to be taken, as the 1st and 5th of Eliz: and the 3^d and 9th of King James, inferring from thence, that they could not admit him without a violation of their own Oathes, which bound them (they said) to the observance of those Statutes, unless he took those Oathes prescribed by them ; he urged likewise, that the takeing a degree, as that of Master of Artes,

T O M.
III.

1687.

was nòt an Ecclesiastical matter, and so not under the cognizance of the Commissioners, and lastly, that by the 16ᵗʰ of King Charles the Second it was order'd, that no such Court as that should be erected; But all thes objections the Commissioners sayd, were answer'd in effect by the objectors themselves, in as much as they did not say one word to shew, that the King had not power to dispense with those Statutes in a particular case, on which the matter soly depended ; nor could the Vice Chancellor thō press'd to it, shew one instance where the King's Mandate had been disobeyd, only that the late King haveing recommended one Fatswell, they had prevail'd with his Majesty, upon his refusal of the Oaths, to recall his Mandate ; which only proved (they Sayd) the King's indulgence in desisting, not his want of power to force a complyance had he persisted in that resolution ; on the contrary one Dᵗʳ Lightfoot was instanced to haue been admited Master of Artes not long before, without takeing the Oaths, to which their only reply was, he had sign'd the 39 Articles, wherein the King's Supremacy was acknowlidg'd ; but this the Court judg'd a poor evasion to saue the consciences of men, who pretended to so nice a scrupulositie as not to admit the King's power of dispensing with the least tittle of a Law or Statute of their Vniuersitie, and yet did it themselves because a man had sign'd the 39 Articles, wherein was contain'd one of the several heads comprised in the Oaths ; whereupon Sentence of depriva- tion was pass'd upon the Vice Chancellor for his contumacy and disobedience, as well as his other crimes and contempts.

Notwithstanding all the reasons which could be alledg'd in justification of these proceedings, the people began to be hugely dissatisfyd not only with the manner of executeing its power, but with the very erecting of his Ecclesiastical court it self; it thwarted, (they sayd) his Majestys promis of protecting the Church of England, and they were no ways satisfyd with the

The Vice Chancellor of Cambridge is deprived May 7ᵗʰ: 1687.

T O M.
III.

1687.

Zouch Jur:
Ecclesi:
part: 1:
Cor: 1. b: 1.
Elie: Cap: 2.
Noys Rep:
Foli: 100.

answers which were given, thō plausible enough, as, that the correcting some disobedient Members of a Church, was not to destroy it, but a necessary means to preserue it; that he stretched not his arme too far in granting a Commission, which (as was sayd already) was provided for by the very Act which was pretended to disanull the extraordinary power; nay, that it was manifest that the King's power extended much further, and that with his Ecclesiastical Commissioners he might haue made new Laws about cerimonys, * without a Parliament, or new constitutions for the government of the Clergie, and deprived the disobedient *ex officio*, and that it had been so adjudged in Cowdreys case; which answer'd also the objection, that the Fellows of Magdalen Colledg could not be lawfully deprived, unless the process had been in due forme as is used by temporal laws: It was therefore urged as a great argument of his Majestys moderation considering the provocation of some hot Churchmen on one hand, and the authoritys and reasons which were alledged by learned men for his power on the other, that all the exercise he made of it, was to suspend one Bisshop, depriue a Vice Chancellor, and punish the insolent disobedience of the Fellows of one Colledge; whereas he was tould, he might by vertue of his Ecclesiastical prerogatiue, haue deprived every one, that would not subscribe the declaration for Libertie of Conscience if he had pleas'd, as

* The Minister and Secretary of State in France, under Louis XVI. *Bertrand de Moleville,* in his *Chronological Abridgment of the History of Great Britain,* (Vol. 3. p. 449.) remarks on this period, " The Royal Power was so much increased at that time, and the revenue managed by James's frugality, so considerable and independent, that, had he embraced any rational party, he might have carried his authority to what length he pleased. But the Catholics, to whom he had entirely devoted himself, composed scarcely the hundredth part of the English Nation, and the Protestant Non Conformists, whom he so much courted, were little more than the twentieth." Editor.

well as the Puritans were in Queen Elizabeth and King James the firsts' time, and the Nonconformist in the late Reign ; but the King was resolued to keep within the limits of that power he conceiued to be incontestible, and therefore notwithstanding the malicious labours to misrepresent his intentions, and moue his passion, he calmcly and steddyly pursued his designes of grace to all, and protection to the Churchmen in particular, togather with the preservation of all that was dear to them, except the sword of persecution, which for the universal peace of the Nation, he thought reasonable to wrest out of their hands : but such justifications as these of his Majestys proceedings, by proveing he had power to extend his arme still further if he pleas'd, instead of satisfying people with what he had done, rais'd new aprehentions he might doe more, and therefore encreased, rather than appeased, the murmurs and jealousies, and ripen'd those discontents, which soon after had so fatal a consequence.

T O M. III. 1687.

But that which rais'd them to an incurable hight, was the Queen's fortuneing to be with child, she had been four years without that prospect of giveing an heire to the Crown, it was conceiud the Bath might conduce to it, and accordingly that journey had been resolued on, early in the year ; but the news of the Dutchess of Modena's death (the Queen's Mother) made it be delayed till August, at which time, the King accompanying her thither, went from thence to Holliwel in Wales, a place much frequented out of deuotion, and it is probable with a view of begging that blessing, which it pleas'd the divine Providence to grant him, for soon after the Queen apear'd to be with Child, which as it was an argument of great joy to them, so it was one of exceeding jealousie and dissatisfaction to the Church of England ; who now aprehending an heire might perpetuate that Religion on the Throne, which they were willing to bear with the remainder of one man's life, they kept no measures

The Queen proues with child.

TOM.
III.

1687.

My Lord
Sunderland
endeavours
to be made
Treasurer.

with their Prince, nor moderation * or decency in their endeavours to screen their Religion from this immaginary danger, and therfore thought no slandrous invention, or calumny unpermited, to render suspected this prospect of an heire to the Crowne, which their true intrest as well as duty should haue made them consider as one of the greatest Blessings of heaven.

His Majesty might haue much better struggled with these discontents in his people, had he been better serued in his family ; but the ambition and extravagant temper of his chief favorite the † Earle of Sunderland, open'd a door not only to divisions in that, but by it bribery, and at last treachery itself, got admittance into his Council too : That Lord, had no sooner got quit of his rival the Earle of Rochester, but he covited his imployment ; he was a man of pleasure, and no niggard in the expence that attends it, which made him always necessitous for mony ; so that his great and beneficial imployments, togather with his forreign pentions, were not sufficient to supply his lavish humour ; it is incredible how a Minister so favour'd by his own Prince, could be so abandon'd as to seek advantages from an other, and from more than one, and they of such opposite intrests, as his most Christian Majesty and the Prince

---

* Lord H. Clarendon in his Diary (page 79) has preserved a singular conversation which he had on this subject. EDITOR.

† Some severe animadversions on Sunderland's Character, with extracts from his Apology, are given by RALPH (Vol: 1. p. 971, 972.) who then adds, " It is said this Nobleman stood so high in his Majesty's Favour, that he would scarce grant any Suit to any person, unless at his Instance, or under his Approbation : that when his Majesty was told he got all the Money of the Court, he replied, *He deserved it ;* and that, when any application was made to him, his usual question, with regard to the solliciting parties, was, *Have they spoke to Sunderland ?*" — The character and views of this Minister are marked by Barillon in writing to his Sovereign." (*Appendix to Fox's History of James 2^d:*) EDITOR.

of Orange were : but it seems he had dexterity enough to keep
up his credit with them both, for as to the fact, no one can
doubt of his haveing been a pentioner to the latter ; but it was
incredible he should haue been so to the former, had not that
King assured his Majesty of it after the reuolution, telling him
he allways looked upon it as a thing done by his privity and
allowance.

But all these supplys falling short of his occasions, he held ”
a private consultation with Father Petre and S^r. Nicolas ”
Butler how to bring about what he had been long medi- ”
tateing, to perswade the King to make him Treasurer, ”
because his Majesty had taken a resolution never to put the ”
management of the Treasury into the hands of one person ”
any more, and had made a declaration in Council accordingly, ”
but My Lord Sunderland dispair'd of nothing, haveing so
many instruments to work with ; This S^r. Nicolas Butler (who
was one of the cheif) was of a gentleman's family, but of no
fortune, however haueing got a place in the customes, and
gain'd some reputation in it, came at last to be one of the
Commissioners, and being a forward actiue man, and a
pretended convert of Father Petre's, gain'd great credit with
him, and by consequence with the King ; and My Lord
Sunderland finding him a proper agent for his purpose too,
brought him into great esteem at Court, and into many private
Caballs, and when any new project was layd, sent him out to
try the ford, contriveing generally (in order to excite his
sollicitude) to turn the matter so, as that he should find his
account in it likewise : To flatter therefore both Father Petre
and him on this occasion, he proposed that Father Petre ”
should succeed him in the Secretary's Office, and S^r. Nicolas ”
Butler be Chancellor of the Exchequer ; accordingly S^r. ”
Nicolas took an occasion a little before Christmas to discours ”

King Jam:M^{en}
To:9. Pag.213.

King Jam: M^{p}
To.9:pag:213.

s 2

TOM.
III.
1687.

" with his Majesty on that Subject, and finding fault with the
" present Commissioners and their management, concluded it
" would be infinitely better in one man's hands, than as it now
" was: the King sayd not much to him, only enough to let him
" see he was not of his judgment; his Majesty Saw very well
" what was aim'd at, and thō he had too good an opinion of
" My Lord Sunderland in other things, he knew very well his
" incapacity for such an imployment; that Lord's cunning lay
in intrigue, not in management, for he scarce knew how to
forme a figure, and the King was too prudent in what concern'd
his revenue, to trust a man with his purs, who never could keep
a penny in his own: but My Lord Sunderland not content
" with this, came soon after to the Queen and tould her, that

Ibid. pag. 214.

" Father Petre and Sʳ. Nicolas Butler had press'd him for
" several months, to think of being Treasurer, finding fault
" with some of the present Commissioners, and that Father
" Petre to facilitate the matter, had proposed that two of them
" might be turn'd out and My lord himself, and an other put
" in, and then it would be easyer to perswade the King to leaue
" the management of the whole to him alone; he assured her
" Majesty it was not of his seeking being very well contented
" as he was; upon which the Queen took him at his word, and
" sayd, She was glad to find him of that mind, for that after
" the King's declaration in Council, and settled resolution in
" the matter, there was no probabilitie of perswadeing him to
" alter it, especially since it was so agreeable to reason as it
" manifestly appear'd to be.

His Lordship was forced to desist when he saw no remedy, and being an artfull dissembler seem'd satisfyd in apearance, thõ tis more than probable this disapointment help'd on those darke contrivances whereby perhaps he thought to better his condition in an other * government ; in respect of which his Master's intrest weigh'd little in the ballance ; his Majesty by this time began to be sencible of the danger, thõ he did not yet see from whence it chiefly flowed, however took some precautions ; and finding that Seditious pamphlets began to fly about, he published a Proclamation pursuant to the Statute made the 14th of the late reign, prohibiting all unlicenced papers or prints ; and to take away all ground of complaint on account of his Troops, he caused a most diligent serch to be made after highway men, and irregularities in their quarters, and indeed as the Kingdom never abounded more in riches and trade, so never was there more security, had the people been sencible of their happiness ; but that restless spirit, which never has an attention to a million of favours, as long as there is but one grievance to complain of, so encreased upon his hands, that he thought it necessary to encreas his Troops too, which he now conceiu'd to be his chief security, by recalling those in the service of the States general, which was done by Proclamation likewise.

T O M. III.

1688.
The King recalls his Troops out of Holland.

February 13th 168[6].

March 14th 168[7].

---

* *Ralph*, says Dr *Smith* in the work already cited, (*Vol.* 2. *p.* 374.) "makes no scruple to declare, that the Revolution was concerted from the Restoration, and a perpetual design carried on to ruin the House of Stuart; into which measures the Prince of Orange seems plainly to have entered very early. . . *Sir Roger North* observes, that the Prince of Orange's actions, through his whole life, if nearly observed, will declare a notable connection of his thoughts with the affairs of England, so early as that memorable, and never to be forgotten overthrow, which King James, when Duke of York, gave the Dutch. They were from that time determined to ruin the Royal Family. . . . We see by *Temple's Memoirs*, that several persons here, and considerable ones too, had formed schemes of a Revolution from that side of the water long before they got it accomplished." EDITOR.

But the Dutch began already to shew their teeth, and contrary to all reason and justice chican'd the King's power of recalling his Subjects; they sayd nothing was more reasonable than that those who were born free, should haue the libertie of settling where they pleas'd, who by puting themselves under the protection of what government they liked best, gave that government the same right of dominion over them, as over their natural Subjects; but the King's Minister there, the Marques of Allbeville (a title given him by the Emperour) had no great difficulty to answer so weak a pretence, he tould them, That since government had been established in the world, such a natural libertie had no more place in it, and that by their pretending, that their election made them as natural Subjects, they shew'd that natural Subjection carryd a duty and obedience along with it; and by consequence they being such to the King of England, were oblig'd to obey his orders, and return to his service when recall'd, which was a common right of Soveraignety, and what the Kings of England had ever layd clame too, prohibiting their Subjects to engage in the Seruice of any forreigne State without permission, and recalling them at pleasure; alledging moreover that it was a point blanc contradiction to the capitulation made betwixt the Earle of Ossery and the Prince of Orange: So the Dutch finding there was no colour to support so manifest a breach of common faith, and right of Nations, submited at last; but had beforehand so debauched the Soldiers from their duty, that few of them chose to return when they were permited to do it.

The Pensioner
of Holland
publishes a
Treaty agains
repealing the
Test.

But this was not the only rub they threw in his Majesty's way, for the King now finding that nothing, which had the least apeerence of novelty, thō never so well warrented by the prerogatiue, would go down with the people, unless it had the Parliamentary Stamp upon it, resolved to try if he could get the penal laws and Test to be taken off by that

.* authority; this design was no sooner made publick, but
Minheer Fagel the Pentioner of Holland writ his thoughts, or
rather those of the Prince and Princess of Orange upon it; and
thō he declar'd it to be both his and their Highnesse's opinion,
that no Christian ought to be persecuted for his conscience, or
ill used because he differ'd from the established Religion, yet
all politick bodys (he sayd) had ever made laws to secure the
established Religion, and their own safety, by excluding the
enemies thereof from all publick imployments; and the Test
being of that nature, declar'd they could not consent to haue
it abrogated; The King wanted not friends who replyd to this,
That it seem'd a little too early for those Princes to meddle
with, and very unbecoming the chief Minister of a Forreign
State to concern himself with, the makeing or abrogating the
laws of an other Country; and that in efect he answer'd his
own argument, when he own'd, That they themselves, did not
shut out Roman Catholicks from military imployments,
because of their services and smallness of their numbers;
which reason houlding much better for England, where their
merit was full as great, and their number much fewer in
proportion; the question was reduced to this, whether any
great danger could acrue to the State, by admiting them into
other imployments likewise? the great aprehention was, that if
they were made capable of being Members of Parliament,
they might in time turn the Laws against the Protestants
themselves; but it was answer'd to that, that if the people

T O M.
III.
1688.
PENTIONER
FAGELS
LETTER dat.
Nou: 4: 1687.

---

* Rapin informs us, under this year, That the King had sounded the inclinations
of the Prince of Orange, without appearing in it, by employing Stewart a Scottish
Lawyer, whom King James had pardoned after a long exile, and who wrote to
Pensionary Fagel. . . . . " The Letters of these Gentlemen have made so much
noise in the world, and are so universally known, that I do not think it necessary
to insert them." EDITOR.

doubted the uprightness of the King's intentions, in his repeated promises of mentaining those of the established Religion in their possessions and priviledges, they had more reason to fear it from an Army (which the Pentioner alow'd Papists might be admited into) than from a Parliament : There were few Subjects in England of that Religion, qualified to be Parliament men, whereas each one was capable of being a Soldier ; the Election also of the former depended on the people, and perhaps Scarce a Catholick in England had an intrest to efect it, whereas the later depended soly on the Prince: but that the King instead of attempting any such thing, which at his first Accession to the Throne he had the fairest opertunity immaginable to promote, had he been so inclined, only by pursuing those methods he found ready disposed to his hand, he published his settled resolution to endeavour the establishment of Libertie of Conscience on such just and equal foundations as should render it unalterable, and leaue it to the wisdome of Parliament to invent and settle what security they thought proper to preserue the Church of England in its possessions and priviledges, intending to rob it of no prerogatiue it then enjoyed, except that of persecuting others, which Fagel himself condemn'd ; there being nothing more obvious to reason, than that every thing is best preserved by the Same cause that produced it, and the Gospel haveing been established by spiritual armes, without the assistance of humain laws ; it was a great argument of diffidence, that men should relaps from such divine grounds of confidence, and depend upon their own weak contrivances for its support, and continuance, and cease to endeavour to gain men by gentleness and patience, which were the genuin methods of true Christianity, unless they thought the Church of England could not be Secure from the attempts of others, unless it had the power to persecute them ; a denyall therefore to repeal the

Test on such grounds, was sayd *by y*^e *King's friends* * to be a
threatening for the future, which might haue endanger'd their
Religion indeed (had the Prince been disposed to take fire at
such menaces) much more, than by abrogateing the penal Laws
and Test.

But it was not to be wonder'd that those who had no
dependence on the King, or the Soldiers, who had been so long
under the Prince of Orange's directions, should be so easily
drawn into that opinion, and be byaced from their duty,
since his Majesty found such a refractory temper, and so much
disobedience, from those who were under his immediate
protection, and so near his person, and of those none more
obstinate than many of the Clergie themselves; who by their
former preaching up so contrary a doctrine, and their pretending
aboue all other Churches in the world to be the patterns of
Loyalty, made the surprise the greater; But his Majesty soon "
found that they of all people could worst bear with a "
Catholick King, forgeting that submission which they vallued "
themselves for in all their writeings, sermons, and declarations, "
particularly in both Vniversitys; pretending that no part "
of the Christian world came so near to the primitiue practice "
of submiting to Princes for conscience sake, as they, which "
brought into his mind what My Lord Halifax had sayd, when "
the late King published his declaration for Libertie of "
Conscience, upon which occasion his Majesty then Duke of "
York sayd, That none but Catholicks, and Protestants of the "
Church of England, made a conscience of submiting to "
their Kings; to which My Lord Halifax reply'd, His Highness "
would soon see the contrary as to the later, who he was sure "
would roare out against this declaration with all their might, "
which proued accordingly: but his Majesty was much "

T O M.
III.
1688.

KING JAM:
LOOSE SHEETS
pag: 8.

---

* Interlined as before mentioned. EDITOR.

TOM.
III.

1688.

more fully convinced of it afterwards, when it came to his turn to try their obedience ; and therefore it had been without doubt more prudent, had he not depended so much upon it, nor given them so much jealousie, since he found they would not bear the least contradiction ; but it was his misfortune to be misguided in that by the weakness of some, and the knavery of others, being pushed for the most part on the most dangerous Councells, *or y*ᵉ *most dangerous ways of executing 'em**; and the future behaviour of his Chief Minister My lord Sunderland shew'd planely enough the views he had in doing it, which will render the memory of him odious to future ages : for thō it be no new thing, for Subjects to demur to their Prince's orders, when they aprehend them opôsite to the Laws ; it is an unheard of treachery for Councellors and favorites who had been loaded with honours, riches, and imployment, to put their Master upon dangerous methods, with intent (as was too much to be suspected) to turn the heartes of the people against him, and to second the attempts of a most unjust and unnatural invader ; this is what comes up the nearest, (of any example we meet with in history) to him, who after the gift of workeing miracles, sayd to the Jews, *quid vultis mihi dare, et ego vobis eum tradam :* However all this malicious craft of false friends, and the natural propention the King had, to shew favour to those of his own Religion, was not able to draw him beyond what he was advised, by the judges of the Land, to be in his power to doe ; and notwithstanding the great clamours against his proceeding in reference to Magdalen Colledge, Father Francis at Cambridg, &c, it was however obserued, that never any Lawier or Divine made it appeare, that what his Majesty had done was either repugnant to the Laws of God or the Land ; for if the King had power to dispense with certain Laws on certain occasion (which all

---

agreed he had) then their disobedience was criminal and their punishment just.

But his Majesty finding that no reason or argument would give content in this dispute, and that Libertie of Conscience, the only thing aimed at by it, began to be loathed even by those who liked the thing, because they suspected the power from whence it was deriued, it quicken'd his resolution of trying to get it settled by Act of Parliament, which was only capable of giveing it a Sanction in the popular acceptation, and reconcile the Kingdom to its own eas and hapiness. The House of Commons which had been assembled at his Accession to the Throne, being ruffled and angry at their parteing, made his Majesty think it necessary to haue it dissolued; and before the writs were issued out for a new one he thought proper likewise to see, if he could convince the people of the reasonableness of his designe, and how far it would be, from prejudiceing, much less endangering, their Religion and Libertie; he knew how industrious the enemies of his government had been to poison the Corporations with those sinister surmises; his first care therefore was, to purge them from that leven which was in danger of corrupting the whole Kingdom; so he apointed certain Regulators to inspect the conduct of several Borrows Townes, to correct abuses where it was practicable; and where not, by forfeiting their Charters to turn out such rotten members as infected the rest: But in this as in most other cases the King had the fortune to chuse persons not too well qualifyd for such an imployment, and extreamly disagreeable to the people, it was a sort of motley Council made up of Catholicks and Presbiterians, a composition which was sure never to hould long togather, or that could probably unite in any method sutable to both their intrests; it serued therfore only to encreas the publick odium, by their too arbitrary ways of turning out and puting in, and yet those who were thus intruded as it were by force, being of the Presbiterian partie, were by this time become as little inclinable to favour the King's intentions, as the excluded Members, which gain'd the King a great deal of ill will from the people and no advantage in the business he aimed at ; his late Progress which had a view towards that likewise, was a more sutable method and had better success, his kind and affable reception of the gentry where he pass'd, had gain'd in some manner upon their stubborn temper; and they seem'd at last to be convinced how just and reasonable it was, to give eas to others, so long as it did not prejudice themselves, it being represented to them that the freedom of Consciences was dearer to men, than all the freedoms and immunitys Magna Charta could possebly secure : Tis certain the King had no reason to be dissatisfyd with his own endeavours herein, for the benignity of his cariage, and the awefull presence of a Sovereign imposed such veneration upon the generality of the people where he pass'd, that their joyfull acclamations and dutifull acknowlidgments seem'd to be pledg's of their complyance, and apear'd as unfained as they were universall; Portsmouth, Salisbury, Bath, Bristol, Glocester, Worcester, Chester, Shrewsbury, Ludlow, Neiuport, Litchfeild, Coventry, Banbury, &c, seem'd to vye with each other in demonstrations of duty and respect, nay Oxford itself, thō the dispute was then depending about Magdelen Colledge, was not behind hand with assurances of the like nature; in fine this kind visite from their Prince so molifyd their hearts, that in most of those places they promised to send such members to the ensuing Parliament, as would be for tákeing off the penal Laws and Test : he haveing dissipated their main prepossession by assureing all, who had the honour to aproach him, that thō he had admited Catholicks into Civill as well as Military imployments, yet he had no intention to introduce them into the House of Commons, whereby all immaginable innovation in Religion would be render'd impossible. There

were many * Addresses likewise from other partes of the
Kingdom, which (thō chiefly design'd to congratulate the
Queen's being with child, as from York, Cantobury, Monmouth,
Carlisle, &c) gaue however the same assurances of their sending
representatiues, who would concurr with his Majestys desire
of abrogateing the penal Laws and Test ; that from Scarborough
deserues for the ingenuity of its stile, as well as the dutifullness
of its expressions to be cited as an example of the rest:

TO M.
III.
1688.

Scarborough
adress Apr: 28.
1688.

The Vnion of York and Lancaster made the inheritance of
this Empire one, the conjunction of England and Scotland
made two Kingdoms one, but your Majestys † Declaration for
Liberty of Conscience has made our intrest one ; thus our
blessings haue risen by degrees to the last perfection, every
happyness was succeeded by a greater, and every Succeeding
Age Stroue as it were to outvy the former. Tis true our Civil
wars haue been renew'd in the time of our Fathers, England
and Scotland haue again been disunited by an unnatural
Rebellion, but Libertie of Conscience is so strong a Cement,
that no Age shall be able to dissolue it, its firmeness will encreas
by its duration, for all men will endeavour to propagate this
blessing which brings a visible reward along with it, and if
the darling argument prevail we haue already an ocular

---

* " The Gazettes," says Sir J. Dalrymple, " of the year 1687 and 1688 are
full of these Addresses. James was so fond of them, that he received one from
the Company of Cooks, in which they said, that the Declaration of Indulgence
resembled the Almighty's manna, which suited every man's *palate*; and that men's
different *gustos* might as well be forced as their different apprehensions about
Religion." (*Memoirs. Vol:* 1. *p*, 169.) The flattering Address that was presented
to the King by the Society of the Middle Temple June 11th 1687, is inserted under
that year by Rapin. See also De Foe's History of Addresses. EDITOR.

† The King repeated and confirmed his former Declaration by a new one
dated from Whitehall, April 27th 1688. It is given at length in Kennet's
History. (*Vol:* 3. *p.* 508.) EDITOR.

experience of our profit, men will not be more studious of transmiting a clear title of their possessions to their Children, than they will be of leaveing an undoubted inheritance of trade, Society, and Brotherly affection. In the first place, therefore on our knees we thank the God of Heaven for your Majesty, who, as a true Father of your people has provided for them so rich a patrimony of immortal happiness, tis a portion put out to use for Posteritie, which in every Seaven years will double and redouble the principal; God Almighty as we hope and pray, will grant you an heire masculine of your body, but you haue already given us one of your mind, in your gracious Declaration, tis to yourself alone O Sacred Majesty, that we Stand oblig'd for it, we own it not to be the Councel or procurement of any other, none but a wise and gracious King could haue found it out, none but a Catholick King has been able to efect it; we hope a Parliament will concurr and ratify this Blessing, for this Blessing has in a manner ratifyd it self by its own success, tis an Act already pass'd in the heartes of all your Loyall Subjects, and what it wants in formality of Law, is supplyd in the concurring Votes of all desinteres'd men; it will spread like the Tree in the Vision of holy Daniel till it overshaddow the three Nations, and the Birds of the air shall not only build in it, but all the beasts of the forest shall be secure beneath it; may your Majesty long enjoy the frutes of so happy a plantation, may it be fenced about with the care of the present age, and made Sacred to all future time as set by your auspicious hands; and as it is in our power, so we solemnly engage ourselves to return your Majesty two such Members to serue in Parliament, as shall Vote for repealing the Test and all penal Laws in matters of Religion, Laws which were begot under a doubtfull title, were bred up in persecution, and would subvert the fundemental freedom of the Conscience, which is God's Magna Charta, to all his reasonable creatures.

But this Seeming complyance in some, rais'd up a greater aprehention and sollicitude in others to oppose it, all hands and heads were at work to instill suspicions into peoples minds, and as men of wit never want topicks and turns of expression to darken the plainest truths, they had already so byaced the generality of the gentry against it, that when his Majesty thought fit to ask many persons of distinction their resolutions therein, he found a much greater reluctancy than could well haue been immagined ; and indeed that method was no ways relish'd by the people, who look'd upon it as a forestalling the liberty of debates, and set many in opposition to the thing, because it seem'd to be extorted, who probably would haue yeilded to the reason of it, had it been proposed in the usual formes; but there lay a suspicion of that mismanagement, as well as of other such like councells, at the chief favorit's door.

There was nothing they dreaded more, than least the Presbiterians, and other Protestant dissenters being fond of their present eas, should join in the undertakeing, and carry it in spight of them all ; this made the Church of England partie neglect no argument, or artifice, to work a sort of reconciliation with those, they own'd they had used too roughly heretofore, but that now the common danger, they sayd, had layd open their mistake, and had forced them to turn their spirit of persecution into a spirit of charity, and therefore hoped the Protestant dissenters being moved with the example, would meet them half way in that happy change; they soothed them up with hopes of haveing tolleration granted them alone, the next Succession, and least they might object, that the Church of England was meek only because it was *weuk,* * *and out of authority, they mixed threats with their wheedles, and tould them it*

T O M. III.

1688.
Great industry used by the discontented partie, to frustate his Majestys endeavours about Liberty of Conscience.

---

* Interlined by the Son of James the Second, having altered the first word into that of *weak.* EDITOR.

T O M.
III.

1688.

was in their power still if they pleased to supplant them in their Court intrest, and by the least glimps of their being willing to comply with the King, bring the royal thunder again upon the dissenters heads, and turn that glair of Sun shine into as gloomy a day as ever, which would bring all the arears of suffring upon them : The infalibility, they sayd, which the Church of Rome pretended too, was incompatible with Libertie of Conscience; and that Roman Catholick Princes being under an obligation of extirpateing herisy, when once they had the power, the dissenters would be the first who would feel the efects of it; the penal Laws and Test, they sayd, haveing been thought necessary to secure the Kingdom from Popery under Protestant Princes, that aprehention was not lessen'd by the King's being a Catholick, and therefore they were not now, to be throwne away ; that thō his Majesty was in such a situation as might make him a terrour to all his Neibors, by his Visible zeal for popery and endeavoring so many things in favour of it, seem'd to content himself with being a terrour only to his own Subjects ; they urged the King of France for a paterne, and that his aid might be made use of, to doe the same thing in England he had done in France; that the King's Councel being influenced by those whose zeal (they sayd) went beyond the aprobation of Rome itself, they aprehended Father Petre might doe the same thing here, which Pere la Chaise did there, especially haveing more fire and passion, with less prudence and conduct; the Judges, they sayd, who had been chozen more for favour than abilities, had not power to set aside positiue Laws so lately made ; nay in some papers published while the clositing was in fashion, the very future Parliament men were threaten'd too, that if that body, which (*they sayd**) was like to haue so

---

* Interlined as before mentioned. EDITOR.

many flaws in its conception went about to repeal Laws made
by legal Parliaments, (insinuateing as if the asking their opinion
before hand had much weaken'd, if not rob'd them of their
authority) that they must not expect so ready a complyance in
the people, as they perhaps immagin'd ; that it would put the
Nation upon an enquiry, who gaue them that authority to
make a rape upon its religion and liberty, and therefore bid
them beware of giveing occasion for such angry questions,
which were easilyer made than answer'd ; [But this doctrine
was soon forgot when the Prince of Orange came, for such
flaws in a Parliament were not only overlook'd, but a tumultuous
convention, assembled without any authority, took upon it not
only to repeal Laws but subvert fundementals, without being
call'd to an account by the people for it. *]

. With such plausible arguments as these, mixed with pert Sallys
of wit, and florishes of Rhetorick, some were wheedled, and
others terrifyd to fly in the face of their Benefactor, and repine
at their libertie, because they enjoyd it in the ill company
of their new friends, as the Catholicks were then term'd. :

The King on the other hand was not wanting to himself, to
obviate those popular appeals, by laying open the Venom and
Shollowness of all their Sophistry, and demonstrating by
unanswerable arguments, the reasonableness of repealing such
Laws as made men lyable to the greatest punishments, for what
it was not in their power to remedy ; for that no man could
force himself to belieue what he realy did not belieue: the
Test, it was sayd, in the first place rob'd the Peers of their birth
right, and without their being guilty of any crime, took that
from them which nothing but treason could haue done before,
which made the Peers reject it in the year 1675 ; that it rob'd

---

* These crotchets appear in the Original MS, and as if made by the Son of
James the Second. EDITOR.

the King of his right, which the law of Nature and the fundamental laws of the land gaue the Sovereign, of makeing use of his Subjects Seruice, from which My Lord Cook sayd, they would not be dispensed ; that it was occasion'd by Oates his Plot, which proveing so gross an impostor, nothing was more unreasonable, than that the Roman Catholicks should haue a penalty continued upon them, for haveing been wrongfully oppress'd at that time, and still treated as criminals, instead of haveing some amends made them for so unjust a persecution ; that it was not in the power of Parliaments to make decrees about divine veritys, which in all ages belong to the Clergie alone, nor did the Bisshops sitting in the House excuse it, because they acted there as temporal Lords, and were capable of being out voted by those who realy were so, and in conjunction with whom they had no such authority ; that it should haue been first done in the Convocation, which alone was vested with the Ecclesiastical power, and then the Parliament might haue abeted or rejected it as they thought good ; that it was a temerarious Oath, in as much, as it obliged people to swear to the truth of so obstruce and uncertain a proposition, and denounce the doctrine of transubstantiation to be false, which till of late years the Church of England divines did in substance agree too : for in all the disputes relateing to that Mistery before the Civil wars, the Church of England Protestant writers owned the real presence, and only abstracted from the *modus*, or manner of Christ's body being present in the Eucharist, and therefore durst not say, but it might be there by * transubstantiation as well as by any other way ; that the other part of that Oath which stigmetizes the veneration of images, and invocation of Saints, with the black

---

* A most able and learned Treatise on this Subject, was written in Latin by Dr Cosin Bishop of Durham, and afterwards published in English, 1676, dedicated to Heneage Lord Finch. EDITOR.

character of Idolatry, was no less temerarious and absurd, for that both those doctrines supposed a superiour diety, which cut off the very being of Idolatry ; and was in reality a direct protestation against it ; that it was only of late years that such principles were crept into the Church of England, which haveing been blown into the Parliament House had rais'd continual tumults about Religion ever since ; that those unlearned and fanatical notions, were never heard of till Doctor Stillingfleet's late invention of them, by which he exposed himself to the lash not only of the Roman Catholicks, but to that of many Church of England Controvertists too, to whom such arguments ought to be left, and not oblige illiterate persons to abjure what it was moraly impossible for them to understand, and an intollerable hardship, not to say Sacraledge, to force them to determine solemnly in the Presence of God, the truth of certain metaphisical notions, which all the subtilties of the Scooles according to their own doctors opinion, had not yet been able to decide: that the design of the Test was the King's destruction when Duke of York, that by striping him of his imployments and friends, those factious spirits might easilyer come at his person, and so run down Monarchy it self in the end ; nothing therefore (they sayd) seem'd more just and equitable, than to take away that intollerable yoake from their shoulders, which considerate and conscientious men of any Religion, must needs haue great difficulty to bear.

As to the penal Laws it was urged, that they were not only terrible for their rigour but their bulke too, being three or four and twenty in number ; which consisted of such variety of clauses and diversity of punishments, that a man had need be a good Lawier, to be a good Subject, or he would unavoidably be caught by some of the tenter hooks those sanguinary Acts had stuck up in his way ; how many fellonys, outlarys, and

T O M.
III.

1688.

treasons, were men made guilty of by them, without any immoral action against God, the King, or their Neibours? but only for not being able to get the master of their reason, or change their opinion concerning the Sence of some points in Holy writ: which being layd open to all men, and no power pretended too by the Church of England, to bind peoples assents, it was highly unreasonable to punish men for not thinking and believeing as some others did, being tould at the same time they were not obliged to it; they were exhorted *to*

THESS:
C:5: v 21.

proue all things and to hould fast what they thought best, and yet were threaten'd with grievous punishments, if they fortune to belieue as the greatest part of the Christian world does. That those laws in their direct sence made a Criminal of the Prince to the very government, over which he presided, by declareing the worship he makes use of to be Idolatrie, and (than which nothing could be more absurd) make him by embraceing that faith, guilty of high treason against himself; that it was contrary to the tenor and spirit of the Gospel, which inspires meekness; and particularly oposite to that great rule of Christian Charity, of not doing to others, what one would not haue done to ones self; that the intent of those Acts was pretended to be the King's safety, which the King being a Roman Catholick himself, could haue no colour now, no more than their reason of State, that all might be of one Religion, for that should Catholicks be extirpated, the divisions, and disputes about Religion, would not ceas for that; they had lately had tragical examples of it, and did not the attention they now had to Popery which they looked upon as their common enemy, quiet their animositys for the present, their old wounds would soon bleed again; why therefore should there be so much cutting and slashing to cure one tumour, in a body cover'd with Vlcers? especially considering how little it recommended the Church, which by this vehement proceeding

declared, how great need it had of such a number of pénal
Laws for its support; that as to reason of State, it was much
more for the repeal than the continuation of those Laws, for
besides the encouragement to Trade which was so obvious,
his Majesty had obserued by Monmouth's rebellion that the
Dissenters would never be easy till they had more liberty;
that a Tolleration had been the cement of the peace of Munster
after such bloody wars about Religion; which made his Majesty
wish to be able to establish the like harmony amongst his
Subjects ; that as to the aprehention, that the Roman
Catholicks (if once in power) might turn the persecuteing.Laws
against the Protestants themselves, in immitation of what was
then practiced in a neiboring nation; besides the impossibility
of such an attempt from so inconsiderable a part of the people,
the King offer'd them any security for their Religion, and the
possession * of Ecclesiastical Benefices, which the wisdome of
Parliament could propose ; whereas on the contrary to bring
for an example the present proceedings in France, were by their
owne practice, to approue the grounds of those regors, they
had of late so lowdly exclaim'd against; nor was the reason of
State the same in England as there, where by suppressing the
Hugenots all the Kingdome was made of one Religion, which
the extinxtion of Catholicks would be far from effecting in
England ; and that as to the objection of infalibility being
incompatible with liberty, the practice of so many Countrys
So evidently shew'd the contrary, that one need but cast an eye
upon Germany, Switzerland, Holland, and even Rome itself,
where the Jews were tollerated, to be convinced that the
beliefe of infalibility does not oblige the forceing all others to
be of the same faith : besides how rediculous would it be, for
so small a party as the Catholicks are, to endeavour the makeing

---

* Inserted by the Son of James the 2ᵈ, instead of the word, *Session.* EDITOR.

theirs, the National Religion, they would be in eminent danger
by such a disproportion'd force. to draw ruin and destruction
upon themselves, so that their own intrest, as well as· the
Princes, run paralell to his solemn promisses. Nor did his
Majestys seeking to haue Liberty of Conscience establish'd by
law, argue the illegality of the Declaration (as had been objected)
for that by the latter, the Laws (he Sayd) were only Suspended,
whereas a total repeal must be the work of a Parliament: In
fine there could be no reason (he Sayd) to aprehend that the
repeal of the Penal Laws and Test would· be an establishing
of Popery, for there would still be Laws· enough in force to
preserue the Church of England in the possession of the tythes,
their dignitys, and Reuenues ; that it did not follow that
people were immediately Masters assoon as they were let. loos
from jails and prisons, that the Catholicks were only formidable
because some people were resolved to be afraid, whereas if the
penal Laws was so necessary for the Church of England's
security, how came it to subsist in former time ? nay the Tests
were counted hurtfull not long before by that very Lord *
who was the first broacher of them afterwards, when his malice
had given an other turn to his reason : for he made so vehement
a speech against the first Test, or Oxford act, in the year 65,
that the Lords yeilded to his arguments and protested against
it, because, as he Sayd, it overthrew in great measure the act
of oblivion, and renew'd distinctions of parties ; that Oathes
about Religion were intricate and darke, and only snares to
consciences, that they were against the propertie of the
Subject, and dirogatory to the dignity of the King; and that
sweareing Subjects in points of Religion, was the highest
invasion of his .Supremacy, that had been offer'd at since the
Reformation : Thus did the Earle of Shaftsbury argue in those
days, which made his Majesty hope, the Peers would not be
against abolishing' the Test, which they had once thought good

to protest against ; nay Minheer Fagel's letter thō maliciously intended to obstruct his Majestys aims, yet by allowing of such a Tolleration in England as was practiced in Holland, where Catholicks were admited into military imployments, infer'd a necessity of abolishing both Tests which excluded both Peer and Commoner from any such in England ; and therefore to talke of permiting Catholicks, their propertie, libertie, and life, while the penal Laws were in force against them, was like inviteing them to Democles his feast, who had no great relish to his meat, while the Sword hung over his head ; it was in efect but telling them to eat and drink for tomorrow they must dy :

These reasons therefore (which the King took care to publish as much as possible) made him hope, that notwithstanding the sullen murmur of the Church partie, the Declaration for Libertie of Conscience, would not be so ill accepted in the main ; and therefore order'd it to be reprinted with some additions, seting forth his reasons for seeing it prosecuted, which, he sayd, he was encouraged too not only by the multitude of addresses, but several other assurances of his Subjects satisfaction, as well as duty in complying therein ; that he did not doubt, but the next Parliament would see the good efects of it; and aproue his endeavours of settling a Libertie of Conscience upon a sure and unalterable foundation, as the most agreeable thing upon earth, not to be constrain'd in matters of Religion ; that he should ever prefer that security, which proceeded from the peoples eas, before the burthen of Oathes and Tests, which had been fram'd by some governments, but never could support any ; which hinder'd the * advancement

T O M.
III.
1688.

TheDeclaration
for Libertie of
Conscience
order'd to be
reprinted.

---

* Sir J. Dalrymple in his Memoirs (Vol: 1. p. 166.) notices the change which the King had made in the Oath taken by a Privy Counsellor : " The Oath of a Privy Counsellor contained these words — I shall, to my utmost, defend all jurisdictions, pre-eminences, and authorities, granted to his Majesty, and annexed to

T O M.
III.

1688. of many men to imployments, which their qualifications and merit render them most capable of, and ought always to be the reward of service, capacity, and desert ; that he had made several changes both in the Ciuil and Military imployments on that account, not thinking such men fit to remain in his seruice who did not concur in, or aproue of, so necessary a thing to the peace and grandure of his Country ; recommending to his Subjects to remember how much peace and security they had enjoyd during the three years already pass'd of his reign, and how far he had been from apearing such a Prince, as his enemys would haue made the world belieue, as if his chief aim had been to be the opressor not the Father of his people.

The Declaration order'd to be read in Churches, which the Bisshops address against. Accordingly it was order'd in Council on the 4th of May, that this Declaration should be read the 20th and 27th of that month in all the Churches and Chappells of the Citie, and within ten miles, and on the 3[d] and 10th of June in all the Churches and Chappells throughout the Kingdom, ordering the Bisshops to make their distribution throughout their Diocesses accordingly ; but the Clergie (hugely alarm'd at this order) had a great assembly at Lambeth upon it, to consult what was fit for them to doe ; where they came to this resolution, That it was illegal to dispense with all sort of Laws, in cases contrary to the very designs of the Law ; they own'd they were not Judges of that any further than as it related to their own consciences, against which they must not go ; that the Declaration of the Judges in reference to S[r] Edward Hales,

---

his Crown by act of Parliament, or otherwise, against all foregn Princes, persons, prelates, states, or potentates. This part of the Oath was, by special order of the King, expunged from the Council Book. (Books of Privy Councel, 1, 13, July 1688.) The words were replaced at the Revolution. (Vide books 16 February 1688.)"
'Editor.

went no further than one Military case; and then they came
off with as nice a Subtility, as that of the Rebellious Parliament's
distinction of the King's person from his authority (to justify
the destruction of the former, as they pretended, by the latter)
so the Bisshops and Clergie agreed, that this being an illegal
order, and it not being in the King's power to doe an illegal
thing (for the Law says The King can do no wrong) they
infer'd from thence, it was not the King's order, and by
consequence they not oblig'd to obey it: by this way of
arguing, if they did but immagin the thing unlawfull (thō they
own'd they were not Judges in the case) there was an end of
the King's authority, and every man left to his own discretion;
then they consider'd the inconuenience and consequence, as
that it would amount to an aprobation and therefore encourage
others to follow their example, and the King to require more
hard things of them; that they had better make a stand at the
first, than when their reputation was lost; they Sayd, it would
not reflect on their Loyalty, for that Loyalty was an obedience
according to Law, nor disgust the Dissenters, for that they
could not be ignorant of their good will to them in the maine,
so resolved to present an adress against it; and accordingly
the Arch Bisshop of Cantorbury, (*Sancroft*) to gather with the
Bisshops of St Asaph, (*Loyd*) Ely, (*Turner*) Chichester, (*Lake*)
Bath and Wells, (*Kenne*) Peterborough (*White*) and Bristol,
(*Trelawny*) came to the * King on the 18th of May with the
following Petition, That the great averseness they found in

The 7 Bisshops
petition the
18 May.

---

* *Lord Henry Clarendon* in his DIARY, (*page 41.*) recorded what had
previously passed: "May 12th *Saturday*. I dined at Lambeth; where likewise
dined the Bishops of London, Ely, and Peterborough, Chester, and St Davids.
The two last discomposed the Company, nobody caring to speak before them.
Quickly after dinner they went away. Then the Arch-bishop and the rest took
into consideration the reading of the Declaration in the churches, according to the

TOM.
III.

1688.

themselves, to the distributing and publishing in all their Churches his Majestys late Declaration for Liberty of Conscience, proceeded not from any want of duty or obedience to his Maȳy (their holy Mother the Church of England being both in her principles and in her constant practice unquestionably Loyal, and haveing to her great honour been more than once publickly acknowlidg'd to be so by his gracious Majesty) nor yet from any want of due tenderness to Dissenters, in relation to whom they were willing to come too such a temper as should be thought fit, when that matter should be consider'd and settled in Parliament, and Convocation ; but, amongst many other considerations, from this especially, because that Declaration was founded upon such a dispenseing power, as had been oft declar'd illegal in Parliament; and particularly in the year 1662, and 1672, and in the begining of his Majestys reign, and was a matter of so great moment and consequence to the whole Nation, both Church and State, that the Petitioners could not in honour or conscience make themselves so far parties to it, as the distribution of it all over the Nation, and the Solemn publication of it once and again even in God's house, and in the time of his divine Seruice, must amount to, in common and reasonable construction : therefore they did most humbly and ernestly beseech his Majesty, that he would be most graciously pleas'd not to insist upon the distribiteing and reading the Said Declaration. The King * was much

order of Council; and, after full deliberation it was resolved, not to do it. Dʳ Tennison was present at all the debate. The resolution was, to petition the King in the matter; but first to get as many Bishops to town as were within reach: and in order thereunto, that the Bishops of Winchester, Norwich, Gloucester, Sᵗ Asaph, Bath and Wells, Bristol, and Chichester, should be written to, to come to town." EDITOR.

* Lord Henry Clarendon in his DIARY, (page 43.) gives some further information, " It was written with the Arch-bishop's own hand, and signed by

Startled at this adress, and tould them, that thō he had heard
of their design, he did not belieue it ; nor did he expect such
usage from the Church of England, especially from some of
the Petitioners, that he had the charity for most of them to
think they were not Sencible of the harme they did him and
themselves, but that they had been imposed upon by ill men,
who design'd his and their ruin ; that it was a sounding of
Shabas trompet, and that the Seditious preachings of the
Puritans in the year 40, was not of so ill consequence as this,
that they had raised a devil they could not lay, and that when
it was too late they would see their errour, and would be the
first that would repent it, [which prophetick expression thō
very little regarded at that time, they had occasion enough to
remember not long after*] and lastly he tould them that if he
changed his mind, they should hear from him, otherwise he
expected his orders should be obey'd.

. The great marke of insincerity in this affair, was, that either
designedly or indiscreetly, they had put it out of his Majestys
power to consult about, and by consequence to grant what they
required ; the Declaration for Liberty of Conscience was no
new thing, it had been published aboue a year before, and this
reiteration of it had been since the 27ᵗʰ of April, which was
time enough to haue consider'd the matter ; and yet the Bisshops

himself and the other six. The King took them into the room within the bed-
chamber : when he had read the Petition, he was angry, and said, He did not
expect such a Petition from them. This the Bishop of Sᵗ Asaph told me, when he
came home."—Under May 20ᵗʰ, the ensuing Sunday, his Lordship adds, "In the
Evening I had an account, that the Declaration was read only in four churches in
the city and liberties. Neither Stillingfleet nor Tillotson were at their Churches;
but as I am told, went yesterday to their country houses. So overwise are some
sort of men." EDITOR.

* These crotchets, like the former ones, seem have been inserted in the MS.
after it had been written. EDITOR.

made no scruple till the 18th of May about ten a clock at night (at which time they gaue their Petition) and the 20th it was apointed to be read: they could not belieue the King would departe from an opinion and resolution he was so settled in, without consultation, and what time was there for that? much less for countermanding his orders (had he alter'd his mind) in the compass of one day: this looked therefore as if they had been numbring the people, to see if they would stick by them, and finding it in their power to whistle up the winds were resolued to rais a storme, thō they seemingly pretended to lay it; they found the people disposed to follow the cry they heard from the Alter; this made his Majesty giue a wors interpretation to it, than that it was meerly scruple of conscience. He knew the Church of England had always preached obedience, but now perceiv'd that doctrine was to be kept cold for a fitter season; notwithstanding that very case had been decided by so eminent a man as Bisshop Taylor, who declar'd that an Edict thō unlawfull in it self, ought to be published by the Clergie when requir'd to do it by a Lawfull Prince, and cited St Gregory, who, when Mauritius directed him to publish a certain Edict in the Churches which he conceiud to be Sinfull, that he remonstrated indeed against it, however obeyd; his Majesty therefore thought he had much more reason to expect a complyance, since he commanded nothing that was Sinfull in it self, and that only publication was required, he neither obliged them to aproue nor recommend it to the people.

There is no doubt but according to humain prudence, his Majesty had done * better in not forceing some wheels, when

---

* Lord H. Clarendon in his Diary (page 49.) says, that the Lord Chancellor Jeffries was favourable to the Bishops, " He was much troubled at their

he found the whole machin stop; but his too great attention
to what he thought just and reasonable, hinder'd him from
reflecting on what (to be sure) had been more safe as the case
then stood; for how could he expect obedience or assistance
from those he had long obserued were sowing tares so
industriously amongst the people, and they so ready to receiue
them? or that those should be the fittest persons to bind up the
wounds, who did all they could to make them bleed a fresh;
but it was the King's misfortune to giue too much ear to the
pernicious advice of those who put him upon such dangerous
councells, with intent (as was suspected) to widen the breach,
and therefore encouraged his persisting in those ways which he
might have seen would not go down with the multitude; but
his prepossession against that yielding temper, which had
proued so dangerous to the King his Brother and so fatal to
the King his Father, fixed him *too obstinately* * in a contrary
method; he had obserued that nothing was more pernitious to
them, than their frequent goings back from such Councells as
had been prudently resolued upon, which determined him, not
to fall into the same errour he had so much preached against
in his Brother's reign; his Majesty saw likewise that other
Bisshops made not the same difficulty, and since many
complyd, it seem'd natural to think those punishable, who did
it not.

prosecution, and made many professions of service for them, which he desired me
to let them know. He said, the King was once resolved to let the business fall,
and not to have proceeded thus against them; that he was grieved to find, he had
changed his mind; that he knew not how it came to pass, but said, there was
no remedy; some men would hurry the King to his destruction." — Sir J. Dalrymple
(page 175.) was of opinion, that Sunderland promoted the Prosecution, "while
underhand he exhorted the Bishopps to stand firm." EDITOR.

* Interlined as before mentioned. EDITOR.

T O M.
III.

1688.
The Bisshops
Summon'd the
9ᵗʰ of June.

Hence it was that he gaue more easily into the Chancellor's advice, who thought his haveing reprimanded them not sufficient, he told him that their way of petitioning was tumultuary, and by consequence lyable to a legal prosecution ; where-upon the Bisshops were summon'd before the Councill on the 9ᵗʰ of June ; at first, they made difficulty to own the petition, but that being proued upon them, they refused to giue bail to answer what should be objected against them, this brought a necessitie of their being commited to the Tower, which otherwise the King would willingly enough haue avoided, for fear of encreasing the ferment which he now perceiued was already grown too high, and he found there was no puting too great a stress upon the peoples obligation of not resisting their Prince, when their leaders were so refractory, and so sencibly fallen away from their former doctrine of obedience, and that what is prudent as well as what is lawfull, ought to make part of a Prince's consideration, and this his Majesty was much more sencible of, when he was once freed from those

KING JAM
LOOS SHEETS
pag: 8.

Sycophants, who cover'd his eys from the light, and therefore when the veil was taken off, he own'd it to haue been a fatal Councell ; for besides the common reasons against it, nothing ought to haue made the King more cautious in the matter, than the present conjuncture on account of the Queen being with child ; it was that which gaue the alarum on all sides, and by consequence required a greater attention to avoid the least suspicion, or occasion of complaint in a thing, on which the future hapiness of the King and Kingdom so much depended : So long as the King had no other Children, but those two who were already disposed of to Protestant Princes, the Church men were less refractory, thinking that if the King encroached a little, it would be of no long continuance, and that at his death things would fall back into their antient track,

and the webb thō never so well wrought would soon be unravel'd
again; but when they saw the Queen with child, then they
grew so jealous of the consequence, that it made a sort of
metamorphosis of the Nation; the old declamers against fears
and jealousies, became the fiercest promotors of them, and the
great enhaunsers of the prerogatiue, now began to talke of
nothing but Magna Charta; it prompted, not only those who
eat his Majestys bread, but his Children too, to spurn against.
him, the two Princesses expected both to succeed to the Crown,
the Princess of Orange as the eldest, and the Princess of
Denmark, because her Sister had no issue, this made the latter
contriue to go to the Bath that she might be absent when she
knew the Queen was to be brought to bed, and it is to be
doubted the Bisshops had the same motiue in forceing the
King to imprison them too, who not only would haue taken
their recognizance but even their word for their apearance;
both which they refused, forseeing that an imprisonment would
not only inflame the more, but prevent the Arch Bisshop of
Cantorbury's being a Witness to the Queen's delivery, which
they knew the Kingdom had already resolued to question and
Cavil with.

It is not to be wonder'd that his Majesty thought not of
those necessary precautions, to obviate the malice of his enemys
on this occasion, it lay too deep to be easily fathom'd, besides
it seem'd as wild a thing to forestall their questioning the
Queen's being with child, as to the Ancient Romans to make a
law against Paricide, but new crimes and new contrivances
enter dayly into the world so wicked and unconceivable, that
they are never dreamt of, till the fact demonstrates their
possibility. It is true the King desir'd the Princess with great
earnestness to differ her journey to the Bath, till after the
Queen's delivery; but in that he had no further view, than the

Queen's comfort in the advice and assistance of so near a Relation on that occasion; but the Princess, who was prepar'd to elude, what the King was not prepared to obviate, pretended, the Doctor's opinion that it would endanger her health, in case she differ'd it; the King, who was the most affectionate Father upon earth, had always more attention to his Children's good, than his own satisfaction, so sayd, If her health was concern'd, all other considerations must yeild to that, and indeed the Queen haveing two reckonings, it was belieud she would goe to the latter, and the King calculated, that the Princess would be back before that, which made him easilyer satifyd with her reasons; so that what was the efect of her own contrivance, and the King's affectionate complyance, was afterwards rumour'd to haue been forced upon her, that she might not be privy to the impostor, which abominable calumny being in like manner published in reference to the Arch bisshop of Cantorbury, gaue reason to suspect there might be the same view in his contrived absence too; thō not perhaps designed by himself (for he was certanly a man, thō easily misguided, yet of a sincerer character) but by the advice and contrivance of others.

The Prince born the 10th June.

They had indeed calculated it to a day. as it fell out; for the very next, being the 10th of June, the Queen fell in labour and was hapely deliver'd of a * Prince, and notwithstanding

---

* *Lord H. Clarendon's* Diary, thus notices this event. "June 10th *Trinity Sunday...* " As I was going home my page told me, the Queen was brought to bed of a Son: I sent presently to St James's, (whither the Court removed but the last night) and word was brought me, it was true, that her Majesty was deliver'd about ten this morning. As soon as I had dined, I went to Court, and found the King shaving: I kissed his hand, and wished him joy. He said, the Queen was so quick in her labour, and he had so much company, that he had not time to dress himself till now. He bid me go and see the Prince. I went into the room, which had

the malicious combination of those who design'd to aspers him, and were industriously absent, there were still more than sufficient in the roome to testify the reality of his birth ; as apear'd afterwards by the testimony of Queen Dowager and the rest, when the King was made sencible that such a publick attestation was necessary.

   The birth of the Prince as it was an argument of the greatest joy to the King and Queen, and to all those who wished them well; so it gaue the greatest agonys immaginable to the generality of the Kingdom, but to none more, than the Prince of Orange, however he was as forward as any with his congratulations, sent Mon^r Cappel with his compliments, and carryd the maske for a considerable time, ordering him to be prayd for in the Princess of Orange's Chappel ; but the King had soon notice that it was done no more, and writ to the Princess of Orange to know the reason of it, which she assured the King, was *omited* * only thorough forgetfullness, and not by order from her, and that the Marques of Allbeville could informe his Majesty that the Prince of Wales was prayd for there, long before it was done in England : This ambiguous answer was only to see whether the Prince would liue or dy, before they thought it proper to shew their teeth, for besides that so many of the King's Children were dead, (and they thought this might haue the same fate) the Prince soon began to be so ill, the world reported it, of him too ; the King's Phisicians it seems, particularly Sr William Walgraue were against the giueing him a nurs, which, they immagin'd had been so prejuditial to the others,

T O M.
III.

1688.

KING JAM:
MEM^{rs}. To: 9:
pag: 215.

---

been formerly the Dutchess's private bed-chamber; and there my Lady Powis (who was made governess) shewed me the Prince : he was asleep in his cradle, and was a very fine child to look upon." (*Page* 48.) EDITOR.

  * Interlined as before mentioned. EDITOR.

but this new method of being brought up by the hand, and even without milk succeeded not long with him ; he soon began to pine away, and was reduced to such extremity that his life was dispair'd of; he had been remoued to Richmond as a better air, whither the King and Queen, upon this ill news, went with great expedition to see him, but before they cross'd the river, sent to know whether he was aliue or no, that they might not haue the additional affliction of seeing him in case he were dead ; and when word was brought that he was yet aliue, they venter'd over, and as a last experiment consent'd that a Nurs should be given him, which he immediately took too, and thō the great weakness he was reduced too, made him receiue very little nurishment at first, yet by degrees he gain'd strength, and became a healthy child and likely for life; which as it gaue the King and Queen the greatest comforte they were capable of upon the earth, so it raised to the highest pitch the jealousies and aprehentions of the people ; thō no body in reality was like to suffer by it but the King and Queen themselves and those few that adhered to them : so little reason had the world to giue credit to that detestable calumny, of their haveing put a supposed Prince upon the Nation; since nothing could contribute more to disturbe the peace of their reign, for by damping the expectation of those who already grasp'd at the Crown, and consummateing the fears and aprehentions of those who were already in a tremble for their Religion, it was sure to redubble the fury of those against him, who had sufficiently exercised his skill and patience already.

The tryal of the Bisshops which happen'd a few days after the Prince's birth, shew'd by the great concours and clamorous comportment of the people, to what a higth the discontent was risen ; on the first day of the terme they were brought by habeas corpus to the King's bench bar to plead to an information of high misdemeanour ; there was some debate at first about the forme of their commitment, and the priviledg of Peerage, which the Bisshops Councel pretended did exempt them from being commited for a misdemeanour, and the Arch Bisshop gaue in a paper to the same effect, and that they could not, as the case stood, be compel'd to plead immediately, but those objections being overruled they pleaded not guilty, and then had till the twenty ninth of June to make their defence; when that day came there was a long contest at first about proveing their hands, or that they were the publishers of the petition, which at last upon My lord Sunderland's evidence, That the Bisshops of St Asaph, and Chichester came to desire an audience of the King to deliver this petition (which they offer'd him to read and then being brought in to the King deliver'd it accordingly) put that matter out of dispute; they then proceeded to the question, whether criminal or no? which brought on a long and learned debate even amongst the Judges themselves about the dispensing power, on which the whole depended; for if the King was legally vested with it, his command was just, and their disobedience punishable: accordingly the Chief Justice Wright, and Judg Allibon argued for it, and the other two, Powel and Holleway as vehemently against it; which latter it seems weighed most with the Jury, who after haveing set up all night, brought them in not guilty. Assoon as the verdict was given there was such prodigious acclamations of joy, as seem'd to set the King's authority at defyance: it spread itself not only into the Citie, but even to Hounslo heath, where the Soldiers upon the news of it, gaue up a great shout, thō the King was then actually at dinner in the Camp; which surprised him extreamly, not on account of the Bisshops acquittal, for his Majesty only desired justice might be done, which he no ways obstructed, nor gave any markes of his displeasure to the two Judges, Powel and Holleway, who arraign'd so publickly his dispensing power; he had been tould the Bisshops had commited a fault, so he left them to the Law, and when the Law had acquited them he remain'd satisfyd with it; but what gaue his Majesty great disquiet was to see such industry used to inflame the multitude, and set the peoples heartes against him, and that this infection had spread it self even amongst those, from whom he expected his chief security, and that the Church partie instead of obedience, and duty which he had hoped for, and which he thought his protection justly merited, should be now the ringleaders of the faction, and that the Bisshops to highten the discontent should use all their little artifices to render his intentions suspected: for as they went through Westminster Hall, the people falling on their knees, in mighty crowds to aske their blessing, they cryd out to them, Keep your Religion; *as if * the* questioning them for a misdemeanour, wherein they had a fair tryall and were juridically acquited, should be such a mighty invasion of their Religion and priviledges, as to force them to cry, To your Tents O Israel. He own'd he had depriued them of one priviledge, which he found went nearer their heart than he immagin'd, he had wrested the sword of persecution out of their hands, and it seems they enjoyd no peace if others had it too, nor could bear an equality in those who had stood so long in awe of their authority; but they soon found their mistake; if they thought the world was made for none but Church of England Protestants, and that the way to preserue their Religion was to dispossess their Prince of his right; which as it had as little *divinity* † as law in it, so it had as little policy and prudence too, for by endeavouring to Secure themselves against a handfull of Papists who were unable to hurt them,

---

* Interlined as before mentioned, after two lines of MS. blotted out. EDITOR.
† Inserted by the same, for what appears to have been the word *Duty.* EDITOR.

they layd themselves at the mercy of a partie, which haveing
as great an enmity, and much greater power, made them feele
the efects of their errour ever since : The King indeed felt the
efects of his, much sooner, by laying too great a stress upon
those empty protestations of fedelity on one hand, and the
weak and treacherous advice of some Councellors on the other,
who perswading him, that since Law and justice was on his
side, there was more danger in yielding, than resisting the
current ; which made him reject that wholsome advice of those
who aprehending the consequence, perswaded his Majesty upon
the birth of the Prince, which happen'd the day after the
Bisshops imprisonment, to haue pardon'd their fault, and set
them at liberty, as a generall Jubileé on so joyfull an occasion,
and by that means shun'd the danger of a Baffle. But thō the
opinion of others overpower'd then, the King now repented
himself he had done it, and began to See a little through the
veil, which those people who were leading him to the precipice
still held before his eyes.

Tis certain the King had much highten'd this dissatisfaction,
not only by takeing Catholicks into imployment, but by the
great countenance he shew'd to many noted Presbiterians, who
were in outward shew gratefull for their present ease ; and as
it is natural for a Prince to be pleas'd with those who are pleas'd
with him, so they were well look'd upon at Court, and their
Councel made use of in the management of several private
affairs, as the regulateing corporations and the like ; but this
was the sequel of that train, which his treacherous Councellors
had traced out for him to set those against him who might
otherwise haue been his friends, and court those they were sure
never would : at first indeed this indulgence apear'd such a
superlatiue favour, and was receiued with such seeming thanks
and gratitude by the Dissenters, that they declar'd, that in case
they could haue foreseen his Majestys clemency, they never

would haue press'd the Bill of Exclusion, nor seconded Monmouth's rebellion; they made a specious shew not only of equalling but exceeding the most complying Subjects, and haveing the same intrest with Catholicks in geting the penal Laws taken off, they gain'd such a credit with several of them, that it was not to be wonder'd the King should giue them so much countenance, when he found the Church of England partie grown so dogged and dissatisfyd; which they, on the other hand counted such a piece of ingratitude in the King, that no attonement could be made for it less than the loss of his Crown and Kingdoms : it had been happy for many of them, if they had not felt a heavyer hand upon them since, for the King depriued none of them of their dignitys or revenue; nay after their acquittal he not only admited them into their former favour, but took their Councel in restoreing corporation Charters, and severall other things for the publick satisfaction; thō they themselves were not disposed to giue him any, nor even declame their aprobation of the Prince of Orange's comeing, which they apear'd (at least most of them) as well pleas'd with, as other people; but it is hard to Say, whether the King or the Bisshops were in a greater mistake in this affair, for if the King was convinced at last that men dó not gather grapes of thornes, or figgs from thistles, and that the Dissenters, whose principles were so opposite to Monarchy and the Catholick doctrine, could never join with one, or support the other; So the Bisshops who saw themselves follow'd with such crowds, and almost adored by the multitude, fancyd it was for their sakes that all that dust was rais'd; whereas it soon apear'd to be faction, not Zeal that gain'd them so much credit; for they who were so follow'd by the people and even cannonized aliue, when they abandon'd their antient doctrine, and duty to their Prince; when most of them suffer'd soon after realy for conscience sake, they found themselves as destitute of admirers, as they had been dazled with them before; and whereas the Archbisshop when he was in the Tower (to highten the animosity against the King) Sayd, he could liue upon * Sixty pounds a year (as if such severitys had been intended) was reduced soon after to liue, and end his days, upon an estate of his own not of much greater value ; when their greate deliverer (who they thought had made that expedition, out of a compliment to their Church) had convinced them that they must not expect to gather figs from thistles, no more than other people.

All this however did not discourage his Majesty from makeing an enquiry how his orders had been complyd with in other places, and the Archdeacons of the different Diocesses were directed by the Ecclesiastical Commissioners to send up an account of such as refused : The King's perseverance in this errour, was not so much to be wonder'd at, considering that several Bisshops had complyd ; that of Durham had carryed it so far as to suspend therty Ministers of his Diocess for their refusall, and a great part of the Clergie of Chester united in an address of thanks for the Declaration it self, wherein they confess'd, that if the matter of it were not according to their wishes, yet the publishing of it was according to their duty ; since it issued out of the express prerogatiue of his supremacy over them, and that they were requir'd by the Statute law as well as the Rubrix of their liturgy, to publish whatever was enjoin'd by the King, or their Bisshops, whose case herein, *they said†*, was remarkable in as much as it was prescribed in the rules of the book, so that they could not but with trouble of mind hear of the proceeding of the Seaven Bisshops, who thō they tenderly promised the dissenters something, yet refused to do their part

T O M.
III.

1688.

The King begins to be disobeyd by Soldiers as well as Churchmen, whereupon Col:Beaumont is tryd.

---

* Granger records an Anecdote respecting Lord Ailesbury's visit, at that time, to the Archbishop. (*Vol:* 4. *p.* 281.) EDITOR.

† Interlined as before mentioned. EDITOR.

about the Declaration least they should be parties to it, which reason the adressors thought insufficient; therefore they, in all submission, became earnest intercessors to his Majesty, in behalf of the Church of England, that the faults of those, and others, might not be layd to their charge, in whose communion there were many, and they hoped would be more, who concurr'd in promoteing the purposes of his mild government; and so concluded with their hearty congratulations, for the happy birth of the young Prince in his hereditary successiue Kingdom &c. Thus his Majesty wanted not abetters amongst the Church of England partie themselves, which made him persist longer in that contest, thō he found himself so over-match'd; for thō some few were pleas'd, many more flew off, and the Bisshop of Rochester fancying the Commissioners went too far, or rather hearing the rumour from the Cost of Holland, thought fit to write a letter to his Collegues to desire to be excus'd from siting any longer amongst them, as a Commis-sioner of the Ecclesiastical Court: and indeed the dissatisfaction had now spread it self so far, and that rumour of the Prince of Orange's comeing so incouraged the faction, that his Majestys orders were little regarded; who insted of being able to punish disobedience in others in favour of Catholicks, or get the penal laws repeal'd, the Kingdom began in defyance of his authority, even to put them in execution: for at the Assises at Shrusbury several Roman Catholicks were presented by the grand jury, and the judges openly countenanced or encouraged any contempt the people thought fit to offer to them, or to his Majestys orders in general; in so much, that neither natural allegiance nor even beneficial imployments, were counted any ty or obligation to keep men to their duty; for the Duke of Berwick haveing directed his Lieftenant Col: Beamont to admit some Irish Soldiers for recrutes, he being already engaged in the Prince of Orange's intrest, was unwilling to haue so many spy's upon him ; so refused it, under pretence, that it was a dishonour to the Subjects of England to haue recours to forreigners (as he term'd them) to fill up their Companys, and proffered to lay down their Commissions rather than comply : this refusal was too insolent to go ūpunished, the Coll: therefore (and such as join'd with him) were tryd at a Council of war and cashired accordingly : but it was obserued; and wonder'd at afterwards, when peoples intentions came to light, that amongst those officers who sat upon them, some, who soon after apear'd to be in the same intrest with those they condemn'd, were nevertheless by much the most severe against them ; particularly My L⁴ *Churchil moued to haue them suffer death for their disobedience, foreseeing that such a piece of severity would reflect upon the King and inflame the people, who still cry out against the Prince for all the ills, which oft times, by the malice, averice, or treachery of his Ministers, are done quite contrary to his intention.

But the Kingdom and Court were fill'd with incendiarys, whose constant endeavours were to scatter fears and jealousies ; and draw suspicions from every step his Majesty made ; and above all, to pervert that Royal and Christian one of granting Libertie of Concience, and to insinuate a belief, that it was only in order to supplant Religion, and then destroy it ; and now the Dissenters too, did not only concur in this, but valued themselves upon the strength and penetration of their judgments, that they could foresee and discover, that, to *haue been yᵉ originall*† motiue and end of it, and that all the mitigations to them, was only for the sake of the Papists, by that means makeing the

T O M.
III.

1688.

The Presbiterians join with Church partie to oppose the King.

---

* What is related in this and other pages of the work, respecting LORD CHURCHILL, afterwards Duke of Marlborough, is worthy of notice. EDITOR.

† Inserted by the Son of James the second, instead of the words, *be the.* EDITOR.

Throne dreadfull even when it was the seat of mercy; they
soon therefore join'd hands and voices with the Church of
England partie, so far at least, as to rail against the Church of
Rome, and talk of nothing but fire and fagot, as if Smithfield
had been all in a blaze, when the King's tendreness made it
his principal care, that there should not be the least fine
inflicted for Religion's sake; but this (they were tould) might
be cathelogued amongst their other thankfull returns, for the
King's snatching them out of the fire, and loosing his credit
with the Church partie, for haveing gather'd those Vipers from
the Dunghill where the Laws had layd them; and cherishing
them in his bosome till they stung him with reproaches, as
false as they were vilanous and ungratefull, for had the King
design'd the overthrow of the Protestant Religion, he could
not haue done a more unpolitick thing, than by granting a
Libertie to all Sects, unite their force against him; besides,
there could not be a more demonstratiue evidence, that this
indulgence proceeded from principle in his Majesty, and that
he realy thought it an evil thing to force people in matters of
conscience, than that, notwithstanding the termes of amity he
stood in with his most Christian Majesty, he both receiud and
relieud the French refugees, thō full frought with rancor against
their Prince; he gaue them a wellcome, and a compationate
entertainment, nor was he satisfyd to take them under his wing,
and make them sharers in his own and peoples bounty, but
entertain'd divers of them in his seruice, and honour'd some of
them with his friendship and confidence; so that had they
been Catholicks banished from some Protestant Country, he
could not haue done more; whereas those people could not
plead priviledges, immunitys, and Magna Charta, and tell the
King he was bound by his coronation oath, to protect them; so
that this, could proceed from no other reason than an antipathy
in his nature against persecution, for how otherwise could he

doe a more unpolitick thing, (if his design had been to root out
the Protestant Religion) than to encreas their numbers even by
forreigners, and those the most pervers of that perswasion, and
disoblige by it the King of France, by whose assistance it was
pretended this great worke of abolishing the Northren Herisie
was to be brought about? and thō soon after those very men,
laying aside all measures of thankfullness and gratitude, became
as warme inflamers of Rebellion as the rest, yet the King
constantly refused the succours his Most Christian Majesty
offer'd him; which was an other demonstration how far it was
from his thoughts to force peoples Consciences, otherwise he
would never haue let slip so fair an opertunity of admitting a
forreign force to execute it, when it was so excusable even for
his own preseruation.

And now the general discontent was grown to such a head,
that the Prince of Orange thought it ripe for his undertakeing;
he had long ambitioned the Crown of England, and bore with
great impatience the delay of a reversion, but now being cut
off even from that expectancy by the birth of a Prince of
Wales, was resolued to wait no longer, finding so favorable a
disposition on all hands to second his attempt; first, from the
factious temper of the people of England, and their inclination
to *. chang; and now especially, by reason of their disgust at

T O M.
III.
1688.

The League
against France,
which the King
is press'd to
enter into.

---

* *Dalrymple* in his Memoirs (*Vol:* 1. *p.* 180, 182.) remarks, "The Whigs
were willing to seize liberty under any leader; and the Tories deemed it not
incompatible with their principles of obedience, to receive it from the hands of a
Prince whose Consort would, in all probability, have a right to their future
allegiance. The Church of England was driven to despair; the dissenters found
out at last, that they were like to be made the forgers of their own chains . . . . . .
All these different parties carried their complaints to the Prince of Orange with
the more freedom; because, although the reserved manner which was natural to
him, together with his opinion of the violence and variableness of the British in
politics, made him cautious of speaking out his own sentiments; yet he was ever ready
to hear the complaints of a people who, beyond all others, are impatient of misery;
and who, even when happy, complain because they are not happier. EDITOR.

the King's favoring Catholicks, and dispensing with certain Laws, which disposed them not only to receiue the Prince of Orange, but invite him to their aid ; however all this would not haue done his work, had not the situation of affairs in other neiboring Countrys seconded his design : The House of Austria had for some time been projecting a formidable League against France, whose former acquisitions had given them great disquiet, and made them aprehend new ones, so were resolued (if possible) to be beforehand with it now. The Prince of Orange's ambition to be at the head of a powerfull army, and his inveterate enmity against that King, made him an earnest stickler in this League, which at last was concluded at Ausburge, betwixt the Empire, the Kingdom of Spain, and the States of Holland, and they had found means to render the Pope himself (who was at that time ill satisfyd with the Court of France) to be more than favorable to their enterprize ; so that nothing was wanting but the conjunction of England to make their force as formidable as they themselves could wish it : But the King (besides the little inclination he had to fall out with a Prince his near relation and antient friend) haveing the prospect of enjoying a perfect peace, and free trade, when all his Neibors should be engaged in war, made him giue no ear to the earnest sollicitations of the Emperour's and King of Spain's Ambassadors, who press'd him violently to enter into this Confederacy; they urged it upon him under the notion of being Guarantee of the peace of Nimeghen ; but that was no reason, he Sayd, why he should side with one partie, and that too, which was resolved to be the agressor ; besides that obligation (if any) was personal and ended with his Brother ; but (as was already obserued) his Majesty made apear, there was no such obligation upon him, for the Dutch haveing clap'd up a seperate peace without the privity of the King's Ministers, they had orders not to sign even as Mediators, much less as

Guarantees; besides, his Majesty looked upon the immagination of an universal Monarchy (with which they stroue to fright him as a thing aim'd at by France) as a fantastical dream, both impolitick and impracticable, as apear'd by Charles the 5th, and Philip the Second, but that were it otherwise, the situation of England still secur'd it so well against a French, or any other encroachment, that newtrality was its true intrest; which made his Majesty graspe at this occasion of eating out the Dutch, the Kingdom's rivals in trade, rather then to eat out his own peoples bowels, in the defence of that Commonwealth, which never fail'd to leaue their Allys in the lurch, at the least faint apearance of advantage by it.

The Prince of Orange knew how to turn this disposition and resolution the King was in, so as to second his intentions; by perswading the Emperour and King of Spain, that certainly the King of England had made a private League with France, and that there remain'd no means, but that of armes, to remoue the remora, which the present misunderstanding betwixt him and his people, gaue a fauorable occasion of efecting; it is not otherwise to be immagin'd that those two Prince's so zealous in their Religion, would haue concurr'd so easily with Rebellious Protestant subjects, to dethrone a Catholick King for no other reason, but because he was so; and against whom, they had not the least ground of quarrell or complaint: however by this stratagem the Prince of Orange drew them in to so unjust an enterprise, which without that turn, they would never haue *given in too, nor without their aid he could never haue* * efected; but he had the dexterity to delude all sides, by shewing them but half his design at first; he made the greatest part of the people of England believe, his comeing was but a compliment to their

The Prince of Orange's dexterity to make all Parties contribute to his designes.

---

* Interlined by the Son of James the second. Editor.

Laws, Religion, and Liberties, and to reduce the King to what they thought the just bounderys of his power; this was the wheedle that deluded the Church of England partie, and made the Seaven Bisshops write to invite him even when they were in the Tower. He easily perswaded the Emperour and the King of Spain, there was no other method of forceing the King of England into the League, and that he had no further aim in the undertakeing; but when once he was possessed of the full power, which the treachery of the English put into his hands, and the Confederate Princes through their enmity to France had so effectually concurr'd too, he forced the former to confirme his usurpation, and the latter finding the Sweet of such vast issues of Englishmen and mony, which the Prince of Orange fail'd not to feed them with, soon framed palleateing reasons to tollerate, what, perhapes at first they would not haue consented too : besides, they knew the King was a lover of his people, and a good husband of his treasure, and therefore would never willingly haue parted with either, but upon an equivalent return of glory and profit; whereas they saw, the Prince of Orange's greedy ambition of Command, avidity of fame, *and enmity to* * *France*, would make him as lavish of the English blood and coin, as they *themselves* * could wish, which he being forreign too in inclination as well as birth, did not disapoint their expectation in; The Hollanders indeed with less reason in apearance contribited to put so great a power into the hands of their Statehoulder, which so easily might haue been turn'd upon themselves, it was what their Pentioner Fagel had long dreaded from his right to the Succession to the Crown of England, and which by consequence they had no reason to anticipate; but his haveing no Children eas'd them

---

* Interlined as before mentioned. EDITOR.

of that aprehention, and his ill health convinced them he might liue long enough to Serue them, but not to annoy them; his loue to his natiue Country would make him (they hoped) favour its intrest on all occasions, and be ready to empty the English treasure into the Dutch excèquer, which was what they sought, and what he fail'd them not in; and his haveing no Children prevented the thoughts of the like usurpation upon Holland, especially they finding their account in letting him govern it as absolutely, as if he had been their King the short time he was like to liue : tis true they had the hipocrisy to cloath their Manifesto with the zeal for Protestant Religion too, and cheated some people with the beliefe, that their disinteressed succours was a sort of Almes to England, to reestablish their Liberties &c; but such*people did not reflect, that zeal and generosity are not the vertues of Merchants, they expected to be reimburs'd every penny they layd out, which was accordingly made good to them afterwards, and thō the account was swell'd high enough otherwise, yet they forgot not intrest, nor the hazard of the principal, which they were satisfyd for, before all was discharg'd ; this made them contribite so heartely to the enterprize, and cause their Ambassador Van Citters, to deliude the King so treacherously, by his repeated protestations, that their preparations were not against him : There is no doubt therefore but the States of Holland knew the bottom of the design, which made the Prince of Orange at his going off assure them, he would liue their friend, or dy their Servant ; thus was the Nation debauched from its duty, and tricked into a manifest undoing of itself, to support a forreign iutrest, and feed those needy Princes of Germany, with mony and troops, for which the English could expect no other recompence, then the honour of establishing their neibours by their own ruin ; yet all these hidden designes pass'd upon the people, under the notion of the Prince of Orange's pangs of conscience for the Protestant Religion, and his tender regard of the expireing libertics of England, whereas all those fair pretences of asserting the peoples liberties and secureing their Religion, were but introductory too, and a cloak, to the real design, of executeing the ends of the confederacy in general, and to serve his own ambition, and unsatiable therst after Empire in particular; nay there were those, who, conceiveing it to be more glorious to be wise than vertuous, and succesfull in wickdness than unfortunate in the pursute of justice, haue thought to ad a lustre to the Prince of Orange's character in afirmeing, that the very League itself against France, was only subservient to this unnatural design; which being first in his view, he put the Princes of Germany, and House of Austria, upon a confederacy against the King of France, to find him business enough at home, and prevent his giveing him any impediment in his attempt upon England : but the Count d'Auaux the French Ambassador at the Hague, who kept a watchfull eye upon his motions, suspected early this design, which he fail'd not to advertice his Master of, and he the King; The Marques of Allbeville did the like from Holland, and Mr Skelton his Majestys Envoy from Paris ; nay the latter got intelligence of the Secret from one Verace, who had formerly been a Servant to the Prince of Orange and extreamly intimate with Bentinck his favorit, but for some mistrust had been lately dismissed and was retired to Geneva, from whence he writ to Mr Skelton (who had formerly befriended him when he was Envoy in Holland) that he had things to communicate to the King of England, of no less concerne than the Crown he wore; which Mr Skelton by reiterated letters press'd the King to permit him to examin into ; but it makeing little impression upon him, the King of France sent over Monsr Bonrepos to convince his Majesty (if possible) of the danger, and to make him an offer of therty thousand men to his assistance, but the

Spanish Ambassador, and My Lord Sunderland found means
to work the King rather into a displeasure at the proposal;
they remonstrated how ungratefull a thing such Troops will
be to the people, and that the French King's magnifying the
Dutch preparations, was but a contrivance to fright his Majesty
into an Allyance with him; So Monsr Bonrepos finding his
Master's kindness so ill accepted, return'd home again, no less
ashtonished than the Court of France itself at his Majestys
surprizing security.

But he was scarce gon when the King began to open his The King began to be Sencible of the Prince of Orange's designe.
eys by the repeated intelligence from abroad, and the visible
defection at home, and so many men of quality haveing lately
left the Kingdom, and retiring to the Prince of Orange, who
by his friends and emisarys had so prepared the heartes of the
rest to receiue him, that at last the King was convinced the
design could be no other than against himself, thō he never gaue King Jam: Mem:^{rs} To:9. pag:227.
any real credit to it, till about the middle of September; for ”
besides the repeated assurances he had from the States, by ”
their Ambassadors or others, and even the Prince of Orange ”
himself, that those preparations were not design'd against ”
him, the Earle of Sunderland and some others about him, ”
whom he trusted most, used all immaginable arguments to ”
perswade the King it was impossible the Prince of Orange ”
could go through with such an undertakeing; and particularly ”
My Ld Sunderland turn'd any one to ridicule, that did but ”
seem to belieue it, and had so great an influence over all ”
those the King most confided in, that not one of them except ”
My Lord Dartmouth sem'd to giue any credit to the report, ”
and he indeed ever since the Duke of Monmouth's invasion ”
always tould the King, that sooner or later he was confident ”
the Prince of Orange would attempt it. ”

But thō the King was thus lull'd asleep by ye treacherous The King Qu^estions the Dutch about it.
Councel of those that ow'd him better service, nevertheless he

T O M.
III.

1688.

Marques
d' Albevilles
memorial
Septemb: 5.

was not altogather negligent in preparations at home, and by his Agents abroad, to Sift as much as possible into the bottom of this armeing in Holland ; he had order'd therefore his Ambassador at the Hague to giue in a * Memorial to the States acquainting them, That the great and surprizing preparations of war, made by their Lordshipps by Sea and Land, and in a Season where all action especially by Sea seem'd to be layd aside, gaue just cause of alarme to Europe, and obliged the King his Master who had nothing so much in his mind, since his Accession to the Throne, as a continuation of that peace and correspondence with their State, to order him his Ambassador Extraordinary to know their Lordshipps intentions thereby ; his Majesty as their antient Ally and Confederate belived it just to demand that knowledg, which he hoped with good reason to haue heard from their Ambassador himself, but that seeing the duty of Allyance and Confederation so neglected, and such power raised without communicateing the intent in the least to him, found himself under a necessity of reinforceing his fleet, to put himself in a condition of mentaining the peace of Christendom : The Dutch were not terrifyd nor moued with this, they knew their friends at the English Court would answer for their neglect, and on the otherhand they were so aprehensiue of the King's great Zeal and industry to encourage trade, that they were resolued to Second the Prince of Orange's ambition, which offer'd them so fit an opertunity of impoverishing and subjugateing the English Nation to that degree, as that it might be no longer an object either of their jealousie or envy ; and so made no difficulty of commenceing a war in violation and contempt of actual and Subsisting treatys.

The Dutch
Answer.

They answer'd therefore, that they armed in imitation of his Britannick Majesty, and other Princes, who were in motion likewise ; and because they were long since convinced of an

---

* This Memorial is given in Kennet's History, Vol: 3. Page 519. EDITOR.

Allyance betwixt the King his Master, and that of France, which they sayd the Count d'Auaux had owned in his late Memorial on the same occasion: *this ye King took to* * *be a dirideing of him rather than* * a rationall answer, since all the world knew who it was that gave the alarme; The Count d'Auaux's Memorial indeed had imprudently given some colour to the latter part of it, for his Most Christian Majesty was too well informed of the League which was made against him, and of the endeavours to draw England into the Allyance, to neglect a thing which concern'd him so near; so he order'd his Ambassador at the Hague to deliver a sort of threatening Memorial, wherein he tould them that their armeing in a time of general peace and tranquility, could haue no other meaning than to invade England, as his Most Christian Majesty was convinced by several circomstances, and therefore thought fit to acquaint them that the bonds of friendship and Allyance were so strict betwixt him and the King of England, that he thought himself not only oblig'd to assist him, but should look upon any act of hostility done either by Sea or Land against his Majesty of Great Brittain, as a manifest rupture of the peace with his Crown: the occasion of this Memorial arose from a conference betwixt M^r. Skelton and Monsr Croisy (then Minister for forreign affairs in the French Court) the former obserued, that notwithstanding the repeated advertisments that had been given of the Dutch intentions, not only the King's ears were stop'd against them, but that the Prince of Orange had got very early notice of several intelligences he had sent relateing to that affair, which naturally led them into a suspicion of My Lord † Sunderland, to whom those letters had

T O M.
III.
1688.

The Count d'Auaux's Memorial Sep: 9th.

---

* Inserted by the Son of James the 2^d, for words he had blotted out. EDITOR.
† *Lord Clarendon* in his *Diary* (Page 66.) relates a conversation which he had with the Princess, Sept^r: 23. " She then spoke with great dissatisfaction of my *Lord* and *Lady Sunderland*; especially of my Lady. I said, *I was much surprised*

been directed, and whose conduct in other things was not too
cleere from jealousy ; hence they concluded it was impracticable to serue the King efectually in the common road : so
without his Majestys privity Mr Skelton venter'd to propose,
that his Most Christian Majesty would pleas to acquaint the
States general, that unless they immediately ceased their
warlick preparations both by Sea and Land, he would look
upon it as design'd either against himself or the King of
England, and would forthwith declare war against them and
invade their Country with an army of forthy thousand men;
wh^{ch} method had it been pursued would haue broke the neck
of the design, and of the League itself ; but as soon as My Lord
Sunderland got wind of it, he (who had hithertoo preuail'd
with the King to reject the advice as well as offers of that
Court, which he pretended was but a French Stratagem who
being jealous of his Majestys power and riches, they did it
only to make him exhaust his treasure in unnecessary preparations) had still the same credit to expose this step, which
M^r. Skelton had made, as a criminal presumption, urging,
that the Dutch rais'd an argument from it for arming, and
that his Majestys own Subjects were alarm'd with it, to that
degree, as to haue already rumour'd it about, that there was
an Allyance betwixt England and France, and that it was
design'd against their Religion, and even to cut all the Protestants
throats ; in so much, that his Majesty thought fit, to disclame

---

*to find her Royal Highness in this mind towards that Lady, whom all the world
thought to have great interest in her ; and asked, If I might presume to enquire,
what the matter was ? She said, she thought her one of the worst women in the
world. After a little pause, I took the liberty to say, that I wished her Royal
Highness had not thought so well of her, as she had done, heretofore ; that, I was sure,
she had a just caution given of her. She then looked upon her watch, and went
into the withdrawing room : she desired, I would see her often."* EDITOR.

the Count d'Auaux's Memorial, both to the Dutch Ambassadors and in all forreign Courts, and to call home Mr Skelton, and at his arrival to Send him to the Tower: but it was not long after ere his Majesty was aprised who was the Traitor; and haveing punished M^r. Skelton's imprudence by comiting him to the Tower, he thought fit to reward his fidelity by comiting the Tower to him (as some persons pleasantly obserued) by makeing him governour of it, in Sr Edward Hales his room, when the King thought fit to put Catholicks out of all imployments except those in the army. T O M.
III.
1688.

However nothing rais'd the King more enemies, than this spitefull and groundless report of a League with France, which had no other origin but this; nor is it to be wonder'd, that the King of France (seeing the design of drawing his Majesty into the Allyance against him, which he had the more reason to aprehend because there was in realitie no such league betwixt them, and by consequence no obligation to the contrary) should endeavour by this flight of generosity, in offering him succours and threatening the Dutch in his behalf, to worke him to his intrest: it was no wonder each party should labour to get England on its side, it was sure to weigh down the ballance wherever it was cast, but the King was too good a Christian to invade a Prince he had no quarrel with, and too much an English man to engage with France against his Subjects inclinations; his intentions were to engrosse the trade of the world, while forreign States destroyd each other, but the want of wit as well as loyalty in his Subjects, would not suffer them to be so happy; fears of Slavery amongst the gentry, and Popery amongst the Clergie, were so artificially spread, as bewitched the people, not only to their ruin, but to be themselues the instruments of it; so the King suffer'd for his good will to the people, and the people were punished sufficiently for their folly and rebellion. The Dutch indeed The rumour of a French League did the King much hurt.

gain'd their point, and drew in the English rather to dethrone their King, than not to haue their share in an expensiue and bloody war, where nothing was to be got for themselves; instead of enjoying peace and a florishing trade which their Prince design'd them, and was thus rewarded by them for *his good* * *will.*

It was hop'd that this generous neglect of all forreign assistance, when his Majesty was so grievously threaten'd both at home and abroad, and his throwing himself thus into the armes of his Subjects, would haue moued their generosity too; and haue reconcil'd the people not only to his mild government, but his charitable design of establishing Liberty of Conscience, especially haveing published to the world so many good reasons for it, declareing he aim'd at nothing † more, and even referring the manner of doing it to the Parliament it self; but it seems the method his Majesty took to know their inclinations beforehand, had so put them out of humour, that no confidence or kindness, no assurance, the King could make them, was able to sweeten that froward disposition they were in: it is not improbable but My Lord Sunderland (by the Prince of Orange's instigation, who aprehended the King and Parliament might agree upon such reasonable termes) endeavour'd to spoil at least what he could not prevent, by puting the King upon a disagreeable method of doing, what if he had been left to

---

* Inserted by the Son of James 2ᵈ, instead of the word *It.* EDITOR.

† In a Conversation which Lord Clarendon had with the Queen during the month of November, " Her Majesty discoursed very freely of the publick affairs, saying, how much the King was misunderstood by his people; that he intended nothing but a general Liberty of Conscience, which she wondered could be opposed; that he always intended to support the Religion established, being well satisfied of the Loyalty of the Church of England. I took the liberty to tell her Majesty, that Liberty of Conscience could never be granted but by Act of Parliament: the Queen did not like what I said . . . ." (*Diary,* Page 91.) EDITOR.

the usual method, might probably haue succeeded; but whether this unpolitick proceeding had its origin from such a treacherous contrivance or no, (which dose not appear) it is certain the King very imprudently asked their opinions beforehand, by Closeting (as they term'd it) all men of distinction not. only Peers but Commoners, giveing directions to the Lord Lieftenants of the respectiue Counties to do the like all over the Kingdom, by interrogating the Corporations and men of intrest, whether they would be for electing such Members as would take off the penal, Laws and Test, and establish a Libertie of Conscience : Tis probable the King thought, or was perswaded, this plain and open dealing would be most likely to incline people to a complyance, when they knew the extent of what was desir'd, and that no harme was intended to their Religion or prop rtie ; it was but an informeing their judgment, or consulting their reason, in order to restore the Crown a priviledg it had been ever in possession of till of late, but it was certain he could not haue don a more ungracious thing than to forestall thus the freedom of debate, which they took to be so essential a point of Parlementary proceedings, that it gaue a fresh handle to the discontented partie to decry the King's conduct ; They sayd the Act of Vniformety was within the number of penal Laws, and should the people engage to a general repeal of them, it would amount to an abolishing the established Religion ; so by these and such like insinuations, notwithstanding the King's repeated assurances, no such thing was intended, most people were terrifyd to giue a flat denyal, many whereof might probably haue been of an other judgment had the thing been fairly proposed in a Parliamentary way, and in the manner the King design'd it ; however to obviate this, his Majesty issued out a Proclamation declareing, that least those who had the power of electing Members of Parliament, should be under

T O M.
III.
1688.

This Proclamation was issued out Sep: 21th.

T O M.
III.

1688.

A Proclamation published upon the noise of an invasion. Septemb: 28th.

any prejudice or mistake through the artifice of disafected persons, he assur'd them it was his purpose to procure a legal establishment of Libertie of Conscience for all his Subjects, but still so as to preserue inviolably the Church of England, by a confirmation of the severall Acts of uniformety; and for the further secureing not only the Church of England but the Protestant Religion in Generall, he was willing the Roman Catholicks should remain incapable of being Members of the House of Commons, and remoue those fears and aprehentions least the legislatiue power should be engross'd by them and turn'd against the Protestants; and further assured them, he would doe any thing els for their safety, that became a King the most indulgent and carefull of his peoples good:

But soon after this the alarme growing stronger from the Cost of Holland, his Majesty published a * Proclamation of an other kind, which was to notify to the Kingdom his haveing receiud undoubted intelligence, that a great and sudden Invasion from Holland was speedily to be made in an hostile manner upon the Kingdom; that the pretence of libertie, propertie, and Religion was made use of as a colour, but that an absolute conquest, and a subduing him and his dominions

* *Lord Clarendon* in his *Diary* (Page 68.) describes what passed at Court on the day previous to the publishing of this Proclamation. " Sept: 27. *Thursday*. I waited on the Princess. .She told me, the King had received another express this Morning, that most of the Dutch Forces were shipped; that the Prince of Orange himself was to embark as on Monday next; that Lord Shrewsbury, Lord Wiltshire, and Mr Sidney were with him. She said, the King seemed much disturbed, and was very melancholy. I took the liberty to say, That it was pity nobody would take this opportunity of speaking freely and honestly to the King; that I humbly thought it very proper for her Royal Highness to say something to him, and to beg him to confer with some of his old Friends; who had always served him faithfully. She answered, she never spoke to the King on business. I said, her Father could not but take it well to see her Royal Highness so concerned for him; to which she replied, He had no reason to doubt her concern." EDITOR.

to a forreign power, was the true designe ; that some restless and wicked spirits whose implacable malice, and desperate attempts, made them forget not only the former intestine distractions and miseries that attended them, but remaining insencible of the reiterated acts of grace and mercy, were endeavouring to embroil the Kingdom again in blood and rapin, that nevertheless he rely'd upon the courage fidelity and allegiance of his people, and as he had formerly venter'd his life for the honor and safety of the Nation, so now he was resolued to liue and dy in the defence thereof ; that this put a necessity upon him contrary to his intention and inclination to recall the writts for the Parliament, because it was impossible for him to assist there, and be at the head of his Army where his presence would be no less necessary, and that he would not be wanting on his part to make such preparations as became him, and which he hoped would make his enemys repent their rash and unjust attempt

For thō the King had little encouragement to hope for success in what he aim'd at in a Parliament, by the answers he had receiued in most parts of the Kingdom, however he had been willing to giue the people the Satisfaction of seeing it assembled, and accordingly had issued out the writts, had his enemys allow'd them time to meet : but their pressing so hard upon him, he thought too reasonable an excuse for his calling them in again ; thō it vext the moderate sorte to see themselves disapointed, of what they hoped might haue set things to rights by a method more sutable to the Laws and constitution, than that, which now the generality were pursuing with such violence ; and which put a necessity upon the King of makeing his whole aplication to the business of his defence: Accordingly ”
orders had already been given, to set out more ships to ”
fortify the Squadron which was actually at Sea; and thō ”
the King thought not fit to accept of his Most Christian ”

T O M.
III.
1688.

The King
recalls the
writts for
assembling the
Parliament,
and encreases
his forces.

KingJam:Mᵉⁿ
Tom:9.pag227:

" Majestys offer of Sixteen Sail to join with his, yet he desir'd
" they might be in readiness at Brest in case he had need of
" them, which Monsr Van Citters being alarm'd at, took
" notice of it to the King, who answer'd, He had no intentions
" to make use of them unless his Masters forced him to it :
" but the King haveing dayly more and more advertissement
" of the intended invasion, gave directions to haue the
" Squadron already out to be made up therty Ships, all 3^d
" and 4th rates as most sutable for the season, togather with
" Sixteen fire Ships, besides the Straights Squadron and what
" was in the west Indys, and augmented all the regiments of
" foot, hors and dragoons (the Guards excepted) ten men in
" each company, gaue out Commissions for raising Several
" new regiments, sent for three battalions of foot, the troop of
" Guards, the regiment of hors, and regiment of Dragoons out
" of Scotland, and three batalions of foot and a regiment of
" Dragoons out of Ireland ; so that he made account his army
" was no less than forty thousand men, which force his Majesty
" thought sufficient to deal with the Prince of Orange either by
" Sea or land, and had realy been so, had the Officers been
" faithfull ; so that finding a general aversion not only in his
" Council but in all his Commanders by sea and land, to the
" assistance proffer'd by France, he thought fit not to send for
" the Sixteen sail of Ships, tho they lay ready at Brest *for that**
" *purpose.*

Had the King harbor'd any dark or ill designe, it had been
natural for him to catch at this occasion to put it in execution,
but haveing no other, than that of makeing his Subjects a free,
rich, and glorious people, he cast himself entirely upon their
loyalty, whilest those who had most reason to be so, as the

---

* Interlined as before mentioned. EDITOR.

Duke of Grafton, My Lord Churchil, and others, had already " T O M.
taken their measures with the Prince of Orange, and had so " III.
great an aprehention of the French Squadron joining, that " 1688.
they industriously fomented the natural aversion the English " *Ibid:* 229.
haue to the French, in order to prevent it, nay they found "
fault with the King's sending for the few Irish, and so "
cunningly insinuated their pretended jealousies, that the "
Council gaue into it, some with designe to betray the King, "
others because their heads turn'd; so that those very men "
who had advised the things, which had given such offence to "
the Church of England, turn'd on the toe and were at once "
for undoing all they had done, even as to Libertie of Conscience "
it self. "

My Lord Sunderland who had long in private pretended " *Ibid:* 229.
to be a Catholick, and now publickly own'd himself to be "
such, was as forward in pressing this retraction as any, with "
this design (as most people belieu'd) that haveing already "
found means to alianate the Church partie from the King, "
this might make all the Nonconformists fly in his face too, "
and so leaue him quite destitute of any friends; this made "
the King begin to suspect his advice, and harken to those "
who assur'd him, that Lord's intentions had been all along "
the same, by pressing those councells which he knew would "
give most offence, and was sure to run the King upon the "
rock on which he Split at last, that he had been brought to "
it by his Wife and his Vncle Coll: Henry Sidney; but y⁰ "
King's tendernesss in forbeareing to censure any man without "
manifest proof, made him prescind from that judgment, "
especially when he reflected that all those contrivances would "
haue signifyd nothing had the army done its duty. "

His Majesty however left nothing undone which he thought "
might set the people right in their notions and obviate the "
groundless aprehentions they were prepossessed with, he "

" sent therefore for the Major and Aldermen of London on
" the 2ᵈ of October, and tould them that out of his tender
" regard for the Citie and to enable them to serue him in this
" conjuncture with that duty and loyalty as became affectionate
" Subjects, he was resolued to restore them their antient
" Charter, which some days after My Lord Chancellor carryd
" them to the inexpressible joy of all the Cittizens, he likewise
" published a general pardon with some few * exceptions,
" and the next day when the Archbisshop and several other
" Bisshops waited upon him with certain heads of advice, he
" receiud them favorably, and gave them satisfaction in the
" most essential things.

On the 3ᵈ of
Octobʳ. the
Bisshops made
proposalls to
the King, which
he grants in
great measure.

It was the seaven Bisshops who had given him the petition
(which shew'd he bore them no ill will) together with the
Bisshops of London and Winchester that came upon this
errand, nor was this the first interview he had with them since
their acquittal : for the Archbisshop tould him, that he
perceiu'd what had already pass'd betwixt his Majesty and
several of his Breethren had been only certain expressions in
generall terms, of his Favorable inclinations to the Church of
England, and of their reciprocall duty and loyalty to him, but
that they were impatient to suggest what they conceiu'd would
be exceeding proper in the present conjuncture ; which the
King condescending to hear, the Archbisshop presented these

* Lord H. Clarendon in his DIARY (page 70) relates what passed on Sunday
Sept': 30, when the Archbishop had been with the King: His Grace had concluded
by observing, " That he must beg leave to acquaint his Majesty with one particular;
which was, that, in the general pardon published yesterday, all the Clergy of
England were excepted out of it, as bodies politick and corporate; which was a
great discouragement at this time. The King said, that must be some mistake in
wording the pardon, for he intended no such thing, as was mentioned; and it
should be explained: that he was now going to Church; but that his Grace, or
any of the Bishops, might come to him, when they would; he would hear them
all he had to say." EDITOR.

Severall heads of advice; Ist that he would pleas to put the managment of the government into the hands of such as were legally quallifyd for it, 2dly that he would annul the Commission of Ecclesiastical affairs, 3^{ly} that he would pleas not to grant any dispensations wherby men not qualifyd by Law might be put into any imployment in Church or State, and that he would pleas to restore Magdalen Colledge to the President and antient fellows, 4^{ly} to recall all licencys wherby those of the Romish religion taught Scools, 5^{ly} that he would pleas to waue his dispenseing power till it were calmely debated and finally settled in Parliament, 6^{ly} that he would be pleased to inhibite the four Romish Vicar Generals, 7^{ly} that he would pleas to fill up the vacant Bishoppricks in England and Ireland, and Particularly York, 8^{ly} that he would pleas to restore the Charters to other Corporations, as he had been pleased to doe to London, 9^{ly} that he would be pleas'd to call a Parliament where the Act of Vniformety might be settled, and provision made for a due Liberty of Conscience; and lastly, that they might haue liberty to lay before him reasons to return to the Protestant Communion, all which they left to his Princely consideration, begging of him who governs the heartes of Kings to direct him, &c:

They would not, it seems, stay till things were settled, when his Majesty proposed to have given them a more disinteress'd testimony of his sincerity, in what he had promised all along; he knew very well that condesentions and favours when ill timed, and extorted from a Prince, argue rather the weakness of his power, than the clemency of his nature, but being they were resolved to haue it now he would not disgust them; accordingly he dissolued the Ecclesiastical Commission two days after, and as a further assurance that he would take nothing from them (tho he thought he might haue justly detain'd

1688,
Magdalen
College was
restored
Oct: 12.

Octob: 17.

one Colledge to punish its disobedience) he order'd Magdalen and Sidney Colledge to be restored, the Charters to be return'd, and all Roman Catholicks to be put out of imployment except in the army, which could not in any reason be expected as things stood ; nor did the Bisshops particularly insist upon it, or positiuely declare against his dispenseing power, or liberty of Conscience, only wished they might be regulated in Parliament, which was all the King desired, so no essentiall difference remain'd betwixt them : and now the King haveing done so much to giue them satisfaction, expected a sutable return, pursuant to their duty and such repeated assurances of their good intentions towards him, but he soon found that haveing forfeited their allegiance, by inviteing a forreign Prince, they made no difficulty of forfeiting their word and engagement to their Lawfull one, for now that the King had done in a manner all that they could wish, they would not so much as declare an abhorrence of the invasion it self, *tho earnestly press'd by ye King to do * it.*

Besides this deceiptfull cariage of the Clergie, the most part of those who were under ingagements to the Prince of Orange, added the basest sort of dissimulation and treachery to their treason : Whitehall was never more crowed'd with people of quality, who came to giue assurances of their fidelity, on which occasion none were more copious in expressions of Loyalty and affection, than those who were deepest engaged in the treason ; and those who durst not venter their persons in the King's presence, had the impudence to send up profers of their seruice at the time they were makeing powerfull intrests in their respectiue Countrys, to join the Prince of Orange at his

---

* Interlined by the Son of James the second. Editor.

landing; the Officers of the Army themselves follow'd this example, and when they kiss'd their Majestys hands to go down to their respective commands, those were most profuse in their proffers of sheding their blood for their Seruice, who were the first that deserted to the enimy : every one contributing thus to lull the King into an immaginary security, that when the Scene open'd, he might be the more surprized and wors prepared, which had its efect as to the first, but hinder'd not the King's aplication to the most proper methods for his defence, and makeing such a disposal of his troops, as he conceiud most necessary for his security.

The first motion his Majesty caus'd his army to make was to the neiborhood of London, to secure that important Citie, not knowing what intelligence the Prince of Orange might haue there, that his first attempt might possebly be upon the river, or at least to make himself Master of Rochester and Chatham, which were not to be defended but by great numbers of men ; and that if they landed in the North or West, his troops might be at an equal distance to march either way, and in the mean time all immaginable diligence was made to fit out the Fleet : My Lord Dartmouth, Sr Roger Strickland, and Sr John Bury were the three flag officers, men came in so fast that greater dispatch was made than well could haue been expected ; his Majesty did not neglect his remoter garisons neither, he left three batalions of foot and two Squadrons of hors at Portsmouth, one Batallion at Plimouth, two at Hull, one at Chester, and one at Carlisle ; and when the Army was drawn closer togather, two Batalions were sent down to Rochester, two more to Gravesend, one to Dartmouth, and two Squadrons of hors to Maidstone.

Amongst these distractions and preparations for war, the King forgot not the Cerimony of nameing the Prince of Wales, which had not been done when he was Christened, but on the

T O M. III.

1688.

King Jam: Mem To: 9. pag. 230.

On the 15 of Oct: The Prince of Wales is named, which

TOM.
III.

1688.
was not done
when he was
baptiz'd.

15 of October was perform'd in the King's Chappel at St James's with great Solemnity, the Pope being Godfather represented by the Nuncio, and Queen Dowager Godmother, who gaue him the names of JAMES, FRANCIS, EDWARD : and now considering the hazardous situation his Majestys affairs were brought too, severall persons about him thought it necessary, something should be done to vindicate himself and the Queen from the blackest of Calumnys ; and the Prince from that horrid imputation of being a suppositious * heire, for the Queen it seems, was no sooner with child but it was rumour'd about, that her big belly was a counterfeat ; the Prince of Orange who dreaded the consequence of it, took care by his emissarys to poison the people with that opinion, all artes were used by scorelous † songs, and underhand insinuations, to delude the Kingdom ; nor was this a new invention,

VIDE Sr ROGER
LESTRANGE
HIS OBSER-
VATORS.

for the like industry had been used when the Queen, then Dutchess, was with child four years before ; as soon therefore. as the Prince was born, pamphlets flew about fill'd with all the ribaldry and calumny that malice and wit was capable of inventing, where under the notion of novells and private relations of what pass'd at Court, the horridest crimes were layd to the Queen's charge, by way of introduction to the grand impostor, and the most virtuous, the most chast Princess in the world, had that additional mortification, of being traduced by a people she loued ; and blacken'd (if it had been possible) by the most execrable falsetys, that Hell it self was

---

* Upon the suspicions expressed concerning the Birth of the Son of James the Second, the reader will find some remarks by Walter Scott in his introductory observations to Dryden's Poem on that subject (*Vol:* 10. *p.* 285.) particularly a quotation from Smollet's History. (*Ibid.* p. 305.) EDITOR.

† *Ralph* has preserved one of these (*Vol:* 1. *p.* 980.) *Partridge*, the Almanac-Soothsayer, in his Predictions for 1688, is said by the same Historian to have availed himself of the temper of the times. EDITOR,

capable ·of inventing: she deserued a much better treatment
from a Country, which (thō a stranger born) was become so
natural to her, that all the hard usage of banishment, persecutions and contradictions, she had met with, could not hinder
her from contending with the King himself in a real affection·
for the people ; but God had destined them both a more
essential reward· than popular applaus, so they met with few
gratefull returns to their real favours, and where they planted
vineš they reap'd nothing but thornes.

The people therefore who too easily credit lys of their Prince,
especially considering his Religion, gaue so roundly into this,
that it was thought indispensably necessary to haue the reality
of the Prince's birth proued, by those who were present at it.
At·first the King was ashtonished at the proposal, not conceiveing how a thing of that nature could be call'd in question, how
impossible it would be, to compass such a cheat were one so
wicked as to endeavour it, and how improbable he himself
should contriue to depriue his own Children of their right, but
most of áll, how senceless an immagination it was, that he
and the Queen should conspire to do so detestable a thing to
endanger the ruin of themselves and all that adher'd to them ;
they saw plainly that nothing rais'd the peoples aprehentions
so much as the prospect of a Prince of the same Religion to
succeed the King, that the Prince of Orange's ambition was
impatient of such an obstacle, and that his birth was the main
origin of all ·their dangers and hazards, and had not only
occasion'd a present great defection in the people, but rais'd
his own Children in opposition to him, and as to the common
calumny, that Papists think all things permitted for the sake
of * Religion, and that their Zeal will expose them to any

The King is advised to proue the Prince of Wales his Birth.

T O M. III. 1688.

---

* It had been written in the MS. *their* Religion. EDITOR.

danger for its advancement, *it appear'd to him* * *as* great a
contradiction as the rest; for since they supposed Religion to
be so dear to them, how could they think that the obseruance
of its morralls, which are as much of divine ordination as its
faith, could be so easily dispensed with? but what apear'd to
him still more absurd, was that in their supposition, the King
and Queen should Visibly contribite to their own destruction
for the sake of a people that was now riseing in armes against
them; and yet, at other times, they sayd, the King had made
a league with France to destroy them and cut all their throats.
For this pretended good of Religion, could haue no relation to
the King himself and the Queen, and the other Catholicks of
the Nation, they were already such and needed not a Prince
of Wales † to make them so, it was therefore for the sakes of
those that profess'd themselves Protestants, and at this time
his enimys, that the King and Queen were supposed to do so
wicked an action; these were, in fine, such Paradoxes as the
King stood amazed at, and indeed none but a people accostomed
to belieue the fables of forty one, and the contradictions of
Oates's plot, could reconcile; ...

This was what occur'd to the King at that time, but when
the immagination was carried further which those wicked
fomenters of it endeavour'd to do *with this* † *design*, that it might
be an obstacle to the Son's Succession, as it had been an
argument for detroneing his Father; the absurdity still
apear'd greater, that the King and Queen should suffer themselves to be expell'd the Nation, to liue in banishment, and
upon a precarious subsistance, for the sake of a Child which
was supposed not to be their own, to see the Catholicks of the
three Nations grievously oppress'd, new laws invented for their

---

* Inserted by the Son of James the second, for some word that had been blotted
out. EDITOR.

† Interlined as before mentioned. EDITOR.

speedyer destruction, and such as would probably extirpate
them in a few years if not repeal'd, and yet to immagin all
this was for the good of Religion; so that by these peoples
reasoning, the King and Queen made themselves most miserable in this world, exposed themselves to be so in the next,
and contribited as much as in them lay to the utter extirpation
of Catholick Religion in all their dominions, and yet this is
supposed to be for the advancement of the Church : it was
much more reasonable to immagin that the King, when he saw
himself in his declineing age, destitute of hopes of regaining
his Kingdoms, would haue accepted a pension from his own
people, which they would willingly haue given him, and so
settled peace to them, and libertie to his Catholick Subjects to
submit to the government, to prevent their present oppression
and future destruction, had not his obligation in conscience
tyd him never to give away the right of his Son; and if the
King was supposed to haue too generous and great a soul to
come to any composition with his people during his life, at
least after his death the Queen who could demand nothing but
her Dower, would never haue refused it, to liue upon the
uncertain relief of a forreign State for the Sake of a Child that
was not hers, But time the best discoverer of such darke
contrivances, has set the falsety of that enormous Calumny in
so clear a light, that the most impudent broachers of it, will
blush at the remembrance of their wickedness, never Child
had a greater resemblance of his parents both in body and
mind, than his present Majesty of the * late King his Father
and the Queen his Mother, no other argument is now needfull
than a sight of his royal person, to fill with confusion the
infamous contrivers of that Hellish Calumny ; who by thus

---

* Proof of the date of the composition of this Biographical Narrative, after the
death of James 2ᵈ and that of his Queen. EDITOR.

traduceing their Prince, haue endeavour'd to ad to their other crimes, that of debarring his present Majesty, his right of Succession to three Kingdoms, upon a senceless story that would not be an obstacle to a man's succeeding to the inheritance of an acre of land; what a condition would the world be in, if the next in remainder to any estate might dispossess the present possessor, or aparent heir, that could not proue his legitimacy by more witnesses than those who were present at the Prince of Wales his birth? how rediculous would such a plea apear in a court of justice, yet no scruple is made of dispossessing one of the greatest Princes in the world upon this groundless fable, so wicked, senceless, and even impossible to be true.

But notwithstanding all the arguments which reason and prudence might suggest against the necessity of such a proof; yet the malice and credulity of the people was rais'd to such a pitch, that it was necessary to follow them in all their laborinths of fears and jealousies, and obviate the most senceless reports and rediculous aprehentions. The King reflected that dureing the Queen's being withchild, the report of her haveing a conterfeat big belly was universally spread, which then indeed was looked upon as a jest, and the talke of a Cussion was the dayly subject of mirth to those who attended upon them, and saw every day the reality of the Queen's being with child; but his Majesty was now convinced that popular conjectures, thō never so groundless, are not always to be cur'd by jests and undervalluing them, and that whereas the Queen's bed-chamber was accessible but to a few, no corner of the Kingdom was impenitrable to the false suggestions of the Prince of Orange's Emissarys; who by this time had caused a certain memorial to be presented to him in the name of the English Protestants, Sayd to be writen by D\u1d57 Burnet, where amongst other grivances, that of putting a supposed Prince

upon the People is principally complaint of. The Queen had
more difficulty than the King to immagin such a proof
necessary, till one day at a visite she made the Princesse *
Anne, speakeing of those reports, the Queen sayd, She
wonder'd how such rediculous falsetys could gain the least
credit; to which the Princess answer'd very couldly, It was
not so much to be wonder'd at, since such persons were not
present, as ought to haue been there; the Queen was hugely
surprised at this, and began as well as the King to suspect the
worst, when his own Daughter who knew so well the reality
of the Queen's being withchild fomented the contrary report:
this made the Queen call to mind how differently the Princess
had carryed herself in that matter, at the begining of her being
withchild, and afterwards; that while she thought the Queen
might probably miscarry as she had done formerly, she was
frequently at her twylet and put on her shift as usually; her
discours and cariage was sutable to the occasion, and particularly at the 7 months end, when the Queen fortuned to be
taken exceeding ill and the King being gon to Chatham, her
aprehention of miscarrying was so great, that she writ for him
immediately to come to her, sent for her Confessor not being
out of fear for her life, so that every body flocking about her,
the Princess fail'd not to be there too; who apear'd so easy and
kind, that nothing could equal it, talked of the Queen's
condition with mighty concern, and was wanting in no manner
of respect and care; but when the Queen had escaped that
danger and drew near her time, the Princess pretended ill
health, apear'd extream Seldom in the Queen's bedchamber,
which usher'd in a pretence of going to the Bath, that she

T O M.
III.
1688.

---

* *Sir J. Dalrymple* amidst the valuable Historical Documents which he has given
in the second Volume of his *Memoirs,* has inserted what are styled *Curious Notes
from the Princess Anne's Letters to her Sister the Princess of Orange,* which Sir John
received from Lord Hardwicke. In most of these Letters (*page* 300-310) her Royal
Highness seems to have doubted the Fact of the Queen's pregnancy. EDITOR.

T O M.
III.

1688.
An extraor-
dinary Council
call'd to proue
the Prince's
birth, Octob.
the 22ᵈ.

might be sure to be absent when the Queen was deliver'd, and not be a witness, to what she was resolved to question.

All these considerations convinced the King and Queen it was necessary to obviate this malicious Calumny, so he summon'd an extraordinary Council the 22ᵈ of October, where was present the Queen Dawager, all the Lords Spiritual and Temporal then in Town, the Lord Major and Aldermen, the Judges, and Kings Councell, to whom his Majesty spoke as follows.

I haue call'd you togather upon a very extraordinary occasion, but extraordinary diseases must haue extraordinary remedys, the malicious endeavours of my enemies, haue so poison'd the minds of some of my Subjects, that by the reports I hear from all hands, I haue reason to belieue that very many do not think this Son, with which God has bless'd me, to be mine, but a supposed Child; but I may say, that by particular providence scarce any Prince was ever born, where there were so many persons present.

I haue taken this time to haue the matter heard and examin'd here, expecting that the Prince of Orange with the first fair easterly wind, will invade this Kingdom, and as I haue oft venter'd my life for the Nation before I came to the Crown, so I think myself more obliged to do it, now I am King, and do intend to go in person against him, whereby I may be exposed to accidents; and therefore I thought it necessary to haue it now done, in order to satisfy the minds of my Subjects, and to prevent this Kingdom's being engaged in blood and confusion after my death, desireing to doe always what may most contribute to the eas and quiet of my Subjects, which I haue shew'd by securing to them their Libertie of Conscience, and the enjoyment of their properties, which I will always preserue; I haue desired the Queen Dowager to giue herself the trouble to come hither and declare what she knows of the birth of my son, and most of the Ladys and Lords, and other persons who were present, are ready likewise to depose upon Oath, their knowlidg of this matter. Vpon which Queen Dawager was pleas'd to Say, that when the King sent for her to the Queen's labour, she came assoon as she could and never stir'd from her, till she was deliver'd of a Prince of Wales ; there were no less than fourthy two persons who were both present and witness (as much as the circumstances and modesty could allow) to the Birth of the Prince ; the men, who were the chief officers of the Crown, as Lord Chancellor, the Earle of Sunderland Lord President of the Council, the Earle of Mulgraue Lord Chamberlin, Lord Arundel Lord Privy Seal, the Earle of Middleton Secretary of State, the Earle's of Craven, Peterborough &c, all deposed, that they Saw the Child immediately after the Queen was deliver'd, and saw it was a Prince and all the markes of being new born : the Ladys who may be supposed to haue had a nearer admittance, both at y⁰ time of the Queens labour and during her being withchild, as Lady Powis, Aran, Peterborough, Sunderland, Roscommon, Bellacis, Lady Sophia Bulkeley &c; and almost all the other Ladys of her family, deposed upon Oath likewise, their haveing frequently seen the milk run out of the Queen's breast, and very often felt her belly, which My Lady Sunderland deposed she did even while the Queen was in labour, for her Majesty being in great pain and the Midwife assureing her she would soon be deliver'd, she sayd, she aprehended the contrary; because the Child lay so high, and My Lady Sunderland being next her she made her feel whereabouts it lay, which she did and deposed it upon Oath accordingly, as did as many other Ladys as could stand round the bed, that they were eye witnesses of his Birth.

Nevertheless such was the weak credulity of some and malice of others, that this was not able to stifle the report, nay there was one who fram'd a sort of Answer to these Depositions after the Revolution, grounded upon redeculous suppositions and manifest falsetys, as that the Papists make no scruple of the greatest wicknesses to compas what they think for their advantage, that it was impossible for the Queen to haue a Child, thō she had had so many, was not then above therty years old, and (as it happen'd) had one four years after ; that the Princess Anne was never permited to see the Queen's belly, whereas she did it frequently in the beginning, and if she absented herself towards the end it was industriously done, as well as her going to the Bath, which it had been impossible for the King to haue forced upon her, had she suspected any thing of what was afterwards pretended, and been desirous to see the truth ; then he says, that the wether being hot there was no need of a warming pan, unless it were to carry the child into the bed, as if linning were not to be air'd at all times, especially on such occasions, and Mⁱˢ Dawson who was a Protestant deposed amongst other things, that she saw fire in the warming pan when it was brought into the room ; then he complains that the Dutch Ambassador was not there, as if the Queen who had always a quick labour, could delay the birth, till people so remote could be sent for ; the same thing, he pretends, was projected by Queen Mary to disapoint Queen Elizabeth's Succession, that the Princess of Orange was hinder'd from being there, that the Arch bisshop of Cantorbury was sent to the Tower for the same reason ; in fine whatever was done by contrivance of the persons themselves to avoid being wittnesses, or happen'd by accident, was all charg'd upon the King and Queen as designedly brought about to cover the cheat, and then for the witnesses, he accuses them either of downright perjúry, or equivocation, not spareing Queen Dowager herself; and thus he rids himself of them all, not regarding that most of them were Protestants and some of them not too well affected to the King and Queen, as apear'd soon after : It were an improper digression thus to take notice of so senceless a Scribler, who supposes without ground, denys without answering, and affirms without proof, were it not necessary to shew what sort of reasoning pass'd current in those days, and how the people were deluded to think or believe the greatest crimes or even impossibilitys of the best of Princes only because he did not think or belieue as they did in matters of Faith ; but the world had been better satisfyd in this matter, had the Prince of Orange complyd with his Sollemn promis in his declaration, of examining the Prince's birth ; he was not indeed wanting in his endeavours, Commissioners amongst the Nobility were nam'd to make an enquiry, and many dark contrivances were set on foot to make the world belieue the accusation well grounded, but after all, neither the cunning, nor malice of those who were imployed about it, could ever frame so much as a probablely, capable of fobbing off the credulous multitude ; and My Lord Danby who was particularly imployd in that affair, being asked why nothing was done to satisfy the world in a thing of that importance, Sayd, the more they examin'd into it the more proof they found of the reality of the Prince's being born of the Queen ; but the Prince of Orange haveing brought about what he aim'd at by that, and other Calumnys, let them moulder away when he had no further use for them.

The Princess * Anne had been desir'd by the King to be present at this Council, both to hear the attestation of others,

T O M. III.

1688.

The Princess Anne waued being at this Council.

---

* In the second volume of *Sir J. Dalrymple's Memoirs*, (page 305.) are the Questions sent by the Princess of Orange to the Princess Anne of Denmark, respecting the state of the Queen, dated July 21, 1688 ; as also the Answers that were returned by the Princess Anne : one of the former, which is styled an Additional Question, was, " *If the King did not use to be nearer the Bed and hold the Queen in former labours.*" EDITOR.

and depose her own knowlidg, which (before so many wittnesses
of her haveing been privy to the Queen's being with child) she
durst not haue disown'd ; but she pretending danger in comeing
abroad, the King had the goodness not only to accept her excuse,
but to acquaint the Lords that she would haue been there, but
that being with child, and not haveing of late stir'd abroad, could
not come so far without hazard ; and then added, And now
My Lords although I did not question but every person here
present was satisfyd before in this matter, yet by what you
haue heard you will be better able to satisfy others ; besides if
I and the Queen could be thought so wicked, as to endeavour
to impose a Child upon the Nation, you see how impossible
it would haue been, neither could I my self be imposed upon,
haveing constantly been with the Queen dureing her being
with Child, and the whole time of her labour, and there is none
of you but will easily belieue me, who haue suffer'd so much
for conscience sake, incapable of so great a villany to the
prejudice of my own Children ; and I thank God those that
know me, know very well, that it is my principle to doe as I
would be done by, for that is the Law and the Prophets ; and
that I would rather dy a thousand deaths, than doe the least
wrong to any of my Children ; and if any of My Lords think
it necessary that the Queen be sent for, it shall be done:
but they thinking it unreasonable to put the Queen to that
confusion, the Council broke up, haveing deputed some Lords
to wait upon the Princess Anne, with the particulars of what
had been done, who being prepar'd with an answer, sayd,
the King's word to her was more than all the rest ; thus by
pretended indispositions on one hand, and an equivocal reply
on the other, she eluded what otherwise it had been impossible
for her not to haue own'd, had not the King's tenderness of
her made him ready to accept any excuse : there remain'd no
more to perfect this affair, but to haue the King's own

declaration, Queen Dowager's, and all the other depositions
enrol'd in Chancery, which the next day being the 23 of
October was done accordingly ; and because that Court takes
no notice of any thing done out of it, each person upon oath
affirm'd their respectiue depositions to be true, to which were
added those of the Earles of Huntington and Peterborough to
the same efect with the others, they not haveing been present
at the great Council : so that no formality was wanting to
obviate, if possible, this injurious and groundless Calumny,
which thō more than sufficient to convince all reasonable and
well meaning men, yet it hinder'd not the wicked framers of it
from endeavouring to support its credit, so long as it was thought
usefull to their further aimes.

By this time the King was fully convinced that My Lord * The Seal taken from My Lord
Sunderland was not the man he took him for, nor any longer Sunderland.
to be trusted, so assoon as they were return'd from the Court
of Chancery, he order'd My Lord Middleton to fetch the
Seals from him : this artefull dissembler thought it too early
yet to pull of his maske, and own to the world the treachery,
he soon after made a merit of ; so to cover as much as in him
lay, the true reason of his disgrace, he pretended it was not
fitting now that any Catholick should be in imployment,
insinuateing, as if his dismission had been on that account,
which as it served to palliate his vilany at that time, it exposed
it the more when he shew'd himself in his naturall colours.

By this time the Prince of Orange had embarked his ” The Prince of Orange sets
army, but lay long wind bound, which at last comeing fair, ” sail, but is driven back.
he set sail the 26th of October, from the Brill and Heluersluce ” KingJam:Mem To:9. pag.231.

---

* In the same volume of Sir J. Dalrymple's Memoirs, are three Letters, two
written by Lord Sunderland and the other by his Wife, to King William,
immediately after the Revolution, which as Sir John well remarks, " Shew the
difficult situation into which the double conduct of Lord and Lady Sunderland (as
double dealing always does) had thrown themselves and King William." EDITOR.

" with all his fleet, consisting of aboue fifty 'men of War,
" and at least four hundred sail of fluts, fly-boats, and other
" transport vessels to carry his men, horses, and artilery, with
" all sorts of amunition and warlike stores necessary for such
an enterprise. He was accompanyd with several English
Lords and people of distinction, who for some time before out
of disafection, or fear of descovery, had retir'd to his Court, at
the head of which was the Earle of Shurwsbury who had
refug'd himself there meerly out of a factious temper, haveing
no personal pretence of disgust ; the Earle of Macclesfeild, who
had likewise quarrell'd with the Court because the reward he
receiued for his Seruices in the late rebellion did not equal his
vain expectation, thō they infinitely surmounted his merit ;
My Lord Mordent who haveing been always of a turbulent
factious spirit and incapable of doing good, sought where he
might do most mischife ; Coll: Henry Sidney a chief instrument
of the whole intrigue, by his constant correspondence with My
Lady Sunderland; Admiral Herbert whose loyalty and gratitude
were no longer liued, than his honours and imployments, he
had been rais'd by the particular fauour of his Prince to a
considerable fortune in the world, the dignity of an Admiral,
Master of his robes, and Collonel of a Regiment of foot, and
when the King asked him one favour in returne of so many,
which was, if he would consent to haue the penal Laws and
Test taken off, his answer was, he could not do it in honour nor
conscience ; at which the King being more moued than
ordinary, could not forbear telling him, That as for his honour,
he had little but what he ow'd to his bounty, and for his
conscience, the puting away his Wife to keep with more liberty
other weomen, gaue a true idea of its niceness, and therefore
thought fit to dismis him from his imployments; which had
this good efect at least, that it made him an open enemy instead
of an hidden one, and anticipated a manifestation of that

treason, which most other creatures of the King's kept longer under cover to work him greater mischief; besides those persons, the Marcchall Schomberg, and severall men of distinction of his own Country accompanyd the Prince: and to impose a belief as if the Religion and liberties of England had been his only aim in this expedition, he carryd a flag with English colours, and this Motto upon it, THE PROTESTANT RELIGION AND LIBERTIES OF ENGLAND, and underneath IE MAINTIENDRAY.

At his first setting out he steered his cours northwards, but the next day the wind comeing contrary and blowing very hard it dispers'd severall of his fleet, and forced the rest back to their harbour with the loss of many horses; the Dutch gazette amplifyd exceedingly the damage sustain'd on this occasion, with intent (as was presumed) to slacken the King's preparations, but that was a dangerous policy, and more likely to haue produced an information of the treasonable practices in England wherein such numbers were concern'd, when, upon such an accident the success of the enterprise might be so reasonably suspected; but what-ever their aim was in it, the King was glad of the time it gaue him, whereof he lost no part, in makeing due preparations; it gaue leasure to the old Regiments to make up their recruts of ten men for each company, as had been order'd; and some of the new ones being in a good forwardness, the King sent Major General Lanier with Aran's and Hamilton's Regiment of hors, and the Queen's regiment of foot commanded by Coll: Cannon to Ipswitch, to endeavour to preserue Landgard fort, and prevent if possible their landing there, but with directions that if they could not hinder the Descent, to draw out the garison which was but a hundred men, and make what opposition they could, so as not to expose that small body too much, and therefore two regiments

T O M.
III.

1688.

King Jam:
Mᵒⁿ. To. 9.
pag. 231.

King Jam.
Mᵒⁿ. Tom: 9.
pag: 231.

TOM.
III.

1688.

pag. 223.

pag. 332.

" of hors more and one of Dragoons were order'd to Coulchester
" to second him if needfull; and in case the Prince of Orange
" directed his cours northwards, then all these Regiment were
" to make the best of their way to Newarke, and if he came to
" the river Theams, or Westward, than to return to London:
" but his Majesty it seems had made chois of an improper man
" for that Seruice, for had the Prince of Orange landed there,
" Lanier had agreed with most of the Officers to haue secured
" My Lord Aran, Coll. Hamilton, and Cannon, and haue
" declared for him, as the King was afterwards inform'd by
" Cap: Powel: His Majesty had given the direction of what
" troops were about Chattam and Sheerness to Major General
" Kerke, and haveing made this disposition by land, he had
" notice the fleet was got togather at the boy of the Nore, and
" My Lord.* Dartmouth writ he was under sail, designing
" to anchor something to the east of the Galoper to be cleer of
" the Sands, and so to be able to stretch it one way or the other
" as he pleas'd, when the wind should come fair for the enimy
" and according to the cours they steer'd; but he stood not

---

* George Legge Lord Dartmouth, had in 1683, after having previously distinguished himself, been sent to Tangeer, where he demolished the Fortifications and blew up the Mole. In *Dalrymple's Memoirs* are some interesting Letters from the noble Admiral to his Sovereign, (*Vol:* 2. *p.* 319-331.) which passed whilst Lord Dartmouth lay with the Fleet at the mouth of the Nore. In one dated Oct': 12, 1688, his Lordship says, " Your Majesty cannot be more desirous to have me from among the Sands, than I am impatiently endeavouring to get out. I judge it much more for your service to unite while we have time, than to drop out in parcels with the hazard of being separated, especially knowing myself here in the best place to do my business while these winds continue; and be assured, Sir, I shall be at Sea upon the first alteration." King JAMES replied to this letter, Oct': 14. " I make no doubt but that God will protect me, and prosper my arms both by land and sea. I need say no more to you, being sure you will do what is best for my service, which you that are on the place are the only judge of, and must govern yourself according to the enemies motions, and as wind and weather will permit." Lord Dartmouth died in the Tower as related at page 209, Oct': 25th: 1691. EDITOR.

out so far, but anchor'd a brest of the long sands head, when "   T O M.
the Easterly wind took him and blew very fresh.   "   III.

The Prince of Orange being so well reassured by the intel- "
ligence he had from the King's army, was no ways dis- "
couraged with his late disaster, nor the loss of so many "
horses, or the sickness of his men, but waiting only for a "
wind which comeing fair, on the therd of November he put "
to sea again, sail'd out of the harbour and steer'd away for "
the Channel; it was sayd he had not resolved which cours "
to take till he was out at Sea, and finding the wind had too "
much of the West to reach Burlington bay upon a stretch, "
determin'd him to go westward; but whether it was that, or "
the intelligence he had that none of the King's forces were "
in that part of England is uncertain, the next morning "
My Lord Dartmouth's Scouts which were a league and a "
half a head of him to the Eastward, saw some of the enimys "
shipps, upon which they made their signal, then gaue them "
chase, and took a flyboat with four companys of English "
in her; what reason the Lord Dartmouth had, not to do the "
same, is yet a mistery, and the King who till then had a "
good opinion of him, would not censure him till he heard "
what he could say for his own justification, but never seeing "
him more, that could not be done, only in general it was "
pretended, he was not able to get about the long sands head "
as the wind and tide stood; on the other side several of the "
Commanders affirm'd, he might haue done it, which if he "
had, and the other Captains been true to him (which then its "
belieud they would) he might haue ruin'd their formidable "
fleet, or at least haue hinder'd their landing and broke the "
whole enterprize.   "

There was no man in whose fidelity the King had greater
confidence than this Lord's; his obligations to his Prince (if
that had been any ty in those days) were infinite, and haveing

1688.
The Prince of
Orange Setts
sail a Second
time, and
Lands in
Torbey.
pag: 231.

pag: 232.

T O M.
III.

1688.

KING JAM:
Mem. TOM: 9.
pag. 219.

still forewarn'd him of the Prince of Orange's designe, seem'd
a demonstration he would not giue a helping hand to it; the
King had likewise suffer'd much by giveing him the command
of the fleet preferrable to the Duke of Grafton who expected
" it, and for vexation at his disapointment, went down to the
" fleet before the Prince of Orange set sail, and endeavour'd
" to corrupt the Commanders (as he afterwards owned to My
" Lord Dover) and that two therds of them had engaged their
" words to join the Prince of Orange; and whether out of
" spight to his Rival, or that he thought My Lord Dartmouth
" true to the King's intrest, they had layd a designe to invite
" him on board Captain Hasting, or Elmore, and there haue

Ibid. 223.

" Seiz'd him; Captain George Churchill confirm'd this relation
" to My Lord Bulkeley, and that My Lord Berkeley and Sʳ
John Berry were privy to it : but this not being to be executed
till just before the Prince of Orange was expected to land, tis
probable they saw reasons before that, not to be so much
dissatisfyd with My Lord Dartmouth's conduct; for besides
the conflicts which My Lady Dartmouth own'd he had betwixt
his Religion and loyalty, the opposition he afterwards gaue to
the Prince of Wales' passing from Portsmouth to France,

Ibid: pag: 219.

" which he made a merite of in a letter he writ to the Prince
" of Orange from Portsmouth, and his ernest sollicitation that
" he might keep his place of Master of the Ordenance, for
" which the Lords Churchill and Godolphin where his inter-
" cessors, doe but too manifestly shew, that whether it was
" Religion, faction, or intrest, that weighed most with him, tis
" certain his loyalty was worsted in that conflict; and that it

Ibid.

" was the Prince of Orange's contempt of his seruice, rather
" than his want of good will to serue him, that hinder'd My
" Lord Dartmouth from falling in with the current as others
" did at the Revolution, thō afterwards he return'd to his
duty, and offer'd his service to the King; of which the Prince

of Orange being inform'd by one Fullam put him in the
Tower where he soon after ended his days, so that thô he
could not repair the mischiefs he had contributed too in reference
to his Prince, he did it in some measure in respect of his own
reputation.

"Assoon as the King had notice from Dover that the
"Enemys fleet had pass'd by there, he order'd three battalions
"of the Guards, his own regiment of Dragoons and a hundred
"Granadiers on horseback, to march with all expedition to
"Portsmouth for the further security of that place, with
"directions to go on towards Salisbury, if the Enemie went
"more Westward, which way all the rest of his Army march'd
"likewise, except three battalions of Guards and Prince
"George's regiment of foot. The Hors and Dragoons were
"divided into different bodys, Sr John Lanier commanded
"that which was order'd to Salisbury, Sr John Fenwick an
"other which marched to Marlborough, and a therd was sent
"to Warminster whether Sr John Lanier was to advance; so
"soon as My Lord Feversham (to whom the King had given
"the Command of the Army under himself) should arriue at
"Salisbury; his Majestys design being, that assoon as these
"different bodys of hors and Dragoons (being twenty
"Squadrons of the former and ten of the latter) were arriued
"at their respectiue quarters, to march on further westward
"and come up as close as possible to the Prince of Orange,
"not only to prevent his advanceing, but to hinder any dis-
"afected persons from joining him till the whole Army could
"come up, which with the train of Artillery and baggage, was
"on its march towards Salisbury; all but the Scoth hors and
"Dragoons; and the Irish Dragoons which being newly
"arrived, and much fatigued, were left for some days behind
"to rest and refresh themselves.

T O M.
III.

1688.

The King
orders his
Army towards
Salisbury.
KING JAM:
M^{em}. To: 9.
pag. 233.

T O M.
III.

1688.
The King
Questions the
Lords, and
Bisshops,
about what
was sayd in
the P. of
Orange's
Declaration.

While this was a doeing, one Capt: Langham was Seiz'd with the Prince of Orange's Declarations about him, wherein he own'd that his comeing was at the earnest invitation of Divers Lords both Spiritual and Temporal; Langham was commited to prison, and his Majesty thought fit to enquire a little into the truth of that Assertion, so sent for such Lords as were then about town, My Lord Marq: of Halifax, the Earles of Notingham, Clarendon, Burlington, My Lord Alington, &c; who being examin'd about it disclaimd any share of that invitation, adding all imaginable protestations of Loyalty: the King thought when honour, Conscience, and Religion, was in every bodys mouth it should haue been in some peoples hearts too, which made him credit what they Said, but a few days more convinced him of his errour, and that the Divines themselves were not exempt from that duplicity; for upon the same occasion sending for the Arch Bisshop of Cantorbury, the Bisshops of London, Winchester, and two or three more, he put the same question he had done to the Lords, Whether they had invited the Prince of Orange as was said in his declaration? they were a little pussled what to answer, not being quite so artefull dissemblers as the others; but sayd at last, they would never own any other King while his Majesty lived, in which (thō some of them indeed kept their word) others shew'd soon after how little regard they had for truth, thō all this contest was about it: The King not too well Satisfyd with this equivocal answer, press'd them to sign an abhorrance at least of the Prince of Orange's invasion, but they demurring to it, he saw what he was like to expect from them,

King Jam:
Mem. Tom: 9.
pag. 229.

" and therefore thought fit to remind them of what he had
" sayd when they first petition'd him, that he belived they
" were not sencible of the harme they had done by it, both to
" him and themselues, but that they had been imposed upon

by ill men, who design'd his and their ruin, that they had "
rais'd a Devil they could not lay, and that when it was too "
late they would repent their errour; and to convince them "
that some of them had done it maliciously, he assur'd them, "
he kept the paper in his pocket, and yet coppies of it was "
spread about which rais'd so furious a ferment against him : "
He bid them therefore take notice, that what he then Sayd to "
them, had in great measure proued true, and that therefore "
they were now at least oblig'd to declare their dislike of the "
invasion; and shew their zeal for Loyalty both in the Pulpits "
and out of them, and proue themselves to be true Sons of "
the Church they profess'd to be Members of; that he "
expected this from them as a thing of the last consequence "
for his seruice, and as some amends for the harme they had "
done him by their petition and behaviour after it; that he "
was a going to head the Army and oppose the invader, and "
that if it pleas'd God to gaue him success and victory over "
his enimies, he assur'd them he would keep his promis; and "
thō he had little reason to be satisfyd with many of them, yet "
it should not hinder him from standing to the engagement he "
had always made, of supporting them in the enjoyment of "
their Religion and possessions, being resolved to mentain "
Libertie of Conscience thō he were absolute Master to doe "
what he pleas'd : but notwithstanding all the King could Say, "
and all he had done, to giue them Satisfaction, he could not "
prevail with the Arch Bp: nor the majority of them to "
declare their dislike of the invasion, thō the Bisshop of Win- "
chester and some others were for doeing it, nor did they take "
care to rectify those errours in the People, they had indus- "
triously contributed too; for the night before the King went "
down to Salisbury, they waited upon him again with further "
proposalls, about assembling a Parliament and treating with "
the Prince of Orange, and had got some temporal Lords to "

" join with them, as the Dukes of Grafton and Ormonde (but
" the M: of Halifax, E: of Notingham, and Several others
" posituely refused) all the King could say to it was, that it
" was too late, being then ten at night, and he to set out next
" morning to Salisbury; and therefore could not giue them an
" answer in writeing; that it was not a time fit to call a
" Parliament, when Armys were in the field, nor proper for
" him to send to treat with the Prince of Orange who had
" invaded him without any provocation, against all the Laws
" of God and man ; and against the duty he ow'd to him as a
" Nephew and Son in law ; and that it would much better
" become them, who were Bisshops of the Church of England
" to perform their obligation by instructing the people in
" their duty to God and the King, than to be presenting
" petitions and giveing rules for government and fomenting
" that rebellious temper they had already begot in the
" Nation, instead of declareing against the invasion; which
" he found they could not be prevail'd upon to doe : By
this the King saw that Religion which is the common cloke
for rebellions, scarce proues a security against one : but
they were not many months older before the Arch Bisshop
and some other of his Breethren became sencible of their
mistake, and repented themselves of haveing dealt so harshly
with their Prince, who had at their request rectifyd in a manner
all they had found fault with, whereas they could not even
then, be prevail'd upon, to doe what both the Law of God and
of the Land, and the positiue tenets of their Church, oblig'd
them too, thō the King had been the greatest Tyrant upon
earth ; who therefore was at last convinced, that the late
Church of England doctrine of passiue Obedience was too
Sandy a foundation for a Prince to build upon, since they
so easily overlooked not only their own writeing but all the
State laws, which if they had been stuck too, would haue

preserued the Constitution from all the convulsions it suffer'd afterwards; the King therefore caus'd a Proclamation to be published in answer to the false assertions of the Prince of Orange's Manifesto, assuring his people, That it was but too evident by a late Declaration published by that Prince, that notwithstanding the many specious and plausible pretences to colour his ambition, his design in the bottom did tend to nothing less, than an absolute usurpeing his Crown and Royal authority; as might fully apear by his assuming to himself in the said Declaration the Regal Stile, requireing the Peers of the Realm both Spiritual and temporal, and all persons of what degree soever to obey and assist him in the execution of his design, a prerogatiue inseperable from the imperial Crown of the Realm; and that for a more undenyable proof of his immoderate Ambition, and that nothing could satisfy it but the immediate possession of the Crown itself, he call'd in question the legitimacy of the Prince of Wales, his Majestys Son and heire aparent; thō by the Providence of God there were present at his birth so many Witnesses of unquestionable credit, as if it seem'd the particular care of heaven, to disapoint so wicked and unparalell'd an attempt: that in order to the efecting his ambitious designs, he seem'd to submit all to the determination of a Parliament, hopeing thereby to ingratiate himself with the people; thō nothing was more evident than that a Parliament could not be free So long as there was an Army of forreigners in the heart of the Kingdom; so that in truth he was the sole obstructer of such a free Parliament, his Majesty being fully resolved as he had already declared, so soon as by the blessing of God his Kingdoms should be deliver'd from this invasion, to call a Parliament; which then could not be lyable to the least objection of not being freely chozen, since his Majesty had actually restored all the Boroughs and Corporations to their antient rights and priviledges: upon which consideration and the obligations of their duty and natural obedience, his Majesty could no ways doubt, but that all his faithfull and loyal Subjects would readily and heartely concur, and join with him in the entire suppressing and repelling of his Enemies and rebellious Subjects.

The King has notice of the Prince of Orange's Landing.

While these things were a doeing the King had advice, that the Prince of Orange was come to anchor in Torbay and on the fifth of November began to put his men ashore, which he did without opposition, that his hors were in a very ill condition, and his common Soldjers in no good one, haveing been so long on shipboard; however he marched with all expedition to Exeter, which being a place of no defence and no garison in it was not in a condition to hinder his entry, thō the Major shut the gates, and clapt up one Hicks whom the Prince of Orange had sent befóre to rais recruts, and thō My Lord Mordent and D^{tr} Burnet press'd him to meet the Prince, he refused it. The Prince of Orange was necessitatd to stay some time there to refreth his troops and put his artillery and stores ashore, after which one of the first things he did, was to make his Declaration be read; in which great pains was taken to enumerate the pretended grievances, which he charged upon the evil Councellors (out of an affected modesty not to blame the King) thō many of those Councellors had acted and put the King upon those very methods, by his direction and instigation; so like Henry the 7th (who as it was sayd, caused those whom he had sent to betray Perkin to be cursed at Paul's cross with other Rebells, the better to cover their design) So the Prince of Orange complain'd of nothing, with more violence, than that a' Papist (meaning My Lord Sunderland) should be an Ecclesiastical Commissioner; but his kindness to him afterwards shew'd in what spirit that was sayd. However the Prince of Orange found himself under a great disapointement, when he perceiv'd that most of those grievances which he

grounded his invasion upon had been redress'd before he
came, so he was forced to make an additional Declaration,
that thō some thing was done as (he Sayd) to prevent the entire
reestablishment of Religion and the Laws in the Kingdom,
under the Shelter of his Armes, there still remain'd a great deal
to perfect the work which he porposed to compleat, but tooke
great care to purge himself from the imputation of haveing any
design to conquer the Nation, assureing them, his sole intent
was to procure a free Parliament, and to Vindicate their Religion and the liberties of England, from Popery, Arbitrary, and
and a dispenseing power, to assert the Succession of the Crown
and examin into the birth of the pretended Prince of Wales;
in fine to redress all irregularitys civil and military and settle
peace and plenty in the Nation: but Notwithstanding all these
fair promises (which he never complyd with in any one point "
afterwards) and notwithstanding the many assurances he had "
receiu'd from people of quality in those parts, of joining him, "
there came not any in, which discouraged him mightely, thō "
there was no force of the King's, nor other reasonable "
impediment to excuse their not performeing what they had "
so solemnly promised; this made it for some time be rumour'd "
in his Army, that nothing was to be done, and even severall "
persons of greatest distinction about him, sayd he was "
certainly betrayd; and that his only cours was to return on "
board his Ship and begon; nay the very circular letters sent "
by Admiral Herbert with the Prince of Orange's Declaration "
in them, which were deliver'd to Coll: Strangways and others, "
instead of being dispers'd, were sent up to the King, and "
not one man of consideration in the four westerne Countrys ."
went in to him, till My Lord Cornsburys treachery began the "
general defection. "

That Lord being come to Salisbury with his own regiment "
of Dragoons, where he found the King's Regiment, St Alban's, "

T O M.
III.
1688.

KING JAM. M⁰ᵈ
TOM:9.pag.234.

My Lord
Cornsburys
defection.
Ibid: pag.235.

" and Fenwick's, but all those Collonels being absent and
" Lanier not yet arrived, he commánded the Quarter; so
" finding this a good occasion to execute the treachery he had
" in his heart, he order'd out his own Regiment, the King's
" Regiment of which Sr Francis Compton * was Lt Collonel,
" and St Alban's which Lt Coll: Langston commanded
" (Fenwick's was commanded by Southerland, who not being
" for his purpose, he left behind) with these three Regiments
" he marched by Blanford to Dorcester where he stayd but
" an hour or two, and so on towards Hunniton : this seem'd
" so surpriseing to the officers, that his own Major Clifford,
" asked the meaning of it, and desired to see his orders, or at
" least some reason for so long a march towards the Enemie,
" he answer'd, it was to beat up a quarters of theirs in those
" parts; and when he came to Axminster he commanded out
" Sixty Dragoons to fall upon the enemy as he pretended at
" Hunniton ; but by this time several of the officers as Major
" Littleton and others suspecting the design, began to question
" My Ld Cornbury something roundly, who not being able to
" dissemble the matter any longer went off with his sixty
" dragoons, togather with his Lt Coll: Hayford, Captain Russell
" and the rest of his Captains then present without letting the
" common men know any thing of his intentions : Langston
" follow'd him with his Regiment he haveing been the chief
" man who had concerted this matter with My Ld Cornbury
" without acquainting his officers till they arriued at Hunniton,
" where they found two Regiment of foot commanded by
" Talmach ready to receiue them, Langston then tould them,

---

* The late Joseph Ritson in his Ancient Songs has inserted a Parody upon
Chevy Chace, in which are recorded as Traitors to James the Second,
" Compton, Langston and the rest
Who basely from him ran."
That industrious Antiquary was unable to find out who Compton was. EDITOR.

he had brought them thither to serue the Prince of Orange, "
which Norton his Major and several Subalterns refuseing, "
they were immediately disarmed, dismounted and plunder'd, "
and with much adoe got liberty to return on foot to the "
Army ; the other two Regiments finding they were betrayd "
march'd back in great disorder, only Cornet Coumpton with "
two or three Subalterns and about ten troopers of the King's "
Regiment of hors diserted, it was belieud the Lᵗ Coll: would "
haue donc so too, but that he was stunn'd, and apprehended "
the Major would haue secur'd him, so he return'd to the "
King, and Clifford the Major of Dragoons, brought off the "
body of the Regiment, nay most of the troopers even of "
Sᵗ Alban's Regiment return'd as they found opertunity ; which "
shew'd a greater honour and fidelity in the common men, "
than in the generality of the officers who usually value "
themselves so much for those qualifications. "

Thō the loss was very inconsiderable in it self yet the "
consequence was exceeding great, for besides that all those "
horses were so harass'd, that they were not fit for seruice of "
a forthnight, it broke the King's measures, dishearten the "
other troops, and created such a jealousie, that each man "
suspected his Neibour, and in efect render'd the Army useles ; "
it also gaue incouragement to the Countrey Gentlemen to go "
in to the Prince of Orange, who hithertoo had been diffident, "
especially upon what happen'd to My Lord Louelace, who "
being of a violent temper and deeply engaged in the design "
had got a few men togather and attempted to join the Prince "
of Orange ; but at Cirencester was stop'd by the militia, and "
thō he made some resistance, where the officer that Commanded "
for the King was kill'd, yet he was seized and sent to prison : "
but now not only the discontented partie but the trimmers, "
and even many that wished well to the King went in, meerly "
for aprehention ; which gaue mighty courage to the Enimy. "

T O M.
III.

1688.
Ibid: pag:236

" who till then were in a dispairing way, and hinder'd many
" of them from comeing over to the King, who otherwise were
" upon the point of doing it.

" My Lord Feversham arriued at Salisbury just as this
" happen'd, and believeing at first all the three Regiments had
" deserted to a man, order'd the hors and Dragoons who were
" at Warminster, and Marleborough to march with all speed
" to Salisbury, and the foot that was already arriued there to
" retire to Andover, believeing the Prince of Orange would
" upon this occasion send his hors and dragoons to fall upon
" some of those advanced quarters ; and because at Andover
" there was not cover for a great body of foot, Stop'd those
" who were on their march towards him, and order'd them
" to quarter about Windsor, Stains, &c.

Assoon as the news of this defection came to Court where
his Majesty yet remain'd, it was not possible to express the
surprize and trouble it occasion'd ; it seem'd to pull up all his
hopes and expectations by the roots, when his chief and only
support began to fail him, haueing reason to suspect he was no
better serued in his Family than in his Army, but so much
the wors, as the enimys about his person bore yet the countenance
of friends, whereas those in the Army began to manifest their
corruption, and indeed many who remain'd at Court, could
scarce contain shewing to the world their inwardpleasure on
this occasion, for the express arriueing just as his Majesty was
going to diner, his concern was too great to think of any thing
but how to remedy the comforthless situation of his affairs, so
calling for a piece of bread and glass of wine, went immediately
to consult what measures was fitest to be taken ; at which time
The Lords Sunderland, Churchil and Godolphin, instead of
compassionateing at least the anguish of so kind and bountifull
a Master, were seen unawares going hand in hand along the
Gallery in the greatest transport of joy immaginable.

The result of this consultation was to delay his Majestys "
going to Salisbury two or three days, that he might see "
peoples minds settled a little ; so the next day he call'd "
togather all the Generall Officers and Collonells that remain'd "
in town, and made them a short discours sutable to the "
occasion : He tould them, he had order'd a Parliament "
to meet assoon as things were a little pacifyd ; that he was "
now resolved to content them in all things relateing to their "
Liberties, Privileges, and Religion, and if they had any thing "
more to ask was ready to grant it, and that if there were any "
amongst them that were not free and willing to serue him, he "
gave them leaue to surrender their Commissions, and to go "
wherever they pleased ; but that he looked upon them as men "
of too much honour, to follow My Lord Corneburys example, "
and was therefore willing to spare them (if they desir'd it) "
the discredit of so base a desertion : They all seem'd to be "
moued at this discours, and vow'd they would serue him to "
the last drop of their blood, the Duke of Grafton and My "
Lord Churchill were the first that made this attestation, and "
the first, who (to their eternal infamy) broke it afterwards, as
well as Kerk, Trelawny, &c, who were no less lavish of their
promises, on this occasion, thō as false and treacherous as the
rest, in the end.

The free and candid disposition the King was naturally of
himself, would not suffer him to think, that men who pretend
to Honour aboue the rest of the world, could be capable of
meaning otherwise than they sayd ; or that when Religion was
the main concern, men should haue so little regard to its
morralls and the practice of it, as to think to do seruice to it
by perjurys and blasphemies, so he comforted himself upon
these assurances that the contagion was not so universall as he
immagin'd, and the more, when hē heard that all those men
were not lost that My Lord Cornbury had carryd off ; so he "

T O M. III.

1688. The King's speech to the general Officers, on occasion of My Lord Corneburys desertion. KING JAM: Mem TOM: 9. pag: 237.

Ibid. pag: 239.

" directed the foot to march westward according to the first
" orders, and apointed the hors and dragoons, with some
" batallions of foot to advance as far as Warminster; and then
" set out himself for Salisbury on the 17th of November where
" he arriued in three days, being conducted thither by a
" detachment of the hors guards and the Irish dragoons.

The Prince of
Wales Sent to
Portsmouth.
Ibid. pag. 255.

" At the same time his Majesty left the Town, he sent the
" Prince of Wales to Portsmouth, not only as a place of more
" Security than London, but that he might with more facility
" be transported to * France (the only place he could be safe
in) if things went wors, thinking also such a separation
necessary for their mutual safety. This was a melancholy
parteing especially to the Queen, who never fear'd danger
when the King was with her, and therefore had all her life
rather chos to share in his hazards and hardships, than to be

---

* See the Letters between King James and Lord Dartmouth already mentioned,
as being in the second Volume of *Sir J. Dalrymple's Memoirs.* (page 326.)
In one dated Nov[r] 29th the King wrote, " 'Tis my Son they aim at, and
'tis my Son I must endeavour to preserve, whatsoever becomes of me;
therefore I conjure you to assist Lord Dover in getting him sent away in the
yatchts, as soon as wind and weather will permit, for the first port they can get to
in France, and that with as much secresy as may be; and so that trusty men may
be put in the yatchts, that he may be exposed to no other danger but that of
the Sea; and know I shall look upon this as one of the greatest pieces of service
you can do me." — Lord Dartmouth replied at great length in a Letter dated,
Spithead, Dec[r] 3. 1688, in which he said, " I need not tell your Majesty how strict
the Laws are in this matter, nor after so many experiences of my Duty, and Loyalty
to your person, lay before you fresh assurances of giving ready obedience to any
commands within my power; but to be guilty of Treason to your Majesty and the
known Laws of the Kingdom, of so high a nature as this, when your Majesty shall
further deliberate on it, I most humbly hope you will not exact it from me, nor
longer entertain so much as a thought of doing that, which will give your enemies
an advantage, tho never so falsely grounded, to distrust your Son's just right, which
you have asserted and manifested to the world (in the matter of his being your real
Son born of the Queen) by the testimonies of so many apparent witnesses. Pardon
me therefore if, on my bended knees, I beg of you to apply yourself to other
Councels, for the doing this looks like nothing less than despair." . . . Editor.

in ye greatest eas and security without him; but that being
now denyd her and he obliged to part from her upon so
dangerous an expedition, and the Prince her Son at the same
time sent from her into a forreign Country, while she was left
in the middle of a mutenous and discontented Citie; it is not
to be wonder'd if she beg'd of the King to be cautious what
steps he made in such suspected company, not knowing but
the ground on which he thought to stand with most security,
might sink from under his feet.

.. Before his Majesty left London he recommended the care of
the Citie to My Lord Major, reiterateing his promis and royal
word, that should it pleas God to grant him Victory, he would
performe his engagement of Secureing their Religion and
liberties, that upon any emergency he might haue recours to
his Council, which were My Lord Chancellor, My Lord
Preston (who had been made Secretary of State in My Lord
Sunderland's room) My Lord Bellasis, Arundel, and Godolphin, the two Catholicks not too agreeable to the people,
and the last (who had the greatest influence) not too faithfull to
the King. He thought to haue dispatch'd likewise at the same
time the Duke of Hamilton into Scotland to inspect affairs
there, and bring more succors from thence if necessary to his
assistance: but upon reflection immagin'd he might proue as
ill chozen for that Seruice, as most others, and as in reality he
had been, for it soon apear'd whose intrest he studyd to
promote, when he arriued in his own Country some time
afterwards. In this general consternation Father * Petre, who
perceiued the sky was too gloomy to think he could wether the
storme, retired beyond seas about the same time that My Lord

* _Granger_ notices (_Vol:_ 4. _Page_ 304.) a Dutch Mezzotinto of FATHER PETRE,
with the devil tempting him to hang himself; Achitophel is representing hanging
at a distance. PETRE was unfortunately Confessor both to the King and Queen.
Dalrymple describes him (_Vol:_ 1. _p._ 151.) " as a man of noble birth, but puffed up
with a vanity and ambition which gave Sunderland an easy hold of him.": EDITOR.

T O M.
III.

1688.
The King
arriues at
Salisbury.
KING JAM:
Mⁿ. TOM: 9.
pag: 239.

Waldgraue went into France, who had been apointed to
succeed Mʳ Skelton in his Embassy at that Court.

"The King got to Salisbury the 19ᵗʰ of November, but it
"was not then possible to put his first project in execution,
"and march his hors and dragoons as far as Axminster, Chard,
"and Lamport; to prevent the Countrys comeing in to the
"Prince of Orange, and close him up in the corner of the
"Kingdom, and then haue advanced the foot as fast as
"possible to their support; where the high ways being narrow,
"and the hedges and ditches exceeding great, would haue been
"as good as retrenchments, to whosoever had first possess'd
"them: but the late treachery had made this impracticable,
"for notwithstanding Clifford and Sarsfield had beaten a
"considerable party of the Enemy, and put some little check
"to their progress; they were by this time advanced as far as
"Axminster, and some other of those postes, besides the King's
"Artillery, with some foot and one troop of Guards with the
"Scotch and Irish Dragoons were not yet come up; he
"resolued therefore in the mean time to visite the advanced

Ibid. 240.

"quarter at Warminster commanded by Major General
"Kerke and the Brigadires Trelauny and Main, where was
"two battalions of Dunbarton's, that of Kerke's, and the
"Queen's, with the third troops of Guards, togather with
"Wearden's and one more Regiment of Hors, and the Queen's
"Regiment of Dragoons; but the evening before his Majesty
"design'd to go his nose fell a bleeding, as it did again next
"morning a considerable quantity, and continued to do so
"Several times that day, which oblig'd him to be let blood,
"and being three days ere it was perfectly stop'd, forced him
"to lay aside the thoughts of going thither at all.

The King's
bleeding at
the nose, pre-
vented being
betrayd into
the Enemys
hands.

This bleeding which the King was not naturally subject too,
"happen'd very providentially, for it was generally belieud
"afterwards, that My Lord Churchill, Kerke, and Trelawny,
"with some others in that quarter, had layd a design to Seize

the King either in his going thither or comeing back, and "
so haue carryd him to the Prince of Orange; which they "
might easily enough haue efected, haveing at that time no "
suspicion of them at all, thō some days after he had so fare "
intimation of their design, that it was proposed to secure "
My lord Churchill and the Duke of Grafton and haue sent "
them to Portsmouth, but upon. further consideration his "
Majesty thought fit not to doe it.   But his clemency therein, "
was as much beyond example, as their treachery; of which
scarce any history can shew a paralell; perhaps they *might*
* *pretend*, it was not with intention to haue done him any personal harme, only force him to consent to what they thought
reasonable: but what could be desir'd of him more than he
had already granted, but his life or Crown? and they had too
much knowlidg of the world, to think, that less than the latter,
would content so ambitious and uñatural an invader.

The misfortunes which had already happen'd, and the
suspicions which threaten'd more, made his Majesty think it
proper to call a Council of Generall Officers, to consider and
resolue what was best to be done, and such was his benignity
as not to exclude from it, even those who in the bottom gaue
the main occasion to this consultation: My Lord Churchill
therefore was of the number, and argued against the King's "
drawing his Army towards London; which My Lord "
Feuersham, the Count de Roye, and My lord Dunbarton "
advised; and the King haveing then more confidence in the "
latter, follow'd their Councel, for besides that it was too late "
now to execute the first project, or to go about takeing the "
Posts beyond Blanford, he now suspected many of the Chief "
Officers and others, and accordingly that very night the "
Duke of Grafton and My Lord Churchill (who seem'd "

Ibid. p. 240.

---

* Inserted by the Son of James 2ᵈ, instead of *will say*.   EDITOR.

T O M.
III.
1688.

"extreamly troubled at the resolution the King had taken)
deserted to the Prince; tis probable that Lord's failing in his
project of seizing the King, and now finding he could not keep
his Majesty there, where perhapes he might haue found means to
haue done it, or at least the proximity of the enimy made it more
favorable to desertion, he durst not venter to stay any longer;
at his arriual in the Enimys camp, all the compliment he
receiud for abandoning the best of Masters and endeavouring
to betray the most gratious of Princes, was to be tould by y^e
Mareshall de Schomberg, that he was the first Lieftenant
Generall he ever heard of, that had deserted from his Colours.

King Jam:
M^m. To: 9:
p: 241.

" The King had intelligence the same day that Rogers
" Leftenant of the Grenadeers on horsback, was gon likewise
" from Warminster, that Coll: Leuson with Cap: St George
" and two and three other officers of the Queen's Regiment of
" Dragoons and some few Commen men had deserted in like
" manner under pretence of following them to bring them
" back, and that Kerke upon a frivolous excuse had disobeyd
" the King's orders to march the Troops under his command
" to the Divises, upon which his Majesty repeated them
" positively to march next day as directed, and from thence
" to Hungerford and so to Reading. After which, the King
" with all the Troops he had in and about Salisbury, marched
" away by severall roots for the convenience of quarteing,
" with design to draw the body of his Army behind the
" Themes and make it good; and left My Lord Feversham
" with most of the hors and Dragoons to eat up the forrage on
" the other side and Remain as long as he could at Reading,
" without exposeing himself to haue his quarters beaten up.

Great deser-
tion, even P.
George
himself.

" The first night the King went to Andover, from whence
" Prince George, the Duke of Ormonde, My Lord Drum-
" lanerick with some others deserted, as Several more Officers
" did from other quarters; which shew'd the King's design

11

of drawing his Armie beyond the river was the prudentest
Councel in his present circomstances, and most likely to
prevent others following the example, and which for the
contrary reason My Lord Churchill had before so vehemently
opposed. The King was hugely surprised when they tould
him the Prince was gon, however could not forbear saying,
That he was more troubled at the unnaturallness of the action
than the want of his seruice, for that the loss of a good trooper
had been of greater * Consequence ; nor could all this change
the King's good nature and generosity, which seem'd to contend
with these peoples ingratitude, for instead of shewing the least "
resentment, he order'd his Servants and equipage to follow "
him. "

When such men as these went off, the King made no doubt "
but Kerke would doe the like, wherefore he sent to haue him "
seiz'd which was done accordingly, thō his clemency was "
too great to use him hardly, so soon after order'd him to be set
at liberty again : but in the mean time directed My Lord "
Dunbarton to take two Squadrons of hors to help to bring "
off the four battallions of foot at Warminster, but before he "
could join them, Brigadeer Trelauny who Commanded them, "
Coll: Charles Churchill and twenty or therty of the Common "
Soldiers had deserted, the rest of the men stuck to their duty : "
It is hard to Say which was most surprising, to see so generall
a defection in the Officers from a Prince that payd them well
and cherished them so much, or so much Loyalty amongst the
Common Soldiers when almost all their Officers gaue them so
ill an example, to see such ingratitude amongst men who

---

* Prince George of Denmark had been accustomed upon every fresh instance
of Desertion from James 2d, to exclaim, *Est il possible !* When the forsaken Monarch
at length missed Prince George himself, he said to one of his attendants, " So *Est
il possible* is gone too." *Kennet* has given (page 530.) Prince George's Letter to
the King. EDITOR.

T O M.
III.
1688.

pretend so much to honour, and so much honour in those, who generally seek nothing but their pay, but this change of characters and humours, run through all ranks of people ; men of the ludest liues talked of nothing but Religion, and the Clergie who should haue had Religion and duty before their eys, were become the trompets of Rebellion.

The Princess
of Denmark
went to the
Prince.
KING JAM:
M^{em} TOM:9.
pag:241.

" Assoon 'as the Army had repass'd the river the King " assign'd the troops to their respectiue quarters of Maidenhead, " Windsor, Stanes, Edgham, Chersea, Colbrook &c. and then " went on to London himself, where he arrived the 26ᵗʰ of " November and was above measure ashtonished, to find that " his daugter the Princess of Denmark had abandon'd him " also, it is uncertain whether she did it by direction from " Prince George her husband, or the advise of My lady " Churchill and Mʳˢ Berkeley who were gon also along with " her ; she had indeed alter'd her way of liveing with the " King and Queen for some time, which was a sufficient " demonstration how ill she stood affected ; but considering her circomstances of being then with child, and exceeding apt to miscarry, it seem'd the efect of a more than ordinary malice to hazard her life, rather than not contribite what she could to the ruin of her Father ; for which end at her going off, care was taken to rais such reports, as would most inflame and enrage

142.

" the people; her Nurs and My Lady Clarendon run about " like people out of their sences, crying out, The Papists had " murther'd her ; and when they met any of the Queen's " servants, asked them what they had done with the Princess ; " which, considering the ferment people were in, and how " susceptible they were of any ill impression against the Queen, " might haue made her been torn in pieces by the rabble : but God preserved her from their malice which was not able to make this contrivance more than one days wonder, for the next morning it was known wither she was gon, and that the Bishop

of London her spiritial Guid, had chozen to be her leader too
in this expedition, that My Lord Dorset had accompanyd her
likewise to Notingham, where My Lord Devonshire met her
with a guard of two hundred hors, and not long after Prince
George came to her at Oxford ; there apear'd in * print a "
day or two after, a letter pretended to haue been left on her "
table and directed to the Queen, but no such letter was "
found, or at least deliver'd to her ; that would haue spoil'd
the contrivance of haveing it believ'd she was murther'd, so
when that was at an end, this letter was published, where
conscience was. pleaded (according to the cant of those times)
for the most unjustifyable actions in the world ; and then to
keep up a seeming respect, she begs the Queen's pardon, that
being so sencibly touched at the news of the Prince her
Husband's being gon, she could not see her Majesty, nor durst
shee bear the King's displeasure against her Husband or her
self, and that being so divided between her duty to her Father
and affection to her Husband, she thought it most expedient
in such unfortunate circomstances to follow the one to preserve
the other.

This pretence of preserveing the King by riseing up in armes
against him, was counted but a scurvy doctrine even in
common † Subjects, dureing the late Rebellion, but what terme
to give it in Children, is hard to Say ; the Prince of Denmark
however had observed the Same method, and at his going off
too, had left a letter for the King worded in the same manner,
which shew'd the matter had been concerted betwixt them, and
by consequence no such surprize upon her ; he tould his

---

* For a curious account of the Princess Anne's Flight, see *Colley Cibber's Apology for his own Life*. The Princess's .Letter to the Queen is in *Kennet* (page 531.) EDITOR.

† Interlined as before mentioned. EDITOR.

Majesty he could no longer disguise his concern for the Religion, wherein he had been educated and in which England (now become his Country by the dearest tye) was so highly concern'd, that while the restless spirit of its enimys back'd with the power of France, had so justly united the Protestant Princes in order to its support, he could not deny his concurrance in endeavouring to disabuse his Majesty, by the reinforcement of those Laws and reestablishment of that government, on which depended the wellbeing of his Majesty, and the protestant Religion in Europe; which was the onely irresistable cause, that could come in competition with his duty. It is probable, the Emperour and King of Spain's Ministers had no hand in penning this letter, thō it seem'd to take the League in which they were engaged so much to heart; but any pretence, as well as any crime was good and allowable in these men's acceptation against an inocent Prince when the world united in his destruction. And now that Concientiousness was grown so much in fassion, My Lord Churchill thought fit to explain the tenderness of his too, in a letter to the King which he left behind him likewise; protesting that his desertion from his Majesty proceeded from no other reason, than the inviolable dutys of Conscience, and a high and necessary concern for his Religion, with which nothing could come in competition; this was decideing the matter like one that had authority, and not like the Scribes and Pharisees, not a word of passiue obedience, thō that was once counted a branck of that Religion he pretended to be so zealous a defender of, nor does he think his duty to his Prince, or obligation to so profuse a benefactor, worth his takeing notice of in the case; so that the King, who had no ways injured their Religion, and had even retracted those things they were offended with, nevertheless must be abandon'd and destroyd, or els these good peoples

Consciences could never be at rest; but this hipocresy and senceless cant was necessary to keep up the immagination of a french League to destroy the protestant Religion, which was the Prince of Orange's main Support in this wicked enterprize, and in which so many of those conscientious souls were forced to concur in expectation of what they never got afterwards, notwithstanding the drudgery and infamy they underwent for his Service.

T O M.
III.
1688.

It was on this occasion that the King finding himself in the like circomstances with holy David, he cryd out with him, *O if my enimys only had curs'd me, I could haue born it,* but it was an unexpressible grief to see those he had favour'd, cherish'd and exalted, nay his own Children rise thus in oposition against him; this was what requir'd a more than natural force to support, those strokes had been less *sencible, had they come from hands* * *less* dear to him, but being deliver'd over to all the contradictions that malice or ingratitude could throw in his way, he saw no hopes of redress; so turn'd his whole attention how to Save the Queen and Prince his Son, and cast about which way to doe it with most Security and Secresy.

When the King went to Salisbury he had sent My Lord Dover to command at Portsmouth, the Duke of Berwick haveing then join'd the Army, but the King's chief design in it, was to haue him there in order to send away the Prince of Wales for France, if he found things went wors, and gaue him dormant orders to that purpose, directed both to the Capt: of the MARY Yacght to transport him, and to My Lord Dartemouth to facilitate his passage; that Lord was then come back with the fleet to Spithead very much shatter'd by ill wether, haueing been to the westward by the King's orders,

KingJam:Mem
To:9. pag.242.

---

* Interlined by the Son of James the second. EDITOR.

" to look out for the enemys fleet and engage them, which then
" lay at Torbay under the command of Admirall Herbert ; he
" got the length of that bay, and saw the enemy at Anchor in
" it, but it growing very bad wether, he could attempt nothing
" against them, but his fleet being much endamaged and
" dispersed, some were forced back into the Downes, and he
" to Spithead, Cap: George Churchill put into Plimouth to
" stop some lakes, and finding that place had declar'd for the
" Prince of Orange he did the like himself.

The E. of Bath declares for the Prince of Orange.

That Towne was under the government of the Earle of
" Bath, whose defection was more wonder'd at by the King
" than any which had happen'd, his obligations to the Crown
" were so great, his family allways esteem'd so loyall, and
" himself till then looked upon as uncapable of being shaken
" or tempted to an ill action ; however getting Lt Coll:
" Ferdanando Hastings, thō Cozen to the Earle of Huntington,
" to join with him (that Earle's Regiment being then in the
" Citadel) they secur'd both him, and all the Catholick Officers
" together with the common Soldjers of that perswasion, and
" kept them prisoner till he had perfected the work, and settled
" the Town in the Prince of Orange's intrest.

The King has news of Risings and defections in all partes.

But by this time the contagion was spread so universally,
" that all partes of England furnished the same news of risings
" and defections, the only strife was who should be forwardest
" in abandoning the King; Sr John Hanmore Lt Coll: to My
" Lord Montgomerys Regiment had done the same thing at
" Hull as had been done at Plimouth, for combineing with
" one Copley the L^t governour, the Protestant Officers and
" some of the Magistrates, surprized My Lord Langdall the
" Governour, and My Lord Montgomery in their beds, then
" seized all the Catholick Officers together with severall
" Catholick gentlemen of the Country who had retired thither,

as a place of Security by reason of the great nois, My Lord *
Danbys riseing had made in those parts.

That Lord had given the greatest shock to the King's
authority in the North of any that apear'd against it ; he had
taken the pains to go about the Country to prepare and sollicit
the gentry in favour of this invasion, and as it was belieud
the Prince of Orange's first intent was to haue landed in those
partes, had the wind serued, so no one was earlyer aprized of,
and forwarder in fomenting the design, and therefore so soon
as things were ripe for an insurrection, he met by apointment ”
at York with a great many people of quality of that Country, ”
seized Sr John Raby the Governor, who was in no condition ”
to defend himself, with one only company of foot he had in ”
the Town, after which he declar'd for a free Parliament and ”
the Prince of Orange, caused a Catholick Chappel in the ”
Town to be demolished, and then fell to raising of men ”
which he formed into Companys and Regiments, and grew ”
soon so formidable that all that great and populous Country ”
gaue perfect obedience to his orders, permiting him to Seize ”
upon the King's mony, which he fail'd not to do wherever he ”
could find it : The Earle of Devonshire was of intelligence ”
with him and had done the same thing in Nolinghamshire, ”
for besides the general disposition to a revolt, that Lord had
conceiv'd a particular disgust on account of a quarrell with one
Coll: Culpeper, whom he had struck in the King's appartement, for which he was fin'd thirty thousand pound and
imprison'd, but had liberty granted him upon giveing security
to the warden of the King's bench to go in and out; which
priviledg he made use of to go down and rais sedition in the

---

* For the particulars of Lord Danby's Rising, see *Reresby's Memoirs*, Ed. 1813.
(P. 356-367.) and for some political remarks and information respecting what passed
at that time, see Memoir of the Reign of Jame 2^d, by *Sir John Lowther*, (*Viscount
Lonsdale*) printed in 1808, but not published. EDITOR.

T O M.
III.

1688.
Ibid: pag. 243.

Ibid:

Country, which thõ the King was not ignorant of, however at
" the same time forgaue him his * fine: which favour, licke
" the rest he rewarded by assembling a great number of
" gentlemen and declareing for the Prince of Orange, and
" then sent to the Duke of Newcastle to join with him, which
" he refuseing, he seized his horses and took a great quantity
" of bright armes from his house at Welbeck, which that good
" Lord had prepar'd and kept in great order for a better use.
" My Lord Delamere was not behind hand with the like
" declaration in Cheshire and Lancashire, a man of no great
esteem amongst the chief gentry of those Countrys, but being
of a factious temper and never too late in any tumult, put
" himself at the head of all the discontented persons he could
" possebly scrap together, with which he ransacked the houses
" of Roman Catholicks, and thus with about four or fiue
hundred disorderly ill armed men he rambled about till he
could join the Prince of Orange; his intrest lay most amongst
the Presbiterians, who had no reason to be disgusted with a
Prince who had given them a freedom they had never yet
enjoyd; he tould them therefore, in a speech he made on that
occasion, That if the King prevail'd, they must bid adieu to
liberty of Conscience, which had been hithertoo granted (he
Sayd) not for the sake of Protestants, but to settle Popery.;
so that the fear of not haveing liberty of Conscience (for which
the King contended even to the loss of his Crown) is here
made an argument to rais the world against him; the Church
of England partie rebelled, because the King granted it, the
Presbiterians least they should loos it, so *that ther appear'd* †

---

* It is said that My Lord Devonshire, upon being informed that his Fine had
been forgiven, declared, " He wished no such favour at his Majesty's hand, but
would willingly play for Double or Quit." EDITOR.

† Inserted by the Son of James the second, instead of the words *the King saw
no.* EDITOR.

little possibility of pleasing such a brane sick people : In fine, T O M. III.
the King hears of nothing but insurrections, disertions, and
treasons, My Lord Colchester and M[r] Wharton were up in 1688.
Buckingham shire, My Lord Northampton in Northampton
shire, in Wales My Lord Herbert of Cherbery, Newcastle
receiud My Lord Lumley and declar'd for the Prince of
Orange, the Duke of Summerset and Earle of Oxford were
gon in to the Prince, My Lord Stamford had join'd My Lord
Shrewsbury at Bristol ; in fine dismal accounts came from all
sides, that the King thought it necessary to hasten what he
had long been thinking of and preserue the Prince of Wales
his Son at least for better days, so he sent again to My Lord
and Lady Powis (under whose care he was) and to My Lord
Dover to put his former order in execution, and in an other
letter to My Lord Dartmouth conjured him to be assisting to it: My Lord Dartmouth
When My Lord Dover deliver'd the first order to him ” will not suffer the Prince of
which had been sign'd at Andover, he seem'd to concur ” Wales to go for France.
readily, but afterwards, thō the Princ's weomen and bagage ” KingJam.M[em]
was put on board the Yacght in the evening, and he design'd ” Tom:9.pag.24.
to be brought next morning, he began to rais difficultys, and ”
sent that day to My Lord Dover to come and dine with him, ”
and told him it was against the Law to cary the Prince out ”
of England without a positiue * order; and that unles he had ”
such an one, he would not suffer it to be done least he should ”
be call'd to account for it afterwards, and in short positively ”
refused to let him go, and as long as the Prince Stayd there ”
were severall·chalops belonging to the fleet armed out, and ”
order'd to ly in the mouth of the harbour together with a ”
Ketch that rid constantly there, to examin all boats and ”
vessels which went out : The King was hugely troubled when ”

---

* See Note in preceding page 220. EDITOR.

H H

TOM.
III.
1688.

" he heard it, thō not surprized, considering the address which
" came from that Lord and the rest of the Mariné Officers a
" little before, wherein they desir'd the King to call a Parlia-
" ment, declareing their resolution of standing by the
" Protestant Religion but not one word of standing by the
" King, which address the Admiral had Sent by My lord
" Berkeley and Capt Hastings, the most factious and disafected
" Officers of the Navy; nevertheless it was the opinion of many
" persons, that had the fleet engaged the Enemy, when it went
" to seek them in Torbay, they would haue fought heartely at
" that time, such was their natural animosity to the Dutch,
" but after they return'd to Spithead, the generality of them
" by one art or other, or for fear of loosing their Command,
" were so chang'd in their opinion and affections, that no
" dependence could be had of them, even Sr John Berry
" himself seem'd of that mind.

Scarce any thing ever went nearer the King's heart, than to
see the English * Mariners, so famed for a braue and loyal
race of people, proue false to a Prince, who had encouraged,
cherished, and promoted that profession, more than any King

---

* There can be no doubt of KING JAMES's regard for the interests and honour
of the British Navy. If any additional Proof were wanting of his great Ability
in the various arrangement of Naval Business, it may easily be collected by a
reference to what has been termed, *Memoirs of the English Affairs, chiefly Naval,
from the year* 1660 *to* 1673, *written by His Royal Highness James Duke of York,
under his Administration of Lord High Admiral,* &c. published from His Original
Letters and other Royal Authorities. 8vo. London. 1729. Campbell, also,
(*Vol: 2. p.* 566.) observes, " The Regulations, in respect to Naval Affairs, when
the King himself acted as Admiral, assisted only by Mr. Pepys, as Secretary, at
five hundred pounds per annum salary, are allowed by all Seamen to be as judicious and effectual, and at the same time as gentle, and as practicable, as can be
desired." It is also due to the memory of JAMES THE SECOND to add, that the
Naval Regulations now in force, are nearly the same as those originally drawn up
by THE DUKE OF YORK. EDITOR.

since the Conquest; who had been all his life a model and
example as well as a Spectator and praiser of their courage:
he gloryd in nothing more, than that he had shar'd with them
in the hardships and dangers of defending the dominion of the
Seas, but the mistaken notions of Religion had been so
managed by angry men, as to stifle all those former sentiments
of honour and duty, and even of Religion and morality too,
when rightly understood.

T O M.
III.
1688.

This cross and perplexing accident was a great addition to
the King's uneasyness, he knew not whether to lay greater "
blame upon My Lord Dartmouth's scruples not to say wors, "
or My Lord Dover's mismanagement, for it is certain the "
Captain of the Yacght would haue done his duty in spight of
My Lord Dartmouth, if the other Lord would haue agreed to
it; in fine there was no remedy but to send for the Prince "
back, which now was become very dangerous and unsafe on "
many accounts, however the King thought it prudenter to "
run any hazard, then to expose his falling into the Prince "
of Orange's hands, which considering the temper of the fleet, "
he was in great danger of, if he stayd there; and to bring him "
back would need a convoy of his troops, which now were as "
little to be trusted to as the Fleet: but their being two "
Catholick Regiments of hors now ready rais'd and cloathed, "
which had been done at the Collonell's expence, the Earle of "
Salisbury and Mr Holman, his Majesty order'd them, and a "
detachment of the Irish Dragoons to march towards Ports- "
mouth and conduct him to London.   "

The King
sends for the
Prince of
Wales back.
Ibid: pag. 25.

Ibid: pag. 245.

But the orders comeing to the Lord and Lady Powis to
bring the Prince away before those troops could reach
Portsmouth, they prepar'd for a journey next morning, and
My Lord Dover command'd Collonell Clifford to be ready by
six a clock with an escorte, but afterwards thinking that too
late an houre perswaded My Lord and Lady Powis to set

out by fiue, so they were got three miles from the Towne ere it was light, when no guards apeareing, they were in great concern; but My Lord Dover perSwadeing them it could not be long ere they came up, they venter'd on till they came to the Forest of Beares, and there were in a mighty perplexity what to doe, so they desir'd one Mr Macarty an Irish Officer who fortuned to accompany them to ride back and hasten up the guards, who in his way meeting a Country fellow, asked him what news? He sayd he knew none, only that a partie of hors had been at Collonell Norton's the night before, where they had refreshed themselves, and was gon that very morning in to the wood; Mr Macarty aprehending it might probably be the Enemy, enquired of the man, if there was no other coach road to mis the wood, he tould him there was, and a better way too, upon which intelligence, they immediately turned into it and arriued at Petrefeild ere the guards over took them.

It was sayd afterwards that the Prince of Orange had notice from Portsmouth of what had pass'd there, and that certainly the Prince would be carryd back to London; and therefore he had detach'd a hundred hors, two Captains, two Leiftenants and two Cornets to intercept him, and that they were then actually in that wood. when the Prince took the other road: so visibly did Prouidence watch over his preservation, as to chang a seeming disapointment to his greater Security, for had the guards been with him, they had probably not light of that guide but follow'd the ordinary road, and fallen, by consequence into the ambuscade; and it is probable his escort had been too weak (supposing them willing) to defend him against so great a partie of the Enimy, from whom he could haue expected no good treatment, since it was his birth that had given the main, if not the only rise to this invasion.

Care had been taken by the King to keep the Prince's comeing as secret as possible, otherwise he might haue met with

greater danger at his arrival at London than he had escaped
on the road, for the very troops *which were sent to meet him* *
could not defend themselves, much less him from the insults
of the Rabble assoon as they enter'd Southwarke; for being
known to be Catholick Regiments were met with such an out-
cry and prodigious multitude of people that they were forced
to disband, and each one shift for himself, but the Prince
passing at † Kingston bridg was met by a Squadron of the
guards who conducted him safe to Whitehall, where the King
had prepar'd every thing ready not only for his, but the Queen's
departure likewise, being resolved to send them both immediately
into France, there being no more safty for them in England ;
but before we mention the particulars of that, it will be
necessary to take notice of what further Steps the King made
at his return from Salisbury, to Saue if possible this sinking
Vessel.

Before his Majesty went thither and indeed before the danger
was capable of terrifying him into a complyance, he had
revoked many displeasing Councells, takeing nothing so much
to heart as the content of his people, and he knew all further
concessions would be now imputed to the ill Situation of his
affairs, however he was resolued to leaue nothing undone that
could in any reason be expected from him ; to the end that if
they persever'd in their disobedience it should ly at their
doors both in the Sight of God and man. The Bisshop of
Exeter therefore who at the Prince of Orange's arrival in that
town had refused to receiue him and had retired to London,
his Majesty to recompence his dutyfull comportment, confer'd
the Archibisshoprick of York upon him, the cerimony was
forthwith perform'd at Lambeth, and the next day after he

T O M.
III.

1688.

The King
issus out writts
again for a
Parliament,
assembles a
great Council,
and Sends to
treat with the
Pᵉᵉ of Orange.

---

* Inserted as before mentioned instead of the words, *that conducted.* EDITOR.
† Knightsbridge had been inserted in pencil in the MS. over Kingston. EDITOR.

did homage to the King for the translation; a great reward
for one single act of duty, and more sutable to the King's
generosity than his real merit, who retracted so soon his short
liued loyalty, and was as ready to fly in his Prince and
Benefactor's face as the rest, when there was no more to be
expected from him : but his Majesty was now become well

" acquainted with Such returns, so it no ways rebuted him, but
" seeing the people Still longing after a Parliament, thõ the
" present circomstances were very unseasonable, however he
" order'd writts to go out for its meeting on the 15ᵗʰ of
" January following, belieuing it might be of some use to him
" in the desperate condition his affairs were in ; issuing out a
Proclamation at the same time so full of clemency and complyance, that if any thing could haue moued the obdurate
hearts of his Subjects, that would haue done it: He tould them
that for the security of all persons both in their elections and
Seruice in Parliament, they should all haue free liberty to
Elect; and all the Peers, and such as should be chozen
members of the House of Commons should haue full liberty
and freedome to sit and serue in Parliament, notwithstanding
they had taken armes or committed any acts of hostility or
been any ways aiding or assisting therein, that for the better
assurance thereof his Majesty had directed a general pardon
for all his Subjects to be forthwith prepared to pass the broad
Seal ; and for the reconciling all publick breaches, and the
obliterateing the very memory of all past miscariages, his
Majesty did hereby exhort and kindly admonish all his Subjects
to dispose themselves to elect such persons for their representatiues in Parliament, as might not be byass'd by prejudice or
passion, but qualifyd with partes, experience and prudence

" proper for the conjuncture ; and in the mean time he order'd
" all the Lords Spiritual and Temporal to wait on him at
" Whitehall in nature of a great Council, as had been usually

practiced in such disorderly times, and thō it was generally "
obserued it scarce ever did any good, however to take away "
all objections, (and that the Lords might not Say, had they "
been call'd upon by the King, they would haue done wonders "
for him) he assembled them accordingly : There were nine "
spirituall and therty or forty temporall Lords whom the "
King in a short discours acquainted with the occasion of "
their being assembled, he tould them, He had issued out "
writts for calling a Parliament, had restored the Charters, and "
given all the assurances that could be desired either in words "
or actions of his intentions to Support the Church of England; "
but that all these concessions haveing hithertoo wrought no "
cure, he desir'd their advice what was best to be done in the "
present posture things were in : My Lord Halifax and "
Notingham speak with great respect and seeming concern, "
especially the last, they thought there was now no remedy "
except it could be had by a Treaty with the Prince of Orange, "
they were sencible (they said) it would proue a bitter draught "
to his Majesty, who must swallow many disagreeable propo- "
sitions, and yeeld to such conditions as would be exceeding "
grievous to him; but My Lord Clarendon flew out into an "
indiscreet and Seditious railing, declameing against Popery, "
exagerateing fears and jealousies, and blameing the King's "
conduct, so that nobody wonder'd at his going a day or two "
after to meet the Prince of Orange at Salisbury; but in "
conclusion it apear'd to be the most general opinion the "
King should send to treat, so his Majesty agreed to it, and "
My Lord Halifax, Notingham, and Godolphin, were named "
for that Service; thō indeed what they were commission'd "
to insist upon, were rather Preliminarys than formed Articles "
for a Treaty ; as that the King haveing observed that all the "
causes of complaint and differences seem'd to be refer'd by "
his Highness to a free Parliament, that his Majesty had "

T O M.
III.

1688.

" resolued some time ago to call one, and that his haveing of
" late put it off, was because the present troubles render'd it
" improper, but that seeing his people still press'd for it, he
had issued out his Proclamations and writts for its siting
accordingly, that he was willing to consent to any thing that
could reasonably be requir'd for their security and freedom
dureing the Sessions; and that in order to it he had commissioned those three Lords to ajust all matters with his
Highness for the freedom of Elections and secure sitting; and
lastly his Majesty proposed, that both Armys might return
within their lines, at such a distance from London as might
prevent the aprehentions of any disturbance; being desirous
its meeting might be free and unmolested and according to its

KING JAM:
MEMꝏ.TOM:9.
pag: 247.

" usual formes: they were particularly instructed also to insist
" in the first place, upon the Prince of Orange's Army not
" comeing nearer than therty or forty miles from London;
" for if he would not harken to that, and agree to so reasonable
" a proposall, it was a sign he woul doe nothing by way of
" Treaty, so charg'd his Commissioners to give him early
" notice how that was accepted, that he might take his measures
" accordingly: When the Commissioners came to Andover,
the Prince of Orange sent them word to go to Ramsbury, where
they should hear further from him, and so by one pretence or
other puting them off for two or three days, at last were admited
at Hungerford, and after Severall Conferences return'd this
answer: We, with the advice of the Lords and gentlemen
assembled with us, haue in answer made these following
proposalls, 1st that all papists and such as are not qualifyd by
law be disarmed, disbanded, and remoued from all imployments Civil and military; 2ly that all proclamations which
reflect on us, or any who haue come in to us, be recall'd; and
that if any persons for haveing assisted us be commited, that
they be forthwith set at libertie; 3ly for the security and safety

of the City of London, that the Custody and government of the Tower be immediately put into the hands of the Said Citie; 4ˡʸ that if his Majesty shall think fit to be in London dureing the Sitting of the Parliament, that we may be there also, with an equal number of our guards, and if his Majesty shall pleas to be in any place out of London whatever distance he thinks fit, that we may be at the same distance, and that the respectiue Armies be distant likewise from London forty miles at least, and that no further force be brought into the Kingdom; 5ˡʸ that for the further security of the Citie of London, and its trade, that Tilbury fort be put into the hands of the Said Citie; 6ˡʸ that a sufficient part of the publick revenue be assign'd as for the Support and maintenance of our troops till the Sitting of a free Parliament; 7ˡʸ that for preventing the French or other forreign troops from landing, Portsmouth be put into such hands as by his Majesty and us may be agreed on.

When the King receiud these proposalls, he saw plainly what was aim'd at and took his measures accordingly, he was too well acquainted with the ambitious views of that Prince to immagin (as many did) that all this undertakeing was out of pangs of conscience for the Religion and liberties of the people; that in those arogant demands he assumed in a manner already the Regal authority, which was so far beneath a Crown'd head to submit too, that they Served only to confirme him in his resolution of sending the Queen and Prince into France, and of following them * himself in 24 hours

T O M. III.

1688.

KING JAM: MEMᵒⁿ TOMꞁ9. p: 247.

---

* Lord *Dartmouth* in a second letter to the King upon his first flight, dated Spithead, thus expressed his Loyalty and Regret. (*Dalrymple's Memoirs, Volꞁ* 2. *p.* 330.) " It is impossible for me to express the grief and anxious cares I am in for your Majesty, and the news of your withdrawing was the greatest surprize of my life; for I did humbly hope, my dutiful Supplications to your Majesty would with your own considerate thoughts have wholly altered your intentions of sending away the Prince of Wales, and did think it impossible ever to enter into any body's

T O M.
III.

1688.
Ibid: pag:255.

The King's
concern to
Secure his
papers, or
Memoirs of
his Life.

" afterwards : for now things were come to that extremity, by
" the generall defection of the nobility, gentry, and Clergie,
" by the scandelous desertion of the Chief Officers and others
" in the Army, as gaue little reason to trust those who
" remain'd ; so that no other Councel could reasonably be
" embraced, but to quit the Kingdom with as much secrecy
" as possebly he could.

This resolution once taken there was nothing his Majesty
was more in pain for than how to saue his papers or Memoirs
of his Life, from whence all that is materiall in this Account
or Relation of it, is in a manner taken ; he could not think of
any one properer to confide such a trust too, than the Count de
Therese the Duke of Tuscanys Envoy, whom his Majesty
knew to be an honest and intelligent person ; he sent for him
therefore, and asked him if he would undertake to secure a box
for him, which he readily engaged to doe ; so the King

thought, that had the least inclination of Duty to your Majesty, to give you so
pernicious and destructive counsel as to go away yourself ; and if your Majesty
had been drove to such a desperate course (which was morally impossible, at least
in my thoughts) as to absent yourself, Sir, could you have been with more honour
and safety, than in your own Fleet, who would always unanimously (I dare say)
have protected and defended your sacred person, from any violence or unhallowed
hands ; but this looks like so great mistrust of me, that many can witness it hath
almost broke my heart. Your Majesty knows what condition you left the Fleet
in, and me in the utmost unsupportable calamity of my life ; what could I do but
send to the Prince of Orange, when I found the whole Nation did, and received
orders from the Lords, which were communicated to the Fleet, and removed all
Roman Catholic Officers. I have had yet no return from the Prince of Orange,
but I hope all will end in your Majestys happy reestablishment . . . . but
withal, my confusion is so great, that I am only able to beg God Almighty's
protection of your Majesty, and to deliver you out of all these troubles, which shall
not only be the prayers, but hearty endeavours of a heart that never studied any
thing but your real service, and will ever do to my unfortunate life's end." — Sir J.
Dalrymple thought (page 223.) " that Lord Dartmouth's error lay in not anchoring
somewhat east of the Gallopper, as he had promised to King James he would do,
in order to be able to stretch which way he pleased." He afterwards changed his
mind, and anchored a-breast of the Long Sands. . . . EDITOR.

haveing just time to thrust them all confusedly into it, sent it
to him, which he immagining to be jewells of great value, was
exceeding carefull of it; thō that immaginatión had like to
haue occasion'd its miscariage, even after it had scap'd the
fury of the Mob (who in their barberous and tumultuous rage
of plundering, had not spared the houses of forreign Ambassadors, nor his amongst the rest) for the Merchant to whose
care he had commited it to be sent to Leghorn, haveing the
same fancy, thō not the same fidelity, design'd to imbezle it;
which an Italian Servant of the Envoys mistrusting, got it out
of his hands, and convey'd it safe to Leghorn as directed;
from whence the Great Duke sent two Gallys on purpose to
convoy it into France, through which Kingdom it was brought
likewise guarded up to St Germains, all persons supposeing it to
be some great treasure: Which thō it was not of that nature as
people immagined, it contain'd what in it self was much more
valuable, being the uncontestable Memoirs of the most Heroical,
the most opressed, and most Christian Prince, the world has
seen for many ages; never Prince had fewer moments of quiet,
yet never Prince left more monuments of what passed in his
time, amounting to Nine Tomes writ in his own hand, and
which by a writeing under his privy seal he apointed to be
lodged in the Scotch Colledg at Paris, where they will remain
not only an eternal and glorious monument of his Actions, but
a standing model both to his own Royal posterity, and to all
Christian Princes, of the most perfect resignation while a
Subject, and the most generous moderation when a King
(whatever aspertions to the contrary the world has cast upon
him.) It will there apear how intrepid he was in the greatest
dangers, how unshaken in the severest persecutions, how
affectionate a lover of his people, and how ill he was requited
for it; how insencible they were of his favours, whilest he by

his moderation and Vertue, apear'd to be so of their ill treatment; they hated him when he sought their good, he loved them when they sought his destruction: they will see there how his Courage had often defended the Nation, his Prudence and Resolution preserv'd it, his Industry encreas'd its riches, his Skill improu'd its trade, and his good Management secured it from taxes; in fine he had all the qualitys which would haue made him adored by the people, had not his Religion differ'd from theirs, which as it embittern'd all he did in their acceptation, so it sweeten'd in him all their unnatural returns From these Memoirs therefore Princes may learn, that their dignity ought not to exempt them from danger in Warrs, nor from pains and sollicitude in times of Peace; and that as the good and wellfare of the people ought to be the cheif concern of Princes in this world, so they must, like him expect their reward for it only in the next.

The Queen and Prince goes for France.

All things being ready by this time for the Queen and Prince's departure, it fell out opertunely enough, that the Count de Lozune a French gentleman was then at the Court of England, whither he came to offer his seruices to the King, but treachery and disertion of so many false friends made the zeal and fidelitie of his true ones useless at least in reference to the war; so his Majesty accepted of his offer an other way, as thinking him a proper person to attend upon the Queen in this Voyage, and that under the notion of his returning to his own Country (there being no business for him in England) a yacght might be prepared, and the Queen and Prince pass unsuspected in his company.

The Queen had a great reluctancy to this journey not so much for the hazards and inconveniencys of it as to leave the King in so doubtfull a Situation; she haveing never done it hitherto in his greatest difficulties and dangers: and therefore

when it was first proposed, her Majesty absolutly refused it
in reference to herself; telling the King she was very willing
the Prince her Son should be sent to France, or where it was
thought most proper for his security, that she could bear such
a separation with patience, but could never endure it in
reference to himself; that she would infinitly rather run his
fortune whatever it should prove than abandon him in that
distrets; that all hardships, hazards, or imprisonments it self
would be more acceptable to her in his company, than the
greatest eas and security in the world without him, unless he
realy purposed to come away himself too, then she was willing
to be sent before him if he thought it a more proper method
to conceal their departure; which the King assuring her he
realy did, her Majesty consent to it at last.

This reluctancy which the Queen had to part from the
King made some persons, who wished him well, and thought
his leaveing the Kingdom too precipitate, suspect her Majesty
to have been the occasion of it, which was the farthest thing
in the world from her thoughts, she neither advised it, nor
urged him to it; on the contrary it was her own staying, not
his going, her Majesty contended for; apprehending that the
King's pretence of following her, was only to make her go
more willingly, and that he had no such design in the bottom,
she press'd only to know the truth that she might dispose of
herself accordingly.

But it was the Queen's hard fate as well as the King's, in
most occurrancies of their life, to haue a false construction
put upon their actions, to be condemned where they merited
greatest prais (as the Queen's so passionate affection for the
King, most deservedly did in this case) and for addition to
the persecution of their enemies, to be continually blamed and
censured for their conduct, by their friends.

This journey and Separation therefore being at last resolv'd on, the Queen * disguising herself cross'd the river upon the 9th of December, takeing only the Prince, his Nurs, and two or three persons more along with her to avoid suspicion, and had sent to haue a coach ready prepar'd on the other side, in which she went down to Grauesend and got safe aboard the Yacght; which considering that the Rabble was up in all partes to intercept and plunder, whoever they thought were makeing their escape, was such a prouidence that nothing but a greater danger could excuse from rashness and temerity in attempting; but in such aflicting circomstances where the government of a distressed Prince is not only overturn'd, but himself and Royal family in just aprehentions of the most barberous treatment, all other hazards and hardships pass unregarded. Otherwise for the Queen to cross the river in a tempestious night, with the Prince not Six months old, to wait in the open air for a considerable time till the Coach was ready, and not only exposed to the could but to the continual danger of being discover'd, which the least cry of the Prince might haue done; to travel in the middle of an inraged people

---

* *Sir J. Dalrymple* in his *Memoirs* (*Vol:* 1. *p.* 238.) gives a more minute account of what the Queen went through on that occasion, in which he probably followed Father Orleans. " On the 6th of December, in the evening, the Queen, with the nurse carrying the Prince, then five months old, in her arms, and accompanied by the Count of Lausune, so famous for his own misfortunes, and by a few attendants, went privately from Whitehall: She crossed the Thames, in an open boat, in a dark night, in a heavy rain, in a high wind, whilst the river was swollen, and at the coldest season of the year. A common coach had been ordered to wait for her upon the opposite side; but, by some accident, it had been delayed for an hour. During this time, she took shelter under the walls of an old church at Lambeth; turning her eyes, streaming with tears, sometimes on the Prince, unconscious of the miseries which attend upon Royalty, and who, upon that account, raised the greater compassion in her breast, and sometimes to the innumerable lights of the City, amidst the glimmerings of which, she in vain explored the Palace in which her husband was left, and started at every sound she heard from thence." EDITOR.

without guards, Servants, or convenience sufficient to preserve
them from common dangers, or even defend them from the
could, had been a tempting of providence on a less pressing
occasion: however it pleased God to bring them through all
these dangers, and indeed much was oweing to the Count de
Lozun's care and conduct, without which considering the
many cross accidents and disapointments they had not got
away: Assoon therefore as the Queen and Prince was on
board the wind proueing fair they had a quick passage and
landed next day at Calais ; where the Queen intended to haue
waited the King's arrival as had been agreed betwixt them,
he haveing promised to follow in 24 hours, but he not apeareing she went on to Boulogne, where an account was brought
that his Majesty had been seized by a rabble of people as he
design'd to follow her, that he had been treated with great
rudness and barbarity by them and remained in effect a
prisoner in their hands : this put her into the last degree of
torment and aprehention ; She immediately resolved to send the
Prince forward and return herself into England ; she consider'd neither the rage of the people, nor the hazards of the
journey, her own safty weighed little with her, in comparison
of the axiety she was in for that of the King's ; but assoon as
the Duke d'Aumont in whose house she lay, and the Count
de Lausun understood her design, they beg'd of her Majesty
not to doe so unadvised an action, that it would be an unpardonable temerity so to expose her life, without any prospect
of doeing the least good by it; that it would only aggravate
the King's troubles and make it more difficult for him to
extrecate himself out of them, that there was no doubt but the
people would soon return so far at least to themselves and their
duty, as not to offer any indignity to his person, and at last
by much arguing and importunity preuail'd upon her to wait
at least a further account; and in a few days after, she hearing

T O M.
III.
1688.

KING JAM:
MEM᷎. To: 9.
pag. 256.

something better news it made her Majesty less sencible of
her other misfortunes, for to her the King's safety did out-
ballance all the good she could expect, or evils she could
suffer.

His most Christian Majesty no sooner heard of the Queen
and Prince's arrival in his Country, but he dispatch'd his
orders and Officers with Coaches and all things necessary for
their jorney up; which was performed with so much order,
magnificence and respect, as suted better with his Princely
generosity and the dignity of his Guests, than the mornfull
condition of the disconsolate Queen. The roads being bad and
the grownd cover'd with Snow, a stright way was marked out
over the Country, which a number of pioneers going before
plain'd, and made even whatever might obstruct their passage;
her Majesty finding the same preparations all along on the
road, as to lodging, diet &c, as if she had been in a Royal
Pallace, till she arrived within a league of St Germains, where
his most Christian Majesty met her himself: Assoon as he
came up to the Prince of Wales takeing him in his armes he
made him a short speech, wherein he promis'd him both
protection and secour, and then going on to the Queen, he
left nothing unsaid which might molify her present suffrings
and encourage the hopes of a speedy redress; so conducting
them to * St Germains (which house he had left some little
time before to make his constant residence at Versailles) he
settled her Majesty and the Prince of Wales there, apointing
guards and all other necessary officers to attend them, waiting
for the King's arrivall, whom the Queen had heard at last (by
an express that overtook her at Baumont) that he was safely
landed in France, after haveing run more dangers, and passed

* Sir John Reresby says, the French King had first prepared the Castle of
Vincennes for their reception and entertainment. EDITOR.

thorough more different Situations, than ever Prince was known to haue done in so short a space of time : the particulars wherof ar too memorable to be omited, especially he haveing racounted em in great part himself, and left them written in his own hand.

Assoon therfore as the Queen had set Sail from Graueend, S͏ᵗ Victor a French gentleman who was with the Count de Lozune, came back to acquaint the King he had seen them on board the Yacght, and that they were gon off with a fair wind, so the King prepar'd to follow them, seeing no security where he was, and well remembring how the King his Father and Several of his predecessors had been used on like occasions ; he was resolved never to consent to those mean things which would haue been imposed upon him, and saw plainly by the Prince of Orange's answer which he receiv'd that night, that nothing but the Crown would satisfy his ambitious Nephew and Son in Law. But notwithstanding the confusion and hurry the King was in, he took care before he went to doe the part of a true Father of his people, thō they were in the highest State of rebellion and ingratitude to him, for being resolved not to resist this torrent any longer, he was afraid some of his Subjects might loos their lives in a quarrell, he yielded for the present, for there had been some Skirmishes in defence of Reading and Maidenhead bridg : but the people every where sided so openly with the invader, that it was not possible for those few forces that were loyal to mentain any Post long ; for which reason his Majesty writ the following letter to My lord Feversham. Things being come to that extremity that I haue been forced to send away the Queen and my Son the Prince of Wales, that they might not fall into my enemys hands, which they must haue done had they stayd ; I am obliged to doe the same thing, and endeavour to secure myself the best I can, in hopes it will pleas God, out

The King resolues to follow the Queen.
K͏ɪɴɢ Jᴀᴍ: Mᴇᴍᵒʳ. Tᴏ: 9: pag: 257.

The King writes My lord Feversham to make no more resistance.

of his infinitie mercy to this unhappy Nation, to touch their hearts again with true loyalty and honour : if I could haue relyd upon all my troops I might not haue been put to this extremity I am in, and would at least haue had one blow for it; but though I know there are many Loyal and braue men amongst you, yet you know, you yourself and Several of the General Officers tould me, it was no ways advisable to venter myself at their head : there remains nothing more for me to doe but to thank you, and all those Officers and Soldiers, who haue stuck to me and been truly Loyal; I hope you will still haue the same fidelity to me, and thō I do not expect you should expose yourselves by resisting a forreign Army and poison'd Nation, yet I hope your former principles are so rooted in you, that you will keep yourselves free from associations, and such pernicious * things.

Assoon as My Lord Feversham receiud this letter, he writ to the Prince of Orange that he had orders from the King to make

---

* The Copy of the Letter in Kennet (Page 532.) ends thus, " Time presseth, so that I can add no more." That Historian also informs us, this Letter was written on Monday Evening, Dec^r: 10th; and subjoins (Page 534.) what passed when the Earl of Feversham received it : " It was read aloud to the Troops, and drew tears from most of them. Hereupon they held a Council of War, and concluded from the words of the Letter, That since the King did not expect they should resist a Foreign Army, his intention was, That the rest of the Army should be disbanded; and accordingly 4000 Men the Earl had then with him, were immediately dismissed : After which he sent the following Letter to the Prince of Orange, subscrib'd by himself and three General Officers :

" Sir,

Having receiv'd this morning a Letter from his Majesty with the unfortunate news of his Resolution to go out of England, I thought myself oblig'd, (being at the head of his Army, and having receiv'd his Orders, to make no opposition against any body) to let your Highness know it, with the advice of the Officers here, so soon as was possible, to hinder the effusion of blood. I have order'd already to that purpose all the Troops that are under my command, which shall be the last order they shall receive from

Feversham, Lanier, Fenwick, Oglethorp." EDITOR.

no opposition, which he sayd he advertised him of, to avoid the efusion of humain blood; and that he had given the like orders to the troops under his Command, which were the last they were like to haue from him: Upon this, each Officer and Soldier being left at his liberty, many of the latter especially, dispers'd and went home, which was no small disapointment to the Prince of Orange (as apear'd afterwards by his resentment of what had been done) who had already fram'd to himself great prospects of aid and advantages from those troops in the further prosecution of his designs against France, whereas by this means (before he was absolute master of them) they were dwindled away to a very small number in comparison of what they were when he landed.

T O M.
III.
1688.

His Majesty haveing thus prudently lessen'd as much as he could, the force, that was now like to be turn'd against him; thought it necessary to perplex his enemys also in the Civil, as he had done in their military affairs, by recalling the writs for assembling the Parliament, which he knew would disconcert the measures and malice of those who sought his ruin, and retard at least the injurys they design'd him; so Sending for " the Chancellor, (whom he had order'd some days before to " bring him the great Seal) he burnt the writts, and then betwixt " twelve and one on munday night the 10ᵗʰ of December he " left his Pallace of Whitehall, and haveing concerted matters " before hand, with Sʳ Edward Hales, he took a Hackney " Coach and went to the hors ferry, where he left Monʳ de la " Badie, who had accompanyd him thither; then takeing a " pare of orès he pass'd over to Foxhall, where horses were " ready layd, and about one on tusday morning the 11ᵗʰ of " December he set out haveing nobody with him but Sʳ " Edward Hales, Sʳ Edward's Quartermaster, and a guide; " he pass'd the river Midway at Alfor bridg about Seaven a " clock, and meeting the relay which Mʳ Ralph Sheldon one "

The King recalls the writts and then went privately away, but is seized in the river.

KING JAMᵉ MEMˢ Tom:9. pag:248.

" of his Queries had ready for him at the Woolpack, he got to
" Emley ferry near Feversham by ten, where the Custome
" house Hoy was hired to attend there by an acquaintance of
" S' Edward Hales, in order to transport them to France. The
" Vessel was not come up when the King arriued, but assoon
" as it came his Majesty, S' Ed: Hales, and M' Sheldon went
" on board, without acquainting the Master who they were;
" the wind was fair, and it blew a fresh gail, but it seems the
" Vessel wanted ballast and the Master telling the King he
" durst not venter to Sea as it was, his Majesty consented to
" haue him stay to take some in being sencible himself she
" could not carry sail without it; so falling down to Sherness
" at the west end of Sheepway ran ashore at half ebb, and
" haveing taken some in intended at half flood (by which
" time the Vessel would be on flote again) to set sail for the
" nearest part of France they could make; but about eleaven
" a clock at night just as the Hoy began to float, the King
" was boarded with three small fisher boats of Feversham
" haveing some fifty or sixty men in them, their Captain with
" his sword and pistol in his hands jump'd down into the
" Cabbine where the King and the two gentlemen were, and
" Seizing on them as suspected persons, pretended he must
" carry them before the Major of Feversham to be examined;
" presuming they might be Papists who were makeing their
" escape, but that no harme should be done to them, nor any
" thing taken from them: The King finding he was not known
" by any that came into the Cabine, thought best not to
" discover himself, hopeing still to find means to get from
" them; and as the Captain whose name was Amis Sat
" examining them in the Cabine, S' Edward Hales took a time
" when none of his men look'd that way, to clap fifty guineas
" into his hand, and tould him in his ear, he should haue a
" hundred more if he would get him and his two friends off,

before they were carryd to Feversham ; he took the mony ”
and promis'd to do it, by this time the Vessel was quite a ”
float, so they turn'd up with her to the mouth of Feversham ”
water and anchor'd there, staying for the top of high water ”
to carry her in; there the Captain left them pretending it was ”
to find means to get them off, but before he went, he tould ”
the King and those with him, that he was afraid his men ”
who were very unruly fellows, might plunder them in his ”
absence, and advised them to put what mony or other things ”
of value they had into his hands, which he promis to keep ”
Safe, and that if they were found free men they should be ”
restored, and if lawfull prize be more equally divided : the ”
King took his advice, and they gaue their watches and what ”
mony they had, before witnesses, takeing his receipt for ”
them; but the King kept the great diamond bodkin which ”
he had of the Queen's and the Coronation ring, which for ”
more security he put within his drawers : this advice of the ”
Captains proued very seasonable, thō he fail'd in his ingage- ”
ment, for he neither got them off, nor did he return in three ”
hours as he promis'd, but kept them there till it was broad ”
day, when he came and tould Sʳ Ed: Hales (who by this time ”
was known) that he must apear before the Major, and that ”
he was geting a Coach to carry them up. In the mean time ”
(it now being light) severall of the Sea men lept down into ”
the Cabine, saying they must Search them, believeing they ”
had not given all their mony to the Captain ; the King and ”
the other two gentlemen bid them search if they pleas'd, ”
immagining by that readyness to perswade them they had ”
nothing more ; but they not satisfyd with that, fell a Searching ”
their pockets and opening their breeches felt all about in a ”
very rude manner, and the more, because they found nothing; ”
but at last one of them feeling about the King's knees, got ”
hould of the diamond bodkin, and cryd out he had found a ”

T O M.
III.

1688.

260.

253.

260.

252.
261.

"prize, but the King faced him down he was in a mistake,
"that he had several things in his pocket, as sizers, a toothpick
"case and little keys, and that perhaps it was one of those
"things he felt; at which the man thrusting his hand suddenly
"into the King's pocket lost hould of the diamond, and
"finding those things there the King had mention'd, remain'd
"satisfyd it was so; by which means the bodkin and the
"ring were preserved: thō indeed they were so ignorant in
"jewells, that finding a pare of diamond buckles lap'd in a
"paper in the King's pocket, they took them for glass, and
"gaue them him again.

The King is
brought to
Feversham.

By this time the Coach was come to the shore side; so geting
into the small boat, they landed and were guarded up to the
"Town by one Edwards and some of the Rabble, and brought
"to an Inne, where, as the King went up staires notwith-
"standing his disguise and black periwig, he perceived several
"people knew him; so he tooke no more pains to conceal
"who he was, upon which the Rabble dispersed, and the King
"being inform'd that My Lord Winchelsea and most of the
"gentlemen of the Country were met at Cantorbury, sent to
"them to come to him : in the mean time his Majesty order'd
"Mʳ Sheldon to go the Master of the Custome house Smack,
"who he was informed was an honest man, to get it ready and
"attend at some distance from the Town, where horses were
"likewise prepared to carry him to it; but that Edwards who
"had guarded the King up, being a factious fellow, and
"Suspecting this, rais'd the Rabble again and beset the Inne,
"so that it was impossible for the King to get away, much
"less to assist others who he heard were seized likewise there
"in their way to Dover, as Judg Genner, Mʳ Burton and
"Greham, the Bisshops Leiborn and Gifford, two Mʳ Arundels,
"Fʳ Pulton a Jesuit, Dʳ Obedia Walker and Several others,
"but the rabble being masters there was no helping them.

By the close of the evening My Lord Winchelsea came *TO M.*
and only two gentlemen with him, so then the King resolved *III.*
to go and lodg at the Major's house, who was a Loyal * man ; " *1688.*
but as his Majesty went down Staires the rabble were very "
rude to him, so that he had much a doe to force his way "
through them, thō My Lord Winchelsea and one or two more "
went before to open the passage : but one reason of it was, "
least S^r Ed: Hales should escape, whom they had a mighty "
spleen against for haveing chang'd his Religion, and at that "
very time the people of the Country were plundering his "
house and killing his deer; and he being sencible how odious "
he was to them, prudently stayd in the Inne and would not "
follow the King least his company might draw a greater "
inconvenience upon him. The King was escorted by the "
Seamen and Rabble, who as he went along cryd out, that a "
hair of his head should not be touched, but still kept a strickt "
eye upon him that he might not escape, and when he cam to "
his lodgings they made his withdrawing room a Sorte of corps "
de guard.   "

The next day Sr Bazil Dixwell and Sr James Oxenden " Two Captains
came to Feversham with their two Militia troops, under " of militia troops detain the King
pretence of secureing the King from the Rabble, but indeed " prisoner at Feversham.

---

* *Sir John Dalrymple* in his *Memoirs,* is of opinion that King James's conduct at this most critical period of his Life, was influenced by a dread of his personal safety from the Prince of Orange, a fiction which Lord Halifax had contrived. (page 238.)—See also *Sir John Reresby's Memoirs.* (pages 382. and 383.) " After the King was brought back, Lord Halifax was one of the Peers that came and admonished him, on behalf of the Prince, to leave Whitehall for Rochester or Ham, within the short space of two hours; and that his Lordship's reason for conveying this ungrateful message to his Majesty was, That he was assured the Prince's Party had in Council resolved to seize on his person, and imprison him. That upon the whole it must be notoriously known to his Lordship, that the King had no manner of inclination to withdraw either the first or the second time ; and that he was compelled thereto out of a principle of mere self-preservation." EDITOR.

" to Secure him to themselves, and to make a merit of it to the
" Prince of Orange, as contribiteing to hinder his escape ; and
" accordingly they ·sent away immediately one Mr Nappleton
" a Lawier and friend of theirs, to informe the Prince of
" Orange they had the King in their power, and to desire his
" orders how to dispose of him ; which Mr Nappleton made
" no difficulty to acquaint the King with before he went, and
" in the mean time, those two gentlemen kept a very strict
" guard upon the King, and had the imprudence to find fault
" with· him, for sending away a letter to London for mony,
" Cloaths &c, without shewing it them before he seal'd it : ·so
" they took care however to guard him very rigorously, for
" which they made use of the Seamen, who had chozen an ill
" looking ill natured fellow one Hunt, to be their Captain,
" whom the King could neither perswade, nor tempt by mony,
" thō he was but the master of a small fisher boat, to let him
" go ; but on the contrary was exceeding rude, and when any
" one came to the King, they took away his sword and
" deliver'd it not till he went out of the house again.

The great
disorder after
the King was
gon.

" In the mean time not only London but all England was
" in the greatest confusion and flame immaginable, assoon as
" the King's departure was known, the Mob (who had begun
" to be unruly even before) was not now to be kept within
" any bounds ; they assembled in great bodys chuseing some
" one amongst them for their leader, ran in the most tumultuous
" manner immaginable through Town and Citie, where first
" they fell upon the Catholick Chappells pulling down and
" destroying all before them, makeing bònefires of the books,
" church stuff and even materials of the buildings ; this not
" Satisfying their rage, they fell upon most noted Catholick
" houses, which they plunder'd and ransack'd in no less rietous
" manner, at last the publick ministers themselves found there
" was no Sanctuary, nor law of nations to be obserued, where

the Rabble govern'd; for haveing once tasted the sweet "   T O M.
of plunder, as their fury abated, their averice encreas'd, "   III.
and they haveing intelligence that many Catholicks, even "   1688.
the King himself, had sent plate, mony, and their most "
valuable goods for security to those houses, were resolved, "
now their hands were in, not to stick at formalitys, so "
the Florentine and even Spanish Ambassadors houses "
far'd like the rest, thō the French and Venetian houses and "
Chappells, were saved by the guards they had the precaution "
to procure; which the Spanish Minister by reason of the "
great credit he had in this affair, thought not necessary; but "
for the same reason, there being most plunder, and parti- "
cularly the plate of the Royal Chappel, that proued no "
protection. Nor was this fury peculiar to London, the same "
spirit rain'd in most partes of England, especially in the "
Southern and Midland Countrys, where the Catholick houses "
were generally plunder'd and gutted (as they then term'd it) "
by the neibouring Rabble, even the high roads were not free "
from this contagion, all passingers were stopp'd, and if "
suspected to be Catholicks plunder'd, and imprison'd; the "
same was done by boats armed out upon the rivers, which
was the occasion of the King's being seized and of almost all
those who thought to haue follow'd him, and were going to
the Sea cost either by land, or water.

But what might probably haue had a much more tragical   The Rumour
efect, was a most malicious * rumour industriously spread   of the Irish were burning
abroad, that the Irish troops were in a desperate rage, killing,   and destroy- ing, had like to
burning and destroying all before them; this report began in   haue occa- sion'd great
London on thursday the 13th of December about one or two   mischeif.

---

* This Rumour of the Irish Insurrection, and a forged Proclamation of the
Prince of Orange, were devised by Speke, who drew up what he styled, *his Secret
History of the Happy Revolution.* See *Somers' Tracts* end of James 2[d]. EDITOR.

in the morning; the cry run So furiously through the Town that in a moment all people were up and in the greatest consternation immaginable, the streets illuminated and even the Militia assembled in many places; the rumour still went that in the next quarter of the Town all was fill'd with blood and ruin, which struck such a terrour that many weomen withchild miscarryd, and some timerous and antient people were sayd to dye with aprehention; and as a mark that this was not purely accedental, the Same was carryd in the space of two days all over England and Scotland too, every town had news that the next Town to it was fired by the Irish, and that they must in a few houres expect the Same fate: which struck such a consternation in most places that people fled from their houses, secured their goods, assembled in great boddys to oppose them, and in many Towns that stood upon rivers were at the point of breaking down their bridges to Stop the supposed torrent; while this handfull of Irish who were thus immagin'd to be burning and destroying all over England at once, were disarmed and dispers'd, not generally knowing where to get a meals meat, or a nights lodging, and lyable themselves to be knocked in the head, in every town they came to.

Whoever was the forger of this report, tis more than probable, his intention was to haue caused a general massacre of the Catholicks all over the Nation; for upon So dismal an alarme that all the Protestant throats were to be cut by the Irish Papists, what could be more natural, than for the Protestants to be beforehand at least with the Papists in their respectiue Towns or neiborhood, supposeing they would join with the Irish when they came? But to the great honour of the English Nation, notwithstanding their turbulent and factious spirite, they are so far from a bloody disposition, that not one Single Catholick, or even Irish man himSelf, was known to loos his life by this wicked and unhuman contrivance; which

is a great argument it sprung from the breast of a forreigner, T O M.
but since the true origine was never yet discover'd, it were III.
temerity to lay it at any man's door: amongst others My Lord 1688.
Chancellor Jeffreys was * seized in this confusion, as he was
endeavoring to escape in a Seaman's habit, and was commited
to the Tower where not long after he dyed.

By this time the rumour of the King's being taken and " KING JAM:
kept at Feversham had brought many of his Servants thither, " MEM^{rr}.TOM:9.
and Several loyal Officers of the army, by whom My Lord " pag. 258.
Feversham sent word, he was comeing with a detatchment of "
the hors guards and grenadeers on hors back to † secure him "
from the Rabble, and conduct him to London, whither his "
Majestys friends advised him to come; this news troubled "
hugely those Seditious Kentish gentlemen, who had pro- "
jected to themselves mighty advantages from their rude and "
rebellious carriage to their Sovereign. "

It seems upon the King's withdrawing from London, the
Lords about Town met at Guildhall to consult what was fit to
be done, they looked upon the present Situation of affairs as
an interregnum, that the government was in a manner devolved
upon them, and were in great hast to make a present of it to

---

* *Sir J. Dalrymple* condenses (*Page* 240.) what *Ralph* narrates more at large
(*Page* 1063.) " Jeffries they seized," says Sir John, " in a Seaman's habit at
Wapping, endeavouring to find a ship to make his escape. Treating him with
that want of mercy which he had shewn to others, they carried him in his blue
jacket, and with his hat flapped down upon his face, before the Lord Mayor;
who, as soon as the hat was lifted up, and he beheld that countenance which was
in use to strike terror wherever it appeared, fell into a faint with the shock of the
surprise, and died next day." EDITOR.

† The Council shewed no great inclination to relieve an insulted Monarch
from his Captivity at Feversham, until they were fairly shamed into sending a
party of the Guards for that purpose, by the remonstrances of the Earl of Mulgrave, afterwards Duke of Buckingham. See his Account of the Revolution, in
the fourth Edition of the Duke of Buckingham's Works (*Vol*: 2. *p.* 77.) This
interesting Memoir was placed amongst the Castrations in the 2^d Edition, at ye end
of the Poetry. EDITOR.

the Prince of Orange : Those who were most zealous in the matter took care to advertise and even press the two Secretarys of State, the Earle of Middleton and Lord Preston to be there, to ad a greater weight to their pretended authority ; but the former absolutely refused, and soon after hearing the King was at Feversham went immediately down to him ; the latter was prevail'd with to meet, but when he saw what was aim'd at refused to concur, whose example several others were sorry they had not follow'd when they heard that there was still a King in England. In the first place therefore to compliment the Citie, they Sent for M. Skelton Governor of the Tower under pretence of business, and then detaining him, commited the governm of the Tower to My Lord Lucas ; then they drew up a Declaration how much they were concern'd for the Protestant religion and the publick good, and that since the King had thought fit to withdraw himself, and recall the writts for a Parliament, whereby they were disapointed of seeing things settled that way, they unanimously agreed, to aply themselves to the Prince of Orange, who (sayd they) had with so much expence and hazard of his person undertaken to rescue them from imminent danger of Popery and Slavery, and declared they would assist him in procureing such a Parliament as might secure their Laws liberties &c, and deputed the Lords Pembrock, Weymouth, Culpeper and Bisshop of Ely to attend the Prince of Orange with this Declaration : the Leiftenancy of London as also the Lord Major and Aldermen sent the same day their adresses to the Prince likewise, all Sides contended who should express most gratitude for their pretended delivery ; but when the Lords heard the King was at Feversham, they were variously affected with the news, considering the advances they had made to the Prince of Orange ; however they thought fit to request his Majesty to return, and directed My Lord Feversham, as has been Sayd,

to attend upon him with guards in order to it; who arriveing " **T O M.**
there himself early on Saturday morning, acquainted the " **III.**
King he had left the guards at Sittinburn, upon which the "
King took his leaue of the Rabble and dismised them, and " 1688.
KING JAM.
MEM⁽ᵒⁿ⁾ TOM:9.
orderʼd the two Militia troops to attend upon him to Sittin- " pag: 259.
burn, where meeting his Guards he dimisʼd them likewise, "
and went that night as far as * Rocheʹster; from whence "
assoon as he arriued, he dispatched away My Lord Feversham "
to the Prince of Orange with a letter of credence, wherein he "
tould him, he would be glad to see him at London on "
munday, to endeavour by a personall conférence to settle the "
distracted Nation, that he had orderʼd S⁺ Jamesʼs to be pre- "
pared for him. Commissioning My Lord Feversham to "
propose Severall other things, which he conceiud proper as "
matters then stood, upon which he parted that very night, "
with orders to be back at London next day, to meet the "
King at his arrival there. "

The King continuing his journey to London was met by " The King
returns to
some Loyal Officers on the road, who informʼd that the " London, where
he is receivʼd
Batallion of the first regiment of Guards, which was left at " with exceeding
great joy of
Whitehall had declarʼd for the Prince of Orange, that they " the people.
belieud the Hors there had done the same, and that by con- "
sequence his Majesty would not be safe at his arrival there in "

---

* " He was conveyed thither," says the Duke of Buckingham, in the Memoir already cited, " by water, under a guard of fifty Dutchmen, whose Officeʹr had private orders to let him escape afterwards to France. I must not," adds the Duke, " omit two things, which shewʼd his temper under such an unexpected change. When the stout Earl of CRAVEN resolved to be rather cut to pieces, than to resign his post at Whitehall to the Princeʼs Guards, the King prevented that unnecessary bloodshed with a great deal of care and kindness : And amidst all that just apprehension of violence to his person, at the sudden entry into his chamber of those three Lords, he at least disguised it so well, as to discourse about the serving of the Tide, and other things relating to his removal as coolly, and uncon-cernedly, as if it had been only a common journey." EDITOR.

" such hands ; which made him resolue to go through the Citie
" that he might not (be) obliged to quit that part of the Guards
" and Grenadeers on hors back, which now were with him and
" would be an awe upon the rest: assoon as he arriued there,
he was hugely surprized with the unexpected testimonys of the
peoples affection to him, it is not to be immagined what
acclamations were made, and what * joy the people express'd
at his Majestys return ; such bonefires, ringing of bells, and
all immaginable markes of love and esteem, as made it look
" liker a day of tryumph than humiliation ; and this was So
" universall amongst all ranks of people, that the King, nor
" none that were with him had ever seen the like before, the
" same crowds of people and crys of joy accompanying him
" to Whitehall, and even to his Bed Chamber door itself,
" wither he was no sooner come, but y* Scene began to Change
" by the Arrival of Mons* Zulistin with a letter from the Prince
" of Orange ; the Substance of which was, That he had receiud
" his by My Lord Feversham, but that what was contain'd in
" it, and what that Lord had proposed to him, was of so great
" consequence that it could not then be answer'd ; and in the
" mean time desired his Majesty to remain at Rochester:
" The King answer'd Mons* Zulestine, that had he receiud
" that letter before he left the place, he should willingly haue
" stayd there, but that now he hoped the Prince of Orange
" would come the next day to S* Jame's, that he might confer
" with him concerning what he had writ by My Lord Fever-
" sham ; but Mons* Zulestine tould the King planely, That the
" Prince of Orange would not come thither till his Majestys
" troops were sent out of the Town ; upon which, the King
perceiving that his Messages, now began to take the air of

---

* The same is noticed by Henry Earl of Clarendon in his Diary (Page 120.)
EDITOR.

commands rather then requests, he made no reply; but ”
answer'd the Prince of Orange's letter, and gaue it to Zules- ”
tine who was not got out of the room when the Count de ”
Roy came in to acquaint the King, that assoon as My Lord ”
Feversham had deliver'd his letter of Credance to the Prince ”
of Orange at Windsor, he order'd him to be made a Prisoner ”
in the Town; upon which the King sent for Mons'ʳ Zulestin ”
back, and tould him he was very much surprized at My ”
Lord Feversham's being made a prisoner; that it was against ”
the Law of Nations and the universall practice to detain a ”
publick minister; that he hoped the Prince of Orange would ”
haue so much consideration for him, as not to keep him in ”
restraint any longer: but the Prince of Orange had no regard ”
to the King's request, but left him prisoner at Windsor when ”
he quited that place to come to Sion; nor did he so much as ”
answer his letter, or indeed keept any sort of measures with ”
his Majesty afterwards; but that the Prince of Orange's harsh ”
and sower temper was known to be proof against civility, as
well as good nature, people would haue wonder'd much more,
how he could haue refused so modest and just a request, and
of so little consequence to his affairs: But he was in such a
surprize at the news of the Lords haveing invited the King
back again to Whitehall, and at the joyfull reception he met
with at his arrival, as made him stand at a gaze in some doubt
with himself what was next to be done; for being of a suspicious and diffident disposition, he aprehended extreamly this
sudden change and the unsettled genious of the people; he
rosolved therefore not to give that inconstant humour of the
English Nation, leasure to reassume those sentiments which
nature and reason generally inspire Subjects with, in reference
to their Sovereign: So he threw off the maske before the end
of the first Scene; for hithertoo the pretence of the Expedition
had been only to bring the King to reason, in reference to the

The Prince of
Orange Sur-
prized at the
King's recep-
tion, sends to
takethe postes
about White-
hall with his
own guards.

T O M.
III.
1688.

Laws, libertie and Religion, and to engage him in a league against France; the one to Satisfy (or rather bubble) the people, the other his Forreign Allys; but now that the King sends message after message to him to disire a personal conference, in order to rectify and settle whatever was amis, and if any thing more were required over and about what he had already granted, that he was ready to debate it with him, or refer it to a free Parliament, that all things might be adjusted to the general Satisfaction of his Subjects, he did not think fit to giue the least ear to all this; the Prince of Orange dreaded nothing now so much as what he gaue out to be the only motiue of his Expedition, for this pretended reconciliation was indeed the first in his pretences, but the last in his intentions: so being terrifyd with the King's welcome back, and seeing the peoples affection so ready to run into their antient Channel, he resolved to outface all his former protestation, and therefore would not voutsafe his Majesty the honour of seeing him, nor

King Jam:
Mem^{ors} Tom:9.
pag. 261.

" so much as an answer to his letter; but sent the Count de
" Solmes that very night, with his Guards to take the postes
" about Whitehall.

" When the King was advertised of this, he could not
" believe it, because he had heard nothing of it he sayd from
" the Prince himself, and therefore supposed they were only
" comeing to take the Portes about St James's to be ready to
" receiue him there next day; but at eleaven a clock My Lord
" Craven came to acquaint his Majesty, just as he was going
" to bed, that the Count de Solmes was in the Parke with
" three battallions of the Prince's foot guards and some hors,
" and Sayd he had orders to take the portes in and about
" Whitehall; upon which the King sent for the Count de
" Solmes and tould him, He believ'd he was mistaken, and
" that his orders were only for St James's; but he was positive
" they were for Whitehall, which he sayd was first named,

and shew'd his Majesty the orders themselves ; upon which the King argued the matter with him for some time, but at last directed My Lord Craven to draw out his men and let Count de Solmes take the postes, which they immediately did.

T O M.
III.
1688.

Things now began to haue a gloomy aspect, his Majesty saw no hopes of a conference, much less of an accommodation, he perceiud he was absolutely the Prince of Orange's prisoner, and at his mercy ; however his usual intrepidity abandon'd him not, so that when some difficulty was made whether he should venter to sleep in the middle of the Dutch guards, he Sayd, He knew not whether those or his own were wors, so went to bed at his usual time, and slept with as much tranquility as he ever did in his life ; for a little after midnight My Lord Middleton, (who lay by the King) was call'd up by My Lord Halifax, Shrusbury, and Delamere, to tell him they had a message to his Majesty from the Prince, which they must immediately impart ; and when My Lord Middleton would haue had them Stay till the King was awake in the morning, they answer'd that their business would admit of no delay : There was no arguing with men who were Masters, so My Lord Middleton went to the King's bed side and found him so fast a sleep, that puting by the curtaine did not wake him, till kneeling down he spoke pretty loud in his ear, by which his Majesty at the first was a little surprized, but immediately composeing himself, asked what was the business? Which when My Lord Middleton tould him, he order'd them to be call'd in, who deliver'd a paper to the King, sign'd by the Prince of Orange; the substance of which was, That to avoid the disorder which his Majestys presence might cause in London, he thought fit he Should go to * Ham that very

The King went to bed tho in the hands of the Dutch, and was waked to be tould, he must leaue the Town next morning.

KING JAM: MEM^rs.TOM:9: pag: 262.

Ibid. 263.

---

* A house belonging to the Dutchess of Lauderdale. EDITOR.

T O M. " morning, he designing to be in town about noon himself,
III. " and this in few but positiue * words : My Lord Halifax
1688. " added he might take *what servants he pleased with him, but must*
" *be gon before ten,* y^t ye P: *of Orange would* † *take* care to apoint
" a sutable guard to attend him there to Secure him from any
" harme. The King Seeing there was no remedy, being
" absolutely in their power, tould them, He was content to go
" out of Town, but that Ham was a very ill winter house, and
" unfurnished ; My Lord Halifax replyd, that his Majestys
" officers might soon doe that ; but upon further discours the
" King tould them, that since he was to goe, he would rather
" be further off, and go to Rochester which was the place the
" Prince of Orange in his letter by Monsr Zulistin express'd a
" desire the King should remain at, and that there was some of
" his own foot Soldiers there who might guard him ; this seem'd
" so reasonable, that they promised to represent it to the
" Prince of Orange, and that his Majesty should know his
" pleasure by nine that morning, but that he must then be
" ready to be gon ; accordingly they came back to the King
" at the time apointed, and tould him the Prince had consented
" he should go to Rochester, but that he would apoint some of
" his own troops, both hors and foot to guard him there, which
" the Count de Solmes order'd accordingly ; so the King's
" barge with the Coaches and pads being ready, he order'd
" them with the Prince of Orange's guards to go over the
" bridg and meet him at Graues end, but My Lord Halifax

---

* The Letter is given in Kennet (page 536.) " We desire you, the Lord Marquis
of Halifax, the Earl of Shrewsbury, and the Lord Delamere, to tell the King, That
it is thought convenient, for the greater quiet of the City, and the greater safety of
his Person, that he do remove to Ham, where he shall be attended by his Guards,
who will be ready to preserve him from any disturbance. W. P. de Orange.
Given at Windsor 17 Dec. 1688." EDITOR.

† Interlined by the Son of James the second. EDITOR.

opposed it, Saying their going through the Citie might "
cause disorder and moue compassion, and was for their "
going over at Lambeth ferry : the King objected that it blew "
so hard they could not well pass ; besides, that it would take "
up too much time and hinder their being at Graves end so "
soon as he should be there by water, but that Lord nothing "
moued with this, press'd earnestly their going by Lambeth, "
and was very unreasonable in his arguing, not to giue it a "
wors name, but My Lord Shrewsbury was fair and civil and "
agreed to what his Majesty sayd; so then the King took "
leave of the forreign Ministers, the Lords and gentlemen "
about him (whereof many could not refrain shedding of "
tears on so moveing an occasion) and so took bargs himself "
and sent the hors guards, coaches &c, over the bridg, and "
had a Captain and a hundred common men of the Prince of "
Orange's foot guards allong with him, who went in ores "
before and behind the barge ; but they were so long of "
embarking, that his Majesty lost the tyde, and got not to "
Graves end till seaven at night, so was forced to lodg there, "
and the next morning receiu'd a blank pass from the Prince "
of Orange, which he had desired, in order to send one over "
to the Queen, believing her Landed before that in France "
with the Prince her Son.   "

The night the King lay at Graues end, the Prince of "   The King
Orange's Guards kept very strict watch about the house, but "   arriues at
the next day when his Majesty arriued at Rochester, they "   Rochester
were not So exact, which confirm'd him in the beliefe he was "   and resolues
of before, that the Prince of Orange would be well enough "   to make his
contented he should get away.; and that the person who "   escape.
brought the afforesaid pass, had orders likewise to the Officer "
that commanded his Guards not to look so strictly after the "
King, for Sentinalls were only set at the fore door towards "
the street, and none at the back door, which went towards the "

" river : by this the King was still farther convinced the Prince
" of Orange had a mind he should be gon, which hinder'd him
" not from continuing in the same mind himself, being per-
" swaded, that should he neglect that opertunity and disapoint
" the Prince of Orange, by not going out of the Kingdom, he
" would probably find means to send him out of it, and the
" world too, by an other way.

" It was the 19th of December that the King arriued at
" Rochester, and stayd till the 22th at night, there came down
" with him Severall of his servants, as Lord Arran, Dunbarton,
" Litchfeild and Alisbury, who were gentlemen of his Bed-
" chamber ; with Fautrey, Biddulph and Griffin, grooms of
" the Bedchamber ; several general officers as Sr Jo: Fenwick,
" Sackville, Sr John Talbot, Sudderland, who gaue up their
" Commissions; as did before his Majesty left London, My
" Lord Newburgh, Lord Griffin, Lord Litchfeild, youn Griffin
" Fautrey and Several others, and the day after his Majesty
" arriued at Rochester, the Earle of Bath's Regiment being
" there, the Major of it Mr Greham, with Captain Mohun,
" Crispt and many subalterns, gaue up their Commissions, and
" so many of the soldiers deserted, that the next day when the
" Regiment marched out, it was not aboue a hundred and fifty
" men, thō it consisted of seaven companys Sixty men each ;
" the same day came thither the Second Regiment of Guards
" with three Companys from Dover, all the officers waited on
" the King, express'd great Loyalty, thō none but Major
" Heuson and his Son in Law who was his Ensigne gaue up
" their Commissions. Every day his Majesty had advice from
" London either by letters or peoples comeing down to him
" how the matters went in Town, in what manner the Prince
" of Orange had been receiud there, his haveing call'd for
" all the Lords Spiritual and Temporal to attend him at
" St James's, which most in Town did expect the Archbishop

of Cantorbury who refused to come at him, or act in any thing so long, he Sayd, as the King was under restraint: That Pelate saw now who he had been working for all this while, that the Church of England, which had only been the Prince of Orange's Stalkeing hors in this expedition, was like to reape no other benifit by it, than the confusion of haveing deserted her celebrated doctrine of non-resistance and adherence to her Prince, and to be dispised by those, she had ruin'd her reputation to assist; and he himself made the first example of the common fate of such as call in forreigners, who like the maid that betrayd the Capitol are generally the first who are oppress'd by them: he found by experience that invaders are never so good natured as to make the Laws, liberties and Religion the ultimate end of such undertakeings, so that the Archbisshop whose authority had contribited more than any ones to the general defection, and who refused to discountenance the invasion after the King had yeilded in a manner to all that he and his Breethren could desire, was the first that felt the heavy hand of the Vsurper (for such Masters are never content to be serued by halues) and for refuseing to swear allegience to him, was dispossessed of his Bisshoprick and reduced to liue upon a small patrimony of about Sixty pounds a year; where he repair'd the dishonour in great measure, of his own fault, but could do little to retrieue the miserys his imprudent zeal had help to bring upon his Prince and his Country.

It was a weak and Childish immagination to think that he, who was so ready to usurpe upon the rights of an Vncle, Brother, Father, and Wife, did it only for the love of truth and justice, or that he would be tyd up to the observance of a verbal promis, and be restain'd by rules of their prescribing, who had so little regard to what nature, duty and Religion required from him. Those Sollemn protestations alas, with which he imposed upon the credulous zealots, when once he was Master of his game, serued only for a Subject of mirth and railery, amongst those who understood him and his intentions better; and were as ready to Sacrifice their King and Country, as he to invade them, provided they might share with him, in the spoils of both.

About three a clock therefore of the same day that the King left London, the Prince of Orange enter'd it in great magnificence, and takeing up his lodgings in S⁺ James's, receiv'd the compliments and congratulations of * almost all the Nobility and gentry about Town; the Citie return'd him thanks by the Recorder, and the Ambassador of Spain and Resident of Venice made him their compliments in private.

" This universal running into the invader, still confirm'd the " King more and more in his resolution not to differ his " withdrawing any longer: Thō Several of the † Bisshops and " others who wished him well advised him against it, or at " least not to go out of England but keep himSelf private in " the Town or Country; Doctor Brady one of his Majestys " Phisicians was sent to him with reasons in writeing to that

---

* Sir J. Dalrymple (Vol: 2. P. 342.) has inserted some Notes of Lord Dartmouth on Bishop Burnet's History. In the Note on page 790 of that History, his Lordship observes, " The Duke of Shrewsbury told me, the Prince was much surprised at his backwardness in joining with him, and began to suspect he was betrayed, and had some thoughts of returning; in which case he resolved to publish the names of all those that had invited him over, which he said would be but a just return for their treachery, folly, and cowardice. Lord Shrewsbury told him he believed the great difficulty amongst them was, who should run the hazard of being the first, but if the ice were once broke, they would be as much afraid of being the last; which proved very true." EDITOR.

† Sir John Dalrymple declares (Vol: 1. P. 300.) that " of the Seven Bishops who had been persecuted by King JAMES, only one, Lloyd of S⁺ Asaph, waited on the new King, or took the Oaths to his Government. When Queen MARY sent to ask Sancroft's blessing, his answer was, That she must ask her Father's, for his would not otherwise be heard in Heaven." EDITOR.

efect, which he press'd very earnestly, but the King was " T O M.
prepared with argument to the contrary, not to be answer'd " III.
any otherwise than by bare suppositions, that they did not " 1688.
believe the Prince of Orange would attempt any thing against "
his Majestys life ; he argued the whole matter with My "
Lord Middleton, whom the King had order'd to stay in "
Town that day he left it himself, and to follow him the next, "
with an account of·what occur'd after the Prince of Orange's
arrival : he own'd it was a hard point to giue councel in ;
that to advise him to stay was extream hazardous, considering
how his Father had been used, thō it began not by much so
violently against him ; only tould the King he was very
confident, that if his Majesty went out of the Kingdom, the " *Ibid.* 268.
door would immediately be shut upon him ; however in "
conclusion own'd, there could be no safety for him to stay, "
and that no reasonable and thinking man could advise him to "
Venter it : Tis certain the King had little reason to hope for
security amongst his Subjects, since upon his first arrival when
he came from Feversham, finding himself so joyfully welcomed
to Town, he sent to Sʳ Thomas Lewis, * *and Sʳ Thomas Stamps*,
two eminent aldermen, proffering to remain in their hands
till he had giuen full satisfaction to his people in all things
relateing to Religion, libertie, &c, provided they would
undertake to secure his person ; he could not (he thought) giue
them greater proof of a sincere proceeding than this, by
makeing the people in a manner Masters of their own terms,
by being so of him ; but Sʳ Robert Clayton so influenced the
Common Council, that this security was denyd, for by this
time, the pretence of the Prince of Orange's comeing to bring
the King to satisfy the people, was become more dreadfull to

---

* Interlined by the Son of James the second. EDITOR.

1688.

him than to the King himself, so all his Agents did what they could to obstruct an accommodation which would haue broke his measures more than any thing, that could happen: This the King saw plain enough, however he made the same offer to the Bisshops, which he sent from Rochester, particularly to the Bisshop of Winchester, but had the Same answer, That they

" could not promis him security ; whereupon his Majesty
" thought it madness not to get away as fast as he could, thō
" he could not compass it till the 22ᵗʰ at night, and therefore
" was a little uneasy in the intrim, not knowing what
" resolutions the assembly of the Lords might produce, nor
" whether the Prince of Orange might not change his measures,
" haveing sent to the Major and Aldermen not to give the
" Oathes of Allegience, Supremacy, and Test to the Common
" Council at their Election on Sᵗ Thomas's day as usual ; but
" order'd them to act without it. This so early a dispensing
" with the Laws and the peoples alligience, was such a manifest
" declaration that nothing less than the Regal * Power would
content him, that the King easily saw he would suffer no delay in the matter ; had the King stayd indeed it would haue ambarasced the Prince of Orange and his partie how to dethrone a Prince, who by the Law could do no wrong, and was so willing to giue full Satisfaction to his people ; but as this was

---

* In another of *Lord Dartmouth's Notes* on Burnet's History, (Dalrymple's Memoirs, Vol: 2. P. 342.) it is observed on page 819 of that history, " There was a great meeting at the Earl of Devonshire's where the dispute ran very high between Lord Halifax and Lord Danby; one for the PRINCE the other for the PRINCESS: At last Lord Halifax said, He thought it would be very proper to know the Prince's own sentiments, and desired Fagel would speak, who defended himself a great while, by saying, He knew nothing of his mind upon that subject, but if they would know his own, he believed the Prince would not like to be his Wife's Gentleman Usher : Upon which Lord Danby said, He hoped they all knew enough now, for his part he knew too much ; and broke up the Assembly, as Sir Michael Wharton who was present told me," EDITOR.

an inducement to his Majcsty not to go, so if he had crossed the Prince's aim therein, it would haue been in his power to
find a shorter way of removeing the obstacle ; and thō no man
could be so brutal, as not to haue a horrour of Sullying the
Crown he grasped at, with a Paricide, if possibly it could be
avoided, yet it would haue been a rash Venter, to trust to his
conscience in that point, and immagin he would loos the frute
of so much labour, and balke his Ambition at the last stage,
rather than ad one crime more, to the many he had already
Commited.

· The reasons being so strong for the King's withdrawing, and
the occasion so favorable (for besides that he was negligently
guarded, the Officer who, commanded was a Catholick, and
near half the Soldiers came next morning to hear Mass with
him after his arrival there) he order'd Captain Travanion and ”
Captain Macdonnel to prepare the Shallop ; which assoon as ”
he heard was come up, and that all things were ready, he ”
resolued to go off about twelve at night, but before he went, ”
thought fit to leaue behind him a paper containing some ”
reasons which obliged . him to take that resolution, with ”
directions to haue it made publick after he was gon : ”

The world (Sayd he) cannot wonder at my withdrawing ”
myself now this Second time ; I might haue expected some ”
what better usage after what I had written to the Prince of ”
Orange by My Lord Feversham, and the instructions I gaue ”
him, but instead of an answer such as I might haue hoped ”
for, what was I not to expect, after the usage I receiud? by ”
his makeing the Said Earle a prisoner against the practice of ”
Law of Nations, the sending his own guards at a eleaven a ”
clock at night, to take the postes at Whitehall, without ”
advertising me in the least manner of it, the sending to me ”
after midnight when I was in bed a kind of order by three ”
Lords, to be gon out of my own Pallas before twelue the ”

T O M.
III.
1688.

KING JAM:
MEM. TOM: 9.
pag 269.

" same day ; after all this, how can I hope to be safe so long
" as I was in the power of one, who had not only done this to
" me, and invaded my Kingdoms without any just occasion
" giuen him for it, but that did by his first Declaration lay the
" greatest aspersion upon me that malice could invent, in that
" claus of it which concerns my Son : I apeal to all that know
" me, nay even to himself, that in their consciences neither
" he, nor they can belieue me in the least capable of so
" unnatural a Villany, nor of so little common Sence, as to be
" imposed on in a thing of such a nature as that ; what had I
" then to expect from one who by all artes had taken such
" pains, to make me apear as black as Hell to my own people,
" as well as to all the world besides ; what efect that hath had
" at home, all mankind hath seen by so general a defection
" in my Army as well as in the Nation amongst all sorts of
" the people.

" I was born free and desire to continue so ; and thō I haue
" venter'd my life very frankly on severall occasions for the
" good and honour of my Country, and am as free to do it
" again (and which I hope I shall yet do, as old as I am to
" redeem it from the Slavery it is like to fall under) yet I
" think it not convenient to expose myself to be secur'd so, as
" not to be at libertie to efect it, and for that reason do with-
" draw, but so as to be within call when the Nation's eyes
" shall be opened, so as to see how they haue been abused
" and imposed upon, by the specious pretences of Religion
" and propertie ; I hope it will pleas God to touch their hearts
" out of his infinite mercy, and to make them Sencible of the
" ill condition they are in, and bring them to Such a temper
" that a legal Parliament may be call'd, and that amongst
" other things which may be necessary to be done, they will
" agree to a libertie of Conscience for all Protestant dissenters ;
" and that those of my own perswasion may be so far

consider'd, and haue such a share of it, as they may liue " T O M.
peaceably and quietly, as Englishmen and Christians ought " III.
to doe, and not to be obliged to transplant themselves, which " 1688.
would be very grievous, especially to such as loue their "
Country; and I apeal to all who are considering men and "
haue had experience, whether any thing can make this "
Nation so great and florishing as Libertie of Conscience, some "
of our Neighbours dread it: I would ad much more to con- "
firme all I haue said, but now is not a proper time. "

This paper the King shew'd My Lord Middleton so soon "
as he had sup'd, and charg'd him to haue it printed when he "
return'd to London; but left it not with him, but My lord "
Dunbarton who was the gentleman of the Bedchamber in "
waiting, to be given to My lord Middleton the next morn- "
ing, the King not being willing the world should then know "
he had sayd any thing to that Lord of his intentions of going "
away; he acquainted also the Earle of Litchfeild with it, he "
being one he coald entirely trust, and a person of great "
honour, and one who on all occasions had served him with "
great stedfastness and fidelity; he could not avoid trusting "
the Secret to My Lord Alisbury likewise, who being to go "
next day to London, had a mind to ly that night in the "
Bedchamber, which would haue made the thing more "
difficult to the King, being to pass through the chamber "
where his Servants lay: the Lord Litchfeild seem'd very "
well pleas'd with the confidence the King had in him, so his "
Majesty went to bed at his usual houre, and when the "
Company was gon got up again, went out by a back pair "
of Stairs and so through the garding, where Captain Mac- "
donnel waited for him to shew him the way to the place "
where Captain Travanion Stayd with the boat; into which "
the King got with those two Captains, the Duke of Berwick "
and Mr Biddulph, about twelve at night, and rowed down "

" designing to go to rights aboard the Smack, which was
" order'd to ly ready to receive them, without the foot of
" Sheerness; but it blew so hard right a head, and the tyde of
" eb being down before they got to the Salt pans, it was
" almost Six in the morning before they could get to the
" Swale, and haveing both wind and tyde against them, it
" was impossible to get out to where they thought the Smack
" lay, so were necessitated to go on board some Vessel that
" lay in the Swale, till the windward tide came, which would
" not be till after day break ; Captain Travanion advised the
" going on board a Hamburger, to refresh their men and stay
" till the tyde served, but the King not likeing of that, pro-
" posed going on board Captain Travanion's own Ship called
" the Harwich, which lay there also ; but the Captain tould
" him, that thō he (*could*) answer for the fidelity of his Officers,
" he was not able to do it for the common Seamen, and there-
" fore would by no means advise his Majesty to it; upon
" which the King resolved to go on board the Eagle fireship
" under the command of Captain Wilford, knowing him to
" be an honest and loyal Officer, and could govern his men

" who had been so many years with him: So on board that
" Ship he went, and stayd till it was broad day, and then
" perceiud the Smack at an anchor within the Swale not far
" from them, being oblig'd to come from the station she was
" order'd to be at, because it overblew, and she not a good
" roader ; the King therefore went immediately on board her
" with his company, notwithstanding the gail did not slacken,
" and took Captains Travannian's boat in a tow and her crew
" with him, So that they were in all aboue twenty men ; and
" Lieftenant Guardiner who had the care of her; provideing
" small armes and hand grenadoes, they would haue been hard
" enough for any of those little Vessels which were watching
" for purchasses : When they were got to the Boy of Nore

they durst not turn down any Lower, the Wind at East " T O M.
North East and East Northesly, but were oblig'd to bear up " III.
the river and anchor on the Essex shoar, under the Lee of " 1688.
the Sand in smooth water till the next tyde flood should be "
done: it blew very heard all that day being Sunday; but as "
it began to be dark the gail slancken'd a little, so that assoon "
as the tyde was broke they got under sail, and turn'd it down "
as far as the red Sand, and anchor'd a mile short of that Boy; "
next morning it proued more reasonable weather, so they "
got under sail before Sun rise and without touching just "
reach'd the Boy of the Narrow, turn'd through it and so to "
the North foreland, and design'd to haue got about the "
North Sand's head and on the back of the Goodwin, and so " Ibid. pag. 274.
scaped the Downs; but being got into the S-en tide which "
ran eb they could not wether it, and so bore up through the "
Downs, chusing rather to venter that, then come to an "
anchor: it was very remarkable that all that day they Saw "
not any Ship nor Vessel under Sail, and only Seaven at "
anchor in the Downs; as it began to be dark they got clear "
of the South Sand's head, about what time it proued little "
wind, and began to Snow about Six, the wind continuing "
still easterly; but about ealeven it clear'd up, and then they "
Saw the high Land of France, about two leagues on head, "
and standing in with it made it to be blackness, and bore up "
to Bolloin bay not being able to fetch Calais, and so came "
to anchor before Ambleteus, where they found a French man "
of War in the road, and so went on shore to that Vilage, "
about three on tuesday morning being Christmas day old "
stile. "

In this small Voyage by Sea the King underwent those
hardships which are never failing attendants of such hasty
and hidden expeditions, if in So calamitous a situation of his
affairs any thing but the loss of his three Kingdoms could be

reckon'd a Suffring; for besides the danger of crossing the Seas in so small a Vessel, and in the depth of winter, he was pen'd up all that while in a small cabbin, where was just room for him and the Duke of Berwick to sit, in continual aprehentions of being attacked and Seized again by his Rebellious Subjects; however it was some cause of mirth to him, when growing very hungry and dry, Captain Travanian went to fry his Majesty some bacon, but by misfortune the frying pan haveing a hole in it, he was forced to stop it with a pitched rag, and to ty an old furr'd Can about with a cord, to make it hould the drink they put in it; however the King never eat or drank more heartely in his life.

Thus did those pretended English Patriots driue out their Sovereign, who had giuen all the markes of loue, care and tenderness of his Subjects, that could be expected from a true father of his people; he had fought their battles, encouraged and encreased their trade, preserued them from taxes, supported their credit, made them a rich, happy and a more powerfull people, than they had ever hithertoo apear'd in the world; yet all these essential benefits were so overshaddow'd and darken'd with certain immaginary fears about Religion, that they chose to abandon them all, and break through the most * Sacred

---

* The subsequent Speech of the *Earl of Arran*, before the Assembly of Peers, and Scottish Gentlemen at Whitehall, in January, seems to claim an exemption from this abandonment: Sir J. Dalrymple in giving this Speech (Vol: 1. P. 255.) adds, *But one Man alone had the spirit to speak out their Sentiments and his own.* " I respect," said his Lordship, " the Prince of Orange as much as any man here does. I think him a brave Prince, and that we all lie under great obligations to him for delivering us from Popery. But, while I bestow these just praises upon him, I cannot violate my Duty to the King, my Master. I must distinguish between his Popery and his Person: I dislike the one; but have sworn and do owe allegiance to the other. This makes it impossible for me to concur in an Address, which gives the administration of his Kingdom to another. We are Scottish not English men. The King's Grandfather and Father did not abdicate

Laws either of divine or humain institution, rather than not
be rid of him, that they might throw themselves at the feet of
a little forreign Prince, who was no less alien by inclination,
than he was by birth and education to the true intrest of the
Kingdom : They pretended, their Religion and Libertys were
on the brink of ruin, and that in such cases Oathes of Allegiance,
and provisions against resistance were no longer binding; but
others no less zealous for the publick good, and much better
discerners of the natural and genuin ways of attaining it, argued
to the contrary, that thō this apprehention had been well
grounded (which certainly it was not) nay thō they had been
actually under a persecution, yet to repel it by perjury and
treason, was to endeavour a cure by conveying poison into the
wound, and to damn themselves only to preserue what they
conceiued the true way to Salvation; without reflecting that
when Religion is thus alledged for a motiue and made the
argument for what is realy evil in it self, it lessens its power
over the Consciences of men, and hinders its Sertue in Subduing incredulous Soules a thousand times more, than all the
Success (that may possebly attend such contriVances) is able
to advantage it : for nothing (they said) could countervail the
real injuries done to Religion, when it was made an inducement
for doing the most irreligious things in the world : but when
on the contrary the only motiue for all these disorderly practices
was only to Shelter themselves from meer aprehentions, of
what, they had all immaginable assurances was never intended
and was in it self as impossible, as for ten men to master a

---

the Crown of Scotland, even by quitting their Native Country : How then can the
King do it by quitting England only ? The Prince asks our advice. My advice is,
That we should address him, to invite the King to return, and call a Free
Parliament, which may provide, in a constitutional way, for the security of our
Property, Liberty, and Religion. All other ways are unconstitutional. By this
alone the Nation can avoid present and prevent future discord." EDITOR.

T O M.
III.

1688.

thousand, made it the highth of imprudence as well as impiety :
but in reality the King consulted Religion and justice alone,
and his intrest too little ; whereas these seeming Zealots
considered their Religion too little, and their intrest too much,
by makeing it the only rule and Standard of morality ; which
however had been some recompence, had they found even that
in this change ; but when wars, taxes, and oppression, succeeded
the riche and peacefull reign of the King, they were forced to
haue recours to the pretence of Religion again to sweeten and
extenuate all the people haue loss'd and suffer'd ever since :
Thus in fine they threw themselves into confusion, miserie, and
dissention, out of which neither reason, nor the example of
former times, gaue them the least hopes of escaping, till they
think fit to return the just and legal Government, into its natural
Channels again.

HERE ENDS THE THIRD VOLUME OF THE MANUSCRIPT.

THE LIFE

OF

H.R.H. JAMES DUKE OF YORK,

JAMES THE SECOND,

FROM HIS WITHDRAWING INTO FRANCE
TO HIS DEATH AT St. GERMAINS

1689—1701.

TOME IV.

———————

∗ Macpherson informs us, in the first Volume of his *Original*
Papers from the Restoration to the Accession of the House
of Hanover, to which he has prefixed occasional Extracts
from the MEMOIRS OF JAMES THE SECOND written by
himself, that " Mr Thomas Carte made no Extracts
from the MEMOIRS OF JAMES concerning the Transactions of 1689, probably for the same reasons which
induced the Editor (Macpherson) to content himself
with the preceding, having found among *Nairne's Papers,*
the original materials from which JAMES composed his
MEMOIRS for the present year. That Prince usually
wrote, with his own hand, all the occurrences of the

times, or examined and corrected what was written by
others. He sometimes wrote down his instant reflections
and conjectures on the state of his affairs, and the
expected effect of his measures, without waiting to see
what time might determine. The pen must have been
constantly in his hand. The first paper which occurs,
relating to the transactions of this year, is a Journal, in
his own hand, containing an account of some intelligence he received, when on his journey from Cork to
Dublin." (Page 170.)

Carte and Macpherson appear only to have seen these
Original Notes, or Memoirs of JAMES THE SECOND,
written by himself, already mentioned by his Secretary
(Page 242.) as being the documents whence all that is
material in this Relation is in a manner taken. The
Abbè Waters, in his Letter in the Preface to the present
Work, declared, That Macpherson had nothing to do
with this account of JAMES.

Mr. Walter Scott is of opinion that the facts in the following
portion of The Life, concerning the Revolution in
Scotland, were chiefly taken from the Earl of Balcarras's
Letter to JAMES II. which may be found in Somers'
Collection of Tracts. (Vol. XI. page 487.) Mr. Scott
there informs us, that " Colin Lindsay, third Earl of
Balcarras, declined to quit the interest of his unfortunate
Master after the Revolution; attached to it by affection,
gratitude, and the delicacy of sentiment which the love
of Letters commonly inspires." EDITOR.

1689.

A SSOON therefore as the King was Landed he went
immediately to Abbeville where he made himself
publickly known, and from thence, post to St Germains; he
had the comfort of meeting there the Queen and Prince his
Son in a place of Safety at least, which with the generous and
cordial reception of his most Christian Majesty, did not a little
alleviate his present affliction; he had the Satisfaction
likewise of seeing many persons of quality both Protestants
and Catholicks, arriue dayly from England, as well out of
inclination and zeal to run the fortune of their Prince, as to
shelter themselves from that Storme, which had droue him from
the Throne and threaten'd all with ruin who had serued him
with fidelity or affection; and even those who perhaps with a
contrary view, had encouraged such methods as was most
displeasing: this undoubtedly was the reason of My Lord
Sunderland's flying too in weamen's cloaths into Holland, it is
probable his timorous disposition in so generall a confusion
(where for some time most men's liues lay at the mercy of the
Mob) made him uneasy, till he was out of their reach, he knew

not what freaks they might take in reference to one who had been the chief Minister in the reign which was now so grievously decry'd, and had always appear'd the most complying and by consequence the most criminall Councellor, whereas the Secret springs of his acting as yet lay hid to the world, which as it occasion'd his flight, so did it his imprisonment at his arrivall in Holland : but the Prince of Orange made as much hast to haue him set at liberty, as he did to proclame his own infamy in that letter he caus'd to be published for his Vindication'; but there was no mean or sordid action which such a slaue to his pleasurs was not ready to doe, to support himself in that state of opulence and eas which (is to be presumed) had generally been the ultimated end of all his actions, as well as of this resolution.

The drift of that letter being to reconcile himself to the favour of the people, he most falsely pretended to haue constanly opposed all those Councells which were now so cryd out against, whereas in reality, he did not only approue them, but generally run before the rest ; he would oft times indeed try the ford by his secret Agents, as Sr Niccolas Butler, Mr Lob, and even Father Petre himself, that he might seem only not to oppose those dangerous methods which had their true origin from him alone ; and the Prince of Orange by excepting him out (*of*) the first general pardon, kept the maske on for a while too, but soon made a mends, by granting an other, which pardon'd nobody but him; and admited him soon after, into the greatest fauour and intimacy immaginable, which shew'd plainly whose seruice he had studyed to promote all along ; for nothing but the transcendent merite of haveing betrayd his Master, could haue induced that Prince, in contempt of common decency, to have imploy'd a man so infamous in his character, who had been a Pentioner of France, and changed his Religion twice in six months, and had in the publick view been the most odious and obnoxious man in the Kingdom : Accordingly when sucess (which seems to giue a Sanction in those men's eyes to the bassest actions) had established the Vsurpation, he made no difficulty to say upon an occasion to General Ginkle, That though the honour of subduing Ireland belong'd to him, he would not however yeild to him in merite, he haveing had the glory of contriveing the provocations to the Revolution, and of laying the first foundations of the Prince of Orange's grandure.

T O M.
IV.
1689.

The King was no sooner arrived at St Germains but every post brought him fresh instances, with what violence all the people run in, to pay their venerations to the new erected Idol ; on such occasions the expectancy of angry and dissatisfyd men (whose numbers are ever greatest) fail not to be rais'd to what they think their due, or at least qualifyd for, and thō all could not expect great imployments, Ducal titles, and blew ribbons, yet no one dispair'd of getting some share in the spoils of a Crown, and shipwrack of a government ; and this it was which layd the way so open to this ambitious Prince : The Lords, for hast, met on Christmas day it self, to request the Prince of Orange to take upon him the administration of the government, who readily accepting the burthen, summon'd such members of Parliament as were about town, and had served in King Charles's time (casting thereby an espersion on his Majestys government, as if nothing had been regular in his days) together with the Lord Major and Aldermen of London, to haue their advice, what methods were best to attain the end of his expedition, and to haue a free Parliament. Their numbers being great, they formed themselves into a sort of House of Commons, where they tooke their places accordingly, and haveing chozen a Speaker, concur'd with the Lords

The Lords desire the P. of Orange to take the Administration upon him.

in desireing the Prince of Orange to take upon him the administration of the government, and to issue out his circular letter for assembling a Convention the 22ᵈ of February next following; at first he sayd it was a matter of great moment and requir'd time to consider (thō he had taken none for the first step he made) nor could his fain'd modesty hould out many houres, so the next day he acquainted them that haveing weighed their advice, he would concur with them in it.

The King writes from Sᵗ Germains to the Lords of his Council.

When the news, of this Conventions being call'd, came to the King, he thought it necessary to obviate all he could, what he saw they were going about to doe, so writ the following letter directed to the Lords and others of his privy Council:
" Wee think our selves oblig'd in conscience to doe all wee can,
" to open our people's eyes that they may see the true intrest
" of the Nation in this important conjuncture, and therefore
" think fit to let you know, that finding we could no longer stay
" with safety, nor act with freedom in what concern'd our
" people, and that it was absolutely necessary for us to retire,
" we left the reasons of our withdrawing under our hand, to
" be communicated to you and our Subjects in the following
terms ; and so including the reasons mentioned before, he goes
" on and says ; But finding it was not taken to be ours by
" some, and that the Prince of Orange's and his adherents did
maliciously suppress it, wee thought fit some time after to renew the same, and likewise to write to such of your number as were of our privy Council, in the * terms following

MY LORDS, when we saw it was no longer safe for us to remain within our Kingdom of England, and thereupon we

---

* This Letter, as *Ralph* observes, is not so much as mentioned by *Bishop Burnet* in his History. EDITOR.

had taken our resolutions to withdraw for some time, we
order'd to be communicated to you and all our Subjects the
reasons of our withdrawing, and we were at the same time
resolued likewise, to leaue such orders behind us, to you of
our Privy Council, as might best sute with the present state
of affairs; but that being altogather unsafe to us at that time,
we now think fit to let you know, that thō it has been our
constant care since our first accession to the Crown, to govern
our people with that justice and moderation as to give (if
possible) no occasion of complaint, yet more particularly
upon the late invasion, seeing how the design was layd, and
fearing least our people (who could not be destroyd but by
themselves) might by little immaginary grievances, be cheated
into a certain ruin; to prevent so great a mischief, and to take
away not only all just cause, but even pretence of discontent,
wee freely and of our own accord redress'd all those things
which were set forth as the causes of the invasion, and that
we might be inform'd by the Council and Advice of our Subjects
themselves, which way to giue them a further and full Satisfaction, we resolved to meet them in a free Parliament, by
restoreing the City of London and the rest of the Corporations
to their antient Charters and priviledges; and afterwards
actually apointed writts to be issued out for its meeting on
the 15ᵗʰ of January : But the Prince of Orange seeing all the
ends of his Declaration answered, the people begining to be
undeceived, and returning a pace to their antient duty and
allegiance, and well foreseeing that if the Parliament should
meet at the time apointed, such a settlement would in all
probability have been made both in Church and State, as
would haue totally defeated his ambitious and unjust designes,
resolved by all means possible to prevent the meeting of it, and
to doe this the most efectual way, he thought fit to lay a

restraint upon our royal person; for as it were absurd to call
that a free Parliament where there is any force upon either of
the Houses, so much less can that Parliament be sayd to act
freely, where the Sovereign by whose authority they meet and
sit, and from whose royal assent all their acts receive their
life and Sanction, is under actual confinement: The hurrying
us under a guard from our City of London (whose returning
loyalty he could no longer trust) and the other indignitys wee
suffer'd in the person of the Earle of Feversham, when sent to
him by us, and in the barberous confinement of our own
person, we shall not here repeat; because they are, we doubt
not, by this time very well known, and may (we hope) if well
consider'd and reflected upon, togather with his other violences
and breaches of the Laws and libertys of England, which by
this invasion he pretended to restore, be sufficient to open the
eyes of all our Subjects, and let them plainly see, what every
one of them may expect, and what treatment they shall find
from him if at any time it may serue his purpose (from whose
hands a Sovereign Prince, an Vncle, and Father, could meet
with no better entertainment). However the sence of these
indignitys, and the just aprehention of further attempts against
our person, by those who endeavour'd already to murther our
reputation, by infamous calumnys, as if we had been capable
of supposing a Prince of Wales, which was incomparably
more injurious than destroying our person itself, togather with
a serious reflection on a saying of our Royal Father of Blessed
memory, when he was in the like circomstances, That there is
generally little distance between the prison and graue of a
Prince (which afterwards proued too true in his case) could
not but perswade us to make use of that, which the Law of
nature gives to the meanest of our Subjects, of freeing our
selues by all means possible, from that unjust confinement and

restraint; and this we did not more for the security of our person, than that thereby we might be in a better capacity of transacting and provideing for every thing, that may contribite to the peace and settlement of our Kingdoms: whereas on the one hand, no change of fortune shall make us forget our selves so far, as to condescend to any thing unbecomeing that high and royall Station in which God Almighty by right of succession has placed us, so on the other hand, neither the provocation or ingratitude of our own Subjects, nor any other consideration whatsoever, shall ever prevail with us, to make the least step contrary to the intrest of the English Nation; which we ever did and ever must look upon as our own. Our Will and pleasure therefore is, that you of our Privy Council take the most effectual care to make these our gracious incli-nations known to the Lords Spiritual and Temporal, in and about the Citys of London and Westminster, and to the Lord Major of the City of London and to all our Subjects in general; and to assure them we desire nothing more, than to return and to hould a free Parliament, wherein we may haue the best opertunity of undeceiveing our people, and shewing the sincerity of these protestations, we haue often made, of preserveing the libertys and propertys of our Subjects, pro-tecting the Professors of the Protestant Religion, more espe-cially those of the Church of England as by Law established, togather with such indulgence for those as dissent from her, as we haue always thought our selves in justice and care of the general welfare of our people, bound to procure for them; and in the mean time, you of our Privy Council (who can judge better by being upon the place) are to send us your advice, what is fit to be done by us towards our returning, and accomplishing those good ends, and we require you in our name and by our authority to endeavour to suppress all el

tumults and disorders; that the Nation in general and every
one of our Subjects in particular, may receive the least prejudice from the present distractions, that is possible: So not
doubting of your dutyfull obedience, to these our Royal
Commands, we bid you heartily fairwell. Given at our Court
at S‌ᵗ Germains en Laye, the ⅙ of January 1689, and of our
Reign the Forth.

And then the King concluded his letter as follows, All
which we sent with a Servant of our own to be deliver'd as was
directed, but as yet we have no account of it, we likewise
directed copies to several of you the Peers of our Realm,
believeing that none durst take upon them to intercept or open
your letters, of which likewise we haue no account; but we
cannot wonder, that all artes are used to hinder you from
knowing our sentiments, since the Prince of Orange chose
rather without Law to imprison the Earl of Feversham, and
to drive us away from our Palace, than receive our invitation
of comeing to us, or to hear what we had to propose to him,
well knowing, that what we had to offer, would content all
reasonable men and what he durst not trust you with the
knowlidg of.

We think it fit now to let you know therefore, that whatever
crimes shall be commited, or whose postcrity soevcr shall come
to suffer for those crimes, we are resolved to be inocent; and
therefore do declare to you, that we are ready to return (when
safely we can) and to redress all the disorders of our Kingdoms,
in a free Parliament called according to Law, and held without
constraint, more especially to secure the Church of England
as by Law established, and by the advice of that Parliament
give such indulgence to discenters, as our people may haue no
reason to be jealous of; we will likewise with the advice of
that Parliament heal all the divisions, cover with oblivion all

past faults, and restore the happyness of our people, which never can be efectually done by any other power, and which we expect you will seriously and speedely consider; and so we bid you heartely farewell. Given at St Germains, the 3^d of Febru: Anno 1689, and of our Reign the forth.

TO M. IV. 1689.

It will be wonder'd at in calmer times, when these heats and animositys are remembred no more, that men imbued with reason and that were so aprehensiue of their Religion and libertys, should let slip such an opertunity of Secureing them all, not only upon a foundation which nothing could ever haue shaken, but of restoreing the honour, and settleing that peace and tranquility, which their posterity may curs them for neglecting to doe accordingly : If the Laws and Franchises they were then in possession of, render'd not their Religion and liberties impregnable, how firmely might they haue been established for the future by embraceing and improueing those offers, which their Lawfull Prince was pleased to make them, of carueing out their own satisfaction and security ; they might haue settled and better'd (if needfull) their priviledges without any trouble, and a great deal of inocence, what millions might haue been spared, and what numbers of liues preserved! But they were corrupted with rebellion and ripe for punishment, and a people is never so severely handled, as when providence suffers them to be their own chastisers.

The King's letter and representation makes little impression on the people.

The Prince of Orange therefore was too jealous to suffer, and Master enough to prevent the publication of these letters, which must have influenced (to some degree at least) all such as were not blindly abandon'd to his wicked aims, and forced them to enter upon measures more agreeable to their true interest, and by consequence fatal to his ambition ; so he found means to blindfould their understanding and nurrish their ressentment, till all rankes of people had concur'd to finish that chain, with

T O M.
IV.

1689.

VIDE EARLE
OF CLARENDON
HISTORY pag:

which, they themselves were fettered and loaded so grievously afterwards.

It is the main drift of all promoters of Sedition and treason, to get possession of those specious titles of being the Assertors and Restorers of Liberty, Property and Religion, and then they are sure the work is more than half perform'd ; for when once they haue appropriated to themselves those good and pleasing words of plausible and popular things, and fasten'd on the government such as are vulgerly odious and contemptible; faction, envy, and desire of novelty, will do the rest : so the Prince of Orange haveing gain'd that point, had no more to doe but with pleasure look on, while the deluded Patriots entangled themselves in the net, he need but spread before them, who to avoid an immaginary servitude embraced a real one, by subjecting themselves and the Kingdom, to the pursute of forreign aims and intrests, which has since drain'd the blood and treasure of the Nation in a most ruinous and expensiue war.

The different
sentiments of
the people
about settling
the govern-
ment.

However things went not on so glebly in his fauour, but that while the Elections were makeing for the Convention, people began to divide into different factions; and opinions; some were for sending to the King, and thō the terms they design to offer, were such, as there was no probability of their being accepted of, however it would satisfy multitudes (they sayd) that they had used their endeavours, and justify in some measure, their declareing the next heire Regent; which they thought would giue the most satisfaction, and put an end to all the troubles : but this the Prince of Orange's partizans saw the danger of, a Treaty was what the King himself had offer'd, and a little time would have cool'd the mighty heat ; men would have been more reasonable and temperate in their present pretentions, and more aprehensiue of the consequences of an absolute breach ; to prevent this therefore, they had recours to their clamerous noisy way of treateing those persons as friends to Popery, and arbitrary Power ; and by false insinuations and unjust calumnys make that apear rediculous, which they had no reason to oppose but that it was too likely to succeed and give universall content; Others were for declareing the government dissolved and begining all de Novo, thō it was but an improper time (they own'd) to lay new foundations in the middest of such earthquakes ; Others were for Crowneing the Prince and Princess of Orange togather, and posponeing the Princess Anne's title, till after the Prince of Orange's death, this was what the generality aim'd at, who never fail to flatter those who have the power in their hands ; however there were not persons wanting to represent the ill consequence of such a resolution, not only as to the illegality of it, but as to the true intrest of the people ; that such a change being made by an authority that was not Legall, could never force an obedience, and by consequence would lay the government open to perpetual concustions, old animositys would be revived, and new ones created, which would give such shocks to a totering State, as must dissolue it in the end ; that the people would never bear taxes and impositions from those who had no authority to lay them, and that it would entangle men's consciences by new oathes and obligations, which sooner or later never fail'd to breed divisions in the State. They were put in mind, that unless those storys were made out of a suppositious Prince of Wales, and of a French league to cut all the Protestants throats (which had contribited more towards the Revolution, than the Prince's Army) the world would be asham'd of what had been done, and make men of honour and resentment much apter to quarrel with their authority than obey their Laws; that if the Scots concur'd not in the same method, the two Nations would be seperated again, and the old quarrel revived in which such an ocean of blood had been formerly spilt : But all these dificultys disapear'd, or were dispised, when the Convention met, who had their work cut out for them by certain proposals printed beforehand, and offer'd to their consideration ; wherein was asserted that the Supream power *Personal* was in the King, Lords, and Commons, which was now dissolved (they Sayd) by the King's submiting to the Church of Rome, his assumeing an arbitrary power, and * withdrawing himself ; but that the Supreame Power *Real* was in the Community or body of the people of England, who might act by their original power, which was not bound up to Laws already made, as every particular person was, that it was this Community of England which first gaue being to its present Constitution, of King, Lords, and Commons, and might either alter it, or renew it as they pleased, but that since the . Same forme of government was still judged the best, they could not doe better than take a Person which heaven and earth pointed out to them ; That the Lords were in being, and certain places had by custome, or charter, the priviledge of chuseing representatives for the Commons, which might doe the work, that this would assert the power of the Said Community of England; that they could not put the Regal power into better hands than the Prince of Orange's in gratitude

---

* *Lord Henry Clarendon* in his *Diary* (page 144.) relates a Conversation which he had on this subject with Dykevelt : " I answered—, that I went in to the Prince of Orange upon his Declaration, which all honest men heartily concurred in ; that, when I went in to him, it was not to be against the King, his Majesty having appointed a Parliament, and Commissioners to treat with the Prince . . . . . Mr. Dykevelt replied, that certainly I must think, the King's going away had totally altered the state of affairs. I said, I could not imagine, why that should alter them, when I looked upon the resolution of the States General of October, the — which I did not doubt was written in great sincerity. At this he seemed a little startled." — Lord Clarendon concluded this Conversation by informing Dykevelt, That their Religion did not allow of the deposing of Kings, that for his part he could not agree to it, nor could he absolve himself from the Oaths he had taken to the King. EDITOR.

for their delivery, as well as his personal qualifications ; and that if the Voice of the people be the Voice of God, that Voice never spoke lowder than now; that the Princess of Orange would share in. the regal dignity which would content her ; and that the Princess of Denmark for the publick good, would not * repine at her being postponed ; that the exerciseing of this power in the people, would be a caution to succeeding Kings, how they govern'd, and support that noble maxim, That a neiboring Nation may arme to rescue a people oppress'd by tyranny; and then foreign Princes would be apt to look to themselves, when they heard by our Nation's example, that they are no longer safe than while just to their Subjects : Thus did these noble English Patriots erect themselves into reformers, not only of their own, but all other governments that should hear of their fame ; a great undertakeing, and which may find them and their posterity work enough, if they think fit to persever in the defence of this doctrine.

However these shallow and superficial arguments, (which made governments dissolvable at pleasure, and layd them open to eternall Strifes) being back'd by the presence of an Army,

The Convocation meets the 22nd of January, and resolve that the King had abdicated, and that the Throne was vacant.

---

* *Lord Henry Clarendon* in his *Diary*, January 17, gives his Conversation on this subject with her Royal Highness. " In the afternoon I was with the Princess of Denmark. I told her of the discourses of the town, that the Prince of Orange and her Sister were to be crowned King and Queen . . . . and that it was said, she had consented to it, that it should be so : To which she said . . . . she was sure, she had given no occasion to have it said, that she had consented to any thing . . . . and she would never consent to any thing, that should be to the prejudice of herself, or her children. She added, that she knew very well, the Commonwealth Party was very busy; but she hoped, the Honest Party would be most prevalent in the Convention, and would not suffer wrong to be done her . . . . I asked her, If she thought her Father could justly be deposed? To which she said, Those were too great points for her to meddle with; that she was very sorry, the King had brought things to the pass they were at; but she was afraid, it would not be safe for him ever to return again. I asked her, what she meant by that? To which she replied nothing." EDITOR.

and the prepossession of the people against reason and justice, served the present purpose; so that when the Convention met on the 22ᵈ of January following, the Commons presently came to this resolution, That King James the 2ᵈ haveing endeavour'd to subvert the Constitution of the Kingdom, by breaking the original contract betwixt King and people, and by the advice of Jesuits and other wicked persons haveing violated the fundemental Laws, and withdrawne himself out of the Kingdom, had abdicated the government, and that the Throne was vacant.

The Lords likewise without much hesitation agreed to this resolve, only tooke exceptions to the word *Abdicated*, in stead of which they put *Deserted*, and would haue the last words, viz: *That the Throne is thereby become vacant*, to be totally left out; but the Commons stiking to their Vote, a conference was apointed wherein the Managers for the Lower house argued, That the word Abdication, did in effect express no more than what the Lords had already agreed to, in owning the King had broke the original contract and withdraw himself out of the Kingdom, which being, the Throne (they Sayd) must need be vacant: And that their Lordships had in efect sayd as much, in desireing the Prince of Orange to take upon him the administration of the government.

To this the Earle of Notingham answered, that Abdication was a word unknown to the Common Law, and by consequence lyable to doubtfull interpretation, that it express'd a voluntary renunciation, which seem'd not agreeable to this case; that as to the Throne's being vacant, he conceiv'd that a contradiction in termes, where the Monarchy is hereditary, and where no act of the King's can bar the heire to the Crown, and that if King James had deserted the next in remainder was possess'd of it.

These reasons when brought to the Commons, were not to be answer'd by any other argument, than puting it to the Vote (the most expeditious way of faceing down the plainest truthes) by which means it was carryd, against agreeing to the Lord's amendment, by a majority of at least 120 voices ; this begot another conference which was managed with great shew of gravity and formal speeches : Mr Hampden open'd it and sayd, That thō their dispute was but about a few words, yet they were of too great consequence to be parted with, that if the Law made not use of the word Abdication, it was its modesty in not supposeing such a case might happen ; and that their Lórdships not telling them who fill'd the Throne, was a plain indication they thought it vacant. Mr Sommers added, that the word *deserted*, was as little known to the Law as *abdicated*, that the latter implyd an entire renunciation, which might be made as well by doing such acts as are inconsistant with houlding a thing, as by a voluntary relinquishing of it, pretending to proue it from Grotius and other Civilians ; and that since the word deserted in the explanation of the Lords, implyd a right of returning, it could not be sufficient, since he conceiv'd the Lords and Commons both design'd to secure the Nation against it in this case ; and so concluded, that the King by subverting the Constitution and breaking the originall contract betwixt King and people, and by violateing the fundamentall Laws and withdrawing himself out of the Kingdom, had renounced to be King according to the Constitution, by avowing to govern by a dispotick power unknown to the Constitution and inconsistant with it ; that he had renounced to be King according to the Law, such a King as he swore to be at the Coronation, such a King to whom the Allegiance of the English Subjects is due, and had set up an other kind of dominion which was to all intents an abandoning or abdication of the legal title as fully as if he had done it by express words. Mr Serjent Holt afferm'd, that the Government and Majestracy was under trust, and any acting contrary to that trust, was a

T O M.
IV.

1689.

renounceing of it, thō it were not a renounceing by formal deed.

This seem'd a wonderfull doctrine to be sustain'd by such eminent Lawiers, who it seems never consider'd what would become of that so oft repeated maxim, That the King can do no wrong, if the least maladministration divests him of his regal authority; they layd themselves open before to furious attacks, had The * Lords been disposed to use those armes, which the antient Laws and true Constitution put into their hands, but they had foreclosed themselves from that, by yeilding in efect at the first onset what was contended for too late; they had heartely concur'd with the Commons in excluding the King, the Bishop of Ely himself allow'd, that a full irremouable perswasion in a false Religion was a moral incapacity, and that thereby the King had forfeited his right, their only care was to preserue a shew of succession in the Monarchy, and that the exercise of the government might devolve on the next heire; nor was that so much for loue of the Constitution, as that the Regal power might rather vest in the Princess, than Prince of Orange, whereby many of those Lords promised themselves a greater share in the government, which render'd the contest in effect, not so much about what was Lawfull, as who should reap most benefit by this breach of the Law: Indeed My Lord Nothingham put them in mind of the afforesaid maxim, That the King can doe no wrong, and that Ministers and Officers

---

* The Duke of Buckingham, in his *Memoir on the Revolution*, describes the State of Parties in the House of Lords, and probably on that day, Jan' 29, when, as Kennet remarks, the Lords began to consider of the Commons voting the Throne to be vacant. " The House of Lords," says the Duke, " was extreamly full, scarce one of them was absent, except the Papists; and it was divided into Three Parties: That of the *High-Church* inclin'd to the two Princesses; those we now call *Whiggs*, assured of good imployments under the Prince; and a third, very much the smallest, inclin'd to the unfortunate King, some out of conscience, but more out of despair of favour from the Prince." EDITOR.

were only punishable for maladministration; but then came off with a nice distinction, that it was only where such violations were in some few points, which was not, he Sayd, the King's case, who had in effect declared he would act wholy contrary to Law : in fine it was decreed amongst them, that no Law or maxim must doe him any good, and the Commons finding the Lords concur'd in substance, agreed to that distinction, and Sr George Trebie own'd that the breach of the Law in a few instances, was not sufficient to call the Prince to account ; but that a total violation of the original contract did ipso facto divest him of his Regal power: however My Lord Clarendon made bould to tell them, that those expressions of breaking the original contract &c, was a language that had not long been used in that place, nor known in our Lawbooks, or publick records; to which Sr George Trebie replyd, it was runing too far back to argue whether any such thing as original contract was known or understood, his Lordships he sayd by concurring to that part of the vote had own'd it, and so it was out of the debate.

Those who will defend maxims and principles by halfes, their arguments are sure to cut their own throats, and so it fared with these Noble Lords, who had yeilded the body of the place, and yet pretended to defend the out workes; but the Commons did not so easily loos their hould, so haveing in a manner gain'd the word Abdication, they proceed to that of the Throne's being vacant, which held a longer contest but had the same fate in the end.

It seem'd to the Lords, a contradiction in termes, as was sayd before, that the Throne should be vacant in an hereditary Monarchy, and that if they yeilded it, they conceiud it would amount to a dissolution of the antient Constitution, and change it into an electiue one ; which they thought would haue an ill aspect when fundamentalls were so much talked of, and the

The Lords let fall the debate about the word Abdication.

The Lords deny that the Throne is, or can be vacant.

pretended necessity of preserveing them, the only excuse for
this barberous usage of their Prince; but the Prince of Orange
had no such care of their reputation, and seeing no way of
attaining his ends but by an election, made the Commons who
he had gain'd, fright the Lords into a complyance, not by
shewing what was right, but by telling them what was necessary
to support the wrongs they had already done: however the
Lords struggled a little ere they gave it up, the King, they
sayd, had only lost the exercise of the government, and that
it was to devolve by consequence on the next heire: Mr
Sacheverel tould them, if so, the King being liveing, he was
King still, and then all they had done was illegal, which would
bring them, and all the Kingdom into a snare; Mr Polexfen
seconded him, and sayd it was as great a crime to take away
from the King the exercise of the government, as the government itself; and Serjt Maynard added, that nemo est heres
viuentis, and that the King being liveing, it must not go by
descent; My Lord Notingham replyd, that whether the King
be dead naturally or civilly, it was the same thing, and that if
one be apointed to succeed according to the humour of the
times, and not according to linial descent, and then King
James dy before him, what would become of the hereditary
government? where must the Succession come in? By this
means (says he) we shall change the Constitution and commit
the same fault we haue layd upon the King.

This was a knotty point to get over; and the Commons were
modest at least in termes, they durst not bouldly own the same
fault they were about punishing in their Prince, so they
abstract from declareing who should succeed, pretending to be
confined to the words of the Vote, which went no further than
to declare the Throne vacant; and Mr Sommers assures them,
it was no new thing to make such a seperation, that in the
first of Henry the 4th the Throne was declared vacant, and then

the Duke of Lancaster layd his clame; to this the Earles of Clarendon and Rochester answer'd, It was the only precedent of that nature, and was follow'd by an election of one who was not the true heire, and was afterwards declar'd in Ed: the 4ᵗʰˢ Reign to be an Vsurper: Sʳ George Trebie replyd, that declaration was again revoked in Henry the 7ᵗʰˢ time, that in all turns of government there were contrary declarations; to which the Earle of Pembrock replyd, that they were not to seek for precedents from former reigns to prove the Monarchy hereditary, there haveing scarce been three descents without an interruption, but that they were to prove it from the established Laws which were confirmed and corroberated by their repeated Oathes of Alligiance and Supremacy, which tyd them up to keep in an hereditary line; the Earl of Notingham demonstrated also, that an interregnum in an hereditary Monarchy was a chimera, and by consequence that no such thing could be, as a Vacancy in this case.

The Commons would haue been hard put to it to get cleer of this objection, had the Lords been uniforme in their arguments; but they had yeilded too much ground, to defend the remainder: So Sʳ Robert Howard put them in mind again, of what they had already been advertised of, that in case the Throne was not vacant, how could the Lords justify their haveing desired the Prince of Orange to take the * Administration

---

* "At this time," says the *Duke of Buckingham* in his *Memoir on the Revolution*, "among other Consultations held in several places about these matters, there was one appointed at *Mr. William Herbert's* lodgings in Sᵗ James's, who was then sick of the gout; and so concerned at the Great Favourite's urging it was best to make the Princess no Sovereign, and only a Queen-Consort, that, rising out of bed with earnestness, he protested against ever drawing a Sword on the Prince's side, if he could have imagin'd him capable of such usage to his Wife. This so alarm'd and convinc'd Mons. *Bentinck*, of the impossibility of obtaining a point, which even so interested a Courtier as *Herbert* refus'd to comply in, that in half

upon him? that they were all manifestly guilty of high treason by it; that they had already limited the Succession by agreeing to that part of the Vote, which declares it inconsistant with the Religion and the Laws of England, to haue a Papist reign over them; and then (which was ashtonishing in this debate) they call for aid even from the Prince of Wales himself: These industrious bees could suck hony or poison as they pleas'd, from every flouer, for by decrying him as a suppositious Prince, they had made him instrumental to the King's destruction, and now thinking themselues sure of that, they set him up again against the Princess of Orange's clame (which they saw the Lords were so fond of) so far at least, as to make it a disputable case, who was in reality King James the 2ds heire; we know, says Sr Robert Howard, that some such thing has been pretended to us as an heire male, of which there are different opinions, and in the mean time we are without a government, and must we stay till the truth of that matter be found out? He was seconded by Sr Thomas Lee, who tould the Lords, they being the persons that usually were, or ought to be present at the delivery of our Queens, and the proper witnesses to the birth of our Princes, if therefore their Lordships knew who was on the Throne, they should certainly haue heard his name from them, and that had been the best reason against the vacancy, that could have been made.

The Lords yield at last to the Vote of the Commons, without any alteration.

In fine the Lords had passed the Rubicon, and the Commons tooke care to admonish them, there was no retreating; if the Throne was not vacant, how could they excuse their haveing desired the Prince of Orange to take the Administration

an hour's time he brought them assurance from the Prince of his not insisting on it, and of his being content with a conjunctive Soyereignty, on condition he might have the sole Administration; which last they consented to, because she herself so desired it." EDITOR.

upon him? or at least they ought to haue declared who it was
that fill'd it; which the Lords not dareing to doe, they were
forced next day to send and acquaint the Commons, they
agreed to their Vote, without any alteration.

Whoever desires to see these Debates at lenght, may read
them in the Appendex, what is here sayd, may be sufficient
to shew by what degrees the inféction spread, and how these
pretended Assertors of the Laws, libertys and Religion of the
people, violated them all under a notions of their preservation;
but the thinking and unbyaced men, thō they could not
oppose, were far from approveing these proceedings; they
knew the Laws of England as well as the Church of England
declared against the deposeing doctrine, and that this notion of
dispossessing the King on pretence of his haveing broke the
original contract, governing dispotically &c, was in reality
such a crying violation of Law, reason and Religion, that
unless these men could blind the eyes or darken the understanding of future Ages, like those whom Tacitus dirides, *qui
presentis potentia credunt se extingui posse sequentis ævi memoriam,*
they would blush at the view of the Character they must leaue
behind them, and at the blemish they would draw upon that
assembly; which first suppòseing manifest falsetys in fact,
raised a pretence from thence, of breaking those very Laws in
the most fundamental points, they were so zealous to preserve.
This it was that made the moderate men stand amazed, and
cry out, that had the King misgovern'd, it was the Ministers,
not he, who were to (*have*) answer'd, but that the King had not
made the least step in those measures from whence the chief
dissatisfaction arose, before he was assured he had power to
do it according to the Constitution, and yet this they call'd
a way of governing unknown unto it; but that supposing he
was mislead, he not only revoked what was ungreatfull, but
proffer'd to make the people juges in their own case, to put

himself entirely into their power, and let them carue out their own security both as to Religion and civil rights, and this they call'd, resolveing to govern dispotically : All his Subjects in a manner rise in opposition to him, the Officers of his Army desert him, his creatures, nay his Children abandon him ; all partes of the Kingdom are in a flame, or ready to take fire, he had nothing left to loos but himself and even that imprison'd by his Son in Law ; and because he made his escape to saue his life and gain his liberty, they call it an abdication or voluntary renunciation, thō he had no sooner set his foot in a place of security, but he writes to his Council, and to those very Lords and Commons, to clame his authority, proffers to returne, and refer all to a Parliament, but they refuse to read his letter, and then cry out he has abdicated ; the Throne is vacant ; but in what sence or acceptation (sayd the true Zealots of the Laws and Liberties) can this be call'd a voluntary neglect or withdrawing of his person, care, and influence from the administration of the government? when he not only exercised it, while he had any power left, but tryd all methods of accommodation, and even struggled when his hands were tyd, by messages, letters &c: This made sober men cry out, his Father was treated with more cruelty, but not with more unjustice ; and that future Ages will say, that vnhappy Prince had fairer quarter in some sence from Cromwell and Bradshaw, than he from his Servants and favorits ; they pretended to proue their charge, and offer'd to hear him, but this King must be condemned without being heard, they refuse to open his letters, attend to his offers, or proue what they alledg against him, and yet they vote him guilty : besides, those few miscreants who dip'd their hands in the blood of their Sovereign, were an inconsiderable part of the Nation, and detested with horrour by the rest ; but here the chief body of the Kingdom, men who assumed to themselves the authority of a Parliament,

and were in ' reality the persons that usually compose that
grave and *renownéd Assembly, suffer their Prince to be * imprisoned
and* blame him for not apeareing, they permit his hands to be
tyd and condemne him for not acting, they stop their ears
and cry out they cannot hear him; never was such a mockery
made of Religion, Laws, and Loyalty, by so famed a body of
men, where under the popular florishes of asserting the
original Contract, all Contracts and obligations betwixt King
and Subject either of divine or humain institution were
trampled on and dispised; men of temper and moderation could
not but call to mind, that Edward the 4th was never said to
have forfeited his right when he fled into a forreing Country,
to shelter himself from the predominant faction of an Earle of
Warwick; or King Charles the 2^{d} when he fled from Worcester; that were, as if a man should forfeit his house to him
that set it on fire, because he would not stay in it to be burnt;
and be oblidged to loos his estate, for endeavouring to save
his life; if Princes are to be thus roughly dealt withall, their
birth is a great misfortune. Yet such were the times and
disposition of the people, that these extravagant things went
down without chewing, the plainest truthes outfaced and
denyd, whilest the greatest contradictions to reason and
justice found a ready admittance, as if evidence had been an
argument against belief, and absurdity the only motiue of
credibility. Men who had a real concerne for the true English
Constitution, began to be afraid of the consequence of such a
Slavish condiscention to satisfy the ambition of an Invader;
the legislative power which the people (they sayd) had trusted
their Delegates with, was only in conjunction with their Prince,
it was never their intention to put it in their power alone, to

---

* Added by the Son of James the second. EDITOR.

T O M.
IV.

1689.

make an entire surrender of their Laws and libertys, and even
overturn fundamentalls, to court the favour or flatter the
ambition of any Prince, much less an Vsurper; that were to
make the Nation as it were capable of being felo de Se:
they aprehended therefore that if a Convention took such an
authority, it might in time be debauched into a Confederacy
to make a Danish compliment of the lives and liberties of the
people, and strike the Constitution dead at a blow; which was
an authority they were never entrusted with, their business
being to preserue the Constitution not to destroy it.

The P. of
Orange carryd
his point with
difficulty
enough.

Thus did impartial men reason and discours upon these
transactions, and indeed many of the Lords themselves did
not so easily fall into the Common Notions; for when the first
part of the Commons Vote was argued in the higher House
concerning the King's haveing broke the original Contract, it
was carryd in the affirmative only by a small majority, and
when they went upon modelling the government, those who
were for establishing a Regency only, were out done but by
three Votes: so that the Prince of Orange's aims were not
droue on so currently, till his friends within the house, made
it be understood, they were backed by an Army without, and
cause certain threats to be insinuated underhand; that if they
satisfyd not his expectation, he would leaue them to satisfy
King James his justice; which prevail'd with them at last to
make this breach upon the Constitution, and hereditary
Monarchy, and declare the Prince and Princess of Orange
King and Queen of England, the Prince to exercise the
Regal power himself, but in the name of them both, and to
continue so for his life in prejudice of the Princess of Denmark's title, if he surviued the Princess his wife; and yet the
Princess of Denmark's Children to take place in the Succession,
of the Prince of Orange's, if he had any by a Second Venter:
thus did they mangle the Succession, chopping and changeing

it at pleasure, inverting the order amongst the Protestant heires, and totally excludeing the Catholick ones, till they had fixed a series of electiue Monarches; and under a notion of preserveing the Laws, unhinged them all at a stroke, even Magna Charta itself: In the first fervor of their zeal they forget what perhapes they may hereafter be more sencible of, how fatal and destructiue it has always been to England, to beget and establish a compitition of titles to the Crown, the Struggles betwixt the two Roses, shews what blood it has cost; and the contest in King Charles the first's time, might have reminded them, how odious it is to mankind, to make Religion a cover to ambitious and private designes, and that from such seeds nothing could be expected but a plentifull harvest of blood and ruin.

But they were taken up with other considerations, thō the very next step they made put them in mind on how weak a foundation their new built government stood, for being forced to abrogate the old Oath of * Allegience they were gravell'd a little what to Substitute in its room, which would not run great riske of being refused by the generality of the Kingdom; they durst

The Prince and Princess of Orange declared King and Queen of England the 13 February.

---

* " Some of the Bishops and Clergy," says *Kennet*, (Vol: 3. page 594.) " were Nonjurors upon very different Principles." Whilst Bishop Ken stayed in Town in order to take the new Oaths, and lodged with his friend D͏ʳ Hooper, who had daily and earnestly discoursed with him on the subject, the Bishop at last thus expressed his scruples, ' I question not but that you and several others have taken the Oaths with as good a Conscience as I my self shall refuse them; and sometimes you have almost persuaded me to comply with the Arguments you have used, but I beg you to urge them no farther; for should I be persuaded to comply, and after see reason to repent, you will make me the most miserable man in the world.' *Kennet* also refers to " The Declaration of John Lord Bishop of Chichester upon his Death Bed, August 25, 1689, putting his Refusal of the Oaths upon the great Doctrine of Passive Obedience, which he always look'd upon as the distinguishing Character of the Church of England; and that therefore he would not have taken the Oath, though the Penalty had been loss of Life." Printed 1689. EDITOR.

not give the title of Rightfull King to the Prince, thō they
pretended so absolute a right to place him on the Throne, but
contented themselves with the expression *of bearing faith and
true allegiance* to him, which each one was left to interpret in
what sence he pleased ; and the Prince of Orange considering
the difficulty of getting more, and how little oathes in general
had benifited his predecessor, was contented with what they
gave him, thō it was in reality rather a publick owning he had
no right to the Crown, than any great security for his peacefull
wearing it : In fine they were so expeditious in the business,
that the 13th of February (the day after the Princess of Orange
arrived from Holland) the Prince and she being seated in the
Banqueting house in two armed chairs under a canopy, the
two Houses of Convention came in a body, and haveing first
enumerated all the pretended miscariages of his Majestys reign,
as that he had endeavour'd to subvert the Protestant Religion,
the Laws and Liberty's, by assumeing and exerciseing a dispenseing power without consent of Parliament, by committing
and prosecuteing divers worthy Prelates for petitioning to be
excused from concurring to the said assumed power ; by erecting a Court of Commissioners for Ecclesiastical Causes, by
levying money for the use of the Crown by pretence of prerogative, for other ends and in other manner than the same was
granted by Parliament ; by raising and keeping a standing
Army in time of peace, and quartering Soldjers contrary to
Law, by disarmeing several Protestants at the same time that
several Papists were armed and employed contrary to Law, by
violateing the freedom of Elections for Members to serue in
Parliament ; by prosecutions in the King's bench for matters
and causes only cognizable in Parliament ; by causing unqua-
lifyd persons to be return'd upon juries ; by requireing excessiue Bail, and imposeing too great fines, and granting fines and
forfeitures before conviction ; all which they sayd were utterly

against the known laws and freedom of the Realm, and whereas the said King James had abdicated the government, and the Throne being thereby vacant, they then out of the fullness of their power vested the Prince and Princesse of Orange with the Regal dignity, and declar'd or acknowlidged them King and Queen of England, France and Ireland.

There are but three titles to a Crown, which are Conquest, Succession, or Election, none of which suted with the present circomstances; the first would have enslaved the Nation, the second a contradiction in termes, the 3ᵈ so opposite to the Standing Laws of the Land, that they had no way to answer (with any forme or species of Law) the Prince of Orange's ambition, but by supposeing the King had abdicated; thō they knew the contrary, and that the Prince of Wales was a supposititious heire, thō they neither dust venter to prove it, nor affirme it, and then by confounding the Prince and Princess of Orange's right, express it by the words, *acknowlidg and declare*.

Many persons were bakeld in their expectation, to find that, in this enumeration of grievances (on which they grounded their unaccountable procedure) no mention was made of a Suppositious Prince, or the French League to cut the Protestants throats, which had been the main provocations to so universal a defection; so that it was not to be wonder'd that several Lords both Spiritual and temporal, enter'd their protestation when they saw their Prince accused of nothing but what was manifestly false, or unquestionably in his power, or at least but dubious and what however he had redress'd; and that thereupon such an unwarrable disposition should be made of the Crown, and a day apointed to place it on the Vsurper's head: but this Glimps of Loyalty soon suffer'd an eclips in most of those Peers, certain views of intrest got the better of their scruples, and they, like the rest, fell down before the Idol

No mention made of a Suppositious Prince, or a French League, in the enumeration of greivances,

T O M.
IV.

1689.

they were against erecting; and those *who afterwards were ye* *
most early converts, who to their honour return'd soonest to
their duty and principles, had leasure to repent, thō they had'
not power to amend the miserys they, at first, so rashly contribited too: The P. of Orange indeed thought it necessary to
sooth them up for a while in a sort of fool's paredice, by a
seeming subordination to their wills; and, till he had linked
them fast in a forreign war, made shew of being content with
the name only of King, and leaveing all to the direction of the
Parliament, especially the House of Commons which carryd
the purstrings of the Nation: so he wheedled them with a
remission of chimney-mony, when he was well assured he
should be no looser by his generosity, and that it would only
be like throwing water into a dry Pump to make it suck better
below, and cast it out with more abundance aboue; but men of
judgment were not deluded by this seeming modesty, for seeing
that Ambition was the origin of his undertakeing, his drift,
they knew, must be to make himself great and them miserable
in the end, and thō it was the people's pretended intrest that
gave birth and rise to his pretended title, yet in a little time it
apear'd that the Prince and People's intrest was never more
distinctly opposite than dureing his usurped reign.

The calumnie
about the P.
of Wales is
now examined
into, as the
P. of Orange
promis'd. And now that the Prince of Orange had bribed or bubbled
those who had been chosen guardians of the people's liberties,
to betray them up into his hands, he made little account of
satisfying the publick expectation in those material points
which had most conduced to make them favour his enterprise,
there was no more talke of that formidable French League,
which had hair'd people out of their sences, as well as their
duty; on the contrary My Lord Sunderland justifyd the King

* Interlined by the Son of James the second. EDITOR.

in that point, who now that he own'd himself an enemy to
his Prince he was credited by the people; nor did the P. of
Orange think fit to propose to the Convention the enquireing
into the Prince of Wales's birth, thō he had solemnly promised
it in his Declaration dat: October 10th 1688, wherein he sayd,
That the want of evidence in that point, was one of the principal motives of his Expedition into England, engageing himself to refer the enquiry into that affair, and of all things
relateing to it, to the heareing of a Parliament: the P. of
Orange wanted not reasons to endeavour the proof (if it had
been possible) of a thing he had not only promised, but (as the
supposition of it had contribited more than any thing to the
Revolution) so it would have settled his Government aboue all
other arguments in the world : The King in his letter from
St Germains desired the Convention to examine it; and by
many printed pamflets the Prince of Orange was reminded of
his engagement, and the Lords and Commons provoked to it,
to whom it was represented, how much those who had given
testimony of his Birth (being aboue forty persons most of them
of the first quality) suffer'd in their reputation, as if they had
been Confederates to the imposture, which their soules abhor'd
as the masterpeece of wickedness ; they therefore besought the
Lords and Commoners to reexamin them, that they might
either rescue their honour and reputation from those calumnys
which were cast upon them, or, if convicted of insincerity,
wer willing to undergo the penaltys due to so vile and unex-
ampled a perjury ; but at the same time tould them, their
testimonys would be (if possible) more plain, particular and
comprehensive than the former, and that they had several
things to offer which before were thought unnecessary, or
omitted out of modesty or reserue ; that there could be no
danger now (they sayd) of being bribed or ouerawed in favour
of the Prince's birth, which had been objected before, but that

on the contrary there was full encouragement to confront the Deponants by counterevidence, if any such were, that expedition was necessary in this matter, because the number of witnesses would be lessening, and exception could not so well be made to their testimony when dead, who might haue been so easily examin'd whilst they were alive : In fine, in case the Deponants were neither disproved, nor the Prince of Wales own'd, the consequence would be very unfortunate ; not only by setting up a contest about the succession, but that since in strictness of Law there is no greater proof required for the legitimacy of the King's Son, than of a private Subject, it might give a handle to letigious people to question the birth of private persons, and entangle property to a great degree; for that thousands were deprived daily of rich inherances by Children whose birth were far from being so well attested as that of the Prince of Wales's.

But notwithstanding all these provocations, and the P. of Orange's former engagements, nothing was done in it; which those persons sayd, they could make no other construction of, than that they were willing to let the Nation believe, the Lords and Commons were fully satisfyd with the evidence already given in the matter; and indeed Bentinck not long after, being asked, Why his Master made not apear the illegitimacy of the Prince of Wales, as he had promised? he answer'd, That they neither questioned his legitimacy, nor were concerned about it, for that his Master being now in possession of the Throne, was resolved to keep it while he lived, and cared not who it went too when he was gone.

This put the Zealots for the government upon other methods of defending their new establishment, and it is wonderfull what sorte of arguing pass'd for reason amongst the petulant writers of those days ; in the first place they recorded it, as an uncontestable fact, that the King endeavour'd the Subversion

of the Established Religion and government, and from thence
inferring that protection and Allegiance being reciprocal,
upon failure of the first, the Second likewise extinguished,
and by this supposition absolved themselves from the Oathes of
Allegiance and Supremacy, and all other tys or obligations to
a natural Sovereign ; the maxim of the King's doing no wrong;
and that the Ministers are only accountable for all transgres-
sions, thō never so many or manifest, was easily got over, by
affermeing it had no other meaning, than that the King's
power could not go so far as to support him in doeing any
unjustice, either by himself or his Ministers ; so that instead of
punishing the Ministers for the King's fault, the King is made
punishable for theirs : others sayd, it signifyd no more, than
that one could not resist the King as to the executiue part,
thō he commited faults in yᵉ administratioh, but that this
obligation was not binding when the Laws themselves were
overthrowne, which they still supposed to be the present case;
and as for treating with him when he offer'd it, they sayd, it
could not be done without disrespect, that the going about to
charge any mismanagement upon him, was an indignity not to
be offer'd to a King in Person, particularly that of proveing an
imposture in reference to the Prince, in which he must have
had (if true) so great a share ; so that (sayd they) either the
proof of that must be laid aside, or an end put to all treating
with him : So by these men's arguing, he was to be dethroned
out of respect, to his person, and for fear they should not have
a fair tryal about the Prince of Wales, which however was
never put to a tryal afterwards.

There was indeed some tentatives made to give a colour to
that, and other calumnys ; severall witnesses were examin'd,
and My Lord Danby employ'd in the matter, but he declared
the more he serch'd into it, the greater evidence he found of
the Prince's being born of the Queen ; so that it was soon

Some offers as proveing the Prince of Wales an imposter, but it proved the contrary.

let drop as well as the enquiry into My Lord Essex's death, upon which indeed some were imprison'd (and as personal peeques or hopes of advantage, never fail to bring in witnesses to swear right or wrong to the humour of the times) accordingly Major Hawley gentleman Porter of the Tower, was accused by one who had an enmity to him, of haveing been instrumental in My Lord Essex's death, by the Duke's directions, as was supposed; upon which he was imprisoned and the Sentinal who fortuned to stand then at My Lord Essex's door was put into Newgate *for refuseing to own he saw Mr Hawley go into his room at yt time**: but notwithstanding a long imprisonment, most unhumain usage, and continual threats of being hang'd if he did not confess, the poor man had the constancy to persist in afferming, that neither Major Hawley nor any man whatever, enter'd into My Lord's lodging when the fact was commited; which with the accusers owning his perjury soon after, on his death bed, and My Lady Essex's message (who knew her Lord's temper and principles better than other people) to those who were appointed to examine the matter, That she was well satisfyd in what manner he dy'd, and therefore desired them to desist further enquiry which might cast unjust suspicions upon others, this matter was let fall too: besides they needed not now such Shifts and contrivances to compas their ends, they were Masters of more powerfull arguments than Law and reason, to keep possession of the authority which was now in their hands; which droue those who were either loyal from the begining, or disabused by these faileurs, of giveing the publick a due Satisfaction in so many material points, to make use *at least*† of such armes as they had left: for the Revolution

---

* Interlined by the Son of James the second. EDITOR.

† Interlined as before mentioned. EDITOR.

with all its terrours and enticements, could not carry men's
pens and Tongues so entirely in subjection to it, as to hinder
their vindicateing oppressed justice, and clameing at least by
smart and judicious treatices their Prince's right, which they
were no otherways able to Support.

These persons were cautious indeed in ye use of their tongues,
but all the strickt enquirys and rigid hands of the government,
could not hinder a multitude of * pamflets from apearing,
which sufficiently dissected the falcetys of those intrested men's
reasonings, who endeavour'd to dress up usurpation with all
the gaudy florishes that appostate eloquence was capable of:
Amongst the Protestant Clergie the King wanted not men of
wit and learning to defend his cause, but we have few instances
now a days of such victorys as Cicero fancyd he had gain'd
over Catelin, it was not to be expected that reason and oratary
would make Vsurpers drop their Swords, or intrested men
prefer truth and justice before advancement and livelyhood;
for when conformety is required upon pain of Sterveing, it is
not to be wonder'd if Religion be exposed to reproach.

---

* Many of these Publications are noticed, and Extracts given from them, by
Ralph (*Vol.* 2. *P.* 21. 30—33.) *Bishop Burnet*, as we are informed in the new
and excellent Ed. of The Biographical Dictionary by *Chalmers*, wrote several
Pamphlets in support of The Prince of Orange's designs, which were reprinted at
London in 1689, in 8vo. under the title of " A Collection of Eighteen Papers
relating to the Affairs of Church and State during the Reign of King James II. &c."
—The 10th Volume of the *Somers' Tracts* is full of papers relating to the
Revolution; in that Volume is the Letter which the Emperor sent from Vienna,
April 9th, 1689, to JAMES THE SECOND, (*Page* 18.); as also " A Modest Apology
for the Loyal Protestant Subjects of KING JAMES, who desire his Restoration,
without Prejudice to our Religion, Laws or Liberties." (*P.* 401.) The 12th
Volume of those valuable Historical Tracts contains (*P.* 382.) " Political Remarks
on the Life and Reign of KING WILLIAM III. First, from his Birth to the
Abdication of KING JAMES; Secondly, from his Accession to the Crown of England to his Death." This Tract, according to Mr. W. Scott, is a favourable, but
by no means a partial, account of the Life of the great Monarch to whom it
refers. EDITOR.

T O M.
IV.

1689.
Endeavours
made by
Protestant
Divines, to
satisfy men's
consciences
about the
Oath of
Allegience.

These writeings therefore thō they could not rectify men's actions, they informed many people's judgments; and will perpetuate the memory of the King's unjust treatment, and the infamy of such as endeavour'd by new Strains of fancy and eloquence to fix the glorious titles of illustrious, deliver and Saviour, upon men who realy were Usurpers, oppressors, and Tyrants; but flattery alway follows fortune, and the change of government; and would be as ready to give those epethets to the contrary persons, as they can alter the signification of the words Right Obedience and Allegiance, under a Lawfull or an Vsurped government: this made the nonjúreing Protestants murmur to See how great a disreputation those very men (who had long cryd out against the Doctrine of some authors of the Church of Rome) had brought upon the Church of England, they need but look (they Sayd) at home to find a much more shamefull dispensation from the most Sacred * Oaths practised amongst themselves, than they complain'd of in others. Doct[r] Burnet aprehending the reasonableness of this accusation, and that it might souren the humours of all such persons towards the government, as had any Zeal for the honour of

---

* *Lord Clarendon* thus expressed, in *His Diary,* his sentiments on this Subject: " *March* 1. 1689. In the afternoon the *Duke of Queensbery* visited me. He seemed much dissatisfied with the treatment he and the honest Party met with here; but was very reserved what he would do, when he came to the Convention. The *Bishop of St. Asaph* was with me; and, in discourse, we quickly fell upon the New Oaths. I told him, I could not take them; thinking myself bound by the Oaths of Allegiance and Supremacy, which I had already taken. He told me, those Oaths did no longer oblige me, than the King, to whom I took them, could protect me, and that I was free from my Allegiance to King James; and that these new Oaths were no more than to live quietly under King William; and he would fain have persuaded me to take them. But I answered, That I was fully satisfied, that I could not be absolved from the Oaths I had taken, to which these new ones were contradictory; that having already taken the former Oaths, my Allegiance was due to KING JAMES, and not in my power to dispose of...." EDITOR.

the Church of England, writ a Pastorall letter, wherein he
gave another turn to the invasion, pretending it was a just war
the Prince of Orange had made against the King, who by
going about to change the government of the Kingdom
wherein that Prince had an expectancy, and by putting a
supposititious heire upon him, had endeavour'd to disapoint
his succession, which he Sayd gàue a juste cause to make war,
and that the Success of a just war gaue a lawful title to whatever was acquired in the progress of it; that King James being
worsted in it, all his right and title did acrue to the P. of
Orange in the right of conquest over him, however the Prince
of Orange (he sayd) in consideration of the Peers and people
of England, was willing to receive the * Crown by their determination, rather than to hould it in the right of Conquest,
by this nice distinction he thought both to flatter the Vsurper,
and satisfy scrupulous Church of England men; but the
Parliament men were more tender of their libertys, than of their
Consciences; and instead of catching at his Sophistical Salvo,
order'd his Pastoral Letter to be burnt by the Hangman, which

---

* The following is the account which *Burnet* has given in his History, of what had
passed in the mind of the Prince of Orange respecting the Crown. (Vol: 2. p. 574.)
" During all these Debates, and the great heat with which they were managed,
the Prince's own behaviour was very mysterious. He staid at St James's : He
went little abroad : Access to him was not very easy. He heard all that was said
to him : but seldom made any answers. He did not affect to be affable or
popular : . . . . After a reservedness, that had continued so close for several weeks,
that no body could certainly tell what he desired, he called for the Marquis of
Hallifax, and the Earls of Shrewsbury and Danby, and some others to explain
himself more distinctly to them." — The Prince then protested against being established as the Regent, and declared, that he would not accept of it. " Others," he
added, " were for putting the Princess singly on the Throne, and that he should
reign by her courtesy : He said, no man could esteem a woman more than he did
the Princess; but he was so made, he could not think of holding any thing by
apron-strings." EDITOR.

T O M.
IV.

cast a grievous blemish upon this mighty stickler for their new settlement, which they gloryd so much in themselves.

There was an other attempt made not long after, to satisfy scruples too, by one who at at first had signalized himself for the King's cause; it was one Doct.ʳ Sherlock dean of Pauls, who haveing for sometime refused to take the Oathes, at last pretended he was convinced of their lawfulness, and gave so new and surprizeing a reason for it, that thō he was a man of wit and erudition, he exposed himself to the lash of all parties; those of the government were displeas'd, that the common notions of preserveing the Religion and liberties of the people (which they supposed were to be destroyd had the King remain'd upon the Throne) should not satisfy him, alwell as it had done the generality of the Kingdom; others, who were realy consciencious in the point, sufficiently layd open the incongruety of his new Sisteme, which constituteing two rights a providential and a legal one, he allow'd that one person might very rightiously *clame and take a thing and an other as* rightiously hould and keep it; and that whoever got the better, had the providential right by possession; and that all authority being from God, people were obliged to tranfer their Alligiance to him, as a King of God's makeing: but this so manifestly overthrew the notions and nature of right, that the learned men of his own perswasion were his fiercest adversarys, they tould him it open'd a gate to all the violence and disorders in the world, that *authority † was* not to be taken by storme no more than temperance or humility, and that right could no more be got by force or armes than rightiousness, otherwise Kingdoms would be thrown up like a ball of strife for the Strongest arme

* Interlined by the Son of James the second. EDITOR.
† Inserted as before mentioned. EDITOR.

to carry away, which in no manner suted with the peace and order Almighty God design'd, in instituteing government, and obligeing all people to be subject to higher powers; so that tho he shew'd a great deal of dexterity in manageing his argument, it only served to give the King's friends a good occasion to lay open the manifest deviations of all those from the Doctrine of the Church of England, who had conform'd to the usurpation, and that intrest and mistaken Zeal had influenced their inconsistant decisions; and that they had only served the turns of a few men who had made use of the King's Religion, and the Prince of Orange's ambition, to bring the honours and profits of the Government into their hands, and instead of mentaining the property of the people, had made a propertie of the Nation itself.

T O M.
IV.

1689.

And now that the King found his voice was no longer heard in the land, and that the people were deaf to all his Offers, as well as blinded in their ways, he betook himself to such methods as reason and justice suggested to do himself and his injured people Right; he knew he could depend upon the fidelity of the Irish, and hoped the Earle of Tyrconel would find means to prevent the Protestants of that Kingdom (who had the greatest power in their hands) from forceing a conformety to what had been done in England: So upon the 12 of January, the King writ to him from St Germains to this efect:

The King writes to the E. of Tyrconel in Ireland, to support his authority there. Jan: 12.

I send this bearer Captain Rooth to you to give notice ”
of my being here, and to be informed how things are with ”
you, that accordingly I may take my measures; hopeing you ”
will be able to defend yourself and support my intrest there, ”
till summer at least. I am sure you will do it to the utmost ”
of your power, and I hope this King here will so press the ”
Hollanders, that the P. of Orange will not have men to spare ”
to attack you; in the mean time (till I heare from you by ”
the bearer) all I can get this King to doe, is to send 7 or 8000 ”

" muskets, he not being willing to venter more armes or any
" men, till he knows the condition you are in, so that it will
" be absolutely necessary that you send back this bearer, as
" soon as may be, with one or two persons more in order
" thereunto; Just before I left Rochester I had a letter from
" you, as I remember it was on the 13ᵗʰ of December, which
" tould me all was quiet with you, and I hope is so still, and
" that the Prince of Orange has sent over no force to invade
" you yet; what more I haue to say I refer to My Lord Mel-
" ford's letter, and to this bearer, who can give you an account
" how wee all got away, and how kindly I have been received
" here. I haue not had any letter from England of a later
" date than the day I left it; you may expect a duplicate of
" this, which I purpose to send for fear of accidents. J: R:

The E. of
Tyrconnel
sends My Lᵈ
Montjoy to
the King, and
then puts
things in order
for a defence.

His Majesty was not deceiu'd in his expectation, thō My
Lord Tyrconnel very prudently made shew at first as if he
waver'd a little in his resolutions; for being sencible how weak
a condition Ireland was in (should any force from abroad join
the ill affected at home) he stroue underhand to amuse the
Prince of Orange's Agents, with a faigned disposition of submiting, till he could put himself and the Kingdom in a condition not to be forced to it: this made the English slight
Ireland for a time, and took away in some measure all kind
of vmbrage from the disaffected there, which gave him both
time and credit, to secure the government from those he
suspected most: My Lord Montjoy was at the head of that
number, he fear'd his power and mustrusted his fidelity, so
under a notion of consultation on so critical a juncture sent for
him up, and found by his way of arguing and even pressing a
submission, he had not been mistaken in his suspicion: My
Lord Tyrconnel therefore, fearing to contradict him, seem'd to
yeild to his opinion, only Sayd, It would but be fair to
acquaint the King and convince him of the necessity, and that

no one was properer to go on that errand than himself, who
could so well represent to his Majesty, the moral impossibility
of houlding out against the power of England; how necessary
it was to yeild to the times at present, and wait a more favorable occasion of demonstateing the loyalty of his Irish Subjects.
My Lord Montjoy could not disaprove the reasonableness of
the thing, but shew'd some reluctancy to the Commission;
which, to make it go down the better, My Lord Tyrconnell
Sayd, he would send Baron Rice along with him, and gave
likewise some assurance there should be no considerable change
made in his absence, either by granting out new commissions,
or sending more forces into the North, and some other particulars in favour of the Protestants, which he perceiv'd My
Lord Montjoy was more concern'd for, than to support the
King's authority; which made My Lord Lieftnant more
earnest to be rid of him, and therefore directed Mr Baron
Rice (in whom he had an entire trust and confidence) to giue
a quite different account to the King; assureing his Majesty of
his utmost endeavours to support his intrest, that My Lord
Montjoy being a dangerous man, he thought this contrivance
necessary, to put him into his Majestys power, and delude the
enemy with an expectation of what he was resolved never to
consent too; and hoped by his Majestys assistance to be able
to prevent being ever forced too: and accordingly this Lord's
back was no sooner turn'd, but he began by degrees to pull off
the maske, he caused all the Protestants in Dublin to surrender
their armes, because they made a manifest shew of disafection to
the King; he began to augment the standing forces, and with as
much prudence as desterity, soon put the Kingdom in a tollerable condition of defence; while the Prince of Orange, either
deluded by that seeming treaty, or with the mean opinion he had
of the force of that Kingdom, and being eager to forme his
designes against France, neglected the Sending a few troops into

that Country ; which had it been done immediately upon the Revolution, had easily effected what cost him afterwards so much blood and treasure, and might haue cost him his usurped crown itself, if the Councells of France thorough too much diffidence, private piques, and personal animositys, had not fail'd in sending such succors thither, as both reason, honour, or their own intrest, so manifestly call'd for.

Assoon as this account came to the King he immediately resolved to pass over into Ireland himself, and to do it with so much expedition, as to give a fresh encouragement to his friends and be a surprize upon his Ennemys; but first thought fit to secure My Lord Montjoy in the Basteel (where he remain'd till the war was ended in Ireland and was then exchanged for Mr. Richard Hamilton) and prevailing with his most Christian Majesty to furnish him with a tollerable quantity of armes, amunition, some little mony, and a few Officers, he made hast to try his fortune once more, at the head of his Subjects, whose fidelity he hoped would make some reperation for the treachery of those who had so lately abandon'd him : Upon news of the King's resolutions herein, Dublin and most other Towns declared for him, so that thō that Kingdom was not free from that spirit of Rebellion which had got so absolute a dominion in England, however it was forced to canton itself in the North, where the Protestants had gain'd the greatest footing; and therefore where they were outnumber'd they made a shew of continuing in their duty, but where they were masters enough to act freely according to their inclination, soon threw off the obedience they owed to their Sovereign, and were the most obstinate and bitter ennemys he ever had.

His Majesty therefore posted down to Brest, leaveing his people to follow as fast as they could, where he arrived before the end of February, and found a Squadron of ships consisting of twenty two Sail ready to escort him, which the good order in the marine affairs and the natural expedition of that Nation, had equiped in so short a time; but before he set Sail his Majesty thought fit to write to his Subjects of Scotland, from whence he had received a sincere acknowlidgment of duty, and affection of many persons of distinction there, and thō on Account of Religion he could not promis himself the same security and assistance he hoped to meet with in Ireland, which made him chuse to go thither in person; yet his former experience of the generous and loyal comportment of the Scotch Nobility and gentry, gave him ground to hope, his cause would not be so entirely abandon'd in that Kingdom, as it had been in England ; and had this letter been sooner dispatched it might haue checked the proceedings of the factious partie there, who he perceived by this messinger was going about to follow the steps of the English Convention:. but whether * *it was done on purpose*, or that the hurry of other business would not give leave, this Messinger had not audience of his Majesty till some time after his arrivall at St Germains; nor was the letter writ and sent away, till after his Majesty was, not only determined to go to Ireland preferrable to Scotland, but was actually on board the St MICHEL in Brest road from whence it bore date; the success of which will appear, when an account is given of what passed in that Kingdom. Besides this, his Majesty, (that he might not be wanting in any thing, either to justify himself to the world, or seek redress where there was any probability of finding it) made his aplication even to those who had given a helping hand to his misfortunes ; and therefore thought fit to write to the Emperour likewise, hopeing that when his Imperial Maty saw the Prince

T O M.
IV.
1689.

---

* Here five lines have been crossed out with such care, that it was impossible to decypher what had been written: The words in Italics had been inserted by the Son of James the second. EDITOR.

T T 2

of Orange make use of his friendship and assistance, to pursue his own unnatural ambition and dethrone a Catholick King, he might relent in some measure on account of Religion at least, and be inclined to redress so crying an unjustice, when he found his honour and conscience engaged beyond what tis probable his intention was in the begining; but to his Majestys great surprize he found, that intrest had blinded .the Austrian Zeal and had overballanced all thoughts of repairing injurys, which if they are profitable, easily pass upon Princes as necessary for self preservation; the prospect therefore of supplys from England (when under the Prince of Orange's direction) which could not be expected from the King who aimed at a newtrality and the eas of the people, made him and other Catholick Princes (if they did not applaud) at least suffer patiently so beneficial an injustice; and accordingly his Imperial Majesty writ the following harsh, and provoking answer, which thō it came not to the King till he was in Ireland, yet not to interrupt the narration of what passed in that Country, shall be inserted in this place.

The Empe-
rour's answer
to the King's
letter.

LEOPOLD, &c: The letter of the 6th of February which your Serenity writ to us from the Castle of St Germains, we receiv'd from the Earl of Carlinford your Ambassador in our Court, in which you gaue us an account into what circomstances your Serenity was reduced, by the desertion not only of your Army, on the Prince of Orange's comeing, but even of your Servants, and those you put most confidence in, which forced you to seek refuge in France, and therefore request our assistance for the regaining your Kingdoms; wee do assure your Serenity, that we no sooner heard that deplorable instance of the instability of humain affairs, but we were sencibly touched, and truly afflicted, not only out of the common motives of humanity, but for our sincere affection to you, to see that happen which (thō we hoped the contrary) we had too much reason to aprehend;

for had your Serenity given more attention to the kind representations we made you, by our Ambassador le Count of Kaunits, instead of harkening to the fraudelent suggestions of France, who by fomenting division betwixt your Serenity and your people, thought to have had a better opertunity of insulting the rest of Europe; and had you thought fit to use your power and authority, as Arbiter of the peace of Nimeghen, to put an end to their continual breaches of faith and agreements, and for that end, had enter'd into the same measures with us, and those who had a right notion how things stood; we doubt not, but your Serenity would by that means have extreamly mollifyd and repress'd the odium, which your people have of our Religion, and haue settled peeace and tranquility not only in your own Kingdom, but in the whole Roman Empire: We leave it therefore now to your own judgment, whether we are in circomstances of affording your Serenity any succour, we being not only engaged in a war with the Turkes, but under a necessity of repressing a cruel and unjust one, which the French, thinking themselves secure of England, haue (against their solemn faith and engagement) lately brought upon us; nor can we forbear puting you in mind, that our Religion suffers no more from any people then the French themselves, who to our unspeakable damage, and that of the whole Christian world, think it lawfull, not only to unite their force with the sworn enemys of the holy Cross, to twart our endeavours for the Glory of God, and put a stop to the Success it had pleased his Omnipotent hand to afford us; but by heaping one perfidy on the back of an other, haue exacted unreasonable contributions from Townes surrender'd upon conditions, even against the engagement signed by the Dauphin's own hand; and not content with that, haue plunder'd them and reduced them at last to ashes or heaps of Rubbish; they have burnt the Pallaces of Princes which the most cruel warrs had spared till now, spoiled Churches, and (like the most barberous Nations) carried away the people into Slavery ; they have made a jest of executing such horrible things to Catholicks, as the very Turks would have been ashamed of; which has put a necessity upon us to exert our power in our own defence, and that of the Romain Empire, no less against them, than the Turks themselves; not doubting but your Serenity is too reasonable to think us worthy of blame, if we endeavour by the force of armes to gain that security, to which hithertoo so many treatys has proved so inefectual, and that we enter into such measures with those who have the same intrest with us, as seems necessary for our common security and defence; beseeching Almighty God to direct all for his glory, and that he will grant your Serenity true Conforth in your afflictions; whom we embrace with a lasting, tender and brotherly affection. Vienna Aprill 9: 1689.

Thō this letter was civil in termes, the King thought it harsh in substance, and very unreasonable in its way of arguing; for he tells the King in effect, he suffer'd deservedly, for not joining with him against France; as if England had been a feuditary to the Empire, or oblidged to fight the Quarrells of the House of Austria; or as if the King, had not as great an obligation to seeke the honour and advantage of his own people (which was to be had by peace not war) as the Emperour of his ; and to be tould so oft of the peace of Nimeghen which neither was made in his reign, nor did the English Ministers sign even as Medeators, because the Hollanders had made a seperate one without their participation, much less as guarantees : but in case they had, and the obligation had descended on the King, it rather tyd him, (he Sayd) to an exact newtrality, till it appear'd more manifestly who was the infringer of that peace, than to run blindly along with the first complainer ; for if a Prince who is Guarantee should forfeit his right to his own teritorys, in the sence of that Partie who thinks himself not sufficiently vindicated by him, no Prince would take that office upon him on such hard and hazerdous termes. Yet that was the treatment his Majesty experienced from the Courts of Vienna, and Madrid, who forgetting the oppressed Prince, made hast to compliment the Vsurper, and enter'd into a stricter league with him than before; and immediately sent away his Majestys Ministers from both places, without being able to assigne the least reason for such an unwarrantable proceeding, which put his Majesty upon a necessity of seeking redress by force too, seeing all the world was deaf to his arguments, and representations.

Accordingly on the 12th of March the King had Landed " at Kingsale, and was received with all immaginable joy by " his Catholick Subjects there, where he stayd till the mony, " armes, and amunition he brought with him was put on shore; " and on the 14th went to Corke, where the Earl of Tyrconnel " met him, and gaue an account of the state and condition of " that Kingdom; that he had sent down Lieftenant General " Hamilton with about 2500 men, being as many as he could " spare from Dublin, to make head against the Rebels in " Ulster, who were masters of all that Province except Charle- " mount and Caricfergus; that most part of the Protestants in " other partes of the Kingdom had been up, that in Munster " they had possessed themselves of Castle Martir and Banden, " but were forced to surrender both places and were totally " reduced in those parts by Lieftenant General Macarty, and " were in a manner totally suppress'd in the other two pro- " vinces; that the bare reputation of an Army had done it, " togather with the diligence of the Catholick Nobility and " gentry, who had raised aboue fifty Regiments of foot, and " seueral troops of hors, and Dragoons, that he had distributed "

T O M.
IV.
1689.

The King
Lands at
Kingsale the
12th March.
KING JAM:
MEM^{rs}. To: 9:
pag: 285.

" amongst them about 20000 armes, but were most so old
" and unserviceable, that not aboue one thousand of the fire
" armes were found afterwards to be of any use; that the old
" troops consisting of one Battalion of Guards, togather with
" Macartys, Clencartys, and Newton's Regiments, were pretty
" well armed, as also seaven Companys of Montjoys, which
" were with him, the other six haveing stayd in Derry with
" Coll: Lundy and Gus: Hamilton, the Leiftenant Coll: and
" Major of that Regiment; that he had three Regiments of
" Hors, Tyrconnell's, Russel's and Galmoy's, and one of
" Dragoons; that the Catholicks of the Country had no arms
" whereas the Protestants had great plenty, and the best
" horses in the Kingdom; that for artillery he had but eight
" small field pieces in a condition to march, the rest not
" mounted, no stores in the magazines, little pouder and
" ball, all the Officers gon for England, and no mony in
" cash.

The Prince
and Princess
of Orange's
surprize, at
the news of
the King
being gone
for Ireland.

KING JAM:
MEMᵐ.TOM: 9.
pag. 219.

This was the condition of Ireland at his Majestys landing,
there was a great deal of goodwill in the Kingdom, but little
means to execute it, which made the P. of Orange slight it to
that degree he did; but as soon as he heard of the King's being
gone thither (who he immagin'd would not come unprovided
" with what they most wanted) was hugely surprized; on
" which occasion the Princess of Orange (as the King was
" informed from a very good hand) seeing her husband in
" great trouble at the news, tould him, He might thank himself
" for it, by letting the King go as he did: When the King
heard this, and perceiv'd that his own Children had lost all
bowells not only of fillial affection, but of common compassion,
and that they were as ready as the rest of that Jewish tribe, to
cry out, tolle de terra hujus-modi, it was the more grievous, because
the hand (from which he receiv'd it) was the more dear to him;
but Providence give her likewise some share of disquiet too, on

this occasion, for this news comeing just before the time apointed for their Coronation, it put a scurvy damp upon those joys, which had left no room in her heart for the remembrance of a fond and loveing Father ; but like another Tullea, under the notion of sacrificeing all to her Country's liberty, she sacrificed her honour, duty, and religion to drive out a peacefull Tullius, and set up a Tarquin in his room.

Nor did her Sister the Princess of Denmarke express a greater sence of duty on this occasion, thō she was rather a sufferer by being postponed to the Prince of Orange, than a sharer in this unnaturall tryumph; for sending for M[rs] Dawson, in the very time she was dressing herself for that day's " solemnity, she asked her if the child which was called her " Brother, was realy the Queen's? which M[is] Dawson answered " her it was, and that she could answer for it as much as she " could, that she herself was the late Dutchesse's daughter, " haveing seen them both born, and sayd she wonder'd very " much at her Royal Highnesse's asking that Question, since " she could not forget that at her going to the Bath, when she " came to take leave of the Queen, she made her feel her belly, " upon which her Highness sayd, Madame by the Child's " stiring so strongly, I fancy you may be brought to bed ere I " return from the Bath. This instance likewise of unnaturelness " in a daughter his Majesty loved so passionetly, he had the mortification of hearing from one, that had it from Mis " Dawson herself.

But while the King's Children were reaping thus, the frutes of their disobediance, his Majesty had a sort of a short lived tryumph himself too, in the loyall and joyfull reception he met with at his first * landing in Ireland; he set out from

T O M.
IV.

1689.

The Princess of Denmark's Discours with Mis Dawson.

KING JAMES 2[d] M. Tom: 9. p. 220.

The King's reception in Ireland and entrance into Dublin.

---

* *The Journal of what passed in Ireland,* inserted by Macpherson (Vol: 1. p. 174.) from Nairne's Papers, informs us, that, " His Majesty arrived in his Kingdom of

T O M.
IV.

1689.

Cork the 20th, and arrived the 24th at Dublin; his entry there was accompanyed with all the markes of duty, honour, and affection immaginable, the streets were lined with Soldiers, and hung with tapestry, evened with gravel, and strowne with flowers and greens, the appearance of the Majestrates, Nobility, gentry, Judges, and of all ranks of people, was sutable to the most solemn cerimony of that kind, and performed with the greatest order, and decency immaginable ; The King rideing on horse back was more discernable to the people, whose lowd and joyfull acclamations made him some sort of recompence for the indignitys he had suffer'd from his other Subjects : As soon

King Jam. 2^d
Mem^{on} To: 9.
p: 286.

" as he arrived at the Castle he met with an account from
" Lieftenant General * Hamilton, of his haveing beat a great
" body of the Rebells at Drummore, that he had forced them
" as far as Colrain, and to the other side of the Ban, and had
" advanced as far as that Towne, but found the Enemy so
" numerous and so well intrenched in it, that he durst not
" attack them, and therefore desired more troops might be
" given him to driue them from that River ; upon which his
" Majesty sent Monsr Puisignan a Major General to Dungan-
" non, with some hors and foot, togather with Orders to march
" to Portlemon, being one of the passes on the Ban water
" which the Rebels defended, and by that means facilate Lief^t
" General Hamilton's passing it; the Duke of Berwick was
" order'd that way too ; and in the mean time the King him-
" self, with Monsr Rozen and the other French Officers he had

Ireland, the 12th of March, O. S. 1689, and was received at Kinsale, where he landed, with all the demonstrations of Joy imaginable." Editor.

* Macpherson has given a Marginal Note to the French Text of The Journal already cited, originally in Lord Melfort's hand, which asserts, that " The Lieu-tenant General Hamilton was advanced to this rank by the Duke of Tyrconnell, before the King's arrival, without the King's knowing any thing about it until he arrived; as also the Viscount Mount Cashell and some brigadiers." Editor.

brought with him, went as far as Armagh to visite and ”
encourage the other troops, and to be nearer Hamilton and ”
Pusignan, leaveing the Duke of Tyrconnel (which honour ”
his Majesty had lately confer'd upon him) at Dublin, with ”
directions to go thorough Lemster and some partes of Mun- ”
ster to inspect and draw togather the new raised men in ”
those two Provinces.   ”

   The eight of April therefore the King went to Charlemont ”   The Rebells
and sent Monsr Rosen and the rest of the General Officers to ”   give way at
                                                the approach
Dungannon, giveing directions to Hamilton and Pusignan to ”   of the King's
march towards Straban, the later with most of the foot and ”   forces.
some few hors and dragoons by the way of Omagh, the former ”
by an other road on the right hand near the Sea, with the ”
body of hors and dragoons and some Companys of foot. ”
When the King came on the 14th to Omagh, he found ”
Puisignan's foot already arriued, and left under the com- ”
mand of Coll: Ramsey, he himself being gon on, with the ”
hors and dragoons some six miles further to Newton Stewart, ”
which the Enemy had quitted as well as Omagh and the Rash ”
too, at the approach of the King's troops: his Majesty ”
therefore finding the Rebells withdrawn, and his own foot ”
extreamly harashed with their long marches and bad wether, ”
made them sejorn the 15th, and order'd Monsr Rosen, Monmont ”
(*Moumont*) and Lery, on, towards Straban with two troops ”
of hors and one of Dragoons; who on his arrival there, find- ”
ing that Hamilton, that very day, had forced the pass at ”
Claliford, his horse swiming cross the water because the ”
Enemy had broke the bridg, he did the like at Lifford, with ”
the three troops he had with him, and a detatchment of eighty ”
men of the foot guards which he accidentally found at ”
Straban, thõ the Rebels were intrenched on the other side; ”
and besides what was at Lifford, had above 5000 Men drawn ’
up a mile beyond the Town; yet upon Monsr Rosen's ”

" marching towards them with this handful of men, they went
" off in disorder and retired to Derry, thō it was believed the
" Rebells had at Clalyford brig, Lifford, and in the Lagon
" (which they designed to desert too) near twenty thousand
" men.

" Vpon the news of these good successes, and that some
" English ships were come into Lough foil, the King resolved
" to make what hast he could back to Dublin ; to prepare for
" the Parliament which had been call'd before he left that
" place, the time of their sitting being now near at hand, and
" likewise to hasten the march of such troops as were readyest
" to join Monsʳ Rosen ; being willing he should haue the
" honour of it, if in the consternation the Rebels were now. in,
" they deliver'd Derry up to him, but that if those ships
" brought supplys to the Town, it was probable it might hould
" out, and then it were decenter for the King not to be there,
" upon which and some other considerations his Majesty
" return'd the 26ᵗʰ to Charlemont.

" But the next day early, the King receiv'd by an express a
" letter from the Duke of Berwick, in the name of all the
" General Officers, as their opinion, That in case his Majesty
" would return to the Army, and but shew himself before
" Derry, it would infallebly surrender ; upon which the King
" took hors and went that night to Newton Stewart, wherè he
" rested a few houres, and on the 28ᵗʰ came to Straban, where
" he met with a letter from Monsʳ Rosen to acquaint him,
" that intending to march very early that morning towards
" Derry, he was confirmed in his resolution by their haveing
" sent to him to treat about the delivery of the Town, which
" he thought his apearing before, would be a means to hasten ;
" accordingly the King on his passing the River found the
" Army was march'd from Lifford, he overtook the foot some
" three miles off with Puisignan and Ramsey at their head, who

tould him Mons' Rosen was marched on before with some " TO M.
hors and dragoons ; so the King went after him, and thō " IV.
he mended his peace, did not overtake him till he was within " 1689.
a mile and half, or two miles of Derry, where he found Mons' "
Rosen marching out of the way, and going up a hill, which "
overlook'd the Town ; as soon as the hors and dragoons were "
drawn up, the King would haue sent to summons it, but "
Mons' * Rosen desired his Majesty to wait the arrival of the "
foot and the other troops with Hamilton, which the King "
agreed too, and indeed contradicted Rosen in nothing: when "
therefore the foot was come up, he posted them and the "
Dragoons, very near the Town, and sent a Trumpeter with a "
summons, who found them in very great disorder haveing "
turn'd out their Governour Lundy upon suspicion, and even "
made him a Prisoner; so they sent back the Trumpeter, "
promising to dispatch a Missinger of their own with an "

---

* An account of what passed on this occasion is given more fully in a passage, which Macpherson informs us (Vol. 1. P. 186.) is in JAMES's hand, on the margin of the French Copy of the *Journal of what passed in Ireland :* and in JAMES's Instruction to Lord Dover on his being sent to France, the Marquis de Rosen's conduct at *Londonderry,* is thus reflected on : (*Macpherson, Vol.* 1. *p.* 312. *from Nairne's Papers.*) " You are to endeavour with all the softness imaginable to have our dearest Brother recall the Marquis de Rosen, as one, after having done what he did at Londonderry, incapable to serve us usefully ; you are to inform, if need be, of his contemning our protections, by ordering to drive in and starve not only those who lived peaceably at home, but likewise those who were protected by us ; so that no promises will be believed from him, nor indeed from our Officers, till the truth of this affair be known by the Rebels. At Inniskillin they are become more numerous by much, every body running there for shelter from so unjust a violence. You shall shew how he required to be recalled, if this his project was not followed, and how he offered himself garant of the Treaty with the Town, and that if any violation of it happened he would put himself on their side ; the which procedure of his, there was nothing but the consideration of his most Christian Majesty could have made us suffer from him ; and therefore, since we will not vindicate our justice by punishing of him, we must show our dislike of his procedure by having him recalled." EDITOR.

TOM.
IV.

1689.

" answer in an houres time; but none comeing, Mons' Rosen
" proposed to the King the drawing of his troops to put them
" under cover, which was done accordingly, the foot into
" Vilages, and the hors and Dragoons into other quarters near
" them.

What made the Town in such different minds, was the arrival
of one Walker a Minister, who had put himself at the head of
the Rebels at Duncannon, and then abandoning of it at the
King's aproach, retired to Londonderry; before his arrival
Lundy the Governour thought the place untenable, and resolved
to leaue the Townesmen at liberty to make such conditions
they thought best; but this fierce Minister of the gospel, being
of the true Cromwelian or Cameronian Stamp, inspir'd them
with boulder resolutions, and thō Coll: Coningham and
Richards who had brought from England two Regiments,
ammunition, provisions &c, were forced to return without
geting that relief into the Town; nevertheless, they resolved to
bid defyance to the King and their allegiance, and chuseing
this Minister and one Baker to be Collegues in the governement
of the place, gave the first check to his Majesty's progress,
who til then, had met with little or no opposition in that
Kingdom.

KING JAM: 2ᵈ
MᴇᴍᵗʰTᴜᴍ:y.
p: 291.
The King
formes the
Siege, and
then goes back
to Dublin.

" The King therefore with the General Officers took up his
" quarters at Sᵗ John's town some fiue miles from Derry, the
" Country was full of all sortes of provisions, corn, meal and
" cattle; and the troops being much fatigued by long marches,
" and rainy wether, he let them rest all the next day to refresh
" them, and then at a Council of war it was resolved they
" should go back to Dublin, to prepare all things for the
" Parliament's meeting, and to hasten more troops to reinforce
" the Army there; that Mons' Rosen and Lery should go along
" with the King; and that Mons' Monmont and Mʳ Richard
" Hamilton, Liefᵗ Generalls; the Duke of Berwick, and Mons'

Puisignan Major generalls, Dominick Sheldon, and Lord ”
Galmoy, Brigadeers of hors, and Ramsay of foot, should ”
stay with the Army, which Monsr Monmont, as eldest Leif^t ”
General was to Command ; that they should march next day ”
to Colmore fort, and by takeing that, hinder any relief from ”
geting into the Town by water ; and after that, left it to them ”
to block it up or attach it, as they thought fit ; and accordingly ”
on the 30th the King went to Straban and the Army marched ”
to Colmore. ”

T O M.
IV.
1689.

On the first of April early in the morning, one Johnson ”
came from Colmore fort to treat about its surrender, and to ”
know whether the King was there ; So Monsr Monmont sent ”
him on to his Majesty, because he sayd they would deliver ”
it up, if they were satisfyd that he was realy there, haveing ”
been assured by those who Commanded in Derry, that the ”
King was not in Ireland ; but being admited into his ”
Majestys presence and satisfyd it was the King, he promised ”
to use his endeavours to perswade them to surrender, which ”
they did accordingly, upon articles, a day or two after : The ”
King haveing dispatched this man continued his journey to ”
Omagh, where came to him in like manner Deputys from ”
Castle Derg a strong and considerable post, which offer'd ”
to surrender too, on certain conditions ; which being granted, ”
the next morning they surrender'd it up to Coll: Lacy, whom ”
the King sent with some foot to take possession of it ; and ”
the same day went to Charlemont himself, the 3^d to Newry, ”
the 4th to Drogadah, and the 5th to Dublin ; where assoon ”
as he arrived, he took all immaginable care to haue the hors, ”
foot, and Dragoons, formed and armed as far as ten thousand ”
muskets would go, haveing sent Monsr de Pointy with some ”
of his under Officers to Kingsale, to hasten the armes from ”
thence ; My Lord Tyrconnel return'd likewise very much ”

TOM.
IV.

1689.
The condition
of Scotland,
and their pro-
ceedings at
the Revo-
lution.

" indisposed from Kilkenny, where he had been a formeing
" the Regiments in those partes.

The King's affairs were thus in a hopefull condition enough
in Ireland, and not altogather desperate in Scotland ; but to
give more perfect notion of the Situation that Kingdom was
in, it is necessary to look back a little, to what passed there
at the Revolution in England; which, not to interrupt the
narration of other passages and to make this more intelligible
was thought proper to be inserted here : When first therefore
the King sent the news of the design'd invasion to the secret
Committee in Scotland (who were the Earl of Perth the Chancellour, the Marquess of Athol, Viscount Tarbet, the Archbishop of Glacow, My Lord Belcaris and Sr George Lochart)
it was looked upon by most, only as a pretext to get mony
and assemble forces in order to other designes, which still
encreased the jealousies about Religion ; but thō the truth too
soon apear'd, yet the Marquess of Athol proueing a rotten
member in that Committee, and conceiveing hopes of raising
himself by the Prince of Orange, to whom by his Lady he had
some affinity ; had all along encouraged the admission of the
Western fanaticks into imployments, under colour of conformety to the King's inclinations, but in reality because he
knew them fit instruments to carry on the Prince of Orange's
intrest : so he obstructed and discountenanced the discoverys,
which otherwise might haue been made of private Correspondance with that Prince, by which means many suspicions, and
undue practices were overlooked, and amongst the rest, My
Lord Lorn's borrowing a great deal of mony procured him by
Sr James Mongomery, which he cuñingly pretending was to
make a present to My Lady Melford, and therefore it passed
unregarded.

But assoon as the troops were call'd out of the Kingdom to
reinforce the English Army; that awe which they had hithertwo

kept the people in, was taken off; and the dissafected partie shew'd their inclinations sooner than otherwise they durst haue done; so that when the King order'd the Chancellor to know, in what disposition the Presbiterian partie was, to acknowlidg the fauours they had experienced from him more than from any of his ancestors, they delayd answering till the Assembly met; and then, owned indeed that God had made use of him to shew them some kindness, but that being convinced it was for the sake of Popery in the bottom, and with intent to ruin them in the end (since so many were put into the highest imployments, who either professed that Religion, or were well afected to it) they therefore resolved for the future to doe, as God should inspire them; and this was all the return the King met with, from that greatfull generation, for haveing lost the Church partie for their sakes, and for haveing placed them in so easy a Situation, and render'd them, by that means, more capable of annoying him.

This had made the King's friends advise his Majesty, rather to let his troops stay in Scotland; which, with the new moddel'd Militia and a detachment from the Highland Clans would have made an Army of 13000 men, and might have laine on the borders of Scotland or North of England, to be an awe upon both; prevented all risings in those partes; and been a retreat, had things gone ill in England: but that Councel being rejected the Kingdom was left at large, which the fannaticks soon got the possession of; and formeing certain Committees or Councills, intercepted letters, and assumed in fine so great an authority, that My Lord Chancellor thought fit to send a Special Messinger, to know the King's orders thereupon; but he being of My Lord Tarbot's chuseing, went directly to the Prince of Orange, which occasion'd the dispatching My Lord Belcarris himself after him, but before any account could be had of his Message, ill news comeing

T O M.
IV.

1689.

*and then of cours ye government would vest in him, as ye next Officer of State; but they stood in awe of ye new moddel'd Militia w^h had some Officers of My Lord Dur... ton's regiment mixed with it; so My Lord Tarbot proposed their being disbanded, as an unnecessary charge, and 'n account also y^t ye P^r: of Orange had urged as a grievance, ye keeping up forces in ye time of peace, to which ye Chancellor,...
Marginal Note in the hand writing of the Son of James the second. EDITOR.

from England, encouraged the Marques of Athol (being govern'd underhand by My Lord Tarbot and Sr John Dalrumple) to declare openly for the Prince of Orange: his first contrivance in order to this, was by animateing the Rabble to dispossess the Chancellor * (being desirous to satisfy them) too easily consented; so they were all dismised except four Companys of foot, and two troops of hors.

The factious Lords being free'd from this terrour, made a further step, and with the Marques of Athol at their head went to tell the Chancellor, That they durst no longer act in concert with him, and other Papists, who were not qualifyd by Law; but that in case he thought fit to withdraw, they would then act strenously for his Majestys service: The Chancellor consulting with the D: of Gordon and others, *thought perhaps he might gain upon those by his condiscention, whom he could not* † *force,* yeilded again to this, and then retired immediately into the Country, leaveing that partie absolute masters to act as they pleased; who instead of asserting the King's right, encouraged all disorders immaginable in opposition to it; for the mob haveing assembled themselves to pull down the Catholick Chappel in the Pallace, and being repulsed by Cap: Wallace who was placed there for its defence, the Marques of Athol and the other factious Councellors signed an order for its delivery; which, thō Cap: Wallace thought not proper to obey, he was however overpower'd by the multitude, who not only plunder'd the Catholick Chappel, but pulled down the Orgain in the Abbey Church, ransacked all the Catholick houses, and had full liberty allowed to act any insollence or disorder, their malice or averice prompted them too. Dureing these bussles, the Chancellor thinking to fly in

† Interlined by the Son of James the 2^d. EDITOR.

6

disguise beyond seas, was discover'd as he went on board, and being pursued by some Seamen in a long boat, they came up with the Ship where he was, seized him, and put him in Prison,

By this time My Lord Belcarris was arrived at London, and finding the King was gon, he assembled such as were of the Council, and waited upon Duke Hamilton to consult what was best to be done for the King's service; but the Duke instead of considering that, only pressed him mightely to get the orriginal letter into his hands, which he brought from the Council to the King, with intention to accuse those who signed it, and had acted in conjunction with Catholicks, as persons not qualifyd, against whom he declamed exceedingly; but when he heard the King was come back, was in great apprehention of what he had sayd, sent for those Lords to excuse it, and no one fawned more upon his Majesty while he Stayd ; but as soon as he tooke water to go down to Rochester, he went immediately to the Prince of Orange, nor did any one contend with greater vehemence than he, to forme and model that Country, to the Vsurper's will; My Lord Arran his son proposed indeed the inviteing the King back, but few concurr'd in that, his enimys for fear of his being reestablished, and his friends for fear of his life, so he being seconded by no partie, that matter fell to the ground.

In the mean time the disafected Lords at Edinburgh, haveing got rid of the Royal partie, began to arme against one an other, all was not at peace amongst themselves, for haveing master'd the common enemy ; so prepareing the way, by addresses to the Prince of Orange, each side hasts to London, to support its credit, and intrest; the great men to be recompensed for their Zeal, the discontented to have grievances redressed, the Presbiterians to get all power into their hands, and the Lithurgie men to save themselves ; the Marques of

Athol stayd a little longer behind the rest, to exercise for a while his new gotten absolute authority which he was exceeding fond of; so haveing turn'd out his enemys, and put in his friends and creatures, he posted away after them. The fannatical partie not doubting but to carry all by their numbers, proposed in the first place, the exclusion of fiue persons, the Duke of Queensbury, the Viscount Tarbot, the Viscount Dundee, Sr George Mackensy, and My Lord Bel-carris; but the Prince of Orange was resolued to try all sides ere he made choice of any, being fearfull of raising enemys before he knew who would be his friends: this coldness made them all for posting down into Scotland again, but he denyd them passes, till he was declared King in England; which he knew would not only be a leading card to Scotland, but supposeing those Lords could not, in civility, but kiss his hand upon it, it would amount to a sort of owneing him, and by that means forestall the liberty of their own election; but he was disapointed of his expectation, for few would doe it, even of the most factious amongst them, til they had tryd the disposition of their own people, so fearefull they were of doing mischief to *themselues, y^t it had been no hard matter* * to have prevented their doing it to the King too, had that affair been more dextrously managed, or taken a more fortunate turn, when the Convention met at Edinburgh.

By this time the Marques of Athol was come up too, but haveing many enemys at the Prince of Orange's Court, was but dryly receiv'd; which put him upon changeing sides once more: so he began to court his old friends again, promising to join with them in the ensuing Convention; and there being so much need of helpe, former faults were easily overlook'd, and

---

* Added by the Son of James the 2^d. Editor.

his offer readily accepted of: But thõ all immaginable endeavours
were used by many of the King's friends and his Majesty
himself, who had sent a person with an express order that no
man should scruple setting in the intended Convention; yet
many refuseing to come, on such a call, was a great weakening
to the King's intrest, whilst on the other hand, several forfeited
persons being admited without a repeal (a thing never before
known) the Loyal partie was out number'd in the end; thõ for
the present the matter hung in suspence, and their enemys stood
in awe of Edinburgh Castle, of which the Duke of Gordon
who was the governor kept possession as yet; but hearing all
other fortes in the Kingdom had surrender'd, began to think it
rashness not to follow so general an example, so neglected
takeing in provisions (which it was always in his power to haue
forced the Towne to give him) and which he found great want
of, when upon My Lord Dundee's and Lord Belcarris's
perswasion, he resolved to hould it out till he saw what the
Convention at least would doe: which by this time was got
togather, and notwithstanding the scrupulosity of many eminent
persons who refused to apear, the Loyal partie however were
full of hopes, so that the Bishop of Edinburgh at the opening
of it, prayd for the King and his restoration; and had not
great irregularitys been used in elections, and the people
terrifyd by threats and even troops secretly brought into the
Citie, the King's cause had not been so desperate, especially
had the Marques of Athol been sincere and resolute; but his
fickle and disponding temper, made him fearfull (when it came
to the pinch) of apeareing at the head of the Loyalists, to whom
he had lately reconciled himself, and who had set him up to be
chozen President of the Convention, in opposition to the Duke
of Hamilton; but instead of forwarding his own election, he
by a servile courtship, and fain'd humility, declined it himself,
and perswaded all who depended on him to vote for his Rival:

so that ye Duke of Hamilton carryd it by 40 voices, and carryed off with him by that means at leas twenty people of distinction in that Assembly, who had purposed to stick to his Majesty's intrest, had they not been terrify'd by the Loyal parties failure in their first tentative; which gaue the Whiggs such a superiority, that there was no need of haveing recours to argument or debate, but puting every thing to the vote, most scandelously carryd all before them, contrary to Law, reason, and Religion it self.

It was about this time, that Mr Crane arrived from France with the King's letter, which was to this effect: MY LORDS AND GENTLEMEN, whereas we have been informed that you the Peers and representative of Shires and Boroughs of that our antient Kingdom, who are to meet togather at our good Town of Edinburgh some time of this instant March, by the usurped authority of the Prince of Orange; we think fit to let you know, that as we haue at all times relyd upon the faith-fullness and affection of you, our antient people, so much, that in our greatest misfortunes heretofore, we had recours to your assistance with good success to our affairs, so now again, we require of you, to support our Royal intrest, expecting from you what becomes faithful and loyal Subjects; generous and honest men; that will neither suffer your selves to be cojol'd nor frighted into any action, not becomeing true hearted Scotchmen. And that to support the honour of the Nation, you will contemn the base example of disloyal men, and eternelize your name by a loyalty sutable to the professions you have ever made to us; in doing thereof you will chuse the safest part, since thereby you will evite the danger you must needs undergo, the infamy and disgrace you bring upon your selves in this world, and the condemnation due to the Rebellious in the next; and you will likewise haue the opertunity to secure to yourselves, and your posterity, the gracious promises which we have so often made of secureing your Religion, Laws, properties and rights, which we are still resolved to performe, as soon as it is possible for us to meet you safely in a Parliament of our antient Kingdom: in the mean time fear not to declare for us your Lawfull Sovereign, who will not fail on our part to give you such speedy and powerfull assistance, as shall not only enable you to defend yourselves from any forreign attempts, but put you in a condition of asserting our right against our enemies, who have depressed the same by the blackest of usurpations, the most unjust as well as most unnaturall attempts, which the Almighty God may for a time permit and let the wicked prosper, yet then must bring confusion upon such workers of inniquity ; we likewise let you know we shall pardon all such as shall return to their duty before the last day of this month inclusiue, and that we will punish with the rigour of our Laws all such as shall stand in rebellion against us or our * authority : So not doubting but that you will declare for us, and suppress whatever may oppose our intrest, and that you will send some of your number to us, with an account of your diligence, and the posture of our affairs, we bid you heartely farewell.   Given on board the St Michel, March the first, An: D: 16⅔.   By his Majestys Command.   MELFORD.

The Prince of Orange had writ likewise to the Convention full of the same cant and hipocresie, which had so successfully

T O M. IV.

1689.

The Prince of Orange writes about the same time, and his letter is first read.

* *Bertrand de Molville* in his *History of Great Britain,* thus delivers his opinion respecting the Legality of those proceedings, which had been opposed to JAMES THE SECOND, on his withdrawing from the Kingdom : (Vol. 3. p. 478.)   " As to the unprecedented measures which were pursued at this critical juncture, and have been sanctioned both by their success and their happy consequences, it is, perhaps not amiss to observe, that had they been properly shaped into Constitutional Questions, and fairly discussed as such, their Legality might have appeared at least doubtful.   There was not indeed a single word in the Constitution, from which any absence of the King out of his Kingdom, might be construed into an Abdication of the Crown."   EDITOR.

deluded one Kingdom already; assureing them, That in as
much as he had nothing before his eyes but the glory of God
and establishing the reformed Religion, togather with the
liberties and properties of the people which had been in such
eminent danger; he doubted not of their concurrence in the
same ends, to which nothing could conduce so much, as their
union with England; being the same Iseland, haveing the
same language, and the same common intrest : This letter was
deliver'd about the same time with that from his Majesty, to
whom they had yet so much respect left, as to suffer a debate
which should haue the precedency and be first read ; that
indeed from the Prince of Orange carryd it, however the King's
was read afterwards : but the Assembly had already taken its
ply, so no further notice was had of it, and the King's partie
declineing dayly, the others went to work without any opposition, to settle the government after the moddel of their Sister
Nation : The Loyalists seeing therefore no hopes of carrying
any thing where they were, they thought of appointing an other
Convention at Sterling, but the Marques of Athol and the Earl
of Mar failing in their engagement, that project fell likewise ;
upon which the Viscount Dundee after a private conference
with the Duke of Gordon*, withdrew, and other of his Majestys

---

* This brave descendant from his ancestor Montrose, remained steadfast in
his Allegiance to James the second. *Sir John Dalrymple* describes the spirit,
with which Lord Dundee had retired from the Convention at Edinburgh, with 50
horsemen, to his followers in the Highlands: " Being asked by one of his friends,
who stopt him, *Where he was going ?* He waved his hat, and is reported to have
answered, *Wherever the spirit of* Montrose *shall direct me.* In passing under the
walls of the Castle, he stopt, scrambled up the Precipice at a place difficult and
dangerous, and held a conference with the Duke of Gordon, at a postern gate,
the marks of which are still to be seen, though the gate itself is built up." (*Vol.* 1.
P. 287.) In the second Volume Sir John Dalrymple has given Lord *Strathnaver's*
Letter to *Dundee,* advising him to make his peace; as also his spirited answer, in
which he said, " My Lord: I am extreamly sensible of the obligation I have to

friends prepared to follow as soon as they were at libertie to
do it.

1689.
My Lord
Dundee and
others who
withdraw, are
summon'd in,
but stand out.

The factious partie were not sorry to be thus freed from all
obstacles and opposition, however had some apprehention of
such as absented, and sent a Summons to My Lord Lewinston
and the Viscount Dundee to apear; the first apear'd, but the
Second excused himself on account of their visible partiality,
he Sayd, in all their proceedings, and instanced his haveing
demanded security from them, against a design to murther him,
(which he engaged to make out), but that no notice had been
taken of it in the Convention, nor could he look upon their
actions (he Sayd) as free, and unconstrain'd, which were over
awed, by such a number of troops, govern'd wholy by faction,
and against the Standing Laws of the Land; but they were
little moued with such representations, and instead of freeing
people from that umbrage, excreased their force and sollicited
the Prince of Orange to send them more from England, in order
to reduce Edinburgh Castle, and all such as should resist their
authority, which they were resolved it seems to exert to the
utmost: So without regard to their own duty, the Laws, and
Constitution of the government, or his Majestys letter, they
prepare to follow the example of England, thō not haveing the
same pretext, were forced to take an other method; they could
not ground a pretended vacansy of the Throne, upon the King's
withdrawing himself, out of a Kingdom he had never resided

---

you, for offering your endeavours for me, and giving me advice in the desperate
estate you thought our affairs were in. I am persuaded it flows from your sincere
goodness and concern for me and mine; and in return, I assure your Lordship,
I have had no less concern for you, and was thinking of making the like address
to you; but delayed it till things should appear more clear to you." . . . .
So, my Lord, having given you a clear and true prospect of affairs, which I am
afraid amongst your folks you are not used with, I leave you to judge if I or you.
your family or myn, be most in danger. EDITOR.

T O M.
IV.

1689.
The Conven-
tion of Scot-
land follows
the example
of Eng.ᵈ but
by an other
method.

in since he was King of it; and where the same forme of government subsisted, whether he was in England or France; so they go roundly to worke and declare that his Religion was a sufficient incapacity, for that being a Papist he had acted as King without takeing the Oathes, that he had invaded the fundamentall Constitution of the Kingdom, altering it from a limited monarchy to an arbitrary and dispotical one, had cass'd and annull'd the Laws at pleasure, in order to the subvertion of the Protestant Religion and liberties of the Subject; for which reasons (say they) he had forfeited his Crown, and that the Throne was thereby become vacant: These pompous words and plausible pretences are never wanting on such occasions; but when they came to an enumeration of particulars in order to proue this charge, they were either false or exceeding trivial, as that the King had erected Popish Scools and Chappels, permited Popish books to be sould, taken Protestant Noblemen's Children to breed them up Catholicks, kept a Standing Army in time of peace, made grants for exacting mony without consent of Parliam'. imposed exorbitant fines, imprison'd persons without expressing the reasons, had strecthed old and absolute Laws to forefault Several persons, particularly the Earl of Argile, subverted the right of Royal Bourroughs by imposeing Majestrats upon them, obstructed the cours of common justice by letters to chief Courts of Judicature, and granted protections against civil debts. These therefore were the crimes for which they declared he had forfeited his Crown; to which several of the King's friends, particularly the Bishop of Edinburgh replyd, That most of what was alledg'd against him, his Majesty was inocent of, and that were they true, the Ministers were to answer for such irregularity's, that they were not supposed competent judges of such matters; but that the only means to rectify abuses was to call the King back, who in gratitude would not fail to mend whatever they thought.

amis; but that in reality scarce any reign was ever exempt
from greater streethes of power than these, especially the King
resideing in an other Kingdom, and acting by his Officers, who
oft times (and in no Country more than that) make their partialitys be felt without the knowlidg, much less the approbation
of the Prince; others aledged that this accusation was in
general heads, back'd only by their bare assertion, not one real
instance made of any thing material but that of the Earl of
Argile, which was done in his Brother's Reign, and that had
they well consider'd how far they themselves contribited to the
building up what they now were so earnest to pull downe, they
could never haue the face to condemn their Prince for a
moderate use of an authority, they themselves had own'd to bě
unlimited; that his Majesty undoubtedly had done more prudently in not pretending to so absolute a power, but that
they were much more unexcusable, for treateing their Sovereign
with so much rigour for acting conformally to their former
determinations; since they could not so soon forget, to what
degree they had flatter'd him in that very point they now condemn'd. We abhor, Sayd they, in the Act for secureing the
Protestant Religion Ap: 28. 1688, all principles and positions,
which are contrary or dirogatory to the King's Sacred,
Supreme, Severeign and *absolute* authority, which none, either
private persons or Collegiate bodys can participate of, any
manner of way, but in dependance of him; and in another
Act ordain every person (when required) to swear that they
would assist, mentain, and defend the King and his Successors, in the exercise of his *absolute* power under pain of
banishment &c: If therefore the King went too far, it was
they that lead him to it, who therefore merited their prais for
going no further; but instead of returning thanks for his
great moderation, in what (if not his due) at least had their
approbation, they dispossess him of his Crown and dignity,

T O M.
IV.

1689.
They elect
the Prince of
Orange and
the Princess,
King and
Queen of
Scotland.
Vide Letters
from the
Council of
Scotland,
p. 679.

for haveing permited certain actions that did but squint that way.

After they had thus rid themselves of their Sovereign, to whom they had once owned, that no man could be an enimy that was not first so to his Country and himself (wherein they found afterwards they had not been mistaken) they proceed to an election, but first take care to vindicate their antient rights and liberties, declareing that no Papist can be King or Queen of Scotland, or bear any imployment therein; and so running through the rest, article by article, in conclusion say, That in regard the Prince of Orange (whom they call King of England) had been the glorious instrument of delivering them from Popery and arbitrary power, they doe resolve that William and Mary, King and Queen of England, be declared King and Queen of Scotland &c; limiting the exercise of the Regal, and the Succession, in the same manner as the English Convention had done, prohibiteing in like manner all correspondance with the King, or owning him as such for the future.

This reassumption of power flatter'd the people's immaginations at first, but alas it soon slip'd through their fingers, into such hands, as made them find they had gain'd nothing by the change of Masters, but the ignominy of their folly, and the guilt of their rebellion; for neither the restrictions with which they cloged the Crowne when they gave it the Prince of Orange, nor his own declameing against those intollerable stretches of power, which he pretended to remedy, hinder'd him from quartering Soldiers upon the people, nominateing Judges without subjecting them to a tryal, puting men to death without any process; nor rejecting adresses with contempt and scorne, thō pursuant to their clame of Right; which were stretches of a higher nature than had been complain'd of in reference to the King: and in a short time, the Liturgie it self, thō settled by law, was counted as idolatrus as the

6

worship of the Church of Rome, and not allow'd so much as a tolleration in the Kingdom.

T O M. IV.

1689.
The Duke of Gordon keeps Edinburgh Castle for the King for awhile, but deliver'd it the 28ᵗʰ of June.

But thō the body of the Scotch Nation were as violent and expiditious in this unjust treatment of their Prince, yet the defection was not so universal as in England ; the Duke of Gordon being still in possession of Edinburgh Castle, was a check upon that Citie, and might have had an influence over the whole Kingdom had he held it out some time longer, but when Mackay came with troops from England, he began to doubt his being able to withstand such a force, and accordingly deliver'd it up, on the 28ᵗʰ of June; which he was censured for by many, not only on account of its natural Strength, but for the hopes of relief from a body of Highlanders, which by that time began to grow so numerous, as to giue no small disquiet to the Usurpers themselves.

The Viscount of Dundee, when he first retired to the Highland, sent to beg his Majestys Commission to authorise a riseing; haveing great hopes, he said, to bring some relief to his cause, from the Loyal Clans, who had always signelized themselves for their duty and courage on such occasions : the Convention finding he stood out against their summons, were alarmed at it, so order'd the Earl of Mar to secure Sterling, and Mackay to leaue the conduct of the Siege of Edinburgh Castle to Sir John Lanier, and march with the rest of his Army against him ; but My Lord Dundee was so expeditious as to secure the Castle of Blaire ere he could come up with him, and to assemble such a number of men, as thō raw and unexperienced, was able however to make head against Mackay, and even push him the whole month of June, till the Rebells were reinforced ; and then My Lord Dundee retired to Lochaber to refresh his men, and wait for Coll: Cannon, and the Irish Regiment, commanded by Coll: Pursel, to join him ; which they no sooner had done, but heareing

My Lord Dundee relieves Blair Castle, and gains a glorious Victory at Gillicranki, but is unfortunately Slain.

that My Lord Murrey, eldest son to the Marques of Athol, had layd siege to Blair Castle, and that Mackay was upon his march to sustain him, he made such diligence to preserve it, that by an advance partie he raised the Seige, forced My Lord Murrey to retreat, and geting into Athol before Mackay arrived, resolved to wait for him there, thō many were against his venturing to engage the enimy who were so much superior, and advised him only to defend the pass; but he convinced them he should never have so good an occasion of doing it, the enemy haveing but two troops of hors which would soon be encreased, and which was what the Highlanders most aprehended; so resolved to try his fortune in the condition he was in : it was wonderful in how little a time he had raised a force able to dispute the fortune of a Kingdom, with his ungreatefull and disloyall contrymen ; it was a marke of more than ordinary prudence and industry, that could carry him through all the difficultys which usually attend such levees, where money, armes, amunition, unity, or at least a sufficient subordination is generally wanting ; however with these troops not consisting of above two thousand foot and fifty hors, he expects Mackay, who had four thousand and five hunderd foot and two troops of hors, most old regiments well officer'd and perfectly well apointed : Assoon as he had intelligence that the enimy had enter'd the pass of Killicranky, he put his men in order of * battle upon the plaine, before the Castle of Blair,

---

* *Macpherson* (Original Papers, Vol: 1. p. 371.) has given from *Nairne's Papers* the Speech which The Lord Dundee addressed on that occasion to his Highlanders : " GENTLEMEN, You are come hither this day to fight, and that in the best of causes : for it is the battle of your King, your Religion, and your Country, against the foulest Usurpation and Rebellion; and having, therefore, so good a Cause in your hands, I doubt not but it will inspire you with an equal courage to maintain it. For there is no proportion betwixt Loyalty and Treason; nor should be any betwixt the Valour of good Subjects and Traitors. Remember,

his right cover'd by the River of Tomel, his left by the Hills
of Blair, and his front by a small rivelet which ran along the
plaine, which by this time Mackay had enter'd also, and
puting his men in order of Battle too, stretched forth his line
so far, that it reached betwixt the two hills : My Lord Dundee
observeing this, did all he could to make an equal front, which
took up so much time that it was near eight a clock at night,
the 27th of July, ere the action began : the Highlanders bore
the enimys fire with great intrepiditie till they came close up
to them, and then discharging their muskets threw them away,
and fell in so furiously with their broad swords and targets, as
disorder'd Mackey's men exceedingly, who not being accustomed to such a method of fighting made but a faint resistance,
especially when their hors gaue way too ; which My Lord
Dundee chargeing in person routed entirely, and then puting
himself at the head of sixteen men only, seized the enimys
cannon and had gain'd a glorious victory, when crossing over
the plaine to give some orders on the left, where the enimy
made the most opposition, was most unfortunately * kill'd by a

---

that to-day begins the fate of your King, your Religion, and your Country.
Behave yourselves, therefore, like true Scotchmen ; and let us, by this action,
redeem the credit of this Nation, that is laid low by the treacheries and cowardice
of some of our Countrymen ; in which I ask nothing of you, that you shall not
see me do before you ; and, if any of us shall fall upon this occasion, we shall have
the honour of dying in our duty, and as becomes true men of valour and conscience : and such of us as shall live and win the battle, shall have the reward of
a Gracious King, and the praise of all Good Men. In God's name, then, let us
go on, and let this be your word, *King James and the Church of Scotland*, which
God long preserve." EDITOR.

* This appears to be a mistake, *Lord Dundee* did not die until the next morning ; and after the Battle wrote the following Letter to JAMES THE SECOND. *Macpherson* has inserted it (Vol: 1. p. 372.) from *Nairne's Papers.*

" SIR,
It has pleased God to give your forces a great Victory over the Rebells, in
which 3-4ths of them are fallen under the weight of our swords. I might say

random shot, which thō it hinder'd not the total defeat of the
Rebells, who had near two thousand men kill'd and five
hunderd taken prisoners, it proved a most fatal stroke to
the King's cause; who by it lost the man in the world the best
qualifyd, not only by his fidelity, courage, and capacity, to
manage such a war, but who knew admirably well the temper
and humours of those he was to Command, and how to
struggle with the wants and disapointments of such difficult
circomstances; he knew where to use rough, and where gentle
means, and how to accompany his punishments and rewards
with so much equity and reason, as made all he did acceptable;
and had got such an esteem and authority amongst his Countrymen, that had he lived, there was little doubt but he had soon
reestablished the King's authority in Scotland, prevented the
Prince of Orange going or sending an Army into Ireland, and
put his Majesty in a fair way of regaining England it self; but
this gave Mackay and his broken troops time to retreat to

much of this Action, if I had not the honour to command in it; but of 5000 men,
which was the best computation I could make of the Rebels, it is certain there
cannot have escaped above 1200 men. We have not lost full out 900. This
absolute Victory made us masters of the field and the Enemy's baggage, which I
gave to the Soldiers; who, to do them all right, both Officers and common men,
Highlands, Lowlands, and Irish, behaved themselves with equal gallantry, to
whatever I saw in the hottest battles fought abroad by disciplined Armies; and
this M'Kay's old Soldiers felt on this occasion. I cannot now, Sir, be more particular; but take leave to assure your Majesty, the Kingdom is generally disposed
for your service, and impatiently wait for your coming; and this success will
bring in the rest of the Nobility and Gentry, having had all their assurances for
it, except the notorious rebels. Therefore, Sir, for God's sake, assist us, though
it be with such another detachment of your Irish Forces as you sent us before,
especially of horse and dragoons; and you will crown our beginnings with a compleat success, and yourself with an entire possession of your antient hereditary
kingdom of Scotland. My wounds forbid me to enlarge to your Majesty at this
time, though they tell me they are not mortal. However, SIR, I beseech your
Majesty to believe, whether I live or die, I am intirely your's, DUNDEE." EDITOR.

Sterling, and repair his loss, which had been aliue, he would never haue suffer'd him to do. My Lord * Dundee

1689.
The affairs of
Scotland go
ill the rest of
the Campain.

When the news of this misfortune came to the King, it gaue him a fresh occasion of adoreing Providence, and contemplateing the instability of humain affairs, when one single shot from a routed and flying Army, decided in all apearance the fate of more than one Kingdom; for upon the first news of the battle many of the Conventioners were shifting for themselves, and the fright of those who fled so augmented the report of the loss, that it put the Town of Edinburgh in the last consternation, which would soon have spread itself further, had not the news of My Lord Dundee's death, moderated their fears and even make them think themselves gainers in the whole; nor were they deceiv'd in their conjecture, for the Command of the Army naturally devoulveing upon Major General Cannon, who thō a good and experienced Officer, not being conversant with the ways and humours of the Highlanders, and unaquainted with their method of makeing war, he Soon lost all the benefit of this Victory, and the advantagious disposition the generality was in on all hands to join him; for after haveing dismised five or six hunderd prisoners for want of provisions, upon their swearing never to bear armes against the King (a weak engagement with people

---

* Sir J. Dalrymple, in his Appendix, (Vol. 2. p. 16.) has inserted the Epitaph which Dr Pitcairn wrote upon The Lord Dundee:

" Ultime Scotorum, potuit quo sospite solo
   Libertas patriæ salva fuisse tuæ :
Te moriente, novas accepit Scotia cives,
   Accepitque novos, te moriente, deos.
Illa tibi superesse negat, tu non potes illi:
   Ergo Caledoniæ nomen inane vale.
Tuque vale, gentis priscæ fortissime ductor,
   Ultime Scotorum, atque ultime Grame, vale." EDITOR.

T O M.
IV.

1689.

so often perjured in point of Allegiance) it was agreed to send a detachment of a 100 foot and 12 hors in pursute of the enimy, too weak a partie to doe any execution; and yet because they found no opposition, ventring too far, were cut in pieces in St John's Town, which encouraged the enimy to rally their forces, and be able to cross Cañon's design of marching to Inverness, which forced him to return to Argile-shire, where heareing that eight hunderd * Cameronians were in Dunkel an open 'Town, he came so unexpectedly upon them with his whole force (which was now encreased to foure thousand men,) that he looked upon them as certain pray; but being a desperate people and imprudently atacked, the Highlanders suffer'd more than the Rebells, for by entring in several places at once the confusion grew so great, which was augmented by the smoke of the Town set on fire in many partes of it, that they fell foule upon one an other, and so many brave gentlemen were lost, that the others mutenying against their Generalls ill conduct, dispersed by degrees, and so put an unfortunate end to this Campaign in Scotland.

The affairs of Ireland both civil and military, thō as hopefull as those of Scotland in the begining, were no less fatall in the end, thō they held out something longer, and had they been better managed, might have had a better fate; but the Irish by reckoning themselves sure of their game, when in reality they had the wors of it, thought of nothing but settling themselves in richess and plenty, by breakeing the Act of Settlement; and by that means rais new enimys, before they were secure of mastering those, they had already on their hands.

---

* The Cameronians were commanded at Dunkeld by Lieut: Col: Cleland, a good Officer, and a man of some Poetical Genius, who was killed in the Action. He was the Father of the Cleland, whose name is subjoined to the prefatory Letter to Pope's Dunciad. EDITOR.

On the 7th of May the Parliament met at Dublin, to whom the King made the following Speech: The exemplary loyalty which this Nation express'd to me, at a time when others of my Subjects So undutifully misbehaued themselves to me, or so basely betrayd me, and your seconding my Deputy as you did in his bould and resolute asserting my Right in preserveing this Kingdom for me, and puting it in a posture of defence; made me resolve to come to you, and venter my life with you in defence of your liberties and my own Right, and to my great satisfaction I have not only found you ready to serve me, but that your courage has equall'd your Zeal.

I have always been for libertie of Conscience, and against invadeing any man's Right or libertie; haveing still in mind the Saying of the holy writ, Doe as you would be done too for this is the Law and the Profets.

. . It was this libertie of Conscience I gaue, which my enimys both at home and abroad dreaded to have established by law in all my Dominions, and made them set themselves up against me, thō for different reasons, seeing that if I had once settled it, my people in the opinion of the one, would haue been too happy; and in the opinion of the other, too great.

. This argument was made use of, to perswade their own people to join with them, and so many of my Subjects to use me as they had done, but nothing shall ever perswade me to change my mind as to that; wheresoever I am Master I design God willing, to establish it by Law, and haue no other test or distinction but that of Loyalty: I expect your concurrence in so Christian a work, and in makeing Laws against profaneness and against all sortes of debauchery.

I shall most readily consent to the makeing such Laws as may be for the good of the Nation, the improuement of trade, and releiveing such as have been injured in the late

T O M.
IV.

1689.
On the 7th of May the Parliament meets in Ireland; the King's Speech to it.

Act. of Settlement, as far forth as may be consistant with reason, justice and the publick good of my people.

And as I shall doe my part to make you happy and Rich, I make no doubt of your assistance by inabling me to oppose the unjust designes of my enemys, and to make this Nation florish.

And to encourage you the more to it, you know with how great generosity and kindness the Most Christian King gaue a sure retreat to the Queen, my Son, and my self, when we were forced out of England, and came to seek protection in his Kingdom; how he embraced my intrest, and gaue me such supplys of all sorts, as enabled me to come to you, which without his obligeing assistance I could not have done; this he did at a time he had so many and so considerable enimys to deal with, and you see still continues so to do.

I shall conclude as I haue begun, and assure you I am as sencible as you can desire of the signal loyalty you have expressed to me, and shall make it my chief study as it has always been to make you and all my Subjects happy.

The Parliament was extreamly Satisfyd with his Majestys Speech; so after haveing return'd him thanks for it, immediately brought in a bill to make a recognition of his title, togather with an abhorrance of the Prince of Orange's usurpation, and the English defection, then fell to work about finding out funds for the expence of the war, and were so liberal as to grant his Majesty 20000 ℔ ꝑ mensem for 13 months; a summe more agreeable to the King's necessitys, and their own good will, than the present abilitys of the people, considering the distruction the Nation was in; however their was little contest in that or any other business, till the bill for repealing the Act of Settlement was brought upon the stage; to which great opposition was given: The Bishop of Meath made a long and

The Parliament of Ireland is for revoking the Act of Settlement, which raised great debates.

elaborate speech against it, contending it was both unjust in it self, prejudiciall to the King and Kingdom's intrest, he thought it dangerous, he sayd, to unsettle a former foundation on which the publick peace relyd, and erect a new one which must needs be of dubious success; he did not contest, he sayd, the right of the old proprietors, but supposed that the present possessors had a better; that the former had only an equitable pretention, the latter both law and equity by means of two Acts of Parliament, the King's letters patent, and their purchasmony, he thought the reprizal offer'd no way eqivalent, as being in many cases but for life in lue of an estate of inheritance; it was, he Sayd, against his Majestys honour to rescind so many Acts of the Kings, his Father and Brother, and his own promis not to consent to it; that it was against his profit to destroy the richest Subjects, who payd the greatest part of the revenue, which the old proprietors being poor would not be able of a long time to answer, that it would ruin his Majestys reputation with his Protestant Subjects of England and Scotland, that it would ruin the trade by a removeall of Protestant Merchants efects, and destroy the publick faith, on which no one would dare to rely, if Acts of Parliament be no security; it was inconveniant, he Sayd, in point of time, as not being seasonable to look after vineards, when civil war was rageing in the Nation, and when an invasion threaten'd it; it was like divideing the skin before the beast was catch'd, that it would draw men from his Majestys service, whose eyes and hearts would be more upon their own concerns, than the King's business; and concludes, that in case there was a Rebellion in King Charles the first's time, (which he sayd he owned in his Eikon Basiliké), and Signed the Act for secureing the the adventurer's mony for suppressing it; then he thought some discrimination ought to be made betwixt the guilty and inocent, but that the bill made no distinction at all.

The Lord Chief justice Keating to back this, drew up a long adress to the King, to the same purpose, enlargeing upon all the hardshipps, inconveniences and distractions it would bring along with it, that it would be the ruin of trade and future improvements, when the foundation of the general settlement was once undone, and that Act render'd void *ex post facto*, which was good security when the purchass was made, that the Catholick purchassors would suffer with others; wherefore he beg'd that some composition might be thought of, by prescribeing more moderate ways than by depriveing so many persons of their all, w^h they had legally and industriously acquired, and that a Committee of both Houses might be appointed to enquire, whether some medium could not be found out, to accommodate as near as possible, both the Purchassers and old Proprietors.

It is certaine that many of the wise and judicious Catholicks thought such an accommodation very practicable; that the great improuements had so enhaunced the value of most estates, as would allow the old Proprietors a share of equal income to what their Ancestors lost, and yet leave a competency for the Purchassers, who might reasonably be allowed the benifit of their own labours; and in such turbulent times and difficult circomstances, it was just that all pretenders should recede (in some degree) from the full of their pretentions for the accommodation of the whole; no side being so apt to grumble, when all men share in the burthen, especially it being of that consequence to prevent an universal discontent, both for the King's present necessitys, the publick quiet and general safety of the people.

There is no doubt but the King's inclinations were the same; he saw the distraction it would breed, how it would inflame the Protestants and rob him of his most serviceable Catholicks, ruin the trade, and sink the revenue, but he cast not his own

intrest into the ballance, he sought to do what he conceiu'd
most just, and in order to it informed himself the best he could
what were their reasons and arguments, to get a true notion of
the pretentions on both sides ; it was represented therefore to
him on the other hand, what unjust grounds that Act of Set_
tlement was founded upon, that thō there might have been
disorders in the begining of those troubles in Ireland, the
greatest part soon came to their duty, and were fellow sufferers
with the King, both at home while the war lasted, and abroad
during his banishment, where they fought his battles and
supported his credit ; that in consideration of this, King Charles
the 2^d during his exile, by way of publick treaty or accommo_
dation, acquited them of all clames or forfeitures on that score ;
to which the Most Christian King was himself a witness, if not
a Guarrantee, insomuch that when King Charles the 2^d passed
the Act of Settlement, that Prince expostulated with him by a
letter (now published to the world) his recedeing from so solemn
an engagement ; that when the Act was made, there was not
time given for heareing, examining, and delivering in the clames,
whereby many inocent persons were foreclosed without being
heard ; that thō the Purchasers had a right, it was posterior to
the antient Proprietors, and that in all clames antiquity takes
place ; besides, that the very first adventerers who certainly
had the best title by vertue of the Acts $17°$ and $18°$ Car: 1: in
justice and equity had very little ; being the mony which was
advanced by them, under that pretence, was realy imployd in
raiseing forces in England to fight against the King, and that
with the consent of the adventerers themselves as was objected
against them at the Treaty of Vxbridg, that others afterwards
advanced their mony only upon votes and ordinances of the
Rebellious Parliament ; that the hardships done to the Irish in
the whole proceeding had been barberous and unhumain, that
in the qualifications required to be esteem'd inocent, any one

T O M.
IV.

1689.
See Irish Stat.
pag. 525.

Irish Stat.
pag. 800.

who had enjoyd his estate in the enimys quarters, thō he had no ways been aiding to them, was excluded; so that those who lived quietly were in reality postponed to the rankest Rebells, for it was such as was then the Possessors; that the clames of several thousands were never heard and then by an Act of explanation debar'd; and at last to disapoint others, who in spight of all the rigours had made out their inocency, or by their signal service abroad had merited justice at least, they were not to be put in possession, till the present Possessors were reprized out of lands of equal value, worth and purchass, which the late King Charles was made to believe might be easily found, but in reality never was; or at least such lands as might have been so disposed of, the great men, as My Lord of Ormonde, Anglesey, Orrery, Coot, Kingston &c, surreptitiously got grants of; so that nothing being left to reprize the Cromwelians, very few or none of the old Proprietors were restored: in fine, those crying unjustices in the origin were so fully represented to the King, and he at the same time as good as tould underhand, that if he consented not to it, the whole Nation would abandon him, there was a sorte of necessity of contenting them, but at the same time for the quiet of his Conscience and to keep cleer from all apearance of unjustice under so harsh an alternatiue, his Majesty consider'd the prospect he had of reprizeing the Purchasers out of the present forfeitures; for in the first place the greatest number of them were in actual rebellion, and their clames extinguished by it, and such as were not, the forfeitures of others might be sufficient to compensate, and accordingly an Act of Attainder was passed against all such as were in actuall Rebellion, or had withdrawn themselves out of the Kingdom, unless they return to their Country and duty in a certain time prefixed, to surrender themselves: so that haveing well weighed the reasons on all sides, the necessity on one hand, of not

disgusting his Irish Subjects on whom he wholy depended, and
the prospect he had on the other hand of recompensing any
one who suffer'd undeservedly, determin'd his Majesty at last
to give his Royal assent, thō he saw plainly it was hugely prejudicial to his intrest.

But this was not the only instance of his Majestys readyness,
to sacrifice his intrest to the publick Satisfaction, for he agreed
also to his being foreclosed in the Act of Attainder from the
power of pardoning those comprized in it; that the Acts of the
English Parliament should not be binding in Ireland, nor that
writs of errour or apeals should be carryed from thence into
England, which were such diminutions of his Prerogative, as
nothing but his unwillingness to disgust those who were otherwise
affectionate Subjects, could have extorted from him: It had
without doubt been more generous in the Irish, not to have
pressed so hard upon their Prince, when he lay so much at
their mercy, and more prudent not to have grasped at regaining
all, before they were sure of keeping what they already possessed; had it been differ'd till they had droue out the Invaders,
the King might have done it with a better grace, and they been
securer of enjoying the benefit: But whatever his Majestys
sentiments or reluctancy might be to the passing these Acts,
tis certain he gave his Royal assent with a good will to that for
Libertie of Conscience, which granted a free exercise of
Religion to all that professed Christianity, without any penalty,
loss, or molestation whatever; which the provocations he then
had from the generality of Protestants in Ireland, as well as
ells where, and the Superiority of his Catholick Subjects in that
Kingdom, was a demonstration that his so much contending
for that liberty, proceeded from a settled judgment, of its being
most conformable to reason, justice and true Christian
moderation.

The King
grants Libertie
of Conscience
by Act of
Parliament in
Ireland.

TOM.
IV.

1689.

A Proclamation
published on
this occasion
in England.

This was thought a fit occasion to remind the English likewise, how unjustly they had traduced the King in misrepresenting his intentions therein ; so a Declaration was published there, to the same efect, which thō it was done without the King's privity, yet being approued of by him afterwards, and giveing a true relation of the King's conduct in those matters, makes it proper to be inserted here : ALTHOUGH the many Calumnies and dismal Stories by which our enimys have endeavour'd to render us and our government *odious to the world, do now apear to have been advanced by them, not

---

* There was however one distinguished Character, who in a manner that reflected the highest honour both on herself and on King William, vindicated the Character of JAMES THE SECOND : The PRINCESS SOPHIA having in a former Letter thanked King William for his intentions of bringing the Family of Hanover into the Line of Succession, thus, in a second, addressed to that Monarch on his elevation to the Throne, delivered her sentiments respecting JAMES. *(Dalrymple's Memoirs, Appendix* V. 2. P. 22.)

" SIR,

" After the profession which I have always made of being an humble servant to your Majesty, I believe you cannot doubt of the part which I take in every thing that contributes to your elevation and your glory : Yet I lament KING JAMES, who honoured me with his friendship. I should be afraid that your Majesty would have a bad opinion of my sincerity, if I concealed from you this sentiment. I am even persuaded that my candour will give you a better opinion of me, and that your Majesty will the more easily believe the protestation which I make you of my prayers for your prosperity, and of the opinion I have, that you deserve the Crown which you wear, in a thousand respects which I am unable to name, from the fear of shocking your modesty. However, as it has pleased God to make your Majesty the Protector of our Religion, I hope you will put it also in a state to have its arms free, to assist us poor mortals, who, by the desolation of our neighbours, are near to that roaring beast which endeavours to devour us, in order that all those who are not Papists may successively maintain the Religion we profess to all eternity, in England and elsewhere ; and that Your Majesty may count among the most zealous, one who shall be all her life,

SIR,

Your Majesty's

(Translation.)   Most humble and most obedient Servant,

SOPHIA, P: PALATINE."

EDITOR.

only without any ground but against their own certain knowlidg, as is evident, by their not ventering to attempt the
proveing those charges to the world which we cannot but hope
have open'd the eyes of our Subjects, to see how they have
been imposed upon by deceiving men, who to promote their
own ambitious ends, care not what Slavery they reduce our
Kingdoms too; yet we cannot but rejoice we have had an
opertunity, to demostrate the falseness and malice of their
pretences, since our arrival in this Kingdom of Ireland, by
makeing it our chief concerne to satisfy the minds of our
Protestant Subjects, that the defence of their Religion, priviledges and properties, is equally our care with the recovery of
our rights; to this end we have prefer'd such of them (of whose
loyalty and affection we are satisfyd) to places both of the
highest honour and trust about our person, as well as in our
Army; we have, by granting our Royal protection to such
whose minds were shaken by the arts of our Rebellious Subjects,
dispell'd their aprehentions and effectually secured them
against the attempts of their private enemys, our ears have
been always open to their just complaints, and so far hath our
Royal mercy extended to those who are in armes against us,
that we have actually pardon'd severall hundreds of them, and
the most notorious criminels are kept in an easy confinement,
as they themselves acknowlidg.

We have taken care that our Subjects of the Church of
England be not disturbed in the exercise of their Religion, the
possessions of their Benefices and properties, and all Protestant
dissenters enjoy libertie of Conscience without any molestation;
and out of our Royal care for the prosperity of our people, we
haue recommended to our Parliament as the first thing necessary
to be dispatched, to settle such a security and libertie both in
temporal and Spiritual matters, as may put an end to those
divisions as have been the source of all our misfortunes, being

resolved, as much as in us lys, to.entail libertie and happiness
upon our people, so far as to put it out of the power of our
Successors to invade the one, or infringe the other ; and this
we take God to witness was always our design, of which wee
see our Subjects here are more and more convinced, by the
great numbers of those who (haveing been seduced or frighted
by the restless importunities of our enimys) are return'd to
their Country and habitations; and who assure us dayly more
would follow, if the Ports were open ; but the Vsurpers know
too well the sincerity of our intentions, to permit a free passage
of our Subjects, fearing nothing more than that their experience
should undeceive the rest, who are restained more by ignorance
than any ill intention, and therefore deny them that libertie
which we afford to all whose designes we are satisfyd tend
not to the disturbance of the peace.

By this our gracious and Royal care of our Protestant
Subjects here (where the greatest part of our Nation is
Catholick), and have as well as we received the highest
provocations from their fellow Subjects of contrary perswasions, so that nothing but our own inclination to justice, and
desire to see our people florish, could move us to such a proceeding, I hope our Subjects of England will make a judgment
of what they expected from us. And we doe hereby promis and
declare, that nothing shall ever alter our resolutions, to pursue
such and all other methods, as by our Subjects in Parliament
shall be found proper for own common security, peace and
happiness. And that none may be debarr'd assisting us in
the recovery of our right, and redeeming our people from
their present Slavery out of any aprehentions from past
miscarriages ; we doe hereby assure all our Subjects of what
quality soever, let their crimes against us be never so
great, that, if in twenty days after our apearing in person
in our Kingdom of England, they return to their obedience,

by deserting our enimys and joining with us, we will grant
them our full pardon, and all past miscariages shall be for-
getten, so little do we delight in the blood or ruin of our
people; but if after this our gracious condescension they
shall Still continue to assist our enimys and Rebells, we do
before God charge all the blood which shall be afterwards
shed, upon them and their adherents; and we doubt not but
by the blessing of God upon our arms to force the most
obstinate to their duty, thō as we haue made apear in reduceing
our Rebellious Subjects in this Kingdom we desire to use no
other remedy than lenity and mercy. Given at our Court in
Dublin Castle, the 18ᵗʰ may 1689 &c.

The Parliamentary business being at an end, the King had
more time to attend to those of armes, the fortune of which
began to ballance a little and rather seem'd to incline to his
enimys; the garison of Derry being very resolute and neer
upon as numerous as those that besieged it, made the enterprize exceeding difficult, they made frequent sallys, and thō
they were beat back with considerable loss *for the most part,*
*yet it was not without * loss* on the King's part likewise, amongst
which was Monsʳ de Monmont, the Commander in Chief of
his Majesties forces; the breach also advanced slowly by the
smallness of the guns, however on the 4ᵗʰ of June the besiegers
made a vigorous assault upon the wind mill worke, and thō
they return'd several time to the charge, were nevertheless
overpower'd at last and forced to retreat, however they continued still battering the Town, and throwing in bombs, which
did considerable damage, but nothing did so much as want of
provisions, the scarcity of which had brought a contagious
distemper amongst them, and made them begin to dispaire of

TOM.
IV.

1689.

What passed
at the Siege
of London-
derry which
the King is
forced to rais
at last.

---

* Interlined by the Son of James the second. EDITOR.

houlding it out, when on the 15ᵗʰ of Juné, they saw a Fleet of
some 30 sail apeàr in the Lough; they not doubting but it
came from England, and that it brought what they wanted, it
gaue new life and vigor to the besieged, and caused Lieftenant
General Hamilton (upon whom the Command of the King's
Army was now devolved) to order the artillery to be brought to
Charles fort, where the river was narrowest, and at the same
time caused a boom to be drawn coss it; this he thought
would so secure the passage that it might be à fit time to offer
them conditions, promising indempnity for what was passed,
with security, and freedom of Religion for the future; but they
were obstinate and deaf to all proposalls, which put Monsʳ
Rosen (who by this time was arrived at the Army) upon
makeing a mighty Severe * Order, it was to assemble togather
all the Protestants in the ajacent parts, and force them into
the Town, thereby to consume the little remains of provisions
the sooner, threatening at the same time to burn and destroy
the Country to prevent any succors from subsisting which
might come from England; and that not only such as were
in actual rebellion should be lyable to military execution, but
their friends and adherents likewise: but this was too harsh an
order to be aproved of by so mercifull a Prince, who when
the news of it came to Dublin, and that the Bisshop of Meath
had represented the Severity of it to his Majesty, he tould him,
he had heard of it before and had sent orders to stop it, that
Monsʳ Rosen was a forreigner, and perhaps used to such

---

* This Order was dated June 30ᵗʰ, and is given at length in *The Life of James
2ᵈ,* that was published in 1702, 8vo, pages 420, the year after his death. It contains some curious papers. During this Siege the Besiegers lost above 8000 men,
and about 100 officers. The Besieged were reduced from 7350 to about 4300,
whereof at least the fourth part were rendered unserviceable. Mareschal Rosen's
Order is also inserted by *Ralph* (Vol. 2. p. 125.) EDITOR.

proceedings as were strange to us, and that if he had been T O M.
his own Subject he would haue call'd him to an account for * it :   IV.
In the mean time the Besieged were reduced to the last   1689.
extremity, the garison diminished nere two thousand men;
and the famin so great, that horsflesh, cats, dogs, and even
rats and mice, were sould at great prices, so that it was
expected every houre when le Town would submit, but it
seems providence order it otherwise : Major General Kerke, a
person hugely favour'd by the King while he was on the
throne, was the man who commanded this intended succour
to the Town, and as he was one of the first examples of that
signal ingratitude of rebelling against so bountifull a Master in
England, so he was the first that gave a check to his Majestys
Successes in Ireland ; Walker the Governor had found means
to acquaint him in what extreamity they were, so he resolved

---

* Macpherson, in his *Original Papers*, (Vol. 1. P. 207.) gives from *Nairne's Papers* the following Letter which JAMES sent to the Mareschal de Rosen :

" JAMES, R.   Trusty and well beloved.   We have received your project, and we wished we had seen it, before you had issued any Orders to put it in execution. We are thoroughly persuaded that you have seen none of the Declarations, in which we have promised our protection, not only to those who chuse to submit to us and live peaceably at home, but also to all those who chuse to return to their habitations, and behave as good subjects for the future; as we are convinced that in that case you would not have issued orders so contrary to our intentions and promises.   It is positively our will, that you do not put your project in execution, as far as it regards the men, women, and children, of whom you speak ; but, on the contrary, that you send them back to their habitations without any injury to their persons; but with regard to your project of pillaging and ravaging the neighbourhood of Londonderry, in case you are obliged to raise the Siege, we approve of it as necessary to distress our Enemies.   We believe your presence so necessary for the success of our arms before Londonderry, that it is our pleasure you remain there till further orders. . . . . Given at our Court, at Dublin Castle, this third day of July 1689."—Macpherson afterwards subjoins the Circular Letter which JAMES issued, forbidding Mareschal de Rosen's order from being obeyed. In a former Note (p: 333.) has been given JAMES's Letter, desiring that Rosen might be recalled.   EDITOR.

T O M.
IV.

1689.

to venter all for their relief, and on the 30th July order'd the
Montjoy, and Phenix, two Ships leaden with provisions, and
the Dartemouth frigat, to force their way if possible ; accordingly when the tyd serued they bore up towards the Town,
and sustaining a furious fire from both sides the river, at last
came up to the boom upon which the Montjoy struck and
rebounded back with the violence of the blow, but at the
Same time broke the chain, So that the three ships got up to
the Town, without any considerable damage, and by that
means took away all hops of forceing the place; where upon
the very next day Monsr Rosen raised the Siege, and withdrew the weak remains of his harashed troops, to put them
for some little time into quarters of refreshment.

My Lord
Montcassel is
worsted, and
taken prisoner
by the Innes-
killingers.

The ill success of this enterprise gaue a turn to his Majestys
fortune, which now began to decline in other places too.
Inneskilling had follow'd the example of Derry and refused
the favorable offers My Lord Galmoy by the King's apointment
had made them, and thō the Duke of * Berwick during the
Siege of Derry had defeated a considerable body of the
Inneskillengers, it made no impression upon their stubborn
temper, or slacken'd their resolution of houlding out ; So My

King Jam: 2^d
Mem^{rs} Tom: 9.
p. 293,

" Lord Montcassel was sent against them with three whole
" regiments of foot, two of Dragoons, and some hors, being
" all the troops the King could draw togather at that time,
" haveing with himself at Dublin but one Battalion of Guards,
" Grace's regiment of foot, and not aboue two troops of hors.
" and Dragoons, besides his troop of Guards which was then
" but begining to be mounted. The Inneskillingers advanced
towards him as far as Neuton Butler, where My Lord.
Montcassel haveing passed a causey in the middle of a

---

* The Duke of Berwick had marched towards Inniskillen July 4th. Editor.

bog, came down upon the enemy in very good order, haveing
so posted his cannon, that it was very seruiceable to him;
for which reason the Rebels made a furious attack on that side,
and made themselves masters of it at last; so that thō the foot
fought with great obstinacy, and the General did all that
could be expected from a braue and experienced Officer,
yet the King's hors soon giveing way, the rest were totally
routed and My Lord Montcassel Very ill wounded, and taken
prisoner.

These disadvantages in the field raised the King more enimys
at home; for thō the Protestants of Dublin and in most other
partes had submitted to him at his first arrival, yet upon these
Successes of their breethren in the North, gave broad signs of
their satisfaction, which made it not safe to trust too much to
their pretended fidelity; so his Majesty order'd them by Proclamation to deliver in their armes, and prohibited their
meeting in great numbers: but to let them see he had no
further end in it, than to provide his own security, without
the least intention to invade their propertie or Religion, he
published soon after a Proclamation for surrendring all the
Protestant Churches which had been seized upon by the
Catholicks, and took great care to have all grievances of that
nature redressed, no misbehaveour on their part forceing him
to recede from those settled maxims of justice and clemency
which he thought due to his Subjects, who were dutifull at
least in their exteriour comportment, thō he had reason to
suspect their inclinations were the same with their Breethren,
who were in actual rebellion against him.

Thō the Situation of the King's Military affairs were declined
sufficiently, yet the civil were much lower, the mighty Scarcety
of silver had forced him with the advice of his Council to
coin a great quantety of brass and coper mony, makeing what
was not above the intrinsick value of halfepenny, to pass for a

shilling and so proportionably ; this put an obligation upon him of regulateing the change of guineas and the price of goods in the markets, which was so prudently done that for sometime it had no ill effect upon the commerce, and was of great relief to the King's necessitys : but this proveing too easy a resource when his Majestys wants excreased, occasion'd the coining twice as much as was ye usual current cash of the Nation, which made it such a drug, that things were soon sould for treble the rate they had formerly been at, and brought a mighty Scarcety of corn, cloath and indeed of all things necessary for life ; because no one was willing to part with his goods for mony of so low a value, if they could any ways subsist without it ; but what quite ruined the credit of this new invention, was the bringing in of some french mony with other necessary succors, which caused such a confusion between the great inequality of coins, that the importation of forraign gold and silver, which generally is the most solid benifit to a Country, proued in some measure the ruin of this.

The Sea fight in Bantry Bay the 1st of May.

This supply had been brought by a Squadron of French Ships commanded by the Count de Chateaurenaud, which the Prince of Orange haveing intelligence of, sent out Admiral Herbert with a sutable number of frigats to intercept ; but they been got to the cost of Ireland ere the English came in sight of them, the French Admiral wisely avoided an engagement till he had executed his Commission, and put a shore what he was charged with ; and the next morning the English standing in to the Bay of Bantry where the French lay at Anchor; they immediately got under sail and bore down upon them with so much fury, that tho the English made a good defence for a while, and several endeavours or efforts to get the wind, were at last forced to give way, leaving the dominion of those seas to the French for whom they had hithertoo bore so great

a contempt*. The world was astonished on one side to see   T O M.
the English not only worsted in the Soldier's part, but in the   IV.
Seaman's too, and on the other hand, that the French let   1689.
slip so favorable an opertunity of transporteing the King and
his Army into England, which now was hardly to be subsisted
in the Country where it was. But the French on this as on
most other occasions, drew no further advantage from their
Victory, than the glory of geting it, otherwise they might at
least have prevented the sending forces from England, till his
Majesty had recruted his Shatter'd · troops, after the late
disadvantages in the North.

But no leasure was allow'd for that, ere the King's intel-   The ill state
ligence from England assured him, of a speedy invasion "   of the King's
affairs in
from thence; the Siege of Derry, as was sayd, being newly "   Ireland.
King Jam: 2ᵈ
raised, the troops which came from thence were in a·very "   Mᴇᴍⁿ. To: 9:
pag: 293.
ill conditions; the length of the Siege, the badness of "
wether, the frequent Sallys (those within being as numerous "
as those without) the unwholsomness of the place where they "
encamped, with the contagious distemper that was got in ·"
amongst them, had in a manner destroyd the Army, so that "
no service could be expected from it of a considerable time; "
My Lord Montcassel entirely routed, Bregadier Sarsfield, "
who commanded at Sligo and had with him two or three "

---

* " The English Officers and Seamen," says *Dalrymple*, (Vol. 1. p. 332.)
" termed it a defeat, not to have been victorious on their own Element; and the
French accounted it a Victory, because they were not defeated. . . . . When the
news of this advantage reached Ireland, D'Avaux, the French Ambassador
hastened to Jᴀᴍᴇѕ to inform him that the English Fleet had been defeated by the
French : Jᴀᴍᴇѕ, with a generous peevishness, answered, *C'est bien la premiere
fois donc.*" — Thus did he exemply the truth of those sentiments, which he had
addressed from Sᵗ Germains to his Privy Council; (page 289.) " Neither the provocation or ingratitude of our own Subjects, nor any other consideration whatsoever,
shall ever prevail with us to make the least step contrary to the intrest of the
English Nation, *which we ever did and ever must look upon as our own.*" Eᴅɪᴛᴏʀ.

" regiments of foot, with a few hors and Dragoons, was obliged
" to quit that post when the Inneskilliners marched towards
" him, after the defeat of My Lord Montcassel; the rest of
" the troops dispersed about the Kingdom ; Major General
" Bohan was left at Charlemont, with a regiment of foot, and
" some of Purcell's Dragoons, Sr Charles Carny at Colrain.
" with one or two Regiments there, and an other higher up
" upon the Ban water to secure that river : Coll: Maxwell
" commanded at Caricfergus, Belfast, and all betwixt that
" and the Newry, haveing but two Regiments of foot in a
" bad condition, one troop of hors and a few ill armed
" Dragoons: In Drogedah was left four Regiments, and
" Monsr D'Anglour at Athlone with some foot, My Lord
" Clare commanded in Munster, Lord Tyrone in Waterford,
" Lord Limerick in Limerick, in which places and Kingsale
" were only the ordinary garison ; all the troops which had
" passed Drogedah were to remain about Dublin to refresh
" and recrute themselves, and were not got into their quarters
" when the King had an account that on the 13th of August,

Schomberg
lands in Ire-
land with an
Army on the
13th of Aug.

" Monsr Schomberg was landed at a place called Bangor
" some few miles from Belfast, that Maxwell not being able
" to oppose the enimy with so small a force, had left in
" Caricfergus Macarty Moor's Regiment, and some companys
" of Cormach Oneal's, and was retired to the Newry.

" The news of so considerable and so well appointed an
" Army's landing, togather with the present ill condition of his
" Majestys troops, So dispersed, and so few of them nere
" Dublin, struck such a consternation amongst the generality,
" as made them giue all for lost; thinking it impossible to resist
" so powerfull an Army, or to hinder their being master of
" Dublin even in a very few days; for besides what Schomberg
" brought with him, the Inneskillingers were much increased
" by their successes, and it was believed the generality of the
" Protestants would rise on this occasion, their disafection

appearing manifestly before : These considerations made "
many propose to the King to think of Securing his person, "
which they Sayd was not to be done but by gathering what "
troops he could togather, and marching Streight to Athlone, "
endeavour to defend the Shannon, and secure the province "
of Connough till winter, by which time he might expect "
succours from France ; that if he did not this, speedily the "
Inneskillingers would cut betwixt (*him*) and Athlone, Schom- "
berg would in the mean time advance towards *Dublin, so y* "
if y King attempted to go * towards* Drogedah, they would "
have him betwixt them. "

   This was what the French Ambassador, Mons* Rosen and "
Severall other of the French Officers were continually repre- " The French Officers dissenting to the King, and were so imprudent (the French " swadetheKing from marching
Ambassador excepted) as to make the same Sort of reasoning " towards the enimie, but he
the Subject of their publick discours, which comeing from " resolves to do it.
men of experience and so well versed in the trade, encreased "
the consternation to a great degree ; but all their arguments "
and aprehentions could not prevail upon his Majesty to take "
any such measures, he was resolved not to be tamely walked "
out of Ireland, but to have one blow for it at least ; My Lord "
Tyrconnel, some of the French Officers, and many of his own "
Subjects concured with his Majesty in this resolution, so he "
dispatched away the Duke of Berwick to command the "
troops about Newry, and keep the place as long as he could, "
and order'd S* Charles Carny to quit Colrain and come off "
by the way of Charlemont for fear of being cut by the enimie; "
and the King himself went on the 26th of August to Drogedagh "
to encourage his own men, and be nearer the enemie that he "
might better observe their motions ; he took with him a "
hundred of his hors guards, two hundred of Parker's regi- "

---

    * Interlined by the Son of James the second. EDITOR.

" ment of hors, which were all that were then in a condition to
" march, and left the Duke of Tyrconnel behind at Dublin
" (who was then not fully recover'd) to hasten the troops after
" him as fast as they could be got into a condition to march.

" Some days after the King set out, one Dean, an Officer
" of Schomberg's Army, belonging to the ordinance, who had
" quited him the day after his landing, came over to him, and
" gave his Majesty an account of the strength of his forces,
" and that the Prince of Orange had sent Bentinck down to
" Chester where Schomberg then was, to hasten him away,
" which made him set sail eight days sooner than he intended ;
" he tould him how many were already come ashore and how
" many to land, that in all they made two and twenty . Bat-
" talions reckoning what Kerk had already brought, of which
" three regiments were french, two Dutch, the other Seaventeen
" English, togather with six Regiments of hors and two of
" Dragoons, a train of Artillery of twenty pieces of ordinance
" and Six mortars, a considerable summe of mony, and all
" other necessary answerable to such an Expedition.

Shomberg
takes Caric-
fergus, and
then marches
towards
Newry.

" While they were puting these things ashore he besieged
" Caricfergus, and thō a very weak place was forced to attack
" it in form, and it defended it self eight days, a much longer
" time than any body could haue immagined, kill'd a great
" many of his men, and had good conditions at last; thō they
" were not kept, for Schomberg suffer'd the Scotch Protestants
" of the Country to take their armes from them, and after that,
" and other barberous usage, to keep them three days near
" Lisnegarvy in the nature of prisoners, before he let them
" come to Newry. Assoon as he was Master of Caricfergus,
" he advanced by easy marches with his whole army, which
" by that time was all come ashore, and Kirk had likewise
" join'd with his body of men too. In the mean while some of
" the King's foot began to come up to him, and had the hors

been in a condition to haue donc the same time enough, his "

Majesty had resolved to haue marched to Dundalke in person, "
and haue disputed that post with the enemie ; which could he "
haue done, would haue bcen of mighty consequence, ·for it "
would not only haue preserued all that plentifull country "
behind him, but haue kept the enemie on the other side the "
mountains, betwixt that and the Newry which was all ruined, "
or haue obliged them to take a great compass about through "
the mountains, and barren Country betwixt that and Armagh, "
if they design'd to march towards Dublin, which it was "
believed Schomberg would not have done ; for he must have "
quited the Sea cost, and by· consequence haue wanted the "
provisions on board his ships.

With this design therefore the King sent Major General "
d'Escô, with two regiments of foot and two hundred of "
Parker's hors to Dundalke to view the Town and Country "
about it, to giue the King an account if it was as good a "
post as was believed and could be made good against the "
enemie ; and his Majesty had this farther prospect in it, to "
secure the Duke of Berwick's retreat from Newry, if he should "
be hard pushed by them, which upon d'Escô's arrival at "
Dundalk, he found the Duke of Berwick had been obliged "
too ; the town being on the other side of the river, and the "
Enemie come. within four miles of it, to prevent their "
receiveing · any benefit from the fourage there, he burnt it "
and retired to Dundalk. Assoon the King was advertised of "
this he ordered him to come to Droghedah, there not being "
troops sufficient to make good the other Post, so the enemie "
possessed themselves of it ; Mons! Schomberg with the general "
Officers and some regiments for their security quarter'd in "
the Town, but his Army remain'd on the North side the river, "
their right towards the mountain Slugnelen and their left "
towards the Sea, where he waited the arrivall of his great "

Schomberg
comes to
Dundalk, and
threatens he
will march
stright to
Dublin.

" artillery, which by reason of the badness of the way, he had
" sent by Sea, from Carickfergus to Dundalk, and then (as
" the discours of the Enemies army was) they intended to
" march Streight to Dublin and were so confident of efecting
" it, without much resistance, that they had marked down
" their marches, and even the day they would be there; and
" to alarm and delude the King's forces still more, they sent
" some ten or twelve Vessels to make a shew of landing, first
" at Sherrys, afterwards at Dublin, and gave it out they ex-
" pected ten thousand Danes, which they pretended were to
" land in Munster, togather with some English forces from
" Bristol and Milford haven; and this most of the Protestants
" of Dublin and other places who were ready to rise, did not
" only believe, but reported about, which gaue occasion to
" the French Ambassador, Monsr Rosen, &c, their pressing
" his Majesty again to secure his retreat to Athlone, that it
" was impossible to defend the Boin which had so many
" fords both aboue and below Droghedagh, against so numerous
" and well apointed an Army, with so weake, so ill armed
" and so raw a boddy of men, as his Majestys forces were
" composed of; that if Monsr Schomberg declined marching
" streight to him, he might take to the right which was an
" open Country, and steal a march towards Trim, and so be
" assoon at Dublin as the King, and by that means cut off his
" retreat to Athlone; they conceiv'd it therefore necessary,
" that his Ma^{t}y should lay aside all thoughts of defending the
" Boin, but chuse some other post betwixt (it) and Dublin, and
" order the Duke of Tyrconnel with the troops which were to
" march from thence, to stop at Swords or some other place
" about half way, so that he might still haue an eye towards
" Athlone; and to reinforce this argument, sayd, If Monsr
" Schomberg sent but two or three thousand men by sea and
" put them ashore near Dublin, they by the help of the

Protestants might be able to master the Town, when all the
King's forces were at such a distance as Droghedagh.

But all these specious reasonings made no impression upon
the King, who tould them, That if once he made a step back,
the whole Country would be so disharten'd as to give all up,
that the new raised troops would dwindle away to nothing,
and that whosoever had any thing to loos would run in to the
Enemy to seeke protection, when they saw the King about
to desert them, which they would haue reason to believe, if
he durst not looke the Enemie in the face, that if he could
not defend the Boin, the same argument would 'hould for any
other place betwixt (*it*) and Dublin.

By this time the King's troops began to come up, so he
formed a camp, and found his men both Officers and Souldiers hearty, resolute, and convinced that nothing but Victory
could secure them from loosing their liberty, their estates,
and Religion ; nevertheless the French ceased not perswadeing
the King to retire towards Athlone and by consequence to
desert Dublin, even the very night before the Duke of Tyrconnel came to Droghedagh (who brought with him the
remainder of the troops) they pressed him with more
vehemence than ever to come to some resolution as they
called it, which was in efect to abandon all : but when the
King tould them, he would not alter his mind till he had
spoke with My Lord Tyrconnel, they then redubbled their
arguments and earnestness, which made the King tell them
with something more warmth than usual, that he would not
doe so irrational a thing, that he was positively resolved to
fight the Enemie, it being neither agreeable to his temper,
nor reputation to abandon Dublin, and make So shamefull
a retreat unless he was forced to do it.

The next day the Duke of Tyrconnel came up and gaue the
King an account of the condition, and number of his troops,

1689.
The King
haveing
assembled his
Army at
Droghedagh,
resolves to
march towards
the Enemy,
thő the French
were hugely
against it.

301.

" and what he had left with Mr Symon Lútterel the governor
" of Dublin, upon which his Majesty called the Ambassador
" and all the generall Officers to consult what was fit to be
" done; the Duke of Tyrconnel and the rest of his own Sub-
" jects were unanimously of his own opinion, the Duke more-
" over assured them, there was not corn enough in Connock
" to Subsist twenty thousand men two months; upon which
" the King resolved now he had got his army togather which
" consisted of near that number, to advance towards the
" enemy, being they came not towards him; but remain'd still
" at Dundalk, thō their Cannon and Stores were put on shore,
" and the Inneskillingers had joined them with two regiments
" of hors, as many of foot and one of Dragoons such as

The King
came to Ardee
the 14th of
Sept^r.

" they were; accordingly upon Holy Rood day the 14^h of
" Septembre they marched to the Town of Ardee, situated upon
" a small river about eight miles from Droghedagh, and the
" same distance from Dundalke, some three miles on the left
" hand of the road in a very plentifull country.

" The French Ambassador was for this march, but not
" Monsr Rosen, who according to his wonted caution, would
" never give any advice but retire and avoid fighting, not
" that he wanted courage, for no man had more, or more
" experience in the war, but it was his misfortune to be over
" cautious; besides he had writ into France (as the King was
" informed) that it was impossible for his Majesty to get an
" Army togather, and when he saw the contrary, had a mind
" it should do nothing.

" The King expected to haue found the Enemies Army
" advanced as far as that place, haveing notice by his parties,
" and spys, that some of the Inneskillingers (whom the Enemie
" still Sent before them) had been there, and had order'd the
" inhabitants, who were most Protestants, to brew and bake
" for their Army; besides it was reasonable to believe, Monsr

Schomberg would advance thither to be master of that plen- "
tifull Country and oblige the King to eat up his own behind "
the Boin, nor could his Majesty immagin, or ever hear any "
reason why he did it not, so he found the cost cleer, and "
haveing made this step, and being informed by deserters that "
many, as well French as his own Subjects, had a mind to "
come over to him, upon the first opertunity, he thought it not "
improper to advance still nearer them, both for that reason "
and to observe their motion more narowly, and finding his "
men in so good heart, was desirous to come to a battle, he "
haveing as many men and better hors than the Enemie, and "
superior to them in Dragoons. Monsr Rosen and severall "
French Officers were likewise against this resolution, but that "
hinder'd not the King from pursuing it; thō considering how "
great a force he had to deal with, and how fortunate as well "
as experienced a General Monsr Schomberg was, he went "
cautiously to work : so marched on the 16 from Ardee with "
his hors and Dragoons only as far as the Bridg of Affain, "
which is within three little Miles of Dundalke, he went over "
the Bridg of Mapletowne, a great pass, and So to Allerstowne, "
ordering his foot and cannon to be in readiness to march at "
an hour's warning, and Coll: Dorrington with the brigade of "
Guards to advance as far as Mappletowne bridg; and after "
haveing view'd the ground, resolued to encamp there, haveing "
his right by Allerstown, aboue Affain bridg upon the hight, "
about a cannon shot from the river that goes down to Largon, "
his left reaching almost as far as the Bridg of Knock, and "
sent immediately for his foot, cañon and bagage to join him; "
the Brigade of Guards, consisting of two Battallions, togather "
with Garmonston's and Creagh's, each of which made a good "
Battallion, came to the camp by eleaven at night and the "
rest next morning before noone.

304.

fol. "

The King
endeavours to
provoke the
Enemie to a
battle, but
they intrench
themselves at
Dundalke.

" The day the King arriued there, he sent a partie over the
" river, which tooke some prisoners amongst which a Lief-
" tenant of foot, who tould him that Mons' Schomberg had
" begun to fortify Dundalke to secure himself there, his Army
" being encamped on the other side the river, keeping with
" him in the Town and within the retrenchments (at which
" they were workeing) two Battallions of the Inneskillingers
" and Lewson's Dragoons, besides which, he had every night
" (after the King's comeing to Allerstown) a battallion of foot
" from the Camp, and some hors upon the by watch : three
" or four days after the King not content with comeing thus
" near, resolved to march over the river with two lines only.
" and six small field pieces, leaveing the reserve which con-
" sisted of three battallions of foot, and the hors which belong
" to it, to guard the camp ; his intention was to offer battle to
" the enemie and provoke them if possible to come out and
" fight him ; this also Mons' Rosen opposed, persisting still
" in his cautious councells, but that hinder'd not the King from
" executeing what he design'd, who marched his right wing of
" hors and Dragoons, with half the foot over at Affain bridg,
" and the rest at the bridg of Knock, and drew up in battle,
" the right within little more than cannon shot of Dundalk,
" and the left all along the hights which are aboue the boggy
" valley, which runs down before Dundalk and so into the Sea ;
" where after haveing stayd aboue three houres, and finding Mons'
" Schomberg kept * close within his retrenchments, haveing

---

* Sir J. Dalrymple in the *Appendix* (Page 23.) has printed some of the Dispatches
of the Duke of Schomberg to King William. In one dated Sept' 27, the Duke
thus speaks respecting JAMES and his Army : " So far as I can judge from the
state of the Enemy, and King JAMES's having collected here all the force that he
could in this Kingdom, he wants to come to a Battle before the Troops separate,
on account of the bad season, which will soon begin ; for this reason it appears to

placed only some advance guards on the pass before him, the
King drew leasurely back into his camp, the enemie not sending
one man after him, to disturb his retreat; not so much as to
scermish, thō some of the King's grenadeers were posted within
less than musket shot of a guard they had behind a causey
way which cross'd the bog. After this the King continued in
his camp at Allerstown till he had eaten up all the forage
thereabouts, and some days before he marched back to Ardee,
sent the Duke of Berwick to make a forage on the other side
of Affain bridg, who haveing the foot to cover the forragers,
advanced with his hors and Dragoons; he stayd there til
the forragers were return'd to the camp, and then burning all
the forrage that was left even within musket shot of their
guards, they were so tame as never to give the least opposition, they only drew up Lewson's regiment of Dragoons
which marched to the pass of ye Causeyway but advanced
no further, and so let him draw off without sending a man
after him.

T O M. IV.

1689.

About this time the King had information that Monsr
Schomberg had made a detachment of some hors, Dragoons,
and granadeers, under the Command of one Russel a
German, who had been Collonel of a regiment of hors in
Ireland, and Governour of Galloway, with orders to go to
Sligo where the enemie had a garison, to command that
Country (which he knew very well) haveing likewise a
private intelligence in Galloway itself; the King thereupon

The King returns to Ardee which he fortifys.

---

me, that we should lie here upon the defensive, if your Majesty approves of it ....".
In a letter dated Octr 12th, the Duke added, "If your Majesty was well informed
of the state of our Army and that of our Enemy, the nature of the Country, and
the situation of the two Camps, I do not believe you would incline to risk an
attack. If we did not succeed, your Majesty's Army would be lost without resource. I make use of that term; for I do not believe if it was once put into
disorder, that it could be re-established." EDITOR.

TOM.
IV.

1689.

" sent brigadier Sarsfield with Henry Lutterell's Regiment of
" hors, S\` Neal Oneal's Dragoons, Charles More's and Ogara's
" Regiments of foot, to prevent their further progress there;
" and then on the 6ᵇ of October march'd with the whole Army
" to Ardee, which place he thought necessary to fortify in
" order to cover the Boin and all the Country betwixt (it) and
" the River; so the King camp'd his foot on two lines, his
" left to the Town and the river of Ardee, behind him his
" hors; and two regiments of Dragoons he posted in some
" vilages on the right with five or six battallions to cover
" them, with a regiment of Dragoons at Mappletown bridg,
" and the other not far from Tallonston highway upon the
" same river; it being necessary by raison of the rains, and
" cold wether comeing on, to put the hors under cover,
" because he foresaw he should be obliged to stay some time
" there, till the works of Ardee were So far advanced as to be
" out of danger of being insulted: this Monsʳ Rosen opposed
" also, even after it was resolved on, and used little artes to
" hinder the works going forward, under colour of preserveing
" the troops, offring no other expedient to prevent the
" Enemies advanceing, but burning and destroying one's own
" Country, which indeed must have been the only remedy,
" had Ardee been slighted and the River of Boin made the
" frontier.

207.

The Enemie
dy exceed-
ing fast, and
are defeated
at Sligo.

" While the King stayd there he was informed by deserters
" and prisoners who were dayly made, that the enemies Army
" was grievously afflicted with the Countrys deseas, and so
" overrun with lice, that vast numbers of them dyed; espe-
" cially the English, not only common men, but Officers, as
" Mʳ Wharton, Son to the Lord of that name, Sʳ Edward
" Deering, Sʳ Henry Ingolsby, Gore, Barrington, Sʳ George
" Erwin, and others; that Sʳ George Hewit, Lord Droghedagh,
" Lord Roscommons, and others were very ill; which with

the keeping of Ardee obliged. Monsʳ Schomberg to think of ”
quiting Dundalke, and gave the King liberty to quarty his ”
Army more at their eas: but before he left Ardee, he had ”
an account from Connough, that Sarsfield haveing marched ”
the stright way to Sligo, by the Boile and so on, he ”
detached Coll: henry Lutterell with about eighty hors, a ”
hundred Dragoons, and two hundred foot, to take a compas ”
about and cut between a certain pass the Enemie kept, and ”
the Town it self of Sligo ; so that when Sarsfield came to ”
attack the bridg with his whole body, the Enemie heareing ”
that Lutterell was got behind them, after some small resist- ”
ance quited it, and marched back to fall upon Lutterell, ”
who was then advanced near · Sligo in presence of the ”
enemie, who haveing notice of his coming had drawn out ”
to fight him ; so that he was forced to face both ways, with ”
the small body he had with him, and first chargeing those ”
who came from the pass, beat them, thō treble his number, ”
and then advanceing against the other partie, which came out ”
of Sligo, he droue them. into the Town thō commanded by ”
Coll: Russell the German, and Coll: LLoyd whom they ”
called their little Cromwel; so when Sarsfield came up, he ”
found they had quited the Town of Sligo, only left some ”
English and French Granadeers in the Castle or new fort ”
which had a stone wall about it, under the command of one ”
Sᵗ Sauveur a french man, who after four days attack was ”
forced to surrender, whereby Sarsfield secured that place for ”
the King, which was the very key of Connough on that ”
side ; and now the Town of Ardee being defenceable, and ”
no possebility of keeping the hors any longer there, for want ”
of forrage, the King broke up his camp on the 3ᵈ of ”
November and went himself to Droghedagh, leaveing Six ”
battallions of foot and 50 hors in Ardee, under the command ”
of Majʳ General Boislau, little garisons of foot in Nobber, ”

" on Loggan water, Caricmancross, on the left of Ardee, and
" some on the right between that and the Sea ; in some Castles
" and houses to preserve the Country on both sides of it, he
" quarter'd also the 3ᵈ old regiments of hors and two of
" Dragoons upon the Boin near Neavan, Trim and Kells, and
" put foot into those Towns, keeping with him in Droghedagh
" Six battallions of foot, and sent the rest into Winter quarters :
" and now haveing further information by deserters and
" prisoners, that Monsʳ Schomberg had embarked his cannon,
" and was prepareing to send his sick men into winter quarters
" in places behind him, and to abandon Dundalke, the King

The King
returns to
Dublin
the 8ᵗʰ of
November.

" went himself to Dublin on the 8ᵗʰ of November, and left
" but three battallions in Droghedagh ; and when he had intel-
" ligence that the Enemie had quitted Dundalke, he sent those
" hors and Dragoons he had left on the Boin to winter
" quarters further into the Country.

1690.

Thus the * Campagne ended very much to the King's honour
and advantage ; two partes of the Enemie's Army was destroyd
at Land, and an infectious distemper had got into the English
Fleet, which in conjunction with the Dutch had a design
upon Corke, but their men dying so fast were forced to lay
aside that enterprise, and soon after the French kept them So
much in awe, that they durst attempt nothing more that year :
ut the Campaign was no sooner ended, when fortune which

―――

* Macpherson has inserted (Original Papers, Vol. 1. p. 222.) *A Journal of the
most remarkable Occurrences that happened between his Majesty's Army, and the
forces under the command of Mareschal de Schomberg, in Ireland, from the 12ᵗʰ of
August to the 23ᵈ of Octʳ, 1689. Faithfully collected by James Nihell Esq. under
Secretary to the Right Honourable the Earl of Melfort, his Majesty's prime Secretary
of State.* Editor.

seem'd hithertoo to declare itself in his Majestys favour, began
to cross all his endeavours, and threw him back into a wors
condition than ever ; misfortunes and temporal calamities are
oft times sent by providence as well to try the just, as to
punish the wicked ; the miserable diseases which afflicted the
Enemie's camp, accompanyed with all the nautious circomstances of nastiness, infection, and lice, which smarmed not
only in the houses, but upon the very boils of trees where the
sick persons had laine, was a visible mark of God's judgment
upon that wicked and Rebellious generation; and now it
pleased the Divine providence to giue the King an occasion of
purifying himself more and more, by the patient and pious
use he made of those humiliations the remainder of his life
was never freed from.

T O M.
IV.
1690.

The first turn of fortune was in the miscarriage upon Belturbat; the preparations of that enterprise were so well
cover'd, that the enemie immagined those troops were
gather'd only with a design to disturb their fronteer garisons,
and Mareschall Schomberg marched himself with a considerable body of hors and foot towards Drummore, to obserue
their motion ; but the Duke of Berwick's real design (who
commanded on that occasion) was, by takeing that place, to
be able to make incursions into the enemies quarters all the
winter ; but Collonell Ousley suspecting it, at last marched
out of Belturbat with a considerable body of hors and foot;
meeting the King's forces near Cavan, attack'd them there,
and thō the Duke of Berwick behaved himself with great
conduct and bravery, haueing his hors shot under him, yet
he was worsted in the action, and the Town fired by the
Enemie, which consumeing a great part of the Amunition and
provision he had design'd for that expedition, he was forced
to retire; Charlemont also a place of great strength and
importance to the King's affairs had been long blocked up,

The King's
forces are
worsted at
Belturbat, the
begining
February.

Charlemont
surrender'd
the 12ᵗʰ of
May.

T O M.
IV.
1690.

and thō Sr Tege O'Regen the Governour of it held out till the 12th of May, was forced by famin to surrender at last; a Squadron of English ships was now also come into the Channel, which insulted the coast at pleasure and took the only man of war the King had, out of the very road of Dublin where it lay at anchor. But these misfortunes at home were nothing in comparison to the disapointments he met with from the Court of France, whence all hope of succour was to come ; there was no endeavours nor industry wanting in the Queen to represent the necessity of transporting the Irish Army into England, and makeing that the seat of war, where it was hoped the conjunction of the King's friends would soon so augment his force, as to make the English weary of resisting God and their duty, when they found the miseries of war brought to their own doors; besides the incapacity Ireland was in of mentaining such an Army, as would be necessary to oppose the mighty force England was prepareing to send over.

The King was in an ill situation, to prepare against the force which was comeing against him.

This seem'd strang to some people, considering how plentifull a Country Ireland is, but the Enemie was master of all Vulster, and the Catholicks who quited it upon Schomberg's landing, brought such prodigious flocks of Cattle with them as eat up the greatest part of the grass and meadows of the other provinces, and destroyd even a great share of the corne too: the County of Lowth the best corn Country in Ireland, togather with that of Meath, Roscommon, Leetrim, and Sligo were ruined with incursions; the great stocks of cattle, sheep, &c, being in the hands of Protestants, and many of them flying into England, they had been embozled, and those that stayd were ruin'd in great measure by the * Raperees ; this brought such a scarcety, that there was neither corn nor meal

---

* The lowest class of the Irish. See *Dalrymple's* account of them, Vol. 1. Page 454. EDITOR.

to feed the Army any considerable time, nó cloth to cloath
them, nor lether for shoos or saddles, and the brass mony put
an absolute stop to importation; so that the Army must either
be transported out of Ireland, or all necessarys for its subsistance imported from France, as also an additional number of
troops proportionable to the vast preperations England was
makeing : But the Court of France seem'd deaf to all these
representations ; the French Officers and Ambassador in
Ireland had sent such disponding relations from thence, that
thō they could not but see the great advantage of such a
diversion, yet the improbability of success made them avers
from ventring more succours than what was absolutely
necessary to keep the war aliue, and that they might not seem
wholy to abandon the King; about Six thousand men therefore and some few cloaths for the Soldiers were obtained at
last, but as all things fell out cross and unlucky to the King,
so in the choice he fortuned to make of a General to command
them, the Minister was disobliged, which perhaps was the true
reason those succours were dispensed with so spareing a hand.

. It apear'd by yᵉ last Campaign that Monsʳ Rosen's notions The Count de Lausun comes in Monsʳ Rosen's steed, and brings 6000 men with him.
no ways suted with the King's, and it had been happy perhaps
for his Majesty if in the cours of his life he had followed his
own judgment as much as he had done in this occasion; but
it was the King's misfortune rather than his fault by a certain
goodness in his temper to belieue too well of others, and by
that means suffer'd himself frequently to be led by weak men,
or which was still more fatal to him, by knaves : Monsʳ Rosen
therefore haveing leave to return, it was necessary to appoint a
Generall in his stead, the Count de Lausun puting in for it,
whose assistance in the Queen's escape from England had
recommended him to her favour ; and thō no great merit was
due from so accidental a piece of seruice, however it had gain'd
him more credit and acquaintance than a meer stranger, and

her Majesty not knowing but he might be as great a General as he affected to apear, made choice of him for this expedition, and perhaps with a view of doing an agreeable thing to Madame de Maintenon in whose good esteem he was at that time, thō in a contrary intrest to the great Minister Monsr de Louuois; who probably aprehending, that should he proue successfull in this enterprize, it might rais his credit again with the King his Master (whose favorit he had formerly been) and that then he might remember the contempt that Minister had all along treated him with; or wheter (as some immagin'd) Monsr de Louuois had designed a Son of his own for that imployment, is uncertain: but whatever in fine was the motiue, that great and powerfull Minister did not concur in giveing such assistance as was in his power and might reasonably haue been expected; so that in effect all the succours which came from France were but in exchange for the like number of the best Irish troops sent over under the Command of My Lord Montcassell, the armes he gaue were so bad that they did little service, and the cloaths he sent so scanty and so cours, that many of the Irish Regiments prefer'd their old ragged ones before them.

The disunion amongst the King's people, is a great obstacle to his affairs.

Besides all these contradictions his Majesty had an other to struggle with, which was discord and disunion amongst his own people, which are never failing concommitants of difficult and dangerous conjunctures; the Count de Lausune was no sooner landed at Corke, but finding a want of those conveniances, which either the unprovidedness of the County, or My Lord Dover's neglect had occasioned (who had been sent thither by the King to prepare all things for the reception of those troops) he fell into passionate complaints against that Lord's conduct, who probably was as ill qualifyd to fill the place of an Intendant, as the other of a Generall: but the King was forced to work with such tools as he had, or such as were put into his hands by others, which requir'd as much dexterity to hinder their hurting one an other, and by consequence himself, as to draw any use from such ill suted and jarring instruments. This had occasion'd his sending away My Lord Melford *before y last * Campagne,* who had come over with him as his sole Secretarie of State, which business he not only managed, but had undertaken even that of the War, the Ordinance, and in a word assumed all power to himself; which created such a dependance upon him as My Lord Tyrconnell could not bear, nor indeed the Irish in generall, who being naturally jealous of Strangers, could not suffer that one so little beloved even in his own Country, should ingross all the power and authority in theirs, and run away with the King's favour from them all. This jealousy communicated itself to the French Ambassador also the Count d'Avaux, who pretending on his side to a generall direction of affairs, could not suffer the confidence or rather preference which the King gaue My Lord Melford on most occasions; these two factions therefore uniteing (at least against him) proued too weighty for him to bear, and brought a necessity upon the King of dismissing him from his imploy. ments, and out of the Kingdom too, and the same reasons obliged the Queen not to keep him at S*t* Germains neither; for had he remain'd there and all affairs gon through his hands, the jealousie would rather haue encreated than abated; wherefore as an only expedient to avoide that, and yet not part with him entirely, he was sent to Rome to negociate the King's affairs there, and his Most Christian Majesty gaue him a pension to support his Character in that Court.

This Lord's actiue undertakeing temper as it had eased the King of much business (which now he being gon, and the rest so disunited, threw all the bulk of it upon his Majestys shoulders) so it had engaged him in many arguments and disputes, which

---

* Interlined by the Son of James the 2ᵈ. EDITOR.

otherwise he would scarce haue follen into of himself, particularly that about presenting to Ecclesiasticall Benefices in such a manner as seem'd to authorise their acting by vertue of his commission; which being conceiued to be an intrenchment upon the spirituall power of the Church, it occasioned some debates: but the King who was allways exceeding cautious and tender in that point in his own nature, went about to rectify the abuse some time before the beginning of the Campaign; as also to prepare all things necessary for takeing the field, which in a manner lay wholly upon himself; wherefore the pains he took were immence, and people were asktonished he was able to support so prodigious a fatigue; and had he been well secconded, or his orders effectually executed, he would haue thought himself happy, but for want of that, the greatest part of what he did was lost labour: There was scarce any magazines upon the frontiers thō he had taken measures for them, so that not only the Armie, but the very Town of Dublin was upon the point of wanting bread, if not supplyd from abroad; he was made to belieue for some time he had 50 thousand men, and paid them accordingly, thō he had not 18 thousand efectiue: his Artillery, amunition &c, which Monsr de Lausune brought from France, remain'd at Cork for want of carriages to make them moue, while the King had the dissatisfaction to see every day the P^{ce} of Orange's shipps pass unmolested through the Channel, with troops and all necessarys for the North:: This made him press the Ministers of the Court of France to send their fleet into St George's Channel, and either transport his small Army into England, or at least intercept the English sending theirs into Ireland; but their ears were still shut to all such proposalls, either thorough the Minister's aversness, or the disponding relations which continually came from Monsr D'Avaux and the French Officers; who generally instead of assisting the King in that extremity, pull'd each a different

11

way; nor were they much aflicted in the bottom, to see things go so ill, because it verifyd their accounts, and recommended their judgment: In fine such were the wants, disunion, and dijection, that the King's affairs looked like the primitive Cahos, and yet his courage and aplication fail'd him not; the Queen on the other hand, finding her sollicitations So fruteless, would have pawned the remainder of her jewells to buy necessarys; she haveing sent a great summe of mony into Ireland already, which had been raised that way, but the King writ to her the matter was now drawn too near a head to wait for supplys from such methods; and therefore notwithstanding all these ill presages of future success, he venterd out with a body of men in great measure newly raised, half disciplined, half armed, and not above half the number of the Enemie, with a weak artillery, and very little mony, to try his fortune once more against an Army of aboue fourty thousand men, most old regiments well apointed, and waited upon by a fleet at sea, with a train of therty pieces of great Cannon: in opposition to which all the King could count upon, was the fidelity of his troops, which haveing been the only thing was wanting in England, had made the rest of no use, so he hoped it might now make amends in great measure for every thing els that was wanting here; he only proposed to himself, since the inequality in numbers was so great, to try if by defending posts, and rivers, he could tire and wast the enemies force, haveing experienced by the foregoing Campagn, that nothing could be more fatal to them than delays, thō his own universall wants made that a hard game to play too.

In this situation were the King's affairs* when he was advertised both by deserters and Spys, that the Prince of

T O M.
IV.

1690.

The King leaves Dublin the 16 of June, and advances as far as Dundalk.
KING JAMES
MEMᵐ.TOM. 9:
png. 315.

---

* "The Spring," says *Sir J. Dalrymple* in his *Memoirs* (Vol. 1. P. 423.) " had been spent in inconsiderable attempts on both sides, because both Princes were pre-

" Orange and that Vast Army would soon be upon him,
" wherefore he thought fit to advance with his troops as far as
" Dundalke and eat up the forrage there about, and preserve
" his own Country behind him ; in pursuance of this he left
" Dublin the 16ᵗʰ of June, and join'd that part of the Army
" which was advanced to Castle Town Bellew under the Com-
" mand of Monsʳ Giraldin one of his Leiftenant Generalls, and
" camped there with his right to the Town, haveing the small
" river before him which runs into the Sea at Dundalke, and
" fronting to the mountain; at this camp the French and
" most of his troops join'd him.   In the mean time the Prince
" of Orange haveing landed at Caricfergus on the 14ᵗʰ of June,
" he drew out his troops from Belturbet, Inneskilling and all
" the other parts of the Country, leaveing few men in any of
" his garisons, and assoon as he had refreshed his Souldiers
" and resolved in his measures he marched to the Newry,
" and finding the King was still near Dundalke, with his
" Army, remain'd there three or four days in expectation of
" his Artilery, and to consider which way to bend his course,
" whether stright to Dundalke or to take a little compas and
" march by Armagh, during which time he sent parties to
" view the Severall ways ; and it being observed that every night
" he sent one to a pass called the Halfway bridg, to press a
" guard of hors and Dragoons the King had there, betwixt
" Dundalk and Newry, his Majesty order'd out a partie of
" hors and foot under the command of Coll: Dempsy and
" Lᵗ Collonell Fitzgerald to ly in ambuscade, and if possible

paring for the great Events of the Summer. But the eyes of all Europe were
now fixed upon Ireland, in which two warlike Kings were to contend, as upon a
public Theatre, for Empire, and where the singular Spectacle was to be exhibited,
of a Nephew fighting against his Uncle, and of two Sons against their Father in
law. Both Kings were the more respectable too, because, although their animosities
were mortal, they maintained the laws of honour to each other." EDITOR.

to surprize them, which was performed with such success, ”
that the Enemies partie of two hundred foot and sixty ”
dragoons fell into it at break of day, and were most of them ”
cut off, the four Captains that commanded and most of the ”
subalterns being either kill'd or taken prisoners, with the ”
loss of a few common men; on the King's side, only Collonell ”
Demsy himself was wonded, on which he dyed in two or three ”
days afterwards : this little advantage heartended the King's ”
troops, and encreased the desire they had of fighting, but that ”
alter'd not the King's resolution of avoiding a battle all he ”
could; and therefore being informed that the Prince of Orange ”
had prepared all things for his march, and resolued to come ”
streight to Dundalke, the King not thinking that post tenable ”
against such an Army, on the 23^d retired towards Ardee, where ”
his Artillery joined him, and haveing notice by his parties and ”
deserters that the Enemy had passed the mountains between ”
Newry and Dundalke, on the 27th he retired to Dumlane, and ”
the next day came to the Boin, and haveing passed that river ”
camped just over against the bridg, his right towards Droghe- ”
dagh and his left up the river, and finding that post an indif- ”
ferent good one, (and indeed the Country afforded no better) ”
he set up his rest there, and resolued to expect the Enemy ”
thō he had not aboue twenty thousand men, and the other ”
between forty and fifty thousand. ”

What induced 'the King to hazard a battle on this * in- ”
equality, was, that if he did it not there, he must loos all ”
without a stroke, and be obliged to quit Dublin and all ”

The King
resolves to
wait for the
Prince of
Orange at the
Boin, and
fight him
there.

---

* This part of the Life, as well as various other passages, appears to have been
written in almost the same words which JAMES had used in those Original Notes
of his, which it is imagined are lost: A reference to the first Volume of Macpherson's Original Papers (Page 222.) will enable the reader to make the comparison. EDITOR.

" Munster, and retire behind the Shannon, and so be reduced
" to the Prouince of Conough, where haveing no magazines,
" he could not subsist very long, it being the worst corn
" Country in Ireland ; besides his men seem'd desirous to fight,
" and being new raised would have been dishearten'd still to
" retire before the Enemie, and see all their Country taken from
" them, without one blow for it, and by consequence be apt to
" disperse and give all for lost, they would haue reproached
" the King with not trusting to their courage, and haue assured
" him of wonders had he but try'd them ; these and other
" reasons determined the King to hazard a battle, and so
" prepared for it the best he could, and though the ford at
" old bridg was not to be mentained, yet to hinder the Enemies
" being master of it as long as possible he posted a Regiment
" of foot in the Village, which intrenched and cover'd them-
" selves as well as they could, the high ground being on the
" Enemies side.

" On the 30ᵗʰ in the morning (being the next day after the
" King had passed) the Enemie appear'd on the other side the
" river, and drew up over against the King's Army, their right
" towards Slane, where the river was fordable allmost every
" where, their foot over against old bridg, and their left towards
" Droghedagh ; their right wing of hors was so near the river
" on a high ground, that the King made some of his Cannon
" advance between his camp and old bridg, which so galed
" that wing, as obliged them to quit their post and encamp
" behind the Eminence out of sight ; it was there the Prince
" of Orange was touched on the shoulder by one of the first
" two * shots, which just fetched off the skin and did him no

---

* *Ralph* informs us, (Vol. 2. P. 219.) in an extract from *The State of Europe* for
August 1690, p. 31. that " It was about midnight that the Court (of France)
receiv'd the news of King William's *death* (on the report of one of King JAMES's

further prejudice; about noon their Cannon came up, and "
began to play upon some partes of our Camp which lay open "
to them, but at such a distance as they did little damage, thō "
they were very numerous, being at least fifty pieces (as was "
sayd) with severall small mortars which they fired also, but to "
no great purpose ; however the King believeing they might "
march by their right up towards Slane to pass the river there, "
or endeavour to force the ford at old bridg, he order'd the "
baggage to be loaden, and be ready to march that the ground "
might be clear on which it camped by morning; and sent S^r "
Neale O'Neal's Regiment of Dragoons to Slane with orders "
to defend that pass as long as he could, without exposeing "
his men to be cut to pieces, believeing the Enemie would "
endeavour to pass there, and then either offer the King battle, "
or march streight towards Dublin ; which they might easily "
haue done, at least with a detached body of hors and dragoons, "
being so much superiour to the King, in them, as well as "
in foot.   "

On tuesday the 1st of July, they heard the Enemy beat "
the general * before day, and assoon as the Sun was up, "

The Battle of
Boine, on the
first of July.

Lackeys). Yet tho' it is not usual to make bonfires for the death of an Enemy
before he is defeated in battle, the Emissaries nevertheless immediately ran about
the streets, awaking up the people of the City, and crying out to them, *Rise and
make Bonfires.*"— *Kennet* details what happened on that occasion, (Vol. 3. P. 599.)
" A bullet having first graz'd on the bank of the River, did in its rising slant upon
the King's right shoulder, took out a piece of his Coat, and tore the Skin and
Flesh, and afterwards broke the head of a gentleman's pistol. My Lord Conningsby
no sooner saw his Majesty wounded, but he rid up and clapt his handkerchief upon
the sore place; while the King himself mounted again and kept on his pace, and
only said, *There was no necessity, the Bullet should have come nearer.*" EDITOR.

* In a small Volume, called THE ROYAL DIARY, part of which was written by
KING WILLIAM and found amongst his papers, the 3^d Ed. of which appeared in
1705, it is said, that King William " rid in person about twelve at night, with
torches, quite through the Army, and then retired to his Tent with *Eager expectation*, to use his own words, *of the glorious approaching day.*" — The watch-

" saw their right wing march towards Slane followed by a
" line of foot; upon which the King order'd the left to march
" up likewise on the other side the water, and the baggage
" towards Dublin with all the cannon but six which were
" directed to follow the left wing. Sr Neale O'Neal's Dragoons
" did their part very well and disputed the passage with the
" Enemie almost an hour till their Cannon came up, and then
" retired in good order with the loss only of fiue or six
" common men, but their Collonel was shot through the
" thigh and an officer or two wounded. No sooner had the
" Enemie passed there, but they strecthed out their line to the
" right as if they designed to take us in the flank, or get
" between us and Dublin, which Monsr de Lausune seeing
" marched with the left to keep up with them, and obsérue
" their motion ; while this was a doing the King went to the
" right to hasten up the troops to follow Lausune, believeing
" the main body of the Enemie's Army was following their
" right which had passed at Slane ; but when the King
" came up, he found the Duke of Tyrconnel with the right
" wing of hors and Dragoons, and the two first brigades of
" the first line drawn up before old bridg, from which post he
" did not think fit to draw them, the Cannon and baggage
" not being far enough advanced on their way towards Dublin ;
" however the rest of the foot march'd by, their flank towards
" Lausune, and the King took the reserue, consisting of
" Purcel's hors and Brown's foot, with which he marched till
" he came up to that rear of the foot that follow'd Lausune,

---

word that night was WESTMINSTER, and his Majesty " gave Orders, that every
Soldier should be provided with a good stock of ammunition, and all to be ready
to march at break of day, with every man a green bough or sprig in his hat, to
distinguish him from the Enemy, who wore pieces of white paper in their hats."
(Page 73.) EDITOR.

and there ordering Sr Charles Carny, who commanded the "
reserue, to post himself at the right of the first line of those "
foot to make a sort of left wing there, and then rid along "
the line where he found Lausune and the Enemie's Right "
drawn up in battle, within half cannon shot, faceing each "
other: the King did not think fit to charge just then, being "
in expectation of the troops he had left at old bridg, but "
while he was discoursing this matter with Lausune, an Aid "
de Camp came to giue the King an account that the Enemie "
had forced the pass at old bridg, and that the right wing was "
beaten; which the King wispering in Lausun's ear, tould "
him, There was now nothing to be done but to charge the "
Enemie forthwith, before his troops knew what had happen'd "
on the right, and by that means try, if they could recover "
the day; and accordingly sent Monsr Hoguette to the head "
of the French foot, made all the Dragoons to light and "
placed them in the intervalls between the hors and order'd "
Lausune to lead on: but just as they were begining to "
moue, Sarsfield and Maxwell who had been to view the "
ground betwixt the two Armys, sayd It was impossible for "
the hors to charg the Enemie, by reason of two dubble "
ditches, with high banks, and a little brook betwixt them, "
that run along the small Valley that divided the two Armys, "
and at the same time the Enemie's Dragoons got on hors "
back and their whole line began to march by their flank to "
their right, and we soon lost sight of their van by a village "
that interposed; only by the dust that ris behind it, they "
seem'd to endeavour to gaine Dublin road; upon which the "
King (since he could not attack them) thought fit to march "
also by his left towards Dublin road too, to pass a small "
brook at Dulick which was impracticable higher up by "
reason of a bog. The King was no sooner on his march, but "
the right wing's being beat was no longer a mistery, for "

" severall of the scatter'd and wounded hors men got in
" amongst them before they rought Dulick; whereupon Monsr
" de Lausun advised the King to take his own regiment of hors
" which had the van of that wing, and some Dragoons, and
" make the best of his way to Dublin, for fear the Enemie,
" who were So strong in hors and Dragoons, should make
" detathments, and get thither before him, which he was
" confident they would endeavour to doe; but that if his
" Majesty arriued there first, he might with the troops he had
" with him, and the garison he found there, prevent their
" possessing themselves of the Town till Monsr Lausun
" could make the retreat, which he prayd him to leaue to his
" conduct, and advised him not to remain at Dublin neither,
" but go with all expedition for France, to prevent his falling
" into the Enemies hands, which would be not only his, but
" the Prince his Son's utter ruin; that as long as there was
" life there was hope, and that if once he was in France again,
" his cause was not so desperate, they being in all probability
" Masters at Sea; that he would giue one of his hands that he
" could haue the honour to accompany him, but he must
" endeavour to make his retreat in the best manner he could,
" or dy with the French if they were beaten: this advice went
" much against the grain, so the King demur'd to it, thō
" reitterated several times; but Monsr Lausun ceased not
" pressing him, til at last he found by a more particular
" account in what manner the business had been carryd on
" the right, that all the enemies Army had passed the river,
" which forced even those troops that were not beaten to
" retreat, and that by consequence it was necessary for him to
" doe so too.

" As for what pass'd at Old brig, it seems the Enemie per-
" ceiveing the left wing and most of the foot had march'd after
" Lausun, attacked the Regiment which was at the Village of

Old brig with a great body of foot all strangers, and soon ”
possessed themselves of it ; upon which the Seaven battallions ”
of the first line, which were left there, and drawn up a little ”
behind the riseing ground which shelter'd them from the ”
Enemies Cannon marched up to charge them, and went on ”
bouldly til they came within a pikes length of the Enemie, ”
notwithstanding their perpetual fire ; so that Major Arthur ”
who was at the head of the first Battallion of the guards run ”
the Officer through the body that commanded the Battallion ”
he march'd up too, but at the same time the Enemies hors ”
began to pass the river, which the King's foot perceiveing, ”
immediately gave way, notwithstanding all that Dorington ”
and the other Officers could doe to stop them, which cost ”
several of the Captains their lives, as Arundel, Ashton, ”
Dungen, Fitzgarald, and two or three more, besides the ”
Marques de Hoquincour, who was kill'd with several others ”
of his brigade ; Barker Lieftenant Collonell of the guards, ”
with Arthur the Major were both wounded, of which the ”
latter dy'd the same day, nor could the Duke of Tyrconnel ”
himself rally them, thō he used his utmost endeavour to do ”
it ; but notwithstanding the foot was thus beaten, the right ”
wing of hors and Dragoons march'd up, and charg'd such ”
of the Enemies hors and foot as passed the river ; but My ”
Lord Dungan being Slaine at their first going on by a great ”
shot, his Dragoons could not be got to doe any thing, nor ”
did Clares doe much better ; nevertheless the hors did their ”
duty with !great bravery, and thō they did not break the ”
Enemies foot, it was more by reason of the ground's not being ”
favorable, than for want of vigor, for after they had been ”
repulsed by the foot, they rally'd again, and charged the ”
Enemies hors and beat them every charg : Tyrconnell's and ”
Parker's troops suffer'd the most on this occasion, Powel and ”
Vaudrey both Lieftenants of the Guards, with most of the ”

" Exempts and Brigadeers of both troops were Slaine, as also
" the Earle of Carlingford, Monsr d'Amande, and several other
" Volunteers that charged with them. Nugent and Casanone
" were wounded of Tyrconnell's, Major Mara and Sr Charles
" Take kill'd, and Bada wounded; of Parker's the Collonel
" wounded, the Leiftenant Coll: Green with Dodington the
" Major and many other officers kill'd, and of the two Squa-
" drons of that Regiment there came but off about theerty
" sound men. Sunderland's regiment (thō wounded himself)
" suffer'd not much, haveing to do only with the Enemies hòrs
" which he soon repulsed; in fine they were so roughly handled
" and overpower'd by numbers, that at last they were quite
" broke. Leiftenant Genl Hamilton being wounded and taken
" prisoner at the last charg, and the Duke of Berwick
" haveing his hors shot under him was some time amongst
" the Enemie, he was rid over and ill brused, however by the
" help of a trooper got off again, Sheldon who commanded
" the hors had two kill'd under him: The Enemie lost some
" men of distinction too, amongst which was the Marechal de
" Schomberg himself, who was sayd to be kill'd by Sr Charles
" Take, or O'Toule an Exempt of the guards as he was passing
" the ford, Calimot with two other Collonels and the Leiftenant
" Coll: of Schomberg's own Regiment was kill'd, which regi-
" ment and the P^{ce} of Orange's guard du corps suffer'd very
" much; but that signify'd little to so numerous an Army, and
" therefore it was a great oversight in the Enemie, that so soon
" as they had beaten the right wing of the King's Army at
" Oldbridg they did not march after them, for had they done
" so, they might have got to Dulick before the King, who was
" with the left, and so have cut off his retreat to Dublin and
" routed the whole Army. But the King had no sooner passed
" the defilé with the van of his left, and was marching towards
" Dublin, but Tyrconnel joined Lausun as he was passing,

334.

334.

at which time the Enemie appear'd and offer'd to attack their "
reer, but they turn'd upon them with some hors and the French "
foot, and made so good a countenance that they suffer'd them "
to pass quietly over the brook, and bring five (of the Six pieces "
of Cannon) which attended the left wing, the other being "
boged was lost; from thence they made their retreat to the "
Neal, an other great defilé in good order, the Enemie how- "
ever waiting still on them without pressing upon them, and "
at last when night came, follow'd no more : however that "
pannick fear which had seized the troops pursued them still, "
for as soon as it began to be darke, the greatest part of the "
Irish foot dispersed, many of them haveing thrown down their "
armes and deserted before, but the French kept in a body, "
and retreated in good order.

The King haveing yeilded at last to Monsr Lausun's advice, "
got to Dublin that night, where he met Major Wilson "
with letters from the Queen, and an account of Prince "
Waldeck's being entirely routed by the Marechal of Luxem- "
bourg at Flerus, which good news encouraged his design of "
going for France ; but before he would resolue upon it, he "
spoke singly with those of his Privy Council he trusted most, "
as the two Chancellors, the Duke of Powis, Secretary Neagle, "
the Marques of Albeville, the Lord Chief Barron, and others, "
who were unanimously of a opinion, he should loos no time in "
going to France, that he run a great risque of being taken by "
the Enemie, who they believed would be there the next "
morning. "

About midnight the Duke of Berwick sent an Aid de Camp "
to acquaint the King he had rallyd about Seaven thousand "
foot at Brasil, and desired he would pleas to send him some "
hors and dragoons to enable him to make his retreat ; upon "
which he order'd six troops of Lutterel's regiment of Dra- "
goons, and three of Abercorn's hors, (which were all he had "

TOM.
IV.
1690.

335.

The King
haveing lost
the Battle,
retires to
Dublin, and
from thence
returns into
France.
346.

" but those newly arriued with the King), to march thither
" to him; but assoon as it was light the Duke of Berwick
" found that most of them were dispersed again, of which he
" sent the King an account, and about the Same time Mr. Taaf
" the Duke of Tyrconnell's Chaplain (a very honest and dis-
" creet Clergie man) came from him, to press the King to leaue
" Dublin, and get into France as soon as ever he could, and
" to send all the troops in Town immediately to meet him and
" Mons' de Lausun at Leslip, whither he was marching with
" what he had left, not designing to come into Dublin at all,
" for fear he should not get his tired troops soon enough out of
" it again; accordingly the King order'd Simon Lutterel to
" march to Leslip, with all the forces in Town except two
" troops of the King's own Regiment of hors, which he kept to
" attend upon himself, who in complyance to the advice of
" all his friends resolued to go for France and try to doe
" something more efectual on that side, than he could hope
" from so shatter'd and dishearten'd a body of men, as now
" remain'd in Ireland.

" Just as the King was geting on hors back, Mons' de la
" Hoguette, with Famshom, Chemeraud and Marode, all general
" officers or Collonels, came to the King and tould him, they
" had been order'd by Mons' de Lausun to meet him and the
" Duke of Tyrconnel at Dunboin, that not finding them there,
" were come to Dublin to look for them; when the King
" asked them What was become of their men, they answer'd,
" They were dispersed for hunger and wearyness, that it was to
" no purpose to keep them togather, all their match being
" burnt out, that the Enemie was so near the Town that his
" Majesty had no time to loos if he intended to secure himself;
" they said their horses were tired, and desired the King to
" lend them others that they might accompany him, but he
" haveing none, left them there, and seting out aboue five in

the morning, marched leasurely to Bray about ten miles from "
Dublin, where he order'd the two troops he had with him to "
stay till twelue at noon to defend that bridg as long as they "
could, if any partie of the Enemie should fortune to follow "
them; and then continued on his journey through the hills "
of Wicklow, with a few persons, till he came to one "
Mr. Hacket's house near Arclo, where he baited his horses "
some two hours, and then follow'd on his journey to "
Duncannon *. "

The King had scarce got two miles from Mr. Hacket's "
house, when the four French Officers he had left at Dublin "
overtook him, and assured him if he made not more hast he "
would certainly be taken, for they had been pushed by a "
partie of the Enemie, who had pursued them very hard for "
aboue a mile, and that they could not be more than a mile "
behind; the King sayd, He could not belieue it, that it was "
impossible any body of the Enemie could be got so far, "
that probably it was some of the Country people they took "
for troops; to which they replyd, They hoped his Majesty "
believed they knew troops when they saw them, that they "
were sure they were such and formed in three or four small "
Squadrons, sending a little partie before by whom they had "
been (they Sayd) pursued and pushed for aboue a mile, who "
still endeavour'd to cut them, and that they were not then "
aboue a mile behind: The King upon their positiueness "
mended his pace, and by their advice left La Rue and a "
Brigadeer of the guards at a bridg when it began to be dark "
to stop the Enemie in case they pursued, where they stayd "
about half an hour, and hearing of no Enemie, followed the "

* *Macpherson* has given Extracts from the Original Notes of JAMES respecting this part of his Life, in the *Original Papers*, (Vol. 1. P. 229.) which Extracts some readers may wish to compare with this work. EDITOR.

" King who travelling all night got to Duncannon about
" sun rise.

   " Monsr de la Hoguette and his companions went streight
" to Passage, where they found the LAUSUN a Malouin of 28
" guns, newly come in there laden with corn and other goods
" for Ireland; they prevail'd with the Captain to get under
" sail, and fall down with the tyde to Duncannon, and came
" to the King there about noon to acquaint him with what
" they had done, adviseing him it would be easier to go on
" board her, and so pass by sea to Kingsale, rather then by
" Waterford, the wind being good and the coast cleere, and
" that if his Majesty could get out that evening he might be
" at Kingsale next morning early ; the King liked the propo-
" sition, and went on board assoon as the ship fell down, and
" got over the bar before night ; as soon as he was at Sea those
" gentlemen would have perswaded the King to haue gon to
" rights for Brest, but the King did not think fit to do that,
" so he got early next morning to Kingsale, where he found
" Monsr Foran a Chef d'Esquadre, with a Squadron of Seven
" small french ships, with some merchant men laden with corn
" and wine, togather with Monsr Du Quesne who had three
" small frigats likewise.

   The Queen had obtain'd these ships to attend the King's
orders in Ireland * (which fell out opertunely enough for this

---

* *Macpherson* has inserted from Mr. Astle's Papers, a translation of the Queen's
Letter, (Vol. 1. P. 230.) which is there dated St. Germain's, 20th July, instead of
the 27th, which she addressed to the Count de Tourville, Commander of the French
Fleet....." After what you have lately done," said the Queen, " I consider the King
as master of the Sea, and in a condition to re-establish the King my Husband in
his Kingdoms, and to free himself thereby from a great part of his Enemies. If we
are lucky enough to return soon to our own Country, I shall always consider that
you was the first to open the way to it; for it was effectually shut against us, before
the success of this Engagement, to which your good conduct has contributed so
much. But, if I do not deceive myself, it appears to me now to be completely

Service) and she had made so great an intrest with Mons' T O M.
Seigneley the French Minister for the Marine, that he was IV.
become exceeding Zealous in the King's cause, and had Set 1690.
out a great fleet able to dispute the dominion of the Seas (as
apear'd soon after) with the Dutch and English both ; so that
had the King been able to haue waued that decisiue stroke at
the Boine a few weeks, he might haue seen that fleet Master of
St George's Channel, and in a condition either to haue transported him and his Army to England, or of hindring any
succours from comeing to the Prince of Orange into Ireland,
which was what that Minister designed : but the King's life
was a chain of misfortunes and disapointments in his latter
days, So that the advantages the French got were no ways
beneficiall to him, and his misfortunes were dubbly such, by
lessening his credit and intrest with his friends as much as it
did with his enemies, as it fair'd with him particularly on this
occasion.

Before the King went on * board he writ to My Lord
Tyrconnel, that pursuant to his, Monsr de Lausune's and the
rest of his friends advice, he was going for France, from whence
he hoped to send them more considerable succours, and left
them in the mean time fifty thousand pistoles which was all
the mony he had ; after which he set sail, and came to Brest
the 20th of July N. S. from whence he sent an express to
the Queen to acquaint her with his arrival there, and his

open, providing the King could gain some little time in Ireland, which I hope he
will. Yet I tremble with fear, lest the Prince of Orange, who sees clearly that it
is his interest to hinder him, should push the King, and oblige him to give
battle."......EDITOR.

* According to Kennet (Vol. 3. p. 601.) JAMES embarked at Waterford, with
the Duke of Berwick, Mr. Fitz James, the Lord Powis, and the Duke of Tyrconnel.
EDITOR.

T O M.
IV.

1690.
King Jam:
Mem". To:9.
P. 338.

misfortune in the Country from whence he came; he tould her
" he was sencible he should be blamed for haveing hazarded a
" battle upon such inequalitys, but sayd, he had no other post
" so advantagious to doe it in, unless he would haue abandon'd
" all without a strok and haue been driven at last into the
" Sea.

The King is
censured for
leaveing Ire-
land So Soon.

But as the actions of the unfortunate are always censured
more ways than one, so as some blamed the King for hazarding
too much, others did it for his not hazarding more, and quiting
Ireland so Soon; that councel was no doubt too precipitate,
and it is wonderful on what grounds My Lord Tyrconnel
thought fit to press it with so much earnestness, unless it was
out of tenderness to the Queen, who he perceiued was so
aprehensiue of the King's person, as to be in a continual agony
about it; she had frequently beg'd of him to haue a special

Queen's
letter to
Lord Tyr-
connel
June 27.

care of the King's safety, and tould him, He must not wonder
at her repeated instances on that head, for unless he saw her
heart he could not immagin the torment it suffer'd on that
account, and must allways continue to doe so, let things goe as

Letters
August 13.

they would; and owned afterwards that thō she was in the
last extremity of grief at the loss of the Battle, and that nothing
could be so afflicting to her as after haveing broke her head
with thinking and her heart with vexation at the King's, her
own, and her friends utter ruin, without being in a condition
to relieue them, yet, that it was an unspeakable alleviation
that the King was safe, for that had she heard of the loss of
the Battle before that of the King's arrivall, she knew not what
would haue become of her, and therefore acknowlidged it
none of the least obligations to him and Mons' Lausun for
pressing his Majesty to it; for thō she confessed it was a
dismal thing to see him So unhappy as he was in France, yet
in spight of her reason, her heart she Sayd was glad he was
there.

Thō this sollicitude for the King's safety which seem'd to stifle in some sort all other considerations, was not only pardonable but commendable in the Queen, yet those who ought to haue made his own well being, and that of his Subjects, togather with his honour and reputation in the world, a part of their concern, should not so rashly haue advised such disheartening Councels, as to make his Majesty seem to abandon a Cause which had still so much * hopes of life in it ; the loss of the Battle did but force him to that which Monsr Rosen and other experienced Officers would haue advised him too long before, he had all the best ports and some of the strongest places still behind him, he had leasure enough to see if the Army (which was very little diminished by the action) might not be rallyd again, which his presence would hugely haue contribited too, and his speedy flight must needs discourage them from ; he might be sure his own people, and especially the Court of France would be hardly induced to mentain a war, which he himself so hastely abandon'd. But on the other hand it was not so much wonder'd, that the King should be prevail'd upon to do it, considering the unanimous advice of his Council, of the Generals themselves, and of all persons about him ; that universal pannick fear which could make those French officers, (men of seruice) see visions of troops, when none could certainly be within twenty miles of them, excused in great measure the King's takeing so wrong a resolution ; however all that would not have determined him to leaue Ireland so soon, had he not conceived it the likelyest expedient to repair his losses,

T O M.
IV.
1690.

---

* *Kennet* informs us in a Note (Vol. 3. p. 604.) that, " At Rome they depended so much on the success of JAMES in Ireland, that an Historian was there employ'd to write a history of it." EDITOR.

T O M.
IV.

1690.
The King's
project of
Landing in
England,
which was the
true cause of
his leaving
Ireland so
soon.

according to a certain scheme he had formed to himself, and which in realitie had been layd by the * Court of France.

The Prince of Orange with the flower of his troops was then in Ireland, which (notwithstanding the late disadvantage) was far from being subdued, he could not therefore leave it of a long time, unless he would loos all the frutes of his Victory; the French on the other hand were presumed masters at Sea, after haveing worsted the English at Bantry bay, and no one could doubt of their being so at land, especially since the entire defeat of Count Waldeck at Flerus : all these considerations made the King immagin, the sooner he got into France the better, not doubting but he could convince his Most Christian Majesty, that the most speedy and efectual way to restore him, and at the same time to break that formidable league against himself, would be to transport him with a sutable body of men into England, which then was so bare and naked of troops, and wher the generality of the people seem'd sufficiently disposed to repair their fault as well as oversight, of which they began to be equally ashamed; and at the same time to send a Squadron of ships into St George's Channel, which might both prevent the Prince of Orange's bringing back his troops from Ireland, and transport some of the Irish troops to Scotland. This it was which principally inclined the King to this speedy retreat from Ireland, and the news of

---

* *Dalrymple* says (Vol. 1. p. 442.) " In his flight he (JAMES) received a Letter written with Lewis the XIV.'s own hand, in which that Monarch informed him of the Victory of Flerus, which had put it in his power to draw his garrisons from Flanders to the Coast, and of the station his Fleet had taken, which prevented his enemies from succouring each other. In this letter, Louis urged him to sail instantly for France, and to leave the conduct of the war to his Generals, with orders to protract it; and promised to land him in England with 30,000 men." EDITOR.

a signal victory which the French had got at Sea over both Dutch and English fleet and (*in*) the Bay of Beachy, which his Majesty met with at his arrival at Brest, made him aplaud himself exceedingly in that resolution.

The King had been acquainted with this project of fighting the English and Dutch in the Channell, and that Monsʳ de Signeley (who was the author of it) intended that Monsʳ de Chateau Renaud should with a Fleet of five and twenty light frigates go at the same time into Sᵗ George's Channell, and burn all the Ships on both sides, except what was necessary to bring off the King and some troops with him, and by that means haue kept the Prince of Orange and his army in Ireland: This was certainly both the best layd scheme and the best provided for, of any that had been thought of in order to the King's restoration, and was the main inducement to the King's passing into France hopeing he might come time enough to be at the execution of it; but the business was over before his arrivall, as was sayd, and thō the French had gain'd a Victory, yet little or no use was made of it either to advantage the King, or the French themselves. Monsᵗ de Signeley's sickness it seems hinder'd him from going on board the Fleet himself, as he had intended, which forced him to giue that commission to the Cheualier de Touruille, which he executed so far at least as to beat the Fleet, but did not pursue his Victorie and burn the English ships, as he had been directed, which Monsʳ de Signeley questioned him for at his return; he alledged for excuse, that the English by pulling up the buoys render'd the entrance into the river so hazardous that he durst not venter up it: but Monsʳ de Signeley who had espoused the King's cause with great earnestness and affection, being vexed to the last degree at this disapointment, tould Monsʳ de Tourville, That nothing but his cowardise could haue let slip so favorable an opertunitie of ruining the English Fleet, and restoring the King; the Admirall (who wanted not courage) took fire at this and began to express his ressentment upon which Monsr de Seignelay to mollify what he had sayd, tould him, He did not intend to reflect upon his personall valour, for that he knew no man had more, but only on his conduct, and that there were many (of which number he tooke him to be) *qui estoient poltrons de teste quoyqúils ne l'estoient point de coeur.*

This battle had been given the day before that of the Boine, and thō the English suffer'd not so much in the engagement, which fell heavyest upon the Dutch, yet the King immagined that since the Naval force of both Nations, had been too weak to the French, the English alone to be sure could not be in a condition to withstand them, especially considering their backwardness in engageing when the French alone were their enemies; which made the King hope they would not be more forward to do it, when he himself was concerned.

Tis more than probable the Prince of Orange had some suspicion of this, when to the surprize of every body he left his Army all of a sudden after he had conducted it as far as Carick towards Limerick, and return'd to Dublin with a design to pass over into England; but haveing an account from thence, that the French had contented themselves after their Victory, with burning one small Village in the West of England, and were gon off again, he was overjoyd to find himself rid of his apprehentions at so cheap a rate, so he return'd to his Army two or three days ere it arrived before the Town, and thō he stayd near two months in Ireland afterwards, tis probable that apprehention haunted him still; otherwise he would not have venter'd to sea in a storme as he did, and left that Kingdom in a greater probability of regaining what they had lost, than of being speedely reduced to his obedience.

The next day after the King's * arrival at St Germains, his Most Christian Majesty came to see him, and in general termes promised all immaginable kindness and support; but when the King layd open his project to him, he receiued it couldly, and sayd, He could doe nothing in it, till he heard from Ireland ; the King not satisfyd with this, desired a further conference about it, there being in reality no need of an account from Ireland to convince the world, that England was naked and disgarnished of troops, or that the French, being now superiour at Sea, had it in their power to transport the King thither, to make that the seat of the war, and so cut the very sinews of the League; but his Most Christian Majesty was in all probability, either of himself, or by the insuation of his prime

T O M. IV.

1690.
The King of France comes to see the King at St Germains, who proposes his project, but it is not agreed too.
KING JA: LETT: to Ld Tyrconnel. July 29.

---

* On JAMES's arrival at St Germains, he formed, according to *Kennet*, (Vol: 1. p. 601.) the following Court:

" 1. The Duke of Powis, *Lord Chamberlain.*

2. Colonel Porter, *Vice Chamberlain.*

3. The Earl of Dunbarton, and the Earl of Abercorn, *Lords of the Bed-Chamber.*

4. Captain Mac Donald, Captain Beadles, Captain Stafford, and Captain Trevanion, *Grooms of the Bed-Chamber.*

5. Fergus Graham, Esq. *Privy Purse.*

6. Edward Sheldon, Esq., ——— Sheldon, Esq., Sir John Sparrow, *Of the Board of Green Cloth.*

7. Mr. Strickland, *Vice Chamberlain to the Queen.*

8. Mr. Brown, *Brother to the Lord Viscount Montacute, Secretary of State for England.*

9. Sir Richard Neagle, *Secretary of State for Ireland.*

10. Father Innes, *The supposed Writer of this Life of James the* 2^d, *President of the Scots College at Paris, and Secretary of State for Scotland.*

11. John Caryl, Esq., *Secretary to the Queen.*

12. ——— Stafford, Esq., *formerly Envoy in Spain.*

These five last were his Junto, his Cabinet Councellors; the Earl of Melfort being sent to Rome, not so much in hopes of getting money from the Pope, as to please the Irish, who had at that time monopoliz'd the King's favour; his ex^- pectation from their assistance being greater than from both the other kingdoms."
(*Secret. Hist. of Europe*, P. xi. p. 244.) EDITOR.

Minister, dissatisfyd with the King's late * conduct, and his too hasty leaveing Ireland, which made him adverse from ventring upon any new expedition, when he saw his Majesty was not of a temper to opiniatre a thing long enough, and that an other attempt might be as hastely relinquished as the last ; and since the present proposal was so reasonable, as that nothing could well be objected against it, but what in civility was not to be urged, his Most Christian Majesty by pretending indisposition waued seeing the King, till it was in effect too late to do any thing ; for expedition had been the life of the undertakeing, and the surprize haue done more than half the work : When the King therefore perceiued the true motiue of this delay, tis certain his patience never underwent So great a tryal in the whole cours of his life, as he afterwards owned to a person entrusted with the secret ; the defection of his Subjects, the loss of battels, and desertion of his favorits, had never thrown him into dispair, but this not suffring him to open his heart and intentions at so critical a time to the Prince who was his only friend and support, was a declareing a dissatisfaction with his conduct as to what was passed, and a

---

* " Upon this occasion," (*Dalrymple*, Vol. i. p. 444.) " JAMES experienced one of those cruel reverses, which made him often think and say, *He was born to be the sport of fortune.* Louis waited upon him, as soon as he arrived at St. Germains. JAMES, buoyed up with the hopes which that Prince's late letter suggested, and with the flatteries which attend upon Kings even when they are Exiles, imagined that so sudden a visit was made, in order to concert the manner of his imbarkation for England ; and was therefore the more severely disappointed, when he understood, that the intention of it was to make apologies for relinquishing the Expedition altogether. The English Monarch in vain reminded the French one, of the assurances which his letter had given him : In vain he offered to go on board the Fleet, either with an Army, or without one, saying, *He was certain his own Sailors would never fight against one, under whom they so often had conquered.* Louis answered, with one of those graceful but insincere compliments which were habitual to him, *It was the first favour he had refused to his friend, and it should be the last.*" EDITOR.

resolution to hazard nothing upon his management for the future, which sunk his hopes and expectations the Lower, by how much the favorable occasion of executing his project had raised them higher in his own conception ; but he was destined to be a victime of patience by providence, which his friends as well as his enemies exercised by turns, and thō the King's designes by this means proued abortiue, those of prouidence did not, for by denying him the least comforth amiddest his afflictions (except in his own family which upon their meeting again was exceeding great) render'd his sacrifice more perfect, and unblemished, which the King fail'd not to make a Christian use of ; and had not his duty as a King, and obligation as a Father, ty'd him up to a continual attention to doe himself, his Son, and his people justice who were no less injured and abused than himself, he would probably haue spent the remainder of his life, as free from the thoughts of regaining an earthly Throne, as they were fixed upon getting that, which is aboue the reach of Vsurpers armes.

When this pretence of not seeing the King could hould out no longer, he made use of the first occasion to press his being allowed to goe aboard the Fleet, but his Most Christian Majesty replyd, That would signify nothing without land forces which he Sayd were not to be spared, because the Duke of Bandenburg threaten'd to join Count Waldeck with his troops; which was a poor evasion to answer a certain demonstration, that the King's landing in England would hinder the P^ce of Orange and fourty thousand men from joining the Enemie in Flanders the ensuing Campaign, would probably breake the neck of the war, and lay his enemies at his mercy, which he fail'd not to urge ; but the Court of France was so disponding in the matter, that all the King could say was not able to procure so much as a small supply of armes, amunition, &c. for Ireland, his Most Christian Majesty gaue all for lost in that Kingdom, sayd,

Marginal notes:

T O M.
IV.
1690.

The King presses to go aboard the Fleet, but is denyd.

KING JAM.
LETT. to Lord Tyrconnel,
July 24.

LETTER Sep:2.

It would be so much throwne away so send any thing thither, and therefore all he thought fit to doe, was to dispatch some empty shipps to bring away his troops, and such as would come along with them ; so that in conformety to this the King was forced to send an order to My Lord Tyrconnel, to come away himself too if he judged it proper, and either name a Commander in chief at his departure, and bring with him as many as were willing to accompany him, or otherwise to make conditions for their remaining if they rather chose that.

The Irish Army retires to Limerick.

But the loss of men was not so considerable in the late action, nor the dijection so great amongst the Irish, as to render the King's cause so desperate as it was taken to be at the French Court ; the Duke of Tyrconnel and Count de Lausun had assembled the greatest part of the Army, and retireing towards Limerick still made head against the Prince of Orange, and struggled so hard with their ill fortune and universal wants, as not only to render the success of that Campaign very various, but to end it much more to the King's advantage, and the honour of the Irish than the world could possibly haue immagined ; the great towns indeed before which the Enemie apear'd, made little resistance, the loss of the battel and the example of Dublin (which sent immediately to the P^{ce} of Orange, so soon as the King had left it) made them consult nothing but their safety, which by reason of the smallness of the garisons and weake fortifications, they dispair'd of secureing any other way, than by a timely submission ; Kilkenny therefore made no resistance, Droghedagh, Waterford and Duncannon surrender'd upon conditions at the very first summons, but Athlone where Coll: Grace commanded, did not only stand a formal Siege, but forced the Enemie to rais it after a considerable loss; this shew'd that if other garisons particularly Droghedagh had done their duty, it would haue much weaken'd the Prince of Orange's force, and retarded his progress ; but the Governor

Kilkenny, Waterford, Duncannon and Droghedagh are Surrender'd.

for his justification sayd, That the Army being defeated in sight
of the Town, so disheartened the garison, as they shew'd little
inclination to a vigorous defence, that their number was not
aboue therteen hundred men fit to do duty, and not aboue
Seven hundred fire Armes amongst them all; but Seven pieces of
iron cannon of four pound ball, the walls old and low, not
lined with rampars, and no one part flanking an other, So
that he thought it imprudence to resist a victorious Army,
and accordly asson as the enemys cannon apear'd, he
surrender'd upon very poor conditions, only capitulateing for
the garison, but gaue up their armes; which besides the
dishonour, was a very great loss, considering the King's wants
of that kind.

The Prince of Orange therefore finding all in a manner fall
before him, had directed his march, as was sayd, towards
Limerick, whither the Duke of Tyrconnel had retreated with
the remainder of the Armie; it was the place of greatest
strenght and consequence that now remain'd in the King's
possession, but very far from such a regular fortification as
those the world of late has been acquainted with, there was
little or no hopes of its houlding out against a numerous and
victorious Army, which wanted no necessarys for a formal
Siege; however they were not disheartened, but on the first
approach of the enemie defended a narrow pass which leads to
the Town, till forced by their great guns to retire, and even
then mentained every hedg and ditch, till the Prince of Orange
by the number of his forces got possession of two advantagious
posts called old Chappel and Cromwel's fort, and then camping
before the Town, on the 9ᵗʰ of August sent to summons it;
there was some debate about their answer which in their present Situation was not to be wonder'd at, but at last it was
resolved to defend the place, and accordingly Monsʳ Boisleau
the Governour writ back to the Prince of Orange's Secretary (to

T O M.
IV.

1690.

avoid shocking that Prince too much, by not giveing him the
title of King) That he hoped he should merit his opinion more,
by a vigorous defence, than a shamefull surrender of a forteress
he had been entrusted with : So prepared himself accordingly,
and in the first place endeavour'd to prevent the enemies
crossing the river, and takeing their post on that side the
Town, but not being able to doe it long, they forced their
passage at Armaghbegs ford, which however the Irish defend'd
till they had raised some forts, one at the South Gate, an other
at the West, which proued of great use to them afterwards :
there was no further progress to be made by the enemie, till
their battering pieces arrived which as yet were not come up ;
this the Irish getting intelligence of, and the way they were to

The English
train of Artil-
lerie surprized
and blown up
by Coll: Sars-
feild, Aug. 12.

pass, Collonel Sarsfeild with a considerable body of hors and
Dragoons was detached to see if he could intercept them; it
was a desperate undertakeing considering the situation of the
enemies Camp, and that he was to pass the river which would
render his retreat exceeding difficult, but being a prudent and
valient Officer, he passed the Shannon nine miles aboue the
Town, and marched with so much secrecy, and expedition,
that he surprized them within Seaven miles of the enemies
camp, at a place called Balancdy ; he soon defeated the
escort, and then gathering all the wagons, carts, and provisions
on a heap, togather with the guns which he filled with pouder,
and puting their mouths to the ground set fire to the train,
which had its intended efect, burst the guns and burnt all the
rest, and notwithstanding the Enemie by this time had taken
the alarme, and had sent out five hundred hors in quest of him,
and the ashtonishing nois and light it made in the air, gaue
sufficient notice whereabouts he was ; however he dexterously
avoided their pursute, and returned safe into the Town to the
grat joy of the garison, which was hugely encouraged by this
signal advantage.

The Enemie however wanted not resources to supply such a disapointment, so thō it occasioned some delay, and arguments amongst those whose business it was to haue provided for their security, however the Prince of Orange resolved to go on with the Siege and sent to Waterford for another train of Artillery, and on the 17th open'd the trenches before the Town : assoon as the great guns arriued they began to batter the place with great fury, which soon liveled the high towers, from whence the besieged could fire into the trenches, and took two redoubts and a strong fort (thō not without loss) for the Garison disputed every inch of ground, with all the vallour and resolution immaginable; on the 20th they made a vigorous sallie which retarded the Enemies works, and were not repulsed till after they had made a great slaughter of the besiegers, who never ceased all the time throwing bombes and red hot bullets into the Town, a thing the inhabitants had been unacquainted with, however were not disheartened, but generously concurred with the troops, to doe, or suffer any thing for so just a cause and rather than fall into the hands of such unnatrual and cruel invaders of their Laws, Liberties, and Religion.

But notwithstanding all the opposition they were able to make, by the 24th the Enemie had finished their battery of 30 pieces of Cannon and in two days more advanced their trenches within therty paces of the ditch; there was by this time a great breach in the wall near St John's gate, and part of the palessados beaten down of the Counterscrap, which layd it So open that the next day being the 27th the Prince of Orange order'd an attack to be made; which was executed with as much conduct and resolution, as could be expected from troops, who besides the common encitements to victory, were animated with a National emulosity betwixt the English, Danes, Brandenburgers, and French Hugenots : they had not only enter'd the cover'd way and taken most of the forts, which they attacked

T O M.
IV.

1690.
The P. of Orange sends for a new train of Artillerie from Waterford, and continues the Siege.

After a furious attack on the 27 Aug. where-in the enemie were repulsed, the P^{ce} of Orange raised the Siege the 31st.

at the same time, but the Earle of Droghedagh's Granadeers were actually on the rampart; however the Irish made so obstinate a resistance, that thō the Enemie was in a manner Master of the breach, and the dispute exceeding hot and bloody (which lasted aboue three houres) yet they forced them to give way at last and beate them back to their trenches, with the loss of at least two thousand men killed and wonded ; which so dishearten'd the English, that three days after the Prince of Orange raised the Siege, and haveing left the government of Ireland to Sidney and Coningsby, and that of the Army to Count Salmes (who quiting that Kingdom soon after consigned his Command to General Ginkle) the P^{ce} of Orange return'd with all immaginable expedition to England, where he arrived the 5th of September following * : This great hast was without doubt both accompanyed and occasioned with some dread and aprehention of what the King had projected, and which the glorious defence of Limerick gave still greater encouragement to attempt; besides which Cork and Kingsale were still in the King's possession, which left a door open to receiue succours from France, and the Prince of Orange had reason to believe, that the late behaviour of the Irish, as well as the manifest advantage of such a diversion would encourage that King to send a speedy relief ; for which reason, thō the Season of the year was

---

* Soon after the King's Arrival, and the very night on which he arrived at Kensington, his Majesty in Council there ordered a Commission to be prepar'd for proroguing the Parliament to the 2d of October: A Proclamation was also issued for a day of Public Thanksgiving, Sunday, Oct. 19. for the Success and Victory over his Majesty's Enemies and rebellious Subjects in Ireland: 2dly, An Order of the King in Council, to annex to the Book of Common Prayer a form of Thanksgiving to be used yearly on the 5th of November, given at Kensington, Oct. 18, 1690: 3dly, A Form of Prayer and Thanksgiving to Almighty God for the wonderful preservation of his Majesty's person, &c. with a Prayer and Thanksgiving to be used on every Lord's-day, Wednesday, and Friday, during the War with the French King. EDITOR.

little proper for such an expedition, he was no sooner arrived
in England, but he equiped out a Fleet with all necessarys for
a Siege under the Command of My Lord Churchill to attack
those two posts, which being ill provided for a defence, thō the
garisons fail'd not in their duty and held out as long as there
was any hope, were forced at last to submit: which was a
great disheartening to the King's friends when they saw such a
bar put to the succours they expected and stood so much in
need of; besides the garison of Cork which was very numerous
being surrender'd prisoners of war, was a great weakening to
the King's forces. Collonel Maceligot who was governour of
it, shew'd more courage than prudence in refuseing the good
conditions which were offer'd him at first, indeed the Duke of
Berwick had so little hopes of its sustaining a Siege that he
had order'd him to burn the town and retire with his garison
into Kerry; but instead of that, (he) suffer'd himself to be
besieged, and thō in no condition to hould it out to the last,
did it however so long, till he could haue no conditions at all,
and being forced to surrender upon discretion found little
compassion at the Enemies hands, who amongst other cruel
usages, were so unhumain as to refuse to bury those who through
misery dyed in prison, till they amounted to 30 or 40 at a time
through a seeming neglect, or to saue trouble, but in reality
that the infection of the dead and corrupting bodys might
poison and destroy the rest.

Sir Edward Scot thō he made a vigorous defence at Kingsale,
yet did not let slip a fit time for capitulateing, whereby he got
better termes, and his men were conducted to Limerick which
brought some augmentation but little comfort to the garison
there; which now began to want every thing else more than a
reinforcement: however the Enemys loss in those two Sieges
was not inconsiderable, in which number was the Duke of
Grafton, who after haveing trecherously abandon'd the King,

who loved him like a father, had no other recompence from
the Vsurper than to be knocked in the head in his service in
quality of a Volunteer; he who thought himself so highly
injured because the King had not given him the command of
the Fleet, preferable to all the antient and experienced Officers
in the Kingdom.

The Count de
Lausune and
the French
troops return
to France, and
the Duke of
Tyrconnel
goes with him
to sollicit
Succours.

Assoon as the Siege of Limerick was raised, the Duke of
Tyrconnel thought it necessary to go in person to France to
sollicite Supplys, which the shamefull retreat of the Prince of
Orange with his victorious Army, from before a place (that
scarce deserued the name of a forteress) encouraged him to hope
for; perswading himself, it would be no hard matter to baffle
him at last, and driue him again out of the Kingdom, if the
Court of France would be prevail'd upon to second his
intentions.

· At the first news indeed of Limerick's standing upon its
defence, and Sarsfeild surprizing the train of Artillery, his
Most Christian Majesty began to conceiue some hopes again
and promised armes, amunition and other necessarys at the
King's entreaty, howeuer order'd his own troops to return on
pretence of a misunderstanding betwixt them and the Irish;
but its probable the origin of that order sprung cheifly from
the uneasiness of the Commander and Officers, for assoon as
the Enemy had apear'd before Limerick, the French Generall
with all his troops marched streight to Galway, takeing with
him a great quantety of amunition &c; so that instead of
assistance during the Siege the Irish were weaken'd by them
in their stores, with might haue been necessary for their
defence, thō indeed after the Siege was raised, the Duke of
Tyrconnel prevail'd with Monsʳ Lausune to return most of the
amunition back, which the late consumption made them
stand in ·present need of; however this piece of conduct in
abandoning a country they were sent to succour, and which it

was so much the intrest of France to support at so critical T O M. IV.
a juncture, when the last stake was engaged, and the Irish
resolved to make a vigorous defence, was such a paredox as 1690.
could Scarce be fathomed; some discontented persons sayd,
that Monsr Lausune and the French being excessiue weary of Stafford's LETTER, 21 Oct. 1690.
the Country, had a mind Limerick should be taken, to excuse
their leaveing it, that therefore they cared not how things
went, nor what disorder they commited; that Boislau dureing
the assault, order'd several Battallions from the breach, which
had he been obeyd in, the Town had been lost; that their
dispiseing the brass mony brought the credit of it so low, as
it never had any sort of currency afterwards, and was one of
the most essential strokes to the King's intrests that had
happen'd of a long time; for it made him depend upon supplys
of mony from France, which was so exceeding hard to be
got, so long a comeing, and so little when it came, that it only
served to make his authority linger a while longer, but could
not preserue it from certain death in the end: the disagreement
also and disunion which now began to shew itself amongst the
Irish themselves, as it made the French more desirous to be
gon, so it made the Irish less troubled to part with them; for
nothing but such personal piques (which make men overlook
all other considerations) could reconcile such contradictions as
willingly to part with succours when they were seeking more,
but perhapes it was not men the Irish wanted, and that if
they had other necessarys it was all they cared for.

These animositys indeed amongst themselves were come to
so great a pitch, that now when the Enemie gaue them some
respit, their whole attention was to make war upon one an
other; there had been a great partie formed against My Lord
Leiftenant, and they were prepareing to send some persons
to represent their grievances and complaints against him, and
if possible to get the King to remoue him; but he, on the other

hand, considering how necessary expedition was, not only for his own defence, but to execute what he went about, took that opertunity of going off with the Count de Lausune, and got the start of his adversaries so far, as to finish his business before the Deputys they sent after him arriued at Sᵗ Germains: the King indeed had done it to his hand before he came, by convinceing the Court of France, how great a pitty it were, not to second the Irish valour, when it gaue such hopes of mentaining that diversion which was so benificial to them; so that My Lord Tyrconnel had nothing remain'd but to get the grant executed, wherein he shewed himself a diligent and actiue Courtier, thō now an old and infirm man, and gain'd so much credit with his Most Christ. Majesty, as to be heard by him jn person (his Minister being present) and to obtain in great measure what he asked, as to cloathes, linnen, corne, arms, officers, and some little mony, upon condition he would return immediately himself, and then they promised these things should follow. Accordingly Monsʳ Sᵗ Ruth, Tessé d'Vson and several other officers were sent some time after, togather with what was promised in great measure; but his Most Christian Majestys Orders therein, were so ill observed, that the Irish receiued not the relief their necessitys required, nor indeed what was intended them by him.

Four Gentle-
men were
sent as Com-
missioners
from the Irish
Army, to
complain of
My Lord
Tyrconnel.

My Lord Tyrconnel's back was no sooner turn'd (when he came from Ireland) but the discontented part of the Army dispatched away the Bishopp of Cork, Coll. Symon, and Henry Lutterell, and Coll: Nicolas Pursel to Sᵗ Germains, with instructions to sollicite his repeal; adressing themselves to his Majesty to this efect, That since with the remains of a broken Army they had stopped a victorious one, and hoped to bring next year an other into the field of aboue twenty thousand foot and neen (*nine*) thousand hors and Dragoons, they desired a Generall fit to command such a body of men, who

might depend upon no orders but his Majestys alone ; that My
Lord Tyrconnel was not qualifyd for such a superintendance
as he had hithertoo exercised, that his age and infermitys made
him require more sleep than was consistant with so much
business, that his want of experience in military affairs render'd
him exceeding slow in his resolves, and uncapable of laying
projects; which no depending General Officers would do for
him, first by takeing a great deal of pains to make him
conceiue it ; and then either haue it rejected, or he to haue the
honour of it, if successfull; whereas they had to do with
enemys who wanted not Commanders of great abilities and
long experience in the war: they insinuated also that mony
and imployments had been given with greater regard to private
ends, than the King's Service, that his management in fine was
universally disaproued of, and that should he return with the
Same authority again, it would utterly dishearten the body of
the Nation ; they complain'd of the disponding Message he
sent to the King, after the battle of the Boin, which occasion'd
his Majestys leaveing the Kingdom, whereas had he but stayd
a few hours longer in Dublin, he had seen such a number of
fine troops, as would haue tempted him not to haue abandon'd
them ; that dureing the Siege of Limerick, nothing but beans
and oates were given to the Soldiers for some time, which they
eat raw out of their pockets, while there was wheat enough
in the Town; they expressed likewise much disatisfaction at
the conduct of those of his partie, particularly Mr Antony and
Richard Hamilton, and had prevail'd with the Duke of
Berwick to displace some, dureing the Lord Leiftenant's
absence, as Collonel Macdonnel from his government of
Galway, and My Lord Riverston from his imployment of
Secretary of war, (which the Duke of Berwick writ to the
King he did upon intelligence of their treateing with the
Enemie about the Surrender of Galway and Limerick)

T O M.
IV.

1690.

My Lord
Tyrconnel
endeavours to
perswade the
King, to keep
those Com-
missioners to
S' Germains.

concluding at last with Several personal reflections, particularly against the Duke of Tyrconnel, and indeed against all that had any ty to his intrest.

Assoon as My Lord Tyrconnel heard of these Deputies from the Army, thō hė had finished his business, and was on his way to Brest, however it alarmed him very much ; he writ to the King, that he wonder'd the Duke of Berwick could be so far overseen as to suffer Henry Lutterel to go to S' Germains, unless it were with the same view he himself had formerly sent My Lord Montjoy ; and so thinking to cross bite them, perswaded the King to keep them there now he had them, not doubting but matters would go on more to his Satisfaction in their absence ; for thō Sarsfield's head (he Sayd) now that it was turn'd to popularity was quite out of its natural Situation, yet he hoped when he came back, to set it right again, if his Councellors Hen: Lutterel and Coll: Pursel were kept from him; so beg'd of his Majesty to do it, assureing him he would use the softest and gentleest means imaginable to bring people to reason, but if that would not do was resolved to secure the proudest amongst them and send him into France : And indeed he put that method in practice ere he was out of it, for while he was waiting for a wind at Brest, hearing of a persón that was sent by M' Randal Macdonnel into Ireland, and suspecting he had instructions for those of the other partie, prevail'd with the Intendant of Brest to clap him up, till his Majestys orders were known about him.

These and other considerations, so prepossessed the King against these Deputys, that at their arrival at S' Germains he refused to see them ; but they being cunning and insinuating people, and back'd not only by men of distinction in the Army, but at Court too, gain'd so much credit at last, as to make the King ballance with himself, whether partie he should endeavour to satisfy ; but My Lord Tyrconnel being actually return'd, he thought it not proper to recall him, nor to alter measures already settled with the Court of France, least that chief Minister might turn such instability in Councells to the King's further prejudice, against whom he was but too much bent already. The King therefore resolved to support his own authority in My Lord Tyrconnel, and let things goe on in the methods already agreed upon, and hoped to send back the Army Ambassadors in such a temper, as would make them live easily with him ; which cost the King a great deal of trouble and. pains, and was lost labour in the end. But it was the King's hard fate not only to suffer by his Rebellious Subjects, but to be ill serued by his Allies, and tormented by divisions amongst his own people; as if his enemies gaue him not disquiet enough, but that his friends must also come into their aid, to exercise his patience, and agrevate his suffrings *by** turns.*

The affairs of Scotland were no less perplexed and unfortunate in the end than those of Ireland, thō in the begining of this year they had a much more hopefull prospect than could haue been expected after the unfortunate conclusion of the last : Coll: Cannon lived prety quietly all that winter in Loughaber, but in the spring when Major General Buchan arriued, seeing no hopes of.,succour some proposed makeing their peace, but others opposed it alledging, that the King was still at the head of an Army in Ireland, and that it would be dishonorable to doe it without his warrant ; besides it was whisper'd about there was hope of relief from an other quarter, even whence it was least expected, which came about in this manner.

Several persons it seems of great credit in the Kingdom amongst the Presbiterian Partie, and who had run in with violence to the Revolution, * *now* finding themselves disapointed

margin note: T O M. IV. 1690.

margin note: The affairs of Scotland this year.

margin note: The Earle of Annendale, My Lord Ross and Sr James Montgomery, beingdisatisfyd

---

* Added by the Son of James the Second. EDITOR.

T O M.

IV.

1690.
with the Pᶜᵉ of
Orange, en-
deavour to
restore the
King's autho-
rity in
Scotland.

of their aims and disoblidged by the Pᶜᵉ of Orange (as men are
easily brought to repent themselves of unsuccessfull crimes)
resolued to unravel if possible that work of iniquity they had
once so heartely contribited too; it was the Earle of Annendale, the Lord Ross, and Sʳ James Montgomery of Scher-
marley, (one of those who carryd the Crown of Scotland to
the Pᶜᵉ of Orange) that put themselves at the head of this
undertakeing; who presumeing upon their great intrest, which
they measured in their own immagination, by their late success,
doubted not but with the conjunction of the King's other
friends, to ruin the Prince of Orange's intrest in Scotland even
in a Parliamentary way: but they did not consider that it is
easier to doe mischief than to repare it, and that those who
can muster thousands when they cry up a false and immaginary
liberty, are generally left alone if upon better information
they seek peace and justice, in which consists the true intrest
of the people as well as the Prince; they apear'd however
sincere enough in the matter, and before they left London
haveing made their design known to many of the King's friends
there, receiued a considerable summe of mony which was sent
over by the Queen to help on the business, they found no
difficulty in perswading the loyal partie of their Sincerity, who
were always ready to catch at any twig thō never so slippery,
because they saw themselves dayly sinking in the way they
were in.

These new converts, to reinforce their partie, had prevail'd
with the government (with whom they kept fair as yet) to send
the E. of Arran, who was prisoner in the Tower, into Scotland,
under pretence of its being against the priviledge of a Scotch
Nobleman to answer in any English Court of justice; and
when they arriued at Edinburgh used all imaginable perswasions and argument to induce the King's friends to qualify
themselves, by takeing the oathes, to set in Parliament in order
to twart the Prince of Orange's designes, particularly as to the

raising of mony; for the custome and excise of Scotland for want of trade being fallen almost to nothing, Maccays Armie had lived in a manner upon free quarter for some time, which had so increased the general dissatisfaction the Country was already in, that if they could but prevent the raising a supply, they doubted not of the whole Kingdom's, in a manner, declareing against the present government.

At the first takeing up this resolution, these three gentlemen who were known by the name of the Club, writ to the King to acquaint him with their intentions, and as intrest was the prime motiue both of their defection and return to their duty, they took care to make their demands before hand, that they might not fail in their expectations now, as they had done before; the King on the other Side had reason to encourage repentance, and thought it wisdom to oblige men of so great power, so he agreed to what they asked, and accordingly apointed the Earle of Annendale to be his Commissioner, and Sʳ James Montgomery Secretary of State, with Several other promises to their friends and creatures; but being they knew it would disgust the King's antient friends, to see those late Enemies, and new converts prefer'd before them, they were cautious in publishing this, but to such as they were sure would sacrifice their own intrest to the King's Service, in that as in all other things.

When the Parliament met they pursued their point with earnestness enough, the Duke of Queensbury, the Marques of Athol, the Earl of Argile and many more of the greatest quality concur'd with them, and had the rest of the King's friends universally done the like, tis probable they might haue succeeded; but a great many Lords and men of quality, some out of conscience, others out of mistrust of their new associates, refused either to take the oathes, or to act in consert with them, which .gaue the Court partie great advantages; but what discouraged these new undertakers most, was to find that their antient followers the Presbiterians (whom they had govern'd formerly) began to abandon them when they perceived their leaders were changed; which Annendale, Ross and Schermarly were no sooner convinced of, and that they could not carry their point that way, but they, who could easiler change sides than governments, made their peace by discovering what had passed, and suffring the very peapers and Commission which came from the King, to fall into Melvin's hands, the then Commissioner for the Prince of Orange. My Lord Ross and Sr James Montgomery thō they informed the government of most they knew, yet refused to be wittnesses, and by that means, the latter especially, kept up his reputation prety tollerably with the King still : My Lord Annendale thō he absconded for a time, at last came in, and not only tould all that had passed at the Club, but even trecherously informed against Mr Ferguson and some others who had been so generous as to conceal him in his troubles ; and then after haveing discover'd also Mr Nevil Pain's business into Scotland (whither he had gon at his sollicitation) he contrived to have him seized even at his own house, upon which he was * tortured according to the then Laws of the Country which he underwent with great courage and constancy : this defection in the Chiefs brought many to follow their example, drew a great jealousie upon those who did it not, and render'd them much less capable of serueing the King afterwards.

The E. of
Dumfermling,
Majr Gen:
Buchan, &c.
keep the war
alive in the
highlands.

This project failing, the King's friends represented to him, there was no method now but that of force, to support his intrest in that Kingdom ; and that then he might be assured

---

* This according to *Dalrymple* (Vol. 1. p. 426.) was the last instance of the use of Torture in Scotland. " An account of it is to be found in the record of the Scottish Privy Council, 10th December 1690." EDITOR.

the greatest part of it would declare for him, who now were so
overawed by the Enemies troops and garisons, that they
neither durst attempt any thing, nor (were they willing) could
they assemble to any considerable body ; that Major General
Buchan, the Earle of Dumferling, * Cannon and others, headed
some small parties still in the highlands, to keep life in the
cause ; but that unless his Majesty sent mony, armes, and a
considerable force, they could never doe any thing to purpose ; to which he replyd, He was not out of hopes of answering their expectation if matters went tollerably in Ireland,
wher he then was, and notwithstanding the difficultys of
provindeing a sutable force to oppose so formidable an armie
as the Prince of Orange was bringing against him, he had
prepared such a number of men, hors and Dragoons, as was
then demanded by the Scotch, but being disapointed of the
Ships which he was promised to transport them, was no less
troubled than they to be out of capacity of giveing them that
assistance : however he sent Sʳ George Berkeley with mony
and some other necessarys to their relief, who at his arrival in
Kintail found the King's friends had been so pressed, that many

* " Upon the death of the Viscount Dundee," says *Macpherson* (Original Papers,
Vol. 1. p. 374.) " the spirit of the Highlanders, who were in arms for JAMES,
declined. Colonel Cannon, who succeeded to the command, was neither loved
for his manner, nor respected for his conduct. The Insurgents, however, remained attached to their principles; and though they retired home for the winter,
they were ready, with the return of summer, to take the field. Major General
Buchan was sent to command them." — *Macpherson* then subjoins a detail of operations after the arrival of that officer in Scotland, a letter from Sir John M‘Lean
to JAMES, with assurances of perpetual fidelity and attachment, and also a letter
from General Buchan to JAMES, informing him, that the Earl of Bredalbin could
not be depended on, and that Lord Tarbat had attempted to buy off the Clans;
this Letter concludes with saying, " Sir George Berkley is an honest, loyal man,
and knows much more than I can write, and it will be very fit that he be dispatched back again, for the Highlanders have a high esteem for him." *Macpherson* inserts also *A General Letter from the Officers and Chiefs of Clans, now in arms
in Scotland, to* JAMES. EDITOR.

of them had either made their peace, or were So blocked up that they could not assemble their small forces, besides there were eight frigats continually cruseing on the coast, which did not only hinder many Clans, as Sr John Maclane's, Sr Donal Macdonald's and others, from sending their men, but made many descents, burned houses, and destroyed Castles of such as refused to come in, or, to giue their words at least, no to disturb the government; the Earle of Seaford, who lay most opertunely to join Buchan, was complained of to the King for his backwardness on this occasion, but he excused himself on the same account as others did ; the enemy he sayd had so many garisons in the heart of his Country, that both his houses were possessed by them, which made it impossible to stir, but that he hoped by his intrest with the Earl of Leven his Kindsman, to get them remoued, and then he should haue two thousand foot, some hors, and six houses garison'd for his Majestys Service, that at present all he could possebly assemble, would not be aboue three hundred men, which would do little good and disapoint his prospect of regaining all. But notwithstanding this backwardness of those who were capable of doing most good, Major Gen: Buchan and the rest had form'd a sort of flying camp dureing the summer, more in expectation of succours from Ireland, than hopes of doeing any thing themselves, being in the last degree of indigence; however the Earl of Melvin being a timerous man and fearfull of haveing any disturbance during his government, made some offers of a cessation which would haue been advantagious enough to the Royal partie, and given time to wait for a better season and a greater supply ; but Buchan being advised to make an inroad into Cromdaile, Sr Thomas Levingston who was then at Inverness had intelligence of it from Some of Buchan's own people and so surprized him in the night, he defended himself better than could be expected and lost very few men, however was

Maj^r Gen:
Buchan
worsted in
Cromdaile.

forced to retire and quit his enterprize with some precipitation.

This ill success in the field as well as in Parliament made
the King's friends harken to the proposalls of a peace which
they had rejected in the begining of the year, for the Prince of
Orange being exceeding desirous to leaue all at quiet in great
Britain ere he passed into Ireland, had profer'd five thousand
pound and several other advantages to the Earl of Bredalbin
to compass it, who then refused the offer, because the King's
friends were avers from any such thoughts; but now their
circomstances and opinions being alter'd, My Lord Bredalbin
went to meet the Prince of Orange at Chester to propose at
least a cessation, but the Prince being gon before he arriued,
nothing was done in it, so the Loyal partie remain'd under the
oppression of their enemies, who growing every day stronger
on their hands, droue them to the last extremity as well as the
most abstruce recesses of the Country.

This they represented to the King who was now return'd into The King's
France, and layd before him the projects of his friends in both friends in
Kingdoms, who were of opinion a landing should be made in Supply, and
Scotland, preferable to England, where the body of the Nation King's landing
was against him, and would be much more when an Army than in
from France was brought in amongst them; whereas in Scot- England.
land it was manifest (they Sayd) that three partes of four
wished his restoration, and would heartely concur in it if there
were a body of men to cover their riseing; that of aboue neen
hundred parishes in the Kingdom, not aboue 90 Ministers had
taken the oathes, that the four Universitys had publickly
declared against the Government, that there was not aboue
twenty of the Nobility that sat in Parliament, and that the
greatest part of the gentry had refused the oathes; that the
gross of his Majestys English friends were in Lancashire,
Yorkeshire, and the Northeren parts, which could easily join,

and that no Nation agreed better with the French than the Scotch; that they only required six thousand foot, a thousand hors, Saddles, bridles &c, for three thousand dragoons, with armes and amunition for ten thousand men more, and that if it suted with his Most Christian M: convenience, would rather the embarkement should be at Brest, than Dunkerk, and be brought into Clide, that the Ships which carryd those men might stop the transportation of the Prince of Orange's troops from Ireland.

The King
sends some
present
relief to the
Highlanders
by a Ship
from Nants.

The King was no less pressing to obtain this supply from the French than they in desireing it, and in the intrim sent them some mony, brandy, armes, corn, salt, pouder, and other necessarys by a Ship from Nants; the Queen also before the King's return from Ireland had order'd five thousand pound Sterling to be payd them from England, and had destined ten thousand pound more to follow it, but as for the forces required, the King was obliged to tell them, That thō he could not hithertoo prevail with his Most Christian Majesty in that point, yet the late advantages he had got at sea and two signal Victorys at land, had given him so great a superiority, as made people hope he would soon be brought to it: and accordingly Monsʳ de Signeley the Secretary for the Marine had layd the project and resolved to put himself on board the fleet to see it executed, but crosses and disapointments pursued the King through all the Laborinthes of his life; for not long after this able Minister, and the onely one affectionate to his intrest, unfortunately dyèd, which put an end to his designs just as he was upon the point of executing them.

Whilest Scotland called thus pressingly for succours, Ireland was no less urgent on the same account, so the King was in a continual state of violence, not knowing what necessitys first to attend too, much less how to procure funds for any; tis true My Lord Tyrconnel had got, as was Sayd, a promis of supply to follow him, but that was long a comeing and in the mean time it was not possible to immagin the hardships the Irish Soldiers were put too, famin within and a numerous enemie without gaue them no eas nor respite: The English made an attempt during the winter to pass the Shannon at Lanesborough, James Town, and Banaker bridg, at one and the same time, but the Duke of Berwick sent out parties which prevented them and endeavour'd what he could to molest them in his turn, all the winter long; but nothing did it so much as the Rapperees * who performed many bould actions, especially one O'Connor, who with sixty men on horsback and as many on foot surprized two companys of Granadeers, whom they cut to pieces, then went to Philips Town in King's country where they killed a hundred and twenty Dragoons, burnt the Town, and carryd away a great booty of horses.

TOM.
IV.
1690.

BUT these acts of hostility brought no real relief to the suffring Troops, and My Lord Leiftenant at his arrival in January $\frac{20}{1}$ found the Soldiers so miserably naked, that it moued compassion, nor were the Officers any better; so he thought in the first place to cloath the latter, which he proportioned to doe for fiue louis d'ors a piece, and that they might not think it too mean a cloath, resolued to wear a sute of the same himself, but they haveing more mind of the mony, he sent a man into France only to buy linen, and distributed the greatest part of the mony he had brought amongst them; he could not giue less than a hundred crowns to a Collonel for Cloaths, equipage, and all necessarys, and so proportionably downwards two hundred crowns to a Brigadeer, and four hundred to a Major General, this tooke theerteen thousand louis d'ors, and he brought but fourteen thousand with him, besides ten thou-

1691.
My Lord Tyrconnel returns to Limerick in January 1691, where he finds the Soldiers in a miserable condition.

* For an account of them, see *Dalrymple's Memoirs*, (Vol. 1. P. 454.) EDITOR.

sand he left at Brest to buy meal &c; so there remain'd but a thousand louis d'ors for all other necessary provisions, caisons, carts, carriages for the artillery &c, nothing of which could be had, or made to moue without mony: in this situation the number of men instead of augmenting the strength, only serued to multiply difficultys, and encreas the burthen. Balderick O'Donnal had set up for a sort of an independant Commander, and haveing got togather no less than eight regiments newly raised, with a crowd of loos men over and aboue, lived in a manner at discretion ; so that these troops were in effect, but a rabble that destroyd the Country, ruin'd the inhabitants, and prevented the regular forces from drawing that subsistance they might otherwise haue had from the people ; nor was this inconvenience to be remedyd unless there had been mony to pay them, however to make things go as far as possible, Commissioners were sent out to regulate the quartering of Soldiers, and that the takeing up Cattle, provisions, &c, for the use of the Army, might be done with as much equality, and as little burthen as possible to the people. The only comforth My Lord Tyrconnel had, was to find himself well enough receiud at his return, notwithstanding the factious endeavours of his Enemies ; for haveing brought a patent of an Earle for Coll: Sarsfeild, it put him in a good temper enough, and he being realy zealous in the King's service, engaged for the quiet comportment of the other muteneers, and acted heartely in conjunction with the Lord Lieftenant while his former Councellors were absent, which made him press the King mightely to keep them where they were ; but his Majesty was under an obligation of disgusting no side, and to treat with tenderness and condiscention people whose aimes and inclinations did not only ly cross to one another, but even to his own intrest and intentions: for My Lord Montcassel who had a great and beneficial command over those Irish who came first into France (where he now was

settled) had always been of an opposite partie to My Lord
Tyrconnel, and did all he could to thwart whatever he aimed
at in that Court; which still made the King's taske the more
difficult, where there were so many different intrests, and con-
current factions to be managed, both of the French and his
own Subjects, and yet a due regard to be had to them all; he
exhorts My Lord Tyrconnel therefore to the same method,
not to use people too roughly, but gain them by gentleness,
which he promised his Majesty to doe, thō he own'd it was not
agreeable to his temper : but the King had an other reason for
this moderation, he was in pain for the Duke of Berwick, with
whose privacy and consent those Commissioners came away,
who did as good as tell the King, they looked upon him as a
sorte of hostage for their good reception and kind treatment;
this made his Majesty resolue to send for him by the first good
convenience, so upon My Lord Tyrconnel's arrival in that
Kingdom, he order'd him to leue it, which he did accordingly,
and return to France.

It was very wonderfull that the extream miserie and universal wants the Irish Army was in, should not deterr the
Enemie from deserting over to it, which they did in great
numbers ; and shew'd so general a disposition to it, that My
Lord Tyrconnel assured the King, that had he but so much
mony to spare, as would reach a pistole a piece, and subsist
them afterwards, he believed a therd part of the Prince of
Orange's Army would haue come over; but he sayd it was in
vain for poor folkes to talke, who were never believed when
they plead'd for mony ; besides the Enemie finding that, used
their Soldiers something better, who hithertoo had a subsistance
indeed, but not one penny of pay, but now were more liberal
towards them ; for they had better resources on such occasions,
it being still in their power to content their people when they
thought proper to doe it, because they cared not what load

they layd upon the inhabitants of the Country (which they were in a manner wholly masters of) and made no difficulty of treating them like slaves for the better relief of their troops ; of which there could not be a greater instance, than the contrivance they made use of to redeem three thousand of those prisoners which the French had lately taken at Flerus and other places, pretending they had so many in Ireland and would send them to be exchanged ; whereas they had not in reality a thousand, the rest were poor people of the Country they gather'd togather and sent away by force, which the Irish complain'd of, as a piece of cruelty they would haue made a scruple of doing to Indians, or the most barberous nation in the world.

The Succours promis'd from France are long a coming, and in the interim the Irish suffer extreamly.

All this while want and miserie encreased amongst the Irish troops, the fleet which Monsr Louuois promised with provisions &c, was not yet arrived, thō it was near the end of March, which forced the Lord Lieftenant to press its departure with great earnestness, and at the same time to represent its insufficiency when it came, their necessitys being greater than immagined, even to occasion mutenys in several places ; the garison of Thureley had unanimously layd down their armes, saying, they would not serue only to be starved, but upon perswasions and promises were prevail'd upon to take them up again, which was become the only method of keeping men to their duty ; for their was no chastizeing nor even reprimanding an Officer, for he presently cryd, He would serue no longer, and there was no obligeing them to it without pay ; nor was it possible to keep the Soldiers togather without subsistance at least, whereas for a long time, ere the fleet arriued from France, they were reduced to halfe a pound a bread a day for each Soldier, and even wood was grown so scarce that the French Intendant at Galway, proposed the sending bisket rather than meal, there not being wherewithall to bake it ; that they had been forced to buy the ruins of houses and old ships for bakeing the flouer they had already, and that now instead of deserters comeing to them, the excessiue misery occásion'd great disertion amongst the Irish themsclues : This was mortifying news to the King, who upon it urged all he could the Fleet's speedy departure, but Mons' de Louuois (a haughty and hardened Minister) took little notice of these complaints, he writ to My Lord Tyrconnel, He was surprized at his seeming dissatisfyd with the supplys which were a comeing, or that he should think them insufficient, much less that he should trouble him with complaints against My Lord Montcassell, or of dissentions amongst themselves ; that he ought to govern things with that prudence as not to let the common cause suffer through personal animositys, and that the succours already received and about to be sent, merited his overlooking a few obstacles that lay in his way, and therefore expected he should make the best use of them ; he promised him indeed, that when the twelve hundred recrutes came, (which were for the Irish troops now in France) he would represent his further demands to the King his Master.

That Minister took care to sell his favours at as high a rate as was possible, so the Irish troops which were already arriued and the recrutes which were now expected, payd in great measure for the supplys he return'd ; but the King was under a necessity of overlooking that, and thought himself happy he had brought him to so good a temper as he now was in ; My Lord Tyrconnel, indirectly indeed, had contribited to this change, by a certain contrivance intended only to secure his own credit, but had this good effect besides : It seems when he and Mons' de Lausune return'd togather from Ireland, My Lord Tyrconnel tould him at their arrival at Brest, that seeing they had both many enemies, their conduct would infallebly be censured to a great degree, and they both run.

the hazard of being ruin'd, if they stuck not to one an other, and justifyd each others actions; this appear'd too reasonable not to be readily embraced by the Count de Lausune, who stood most in need of a support in this case; so then he tould him, that on account of his own age and infirmity he could not travel fast, that on the other hand delays might be dangerous, so desired the Count not to stay for him, but make what expedition he could to Court, where when he arrived, according to the plan already agreed betwixt them, he justifyd the Duke of Tyrconnel's conduct in every particular, which so prepared the way for him, that he found a very gracious reception (as was sayd) at his arrival ; but when it came to his turn, to answer certain questions concerning Monsr de Lausun's behaveour, he sayd, indeed he believed he meant well and did his best, but could not excuse certain failures which were too manifest to be palliated : when Monsr de Lausun heard this, he was in a mighty rage, but there was no retracting what he had sayd in My Lord Tyrconnel's justification, who little vallued his ressentment, haveing so dextrously made use of him, to establish his own credit with the Minister, who was charmed to find the blame cast upon a person he affected so little; and the King might haue reaped no small benefit too from this contrivance, had not fortune ever cross'd to his expectation, for as the King had lost that Minister by the chois he had formerly made of Lausun, so he gained him in some measure again, by this accidental humiliation : but Monsr de Louuois' suddain death soon after, put an end to those hopes; whereas his Son, who succeeded in his employment, inherited his father's harsh and imperious temper, and aversness to his Majesty and his intrest.

It was now the begining of May and there was yet no news of the Fleet, thō for a month they had been reduced to eat hors flesh, nor had the Soldiers seen a bit of bread, nor any sort of

drink but water, for aboue that time; besides by the account
which My Lord Tyrconnel had of what this Fleet would bring
when it came, he perceiued it would fall infinitly short of
supplying them with those necessarys, that were in a manner
indispensebly required ; there was so little mony, and so small
a quantity of provisions, that all My Lord Tyrconnel aimed
at was only to giue the Soldiers, each a penny a day, and
their bread, with rations to the Officers in proportion, yet
upon computation he found it would not reach for two months,
unless the King sent a thousand pistoles more, which he ear‑
nestly beg'd of his Majesty to doe, thō he spared it out of his
small allowance, and retrenched it from the necessary expence
of his family.

Thus was the King press'd and teazed with more vehemence,
as the difficulty of answering their expectations encreased ; it
was a grievous affliction to him, not (to) be able to relieve them,
but he could not do impossible things, however he did infinitely
more in supplys of that nature, than could haue been expected
in his circomstances, never Prince knew better how to struggle
with want and poverty, nor how to put that little he had, to
the most proper, Charitable, and benificial uses, and would
haue counted himself happy had that been the only burthen
upon him; but the continual complaints, dissentions, and
animositys amongst his own people perplexed him more than
all the rest, where it was of the greatest importance to mentain
an unity : The Duke of Tyrconnel's signal services clamed a
right to a continuation in the high station he had put him ; and
yet not being so versed in the leading of an Army, and management of Military Affairs, as many whose sole profession it was
(which his illwillers failled not to represent, togather with
certain partialitys which it was hard for a man in so much
power and so many provocations to keep entirely free from)
put the King in great doubts, which side to incline too, or how

to keep the ballance so even, as that though he could not make
them friends to one an other, at least he might keep all sides
in amity with himself; for besides the four Envoys from the
Army, others had sent up remonstrances against his conduct :
The Count de Lausun sided openly with the Complainers, but
that My Lord Tyrconnel was not much ashtonished at; thō
they had agreed well enough in Ireland, he knew the occasion
of the change, but what gaue him most disquiet, he sayd, was
to find by his Majestys couldness to him, he had giuen toò
much credit to the insinuation of his enemys ; whilst they, on
the other hand, were dissatisfyd he did not giue more, and the
Court of France the less inclined to giue a helping hand to
people that pulled so many different ways; all which contradictions and disunions fell still upon the King in the end, he
was called upon for justice by those who thought themselves
injuried, for supplys to all their wants, and redress of all their
grivances, while those from whom he could only expect assistance were prepossessed against him and against those methods
which alone were capable of relieveing them : this put the
Irish under a necessity of equiping, paying, cloathing and
provideing for an Army, in a manner without mony, cloaths,
amunition, or provisions, except what came from France,
which was so little, and so long a comeing, that they had all
like to haue perished ere it arriued, and yet were under a
necessity all the while of repaireing their fortifications, thō
the poor Soldiers had scarce a piece of bread to eat, or a
handful of straw to ly upon, when they return'd tired from
their worke; so that under such an universal indigence,
togather with want of discipline, and union amongst themselves,
it was a miracle they brought it so far as they did.

The afflicting accounts of these things, were grievious to the
King, but were not the only ones he had; it seemed as if the
extent of his dominions had been ordained by providence only

The attempts
made in Eng-
land for the
King's resto-
ration, proue
unsuccessfull
likewise.

to serue for an augmention of his Crosses, for England brought in its quota to this account too ; the King's friends there were in no condition to resist the government, yet their numbers encreased dayly with such as began to be dissatisfyd with the Change, this drew many of them to consult how to redress the miseries they had brought upon themselves ; but those struggles proueing too weake to disingage them, serued only to intangle them the more, and afflict the King with the news of continual disapointments, the oppression and ruin of his friends by courts of pretended justice in England, as they were by famin and the Sword in Scotland and Ireland.

There had been many conferences held by the King's Protestant friends in England how to restore him, so as to retriue the Church of England's honour and yet prouide for its security, and that his return might be without danger to the Protestant Religion, which they had an equal concern for with that of their duty to their Prince ; this made them aprehend a French power and yet they found it impracticable to compas the King's restoration without it ; for they owned the greatest part of England was still the same fooles or knaues, and that nothing would make them other but fear, so that unless the King (they sayd) would shew them some cause for that, he must not expect they would ever be his again, or that the people would be gained by obligations alone ; but on the other hand he was to consider, that a french power was hugely disagreeable to the Nation, and that there was no offring at an absolute conquest, which, if he did, would prove a more bloody business than the Romans, Saxons, or Normans found it : in order therefore to accommodate these seeming contradictions, it was resolved My Lord Preston should goe to the King, togather with Mr John Ashton, and Mr Elliot, to propose the embraceing in the first place such methods as would pleas the people, by bestowing imployments about him to Protestants preferable to Catholicks, and by that means tell the Nation what they may expect when he comes amongst them; that he might liue a Catholick in devotion, but must reign a Protestant in government, that the utmost he could expect for Catholicks was a legal libertie of Conscience, and that the least he must think of for the Protestants, was to put the administration into their hands, who being at least two hundred to one, had the wealth, heads, and power of the Nation on their side, that he must haue (even during his abode in France) at least eight or nine Protestants Lords or Gentlemen in his Council, that he might apear to be, so far theirs again : then on the other hand their business was to obtain a force, but upon these conditions, that the most Christian King would engage his word, only to *assist* * his Majesty as a friend and Mediator and not send the offended Prince back with the ungratefull character of a Conquerour ; that he would pleas to permit the English Protestants to haue Chappels at their own cost, which would convince the world that his late severity to the Hugenots proceeded more from the hazard he thought himself in, from their Antemonarchical and resisting principle, than a desire of persecution ; and that the King would pleas to publish in his Declaration, that he brought only so much power with him, as was necessary for his defence, and (*to*) secure his Subject's resort to him, but would dismis them assoon as he had rid the Kingdom of the foreigners that had invaded it ; this was the substance of what they were to negotiate, but the design being discover'd, they were seized on board the Vessel they had hired for that purpose, before it got out of the river : In the hurry of this surprize, My Lord Preston fortuned to leaue the instructions and other papers as they were tyd up togather to a piece of lead, in the place where he lay, which Mr Ashton

---

* Interlined as before mentioned. EDITOR.

perceiveing, tooke up as privately as he could, and puting them in his brest, endeavour'd to get to the side of the Ship, with intent to drop them gently into the river ; but being observed, was prevented, and they seized upon, ere he could do it, which proved fatal to them as being the only evidence of their design : accordingly My Lord Preston and Mr Ashton (there not appearing evidence enough against Mr Elliot) were brought to their tryals, condemned, and the later executed, being the first that suffer'd by a court of justice for the Royal cause, which was a new subject of grief to the King for he knew not what would be the Consequence, when he found the Laws, as well the sword, turn'd against him ; and those suffer as traitors who were most distinguished for their fidelity and Loyalty. My Lord Preston indeed obtained his pardon, but it was by confessing most, if not all he knew, he own'd he had consulted with My Lord Clarendon, the Bishop of Ely, and Mr Pen about restoreing the King, and that Mr Pen had tould him, the Duke of Ormonde, ye Earles of Devonshire, Dorset, Maclesfeild, Lord Brandon &c, were well affected to it, he confirmed the account the Government had already of the Scoth Plot, wherein Nevil Pain had been concerned, that My Lord Dartemouth had given him that account of the Fleet which was found in his papers ; but My Lord Danby (to whose examination he was left) was not satisfyd with this discovery, he thought he could accuse those persons more fully if he pleased, whose names he pretended he have learn'd only by hearsay from Mr Pen and therefore was against his being pardonned, unless he did it ; but it is probable the Prince of Orange thought it not prudent to attack so great a body of the Nobility at once, that what he knew, was sufficient either to be a ware of them, or by forgiveness and a seeming clemency gain them to his intrest, which method succeeded so well, that what ever sentiments those Lords, (which Mr Pen had named) might

My Lord
Preston and
Mr Ashton are
tryd the 16th,
and 19th of
Janu: and
condem^d.

Mr Ashton
executed the
28th of janu:

T O M.
IV.

1691.
Mʳ Bulkeley's
negociation
with My Lᵈ
Churchil and
Lord Godol-
phin, Marques
of Halifax, &cᵉ.

haue had at that time, they proued in effect most bitter enemies to his Majestys cause afterwards.

But notwithstanding this discovery, others were not discouraged from owneing their inclination to return to their duty; and to the King's greater surprize My Lord Churchill and Lord Godolphin themselves were of the number: It is hard (considering what has happen'd since) to make a right judgment of their intentions, and whether they had any further aim in what they did, than to secure themselves from the just resentment of an offended Prince, should he fortune to return by other means, which the successes of France, the distraction of the Prince of Orange's affairs, and the general discontent, made them reasonably apprehend; however tis certain their seemeing repentance (especially My Lord Churchill) had all the markes immaginable of sincerity. Mʳ Bulkley being lately return'd from France, assoon as by the mediation of friends he had obtained his libertie, went to see My Lord Godolphin, and finding he sayd nothing of the King at his first visite, resolved to try him at least the next; so tould him, He was in admiration to find his Lordship in imployment again, he haveing assured him before he left England, he was resolved never to take any for the future: to which My Lord replyd, He had promised the Pᶜᵉ of Orange to come in again at his return from Ireland, and that he kept him to his word; however he enquired after the Court of Sᵗ Germains, but with a Seeming dispondency; which opinion Mʳ Bulkeley endeavouring to disabuse him of, pressed him a little further on the point to know what assurance he might giue the King of his willingness to serue him; at which My Lord raising himself from his chair, sayd, He would quit his imployment assoon as he could, and so left him: This was a coy begining, but it disincouraged him not from trying others at least; so he went to My Lord Halifax next, who received him with

11

open armes, and laying his brest naked, sayd, He would doe all that lay in his power to serue his Majesty, and forward his return : this Lord it seems was of a temper never to be Satisfyd, if he was controwled in any thing, this had alianated him formerly from the King *when on y͏ᵉ * Throne*, and now the Prince of Orange finding his Politicks, thō nice and subtil in speculation, yet seldom good in practice, they two did not hit it long; however this free assurance, whatever motive it came from, togather with that of several other discontented Noblemen encouraged such as were more diffident, and My Lord Halifax giveing Mͬ Bulkely leave to acquaint My Lord Godolphin with his sentiments, and that he would concur with him in any thing for the King's good, made that Lord boulder likewise upon the matter ; so that afterwards he made all the protestations immaginable of his good will to the King, and that so soon as the Prince of Orange returned from Holland (who was then gon to the Congress at the Hague) he would quit all, and then be entirely at his Majestys service and disposal ; for that he made a conscience (he sayd) of be-traying his trust (it had been happy if he had always been so scrupulous) he therefore resolved (he sayd) to disingage himself from any such tye, notwithstanding the Prince of Orange had writ to him from the Hague (which letter he shew'd Mͬ Bulkeley) complaining how many difficultys lay hevy upon him at present, in reference to the Confederates as well as other affairs, but that nothing troubled him so much as his thoughts of leaveing his service in such a conjuncture, he being the person he had most confidence in, and most kindness for of any English man, and therefore charges him not to think of doing it; but he made shew as if all this weighed little with him in respect of his duty to his lawfull Sovereign.

---

* Interlined by the Son of James the Second. Eᴅɪᴛᴏʀ.

1691.
My Lord
Churchil
seems ex-
treame peni-
tent, and
proposes to
serue the
King the best
he can.

Dureing these private conferences with My Lord Godolphin
Mr Bulkeley met him and My Lord Churchil one day togather
in the Park, who seeming mighty glad to see him, invited them
both to dine at his lodgings, where he received him frankely
and made such advances as he resolved to try him likewise;
but it seems My Lord Churchil was so forward in the matter
as to prevent him, by sending soon after for Coll: Sackville,
who waiting on him (thō with some reluctancy) was hugely
surprized to find him in apearance the greatest penitant
immaginable; he beg'd of him to go to the King and aquaint
him with his sincere repentance, and to intercede for mercy,
that he was ready to redeém his apostasy with the hazard of
his utter ruine, his crimes apeareing so horrid to him that he
could neither sleep, nor eat but in continual anguish, and a
great deal to that purpose; upon which they parted, and
Collonel Sackville acquainting his friends with what had
happen'd, who thought it proper to giue him what encouragement they could conceiveing that a person of so great credit
in the Army and so considerable a post in the Council, would
be of mighty consequence to the King's affairs, but resolued
at the same time to search him to the Quick, and try whether
by informeing them readily of what he knew, they might
depend upon his sincerity as to what he pretended: accordingly Coll: Sackville and M^r LLoyd had several meetings with
him (for the former finding their being togather had been
obserued, tould him, it would create a suspicion should he be
missing so soon after, but nameing M^r LLoyd for that service).
My Lord readily agreed to it, and without the least hezitation
gaue them both an account of all the forces, preparations,
and designes both in England, Scotland, and Ireland, whither,
he Sayd, the Prince of Orange intended to go himself, if the
French pressed not too hard upon the Confederates in
Flanders, and that he hoped to reduce Ireland so soon as to

be able to bring part of that Army into the Low Countrys that
very Campaign; he gave likewise an account of the Fleet,
and in fine of whatever was intended either by Sea or land,
which concurring with the informations they had from other
hands was a great argument of his sincerity ; as was also the
constant intelligence he gaue of several incident informations
brought dayly to the Secretaries office, in relation to Jacobites,
and they themselves amongst the rest ; whereby they avoided
many inconveniences and troubles, which otherwise would
haue fallen upon them; he desired instructions which way he
might be serviceable, without being admited into the King's
secrets, owning, that the vilanies he had commited, did but
too justly debar him from expecting any such confidence ; he
doubted not, he sayd, but he could bring over many great
men to the King's partie; and desired to know whether he
should endeavour that, in reference to My Lord Danby, who,
he sayd, was the main stay to the present government, or join
with those Lords and Commoners who were contriveing his
ruin, that hopes of pardon would bring many back to their
duty, it being a desperation of it which made that Lord as
well as many others so vehement, who wrought as it were for
their lives, hopeing for no mercy after the ills they had done;
he proffer'd to bring over the English troops that were in
Flanders if the King required it, but rather proposed he should
act in consert with many more who were intent upon the same
thing, that is, to endeavour next Sessions to get all the
foreigners sent out of the Kingdom which would bring home
more English troops, and those he hoped he could influence
to better purpose ; that in case the French were successfull in
Flanders, or any ill accident should happen to the Prince of
Orange, he believed his restoration would be very easy, that
the Commonwealth partie might probably attempt something,
but that would be rather advantagious than prejudicial to his

Majestys intrest; he advised him when he came, not to bring too numerous an Army, a French power, he sayd, was terrifying to the people; nevertheless he was so sensible that a competent force was necessary, that it would neither be fair in him to propose, nor prudent in his Majesty to trust, to those alone who had used him so treacherously already; that he supposed twenty thousand men might be sufficient to restore the King, and yet not so great a number as to terrify the people, if his Majesty promised to return them when settled in his Throne; that it was necessary for him to support Ireland which the Prince of Orange would make a great effort to reduce, to be more at leasure to attack France; he thought it proper, he Sayd, the King should enjoin My Lord Godolphin not to lay down, who being a Commissioner of the Treasure and one of the Cabinet Council, must needs be more serviceable in that post, than in a private capacity; and upon the whole, he appeared the most Sollicitous immaginable for the King's intrest, and the most penitant man upon earth for his own fault, sayd a thousand things to express the horrour he *had of his vilanies to ye best of Kings, and y^t it would be impossible for him to be at rest * till he* had in some measure made an attonement, by endeavouring (thō with the utmost peril of his life) to restore his injured Prince and beloved Master. His comportement in fine seem'd so candid, and his penitence so sincere, that the King's friends thought it necessary that his Majesty should be acquainted with it; accordingly M^r LLoid went to St Germains upon this errand, by whome all this particulars were related.

The King's mercyfull disposition inclined him to forget the greatest injurys upon the least shew of amendement, and tis

---

* Interlined by the Son of James the Second. EDITOR.

probable this was no more ; for thō in his letters afterwards he
kept up to the same termes in expressing his sorrow for what
was past and Zeale to repaire it, as that he would giue up
his life with pleasure if he could thereby recall the fault he
had commited ; that he was So entirely return'd to his duty,
and loue to his Majestys person that he should be ready with
joy upon the least command to abandon Wife, Children and
Contry to regain and preserue his esteem ; nevertheless the
King found no efects of these mighty promisses, for his Majesty
insisting upon his offer of bringing over the English troops in
Flanders, as the greatest service he could doe him, he excused
himself under pretence there was some mistake in the message,
that it would ruin all to make the troops come over by parcells,
that his business was to gain an absolute power over them,
then to doe all the business at once; however, as if he had
merited great matters he grows upon the King in his demands,
for his first request was only two lines under his hand, thō not
signed, to testify that he would extend his pardon to him, or
any other thō the greatest offenders, who by their future
behaviour should giue him proofs of their deserueing it, which
he sayd would influence the . . . . Self, My Lady
Churchill, and others : This the King readily complyd with ;
but his Lordshipp stoped not there, when he found the King so
good neatured, his next request was, That he would pleas to
write to My Lord Godolphin and assure him of forgiveness too;
in which letter the Queen must insert a few words likewise to
testify her being reconciled to him, and yet at the same time to
order him to keep his imployments, to be more serviceable as
was pretended (it seems he had soon forgot his friends scrupulosity, and that he made a conscience of betraying his trust)
So that in fine, they were to be pardon'd, and in security in
case the King return'd, and yet to suffer nothing in the intrim,
nor to giue any other proofs of their sincerity *in case the King*

T O M.
IV.

1691.
LORD
CHURCHIL's
LETTER TO
THE KING.
- - Jan: 169\frac{0}{1}.
IDEM LETTER,
May 30 1691.

THE KING's
LETTER TO
MY LORD
CHURCHIL.
Apr: 20 1691.

return'd*, than bare words and empty promises, which under
pretence of being suspected, or of doing greater service afterwards, there never was found a sutable time to put the least of
them in execution; however the King thought fit to bear with
this sorte of dubble dealing, and seeing him begin to decline
in the Prince of Orange's favour, still hoped he might doe
service in the end, so accepted his excuses, and continued
his correspondance from time to time as long as he lived, thō
with scarce any other effect than to bring an additional expence
upon him by apointing persons in England to act under his
directions; and an additional trouble from the continual complaints of the King's other friends, who being of different
religions and haveing different views, instead of uniteing their
force for the King's seruice studyed all they could to twart
each others methods.

My Lord Dartmouth's profer of seruice which he sent likewise
by M^r LLoid, thō it was probably more sincere, proued of as
little use as the rest; for not being able to bring over any ships,
all he could doe, he say'd, was to come himself, which he
readily profer'd in case he could haue a command of Squadron
of French men of war, which he engaged to Officer and man
with English; but the Court of France were not for trusting
their ships in such slippery hands, so that this profer came to
nothing too, besides he was soon after clap'd up in the Tower,
as it was supposed upon My Lord Preston's information.

The Armys
take the field
in Ireland at
last, and on the
8th of May the
French fleet
came with
supplys to
Limerick. Before this the English Army was prepareing to take the
field in Ireland, and the Irish as yet heard nothing of the Fleet
from France, thō they were at the last extremity, and writ to
the King in case it came not in a few days they would need
no enemy to destroy them. The Duke of Tyrconnel had

---

* The words in Italics have been crossed with a pen. EDITOR.

however been makeing all the preparation he could in the intrim, and had found means with great difficulty to get two pare of broagues, a pare of breeches, and a pare of stockings for each foot Souldier, which with the coats and shirts they expected from France, would cover them at least; he had distribited the little he had as long as it lasted, with as much equality as possible; haveing sent part of what was at Galway to Sligo by sea, and to Athlone upon men's backs, for want of Carriages. At last upon the 8th of May the French fleet appeared in the river of Limerick, it was like the gaining of a victory to people in so great distress; they sung Te Deum as soon as it arriued and went heartely to work to put things in redyness to take the field, but thō this Fleet brought some armes, cloaths, ammunition, and provisions, it brought it seems no mony, for want of which they were hard put to it to get carriages and other necessarys which were still wanting, but by paying tradesmen and workemen, part mony, part little necessarys of apparrel, part fair words, and part promises, in which they were liberal enough, workemen were prevail'd upon to do their best and at last they got to gather 170 caissons, four hundred small cartes, and carriages for ten field pieces; they proportioned the little mony they had left to pay a penny a day to each Soldier for three weeks, which was all infine it would reach too, so My Lord Leiftenant repeated his earnest petition to the King, to send him a thousand pistoles more, which would continue that pay three months, by which time, he sayd, the matter would be decided, and that since the fate of a Kingdom depended upon it, he took the freedom to tell him, He·ought to sell his shirt from his back rather than fail: The King needed not so much sollicitation to be touched both with their necessitys, and the consequence of it, nor to labour all he could towards procureing a further supply, but in the mean time being as much pressed from an other side, his Majesty order'd My Lord Tyrconnel to pay the value of a 1000 ₶ Ster: to a Scotch gentleman, who was apointed to come thither for it, which My Lord Tyrconnel seem'd hugely surprised at; and thō impossebility pleaded his excuse, yet the want of so necessary a relief to the King's friends in the Hightlands of Scotland, consummated their misery and put an end, to his hopes in a manner, on that side.

Sᵗ Ruth and other Officers came in this Fleet.

On this Fleet came Monsʳ Sᵗ Ruth with other French Officers, as also those gentlemen who had been in France to sollicite the Duke of Tyrconnel's removeal; which thō the King had not yeelded too, however had so far given way to their advice as to abridg his power in reference to the military affairs, the direction of which was vested in a manner wholy in Sᵗ Ruth. So that My Lord Tyrconnel who before could haue made a Lieftenant General, had not power now to make a Collonel, which so lower'd his credit in the Army that little regard was had to his authority; but he prudently submited, and left the whole management of it to Sᵗ Ruth, who seemingly carryd fair, but in the bottom was prepossessed against him, which those gentlemen that came with him from France had leasure and opertunity to doe, so that when Sᵗ Ruth writ to the King for more mony, he desired it might not be remitted to My Lord Tyrconnel's hands.

The Enemie apear before Balimore the 6ᵗʰ June, which is surrenderd next day.

While the Irish were thus in the middle of their preparations, and disputes, intelligence was brought them that the enemie being considerably augmented with the addition of Mackày's troops from Scotland, came before Ballimore the 6ᵗʰ of June, and that the very next day Vlick Burke the governour either out of treachery or cowardice surrendred it at discretion, without any considerable opposition; thō he had near eight hundred well armed men in the place, which were all made prisoners of war to the great weakening of those regiments out of which they were detached. General Ginkle remain'd there till the

Duke of Wirtemberge and the rest of the Troops had joined him, and then on the 18th of June apear'd before Athlone: Coll: Fitzgerald the Governour sent out some Granadeers to dispute the Passes and defilés, to retard their aproach, which was done with courage and prudence enough, still retireing before them, which cost the enemie many men; but at last their whole Army and Artillery comeing up, they raised a battery the next day and had soon made a breach in the slender wall, so that on the 20th the Enemie apointed foure thousand detached men to make an assault; there was not aboue three or four hundred in the town on Limpster side, however they defended the breach for some time, till at least two hundred of their men were kill'd or wounded, and the rest so exhausted with eight and forty houres continual action (whereas the Enemie were relieved by their whole Army) that they were forced to retire to the bridg, where they sustain'd all the power of the Rebells till they had broaken down two Arches of it, and thereby stoped at least all communication with the other * Town.

The Irish Army by this time was got into a tollerable readiness to march, and as this action happen'd, came and encamped at a little distance from the Town on Connoagh side; had it been in a condition to take the field sooner it had prevented the loss of the other Town, but the late arrival of the Fleet with other unavoidable impediments, made that impracticable, however they doubted not but to put a stop to the Enemies further progress, and prevent their passing the

---

* " Athlone," says *Dalrymple* (Vol. 1. p. 470, 471.) " consisted of two Towns, one on the English and the other on the Irish side of the Shannon, which were joined together by a stone bridge, and by a ford a little space below the bridge. . . During nine days, one of the most singular spectacles in history was exhibited, that of two Armies waging war upon each other within the walls of a Town, and amidst the ruins they made, where every bullet that was shot brought the imprecations of the inhabitants upon both Armies." Editor.

T O M.
IV.

1691.

On the 18th of June they appear before Athlone.

Athlone makes a good defence.

river: but they on the other hand, encouraged by the Success, pursued the advantage, and fell immediately upon makeing a bridg of boats under the cover of their Cannon, which batter'd the Castle all the while very furiously; nevertheless the Irish, thõ they had no other Artillery but a few field pieces, prevented that design; this put the Enemie upon endeavouring to throw planks over the broken arches of the bridg, which they had in great measure effected, when one Custume with eight or ten men proffer'd to pull them down again; this was joyfully accepted, and accordingly with courage and strength even beyond what men were thought capable of, they threw down the Planks and beams, notwith-standing the continual fire of the Enemy and held it out till they had finished their worke, thõ most of them were killed in the action.

This forced the Enemie to try an other method, and endeavour to carry on their work, by a close gallerie upon the bridg, but the Irish found means to set it on fire, which so disheartned the English, that they held a council of war whether they should not rais the Siege; and had they not, by great fortune just at that time, found a fordable place in the river, they had certainly done it, but that encouraged them to a fresh attempt, haveing already made such breaches in the wall by three batteries which playd cross the water, that the river was become the Sole defence: they resolved therefore to attempt it with all their force, so haveing disposed all things for the attack on the 30ᵗʰ rushed out of a sudden from the English Town, and marching down by the river side, began to pass the ford, and at the same time fired with great fury from all the batteries; which so distracted the garison, that thõ they galled extreamly those who were passing the river, yet others profitting by that diversion, layd planks over the broken arches, and at the same time made a bridg of boats in

an other place, so that the Irish began to giue way. It was
an additional misfortune to the King's affairs (which always
contributed more to the enemies success than their own vallour
or experience) that there happen'd that day to be upon the
guard two regiments which consisted most of recruts, who
makeing but a feeble resistance, the enemie soon made good
the passage, enter'd the Town and obliged the garison to retire
to the camp.

The begining of this misfortune was oweing in great measure
to that spirit of opposition and contradiction, which different
humours and intrest are sure to rais when there is no one that
has authority sufficient to make himself be obeyd ; on one
hand Monsr d'Vson the governour, would haue had a regular
garison of choice men fixed in the place proper to sustain an
attack, but St Ruth had a mind to accustom his new raised
troops to fire and discipline, so made them rowle by turns,
and as an other expedient proposed, that considering the
slightness of the work and the armys being so near, to demollish
the Curtin on their own side, that a whole battallion might
march into the place at once to relieve the garison and mentain
the pass : but Monsr d'Vson in his turn opposed that, saying,
Their business was to defend not demolish forteresses, and
was so confident the English would never attempt so bould an
action, that he was at breakefast a cannon shot from the Town
when the Enemy made the assault ; for which St Ruth (had he
lived) would haue called him to an account ; he made hast
indeed to the Town upon the first alarme, but was born down
and run over by the men that fled, and those detachments
likewise which St Ruth sent to their succour arriveing not till
the Enemie were masters of the Pass and place itselfe, were
easily repulsed. St Ruth upon this thought fit to decamp, and
marched that night a mile towards Balinasto, and haveing

T O M.
IV.

1691.
The Duke of
Tyrconnel
leaves the
Camp and
returns to
Limerick.

passed the river Suck, stayd there three days, from whence he continued his march to Acrim.

Here My Lord Tyrconnel left the Camp and return'd to Limerick, those animositys encreasing (as usually they do by misfortune) he thought it more prudent to yeild a while, than by opiniatring encreas the distemper: in this retreat the Conough Regiments grew very thin, so that the foot by desertion and maroding was reduced from 17000 to about 11000 men; some therefore advised passing the Shannon at Banacker, which would haue brought in all the maroders, who durst not stay behind, and by that means cut betwixt the Enemie and Dublin, made them masters of the plentifull province of Limster, and encreased the Army to 50000 men, nor could the Enemy have follow'd with their cannon, in which consisted their great superiority and advantage; besides they must haue diminished by garisons as well as other accidents, and to be sure delay would haue been more ruinous to Strangers than to the Natiues: the only objection against this, was leaveing Galway uncover'd, but it could not be presumed that for the sake of that Town, the Enemie would have abandoned Dublin, besides all the Country was eaten up about it: but some French

The Battle
of Acrim
the 12 july.

Officers opposeing this advice, and Monsr St Ruth being a little piqued at the late disgrace resolved to wait for the Enemie at Acrim which he found an advantagious post, so encamp'd himself there in two lines upon a riseing ground, with a bog before him, on which there was but two passes, the one at the old Castle of Acrim on the left of the foot, the other about three hundred yards advanced from the right, and because he put his greatest trust in the hors drew the right wing of hors of the first line, in rear of the right of the first line of foot: On Sunday the 12th of july the Enemy advanced with their foot in collums to the bog side, while their hors took a

great round to flank the right; they had no positiue design to
come to a generall action, but to try the countenance of the
King's army, and to driue them if possible from that post with
their cannon, but being once engaged and encouraged by their
former successes soon brought it to a decisiue point: on the
other hand the Irish considering that this was like to proue the
last effort for restablishing the King's authority, and secureing
the estates and liberties of an oppressed people, expected them
with great constancy, and convinced the English troops, they
had to doe with men no less resolute than themselves; so that
never was assault made with greater fury, or sustain'd with
greater obstinacy, especially by the foot, who not only
mentain'd their posts and defended the hedges with great
valour, but repulsed the enemie several times, particularly in
the center, and took some prisoners of distinction; in so much
that they looked upon the victory as in a manner certain, and
St Ruth was in a transport of joy to see the foot of which he
had so mean an opinion behaue themselves so well, and
performe action worthy of a better fate: But it seems in the
begining of the day, St Ruth (perceiveing that the enemie, who
outnumber'd him, stretched out their left so far that he fear'd
being flank'd) order'd the second line of the left to march to
the right; but he, who was to execute that order, caused a
battallion of the first line to file off with the rest, supposeing
the bog in the front would prevent the enemies advanceing,
but they who stood in awe of that Battallion while it faced
them, took courage when it was gon, and by the help of
hurdles made a shift to get over the bog, and at the same time
four Squadrons of the enemies hors, passing a causey, began to
forme themselves on the other side of the defilé: assoon as the
General was informed of the fault that had been made, he
order'd all the Cavalerie to march, puting himself at the head
of it, which being extream good would soon haue dispersed

T O M.
IV.

1691.
S¹ Ruth the
General is
kill'd, and the
battle lost.

those few squadrons of the Enemie, who as yet were but
a formeing, when by a cannon shot he was unfortunately kill'd,
just as * he was saying to those about him, They are beaten,
let us beat them to the purpose : this accident caused a great
confusion, and thō endeavours were made to conceal his death,
yet the first Squadron of the life guard, who was next him,
stoping upon it, the rest did the same and occasion'd a great
delay, which the enemie tooke care to profit by, and passing in
the intrim a considerable body of hors through the defiles,
attack'd and broke both the lines of the Irish foot, the hors
not advanceing in time to their assistance; but instead of that,
giveing all for lost, thought of nothing but saveing themselves
and so gaue an entire victory to the English : The night indeed
comeing on prevented the pursute, however the Irish lost near
four thousand men, nor was that of the English much inferior,
who had they pursued their victory and marched streight to
Limerick had finished the war at one blow ; for the great
consternation the Irish were then in, the fortifications of that
town not finished, the troops dispersed in the mountains and
bogs, there had been no possibility of houlding out before a
victorious Army ; but by the enemies turning their march
towards Galway, they gaue the Irish time to reassemble
their scatered forces and delay their destiny some months
longer.

---

* St. Ruth was a French General who had been sent by James, with the hope
of destroying the competition that had arisen between Tyrconnel and Sarsfield.
" St. Ruth," adds *Dalrymple*, (Vol. 1. p. 469.) was a good Officer, who had been
" sent in the spring to command the Army: a man who, it was thought, would
be agreeable to the Irish, because he had signalized himself against the Protestants
in France. But, although a great part of the Irish Army had, from want of money,
stores, and provisions, been dispersed, S¹ Ruth was furnished with none of these
necessaries. And the Irish complained equally of the ill-timed parsimony of the
French, and of James's want of respect, who, in return for all their services, had
put a foreigner at last over the heads of all their countrymen." Editor.

It was not to be expected that after this defeat Galway
could make any great resistance, however it might well haue
retarded the enemies progress some days, and given time to
perfect the fortifications of Limerick; which, with the help of
the rainy season then near at hand, would infallibly haue saued
it that campaign, but My Lord Clanrickard and others considering nothing but their own security, made such hast to
surrender it, that they would not wait the comeing up of the
enemies cannon, which was yet at Athlone and without which
there was no forceing the place, but gaue it up and themselves
with it, for he and several others 'both Officers and soldiers
remain'd in the Town thō the garison had libertie to march
out, which was conducted to Limerick accordingly.

My Lord Tyrconnel was got to Limerick before this, and
was makeing all the preparations he could for a defence, for
upon the death of St Ruth he began to reassume his former
authority, so immediately dispatched an express to S^{t}Germains,
to beg either a speedy succour or leaue to make conditions for
themselves. The King who was hugely afflicted at this
misfortune, and abundantly sencible of the hard circomstances
the Irish were reduced too, fail'd not to lay their necessities
open to his Most Christian Majesty, telling him, That after
the many hardships they had suffer'd, and difficultys they had
struggled with, it was necessary some speedy resolution should
be taken in reference to them ; that as he was resolved, on one
hand, not to consent to any thing that was disadvantagious to
France, so it was neither sutable to his inclination, nor the
cause for which he sufferd, to let the best and faithfullest of
his subjects labour in vain against such a superiour strength,
with no other prospect than to be most cruelly butcher'd in the
end by the declared enemies both of England and France.
This was too reasonable a request not to be complyd with
and accordingly some succours were prepared, and some mony

Margin notes:
1691.
Galloway surrendred the 20th July.

My Lord Tyrconnel reassumes his authority on St Ruth's death, and prepares to defend Limerick, and on the 25th of Aug: the Enemie apearbeforeit.

order'd to be sent, but the Enemie pressed too hard to giue
any great hopes they could wait the relief which was to come
from a Country so remote; this made My Lord Tyrconnel
aprehend the Army would capitulate in spite of his teeth, and
many persons of distinction were so much inclined that way, as
had like to haue brought it about even before the enemie
apear'd in sight of the Town.

Coll. Henry
Lutterel treats
with the
Enemie about
surrendring
the Town.

Collonell Lutterell was at the head of those disponders, who
fortuned it seems to be sent out with a partie towards six mile
bridg, just as the garison of Galway arrived there, which being
conducted by an escort of the Enemies, he enter'd into a sorte
of negociation with the Officer that commanded it, to know
what conditions would be granted in case they submited ; this
went on some time ere it was discover'd, which by the Partizans
he had in the Army raised a mighty inclination to make terms
and submit : My Lord Tyrconnel thō not aprized of the
treachery was sensible of the evil, so now that he was in a
manner reestateed in his former power, knew it could. spring
from no other fountain than those factious spirits he had long
complain'd of, so writ again to the King, It would be
impossible to do any thing as he ought, if those men were
sufferd amongst them ; that they had misguided St Ruth to
the loss of his life and the Kingdom's ruin ; that they had cryd
up My Lord Lucan only in opposition to him, and in such a
manner as to insult his Majestys authority : and indeed there
happen'd a passage a little before the battle of Acrim, which
gaue broad signs of some ill intention of that nature ; a
Collonel of the army came one day into My Lord Trimilston's
tent, and discoursing of those dissentions, sayd, He would obey
My Lord Lucan independant of the King's authority, in so much,
that should that Lord command him to kill any man in the
Army, he would readily do it : My Lord Trimilston thought it
his duty to acquaint the General with this treasonable expression,.

but the matter was hushed up, and the Collonel went unpu-
nished ; by which however, togather with the seditious petitions
(which were at that time handed about the Army) and Balderic
O'Donnel's hidden practices, it apear'd afterwards that there
was a design of puting the Kingdom into the hands of the
antient Irish, and upon an equal foot with England ; this it
was made O'Donnel so popular, and had raised him that mighty
crowd of followers with which he liued in a manner at discretion while the war lasted, and then made his peace with the
enemie without the King's privity or consent.

But My Lord Lucan, whose intentions were allways right,
and he zealous for the King's seruice, was the first that opposed
his old friends when he found they went beyond the limits of
their duty and allegiance to the King, and it was by his means
that Lutterel's secret correspondence was discover'd ; for one
day a letter comeing from the enemies quarters directed to
Coll: Lutterel, and being accedentely put into My Lord Lucan's
hands, he, suspecting some indirect dealing, open'd it, and
found it came from one Sebastian a favorite of Ginkle's, and
about that treaty he had set on foot with Coll: Lutterel at six
mile bridg ; so he went immediately with it to My Lord Lieftenant, upon which Lutterel was seized, and apointed to be
tryd, which was done as speedely as possible, but he had too
many friends to be condemn'd, so was sentenced only to continue in prison during his Majestys pleasure, but the reduction
of the place soon after, gaue him his libertie, before the King's
resolutions could be known in the matter.

It was supposed this act of justice would haue united the
wavering spirits, and appeas'd that mutenous temper in the
troops, but the fire was rather smother'd over by the late
misfortunes than extinguished, and even My Lord Lucan's
credit now that he sided with My Lord Tyrconnel began to be
as low as his ; however all these obstacles hinder'd not the Lord

Lieftenant (thō he was now very infirme, and naturally slow in his motions as well as his resolutions) to doe all that was possible to put the Town in a condition of defence; he assembled the troops and formed a Camp under the Canon of the place, encompassing it by a line, and sent out parties to fetch in beef, &c, and made the Officers and Soldiers (first shewing the example himself) to take an Oath of fidelity which contain'd a resolution to defend his Majestys right to the last, and never to surrender without his consent; but notwithstanding this Oath and engagement, many Officers soon began to moue for a treaty, alledging that in all probability the affair would be determined one way or the other before the King's mind could be known; but he press'd them only to haue patience twenty days, their being no likelyhood of their being forced so soon, and that in so much time an answer might be had from the King: but while he was thus struggleing with the cálamitous circomstances of his Country, he was seized with a fit of an Apoplexy upon St Lawrence's day, soon after he had done his devotions, and thō he came to his sences and speech again, yet he only languished two or three days and then dy'd, just when he was upon the point of procureing an unity at least amongst themselves, the want of which was the greatest of the many evils they labour'd under.

The Duke of Tyrconnel dys, being seiz'd with an Apoplexi on St Lawrence's day.

The Enemie press the Town, and by Clifford's neglect pass'd the river.

In the mean time the Enemie had blocked up the haven, and were come with their Army within fiue miles of the Town, expecting a battle, because the Irish were still on the same side the river, thō within the lines, and their hors at no great distance, so Ginkle, for greater expedition, was come up without his cannon, which tis probable the success he expected from the private negociation with Mr Henry Lutterell made him think might be needless; but that failing, and Monsr D'Vson (upon whom the command of the troops was now fallen) ordering the foot into the Town and the hors to Clare side, the

Enemie was obliged to prepare for a formal Siege, and wait
their Artillerys comeing up; this delay made it the 25th of
August ere they could post themselves before the place, which,
considering how far the Season was advanced, that the Irish
had 35 battallions tollerably armed, one side of the Town still
open, unless the enemie divided their forces, and then they had
been strong enough to atack either part, the fortifications in a
better condition than the last Siege, the Enemy weaker, and
the wether begining to be rainy, it was presumed Ginkle would
not opiniatre the matter; and Monsr D'Vson with the Frinch
Officers very generously declared, that what mony they had of
their own amounting to 50000 liures should be distribited
amongst the Soldiers, which gaue great satisfaction and encouragement: The enemie on the other hand, by not opening
trenches before the place, seemed as if they design'd only to
bombard it, which they performed indeed with all the violence
immaginable, battering it at the same time with forty pieces of
cannon which ruined abundance of houses, Churches, and at
last open'd a breach near St Dominick's Abbey, so large, that
they made shew of comeing to an assault; but finding the
garison too well prepared to receiue them, and they too well
informed to hazard so desperate an attempt, were upon the
point of quiting the enterprize, when by Clifford's neglect, not
to say wors, the Enemie made a bridg of boats and passed
their hors and dragoons over the Shannor near Annoghbeg,
and so cut between the Irish hors and the Town; the danger of
this haveing been foreseen, was the occasion of Clifford's being
posted with 1500 Dragoons to oppose any such attempt,
haveing the hors Camp (commanded by Major General Sheldon)
within two miles of him, and the Town within three; but instead
of giveing either opposition, or so much as notice of what was
a doeing, suffer'd the Enemie to make their bridg under his nose,
so that the first news which Maj: Gen: Sheldon had of it, was

that they were actually passed, and Clifford retireing towards him: all therefore he could doe upon such a surprize, was by advanceing the Picket to stop the Enemie at a pass, till he could gain the mountains with his hors, Dragoons, and some foot, and so make their way to six mile bridg, which with great difficulty was performed at last; but not being able to subsist there, were order'd back towards Clare, upon which the Enemie passed a great body of hors and dragoons over their new bridg and came before Thomond gate; at their first apearance Coll: Lacy with 6 or 700 men was order'd out to dispute their aproach, which he did with great valour and good success for a time, till overpower'd by a continual supply of fresh men, he was forced to giue way, however rallyed again and repossessed himself of the ground he had lost, but the enemie was too numerous to be resisted by soe small a partie, soe bringing on still fresh troops obliged him to retire towards the gate, which the Major of the Town (aprehending the English might enter pell mell with them) imprudently shut against his own people, whereby the greatest part were cut in pieces. This so dishearten'd the General Officers that they began to dispair, they saw the Enemie now betwixt them and the hors, which being ready to perish for want of fourage, must have surrender'd at discretion; and what possiblity (said they) was there (suposeing the Town could hould out) of makeing war the ensuing campaign without hors or dragoons, nor was their any means of feeding the foot (had the Siege been raised) the Enemie being master of all the Country, nor hopes of succour from Balderic O'Donnal, who had made his peace with Ginkle tho' few of his men would follow him, there was no news of supplys from France, besides 40 English men of war had enter'd the river; so that Mons'r D'Vson and the other French Officers proposed treateing, but the Irish Officers and Lords Justices made some difficulty at first on account of their Oath,

II

till they had consulted the Bishopps and Divines, who tould them, That being blocked up on all sides, it was impossible to hear from the King should any answer come, which being the thing their Oath obliged them too, there was no possibility of keeping to the letter of it; but that the King's permission to treat, considering the extream want they were in, might rea‑ sonably be presumed, since it could not be known : So they agreed to demand a pass from Monsr Ginkle for some of their hors Officers to come into the Town, which being granted, a treaty * was immediately set on foot, and notwithstanding the ill Situation they were in, their forts taken, a breach made, and their condition, in short, desperate ; yet they had the courage to insist upon, and the dexterity to obtain, articles not only for their own security, but which had a respect to the whole King‑ dom, consulting in the first place the King's honour and advantage in getting permission to go, and even Ships to transport them and all others into France who were desirous to follow their Prince's fortune and adhere to his Seruice ; which, with what went before, brought into that Kingdom first and last near 30000 men ; in the next place they articled for as free an exercise of the Catholick religion as in King Charles the Second's time, and a promis to procure a further security from any disturbance on that account ; that all the inhabitants of Limerick, all Officers, Soldiers &c, in the Army, Garisons, or Countys of Limerick, Clare, Kerry, Corke, and Mayo, should, upon submission, be restored to their Estates they were in possession of in King Charles the Second's time ; all persons to

---

* " A few days after the Capitulation," (*Dalrymple*, Vol. 1. p. 481.) " a French Fleet of 18 Ships of the Line, with 30,000 arms, and with stores of provisions and ammunition, arrived upon the Coast, imbittering, by the sight of assistance, the reflec‑ tion in the minds of those to whom it was brought, that, by their mutual jealousies and impatience, it was now become useless." EDITOR.

T O M.
IV.

1691.

exercise their trads, and follow their professions, possess their goods, Cattles &c, as before the war, and in fine a general indempnity for all such as had been concerned in it; which had the English kept as religiously, as such agreements ought to be observed, the world had not seen so many crying examples of antient and noble famelys reduced to the last degree of indigence, only for adhereing to their Prince in just defence of his right, when he came in person to demand their succour, which all Laws both humain and divine obliged them too : for even that senceless cant word of Abdication, which was the poor and only excuse for their unnatural rebellion in England, had not the least shaddow of pretext in Ireland, unless the King's comeing into a Country he had never been in before, and governing a Kingdom in person he had hithertoo govern'd by a deputy, must be counted an abandoning of it by the Parliamentary Logick of our days.

The Irish Army is transported into France.

Thus was Ireland after an obstinate resistance in three years campagns, by the power and riches of England and the revolt of almost all its own protestant Subjects torn from its natural Sovereign; who, thō he was divested of the Country he was not wholly deprived of yᵉ people, for the greatest part of those, who were then in armes for defence of his right, not content with the Seruice already render'd, got leaue (as was sayd) to come and loos their liues, after haveing lost their estates, in defence of his title, and brought by that means such a body of * men into France, as by their generous comportment in

---

* Amongst these were probably a part of the brave followers of DUNDEE, whose attachment to JAMES has been well described by *Dalrymple*, (Vol. 1. p. 358.) " Their adventures," says that Historian, " were worthy of the happiest days of Athens or Sparta." They consisted of 150 Officers, " all of honôurable birth, attached to their Chieftains and to each other ; in their political principles only to blame, yet glorying in them.........Finding themselves a load upon the late King, whose finances could scarcely suffice for himself, they petitioned that Prince for leave to form themselves into a Company of Private Cen-

accepting the pay of the Country, instead of that which is usually allowed there, to strangers, and their unimitable valour and service during the whole cours of the war, might justly make their Prince pass for an Ally rather than a Pentioner or burthen to his Most Christian Majesty, whose pay indeed they received, but acted by the King their Master's Commission, according to the common method of other auxilliary troops.

Assoon as the King heard of their arrival, he writ to the Commander to assure him, How well he was Satisfyd with the behaviour and conduct of the Officers, and the valour and fidelity of the Soldiers, and how sencible he should ever be of their service, which he would not fail to reward when it should pleas God to put him in a capacity of doing it; it was an additional mortification to him in this conjuncture, to see his people so willing to overlook such stretches of power and pretended prerogatiue in an Vsurper, they had so vehemently resisted in their Lawfull Prince, for the Prince of Orange's

tinels, asking no other favour than that they might be permitted to chuse their own Officers. JAMES assented. They repaired to S' Germains, to be reviewed by him, before they were modelled in the French Army. A few days after they came, they posted themselves in accoutrements borrowed from a French Regiment, and drawn up in order, in a place through which he was to pass, as he went to the Chace.....He asked, who they were? and was surprised to find, they were the same men, with whom, in garbs better suited to their ranks, he had the day before conversed at his Levee. Struck with the levity of his own amusement, contrasted with the misery of those who were suffering for him, he returned pensive to the Palace. The day he reviewed them, he passed along the ranks, wrote in his pocket book, with his own hand, every gentleman's name, and gave him his thanks in particular; and then removing to the front, bowed to the body, with his hat off. After he had gone away, still thinking honour enough was not done them, he returned, bowed again, but burst into tears. The body kneeled, bent their heads and eyes stedfast upon the ground, and then passed him with the usual honours of War.".....In the *Appendix* (Vol. 2. p. 18.) Dalrymple subjoins the Speech which JAMES made at S' Germains to these faithful adherents, which is too long for insertion: it thus concludes, *Fear God and love one another. Write your wants particularly to me, and depend upon it always to find me your Parent and King.*" EDITOR.

granting on this occasion, by his sole authority, such priviledges in relation to the exercise of Religion, preserveing armes,
excuseing from Oaths, and such like concession in the Treaty
of Limerick, was taking much larger steps towards a dispenseing power, than what he himself was now so grievously
persecuted for, and which it seems could never be forgotten or
attoned for; however, being afterwards confirmed by Act of
Parliament ought to haue been more duly obserued, and
exactly complyd with, than the Irish experienced them on
many occasions.

The Highland-
ers of Scotland
lay down their
armes, the
King not being
able to sustain
them.

This malencoly extinction of the King's hopes and authority
in Ireland, was accompanyed with the like success in its Sister
Nation, the begining of this year the Loyal Highlanders who
had continued in armes for him in Scotland, had sent My Lord
Dumfermeling to giue the King an account how affairs stood
in that Kingdom; they complain'd of the backwardness of the
great men, with whose concurrance much might haue been
done, and that unless those of the South join'd them, or that
his Majesty sent speedy succours, it would be impossible to
hould out any longer: before he receiued this relation he was
so sencible of their condition, that thō his abilities and intrest
was exhausted with the pressing necessitys of Ireland, however
he had made a shift to send them some present relief of flower,
salt, brandy, tobacco, medecinal droggs, flints &c, in a Ship
from Nants, which ship had been order'd (as was sayd) to call
in at Galway, or Limerick where the Duke of Tyrconnel had
directions also to pay ten thousand liures, (but that Article
(thō the main,) could not be complyd with) and to deliver twenty
barrils of pouder to Coll: Charters, who was sent on board that
ship and commissioned to carry it to the Isles of Sky, or where-
ever he found Buckan, Cannon, and the Earle of Dumfirmeling,
or most of the other Officers; to be distributed by directions of
the Council of war there; but thō the King out of compassion

to their hard circomstances was willing to assist them, yet he
was too tender of their liues to expose them to any desperate
action, by pretending to doe more than he was realy able, so
he gaue them at the same time a true state of his affairs, That
it was not possible for him to doe more, or send them any force,
till his Most Christian Majesty was Master at Sea, and disposed
to venter his ships on an attempt at such a distance, which
when he was, would giue them timely notice; and that if in
the interim his friends could Stand out no longer against the
pursute and vexation of the Rebels, but were forced by some
kind of outward submission to keep quiet, that he should compassionate, not condemn their suffrings, being perfectly assured
of their hearts at all times, and doubted not of their hands too,
when the condition of his affairs should require them to apear
for him; and that as for such Officers as could not bend to any
sort of outward complyance, or were in danger not to be
receiued by the Rebels thō they did, he desired them to make
use of the opertunity that Ship offer'd, by going in it to Ireland
and serueing there til further orders; and as a marke of his
impartial loue and charity to his Subjects without distinction
on account of Religion or different perswasions, he sent two
hunderd pounds Sterling to be distributed amongst the suffring
Episcopal Ministers by the directions of the Archbishopps of
St Andrews and Glascow; and so left them at libertie either to
continue the war, or wait patiently a fitter occasion (if they
thought it more proper) to assert their Loyalty * *afterwards.*
Accordingly the King's intrest faded away by degrees, and
his friends soon after were forced to submit, who upon laying
down their armes and promisin to liue peaceably were assured
at least of indemnety and protection, yet contrary to that, by

---

* Interlined as before mentioned. EDITOR.

T O M.
IV.

1691.

an order, which Nero himself would haue had a horror of, the Prince of Orange commanded one Coll. Hill and Lieft' Coll. Hamilton to put * Glenco to death, and all the males of his line not exceeding 70 : accordingly the old gentleman was unhumainly murther'd in his bed, and most of the number most barberously bucher'd in cold blood, by the Soldiers who were peaceably quarter'd in those parts, at a time they least suspected such a treatment, haueing all of them either taken the benefit of the immunity, or had protections in their pockets, which put them under the care and saufguard of the government : it was hard to immagin the Prince of Orange could aprehend danger from such a handfull of people, but wether he thought this severity necessary to terrify others, or that he had some particular pique against that Clan was uncertain ; but either of those reasons (tis probable) was a sufficient motiue according to his morality to do so unhumain

---

* *Dalrymple* having detailed what preceded this event, describes what he says is commonly known by the name of *The Massacre of Glenco* (Vol. 1. p. 485—489.) " This Warrant was executed with many circumstances of extreme rigour. Sir John Dalrymple gave orders, that the execution should be effectual, and without any previous warning. For this purpose, in the month of February, twó Companies went, not as enemies, but as friends, to take quarters in The Valley of Glenco, where all the Clan lived ; a Valley famous, in the traditions of Highlanders, for the residence of FINGAL, and which, by an odd coincidence, signifies in the Celtic language, *The Valley of Tears.* To conceal the intention the better, the soldiers were of their own lineage, Highlanders of Lord Argyle's Regiment, and the Commanding Officer, Captain Campbell of Glenlyon, was uncle to the wife of one of Glenco's Sons. All were received with the rude but kind hospitality of the Country. They continued in the Valley near a fortnight ; and then in the night time, rose to butcher their hosts. Captain Campbell had supped and played at cards with Glenco's family the evening before. Thirty-eight men were slain. The rest would have shared the same fate, had not the alarm been given by one of Glenco's sons, who overheard one of the soldiers say to another, *He liked not the work : He feared not to fight the Macdonalds in the field, but had scarcely courage to kill them in their sleep : but their Officers were answerable for the deed, not they.* EDITOR.

a thing, for to obstruct his ambition, or to giue him a personal
offence, exposed men equally to his mercyless reveng; yet
this was the pretended assertor of the liues and liberties of the
English Nation, to whom all Oathes and obligations of duty
and Religion were made a sacrifice of, rather than he should
not reign over it.

By this means the Bass (a small fort upon a rock in Leith
road) was the only foot of land, if it may be so call'd, that the
King remain'd in possession of; where a few Loyal and
resolute persons set all the Kingdom at defyance, but being
in great necessity for want of provisions his Majesty found
means by some French Privateers of supplying their wants:
it was a plesant sort of independant state, consisting of about
15 or 20 souls, and their way of subsisting a subject of great
curiosity to all sort of people; they had a boat which was of
great use to them for makeing descents, in order to bring off
provisions or to get intelligence from their friend; this boat
they frequently changed as they found occasion, till at last
they got one which was very large and more usefull on that
account, but too heavy to be hoised up by their crain, as they
were used to do the others, so being forced to leaue it floating
at the foot of the Rock, it was taken from them in the night
by surprize; this made the Government think, they would be
more inclined to surrender, so sent a Sergent and some
Soldiers to offer them an indempnity if they would submit,
but instead of that they had the dexterity to repair their loss
by it, for desireing them to come nearer under pretence of
not hearing well what they sayd, brought them at last within
reach of their fire armes; by the terrour of which they forced
them in, and disarmeing the Soldiers, seized the boat, and
made the prisoners themselves help them up with it so far as
to put it out of danger of being retaken as the other had been,
and soon after a Danish Ship passing within reach of their

cannon, they forced her in also, and haveing taken a small tribite of provisions and what els they wanted as due to their little independant state, they put their prisoners on board, that they might not help to consume what now began to be too little for themselves, and in this manner they held out till the begining of the year 1694, when they were forced by famin to surrender at last.

1692.

The King settles himself and his way of liveing, sutable to his pention.

THE War being thus unsuccessfully ended, both in Scotland and Ireland, the King submiting patiently to his fate began to think of setling himslelf at St Germains, and of modeling his family and way of liveing sutable to the pension of Six hundred thousand liures a year, which he receiued from the Court of France; and which he managed with that prudence and frugality, as not only to keep up the forme of a Court by mentaining the greatest part of those Officers that usually attend upon his person in England, but relieued an infinite number of distresed people, antient and wonded Officers, widdows, and Children of such as had lost their liues in his service; so that tho the Salleries and pensions he allowed were but low, yet scarce any merit ever went without some reward, and his servants had wherewithall to make a decent apearance: so that with the help of the guards (which his Most Christian Majesty apointed to attend him as also upon the Queen and Prince) his Court notwithstanding his exil, had still an air and dignity agreeable to that of a Prince; for besides those of his famely and severall other loyal persons both Catholicks and Protestants, who chose to follow his fortune, there was for the most part such an apearance of Officers of the Armie espe-cially in the winter, as would haue made a stranger forget the King's condition and haue fancyd him still at Whitehall; nor was this the only resemblance it böre of former days, his

comportment to those about him had the same apearance as
in England, there was no distinction made of persons on
account of their Religion, Protestants were coutenanced,
cherished and imployd as much as others; indeed the Laws
of the Country would not permit the same priviledges as to
publick prayers, burials, and the like, but the King found
means of mollifying what he could not obtain a total relaxation
of. His conversation likewise had so great a resemblance of
what it formerly had been, that one would haue thought him
in that respect in the middle of those persons still who had
abandon'd and betrayd him, no sharp or reflecting expressions
on the people or Country which had treated him with that
indignity, one could not make one's court wors than by
declameing against the ingratitude of such as were most
signally criminal in that point, if any appearance of excuse
could be immagined his Majesty fail'd not to instance it
himself, and was, on most occasions, a professed advocate of
his greatest enemies ; he discoursed upon the transactions and
Government of England, the Votes and proceedings of Parliament, the valour and conduct of their forces, with the same
temper and moderation as if they had been still under his
command, and seem'd no less concerned for the reputation of
the Soldiers and Seamen, then when he was himself a witness
of their behaviour and a sharer of their glory : he could not
so easily divest himself of that tenderness and affection he had
for his people, as they could of their Loyalty and duty to him ;
so that when in any publick instrument or declaration, he was
under a necessity of laying open the misbehaviour of his
Sujects, it was the obligation he lay under of justifying himself,
that forced it from him, and not the effect of any acrimony or
bitterness in his temper, from the remembrance of past
disorders ; and therefore thō it was necessary at certain time
to convince the world he was not insencible of the injuries they

T O M.
IV.

1692.
The Queen
proveing
withchild, the
King invites
several out of
England to
be at her
Majesties
labour.

had done him, yet he shew'd by the whole conduct of his life and actions, it was their repentance he sought, not their ruin, or his own reveng.

The Queen proveing withchild soon after the King's return from Ireland, gaue him a fit occasion of convinceing his Subjects, of the falsety of one important calumny, which had so much contribited to delude them into a concurrance with the Prince of Orange's designes ; he thought an invitation to his Privy Council, and several other persons of quality to be present at the Queen's delivery, would be the most effectual means of demonstrateing that her Majesty was not past child bearing four years before; so he writ to the Lords and others of his Privy Council to this efect. RIGHT TRUSTY &c, Whereas our royal predecessors used to call such of their Privy Council as could conveniently be had, to be present at the labour of their Queens, and be witnesses to the birth of their Children, and whereas we followed their example at the birth of our dearest Son the Prince of Wales, thō even that precaution was not enough to hinder us from the malicious aspertion of those who were resolved to depriue us of our royal right ; that we may not be wanting to our Selves now it had pleased Almighty God, the supporter of truth, to giue us the hopes of further issue, our dearest consort the Queen being big, and drawing neear her time, we haue thought fit to require such of our Privy Council as can possebly come to attend us here at St Germains, to be witness at our dearest Consort the Queen her labour.

We doe therefore hereby signify our royal pleasure to you, that you may use all possible means to come with what conveniant hast you can, the Queen looking about the middle of May next, English account, and that you may haue no scruple on our side, our dearest Brother the most Christian King has given his consent, to promis you, as we hereby doe, that you shall haue leaue to come, and (the Queen's labour over) to return with safety; thō the iniquity of the times, the tyrannie of Strangers, and a misled partie of our own Subjects, haue brought us under a necessity of useing this unusual way, yet we hope it will convince the world of the truth and candour of our proceedings, to the confusion of our enemies; so not doubting of your complyance herewith, wee bid you heartely farewell. Given at our Court of St Germains, the 2^d of April, 1692, and the 8 year of our Reign.

This or Letters to this effect were directed to the Duchesse of Sommerset, Bauford, the Lady Derby, Mulgraue, Rutland, Danby, Notingham, Brooks, Lumley, Fitzharding and Fretzwell, Sr John Trevors his Lady, he being then speaker to the House of Commons, the Lady Seymour, Musgraue, Blunt, Guise, and Foly, the Lady Mairess of London, the two Sherifs Ladys, and to D^{tr} Hugh Chamberlin. But the Prince of Orange who had compassed what he aimed at by that infamous calumny, was now little concerned whether it was thought true or false, and therefore instead of going about to satisfy the world in a point of so high importance, took all the care he could to haue these letters stifled; and was so far from granting a free conduct which was offer'd on the other side, that whether any one was willing or no, tis certain, no one durst venter to undertake such a journey, which they saw the Prince and Princesse of Orange so avers too: this furnished indeed a good occasion to many of his Majestys friends, of publishing the crying injustices he had suffer'd on this and other accounts, but it was not by argument and reasoning that the King could hope to wrest the Scepter out of the Vsurper's hands, there was nothing but force could doe the work, nor was his Majesty quite out of hopes of procureing it even yet.

Notwithstanding the violent Current which had bore down all before it in England at the Revolution, there were many

Many begin to be dissatisfyd with the P^{ce} of Orange's governement.

persons however in that Kingdom so principled in Loyalty as
to keep their hearts true to their duty, thō their hands were tyd
from asserting it, besides every day clear'd up more and more
those dark and hidden contrivances which had wrough so dire
an efect; this made the number of his Majestys friends encreas
dayly, who fail'd not to propose methods, and promis assistance
if he attempted their relief. The correspondance with My
Lord * Churchil was still kept up, for thō so much former
treachery, and so little other proofs of a change, than words
and protestation, made his intentions lyable to suspicion; yet
he put so plausible a face upon his reasons, and actions, that
if they were not accompanyed with truth and sincerity, they
had at least a specious appearance of fair and honest dealing;
and had this reason aboue all others to be credited, that not
only he but his   † was out of
favour with the Prince of Orange, and reap'd no other benefit
from their past infidelitys, than the infamy of haveing commited them; and the most intrested men's repentance may be
credited, when they can reasonably hope to mend their fortune
by repairing their fault, and better their condition by returning
to their duty.

who could not be presumed to dissemble at that time (how
little soever *she complyd with her engagement afterwards) had
writ to the King a most penitential and dutyfull Letter; which
considering the great power my Lord and Lady Churchil * had
with * her, was a more than ordinary marke of that Lord's

---

* These words have been inserted by a different hand, and apparently at a
much later period, both in the above page and in this Letter from H. R. H. the
Princess Anne. Editor.

† This and the succeeding vacant Spaces occur in the original MS. Editor.

sincerity in what he professed. M^r *LLoid* * who was lately return'd into England from St Germains with instructions to the King's friends, was the Messinger entrusted with it, and thō by cross winds and the strict watch which was kept upon the cost, he was hinder'd from delivering it till his Majesty was come to la Hogue, yet * *her* sence in that matter and * *her* inclination to that undertakeing was so far understood, as to giue great life and encouragement to it :

I haue been (says * *she*) very desirous of some safe opertunity to make you a sincere and humble offer of my duty and submission to you, and to beg you will be assured that I am both truly concern'd for the misfortune of your condition, and sencible as I ought to be, of my own unhappiness as to what you may think I haue contribited to it; if wishes could recall what is past, I had long since redeem'd my fault. I am sencible it would haue been a great relief to me, if I could haue found means to haue acquainted you earlyer with my repenting thoughts, but I hope they may find the aduantage by comeing late of being less suspected of insincerity, than perhaps they would haue been at any time before : It will be a great addition to the eas I propose to my own mind by this plain confession, if I am so happy as to find it brings any real satisfaction to yours, and that you are as indulgent and easy to receiue my humble submissions, as I am truly desirous to make them, in a free disistressed acknowlidgment of my fault, for no other end but to deserue and receiue your pardon.

I haue had a great mind to beg of you to make one compliment for me, but feareing that the expressions which would be the properest for me to make use of, might be perhapes the least conveniant for a letter, I must content my self at present

---

* This name and words have been inserted, and by a different hand. EDITOR.

T O M.
IV.

with hopeing the Bearer will be able to supply it for me. Decem ye 1. 1691.

The King
prepares for
an Invasion.

Whether the preparations which were now a makeing for a descent in England, begot this penitent disposition in the , or on the contrary * her return to * her duty who had so great an influence over the Church partie, or was so much influenced by it, (which in this case was the same thing) induced the French to make this tentatiue, is hard to Say; however at last they began to open their ears to his Majestys representations, and resolved to lend him such a force as was judged sutable to the undertakeing. The manifest advantage it would be to France, as well as glorious to its King to restore an injured Prince, and break that formidable league against them, prevail'd upon the Ministers to make one tryal more, being now become sencible how great a reinforcement of power they had suffer'd their enemies to draw from their sterueing the war in Ireland, and neglecting that in Scotland. And thō the papers which had been taken about † Mr Ashton, had allarm'd the government, and put them upon their guard, and My Lord Preston's triming, to say no wors, had discover'd many which were well wishers to this enterprise, yet the French went on with their preparations; and the troops design'd for this Expedition were assembled about the begining of April at Cherbùrg and La Hogue in Normandie, with Ships and other necessarys for transporting 15 or 20 thousand men into England, whither several persons had been sent over to put such as were disposed to assist the King at his landing in a readiness to do it, and to command them when they ris: accordingly great

---

* Inserted as before mentioned. EDITOR.

† *Dalrymple* gives a more detailed account in his Memoirs, (Vol. 1. p. 460-467.) and adds (Page 494.) " At last all things were settled; and the French King got assurances, that the Army would be directed by Marlborough, the Fleet by Russel, and a great part of the Church by the Princess Anne. EDITOR.

numbers of armes were privately brought by Catholicks and other Loyal persons, men listed and Regiments formed ; so that in some of the Northern Countys particularly Lancashire they were so zealous, that there were eight Regiments of horse and dragoons compleatly formed, Officers named, and men listed, and a tollerable provision of armes made for them by the Captains of each troop : and now that every thing was in that forwardness as to require the King's speedy leaving St Germains and comeing to the Sea Coast, he thought it necessary, in order to prepare his way, and to quiet people's minds about libertie and Religion, to publish and send before him into England the following Declaration :

WHEREAS The most Christian King in pursuance of the many obligeing promisses he had made us, of giueing us his efectual assistance for the recovering of our Kingdoms, assoon as the condition of his affairs would permit, has put us in a way of endeavouring it at this time, and in order to it has lent us so many troops as may be abundantly sufficient to untie the hands of our Subjects, and make it safe for them to return to their Duty and repair to our Standard ; and has notwithstanding for the present, according to our desire (unless there should apear further necessity for it) purposely declined sending out forces so numerous as might rais any jealousie in the minds of our good Subjects of his intending to take the work out of our hands, or depriue any Englishman of the part he may hope to haue in so glorious an action, as that of restoring his lawfull King, and his antient government, all which forreign troops assoon as we shall be fully settled in the quiet and peacable possession of our Kingdoms we do hereby promis to send back; and in the mean time to keep them in such exact order, and discipline that none of our Subjects shall receiue the least injurie in their persons or possessions by any Soldier or Officer whatever. Thō an affair of this nature speaks for itself, nor do

T O M.
IV.

1691.

we think our selves obliged to say any thing more on this occasion, than that we come to assert our own just rights and
deliver our people from the oppression they ly under; yet when
we consider how miserably many of our Subjects were cheated
into the late Revolution, by the arts of ill men, particularly
the Prince of Orange's Declaration, which was taken upon
trust and easily beleived then, but since appears notoriously
false in all the parts of it, consisting no less of assertions which
haue been manifestly disproued, than of promisses that were
never intended to be performed : To prevent therefore the like
delusions for the time to come, and to do as much as lys in our
power, to open the eyes of all our Subjects, we are willing to
lay the whole matter before them, in as plain and short a
manner as is possible, that they may not pretend mistakes or
haue ignorance to plead for any false steps they shall hereafter
make towards the ruin of their own and Countrys happiness.

And therefore to take the matter from the begining; it cannot
be forgotten that assoon as we had certain notice of the Prince
of Orange's unnaturall design of invadeing our Kingdoms
with the whole power of the Vnited Provinces, we first took the
best care we could to provide for our defence; which we seem'd
effectually to haue done, when we had put our Fleet and Army
into such a condition, that thō his Most Christian Majesty who
well saw the bottom of the design against us, against himself,
and indeed against the peace of Europe, offer'd us considerable
succours both by land and Sea, we did not think it at all
necessary to accept 'em, at that time, as resolveing to cast our
selves wholy (next to the divine protection) upon the courage
and fidelity of our English Army, which had been with so much
care and tenderness form'd and oblig'd by us; and haveing
thus prepared to oppose force to force, we did in the next place
apply our selves to giue all reasonable satisfaction to the minds
of our good Subjects, by endeavouring to undeceiue them, and

to let them see betimes, and whilst the mischeif might easily haue been prevented, how fatal a ruin they must bring upon their country, if they suffer'd themselves to be seducced by the vain pretences of the Prince of Orange's invasion; however So great was the infatuation of that time, that we were not beleived till it was too late.   But when he was obligcd to throw off the maske by degrees, and that it began to apear plainly, that it was not the reformation of the government (which yet was a matter that did not at all belong to him to meddle with) but the subversion of it, which he aim'd at, that so he might build his own ambitious designs upon the ruins of the English Nation; and when the poison had insinuated itself into the vital parts of the Kingdom, when it had spread over our whole Army, and so far got into our Court and family, as not only to corrupt some of our Scrvants that were nearest our person, and had been most highly obliged by us, but not even to leaue our own Children at that time uninfected; when our Army dayly deserted on the one hand, and on the other hand tumults and disorders encreased in all parts of the Kingdom; and especially, when shortely after the Revolution came on So fast, that we found our selves wholy in our enemys power, being at first confined by them in our Palace, and afterwards rudely forced out of it under a guard of forraigners; we could not then but be admonish'd by the fate of some of our Pre-decessors, in the like circomstances, of the danger we were in, and that it was high time to provide for the security of our person (which was happely effected by our geting from the guard that was set upon us at Rochester and our arrival in France, the only part of Europe to which we could retire with safety,) that so we might preserue our selves for better times and for a more happy oppertunity, such as is that, which, by the blessing of God, is at present put into our hands. Vpon what foundation of justice or common sence the Prince of Orange's faction in England, were pleas'd to treat this escape of ours out of the hands of our Enemies, in the stile of an Abdication, a word, when applyd to a Sovereign Prince's, that was never before used to signify any thing, but a free and voluntary resignation of a crown, as in the case of the Emperour Charles the first and the late Queen of Sweden; and what a strang superstructure they raised upon this weak foundation, that a company of men illegally met togather, who had not power even by their own confession at that time (for it was before they had voted themselves a Parliament) to charge the intrest of the meanest Subject, should yet take upon them to destroy the whole constitution of the Government, to make an ancient hereditary Monarchy turn electiue, and then assumeing to themselves the right of Election, should proceed to settle the succession in so od and extravagant a manner, are transactions that need not to be repeated; they are too well known to the world, to y^e *great reproach of the English Nation, * and* the grounds upon which they are built are too vain and frivolous to deserue a confutation; every free houlder of England is in this case able to make his own observations, and will no doubt examin a little better than hithertoo he has done, what assurance any private man can haue of keeping his estate, if the King himself shall hould his Crown by no better title.

But since some men, that could not say one word in defence of the justice of these proceedings, would yet take great pains to shew the necessity of them, and set forth the extraordinary good effects (*which*) were to be expected from so very bad a cause; we do not doubt but the Nation has by this time cast up the account, and when they shall haue well consider'd, what

---

* Inserted by the Son of James the 2^d. Editor.

wonders might haue been performed with less expence of English blood, than that which has been unnecessaryly trifled away in this quarrel, that such a number of Shipps of war haue been lost and destroyd in the three years last past, as might alone haue been sufficient to haue made a considerable Fleet; that more mony has been drained out of the purses of our Subjects, in the compass of that time, than dureing the whole reign of many of our predecessors put togather, and that, not as formerly, spent again, and circulateing amongst them, but transported in specie into forreign parts and for ever lost to the Nation ; when these and many other particulars of this nature are cast up, it must certainly apear at the foot of the account, how much wors the remedy is, than the fancyed desease, and that at least hithertoo the Kingdom is no great gainer by the change.

The next consideration is what may reasonably be expected for the time to come, and as to that no better judgment can be made of any future events, than by reflecting upon what is past; and doubtless upon the obseruation of the temper and complexion, the method and maxims of the present usurper, from the Steps he has already taken, when it was most necessary for him to give no distrust to the people, as well as from the nature of all usurpations, which can never be supported but by the Same ways of fraude and violence, by which it was first set up ; there is all the reason in the world to belieue, that the begining of this tyranny, like the first years of Nero, is like to proue by much the mildest part of it, and all they haue yet suffer'd, is but the begining of the miseries these very men, who were the great promoters of the Revolution, may yet liue to see and feel, as the efects of that tyrannical government which they themselves first imposed upon the Kingdom.

And yet the consideration must not rest here neither, for all wise men ought, and all good men will take care of their posteritie; and therefore it is to be remember'd, that if it should pleas Almighty God, as one of the severest judgments upon this Kingdom, for the many rebellions and perjuries they haue been guilty of, so far to permit the contrivance of this present vsurpation, that we should not be restored dureing our lifetime; yet an indisputable title to the Crown will survive in the person of our dearest Son the Prince of Wales, our present heir apparent and his issue, and for default of that in the issue of such other Sons as we haue great reason to hope (the Queen being now withchild) we may yet leaue behind us; and what the consequence of that is like to be, may easily be understood by all who are not Strangers to the long and bloody contentions between the houses of York and Lancaster, and whosoever shall read the histories of those times, and there shall haue presented to them, as at one view, a Scene of all the miseries of an intestine war, the perpetual harassing of the poor Commons by plunder and free quarter, the ruin of so many noble families by the frequent executions and attainders, the weakening of the whole Kingdom in general at home, and the loosing those advantages they might in the mean time haue procured for themselves abroad, can not but conclude, that these are the naturall efects of those Strugglings and convulsions, that must necessarily happen in every State, where there is a dispute entail'd against an injured right and an unjust possession.

There is an other consideration which ought to be of weight with all Christians, and that is the calamitious condition of Europe, now almost universally engaged in a war amongst themselves, at a time when there was the greatest hopes of Success against a common Enemie, and the fairest prospect of enlargeing the bounds of the Christian Empire that ever was in any age since the declineing of the Roman: and so far from a general peace before our restoration, that no national project

of a treaty can be formed in order to it; but that once done
will be easy, and we shall be ready to offer our mediation, and
interpose all the good Offices we can with his Most Christian
Majestie for the obtaining of it.

Since therefore we come with so good purposes and so good
a cause, the justice of which is founded upon the Laws both of
God and man, since the peace of Europe as well as of all our
Kingdoms, the prosperitie of the present and future ages is
concern'd in the Success of it, we hope we shall meet with
little opposition; but that all loveing Subjects according to
their duty, and the oath of their Allegiance, and as we hereby
require and command them to do, will join with us and assist
us to the utmost of their power.

And we do hereby strictly forewarn and prohibit any of our
own Subjects whatsoever, either by collecting or paying any
of the illegal taxes lately imposed upon the Nation, or any
part of our revenue; or by any other ways to abet or support
the present usurpation, and that we may do all that can be
thought of to win over all our Subjects to our Service, that
so if it be possible we may haue none but the Vsurper and his
forreign troops to deal with; and that none may be forced to
continue in their rebellion, by despair of our mercy for what
they haue already done; we do hereby declare and promis on
the word of a King, that all persons whatsoever, how guilty
soever they may haue been (except the persons following, viz:
the Duke of Ormonde, Marques of Winchester, Earle of Sunderland, Earle of Danby; Earle of Notingham, Lord Newport,
Bishop of S* Asaph, Lord Delamère, Lord Wiltshire, Lord
Coulchester, Lord Cornbury, Lord Dunblain, John Lord
Churchil, S* Robert Howard, S* John Worden, S* Samuel
Grimston, S* Stephen Fox, S* George Treby, S* Basil Dixwell,
S* James Oxenden, D* Tilletson Dean of Conterbury, D*
Gilbert Burnet, Francis Russel, Richard Levison, John

Trenchard Esqr, Charles Duncomb citizen of London, Edwards, Napleton, Hunt, Fishermen, and all others who offer'd personal indignities to us at Feversham, except also all persons who as judges, or jury men, or otherwise had a hand in the barberous murther of Mr John Ashton and of Mr Cross, or of any others who haue been illegally condemned and executed for their loyalty to us, and all spies and such as haue betrayed our Councils dureing our late absence from England; that by an early return to their dutys and by any signal mark of it, as by seizing to our use, or delivering into our hands any of our forts, or by bringing over to us. any ships of war, or troops in the Vsurper's Army, or any new rais'd and armed, by themselves, or by any other eminent good service, according to the Several opertunitys and capacities, shall manifest the Sincerity of their repentance; Shall not only haue their respectiue pardons immediately passed under the great Seals of England, but shall otherwise be consider'd and rewarded by us as the merite of the case shall require. And for all others who after the time of our Landing shall not appear in armes against us, nor do any act or thing in opposition to our restoration (the persons before mentioned only excepted) we shall provide for in our first Parliament (which we intend to call with all convenient speed) by a general act of indempnity, that so the minds of all our Subjects may be at quiet and as much at eas as their persons and properties will be secure and inviolable under our government.

Provided always that all Majestrates, that expect any benefit by our gracious pardon, shall immediately after notice of our Landing, make such publick manifestation of their Loyalty to us, and of their Submission to our authority; and also publish and cause to be proclamed this our Declaration assoon as it shall come to their hands, and also that all keepers of prisons do immediately set at libertie all persons commited to their

Custody upon account of their allegiance, and affection to us, or be excluded from any benefit of our pardon.

And we hereby further declare and promis, that we will protect and mentain the Church of England as it is now by law established, in all their rights, priviledges and possessions, and that upon vacancies of Bisshoppricks and other dignities or benefices within our disposal, care shall be taken to haue them fill'd with the most worthy of their own Communion.

And whereas more tumults and rebellions haue been raised in all nations upon the account of Religion than on all other pretences put togather, and more in England than in all the rest of the World besides; that therefore men of all opinions in matter of Religion may be reconciled to the government and that they may no longer look upon it as their enemie, but may therefore look upon themselves as equally concerned in its preservation with the rest of their fellow Subjects, becaus they are equally well treated by it, and being convinced in our judgment that libertie of conscience is most agreeable to the Laws and Spirit of the Christian Religion, and most conduceing to the wealth and prosperity of our Kingdoms, by encourageing men of all Contries and perswasions to come and trade with us and settle amongst us; for these reasons we are resolved most earnestly to recommend to our Parliament the setling libertie of Conscience in so beneficial a manner that it may remain a lasting blessing to the Kingdom.

Lastly it shall be our great care by the advice and assistance of our Parliament, to repare the breaches and heal the wounds of the late distractions, to restore the trade, by putting the Acts of Navigation in efectual execution, which has been so much violated of late in favour of Strangers, to put our Navie and stores into as good a condition as we left them, to find the best ways of bringing back wealth and Bullion into the Kingdom, which of late has been so much exhausted; and generally we shall delight to spend the remainder of our reign (as we always design'd since our first comeing to the Crown) in studying to do every thing, that may contribite to the reestablishment of the greatness of the English Monarchy upon its old foundation, the united intrest and affection of our people.

Thus haueing endeavour'd to answer all objections and giue all the Satisfaction we can think of, to all parties and degrees of men, we cannot want ourselves the Satisfaction of haveing done all that can be done on our part, whatever the event shall be, the disposal of which we commit with great resignation and dependance to that God that judges right; and of the other side, if any of our Subjects shall after all this remain so obstinate as to apear in arms against us, as they must need fall unpitied under the Severity of our justice, after haveing refused such gracious offers of mercy, so they must be answerable to Almighty God for all the Blood that shall be spilt, and all the miseries and confusion in which these Kingdoms may happen to be involved by their desperate and unreasonable opposition. Given &c, the 20th of April 1692 in the 8th year of our Reign.

Many are dis-
pleas'd at this
Declaration.

This Declaration was drawn by My Lord Chancellor Herbert who was sure to take care of the Protestant Intrest, a man far from a vindictiue spirit, and in the opinion of some was much more indulgent than could reasonably haue been expected, considering the provocations the King had receiued from all ranks of people; and yet some were excepted more for forme than any design of punishment, as his Majesty took care to advertice My Lord * Churchil in particular, whom he had not only promised to pardon, but looked upon him as his principall agent at that very time, as he always term'd him in his letters, and therefore writ to him then, that had he not been excepted it would haue discover'd too plainly in whose intrest he was:

---

* Inserted afterwards, and in a different hand. EDITOR.

however many objections were made against this Declaration afterwards, as that it should haue mention'd the King's being encouraged to this undertakeing, rather by the invitation of his Subjects, than the promised assistance of the French King; that no particular notice was had of the falsetys of the Prince of Orange's Declaration, nor no reason alledged for the King's first going from London, on which they principally grounded the pretended Abdication; they thought his Majestys resentment descended too low to except the Feversham Mob, that fiue hundred men were excluded, and no man realy pardon'd except he should merit it by som service, and then the Pardons being to pass the Seals, look'd as if it were to bring mony into the pocket of some favorits: in fine, its not being published in time made severall dissatisfyd with it; but no one seem'd to be more so than * *Admiral Russel*, who now haveing the command of the English Fleet, and still pretending to be in the King's intrest, there apear'd a necessity of doing all that was possible to content a person, who held the crown of England so far in his hands as that it was in his power to set it again on his Majestys head, if he realy designed it.

M^r LLoyd was his particular friend with whom he had several conferences before he came away with the

      letter; he express'd an earnest desire to serue the King, sayd the people were inclined enough to be of his side again if his Majesty took a right way to make them so, but that if he would reign a Catholick King over a Protestant people he must forget all past misdemeanors and grant a general pardon, and that then he would contribute what he could to his restoration, without insisting upon any terms for himself; and when M^r LLoyd made some proposalls of that kind, he would not hear him, saying It was the publick good not private advantage he

Marginalia: T O M. IV. 1692.

Marginalia: M^r LLoyd comes away.

---

* Inserted afterwards, and by a different hand. EDITOR.

look'd for in this affair : he tould him therefore If he met the French Fleet he would feight it, even thō the King himself were on board, but that method he proposed to Serue the King was by going out of the way with the English Fleet, to giue the King an opertunity of Landing, or els by makeing choice of ships for a winter Squadron, whose Officers he could influence and by that means do what he pleased.

This resolution of fighting even against the King himself, was an od method of restoreing him, and thō he might pretend an impossibility of influenceing the whole Navy to do otherwise, yet this seem'd rather a contrivance, to rais his fortune which way soever the ballance inclined, which by the King's preparations abroad, and the discontents at home began to be dubious ; he was sure to keep his credit with the present government by engageing the French, and if he missed of them by chance or should fortune to be worsted, he would make a merite to the King of what either happen'd by accident or against his will, but the King was forced to seem well contented with what those men were pleas'd to promis, and make use of such instruments, without urging them too much, as far as they would go with eas.

It is more than probable that many Officers of the English Fleet, when they saw his Most Christ: Majesty was in earnest, began to waver, at least the Princess of Orange (the Prince being in Flanders) was sensible of it ; and seeming by an affected generosity not to credit what she could not remedy, sent them word she reposed an entire confidence in their fidelity and zeal, and that she looked upon the contrary reports as industriously rais'd by her Enemies : This drew an Address from the Fleet, wherein they declar'd they would defend with the utmost perils of their liues their Majestys (meaning the Prince and Princess of Orange) undoubted right togather with the Religion and liberties of their Country,

against all forreign and Popish invadors whatsoever; This, thō
perhaps no more cordially meant by many that signed it, than
Addresses usually were in those days, might however create
so much diffidence in those who intended well, as to prevent
their ventering at what they might reasonably doubt would be
generally opposed by others; nevertheless the King had good
hopes of many Officers particularly * Carter rear Admiral of
the Blew, but endeavour'd to haue matters so order'd as not to
depend upon so dubious a foundation, especially the faint
assurances of † *Admiral Russel* himself, for he knew that fear
alone would make those mercinary soules his friends, and that
nothing but the preparations where he was, could produce that
effect.

The design therefore was so well layd that had not fortune
cross'd him (as it ever did) so many different ways, there was
no reason to apprehend a miscarriage; nothing but a particular
providence of punishing the English by a seeming success,
and of Sanctifying the King by continual suffrings could
have order'd it in the manner it fell out; for first the French
Fleet was fitted out at Brest so early in the yar, that had it
not been prevented by contrary winds and violent stormes for
near six weeks togather, it had been in the Channel before the
English Fleet could be ready, or at least the Dutch had join'd
it, without which the French had been strong enough for
them; or had not the Toulon Squadron been likewise detain'd
by contrary winds from passing the Straits, the French had
been able to dispute the matter with the united forces of the

---

* " The Government," (says *Bertrand de Molleville*) " was acquainted with all
these particulars, partly by some agents of King James who betrayed his cause,
partly by Admiral Carter himself, who informed the Queen that he had been tam-
pered with." (History of Great Britain, Vol. 3. p. 551.) EDITOR.

† Inserted afterwards. EDITOR

T O M.
IV.
1692.

Encmie; but all things falling cross to the French and
fortunately to the English, those winds which kept the French
assunder, brought the others togather, which so intimidated
those Officers of the English Fleet that had any good intentions
towards the King's service, that his succours fail'd him in all
sides; for such was his Majestys hard circomstances (as his
friends assured him) that unless he had force enough to do his
business alone, he was not like to haue more than what he brought;
nor must he promis himself any assistance from his hidden well
wishers, unless he were strong enough not to need them.

The Prince of
Wales is made
Knight of the
garter.

Before the King set out for this expedition, the Prince of
Wales being near four years old, he thought fit to invest him
with the Order of the Garter, giveing it at the same time to
the Duke of Powis and Earle of Melford, which honour he
had confer'd also some time before upon the Count de Lausune,
for his service in Ireland and assistance given the Queen in
her escape from England: this Cerimony being over his

The King
arriues at Cane
in Normandy,
the 24th April.

Majesty set out for Cane in * Normandy, where he arrived
the 24th of April N.S. accompanyed with the Mareshall de
Belfont and follow'd by the Duke of Berwick and several
other Officers of distinction; he began to embarke his men
the day after he came to the Sea cost, but the transport ships
were so † long in geting togather, and those which came

---

* " At length, all things were settled: And the French King got assurances, that
the Army would be directed by Marlborough, the Fleet by Russel, and a great
part of the Church by the Princess ANNE." (*Dalrymple*, Vol. i. p. 494.) EDITOR.

† " During this interval, Admiral Russel got time to renew his Correspondence
with JAMES. He made two proposals to that Prince, desiring him to make his
choice. One was, that the Invasion should be delayed until winter; and he
promised, if that was complied with, that he would, in the intermediate space,
dismiss several of his Captains, and give their commands to Officers who were
better affected to JAMES. The other was, if the intended Invasion should proceed just now, that Russel would give an opportunity to the French Fleet to·
sail for England, by employing his own in a disembarkation of Troops upon the

from Havre de Grace so cruelly batter'd by a storme, that they were not in a condition to sail, till they had notice of the English and Dutch Fleet being joined; upon which Curvetts were sent to acquaint Monsr Tourville the French Admiral, but he haveing orders to seek out the English (then supposed to be alone) came in presence of the Enemie before that intel-ligence rought him, and being piquet at those reflections mentioned before of his not pursuing the victory at Bechy bay, thought fit to obserue his orders to the letter, thō the Dutch were join'd ; so notwithstanding the great inequality bore down upon them the * 19th of May in the morning S. W. off of Cape Barfleur, and mentain'd the fight with equality enough, till about four in the afternoon, and then the wether comeing calme, the French thought fit to tow away with their boats, considering how much they were out number'd and that no defection appear'd on the English part : Whether Admiral Carter had any real design for the King's service (as was reported) he being kill'd at the begining of the engagement, left that matter in doubt as well as by what hand he dy'd ; however the dammage the French had undergon hithertoo, was not considerable, but the wind springing up a fresh gail about six the English renew'd the engagement, which the unseason-able bravour of Admiral Tourville hinder'd the French from

T O M.
IV.

1692.
The French
Fleet is beaten;
and 17 great
ships burnt at
La Hogue the
* 23.th of May.

---

coast of France. In testimony of his sincerity in the last of these proposals, he applied in England for leave to make a descent at St Maloes. But, in all his Correspondence, he entreated JAMES to prevent the two Fleets from meeting, and gave warning, that, as he was an Officer and an Englishman, it behoved him to fire upon the first French Ship that he met, although he saw JAMES upon the quarter deck." (*Dalrymple*, Vol. 1. p. 497.) EDITOR.

* In the MS. the date is the 20th ; and in the side note appears to be an error respecting the number of ships destroyed on the 23d. Admiral Russel, in his letter to the Earl of Nottingham, (*Campbell*, Vol. 3. P. 69.) says, that the boats burnt six of them. EDITOR.

declineing, and was the occasion of a mighty loss soon after; for he counting it too great a dishonour to shew his stern to an enemie, and trusting to the strength of his own ship the ROYAL SUN a mighty vessel of a 120 gunns, resolued to stand the brunt and lay like a Castle in the Sea, thō attack'd on all sides, being too well man'd to be boarded by the Enemie: but by this means both he, and those who thought it their duty not to abandon their Admiral, loosing their opertunity, could never after get cleer of the English, but were forced to that Scurvy alternatiue, either to be taken or run ashore; part indeed of the French Fleet got into the race of Aldernee betwixt the promentory and the Isle of Guarnsey, and so saued themselves at Sᵗ Malo's, but Tourville with sixteen great vessels, was necessitated to run a ground, and yet even then it had not been impracticable to saue them, if the King's Council had been follow'd; for the frigats and fire ships which Russel sent to destroy them could not come near enough to doe them any mischief, upon which the King proposed to put land men on board who would undertake their defence against the Enemies armed boats, which was the only way they had to attack them in the shallow water where they lay: but the Admiral thought it a dishonour to commit the care and defence of his Ships to any but the Seamen themselves, who being dishearten'd by the late defeat soon abandon'd their Posts, at the first approach of the English (thō but in Chalops) who notwithstanding the continual fire of several batteries rais'd on the shore burnt all those men of War that had run upon it.

This malencoly prospect tryd the utmost extent of the King's patience and resolution, his own disapointement occasioned by such a number of cross accidents, was the least part of his trouble at this time; to see the King of France who had always been happy and victorious drawn in to be a sharer of his misfortunes, was what he had scarce con-

stancy to support, had not the * hand of God which thought
fit to Sanctify him by the way of afflictions, given him a
patience and resignation sutable to those tryalls.   We haue "
not yet (sayd he in a letter to the Abbè de la TRAPPE) "
suffer'd enough for our sinns, I mean my Self and my Subjects; "
whos misfortune he lamented in their seeming success, full as
much as his own, he considered the bloodshed, taxes, oppressions and the other necessary consequences of war, which
they unthinkingly gloryd in, and thō in the bitterness of his
Soule, he could not refrain acquainting the most Christian
King with what trouble he reflected upon the loss, he had
been the occasion of, yet he knew his duty too well to declare
he would abandon his own cause, because he found himself
unfortunate; or that he should be contented his Most Cristian
Majestie should do so too, as by a letter then published as
was thought by a French Hugenot was confidently said,
which obliged the King not long after, being asked by a
Religious person if that letter was writ by him, to make this
reply: I can never sufficiently acknowlidg the obligations "
I haue to his Most Christian Majesty, but I am a Father and "
a King, and under obligations never to abandon the intrest "
either of my Children or my Subjects.   I will doe therefore "
what I am able and submit the success to Providence, to "
which I will ever bear a perfect resignation.   He needed not "
this accident to haue driven him into a retreat from the world;

---

* " Whoever," (says *Dalrymple* in concluding his account of this year, 1692,)
" perceives not, in the Events of the Period to which these Memoirs relate, the
hand of an Almighty Providence, which, upon the ruins of an illustrious but
misguided Family, raised up a mighty Nation, to show mankind the sublime
heights to which Liberty may conduct them, must be blind indeed ! May that
Providence, which conferred Liberty upon our Ancestors at the Revolution,
grant that their posterity may never either lose the love of it upon the one hand,
or abuse the enjoyment of it upon the other."   EDITOR.

if his circomstances had permited it, his inclinations led him
" thither long before : You have left the world (says he to the
" Abbè de la TRAPPE,) to worke your salvation, happy are
" those who can do it, those are the only people I envy. It
was a true sence of his duty, therefore, not his desire of
worldly greatness, that forced him thus to struggle with his
fortune, which, wether successfull or not, his obligation he
knew was still the same.

The King was
in danger from
his own guns.

This defeat was too considerable to be redress'd, and too
afflicting to be look'd upon, nor was it even safe to do it long,
for as if every thing conspired to encreas the King's misfortune
and hazard, his own Ships, as it were with their dying groans
would have endanger'd his life, had he not been timely advertised to remoue from the place where he fortuned to stand ;
for assoon as they were burnt to the guns, which were most of
them loaden, they fired on all hand, which raked the very
place where the King had been, and did some small damage
on shore, so little was such an accident foreseen.

This Expedition being thus unfortunately ended, the Troops
were remanded to their respectiue posts, and the King return'd
to St Germains where his Most Christian Majesty according to
his wonted generositie, gaue him fresh assurances of his protection and assistance, notwithstanding this and all his other
crosses and misfortunes ; and to shew that he was neither
dejected nor disabled by that loss, notwithstanding the expence
of the war gaue orders for rebulding as many Ships as had
been burnt, which in a year time was done accordingly of the
same bulk, and burthen, to the great admiration of the riches,
power, and eoconomie of his State.

A Week after the King return'd from La Hogue the Queen
was deliver'd of a Princess, which gaue him at least some
domestick comforth. She was Christen'd LOUISE MARY, the
Most Christian King being her Godfather, which cerimony was

performed with great magnificence and solemnity; and thō no one came out of England according to the King's invitation, however, besides the Princesses and Cheefe Ladys of the Court of France, the Chancellor the first President of the Parliament of Paris, the Archbishop, &c, the Wife of the Danish Ambassad^r Madame Meereroon, as a person on whose testimony the people of England might reasonably rely, was present at the Queen's labour and delivery, and notwith. standing her aversness to the King's intrest, could not refuse owning the rediculousness of that false and malicious insinuation which had wrought him so much mischief, she being an eye wittness of the contrary herself.

The continual contradictions the King had met with, so weaned him from all thoughts of present happyness, as made him in a manner now attend soly to the business of gaining a future one, to which he perceiued Providence design'd to lead him by the paths of affliction and suffring; the surest road for all, but especially such, who are penetrated with a grief and detestation of their former disorders, which the King was too humble not to acknowlidg himself guilty of, and too just not to think a punishment due too; which made him embrace even with chearfullness and alacrity such as it pleased God to send, and even ad many of his own, which had not the discretion of his Director restrain'd him in, might haue gon to excess. However this hinder'd not a due attention to any occasion which Providence might offer to the regaining his right, he knew how to reconcile the suffring with patience, the ill success of his endeavours with a due perseverance in them; for this reason the late disapointment hinder'd not a continuance of that correspondance with his friends in England, who (especially before the business of La Hogue) were, or pretended to be very numerous, not only persons of the greatest rank, but even many who were in actual imployment in the government:

T O M.
IV.

1692.

perhaps it was not purely a zeal for the King's restoration that stuck so much with many of them, as the prospect they had of an endless war and an unsettled government, till things run in their natural Channel again; they saw the most Christian King espoused his Majestys intrest heartely, and the late success (barring that disaster at Sea) against the united power of almost all Europe, shew'd what he was able to doe, even while he had such enemies to struggle with, and by consequence how much more, if that Confedracy should break a Sunder, which being a chain of so many different links, could not be hoped would hould long togather. Since therefore there was some apearance of their being forced to their duty, many of them thought it more eligible to return voluntarily, and by offring certain conditions to the King, not only secure whatever they had any aprehention of, either relateing to Religion, Laws or Liberties of the people; but procure further concessions from the King in reference to those heads, which his present low condition might make him more inclined to grant: upon this errand

King Jam:
Mⁿ. To: 9.
pag. 369.

" therefore, (as was sayd before) Mʳ LLoyd was sent to the
" King about two months before the battle of La Hogue, but
" was so long retarded by the strict observance of the Ports at
" that time, as he came not to him till just after the French
" were beaten, so nothing could be done then, however the
" correspondance was kept up with

&c:

" as well as the rest from whom he came, but he haveing been
" seen accedentally by some of his acquaintance at La Hogue,
" durst not return for England as was designed; for which
" reason some time after the King came back to Sᵗ Germains,
" finding it necessary some body should go in his stead, made

Mʳ Cary is sent
into England,
and the corre-

" choice of Mʳ Cary whom (thō a Priest) those persons were
" willing to trust, and therefore was dispatched with instruc-

tions to the Earle of * Middleton accordingly. And in the
mean time M^r LLoyd by the King's directions writ to †Admiral
Russel to see whether after this Victory at Sea, (thō but a
scurvy proof of his sincerity) he pretended (at least) to continue
in the same mind; he was order'd to tell him, That the King
according to what was desired was contented to grant a general
pardon, or leaue the exceptions to the Parliament itself, that
such a clemency suted best with his inclinations and had
accordingly been shewn in his late Declaration, but that he
was perswaded by others, that some marks of ressentment were
necessary, and that in case it apear'd by his answer he persever'd in the same professions of duty to the King, and desire
of his return, he should be commission'd to assure all his
friends that the King would in a new Declaration doe it effectually; he put him in mind of his haveing sayd, It would be
no wors for the King that the French should be beaten, and
that being so he therefore had it now he sayd in his Power, to
be an other General Monk, in restoreing not only the Prince
to his Throne, but the people to plenty, and a Secure possession of their own : To this †Admiral Russel replyd, He was still
of the Same mind, and that if any way could be shewn him
to appear in the King's favour without reproach, he would
readily embrace it, but upon condition that such a restriction
were put upon the Regal power as to prevent for the future
any undue practices, or the like steps as had been formerly

T O M.
IV.
1692.
spondance
kept on foot
with

---

* " King William, (says Dalrymple in a Note, Vol. 1. p. 500.) probably knew of
the Intrigues of Bulkely, Lloyd, and Lord Middleton. For in the books of the
Privy Council, May 3, 1692, there is a warrant to seize them. In the same books,
23d June of that year, the names of Halifax, Shrewsbury, and Marlborough, are
struck out of the Council Book. And the warrant for seizing Marlborough in the
books, May 3. of that year, bears, ' That he was charged with high treason, and
for abetting and adhering to their Majesties enemies." EDITOR.

† Inserted afterwards. EDITOR.

500

T O M.
IV.

1692.

made; which he conceiued to be neither just in themselves, nor for the intrest of the King: To this it was replyd that care should be taken to giue him and all the Kingdom full satisfaction and security against any unreasonable exercise of Regal power, or of whatever might be disagreeable to the people; and beg'd he would send his thoughts of the whole, which he accordingly promised when a good occasion could be had of transmitting so long a letter as that would require. But whatever *Admiral Russel's intentions were in this correspondance, it was soon out of his power (for a time) to doe more in the matter than a private person, for immediately after his Victory at Sea, haveing proposed a Descent in France, it was agreed too by the government, and Land forces put on board under the command of Mons' Schomberg; but being so long a doing, and the place designed for landing proueing the bayé of Biscay, *Admiral Russel and the other Officers, upon opening the Commission (which was not to be done till they were at Sea) resolved to return to St Helen's road; This made a great nois in the ensuing Parliament, and thō it was own'd the season of the year was too far spent, for such great Ships to liue in the bay of Biscay and *Admiral Russel thank'd by the Commons for his care in that, as well as his victory before, however the Prince of Orange discharged him from his imployment, and gaue the command of the Fleet to Killigrew, Dela val, and Ashley.

Mr Cary returns with certain heads from * Ld Churchil, Admiral Russel, &c.

While this negociation was on foot with *Admiral Russel, others were not neglected and particularly My Lord * Churchil, who in like manner pretended no less sincerity after La Hogue than before, and indeed his being sent this year to the Tower with My Lord Huntingdon, Scarsdell &c, was some proof of

---

* Inserted afterwards, and by a different writer. EDITOR.

it; but that being complain'd of by the Upper House, as a breach of priviledg to imprison a Peer without two witnesses against him, he was soon released; this little suffring however encouraged My Lord Middleton, who had likewise been put in the Tower too (on whose management the King principally relyd to try the strength and stability of these shatter'd reeds) to treat with him again, who found him so frank and cordial in the matter, that he not only consented readily to any thing that was proposed, but generally run before all overturs that could be made in his Majestys favour, he consulted likewise My Lord

T O M.
IV.
1692.

and others who all seem'd desirous the King should be restored, but were hard in the terms they stood upon in order to ·it, without which they pretended an impossibility of doing any thing; but that if such and such conditions were complyd with, they gaue all immaginable assurance of success. My Lord Middleton did not altogather aproue of what these Lords so positively insisted upon, however thought it his duty to giue the King an account of their demands; accordingly M' Cary was dispatched back, but arriued not at S' Germains till January following 1693 and brought eight proposals " from them togather with an assurance that if his Majesty " pleas'd to agree to them, they made no doubt but to restore " him immediately, and assoon as notice was giuen of his " consenting to them, they would send My Lord Middleton to " him fully instructed in the whole affair: the very next day " after M' Carys arrival, the King sent My Lord Melfort to " Versailles to shew these proposalls to his Most Christian " Majesty, and to haue his advice, which was to agree to them " all; the next day the King order'd M' Cary to attend Mons' " Croisy to informe him more particularly of the whole, who " was of the same opinion with his Master, and sayd The "

1693.

KING JAM:
MEM". To:19.
pag: 269.

T O M.
IV.

1693.

"King had no other cours to take but to sign them, and
"accordingly the following post which was munday the 12ʰ of
"January, the King writ to My Lord Middleton to let him
"know he agreed to the Articles he had sent him.

The Earle of
Middleton
comes over.

Vpon this My Lord Middleton sent over a Declaration
which had been formed by the afforesaid Lords conformable to
the articles Mʳ Cary brought, and then follow'd it soon after
himself, which the King thought fit to publish in this following
termes. WHERAS we are most sensible that nothing has
contribited so much to our misfortunes and our peoples
miseries, as the false and malitious calumnies of our enemies,
therefore we haue always been, and stil are most willing to
condescend to such things as after mature deliberation we
haue thought most proper for removeing thereof, and most
likely to giue the fullest Satisfaction and clearest prospect of
the greatest security to all ranks and degrees of our people ;
and because we desire rather to be behoulding to our Subject's
loue to us than to any other expedient whatever for our
restoration, we haue thought fit to let them know beforehand
our Royal and sincere intentions ; and that whenever our
people's united desires and our circomstances giue us the
opertunity to come and assert our right, we will come with the

The King
publishes
an other
Declaration,
April 17.

Declaration that follows. When we reflect upon the
calamities of our Kingdoms we are not willing to leaue any
thing unatempted wherby we may reconcile our Subjects to
their duty, and thō we cannot enter into all the particulars of
grace and goodness, which we shall be willing to grant, yet we
do hereby assure all our loveing Subjects, that they may
depend upon every thing their own representatiues shall offer
to make our Kingdoms happy ; for we haue set it before our
eyes as our noblest aim to do yet more for their constitution,
than the most renowned of our Ancestors, and as our chiefest

intrest, to leaue no umbrage for jealousie in relation to Religion,
Libertie and propertie.

And to encourage all our Loveing Subjects of what degree
or qualitie soever, to set their hearts and hands to the encourageing so good a work, and to unite themselves in this only
means of establishing the future peace and prosperity of these
Kingdoms, we haue thought fit to publish and declare, That
on our part we are willing to lay aside all thoughts of animosity and resentment for what is past, desireing nothing more
than that it should be buried in perpetual oblivion, and do
therefore by this our Declaration under our great Seal, sollemly
promis our free pardon and indempnity to all our loveing
Subjects, of what degree or quality Soever, who shall not by
Sea or land oppose us ; and those who shall think necessary
to accompany our own person in this just attempt to recover
our right, or (in such a number of days after our landing as
we shall hereafter express) shal not resist those who in any
parts of our dominions shall according to their duty, assert and
mentain the justice of our cause : beseecking God to incline
the hearts of our people that all efusion of blood may be
prevented, and Rightieousness and mercy take place ; and for
that end we further promis to all such, as shall come to and
assist us, that we will reward them according to their respectiue
degrees and merits.

We do further declare that we will with all speed call
togather the representatiue body of our Kingdom, and therein
will inform ourselves, what are the united intrests and inclinations of our people ; and with their concurrance will be
ready to redress all their grievances, and giue all those secu-
rities of which they shall stand in need.

We likewise declare upon our Royal word, that we will
protect and defend the Church of England, as it is now
established by law, and secure to the members of it all the

Churches, Vniversities, Colleges and Scools, togather with the immunities, rights and priviledges.

We also declare we will with all earnestness recommend to that Parliament such an impartial libertie of conscience as they shall think necessary for the happiness of the Nations.

We further declare we will not dispense with, or violate the Test, and as for the dispensing power in other matters we leave it to be explain'd and limited by that Parliament.

We declare also that we will giue our Royall assent to all such bills as are necessary to secure the frequent calling and houlding of Parliaments, the free elections and fair returns of Members, and provide for impartial tryals, and we will ratify and confirm all such Laws made under the present usurpation as shall be tender'd to us by that Parliament.

And in that Parliament we will also consent to every thing, they shall think necessary to reestablish the late Act of Settlement in Ireland, made in the reign of our Dearest Brother; and will advise with them how to recompence such of that Nation as haue follow'd us to the last, and who may suffer by the said reestablishment according to the degrees of their suffrings thereby, yet so as the said act of Settlement may always remain entire.

And if Chimney mony or any other part of ye revenue of the Crown has been burthensome to our Subjects, we shall be ready to exchang it for any other assessment that shall be thought more easy.

Thus we haue sincerely declared our Royal intentions in terms we think necessary for settling our Subject's minds, and according to the advice and intimation we haue receiued from great numbers of our loveing Subjects, of all ranks and degrees, who have adjusted the manner of our comeing to regain our right, and to relieve our people from oppression and Slavery.

After this we suppose it will not be necessary to enumerate the tyrannical violations and burthens with which our Kingdoms have been oppress'd, and are now to be destroyed.

And whereas our Enemies endeavour to affright our Subjects, with the apprehentions of great summs which must be repayd to France, we positively assure them that our dearest Brother the Most Christian King expects no other compensation for what he has done for us, than meerly the glory of haveing succor'd an injuried Prince.

We only ad that we come to vindicate our own right, and to establish the liberties of our people, and may God giue us success in the prosecution of the one as we sincerely intend the confirmation of the other. Given &c: April 17^h 1693·

The King was sencible he should be blamed by several of " his friends for submiting to such hard termes, nor was it to " be wonder'd at (he sayd) if those who knew not the true " condition of his affairs were scandalized at it, but that after " all he had nothing els to doe: first, resonably speakeing " none but those persons could doe the work, the Jacobits not " haveing it in their power to begin, thō they might be able to " draw togather considerable numbers of men if once the " business were set on foot by others; that as to France, the " whole Kingdom was weary of the war as well as the " Ministers, the Country being almost ruin'd by the great " taxes, togather with the scarcety of wine and corn, occasioned " by the great rains which fell the Summer before, so that " nothing but his Most Christian Majestys personal vigor and " friendship to the King, supported it; and should the King " haue refused those proposals how hard soever they apear'd, " the clamor of the whole Country would haue been so great " his Most Christian Majesty could not haue been able to haue " resisted it, and probably the King would haue been sent out " of the Kingdom as an opiniatre bigot, who prefer'd some "

T O M.
IV.
1693.

KING JAM: MEMᴿ. To: 9: pag: 370. The King was blamed for this Declaration, thō he used his endeavour to be inform'd of his duty therein.

T O M.
IV.

1693.

King Jam:
Mem⁰. To:9:
pag. 447.

" points of his prerogatiue, which his people perhaps might
" haue afterwards restored, before the peace and quiet of all
" Christendom.

" The King aprehended also that his most Christian Majesty
" might be shocked at an other denyal, he haveing refused, in
" November before, to writ a letter to the English Parliament
" (a copie of which he then shew'd him) and which he was
" assured (he sayd) by those who proposed it, that it would in
" all apearance hinder them from settling a general excise upon
" the Prince of Orange, (a thing which was then apprehended);
" and this his Most Christian Majesty introduced by a long
" preamble how necessary it was to obstruct the Prince of
" Orange's affairs, especially in mony matters, and was so
" cautious in the thing as to desire the King would neither
" mention what he then moued him in, nor press to know the
" proposer unless he approued of it : but assoon as the King
" had read the letter he was surprized, and tould his most
" Christian Majesty, He could not help belieueing that the
" projectors of that affair, were inconsiderable people, and
" unable to perform what they undertook, and so the business
" fell ; however the King gather'd from thence, how uneasy
the Most Christian King was under the burthen he now bore,
when he grasped at such shaddows for support ; and by
consequence how necessary it was for him to make any concessions, that were not point blanc against his dignity or his
conscience, that he might not be obraded with refuseing to
giue a helping hand to his own reinthronement.

Thus did his Majesty argue in his own justification, nor did
he rest upon his private judgment in the matter ; he consulted
learned Divines of the French Nation, who thō they com-
miserated the meanness of his condescention, yet they saw not
(they sayd) as the case was proposed, but he might in conscience do it ; thō tis certain others who understook the case

II

much better were of a different opinion, as indeed most of those French Divines were likewise afterwards when they came to be rightly informed of the true state of the case.

But what hurryd the King on too fast in this affair, was first the little probability or hopes he had of prevailing with his Most Christian Majesty to undertake any thing in his favour, after such losses, and so signal a defeat at Sea ; which made him listen more readily to any propositions which came from his own people, dispairing in a manner now of being restored any other way than by their consent and procure. ment: besides this, his then Minister, the Earle of Melford found himself extreamly maligned by the generallity of his Majestys Subjects ; the Scotch thō his Countrymen, had shewn a mighty dissatisfaction with his conduct, the Irish had obliged the King to dismis him from business in that short time he remain'd amongst them, and the English especially Protestants had as mean an opinion of his abilities, and as great an aversion to his person as the rest ; how justly or unjustly is not to the present purpos to determin, for thō a general dislike be a heavy prejudice, yet it dose not always hould in the case of a Minister, whom Cardinal Richelieu compareing to Male- factors says, As the liues of these are sacrificed to publick justice, so are the liues and reputation of the others to the publick safety, and are oft times as much maligned when they doe their duty, as when they do amis. In fine the fact being thus, My Lord Melfort thought this a good occasion to gain credit with the English Protestants, his endeavours of that kind had hithertoo only produced complaints ; that no one came into England from the King, who had not particular instructions in favour of My Lord Melford, as if the establishing of his credit there, were of equal concern with that of his Majesty on the Throne, whereas they sayd, the King had sent

them word out of Ireland, he would never make use of him or
Father Petre any more ; they loked upon it, they sayd, as a
piece of hardship upon the Queen, that by his pretending to
the Protestants in England, that they were behoulden to him
for all the good will the King of late had towards them, he
should suffer them to attribite the King's former coldness to
her Majestys power: This occasion therefore (besides the
conviction he might be in, of its being the only means to
reestablish the King) seem'd the most favorable in the world to
gain an reputation and esteem amongst them, who had indeed
as a preliminary to their other demands insisted upon his
remoueal, but he assured them they should find by his endeavours to bring his Majesty to what they desired, that he merited
a better place in their esteem and favour ; so he hurryd it on
with more precipitation and Secrecy, than was fitting in a
matter of so much nicety and, so great consequence, and
without a previous enquiry, which way the proposers design'd
to performe their engagement, and effect the great work of a
restoration, in case the King complyd with what they required
of him.

The English
Divines dis-
aproued of the
Declaration.

Tis true he proposed to four English Divines whether the
King might make the following promis's, WE declare and
promis that wee will protect and mentain the Church of England as it is now by law established, and that upon all vacancies
of Bishopricks and other dignities or benefices within our disposal, care should be taken to haue them fill'd with the most
worthy of their own communion. 2ly: We likewise declare upon
our Royal word, that we will protect and defend the Church of
England as it is now established by Law, and secure to the
members of it all the Churches, Vniversities, Colleges and
Scools, together with their immunities, rights and privileges.
3ly Whether the King could promis to agree to any laws that
should be desired for the further security of the Church of

England? The persons to whom these Quere's were proposed, were Father Sanders the King's Confessor, D^{tr} Betham the Prince's Preceptor, Mr Inness the Queen's Almoner, and D^{tr} Fenwick; who all answer'd in the negatiue, and that the matter was improperly worded, but that what resonably could be expected, might be granted in other terms : for first they sayd, The King could not promis to protect and defend a Religion he belieud erroneous, which was the substance of the first and second Queré, nor could he make the promis requir'd in the 3^d, because they might think the educateing the Prince of Wales in the Protestant Religion, necessary for its preservation, or to exclude any Catholick from succeeding, which had once been thought necessary even in respect of himself. But they agreed that the King might promis to secure and protect his Subjects of the Church of England as by law established, in the free and full exercise of their Religion, and in the quiet and peacable possession and enjoyment of their Bisshopricks, Ecclesiastical dignities and other benefices ; and that upon all vacancies care should be taken to fill them up with fit members of their own perswasion, it being they sayd, a quite different case to promis to mentain the Religion it self, or to mentain the pro-fessors of it in their possessions, benefices, &c, which being all the security the Protestants desired, might reasonably haue satisfyd the Minister: but he not content with this, proposed the two first Queres only to fiue French Divines, who not haueing a right notion of the case, nor understanding the Laws of the Kingdom, gaue their approbation too hastely ; upon which the Declaration was dispatch'd away into England, and put past being recall'd, thō soon after those French Divines themselves recall'd their judgment, when they were more fully apprised of the case, and saw the Declaration itself, togather with the Test act, and thought fit to writ a long paper of reasons for their retraction. The Bisshop of Meaux (who had been

T O M.
IV.

1693.

consulted also) had given his opinion for its legallity, compareing it to what the Most Christian King had promised to
the Huguenots in the Edit of Nantes, and writ his reasons · to
Cardinal Janson at Rome, to which no reply was made either
pro or con ; but thō he persisted something longer in his opinion
than the rest, he own'd his mistake at last but did not think
it necessary to doe it by a writeing or publick instrument, the
matter being then at an end, and all expectancys on that
account determined.

It was not therefore to be wonder'd that the reasons the
King had given for publishing such a Declaration, were not so
universally relished as to prevent the clamor of many of his
friends, Servants, and fellow sufferers ; which rais'd him another
sort of persecution than he had yet been acquainted with ; but
the difficulty of proportioning his Councells to the vast variety
of Sects and intrests which possessed the Kingdom, cast him
into these intricacys, and layd him open to continual contradictions which way soever he turn'd himself : but he was the
first that condemn'd his own hastiness in the matter, and so
made the same pious use of this, as of his other Suffrings ; he

Letter to
Abbe De La
Trap, Dec.
1693.

" own'd there was too much precipitation in printing it, that
" it might haue been better worded, and Some harsh terms
" left out, but he was so press'd he Sayd, by those who sent
" the proposalls, and the Ministers of the French Court who
" thought the occasion So favorable, as not to be neglected ;
" that he had not time to correct it as it ought to haue been,
" that he hoped by keeping as neer as his conscience would
" permit to the terms and letter of what was riquired, would
" be a great motiue to those who sent them, to doe their part
" too ; that by conserueing the Test there was no injury done
to Catholicks, but the keeping them out of imployments, whereas
it would certainly be a great advantage to them to haue a
Catholick King upon the Throne.

But the little success this Declaration had, gaue discontented persons a more specious handle to complain, which was what he could not foresee, and he thought it his duty to ketch at every twige when he found himself so evidently a sinking. But whether it was that the circomstances of affairs were so suddenly changed, as that those who promised so largely should not be able to make the least step towards what they under.took ; or whether they were disgusted with some false insinua.tions, as if there had been underhand assurances from the Court at St Germains, to certain persons that were dissatisfyd with it, that means would be found to elude what had been promised ; or whether assoon as My Lord Middleton's back was turn'd (who had been the chief moulder of those Lords and gentlemen into a loyal disposition) they relapsed again into their former infidelity ; or that they ment no good from the begining but to secure themselves let what will happen, this is certain, That all the frute the King reap'd from this Declaration was. blame from his friends, contempt from his enemies, and repentance in himself ; which instead of reconcileing the Protestants at home alienated Catholick Princes abroad ; for Prince Vaudemont a great favorit of the Prince of Orange's, did not only prone this up at Vienna (which Court was but too Succeptable of any ill impressions *against y$_e$* * *King*) but going soon after to Rome (and perhapes it was part of his errand) made great use of it there, to convince his Holyness how little Religion suffer'd in England by the King's being out of it, or would gain by his restoration, he haveing by this Declaration foreclosed himself from endeavouring the least thing in its favour, So that amongst Catholicks where the King's veracity and sincerity was known, it did him great prejudice, and amongst Protestants

T O M.
IV.

1693.
This Declara-
tion had not
the proposed
efect.

---

* Interlined by the Son of James the Second. Editor.

where it was suspected, it did him no good ; nay even some of those very men who had sollicited the thing, were the first that dispised him for it ; My Lord Danby sayd, He could not see what he and others had done since the last Declaration, to merite so much favour, who were so ill treated before, and in that truly he was in the right as well as most of the rest; nor was this all the mischief that sprung from this root, it createed misunderstandings in the King's family at home as well as lessen'd his credit abroad. My Lord Middleton was blamed for haveing handed such harsh proposalls to the King, but he answer'd, He had less regard to the termes and expressions that were offer'd, because he doubted not, but the King would word and mould them to his own likeing for the support of which he reserued himself, that he might be sure to abet what the King aproued of, and therefore threw the blame upon My Lord Melford, who being a Catholick was best qualifyd to make objections ; and My Lord * Churchil himself shew'd manifestly it was expected the King would do so : If there be any thing, " says † he, proposed, you may think a little hard, you will pleas

---

* Interlined by the Son of James the second. EDITOR.

† *Dalrymple* in giving a view of the State of Parties in 1693, (Vol. 3. p. 38.) inserts the following account of what had passed between Lord Churchill and Captain Lloyd, from *Macpherson*'s State Papers, (Vol. 1. p. 480.) " Captain Lloyd's Report to King JAMES, of 1ˢᵗ of May, 1694, contains these words, ' The first person they brought me was Lord Churchill, to whom I showed my Instructions; at the same time informing him, that your Majesty having heard that he was to have an employment, had commanded me to assure him from you, that you was highly pleased at this, and gave him your consent to accept of it; and left him at liberty to employ the properest means for obtaining it, having no doubts of his fidelity, &c.'

" Lord Churchill answered me, that it was true, that he had been solicited some time ago to accept of an employment ; but that he did not choose to accept of it without your Majesty's consent, which he had demanded, by the means of Major General Sackville, without whom he did not move a step : That the affair was now

not to shew yourself much offended with it, and what you "
cannot comply with, make it apear it is from the impracti- "
cableness of it; for should you positively refuse to agree to "
what is proposed, you will loos some of the ablest of your "
Council which may endanger the loosing all : It was there- "
fore an absolute refusal only of what was requir'd which was
aprehended dangerous, and yet even in that case he acquaints
his Majesty, That he would not haue taken the libertie of "
giveing him that advice, but that he had already and did "
again assure him, that for himself he would go on, in whatever "
measures should be taken ; whether he was to be credited or "
no in this generous assurance, is doubtfull, however he might
haue been in what related to any alterations that did not
change the main drift of what was aim'd at, and for which some
good reason might haue been given ; but the King was made
belieue, that by altering nothing, he would incline the undertakers to a readyer performance, but it had rather a contrary
effect, for they suspected that easy complyance as a mark of
some intention to evade all : so the witty men made satyrs upon
it, and the States men endeavour'd to perswade the world, that
such mutations of Councils argued a design of Standing to
nothing, the usual calumnie they charg'd upon the King ;
answers were published to it with sharp reflections and plausible
insinuations, and to create a diffidence and mistrust of his
performance, should it ever come to a tryal, they layd it down
for a principle, That one who broke his word once, and even
his Coronation Oath (as they had the confidence to assert) was
not to be trusted any more, they were not to seeke for specious
calumnys to pursue the same imposter they had set out with at

---

passed, but, if it occurred again, which might well happen, he would not accept,
but from a design of serving Your Majesty; for whose re-establishment he was
determined to resign his life, for expiating his crimes, &c." EDITOR.

the Revolution, and rather then want they raised arguments against it (in private conversation) from the Prince of Orange's not keeping a word of his Declaration, which they hoped would make people never mind (they Sayd) what Princes promis'd on such occasions. But those who knew the King better were of another opinion, seeing the Sollicitude he was in to be well informed what he might in conscience promis, which shew'd a design of sticking to it (for he who scruples not the breaking his word, will never scruple what he promisses) nor did they conclud that because these concessions were in some sence extorted from him, that therefore they would not be comply'd with; for just and religious Princes in such circomstances, are like towns besieg'd, which accept or reject articles according to their different situations, which wether good or bad, in conclusion ought to be alike religiously kept. And therefore many of his Protestant friends were no less displeased with this Declaration than others, thō so favorable to their Religion, they were concern'd for the prerogatiue which they thought the King had been too liberal of, and that these concessions had been wrested from him by men, the greatest part of which, they sayd, neither loued the King nor Kingship itself, and who thought that a good occasion to sap the foundation of the Monarchy either by keeping it in their power to elect whom they pleased, who would still be Subject to the conditions they thought fit to impose, or if the King return'd to foreclose him from exerting his power and punishing their delinquency.

The Church of England partie dis-aproued of the Declaration.
KING JAM: M™
To: 9: pag: 389.

" Pursuant to this one Mʳ Tayler a nonjureing Minister
" comeing some time after out of England, gaue the King an
" account that the Bishops of Norwich, Bath and Wells, Ely,
" and Peterborrough, togather with the Marques of Worcester,
" Earls of   Clarendon,
" and the rest (of) the Church of England partie, desired his
" Majesty not to make any further engagements to the

Republicans; whose designes, they Sayd, in the bottom were " T O M.
to destroy the Monarchy, or at least make the King of " IV.
England no more than a Duke of Venice; that should he " 1693.
come in upon the foot of the Declaration, both he and all "
his loyal Subjects would be ruin'd, and that in the mean "
time the pardoning claus in it, made the loyal men run great "
hazards, the Judges haveing declared, they had their pardons "
in their pockets let them act as they would in the mean "
time. And in reality should they or any one els haue "
commited all the enormities immaginable dureing the King's
absence, they needed but sit still when he return'd (if that ever
happen'd) and they were washed as clean in the eye of the law
as if they had never been guilty of the least misdemeanour.

By this the King saw, he had out shot himself more ways
than one in this Declaration, and therefore what expedient he
would haue found in case he had been restored, not to put a
force either upon his conscience, or honour, dose not apear,
because it never came to a tryal; but this is certain, his Church
of England friends absolued him before hand and sent him
word, That if he consider'd the Preamble and the very terms " KING JAM.
MEM^m. To: 9.
of the Declaration, he was not bound to stand by it, or to " pag. 390.
put it out verbatim as it was worded; that the changeing "
some expressions and ambiguus terms (so long as what was
principally aim'd at had been kept too) could not be call'd a
recedeing from his Declaration, no more than a new edition of
a book can be counted a different work, thō corrected and
amended. And indeed the Preamble shew'd his promis was
conditional, which they not performeing, the King could not
be ty'd, for My Lord Middleton had writ that if the King
signed the Declaration, those who sent it engaged to restore him
in three or four months after; the King did his part, but their
faileur must needs take off the King's future obligation.

The King now perceiued that the fewer friends he had left,
the harder it was to content them, those jarrings, and animosities of parties, made it exceeding difficult to propose or
embrace any thing, which did not meet with contradiction and
opposition from one side or other, there was no makeing a step
that did not displeas many : Nevertheless had the Court of
France been zealous in the matter, there never was greater
hopes of terrifying the English into their duty than at this time,
the great advantages they had got over the Allys at the famous

The battle of
Landen or
Nerwind,
July 29, S:N:
The battle of
Marsalia,—4:
Charleroy
taken, Oct. 10.
Roses surren-
der'd June 5.
Heidelberg
surrender'd
june 2.
The English
Smirna Fleet
attacked in
Lagos bay
june 16.

battle of Landen or Nerwend in Flanders, by that of Marsaglia
in Piedmont, by takeing Charleroy, Roses and Heidelberg, and
the destruction in a manner of the English Smerna Fleet in
Lagos bay, gaue a most favorable occasion to his Most Christian
Majesty of seconding the desires and good will of the King's
friends, and then perhapes one might haue seen a better effect
of those promises which had extorted this Declaration ; but
instead of that the French began to be so weary of the war and
were indeed so terrifyd themselves by the great scarcety which
happen'd that year, that his Most Christian Majesty thought fit
to makes offers of peace by mediation of the Crown of Denmark,
first to the Emperour and then to the P^ce of Orange, and thō
he offer'd to restore many fortifyd towns and quit his pretentions to Flanders in case the King of Spain dyd without issue,
yet they were rejected in both places; and it is not improbable
but when the English saw the French so dishearten'd after such
mighty advantages, that it allay'd their apprehentions of the
King's being forced upon them, and consequently their endeavours of restoreing him themselves, for to be sure it was fear
not affection that made up the main ingredient of those men's
Loyalty, who had so lately engaged to do such wonders for
him; so when they saw no more reason to be affraid, they soon
forgot, what (for that reason alone) they had so solemnly
promised.

However the King thought it his duty not to neglect the least glimering of hopes, and heareing that *Admiral Russel* was restored to the command of the Fleet, resolued to try him once more; so sent M[r] LLoid privately from S[t] Germains about the middle of March, to see whether now that he was in the same power he continued in the same † mind, in relation to his seruice; and whether he was willing to go out of the way with the English Fleet, and by that means giue his Majesty an opertunity of Landing as he had formerly proposed. The Admiral gaue him severall meetings, pretended to haue the same good will for the King, but refused that method now, and sayd, He was resolved to do the thing himself; This was so wide a promis that M[r] LLoyd pressed him to know what method he proposed of doing it, he answer'd, He could not tell, but swore claping his hand upon his breast, he would do all he could; M[r] LLoid still dissatisfyd, urged him to propose some Scheme or means of bringing it about, upon which he asked M[r] LLoid, What he would do were he in his case, and had the command of the Fleet? He answer'd, that the most reasonable project he could propose, was to make as many Captains as he could dureing the

T O M.
IV.

1694.
The King
Sends again to
*Ad[l] Russel.

---

* Inserted afterwards. EDITOR.

† "One of the first steps," (*Campbell's* Nav. Hist. Vol. 3. p. 116.) "taken by King William after his return from Flanders, and his hearing of the unfortunate affair of the Smyrna Fleet, was. the appointing EDWARD RUSSEL, Esq. Admiral and Commander in Chief of the Fleet which should put to sea the next spring. As a further testimony of his Majesty's confidence in that great man, he directed a new commission of Admiralty, wherein Edward Russel, Esq., Sir John Lowther, Henry Priestman, Esq., Robert Austen, Esq., Sir Robert Rich, Sir George Rooke, and Sir John Hoblon, were included..... In the first place it was resolved, that a formidable descent should be actually made on the French Coast, in order to effect what had been long ago proposed, the erecting a Fort on a certain promontory near Brest, which should command that Haven, and entirely prevent the assembling, as the French were wont to do, their grand Fleets there." EDITOR.

summer, and towards the end of it get those ships sent out for
Convoys, which he perceiud were least inclinable to serue his
purpose, reserueing for the Winter Squadron such as were
commanded by his creatures, that the Fleet's apeareing on the
French cost dureing the Summer would naturally draw troops
to the Sea side, which might be design'd for the expedition, thō
under pretence of preventing a descent; and then assoon as the
English Fleet was layd up, and the Convoys gon, might
prepare to embarke, the first rumour of which would certainly
occasion the winters Squadron being sent out, and that being
gain'd before by the Admiral, he might declare for the King,
and so the project could not fail. M^r * *Russel* could make no
objection to this, however would not engage to do it. All he
promis'd was in general termes to do all he could, which he
confirmed by an oath, and that was the utmost M^r LLoid
could bring him too. He had several conferences likewise
with My Lord   * *Godolphin* and *Churchil*, he represented
to them the faileur of what had been promised, in reply
to which they pretended letters had been writ from St Germains, and instanced one from the Queen to the Earle of
Peterborough, assureing him that means would be found to
elude what had been seemingly promised : nothing in reality
could be more false then this, and if any such letter was produced it was certainly forged for an excuse; the Queen
protesting she never writ or thought any such thing; this
however they pretended had so disgusted those engaged in the
affair, that they resolved never to moue their hand for the
King's seruice: but besides (that this had so much the air of
an evasion on their side, who knew both King and Queen
were far from such a duplicity) My Lord * *Churchil* himself in

---

* Inserted afterwards. Editor.

his letter the 13 of december before, alledged no such reason, but tells the King, That he must not depend upon any other advantage by his Declaration, than to dispose the people to receiue him when he came with a sutable force, and therefore begs of his Majesty, not to venter with less than fiue and twenty thousand men, besides arms &c, for Seven thousand more. These were the * *putts* off the King met with from these pretended friends, who never did him any essential good or themselves any harme, for if they were out of imployment, it passed for aversion to the government, and they made a merit of it; and if they found means of being readmited, then it was represented as a mighty advantage to the King, their being in a better capacity of serveing him : accordingly the next letter which My Lord * *Churchil* writ, he tells the King, That My Lord † was so press'd to accept of his former imployment of Secretary of State, that he fear'd he could not resist, but that thō he alter'd his condition he assured him he would never alter his inclinations; whereas in reality one of my Lord principal advisers to this, was My Lord * *Churchil* himself, that he might do him the like good turn, and procure his readmission into favour too, and therefore in the same letter after haueing assured the King that whatever he might think of those proceedings, it was his Majestys real intrest to haue My Lord
Secretary of State again ; he then goes on and tells him, that he is assured by his friends that if he himself will giue them leaue to Sollicite for it, he may be restored to the command he formerly had in the Army, but would do nothing in it, till he had his Majestys permission and aprobation and unless he

T O M.
IV.

1694.
LETTER TO
THE KING.
Dec. 13, 169¾.

LORD
CHURCHIL'S
LETTER TO
THE KING,
Febr: 28 169¾.

---

* Inserted afterwards. EDITOR.
† Lord Shrewsbury. EDITOR.

T O M.
IV.

1694.
Ibid.

My Lord

is sollicited to accept of the Seals by the Prince of Orange.

" thought it for his intrest; for I haue already been so unhappy
" (Says he) and you so good, that it were impossible for me
" to take pleasure in any thing, but what I was sure you
" approued of.

My Lord   did it indeed with some reluctancy, but whether that was occasion'd from any inclination to the King's seruice or no, did not apear; he had other reason sufficient besides, and the Prince of Orange was forced to set several engins on work to perswade him to it, by which some discoverys were made either of a certain tendency to return to his duty, or at least of a dissatisfaction with the ill success of his former disloyalty: For that Lord it seems had lately admitted of a visite from Sr James Montgomery, who had discours'd with much concern (in aperance) for the King's misfortune; and thō My Lord answer'd him with great caution yet the Prince of Orange who soon had intelligence of it, took umbrage at it, and thought it a fit occasion at least to make a last efort to gain him; so sending for him he tould him, He had given great occasion of admiration to the world, that he should so often have offer'd to make him Secretary again, and that he should so oft refuse it, for it shew'd how little he vallued his Seruice. My Lord   replyd, He had ill health, and that hinder'd him; That is not the only reason, replyd the Prince of Orange: No S^r, sayd he, to deal plainly with you, it is not; for you receieud the Crown upon certain conditions which haue not been complyd with, and I cannot goe the same lengths that others will; the Prince of Orange not thinking fit to argue that point, pased it by, and sayd,There was yet an other reason,and at the Same time asked him, when he had seen Sr James * Montgomery? He had seen

---

* This Conversation between King WILLIAM and Lord *Shrewsbury,* is noticed by

him often, he replyd, since he brought the Crown of Scotland :
but the Prince of Orange telling him when he saw him last,
and what discours they had, amazed him very much ; but after
some recollection My Lord   sayd, By that you
may see, S^r, I gaue no encouragement to a man that would
tempt me from my Loyalty : to which the P^{ce} of Orange
replyd, No, I know you are a man of honour, and if you
undertake it, you'l serue me honestly ; and in fine so wrought
upon him, that he promised to accept the Seals at his return
out of the Country, whither he was then going ; which he did
accordingly, and when he was in, endeavour'd to bring in My
Lord * *Churchil* too : but the Prince of Orange not haveing the
same kindness for his person, or opinion of his sinceritie, it
fail'd on his side, and indeed that was the main pledg of that
Lord's † fidelity to the King, of which however he gaue him

Dalrymple, (Vol. I. p. 499.) But a more detailed account is given in his third
Vol. (p. 40.) from *Macpherson's* Original Papers, (Vol. I. p. 480.)

" I went to wait on the Countess of Shrewsbury, who was sick. I made
her the compliments I was ordered by your Majesty and the Queen. In return to
which, she answered me with all the sentiments of duty and affection for your
interests. She afterwards told me, how her son the Earl of Shrewsbury had been
obliged to accept of an employment ; the Prince of Orange having sent for him,
to offer him the post of Secretary of State, which he refused, on account of his
bad health. But the Prince of Orange showed him, that he had a very different
reason, by repeating to him a discourse which he held about your Majesty. This
surprised the Earl of Shrewsbury much, and convinced him of the danger of
refusing the employment ; but, as he expected a descent in England in a few days,
he demanded some time to go to the Country, on account of his health and other
pressing business, before he received the Seals. The Prince of Orange having
granted this, he went to the Country, accompanied by some friends, well mounted,
with an intention of joining your Majesty, in case you had come as was expected
and wished. But that having failed, to his great regret, he was obliged on his
return, to accept of the Seals ; which she told me, from him, he did only in order
to serve your Majesty more effectually here after." EDITOR.

* Inserted afterwards. EDITOR.

† " It is a singular circumstance," says *Dalrymple*, (Vol. I. p. 498.) " that, at this

My Lord *Churchil* give notice to the King of the design upon Brest.

LORD *Churchil's* LETTER TO THE KING, *May 4: 1694.*

some instances, or at least that he was no friend to the Prince of Orange and his government:

"It is but this day (says he in his * letter of the 4ᵗʰ of May) "that it came to my knowlidg what I now send you; which is, "That the Bomb Vessells and the twelve regiments, that are "now encamped at Portsmouth togather with the two Marine "Regiments, are to be commanded by Talmach, and design'd "to burn the harbour of Brest, and to destroy the men of war "that are there; this would be a great advantage to England, "but no consideration can, or ever shall, hinder me, from "letting you know what I think may be for your service, so "you may make what use you think best of this intelligence,

---

period, JAMES distrusted the sincerity of the men, on whose assurances he proceeded, and that WILLIAM made use of the services of some, of whose insincerity he had intelligence. When JAMES considered the justness of the information with which Marlborough supplied him, he believed that Lord to be sincerely attached to him: But, when he reflected upon the breach of his promises, with regard to the revolt of the Army, he suspected, that he meant a second time to betray him. He sometimes believed, that Russel's views were not so much directed to serve him, as from Republican Principles to degrade Monarchy in his person: And, at other times, he suspected, that Russel played a double game; if he missed the French Fleet to plead merit with him, and if he met it, to secure the same advantage with his Rival." EDITOR.

* This Letter, which is also noticed by Bertrand de Moleville, (Vol. 3. p. 571.) is given at greater length by *Macpherson* (Original Papers, Vol. 1. p. 487.) who inserts the following previous remarks: "WILLIAM, probably, though he knew not particulars, suspected in general the secret intrigues of *Marlborough*, when he sent him to the Tower, in the year 1692. JAMES, from a diffidence of his former favourite, required actions, as the proof of his sincerity. He had done considerable service to the Party, before this period. But the most capital instance of his thorough repentance, was the intelligence of the design against Brest, transmitted by him in the following letter to JAMES, inclosed in one from Colonel Sackville. *Marlborough* is supposed to have more designs than one, in this part of his conduct. He wished to serve JAMES with Lewis the Fourteenth, and to ruin General Talmash, as well as to be revenged of WILLIAM. In King JAMES' MEMOIRS, there is the following Memorandum, written, upon receipt of the letter, in his own hand, *May 4th, Lord Churchill informed the King of the design on Brest.*" EDITOR.

which you may depend on to be * true. The ill success of "   T O M. that enterprise was a great argument that this notice (which   IV. the King had receiued likewise from My Lord † *Arran,* was   1694. advantageous to the French, and the mistrust which My Lord   This attack upon Brest † *Churchill* complains he had of Admiral † *Russel* (who in all   was the 8ᵗʰ june O: S: probability did but delude the King, by the Prince of Orange's permission) was a signe he did not intend the same thing himself, at that time at least; but such men being steer'd by intrest, are no longer to be counted upon than that motiue houlds: however he continued his correspondence with the King, if not by letters at least by messages as long as his Majesty liued, but the Prince of Orange dying soon after, a new scene was open'd to him, in which he amazed the world with his conduct, and fortune; however he still pretend'd a good will to make some reparation to the Son, for the former infidelities to the Father.

While the King was thus born in hand with assurances of   Several Gentlemen imprifuture services, by his former Enemies, he had the mortification   son'd and tryd on a pretended to hear continually of the suffring and oppression of his real   Lancashire Plot. friends; the great numbers which had venter'd to Regiment

---

* In the Translation of this Letter inserted by *Macpherson,* the following is added, " But I must conjure you, for your own interest, to let no one know it but the Queen and the bearer of this letter.

" Russel sails to morrow, with forty ships, the rest being not yet paid; but it is said, that in ten days the rest of the Fleet will follow; and, at the same time, the land forcés. I have endeavourèd to learn this some time ago from Admiral Russel. But he always denied it to me, though I am very sure, that he knew the design for more than six weeks. This gives me a bad sign of this man's intentions. I shall be very well pleaséd to learn, that this letter comes safe to your hands." *Macpherson* adds, that " from one of the Earl of Middleton's Letters addressed to a correspondent in England, a part of which is inserted in a following page, there is reason to believe, That about this time, Marlborough had engaged the Prince and Princess of Denmark to enter heartily into terms with their exiled Father." EDITOR.

 . † Inserted afterwards. EDITOR.

themselves, list men, and buy arms, in expectation of the
King's landing when he came to La Hogue, had wunderfully
escaped the Vsurper's resentment, there not being found two
persons of some thousands, (who were privy to all that contrivance) that were tempted to make a fortune by betraying the
rest; so that no one suffer'd for it then : but thō the government
had not witnesses sufficient to bring any one to a tryal, they
were so far apprized of the thing, as disposed them to credit
any story thō never so absurd to those persons disadvantage;
for which reason (thō two years after) some indigent fellows
pretending to make a great discovery of a Plot, linked themselves into a confederacy to frame at least a probable Story (a
proceeding much practiced and countenanced in those days,
there being a considerable number of such bloody instruments
kept in constant pay by the government to serve a State turn).
These people accordingly accused no less than 160 persons of
a formed Conspiracy to rise for the King, chargeing each
particular with some overt act of what they call'd treason,
which the suspicion the government had of them already, made
them easily giue credit too, and prosecute with great heat and
bitterness ; but some gentlemen of Lancashire and Cheshire
who were first aprehended and brought to their tryal, getting
knowlidg of what they were accused of by sending a friend or
two in amongst the witnesses, under pretence of joining in the
accusation, were prepared with undenyable proofs to shew the
falsety of what was sworn against them ; so notwithstanding
many hardships, and several undue practices in their tryals,
they brought themselves off, and stop'd the prosecution of the
rest, which would otherwise in all probability haue left bloody
marks behind it : for the government seem'd disposed enough
to such severities, and beeing otherways satisfyd of those gentlemen's tampering, were the lesse scrupulous as to the credit
of the witnesses, which made their case more hazardous ; for

thō tis easy to purge one's self of an erroneous accusation when
known, it is harder without such a fore knowlidg and contrivance, to make a defence against a false oath than a true one,
because no man can prepare evidence to disproue he knows
not what, and it is too late to send for witnesses at a distance
to confront those, who are already produced in Court.

The dangers therefore which the King saw he exposed his
friends too, and the mercyless temper of the P^{ce} of Orange,
made him exceeding cautious how he engaged them in any
new attempt; so that thō the Princess of Orange dyd soon
after, which might reasonably haue produced a change, his
Majesty made no particular effort on so favorable an occasion,
being fearfull on one side for them, and not out of hopes, but
that now the Princess was dead (whose pretended title or
proximity in blood had been the chief ground work of all their
determinations) the government might shake and unhinge of
it self; and make them more inclined to admit of him, on
whom it could only rest as on a sure and unalterable basis:
but he found that time and continuance had harden'd people
in their evil ways, and the Princess of Denmark (notwithstanding her late pretence of repentance) was better contented,
or at least * apear'd to be so, to let the P^{ce} of Orange thō he
had used her ill, usurp upon her right, than that her Father
who had always cherished her beyond expression should be
restored to the possession of his; so that all the King got by it,
was an additional affliction to those he already underwent, by
seeing a child he loued so tenderly persever to her death in
such a signal state of disobedience and disloyalty, and to
hear her extoll'd and set out for it in the brightest colours, as
the highest vertue, by the mercenary flatterers of those times;

---

* *Kennet* inserts the letter (Vol. 3. P. 668.) which the Princess ANNE sent to
King William on the death of her Sister. EDITOR.

even that dull man Dr Tennison then Arch Bishop of Cantorbury, who with his languid oration at her funeral, rather
diverted than .edifyd the compagny, ranked it amongst her
highest praises that by long and laborious contradictions, she
had got the better of her * duty to her Parents, in consideration
of her obligation to her Religion and her Country : thus she
was cannonised for a sort of Paricide, by usurpeing her Father's
throne, and sending him togather with the Queen and Prince
her Brother to be vagabons in the world, had not the generosity
of a neibouring Monarch receiu'd, entertain'd, and succor'd
them, when their own Subjects and even Children had lost all
bowells of compassion and duty.

The King is
much afflicted
at her manner
of dying.
THE KING'S
LETTER TO
THE ABBE DE
LA TRAPPE.

If any thing had been able to trouble the tranquillity which
the King's resignation afforded him, this would haue done it,
especially when he heard his poor Daughter had been so
" deluded, as to declare at her death, That her conscience no
" ways troubled her, that if she had done any thing which the
" world might blame her for, it was with the advice of the
" most learned men of her Church who were to answer for it
" not she ; this made the King cry out, O miserable way of
" arguing so fatal both to the deceiver and those that suffer

---

* " MARY could never bear any jest to be made, or any thing said disrespect-
ful of her Father. Her anxiety for his personal safety was extreme. When she
was reproved for having too cheerful an appearance when she came first to the
royal residence, she said, None knew what she felt; but in compliance with her
Husband's commands, she affected what cost her much.... She seemed meant for
Empire, ANNE for private life." (*Noble's* Contin. of Granger, Vol.I. P. 14.) *Kennet*
(Vol. 3. P. 667.) inserts the following note : " The Bishop of Glocester, Dr Fowler,
in a preface to his Discourse on occasion of the Queen's death, writes thus:—" Upon
having the first intimation of the danger she was in, she replied to this effect :
*I have been instructed by the Divines of our Church, how very hazardous a thing it is
to rely upon a Death-Bed Repentance ; and I am not now to begin the great work of
preparing for Death ; and I praise God, I am not afraid of it.*" According to Burnet,
Ralph adds, (Vol. 2. p. 540.) " That in all which related to the Public, she *play'd
a part* that was not very natural to her ; for so much in effect does his acknowledg-
ment amount to, and if this is admitted it will follow, *That in all political matters
at least, she had no Will nor direction of her own.*" EDITOR.

themselves to be deceiu'd. She discover'd, it seems by this, her scruple and aprehention, yet blindly follow'd those guides, whose tragical end as well as of those who are guided by them, the Scripture it self forewans us of.

AND now that the Prince of Orange found the people gaue so readily into all his measures of ambition and cruelty, he was not content to make them renounce their subjection to the King, but denyd him the priviledg of a forreign Prince; his Majesty it seems had granted Commissions to several of his Subjects to act as Privateers, according to the formes observed in those cases, some of which being taken by the English, the Prince of Orange order'd one Golding thō he had the King's Comission to be prosecuted as a Pirate; and thō Mr Oldish (I think) a Civilian of greatest esteem in the Kingdom, declared it to be against all law and justice, to repute those persons robbers who in time of war acted by Commission from a crowned head, the Prince of Orange not used to such contradictions in the ways of his reveng turn'd him out of his imployment, and put one in, that could easilyer mould his doctriñe to the usurper's views; upon which, contrary to the law of God and nations he suffer'd an unjust but glorious death: thō in one respect the hardship done him mitigated his unjust punishment, for those who had the Most Christian King's Commission were hanged, drawn and quarter'd as traitors, whereas Golding being judged to haue none, was only hanged as a Pirate, without those other circomstances of drawing and quartering, which thō they add little to the suffrings of a dying man, yet are counted an additional punishment in the eye of the Law.

These constant ill successes of all the King's endeavours, had long convinced him, that Providence had marked out no other

way for his sanctification than that of suffring, for which
reason those attempts he had made of late were rather at the
Sollicitation of his Subjects, or that he might not be defectiue
in his Duty to the Prince his Son and his people, than out of
any earnest desire to make the same figure in the world, he had
formerly done; on the contrary he sought rather, than avoided,
those humiliations which affected his own person, and was not
content with that * abjection the malice of his enemies had
reduced him too: but by contemplateing his own former
failings as to his morral life, more than the indignities he had
suffer'd in respect of his character, he was much more intent
to doe penance for the one, then to be deliver'd from the other;
this made him turn St Germains into a sort of Solitude, and not
content with that, went to seek it at certain times where it was
to be found in its greatest perfection.

It was not only curiosity (thō that might haue some share in
the first voyage) which made the King go to LÁ TRAPPE, a
Convent of reformed Bernardins, who liveing up to the rigour
of that most penetential Father's rule, had appear'd of late an
ashtonishing example, what corporal austeritys, self denyals,
and eminent perfection, men, who seek the glory of God, and
their own salvation with a true Christian fervour, with the
assistance of his grace, are capable of arriveing too: perpetual

---

* There is a curious letter amongst *Macpherson's* Original Papers, (Vol. 1.
p. 488.) from *Nairne's* Papers, dated July 15th, 1694, which describes the poverty
JAMES had to struggle with at that time. This letter was written by the Earl of
Middleton to a member of the House of Commons: " I have received yours of
the 23^d of May. It is most certainly true that The Merchant who owns the
goods, 368 (*King James*) stands in great need of money, and indeed it is not to be
wondered at, considering his great losses and his numerous family; and would
therefore be glad if any of his friends or old customers would advance him what
they can spare, which shall be punctually repaid, with interest, as soon as he is in
a condition to appear on the exchange. In the mean time, he might be put in a
condition to maintain his poor workmen, who are in great misery." EDITOR.

silence, except when they sing the office in the Church, keeps their thoughts as continually fixed upon God, as their tongues are permited to utter nothing but his praises ; their surprising abstenence from flesh, fish, eggs, milk, wine, in fine all but herbes, roots, and cider, makes a numerous Community liue in a manner by their own manuel labour, and out of the product of a garding ; this with their other mortifications in watching, habit, labour, could and heat, togather with their obedience, abjection, constant attendance at their duty thō almost con_ tinually sick, made the King think it a proper Scoole of Christian patience, and so resolued to make a spiritual retreat there the first year after his return from Ireland, notwith. standing the private dirision he was sencible it exposed him too ; but the spiritual profit he reaped from it made him continue it every year, and overlook the censures of worldly men, whose judgments are seldom true, generally ill grounded, and always to be dispised in such cases as those : and thō it seem'd impossible to rais those pious Monks to a higher pitch of vertue than they were already arriued too, yet they confessed it gaue them an additional fervour, to see so great a * Prince accommodate himself not only to their long offices, meditations and spiritual conferences, but to their very corporal austerys ; for unless the King was indisposed, he always eat in the refectory, suffring no addition but that of eggs, to the pene- tential diet the Community liued upon, which the Abbot could not refrain expressing his ashtonishment at, in his edefying and elegant letter to the Mareshall Belfont on that occasion.

---

* They who may be disposed to blame the conduct of JAMES for retiring to La Trappe, should remember, that in the solitude of that celebrated Convent JAMES was still considered as a King, and perhaps as little less than a Martyr to his Religion. EDITOR.

T O M.
IV.

1696.
The King is
again press'd
to make an
other attempt.

THUS the King imployd his time and thoughts, till awaked again about the beginning of the year 1696 by fresh sollicitations from his friends in England, he was prevail'd upon to try his fortune once more ; they conceiveing the Kingdom to be much better disposed, and the conjuncture favorable for such an undertakeing. They were continually adverticeing him from thence, that the Parliament began to jarr with the Vsurper*, that the people were cured of their fondness, with a tedious war and heavy taxes ; that the seeming zeal of so many pretended patriots to deliver the Kingdom from Popery and Slavery, and those other noisy words which had amused the publick for a while, was now discover'd to be a real endeavour to deliver the people only of their mony, whereof the greatest share had been divided amongst themselves; which made them more industrious to remoue men than grievances, and made them regard very little who got most by the war, whether England, the Allys, or even the Enemie themselves, so long as they had the plumeing of the people and enjoyd such honorable and profitable places, as made them unsencible of those oppressions with which the Nation groaned ; that most men saw how unequally the burden was divided betwixt the Dutch and them, that the former had the knack of trading with their enemies, and of drawing only warmth from that fire, which consumed others to ashes, and that haveing so good an occasion

---

* JAMES considered his Son in Law more in this point of view, after the death of Queen Mary, as appears by a curious document amongst Macpherson's Original Papers, (Vol. 1. p. 508.) entitled " An examination of the P. of O——'s right to the Crown at Queen Mary's death." From Nairne's Papers. It thus begins, " All the people of England must necessarily be, at this time, convinced, that the title of the Prince of Orange to the possession of the Crown is not only unjust, in reference to the King and to the Prince of Wales, but also to the Princess of Denmark, according to their own new Law, though his Majesty was, as they pretend, excluded by Abdication ; for none of our new Law-Makers ever pretended, or durst say That the Crown of England is elective." EDITOR.

of draining the English coin, they made no difficulty of shewing they aim'd at something more than of being a meer buttress to the Netherlands, and a barrier to England; that in the management of this affair the Prince of Orange was in effect their Factor, and never served them so well when he was their Subject as now that he was a Sovereign, who by makeing the Kingship truckle to the Statehoulder, render'd three Kingdoms in effect but Provinces to the seauen he came from; that the English merchants for that reason were forced to stay for convoys till the Dutch were ready; through whose hands all letters and intelligence passing, gaue them the first advice and best market: These partialities abroad and oppressions at home, would (as the King's friends immagin'd) bring people to their witts, when they saw nothing amended that was sayd to be amis, nor any thing complyd with that had been promised, but on the contrary their mony made use of to bribe those who were entrusted with the power of giveing it; or otherwise the Prince of Orange durst not haue denyd so many bills in confirmity to his Declaration, or spoke so resolutely as he did on those occasions, but that he thought he might take an authority over those he payd so well; that many who relying on the Prince of Orange's sincerity gaue in too readily into his designes at first, but now seing how little he complyd with his engagement, and the fatal consequences of the Revolution, repented themselves heartely of the loss of peace, plenty and the antient laws, longed for nothing more than to see the Kingdom free again from Dutch seruitude and the prospect of an expensiue, bloody and endless war: the late calling in of the Coing had added to the people's uneasiness too, who when they are uneasy in themselves are generally so with their Masters: in fine the * King was at last convinced it was reasonable to

---

* " There were two Parties in JAMES's Cabinet, the Compounders and the

1696.
Some diffi-
cultys about
wording the
Declaration
for the Calais
Expedition.

try again, especially when he found his Most Christian Majesty fall into the same opinion.

But before the King enter'd upon this expedition, he was in some perplexity what method to obserue, in the Promisses *he was to * make* in his Declaration, the forces he was to procure and depend upon, since so much exception had been made of late to allmost every thing he had sayd or done, by one partie or other, even of his friends; and therefore he took great care to avoid as much as possible the Shocking anny of them, since they all pretended a good will to him, but no ways shew'd it to one another; each one of these parties pull'd a different way, had different prospects and contrary views, whilst his Majesty was under a necessity of not espousing any one so as not to neglect or disgust an other: The Catholicks had little power but the surest to be relyd on, his old friends of the Church of England had talked six years and done nothing, the new ones of the Common wealth or Presbiterian Partie, had promised as largely but done no more; these Parties hated one an other by fits, and consulted togather by fitts, were jealous and prying to see if the King favour'd not one more than an

Non-compounders. Middleton was at the head of the first, and Melfort of the last. The Compounders advised him to offer a general pardon, in his Declarations, and proposed to bring him back only upon certain conditions; the Non-compounders were willing to receive him, without any restrictions, and to except several persons in his offers of pardon. These probably were JAMES's favourites. But, to please the other party, Melfort was dismissed, as if under some disgrace, and ordered to withdraw from Court; and Mr. Carryll was made Secretary of State, in his room......Melfort was as obnoxious to the French Ministry as to JAMES's friends in England; for, on the third of October, (1694) Middleton writes to Mr. Carryll, from Fontainbleau, *I wish the Lord Melfort does not come to spit in our potage: for if the Ministers believe, that he will be acquainted with what hath been proposed, we need think no more about it.*" (Macpherson's Original Papers, Vol. I. p. 494. 497.) EDITOR.

* Interlined by the Son of James the Second. EDITOR.

other, and if he seem'd to contradict himself in any promis, it T O M.
did him much harme, alienated one side and reconciled not IV.
the other; for most of those that desired to treat, did it more 1696.
fore their own ends than the King's advantage, and more
out of weareness of the present government, than fondness
of his; others were against the King's treating at all, they
apprehended he would follow the late Chancellor Hide's
principle, Neglect his true friends and giue all to his pretended
ones, who (they sayd) forsook the government but as ratts
doe a ship when they think it a sinking: These people tould
the King, that he must not depend upon any Treaty, but
come with such a * force as would doe the work without it, or
els he would find little effects of their promisses, no more than
they regarded his, in the circomstances he was in, for that
when his Majesty was in England one act of Grace, or popular
speech would doe more good, than forty promisses he should
make before; so they advised him to keep as much as possible
to generall terms, and refer particulars to an ensuing Parliament
to be well advised for the quiet of his mind, what he might
promis safely, for that his enemies knew as well as he, what he
could say in conscience, and what not; and that if he stretched
in any point, they would mistrust equivocation, which would
dampe the credit of all the rest.

---

* Macpherson has given from Nairne's Papers, under the preceding year, 1695,
*Reasons most humbly offered, why ten thousand men are sufficient and safe for the
King in person to make, at this time, a descent upon England; with a proposal for
making the said descent.* The following is given as the 3d Reason: " That the
Nation being thus divided into three parts, the Prince of Orange's must certainly
be the least, for many plain reasons; but especially this, that no man will be so
mad as to oppose himself to the King and his Son, the Princess of Denmark and
her Son, for the single life of the Prince of Orange, since, after his death, they
must unavoidably fall into some of their hands, even though they were secure
during his life, which no man will think himself." (Original Papers, Vol. 1. p. 520.)
EDITOR.

The Earle of Middleton acting now as sole Secretary of State,
My Lord Melford being out (whom the King at the sollicitations
of his friends in England had thought fit to dismiss) was of
opinion the King ought as much as possible to keep to the
terms of the last Declaration, that he might change, what in
conscience he could not comply with, without recedeing from
the substance of what he had promised ; that the whole people
of England haveing an intrest in what he had engaged to doe,
his Majesty was under an obligation of keeping his promis to
them, thō those who advised the Declaration had not done so
to him, that France could not afford a force to doe the worke
alone, and that the King had no other way of armeing thousands for him, who otherwise would with all their power oppose
him, that the main scope of the late Declaration being security
to the people in promising pardon for what was past, and to
govern by Law for the future ; as to the first his Majestys
conscience could be no way intrested, and haveing once forgiven, it would be harsh to retract ; that a Prince's word is
sacred, and publick faith inviolable, especially in a case where
an honest man is lyable to be punished as a traitor, for paying
taxes might be construed an aiding, comforteing, and abetting,
which all Subjects had done, since the Revolution, and the
best had payd them double.   And as to the difficultys which
were urged against the latter, as that it might imply a necessity
of breeding up the Prince of Wales a Protestant, he answer'd,
That those who had treated, had pass'd from it, and that since
it was not necessary his Servants should be sworn to the King,
they would not fall within the Test Act ; that as to Catholicks
going to Court, it had never been taken notice of, or reckon'd
amongst the pretended infractions, and as for a certain number
of them being imployd, there was no doubt but it would be
allow'd of now, since it had been offer'd before, nor was it ever
complain'd of that his Majesty had a Chappell ; that must be

understood as necessary for a Catholick King, nay the setting
it up as his Majesty did it, was counted one of the best advised
and most applauded actions of his reign, for by his sincerity
and open dealing in that, he gaue the greatest assurance
immaginable, of his being so in the rest ; that the dispenseing
power was what gaue the greatest apprehention, which however
they did not think proper to bereaue him of quite, as they had
done the Prince of Orange, therefore they thought it necessary
to prelimit him, against dispenseing with the Test, for that
otherwise if his Majesty promised only in general terms to
govern by Law, and that the dispensing power should be judged
a part of the Law, then would the people say, It is in his
Majestys power to suspend what Law or as many as he pleases,
and so by Law govern in efect without it; which they call
arbitrary power, and which aboue all things upon earth they
dreaded the most ; that the promising to pass what bills should
be presented to him, was intended only as to judicial proceedings, and civil causes; that the promising in general termes
would induce more people to return to their duty, and that the
more the Prince trusted the People, the more they would trust
him, as appear'd in Queen Elizabeth's time.

The King was perplexed with this diversity of opinions, and
thought the best way to shock none, was to draw the Declaration
as favorable to the people's Libertie and Religion as in conscience
he could, but not to dispers it till he landed ; which *never

---

* " A Mistake, in a conversation between Lewis XIV. and the late King,
defeated the Invasion intended for this year, (1696): Mr. Powel, who had been
sent by the adherents of the latter Prince from England, through the vehemence of
his zeal, produced this mistake. He seemed to insinuate, that the Jacobites in
Britain were first to take arms, and then expected to be supported by France.
On this state of the case, his most Christian Majesty proceeded to make preparations for transporting a force into England..............The King of France insisted,
that JAMES's friends, in England, should take arms, before the French Troops embarked." (Macpherson's Original Papers, Vol. 1. p. 541. 543.) EDITOR.

T O M.
IV.

1696.
The King
went from
S⁺ Germains
towards Calais
18 Febru: S:N:

happening, it never became publick and prevented at least doeing harme since it did no good, and scaped being censured as the others had been.

The attempt being at last resolved on and the Court of France concurring in the thing, the troops design'd for this Expedition began to draw towards Dunkirk and Calais, from whence this invasion was to be made, and on the 28ᵗʰ of February the King himself parted from S⁺ Germains, being hasten'd away from the Court of France sooner than otherwise he intended ; which giveing too early an alarme, hinder'd his friends in England from performeing their part, and in the end ruin'd the whole designe : but besides the ill success this Expedition had in common with the rest, it fortuned to draw over and aboue, a certain obliquy upon the King, as if he had consented to, or approued, a designed attempt upon the Prince of * Orange's person ; which it seems certain gentlemen (thinking to do the King good service by it) had combined amongst themselves to endeavour accordingly. Their first project was to surprize and

---

* " Though JAMES was, at the time, accused by his Enemies of abetting Plots for assassinating King William, it now appears, that he never harboured any such design. The following may serve as an additional proof of the innocence of that unfortunate Prince, upon that head :

" *The Earl of Middleton to the Marquis de Torcy.*

" There is an Englishman arrived here, who calls himself Vane, without a passport and without recommendations ; and there is not one man in the place who knows him. This fellow has had the impudence to propose to me, an attempt on the Prince of Orange's Life ; and, as I rejected this proposal, with aversion, the conversation finished. But when I gave an account of it to the King, my Master, lest the man should make his escape, he spoke to the Count de Druis, to secure his person, until The King's orders about him should be received. It is for this reason, the King of England desires you to inform his Majesty of this adventure immediately ; it being his opinion, That the said Vane should be closely imprisoned, but in other respects, well treated ; because we cannot prove whether he has been instigated to this, by our enemies, or by an indiscreet Zeal." (*Macpherson's* Original Papers, Vol. 1. p. 561.) EDITOR.

seize the Prince of Orange and carry him into France, but finding that impracticable if they scrupled his life, by degrees were drawn in to a resolution of attacking him as he came from Hampton Court, or from hunting, and if they found no possibility of carrying him off aliue, to make no difficulty of killing him. It is not to the present purpose to shew how far such an undertakeing, as the case stood, might sute with the rules of Conscience and honour, or to answer or support the arguments of a certain Treatice published in Cromwel's days, called Killing no murther; for in as much as the King was no ways privy to the design, neither commission'd the persons nor approued the thing, his Majesty was no farther concern'd in the matter then to suffer most undeservedly by it, both in his reputation and intrest, for those unfortunate gentlemen by mistakeing messages on one hand, and their too forward zeal on the other, most of them lost their own lives, and furnished an opertunity to the King's enemies of renewing their calumnys against him, and fix'd the People and Parliament (who otherwise began to waver) in the Prince of Orange's intrest more than ever: so that many suspected * *that* Prince to haue been in the bottom of it himself, since no one reaped more advantage from it than he; and it is more than probable, that Crosbie who was a main mouer of this project, was employ'd by the P^{ce} of Orange to perswade his Majesty to it: for this man haveing been sent to St Germains by the King's friends, was clapt up at his return to England; and assoon as he was out, thō but upon bail, return'd thither again and pressed the King mightely to grant a Commission for seizing the Prince of Orange &c: which thō his Majesty positively denyd, hinder'd him not from writeing to the same purpose out of England, to which all the answer the King order'd should be given him, was, That he thought he was mad,

---

* Inserted by the King's Son, instead of the word *him*. EDITOR.

and made the King suspect his fidelitie, it not being natural
to immagin that after haveing been imprison'd and tryd for his
life, and even still upon bail, he should venter upon an other
voyage and on so desperate an errand, if he had not been
gain'd by the Prince of Orange ; nor that his tryal should haue
gon so glibly in his favour, without a previous engagement of
doing service worthy of such an unusual indulgence.

The Commission the King gaue to S[r] George Berkeley and
others, was in order to a general insurrection of the Jacobits,
which he understood they were ready to make assoon as he
appear'd on the French cost with such a force as was agreed
on ; the Court of France was in the same belief, and had
order'd their troops not to put to Sea till they had news of it,
but the King's friends it seems, meaning the King should land
first (which his Majesty understood too afterwards) the matter
was like to come to nothing while they waited thus for each
others giveing the leading ; so some persons stretched the sence
of certain words, in the King's Commission, which was for
levying war upon the Prince of Orange and attacking him in
his winter quarters, to impower them to do it by surprize,
when he was no otherwise accompanyed then with his ordinary
guards : but to giue a more perfect account how these different
mistakes came about, it will be necessary to relate the fact from
its first origin.

King Jam:
Mem[n].Tom:9.
pag. 39...
The Relation
of this Expe-
dition, and his
miscariage.

" The King being informed in the begining of the year
" 1696, that the Prince of Orange's affairs began not to haue so
" favorable an aspect as formerly, that the new called Parlia-
" ment did not answer his expectation, were reasty and
" refractory in several points ; and that notwithstanding he
" had so many of his domestick servants, Officers of his Army,
" dependers and pentioners in it to influence their turbulent
" spirit, yet the Country partie had got the upper hand, and
" gaue him so much trouble and vexation, that My Lord
" Sunderland and others, who had advised and at last had

prevail'd with him to break the old Parliament, began to "   T O M.
loos his favour and to be ill looked upon by him. This the "   IV.
King's *friends who were then call'd Jacobits by the Countrie "   1696.
partie and indeed by every body els for distinction sake, "
thought a good occasion to blow the coles as much as in them "
lay ; and notwithstanding all their former disapointements, "
and the neglect (as they thought) of so many good occasions "
by his Most Christian Majesty, however now took courage "
again, and press'd hard to haue men and ships made ready "
for the begining of the Spring, in order to lay hould of any "
opertunity which might fortune to offer it self; and whereas "
heretofore they had insisted upon haueing no less then 25 or "
30000 men, they now proposed no more than ten or twelve, "
that the King should land with them as near London as he "
could ; they doubted not but this force would be sufficient "
to recover his Kingdoms, there not being at that time aboue "
fourteen thousand regular troops in England, so that the "
Prince of Orange could not possibly draw togather aboue Six "

* *Dalrymple*, in the beginning of that very scarce Volume of his Memoirs, the third, has drawn the Characters of some of the principal Friends of JAMES. (Page 9.) *Lord Nottingham*, who possessed clear parts and a clear expression, was ignorant of Sea Affairs, though all orders to the Fleet had been sent through him when Secretary of State. " *Lord Rochester* was a man of confused parts, and confused expression. The natural abilities of the *Marquis of Caermarthen* were great, but distracted, and perhaps lost in the detail of packing Parties, in which his youth and his age had been spent. And *Admiral Russel*, at the head of the Fleet, well knew, that, from his own private Correspondence with the late King, his life was in the hands of that Prince, and of Lewis, if he should add injury to injury, by invading the coast of France, after defeating its Fleet. Besides, *Lord Caermarthen* and *Lord Rochester* were in a secret Correspondence with King JAMES. Mr. M'Pherson has published the evidence of *Lord Caermarthen*'s Correspondence; and although, in the former volume of these Memoirs, I had represented *Lord Rochester* as one of the few of the great who stood clear of it, yet I have since seen evidence that I was mistaken. For when I was last at Paris I saw in the Scotch College there, a letter from *Lord Rochester* to King JAMES, written on silk, which, from the form of the piece, had been the inside of a woman's stomacher; and I was told there were others of his letters in the House." EDITOR.

" thousand in a forthnight's time, into .the neibourhood of
" London, and in so doing must leaue the Country naked too,
" and free by consequehce to rise if so inclined; that they
" knew many of those troops both Soldiers and Officers to be
" well inclined, and upon certain news of the King's being
" landed, would immediately join him, and that should once
" the Prince of Orange's people begin to abandon him, the
" tyde would run as violently to the King as it did to that
" Prince heretofore; and the King's friends encreas by the
" same proportion they had formerly fallen away : there were
" some very sobermen amongst the Jacobits, who were so san-
" guin in the point that they writ to the King, that thō they
" durst not advise him to come alone and without troops,
" yet they were perswaded that could his Majesty but once
" get to London, or some other considerable town in England,
" that the greatest part of the Nation would rise and restore
" him. The King gaue his Most Christian Majesty from time
" to time notice of these advices, which at last so encouraged
" him that he resolued to grant the men that were asked, and
" gaue order to haue all things necessary for a descent by the
" end of february S: N: but still press'd that the King's friends
" would rise first and possess themselves of some considerable
" town or at least embody themselves in some good post,
" where they might stand upon their defence till the King
" could come to their relief.

" Vpon this the Duke of Berwick was sent over to head
" them in case they could be perswaded to rise first, and about
" the same time several Officers and other persons who had
" served, disired leaue to go over into England and Scotland
" upon their private concerns, amongst which were several
" gentlemen of the guards, who were weary with serveing as
" common men; and such as could not obtain leaue of the
" government in England to return, were permited to make

use of the owlers or any secret way to get over, and had "
directions to join themselves with any that should rise and "
declare for the King, being most of them men of experience. "

When the Duke of Berwick got to London he saw only "
one or two of those the King could most * confide in, by "
whom he sent to the most considerable Jacobits and pro- "
posed their riseing first, upon an assurance of being seconded "
by the King himself with twelve thousand men, which "
togather with the transport Ships were all ready at Calais, "
and would embark immediately upon notice of their being "
in arms; but they answer'd, It would be impossible for them "
to rise as things then stood, till the King was landed, for that "
should they assemble and the enemies ships interpose, they "
would certainly be cut in pieces, and so never more be in a "
condition to Serue the King, but that the moment he was "
on shore they would all immediately run to their arms in their "
several Countys, and join him without delay. "

This reply was so reasonable, it could not be answer'd, and "
indeed might well haue been foreseen; but what prevail'd "
on the King to moue them to it, was a mistake of his upon "
discours with Mr Powel who was sent over by the most con- "
siderable Jacobits to giue an account of the true state of "
England, and to shew the reasonableness of the King's ven- "
turing over at that time with the number aboue mentioned. "

It was about the end of January or the begining of "
February 1696, when he arriued at St Germains. In "
the first conversation the King had with him before the "
Queen, he was so very earnest for attempting something "

---

* " The Duke of Berwick, shocked to find that he was amidst Assassins instead
of Loyalists, and that his reputation might be involved in theirs, returned to
France, and thereby disappointed Insurrections in England." (*Dalrymple*, Vol. 3.
p. 77.) EDITOR.

" forthwith, and talk'd with so much warmth, that both
" the King and Queen understood him That the Jacobits
" offer'd to rise out of hand, if the King were but ready to
" pass; and his Majesty not haveing leasure to stay long with
" him at that time, so as to come to a fuller explanation, bid
" him put in writeing the substance of his message that he
" might communicate it to his Most Christ: Majesty : but the
" two Kings fortuneing to meet before that was done, his
" Majesty gaue a short account of what had passed, and
" assured him England was ready to rise when ever required ;
" but some days after when Mr Powel gaue in his paper the
" King found his mistake, but not till then ; however it was
" not thought fit to unsay what had been already tould his
" Most Christian Majesty, or alarme the French Ministers,
" which would certainly retard at least the preparations, if
" not make them be quite layd aside, and the King hoped
" that the misunderstanding betwixt the Prince of Orange and
" Parliament might encreas, and afford perhaps an occasion,

" that might encourage the French to send the King over first :
" and indeed the preparations were So forward, and his Most
" Christian Majestys orders so well obeyd, by Monsr Pont-
" chartrain in his departement relateing to the marine, and
" Monsr Barbesieux to land, that things were in readiness at
" the time appointed, which was the end of February ; yet
" thō the preparations were carryd on with all the Secresie
" immaginable, the Naval ones gaue jealousie to the Dutch, it
" not being possible to fit out and assemble three or four
" hundred sail of great and small vessels, thō in several Ports,
" without makeing some sort of nois : upon which the Dutch
" order'd troops to be sent into Zealand, thinking the French
" might haue a design upon some of those Islands, because
" they understood by their spys, that more force than usual
" was drawn towards the Sea coasts ; not suspecting any

design upon England till they heard that the King was gon "
for * Calais, which his Most Christian Majesty thought "
necessary he should doe, being all the transport ships were "
sail'd from their different ports, and were to rendevouz there "
on the 25th of February; on which very day his Most Christian "
Majesty sent Monsr Pontchartrain to the King to let him "
know that he thought the secret could be no longer kept, "
and that in case he approued of it, he thought it fit his "
Majesty should go down forthwith to the Sea side, but not "
to let the men embarke till he was sure the Jacobits were up "
in England; that the next day his most Christian Majesty "
would come himself to St Germains to take the last measures "
concerneing that affair; who came accordingly and repeated "
what his Minister had sayd, and stil takeing it for granted, "
the riseing would be begun by that time the King would "
reach Calais, pressed for that reason his setting out imme- "
diately: but thō the King had no great mind to go till he "
had a return of the Duke of Berwick's message, who had not "
been gon aboue a forthnight, yet for certain reasons he "
thought not fit to mention it, but acquiesed to the proposal "
of his setting out within two days, which he did and arriued "
at † Callais the 2^d of March S. N. "

T O M.
IV.

1696.

Ibid. pag: 399.

---

* "At Calais, on the 5th and 6th of March, JAMES gave Commissions to the Marquis of Harcourt, as Captain General, and to Richard Hamilton as Lieutenant General of his Forces; and on the 22^d of March he appointed Hamilton to the place of master of the robes. On the 23^d he went to Boulogne." (*Macpherson's* Original Papers, Vol. 1. p. 545.) EDITOR.

† "We can scarcely conceive a situation more disagreeable than that, to which JAMES was reduced at this time. Detained on shore, and deprived of intelligence from England, by contrary winds; dreading every moment to hear, that the two Fleets of the Enemy had joined; and warned constantly by the French Ministers to be cautious in exposing their Fleet and Army. Middleton mentions this in his letters from Boulogne and Calais." (*Macpherson's* Original Papers, Vol. 1. p. 547.) EDITOR.

" The day his Majesty left St Germains being the 28 of
" February, he met at St Denis a Servant of the Duke of
" Berwicks, with a letter from his master to the Earle of Mid-
" dleton, which gaue an account of his being come back;
" but that his chair being broke at Clermont he was forced to
" stay till it was mended, and then would make all the hast he
" could to giue a full account of his Negociation, and by some
" expressions in his letter, it was plain he had not succeeded
" in it as expected: upon this the King was in some doubt
" whether he should not return to St Germains or go on, but
" at last resolved to proceed, giueing his Most Christian
" Majesty an account from St Denis of what he then knew,
" and promised a further relation when he had seen the Duke
" of Berwick, which he did not do till he came to Clermont
" that night, where after haveing heard the relation and what
" condition he had left things in England, togather with the
" occasion of his sudden departure, his Majesty sent him on
" and continued his own journey to Calais.

It was a great misfortune to the King that his Most Christian
Majesty had not a right notion of the business from the
begining, and that he durst not disabuse him, for fear his
Ministers who were ever avers from those expeditions, should
quash all, without so much as a tryal; so he still hoped something might happen, on which he could rais a request to let the
troops embarke first, and for that reason continued his journey
to Calais; wher he was no sooner arriued, but according to
his usual fortune found himself at an end of his expectation,
by meeting the news of severall gentlemens being seized on
account of an * attempt upon the Prince of Orange's person,

It was thought
the French
intended
nothing but a
faint.

---

* " The Conspirators in England were seized, tried and executed. The
English Fleet put to sea, while contrary winds detained the French Fleet in their
harbours; and James returned to St. Germains to make fruitless representations to

which put the Kingdom into such a ferment, that now there
was no thinking of the Jacobits ventring to rise, much less of
the King's landing, thō the French had been willing; but
besides their aversnéss to hazard their troops it was sayd
afterwards, that the whole design on the French side was only
a faint to amuse the English, while they made a junction of
their Fleets.

It was a more than usual trouble to the King to see his
project broke, his hopes blasted, and his friends ruin'd, by their
pursuing methods contrary to his judgment, and without his
consent, for he had (as was sayd) been long sollicited to agree
to something of that nature, but had still rejected it: About
the end of the year 1693 a proposal had been made to the "
King by one newly come out of England, of seizeing and "
bringing away the Prince of Orange, and of makeing a riseing "
in and about London, but his Majesty would not hear of it, "
looking upon the project as impracticable, and exposeing his "
friends when he had no prospect of seconding them; the same "
thing, some time after was proposed again, and again rejected, "
notwithstanding which in the begining of the year 1695, it "
was a therd time moued by one Crosbie or Clench, (as was "
mention'd before) who came from people that whished the " ‹
King well (as he pretended), thō an other set of men than "
those the King had hithertoo corresponded with: these persons "
he sayd mad no doubt of seizing the Prince of Orange and "
bringing him off, but desired a warrant signed by his Majesty "
to empower them to do it; this the King again rejected, and· "

Right margin notes:

T O M.
IV.
1696.

The design'd
attempt upon
the P. of
Orange's per-
son, was with-
out the King's
privity, and
against his
will.

KING JAM:
MEMᵐ. To:9.
pag: 400.

Lewis the XIVth and the Pope, against the Peace. The first paper on this subject,
in Nairne's Collection, is the following Memorial, which is in his own hand. It
appears from it that JAMES's friends had advised him to be satisfied, if the Succession was secured to his Son, after the death of King William. (*Macpherson's*
Original Papers, Vol. 1. p. 551.) EDITOR.

" charged him not to meddle in any such matter, nor so much
" as to mention it any more when he return'd for England,
" which he was then obliged too very soon, being only out
" upon bail; but notwithstanding this injunction, at his arriual
" in London he droue it on what he could, and was so indes-
" creet and insolent, as to encourage not only those people of his
" Club to prepare, assureing them an order would soon be sent
" accordingly, but haveing by some means or other found out
" several of the other Club, as Mr George Porter, Goodman,
" Sr William Perkins, and Charnock, engaged them to join
" with him, and to gain the greater credit and reputation with
" them, assured them an order would speedely be sent to him
" for the executeing of it : some of them indeed gaue no credit
" to what he sayd, but others more credulous and zealous sent
" about to hire a vessel for the purpose, but Mr Charnock
" doubting of the truth of what Crosbie pretended, writ over to
" know, and was assured the contrary, upon which the project
" was layd quite aside by that Club; but upon Sr George
" Berkleys being at London privately, to whom and others,
" a power had been given to Levy war and to head the riseing
" as was mentioned before, they proposed their old project to
" him, which it seems he accepted of, and prepared to attack
" the P^{ce} of Orange with fortie hors on the road as he went too,
" or came from hunting at Richmond, whereas his Commission
" imported no such thing. But to giue a clear and unquestion-
" able account of this Attempt which made so much nois in

Sr George
Barkley's
Relation of
designed at-
tempt against
the P^{ce} of
Orange.

the world, it will be necessary to insert Sr George Barkleys
relation of it written in his own hand :

IN NOVEMBER 1695 the King haveing call'd me into his
closet, was pleas'd to tell me he was resolved to make an attempt
for recovering his Kingdoms next winter, that his friends in
England had satisfyd him that the dispositions ther were great
and the time seasonable, but that the forces the King of France

could spare would not be sufficient without the help of his own subjects, that many of them had promised to rise especially in and about London, but that they would want Officers who had some experience in the war; that he intended therefore to send me privately to London some time before, to discours with his friends, and to take measures conjunctly with them, to haue all in a readiness to rise so soon as notice should be given; and that for heading those raw and unexperienced men, he intended to send over a number of Officers, who should be enjoined to follow such orders as I should giue them.

Before I parted from St Germains the King guaue me a Commission, to authorise me and all those who should joine me in his Majesties cause to rise in arms and make war upon the Prince of Orange and all his adherents. Which Commission was exactly as follows:

JAMES R.

OUR WILL and pleasure is and we do hereby fully autherise, strictly require, and expressly command our loveing Subjects to rise in armes and make war upon the Prince of Orange the Vsurper of our throne and all his adherents, and so Seize for our use all such fortes, Towns, Strong houlds within our dominion of England, as may serue to further our intrest, and to do from time to time such other acts of hostilitie against the P^{ce} of Orange and his adherents, as may conduce most to our seruice, we judging this the properest, justest, and most effectual means of procureing our restoration and their deliurance; and we do hereby indempnify them for what they shall act in pursuance of this our Royal command. Given at our Court of St Germains en Laye, the 27th of December 1695. Which day I parted from St Germains, haveing none with me but Major Holmes, and about the 27th old stile I arriued at London.

Soon after my arriuall there I came acquainted with Mr Charnock, who at our first meeting complain'd to me, that he, and some others had a design on foot, which would haue undoubtedly facilitated the King's return, but that his Majestie would never permit them to put it in execution.

A few days after that, Mr Charnock made me acquainted with Sr William Perkins who was concerned with him in all their proposalls, who then open'd the designe to me and assured me they wánted nothing for perfecting of it, but his Majestys leaue; it was to forme a partie to fall upon the Prince of Orange, which I did much approve of, if it could be carryed on with that secresie and conduct as a thing of that consequence ought to be; upon which I immediately asked them, if it was possible to find so many good men as would be requisite, and would undertake a braue action without asking of questions, and urged severall other difficulties which then occur'd; upon which they assured me that they knew severall of their opinion, that would be glad of any occasion to serue the King, though at the utmost peril of their liues.

Presumeing therefore upon the Commission I had from his Májesty, to make war upon the P[ce] of Orange and all his adherents, I thought myself sufficiently authorized to engage with them to attack that Prince when his Guards were about him; upon which I shew'd them my Commission which they were much pleased with, but tould me, it was absolutely necessary I should see M[r] Porter who lodged in the same house with them, and was privy to all their designes, but I did not condescend to it for some time, not that I mistrusted his loyaltie, but that I heard he was much given to drink, and open minded and therefore not so fit to be trusted with a thing of that great consequence; upon which they tould me their liues were as dear to them as I could esteeme my own, and that if he were such as I represented him to be, they would never haue been concerned with him : at last I got Major Holmes to bring me to his lodging where he had kept his bed for some time, but we

did not talk of any thing of consequence at that time, but soon
after I had a meeting with them all three and a great many
times afterwards.

By this time Captain Knightely had heard of me and was
very desirous to speak with me, so I made an appointment
with him and Captain Hungate. At our meeting Capt Knightly
tould me he and some others had a designe of makeing a partie
to fall upon the Prince of Orange, and that he and Durance
(a good Partisan) had viewed the ground severall times, and
that they found it fit for their purpos, and desired me to see
Durance, which I did, to try what I could learn from him
and then went to see the ground; where I was conducted to a
Hunting house kept by one Mr. Latten, and wher the Prince used
to go often a hunting, ther it was they proposed to me to lay
an ambuscade, but I could not agree to their designe : not but
y^t the place was to my minde, but my objection was, that the
men must have been placed there overnight, and if the Prince
of Orange did not come, they could not remoue till the night
following, and in so little a spot of ground they might haue
been discover'd by the Rangers, and if the designe had fail'd,
twenty men would haue been let into the Secret.

I was severall times tould from good hands that one Captain
Fisher who liued in Kingstreet Westminster had made severall
great proposalls of raising men for the King's service in case
any thing could be done, upon which I thought it not improper to see him, hopeing he could not know me in my disguise, and that I might hear his opinion, which seem'd to me
so extrauagant as made me mistrust him. He proposed to me
to Attack the P^ce of Orange between the two Gates as he passed
from Hyde Parke to St James's Parke, that is to say, immediately after the Coach had passed the gate to haue a partie
ready to attack the Coach, and an other Partie to haue shut the
gate, that the Guards might haue been kept out till the affair

had been ended; I owne that had the Prince passed in the
night, it had not been a hard matter to haue done it, but in
the day it was not to be undertaken: after Capt Fisher had
tould me his opinion in this affaire, and that he, if undertaken,
would kill one of the Coachorses thō he should fall down dead
in the doing it, yet notwithstanding that, and severall other
proposalls, I never let him know of any designe I had on foot,
but only asked him to giue me notice when the Prince of Orange
went a hunting, pretending I had a mind to see him hunt;
which he promised, and accordingly sent me word when he
intended to go, and also afterwards, how he had altered his
mind, and that ther was one taken notice of at Kinsington
and suspected to be a Spye, which I beliue was Durance, for
I had him and an other to giue me notice of what they could
learn at that Court: for immediately after my arrival in London, I made it my business to know that Prince's days of
Council, and recreation, and how many Guards he had when
he went a broad, but after we were in readyness I could never
learn he was any where abroad at night or a hunting.

I haveing once engaged in this affair I was resolved to try
every way how to bring it about, but could not find any opertunity of meeting with that Prince unless he went a hunting;
I was at Kinsington itself and Major Holmes with me, and
every wher els about London where that Prince used to go,
both to know the ground and what judgment I could make of
it, in case any occasion should offer, but could find no place
so fit for our purpos as Totnam green ; that, therefore, was the
place we agreed on.

Then Sr William Perkins was to get fiue men well mounted
but not be ther himself, Mr Porter and Mr Charnock the
like number each, and to be ther themselves, giveing me at
the same time their paroles of honour not to name me to any
they should engage in this affaire, but to giue me a list of their

names, that I might not pitch upon the same I being to make them up twenty men; assureing me also not to let our intentions be known to any, only that they were to do a braue action for the King's seruice.

Every thing being thus agreed upon, I gaue mony to Major Holmes and Mr Charnock to buy me twenty horses and furniture which they did in a few days; the men I had ready and most of them under pay with a list of their lodging, who were to be ready when call'd for, they were not so much as to know I had horses for them till they were to mount them, which for that end were taken care of in different stables.

One morning they brought me word that the Prince of Orange was for certain to go a hunting and that his Cooke was parted, Mr Charnock had notice of it also, and sent me word he was ready; upon which I took coach to see if Mr Porter was so too, who had changed his lodging from near the Strand to Berry-Street near St Jaines. I tould him what word I had from Kinsington, and desired to know if he and his men would be ready for the afternoon; he sayd they would, but seem'd to me, to haue a great concern upon him, and tould me, That if the Prince did not go that afternoon, he would go into the Country. I sayd, I believ'd for certain he would go, but that at my return to my lodgings I should know further and should acquaint him accordingly; then they brought me word that the Prince of Orange was getting into his Coach, and that it was belieued he was going to that hunting house where Mr Latten was keeper, which is over against Bramford on the other side the river Theames.

The Gentlemen being thus in a readiness they were to haue parted that afternoon, and not to haue been at most aboue two or three togather, one half was to haue gon to Bramford to such taverns or Inns as should haue been appointed them, the rest to haue staid at Totnam green in the like manner; those who were at Branford could see when the Prince came to the Boate, upon which they were to return as they went, so as the two last were to haue an eye upon the coach, and so those at Totnam green upon the first appearance of those from Branford was to join them.

The road from Branford before one enters upon Totnam green is something narrow with hedges and ditches on each hand, so that a Coach and six horses cannot easily turn at least on a sudden, and at the very entrance of the green there are some little shrubbs and bushes which would put men under some sort of cover, so that those who came from Branford cannot see them till just upon 'em, and that was the place which we were to meet at, and not to haue suffer'd any to haue gone towards Brandford for fear of giveing notice of us; of those therty five men (*for they were brought to y*[t] * *number*) ther were eight to haue taken care of the Prince, and the rest to haue dealt with the Guards: Now every thing being thus order'd to put in execution what we designed, word was brought me, the Prince was come back to Kingsinton in great hast, his horses being in a top sweat; which I no sooner heard, than I suspected a discovery of what we were about. And so it proued, for next day ther was a Proclamation out to apprehend us.

Now I declare that I never saw la Rue or Pendergrast so as to know them.

The Original is eleaven pages.

This Relation written with my own hand consisting of eleaven pages, I declare in my Conscience and as I shall answer to God, to be all true and of my own knowlidg, in wittness whereof I haue signed and seal'd it at Paris, the 4th of August in y[e] year 1697.   GEORGE BARKLEY.

---

* Interlined by the Son of James the Second. EDITOR.

This intended attempt being thus discover'd it raised such
a ferment in the Nation, as put an end to the King's real
designe of Landing, by makeing it impossible for his friends
to assemble, they haveing enough to do to secure themselves
from the strict and universall serch which this discovery occasioned. So the King who was hugely surprized at the news
of it, finding nothing more was to be done, return'd to S^t "
Germains longing to see Sr George Barkeley to know what "
he could Say for himself, being his power for levying war "
was in generall termes only, and therefore however compre- "
hensiue the words might seem to him, he had no reason to
extend them to what the King had so often and so positeuely
refused his consent to ; but his and the other gentlemen's Zeal
carried them beyond those considerations, they first resolued
on the thing and then thought how to put the best colour upon
it, by stretching that expression in the Commission beyond its
natural sence, which gaue the King a dubble vexation, to see
himself thus disapointed for want of a due observance of his
orders, and to loos so many friends which was ever a greater
affliction to him than what regarded himself alone.

It seems one Pendergrast and * La Rue were of the number
of those chozen men, but for want of courage, or hopes of
advantage, gaue information to the government of all that
had passed in order to this attempt, nor is it improbable but
Crosbie had done it before himself; however the Prince of
Orange thought fit not to take notice of it immediately, but
by drawing in more, make nois when it should be made
publick, so he order'd them to continue their meetings as

---

* *Dalrymple* (Vol. 3. p. 75.) says, That Captain Fisher and Pendergrass, a man of family in Ireland, unknown to each other, gave the first information to Lord Portland ; and that King William paid but little attention to it, until a third Informer some days after presented himself. EDITOR.

T O M.
IV.
1696.

formerly, till he thought the conjuncture proper to fix the weavering temper of his Parliament, and stop by the discovery of the * Plot, the mouths of a clamerous † Country partie in the House; which contrivance he ever found the best expedient to ward himself from the displeasure of the people, and turn it upon him who alone could redress the grivances they were then so extreamly oppressed with : so out comes a Proclamation on the sudden with a long account of the designe, and a list of those person's ‡ names who were said to be concerned in it, and a thousand pound reward for who soever should apprehend any one of them ; which temptation Several of those gentlemen found their former friends were not proof against ; and Mr Porter and Goodman fortuneing to be amongst the first that were taken, and not haveing courage to

---

* *Kennet,* (Vol, 3. p. 703. 711.) gives a long account of this Plot, which JAMES so much disclaimed. The language of both Houses on this event was very strong against him : they declared, " And we take this occasion to assure your Majesty of our utmost Assistance to defend your person, and support your Government against the late King JAMES, and all other your Enemies both at home and abroad ; hereby declaring to all the world, That in case your Majesty shall come to any violent death (which God forbid) we will revenge the same upon all your Enemies, and their adherents." EDITOR.

† " And now the Earl of Sunderland and Marlborough, and the Lord Godolphin, who were closely united, not only by ancient familiarity, but by good offices and intermarriages, joined themselves to Mynheer Keppel, newly created Earl of Albemarle. Into their Party, also, came all those who were in opposition to the King or his Ministers, calling themselves the Country Party, and Patriots." (*Cunningham's* History of Great Britain, Vol. 1. p. 165.) EDITOR.

‡ " As the most daring in wickedness are commonly the most cowardly upon the detection of it, *Captain Porter,* who had solicited to be allowed to strike the first blow at the King, now solicited to turn evidence ; and *Charnock,* who had gone much between France and England in Negociations with the Court of St Germains, sent a message to the King, That he would disclose the names of all those who had employed him in England, if his punishment was changed from death into perpetual imprisonment.....The King generously answered, *I wish not to know them.*" (*Dalrymple,* Vol. 3. p. 75.) EDITOR.

look upon death, which then Stare'd them in the face (thō they T O M. had often dispised it at a distance) confessed all they knew ; IV. and the first informers haveing made it their bargaing, not to 1696. be witnesses, those two had not their pardons promised but upon condition they would do that scruice, nor was that granted them till they had drugged on a long time in that ignominious trade, of evidenceing against their late boosom friends, and even those very persons they themselves had drawn into the Plot; for Mr Porter was one of the chief promaters of the design, and a principal adviser of makeing use of Sr George Barkeleys Commission as a warrent for the attempt.

The Government made hast to bring those they had appre- hended to a triall. So Mr Charnock, Mr King, Sr William Perkins, Mr Rookwood, Mr Lowick, Mr Keys and several others suffer'd on this account, who all possitively affirmed (at least such as made speeches) that the King was no ways privy to the design of seizing the P^{ce} of Orange, and Mr Charnock sollemnly declared in a letter to a friend after his own condem- nation, upon the word of a Christian and dying man, That when he was sent to St Germains with proposalls about the King's landing, there was not the least mention made there on any side of an attempt upon the Prince of Orange's person, and that in all probabilitie the reason of it was, because (as he sayd before) when such offers had been formerly made, they were still rejected by his Majesty, and that therefore it was purely on their own heads they venter'd upon it; which Mr Charnock in the sayd letter endeavours to justify the lawfullness of, and that every Loyal Subject was autherized in such a case to rid the Kingdom of so publick an enemie, who in the most trecherous and perfidious manner immaginable, had by false and malicious calumnys debauched his Majestys Subjects

Several gen- tlemen exe- cuted ; who all declare at their death the King was no way privy to the design upon the P. of Orange's person.

M^rCharnock s reason to justify himself.

4 B 2

and even his own Children from him ; and that being himself only the Subject of a forreign State, and under the strictest laws of friendship and consanguinitie, should take upon him to invade a lawfull King his Vncle and father in law, driue him from his Pallace and Kingdom, usurp his Throne, hang, draw and quarter all his loyal Subjects that apear'd for him ; he sayd, against such a publick enemie according to Tertullian, every man had a right of makeing war, *in publicos hostes omnis homo miles*, that his ursurpation was as unjust, and more perfidious than that of Cromwell, who was recognized and dreaded by forreign States as much, or more than he : and yet he thought either of them might be treated as one would do a thief or a Robber, whom it is lawfull in one's own defence to attack, and to kill too, if nothing ells will do ; he bids the Prince of Orange's partisans giue him a reason, why it was lawfull for him in the middle of an established peace, fraudilently and treacherously to set upon the King, thō but a Subject himself, and not lawfull for any of his Majestys Subjects, after such an unjust oppression, to take any occasion of attacking him, especially in the middle of his guards, that Grotius himself, in his book *de jure Belli*, says, It is lawfull for any private Subject of a dispossess'd Prince, to kill the usurper of the supreme power, *Jure potest occidi a quolibet privato ;* that indeed he requirs the legal proprietor's commission, which Mr Charnock sayd, they had in general terms, and in fine, brings many arguments to justify the doing of that, which at the same time he owns the King's exceeding mild temper, and good nature (for which he was so conspicuous aboue all the Princes in the World) would not suffer him to consent too, but Says that his Majestys great tenderness in that point was not soly to be regarded, when his own and the publick good so manifestly requir'd the contrary.

Nor wear these gentlemen the only persons that suffer'd on this account, Sʳ John Frend thō but privy to the general design of riseing, underwent the same fate, and at last *Sʳ John Fenwick, a person of a very antient family of the North was apprehended likewise; but before they could bring him to a tryal, some of the King's friends had prevail'd with Mʳ Good_ man to withdraw himself into France; and two wittnesses being necessary to condemn a man for treason, it perplexed the Prince of Orange how to bring it about, for haveing a personal peeque against him, for some reflecting expressions when he formerly serued in Holland, was resolued, (according to his wonted clemency) to moue heaven and earth but he would haue his life: he caused therefore a bill of attainder to be brought against him in the house of Commons, and thō he was only accused of a general design to rise, and that a great part of that Assembly thought it highly unreasonable to use the utmost extent of the legislatiue power to take away one man's life, which could not be of such consequence to the publick quiet, yet the court partie prevailing, the act was passed, and he suffer'd death accordingly; to the great regret of almost all men, but the usurper, and such as were ready to Sacrifice their con_ sciences, duty and honour, to serue the ambitious and revengefull aims of the Prince of Orange.

The condemnation of this gentleman had an other ill efect upon his Majestys affairs; he had been tamper'd with dureing his imprisonment to make a discovery, and particularly who kept correspondence with Sᵗ Germains, (which whether he did out of hopes to saue his life, or that he thought those gentlemen trecherous to the King, and that it would do him good seruice to reveale them) he went so far as to name My Lord Godolphin, My Lord Churchill, Admiral

Marginal notes:

TOM. IV.

1696. Sʳ John Frend is executed, and Sʳ John Fenwick condemned by act of attainder and executed upon it.

Sʳ John Fenwick's accusation of several Lords, did the King great prejudice.

---

* See Cunningham's History, for Sir John Fenwick's Case. (Vol. 1. p. 165.) EDITOR.

TOM.
IV.

1696.

Russell, and severall others; which instead of appeasing, hightened the Prince of Orange's rage against him, and added the weight of those powerfull men to the heavy hand of their Master; for their reputation was too well established in the government, to be suspected of infidelitie to it, whereas their intrest, and endeavours encreased the animosity with which hé was prosecuted, which till then began to slacken in both Houses: however Sr John in a speech (he published at his * death) per-sisting in the truth of what he had sayd, and that he had it by letters from St Germains it self, it was a demonstration to those who had realy corresponded with that Court, that the secret had not been kept there so well as they expected ; so ever after gaue that for a reason why they would correspond no more, which whether it was any disadvantage to the King in respect of them, is hard to Say, for the Prince of Orange looking never the wors upon †*My Ld Godolphin, & Ad^l Russell,* was an argument he had been no stranger to their practices, but it was a check however upon others, who perhaps meant better, of which number whether My Lord † *Churchil* was to be counted or no, is still a mistery, and the Vail is like to remain upon it.

---

* *Kennet* inserts the Letter which Sir John Fenwicke sent to his wife, on being committed to Newgate, (Vol. 3. p. 725.) with the Speeches of Mr. Methwen and Sir Godfrey Copley on the Bill of Attainder against him, (page 726.) and also the Justification of himself which he delivered to the Sheriffs on the day of his execu-tion. (page 730.) The following is an Extract from the Letter to his wife, " I know nothing can save my life, but my Lord Carlisle's going over to him (King William) backed by the rest of the family of the Howards to beg it. . . . All friends must be made. My Lord Devonshire may perhaps by my Lady; my Lord Godol-phin and my Lord Pembroke by my Lady Montgomery. Mr. Nelson by the Bishop of Canterbury. My Lord Arran might engage his brother Selkirk to use his interest with Keppel. . . . Engage Sir John Lowther, the new Lord, who has more interest than any body. Let my Lord Searsdale engage Jermaine to engage Overkirk for me. Speak to my Lady Arlington."—This Letter was intercepted by the Mayor of Romney, and brought to the Lords Justices. EDITOR.

† Inserted afterwards. EDITOR.

These èxecutions were much more afflicting to the King, than what regarded himself, in particular he lamented the persecution it raised against the Catholicks, their imprisonments and hard usage, and therefore after so many tryals and as many faileeurs to do himself and his Subjects justice, he was more and more convinced that afflictions were necessary for him ; so all those attempts which seem'd to be lost labour in the eye of the world, were great advantages as he managed them in order to that great end which now was become his sole concern : he had indeed some glimering views towards a Restoration, on account of the Prince of Orange's ill health, whom he conceiu'd to be the only obstacle, who bein grown So dropsical, it was manifest he could be of no long continuance ; and the King had resolued with himself, in case he out liued him, to try the good nature of his Subjects, and return into England thō three men had not follow'd him ; it would not enter into his brest that the people of England could offer any indignitys to a heart that loued them so tenderly, but that if it was God's will he should consummate his sufferings, without any mixture of prosperity, and end his days in banishment, in which so great a part of his life had been spent, he resign'd himself most willingly to it : but this ill health of the Prince of Orange which still kept up the prospect of a Restoration, raised a new obstacle which proued as fatal as the other in the end ;   upon the Same Views and considerations, thō she had all along kept up a fair correspondence with the King full of assurances of duty and repentance, however now began to be allured with the hopes of .   . So writ to the King, to know whether he would pleas to permit her to accept it should the Prince of Orange * dye, and it be offer'd * to her — according

T O M.
IV.
1696.

KING JA:
LETTER TO
ABBE DE LA
TRAPPE,
12 May 1696.

The P. of Orange's ill health made people beliue he would not liue long. The King if he had surviued him, design'd to haue gon into Eng^d,thō three men had not follow'd him.

desired leave of the King if the P. of Orange

---

* Inserted afterwards. EDITOR.

to the

accompanyd this request with a seeming sence of * *her* duty, and a readiness to make * *restitution* when opertunitys should Serue; and that should * *she* refuse it, considering the present disposition the Kingdom was in, it would only remoue his Majesty the further from the hopes of recovering his right, by puting the government into wors hands, out of which he would not so easily retriue it : but this suted no ways with the King's temper, he was not for permiting ill that good might come of it, he could suffer indeed injustice not only with patience but pleasure, but could never be brought to countenance or allow it ; besides he knew, that of all * *restitutions* none is harder to make, than that of a * *Crowne;* so his Majesty excused himself from that, and indeed the resolution he was in of hazarding himself in the hands of his Subjects should that case have happen'd, put an end to the proposal.

But these being views at a distance only, his present concern was, to reap a Christian frute from these seeds of affliction, which providence had sent. To which he had gain'd so great a conformity, that he received crosses not only with submission but joy, as apears by a † Prayer he repeated every day and left under his hand in these terms

" I giue Thee O my God most humble thanks for takeing
" my three Kingdoms from me, thou didest awake me by that

---

* Inserted afterwards. EDITOR.

† In the Stuart MSS. which the Archbishop of Canterbury communicated to Mr. Birch the Editor of THE THURLOE PAPERS, and which are inserted at the end of the first Volume of that valuable Collection, are the Morning and Evening Prayers which the Duke of York was thought to have used. The language is excellent, that for the morning thus begins, " O Lord God eternall, whome to know is the greatest wisdome, and to serve the greatest happyness, give unto me, I pray thee, an understanding to discerne, and a heart to imbrace thy Truth." EDITOR.

from the Lethargie of sin, had not thy goodness drawn me " T O M.
from that wretched state, I had been for ever lost. I return " IV.
thee also my most humble thanks for that out of thy infinite " 1696.
bounty thou didst banish me into a forreign Country, wher I "
learn'd my duty and how to practice it. "

But whilest the King was thus turning his whole attention The Crown of Poland offer'd
to the gaining a heavenly Crown, to his great surprise an earthly to the King by some, which
one was offer'd him, not that which was his due and which, his Majesty refuses.
for that reason alone, he desired, but one which gaue the world
a just Idea of his merit, and how well he deserued to wear that,
which had been so unjustly torn from his head : Towards the " King Ja:
end of this summer his Most Ch: Majesty sent Mons' Pompone " Letter to Abbe de
to the King to acquaint him, he had receiued an account " la Traf, ..8th Sep.1696.
from Abbé Poliniac who was then Ambassador in Poland, "
that the people of that Country had some thoughts of him in "
the Election they were about to make of a new King, and "
that some particular Diets had already neamed him; this "
at the first sight, seemed not to be dispised, and many of his "
Majestys friends of the Court of France perswaded him to "
giue into it, but he made no other reply at that time than that "
he should ever retain a gratefull remembrance of the esteem "
and kindness those persons had shewn him; but assoon as he "
saw his Most Ch: Majesty, (he) tould him he could not possebly "
accept it, were it offer'd, much less use any endeavours to "
obtain it, that it would amount to an abdication indeed, of "
what was realy his due, and therefore was resolued to remain "
as he was, thō he had less hopes of being restored than ever, "
rather than do the least act which might prejudice his family "
or be hurtfull to Religion. There could not be a greater instance
that it was the publick good and his obligation to the Prince
his Sòn and family, and not a thirst after rule and dominion,
that made the King never lay aside the endeavours of regaining
his right; which as it will render his memory glorious, so it

will bring an eternal blemish upon the people of England, for haveing rejected their lawfull hereditary Monarch, thō he was so well qualifyd to govern them, that an electiue Kingdom was disposed to make choice of him preferable to all the world besides.

This disinteresedness of the King was more signal at this time, by reason his hopes were in a manner estinguished of being ever " restored; for some weeks before this offer was made him, " the King had intelligence that the Treaty which was then " concluded betwixt France and Savoy, would haue an ill " influence upon his affairs. One would on the contrary haue " thought, according to reason, that nothing could haue been " more beneficial to the King's cause; that by ridding his Most Christ. Majesty of so expensiue a war, he would be more at libertie, and better able, to press his enemies and pursue his views in other places: but the King saw whither that accommodation tended, for as he sayd in the same letter,

" Thō his Most Christian Majesty had the same affection and " consideration for me he ever had, yet he may perhaps think " his condition such, as to oblige him to make a certain step " for the good and peace of his Kingdom, which I am confi- " dént hé will haue a great reluctancy too, upon my account; " and therefore I belieue it will giue him full as much, or more " trouble than it will to me, who haue been so inured to con- " tradictions all my life.

Nor was the King mistaken in his conjecture it not being long after, ere a secret negociation was set on foot, which ended in a general Treaty; it is true that the winter passed in preparations for war more than peace, and the matter remained for some time doubtfull, but the Plenipotentiarys being sent away in March, and Riswick named, (a house belonging to the

Prince of Orange) there was no more doubt but a Peace would be, and that it would be to the exclusion of the King. The world was indeed no less ashtonished than the King, that when his most Christian Majesty seem'd to haue got a perfect supe-riority over his enemies by so many victories, and now a seperate peace with Savoy, he should however grasp so greedely at a general one, as to abandon for the sake of it the cause of a Prince his near relation, his friend and Ally, whose protection as it gaue a lustre to his actions, so the glory of his restoration seem'd to be what was only wanting to compleat his Character, and crown the history of his prosperous reign : the King had lost three Kingdoms rather than be forced into a confederacy against him, his Subjects that follow'd him had merited hugely of the Court of France by their signal service in the war, besides his word was in a manner out against himself, for when his circomstances appear'd more difficult and his enemys pressed hardest upon him, yet still he published to the world a steady resolution of standing by the King of England and supporting him to the last ; yet all these reasons and resolutions (by I know not what fatality to his Majestys cause) vanished of a sudden, which whether it proceeded from secret Court intrigues, or aims at popularity in some persons of greatest credit about him, or that the old and experienced Ministers being dead, the yong ones thirsted after eas and pleasure more than the glory of their Master, or well-being of the State, is still a Mistery ; the only visible reason for such a proceeding, was, that providence had hithertoo led the King to perfection thorough all the rugged paths of contradictions and misfortunes, and seem'd to destine him to end his career in the same track, and that the people of England were not worthy to haue so good a King reign over them ; so God gaue them success in his wrath, a truth which is misterious and unintelligible, to those whose eyes are only open to temporal happiness, but precious and of infinite esteem, to such, who, like our holy King, needed not that example to be convinced of the instabilitie of all humain affairs, and had therefore fixed his views upon a much more Stable and secure felicity.

The King
sends an Agent
to Vienna in
december
1696.

And now that the King saw the storme comeing so fast upon him, he thought it his duty to struggle while there was life and seek shelter on all hands; in December therefore before the place of Treaty was named, he dispatched an Agent privately away to Vienna with the aprobation of the Court of France, first to lay before the Emperour what he had suffer'd, and how unjustly he had been oppressed by this Confederacy, how shocking and misterious it apear'd to the Christian world, that his Imperial Majesty and other Princes of the house of Austria, so famed for their piety and religious zeal, should contribute to the dethroneing a Catholick Prince, and substitute in his place a professed enemie of the Church; and therefore now that a peace was about to be treated of, to shew how conformable his Majesty's restoration would be not only to justice and the intrest of Religion, but to that very peace they so much thirsted after, and was about to treat of; and in case the Emperour was deaf to these arguments, to propose the seting up of a seperate Treaty with his Most Christian Majesty, who promised better terms than could be expected by a general one, if his Imperial Majesty thought fit to harken to them.

The Emperour
deaf to the
King's reasons.

When the King's Agent arriued at Vienna he addressed himself to one Father Edera a Jesuit of his acquaintance, who had great credit there, to whom he gaue a Memorial of the King's case, desireing he might haue a private audiance of the Emperour himself; but that was denyd him under pretence of a letter leately writ to that Court, full of deep ressentment from the Prince of Orange, for their haueing admited a person from St Germains with the privacy of the Court of France to

treat of affairs very prejudicial to his intrest. So he appointed
his Confessor, Father Millingatti to acquaint him, that he had
done nothing but what was both conscientious and allow'd of
by common practice of Christian Princes, that he enter'd into
that league against France for Self preservation, against an
unjust agressor, that he did not attack King James, or go
about to invade his right, but made use of the force of a man
in power to preserue his own state from oppression and ruin ;
that in acknowlidging the Prince of Orange for King, he
follow'd the consent of the whole Nation and the example of
other Princes, who had done the like to Queen Elizabeth and
Cromwel, that he enter'd not into any league with the Prince
of Orange till that Prince was settled in England ; that it was
not the first time Catholick Princes had made such leagues,
and that he never engaged (in his agreement with that Prince)
to settle him in his usurpation, but only to unite against
France : that he always looked upon his invasion as unjust
and impious, and heartely prayd for King James's restoration.

I leaue to such Divines, as pretend to understand reasons of
state, to judg of this misterious casuistry, but it looked like
Charles the 5th makeing publick prayers for the Pope's
delivery, whilst he himself kept him prisoner in the Castle of
St Angelo, however this was all the answer could be obtain'd ;
and as to the second proposal of a seperate Treaty, thō the
restitution of Lorain seem'd to be what the Emperour most
insisted upon, yet there was so much diffidence in both sides,
and the person sent by the King not sufficiently instructed, or
entrusted by the Court of France, that it vanished likewise ;
and the King left to the considerations of a generall Treaty,
the meaning of which was easily understood : however since
he had no other handle left, he was resolued to stretch it as far
as it would reach, and therefore press'd hard to haue his
Minister receiued at least at the general Treaty ; but that being

1697.
The King
presses to haue
his Minister at
the Treaty,
but it is
refused.

So he pub-
lishes a sort of
Manifesto to
shew his hard
treatment.

Vide: *Memoir
summaire con-
tenant les
raisons qui
doiuent obliger
les Princes
confederez
Catholiques a
contribuer au
retablissement
de sa Ma^{te}
Britannique.*

refused him, he published a summery account of the Revolution
by way of representation of his case to the Princes of the
Confederacy, to convince them of the crying injustice he
had suffer'd all along, which he sayd, he had hithertoo delayd
because so long as he perceiued they were still deluded by the
vain hopes the Prince of Orange gaue them, of reduceing
France by force to the terms they wished, they would be deaf
to all his arguments; but that now seeing the vanity of his
promisses, they were forced to haue a recours to a treaty of
peace to seek an end of the publick calamities, he hoped they
would be more inclined to hear his reasons, redress what had
been done amiss, and contribut to his restablishment on the
throne of his Ancestors of which he had been so unjustly dispossessed. And first addressing himself to the Catholick
Princes, he acquaints them what he had suffer'd for Religion
when Duke of York, that nevertheless his accession to the
throne was accompanyed with the joy and acclamations of the
people, that he endeavour'd to make a sutable return to their
kindness and fidelitie, by pardoning his enemies even those
who would haue excluded him from the throne; that he was
in perfect amitie with all the neibouring Princes and States, as
well as in great tranquillity at home, till the jealousies about
Religion (tho he gaue no real cause for them) fomented by the
Prince of Orange, began to make the people uneasy, that
those apprehentions were much encreased by the birth of the
Prince of Wales, as well as the Prince of Orange's impatience
to possess the throne, who seem'd not disposed before to wait
his turn, much less then, when he was remoued so much
farther from it; that upon his descent in England when his
Majestys Subjects abandon'd him and betrayd him, the Confederate Princes seconded the Prince of Orange's usurpation
by sending away his Ministers from their Courts, against the
right of Nations or the respect due to Crowned heads, without

any previous declaration of war, or the least shaddow of a
reason for useing him thus like an enemie.

That this unjust treatment both from his own Subjects and
forreign States, which obliged him to take refuge in France,
was occasioned by false and wicked calumnies which the
Prince of Orange and his emissaries industriously spread; as
that he had broke the Laws of the Land, and put a suppositious Prince upon the Nation, had fail'd in his duty as
Guarantee of the Peace of Nimeghen, and that he had made
a league with France against the house of Austria and
Holland; that as to the first he had acted nothing, but what
the Judges of the Land had determined to be in his power,
who were answerable by law (not the Prince) if they gaue pernicious advice, yet the Prince of Orange or the people never
called any of them to account for it. As to the second, that
it was so black and rediculous a calumnie, that all mankind
stood amazed how it could gain the least credit, that never
Prince had more witnesses of his birth, nor durst the Prince
of Orange (thō he had solemnly promised it in his Declaration)
ever go about to proue so infamous a charge. As to the therd,
he sayd, it was manifest his Majesty had no such obligation,
that first the Holanders made a seperate peace at Nimeghen
without the privity of the English Ambassadors, whose example
the Spaniards follow'd, so that King Charles the Second
order'd his Plenepotentiaries not to sign so much as Mediators:
nevertheless, that if he had been Guarantee, he had done
nothing against it; that he was in a defensiue League with the
Hollanders, who instead of complying with their duty therein,
assisted the Prince of Orange in his unjust invasion, and
deluded the King by their Ambassador's constant asseveration,
That their arming was not design'd against him. And that as to
the pretended League with France, there needed no other proof
how false and groundless it was, than My Lord Sunderland's

owning the contrary, in that very letter he published to *
reconcile himself to the Nation, and cast all the odium he
could upon the King his Master. That on the contrary he
refused the French offers of troops when threatned with an
invasion, rather then giue the least umbrage to his people or
his Neibours, he had indeed denyd to enter into a League
against whom he had no just cause of complaint, wherein he
had this further aim of spareing his people their share of that
expensiue and bloody war, which he saw was about to fall
upon the rest of Europe; he thought therefore the Emperour
and King of Spain should haue required better reasons, and
they better proued, than such vain pretences, to join with an
Heretical Vsurper to dethrone a Catholick Prince, his Vncle,
and father in law, but he did them the justice to belieue, their
first design was only to force him into a league, without entring
into the measures the Prince of Orange should make use of, to
bring it about; and that they were as cautious at least as the
Holanders, who in their Memorial published October, 1688,
declared they lent him their troops upon condition he should
not attempt to dethrone the King of England, nor alter the

---

* *Ralph* (Vol. 2. p. 541.) gives from the Dutchess of Marlborough's Account,
the following testimony of Lord Sunderland's having been the principal person, who
promoted the Reconciliation of KING WILLIAM and the PRINCESS ANNE. " I never
heard of any body (says the Dutchess) that oppos'd this Reconciliation, except
my Lord Portland: But the person who wholly manag'd the Affair, between the
King and Princess, was my Lord Sunderland. He had, upon all occasions relating
to her, shewed himself a man of sense and breeding: and before there was any
thought of the Queen's dying, had design'd to use his utmost endeavours to make
up the breach; in which, however I am persuaded, he could not have succeeded
during the Queen's life. Her death made it easy to him, (for the reasons I have
mentioned) to bring the King to a Reconcilement; and he also persuaded his
Majesty to give the Princess St. James's House. But this, and some other Favours
(a great part of the Queen's Jewels) granted her, at his Lordship's request, were
only to save *Appearances*, and for *Political Views*." EDITOR.

succession, which nevertheless was the first thing he went about; for he imprisoned him and forced him to fly to saue his life, and then caused his escape to be term'd an abdication: his Majesty therefore hoped that the confederate Princes, would haue some regard to their own security, in discountenanceing such wicked attempts on the right of Soveraignity, and that they would for the sake of truth, and justice, (which had been so visibly abused) their own honour, the publick peace, and good of Religion, endeavour his restoration, as the only reperation sutable to so cruel an oppression.

They would perhaps pretend (he sayd) that Religion suffer'd nothing by the change, but that the bare narration of what had happen'd since, sufficiently shew'd the contrary, that the very groundwork of the Revolution was the pretended fear of Popery, and the destruction of that Religion the ultimate end of it. For that had the King been willing to haue given the Prince his Son to be educated a Protestant, the Prince of Orange had been disapointed, and that therefore not only the King, and the Prince his Son, suffer'd in this case for Religion, but all other Catholick Princes, or even such as shall marry Catholicks, are made uncapable of succeeding to the throne of England, by which the very fundamental Laws of the Nation are changed in perfect hatred of Religion; that libertie of conscience since the Revolution had been granted to all Sects but Catholicks, and that thō the Prince of Orange pretended not to persecute any English Catholick purely for Religion (thō they are dayly ruin'd and put to death for their Loyalty which their conscience obliges them too and is part of their Religion) tis because they are under the nose of the forreign Ministers, with whom he thinks it necessary to keep some measures; but that in Scotland which was more remote, Priests had been imprison'd for several years togather, been

T O M.
IV.
1697.

banished or had perished by a cruel oppression; that in Ireland (thō it was always looked upon as a sort of Catholick Country) those of that Religion had by new Laws been prevented sitting in Parliament, and not permited to send their Children to forreign Vniversities for education, which in time would infallebly make Religion fall to nothing in that Country, and that even that outward shew of Lenity, which hithertoo he had in some cases obserued out of respect to Catholick Princes, when once a peace should be made, and he more master of his actions, would soon vanish, especially when press'd to it by the people themselves.

If (sayd he) the Protestant Allies will object that the Prince of Orange is irreconciliable with France, and therefore must be supported, they could not however justify the violateing all Laws, both humain and Divine, oppress the innocent, and autherise all manner of crimes, for such politick views, which even upon the least consideration vanish into smoke: for what reason had the Allies to apprehend the sincerity of France, which thō. in so good a situation of their affairs, after haveing been victorious dureing the whole cours of the war, after a seperate peace with Savoy, and a newtrality in Italye, abunding with all things, while England, Holland and the Empire were exhausted, yet offers honorable terms of peace? what motiue therefore could that come from but a sincere desire of keeping it? That therefore the Confederats had no need of supporting their Vsurper for more security, for that nothing would giue, on the contrary, greater cause of jealousie to France, than their conjunction with a man of so turbulent a spirit, who owed his unjust dignity to wars, divisions, and unhumain oppressions, and must support it by the same means; that they might much more reasonably build their hopes of a lasting peace, by resettling a peacefull Prince on the throne, than by supporting an ambitious Vsurper, who had made

11

a constant practice of sacrificeing honour, Religion, and Conscience to attain his ends.

That as to the pretended expedient of permiting the Prince of Orange to possess the throne for his life, and the Prince of Wales to succeed him, nothing could be more contradictory to reason, and the duty his Majesty ow'd himself, his posterity, and his people; that it were to suffer the fundamental Laws of the Kingdom to be alter'd by a tumultuous assembly of revolted Subjects, to suffer himself to be deposed, and his Son to owe that to their gift, which is his own by right of inheritance, and the uncontested Laws of a successiue Monarchy: and therefore his Majesty was incapable, he sayd, of so low and degenerate an action, he was sencible that a Prince ought to haue a mind superiour to a crown to be worthy of wearing it; and that if he must be depriued of it still, and suffer endways, he was resolued to suffer, at least, like a King, and hoped that the invisible hand which sent him that affliction, would support him in it, and never permit him, either to offend his own conscience, betray the justice of his cause, or debase the dignity of his character by any action unworthy of it.

One might reasonably haue hoped, that so plain a representation of those crying injustices, and the manifest falsety of those reasons, where on they were grounded, should haue moued the Confederate Princes to haue made the King some reperation; but by certain rules of Policy (whose reasons are best understood by those that practice them, and must answer for them) he was totally neglected: the confederates adhered to the Vsurper, they had help'd up into the throne; and his Most Christian Majesty himself, was so bent upon a peace, that he forgot his former resolutions, and own'd him as King of England like the rest. So that now his Majesty had nothing more to do, but by some publick Act to disclame

But no regard is had by the Confederate Princes to the King's repre-sentations.

T O M.
IV.

1697.

The King
by a publick
Act disclames
all proceedings
at the Treaty.
June 8:

their proceeding and enter his protestation in forme against all conventions, or agreements, made to his disadvantage, or without his participation in any kind, which was done in the following termes:

JAMES by the Grace of God King of England &c, to all Princes Potentates &c:

After so long and ruinous a war to Christindom, being convinced that all the contending parties are disposed to peace, and even on the point of concluding it, without our participation, we think it requisite in this conjuncture, to make use of the only means remaining in our power to assert our undoubted right by a Sollemn Protestation against whatever may be done to our prejudice.

It is not our design to enter into a discussion of what is past, since the notority of what has happen'd to us had render'd it unnecessary, nor can we suppose, that any one can doubt of the justice of our cause; the condition we are reduced too since the Prince of Orange got possession of our Kingdoms is not our only trouble, for such is our unalterable loue to our people, that we cannot without sorrow see their blood and treasure lavished in so unjustifyable a cause, nor can we but further reflect, that if any peace be made in our wrong, that they must become a pray to forreigners, for to such they must be subject while this usurpation lasts; we are likewise sencibly concern'd not to haue been in a condition of pursuing our inclinations and intrest in preserveing the peace of Christendom, and preventing the many unavoidable mischeifs of war; and whereas it was maliciously pretended by our enemies, that we had made a secret League with France, we declare on the word of a King we never made any League with that Crown, much less against the Princes Confederates in this war.

We desire those Princes will weigh how dangerous, the

president they make, may proue to themselves, and since ours is the common cause of all Sovereigns, we call for their assist- ance in the recovery of our Kingdoms: let them reflect how glorious such a resolution would be, and how sutable to the true intrest of those who are born to govern, let them judg whether the former Treatys (which we offer to renew with them) will not proue more lasting; and whether the peace now treated of, will not be better secured by our guarante̍, than if they accept of the like offers from a Prince, who has neither title nor succession, for should he haue Children hereafter, they stand excluded from the immediate claime to those Crowns even by the pretend'd present settlement made since his Vsurpation; but since we perceiue the Confederate Potentates insist to have that Vsurpation made as a ground of a future peace, we find ourselves obliged not to let our silence be interpreted as a tacit acquiescence, to what may be concluded in prejudice of us or our Lawfull heirs.

We therefore sollemny protest (and in the strongest manner we are able) against all what-soever may be treated of, regulated, or stipulated with the Vsurper of our Kingdoms, as being null by default of a Lawfull authority.

We protest in particular against all Treatys of Allyance, confederation and commerce, made with England since the Vsurpation, as being null by the same want of authority, and consequently uncapable of binding us, our lawful heires, Successors, or Subjects.

We further protest in general, against all Acts whatsoever that pretend to confirme, autherise, or approue directly or indirectly the Vsurpation of the Prince of Orange, against all the proceedings of his pretended Parliaments and whatever tends to the subvertion of the fundamentall Laws of our Kingdom, particularly those relateing to the Succession to our Crowns.

.T O M.
IV.

1697.
We protest likewise and declare, that no ommission or defect in forms, are, or can be of prejudice to us, our lawfull heirs, Crowns, or Subjects, reserueing and asserting by these presents under our great Seal all our rights, and clams which remain, and shall remain in their full force, and no extremity shall oblige us to renounce or compromise.

To conclude, we protest that after this we shall not think ourselves answerable before God, nor men, for the ill consequences, the unjustices already done, or hereafter may be done to us, will draw on our Kingdoms and all Chritendom. GIVEN &c: the 8ᵗʰ june 1697.

It was thought by some, that the King was too precipitate in rejecting a proposal of the Pᶜᵉ of Wales succeeding the Pᶜᵉ of Orange. Thō no one could blame the King's conduct in this total disclameing all treatys and accommodations, when he found the Confederate Princes no ways disposed to do him justice, yet there was one.* Article privately stipulated which had not the King too hastely rejected, might haue rended his Posterity easy and his people happy in a short time after; his Most Christ: Majesty had underhand prevailed with the Prince of Orange to consent, that the Prince of Wales should succeed to the throne of England after his death. That mercenary Prince it seems, had no great regard to the pretended ends of his comeing, nor to the Acts of Parliament which excluded the Prince of Wales and all of that perswasion from the Succession:

---

* " The Peace was accompanied with two pieces of intended generosity by the King (William) to the exiled Family. By the one, he obliged himself to pay fifty thousand pounds a year to King JAMES's Queen, the jointure to which she would have been entitled had her husband died King of England. By the other, he consented that the young Son of King JAMES should be educated a Protestant in England, and succeed to the Crown at the end of the present Reign. The evidence of this last fact, though long known to some, came only lately to the knowledge of all, from JAMES's OWN MEMOIRS in the Scots College at Paris: and the merit or demerit of no action of WILLIAM's Life has been more the subject of difference, in private opinion at least, than this one." (*Dalrymple's Memoirs*, Vol. 3. p. 87.) EDITOR.

he had under the notion of preserving the Church of England, usurped the Kingdom, so now (that the work was done) those pangs of conscience wer vanished, he was very easy on that head, and ready to leave that Church to providence for the future, not careing under whose government it fell afterwards, so he was but secure of the throne for his life; for this reason he shew'd no great aversness to the Prince of Wales's haveing the preference to those, who were named by the pretended act of Settlement; how he would have brought this matter about in a Parliament does not appear, because it never came to a tryal; but when this seeming advantage to his Famely was proposed to the King, he could not support the thoughts (he Sayd) of makeing his own Child a complice to his unjust dethronement, so immediately tould his Most Christ: Majesty (who had first made the overture to him) that thō he could suffer with Christian patience the Prince of Orange's usurpation upon him, he could never consent that his own Son should do it too : this was too nice a point to be pressed in case of the least reluctancy, so nothing more was sayd upon it ; but had the King taken leasure to weigh the matter more maturely, he might haue found means perhaps of reconcileing that apparent incongruity, and for the sake of his Son and posterity, haue overlooked the jnjustice done to himself, but the King was better at suffring injuries than a conneiveing at them, and the least shaddow of jnjustice·was enough to damp in his acceptation, the best layd project in the world.

On would have thought the King had now gon through all the Stages of contradiction, yet one remain'd which nothing but an absolute Dominion over himself, could haue made him bear with so good a grace: this Peace fortuned to be concluded about that time of the year his Most Ch: Majesty was used to go to Fontainebleau, and whither he was always accustomed to invite the King and Queen for ten or fifteen days,· which

The news of the Peace being concluded, came when the King was at Fontainebleau.

inuitation his Majesty receiveing as formerly, arrived there the very day the news was brought of the Peace being signed. The King haveing long foreseen the stroke was the less surprized with it, and so far from bursting out into expostulations and complaints, that forgeting himself he seem'd only to compassionate his Most Ch: Majesty, as if he had been the great and only sufferer in the point: I am sure says he, in a letter on " that occasion, his Most Ch: Majesty was more mortifyd in " telling it me, than I in hearing it, he sayd indeed he would " do all he could to sweeten the bitter draught, but if the " King of Kings did not voutsafe me a due resignation to his " will, I should not be so easy in the matter as I am. But besides this, his being there put an obligation upon him, not only of comporting himself with his usual contentedness, but of joining with that Court in their publick rejoiceings on account of the Peace itself; it was hard to gild over such a pill, but nothing of that kind was difficult to a Prince so inured to affliction; peace and publick good was what he ever wished and sought, and he had so great a reluctancy to the effusion of humain blood, that his affairs had suffer'd exceedingly dureing the whole cours of his misfortunes, because his mercifull temper would not permit him to burn and destroy, nor expose people's lives when the hopes of doing good by it was weak and ill grounded ; he rejoiced therefore in his heart that a stop was put to those disorders which are the necessary concomitants of a war, and was so sincere and disinteressed as to make his Most Christ: Majestys case his own ; to consider him as Father of his own people whose tranquility and happiness he was to seek preferrable to any other considerations in the world, and that since he believed such a peace most conduceing to it, was far from blameing him that he thought fit to conclude it ; in his own private judgment he was of an other opinion, he knew his restoration would haue been a surer foundation both for the

Kingdome of France, and all Europe to build the hopes of future quiet upon ; but he knew likewise how to submit his judgment to that of others, where he was much more master than he was in this case ; the impression therefore which the sence of his own misfortunes made upon him, alter'd not in the least his usual serenity and cheerfull comportment, he knew not only how to suffer, but how to conform himself to those that knew it not : in so much, that as the most shineing vertues are not exempt from censure, so the King's patience and seem- ing easiness was term'd an insencibility and he in some measure dispised, for what he merited the highest praises ; but he was no less apprized of that, than of the rest, and upon occasion speakeing of it, to a person of great piety, sayd, He was glad that haveing lost every thing els, he had such frequent occasions given him, of makeing a sacrifice of his reputation too.

But his enemies could not so easily lay aside their malice, as he the remembrance of it, for immediately after the peace the Prince of Orange sending his great favorit Bentinck in quality of Ambassador into * France, made use of that occasion

---

* *Ralph,* (from Kennet, Boyer's Life of King William, &c.) gives in a Note some account of what passed during the stay of the Ambassador, who arrived there with his Secretary Matthew Prior, May 21 : " On the 27th, there being a Review of the Troops of the Household in the Plain of Archers, where the King and the Dauphin, the young Princes of France, and divers persons of quality were present, his Excellency went thither also ; but would, perhaps, have forborn coming, if he had known that King JAMES and the titular Prince of Wales had likewise been there. The Prince of Wales, by his Father's directions, endeavoured to join conversation with the Lord Woodstock, but the Lord Portland, his Father, knowing the young Prince's design, order'd his son to avoid him ; as he did him- self all those that belong'd to the Court of St. Germains ; tho' it was reported, King JAMES had caused it to be insinuated to his Excellency, that he never pre-

T O M.
IV.

1698.

King Jam.
Letter to
Abbe de la
Trappe.
March 15 1698.

to press further hardships against the King. It seems at the
" first conference betwixt that Minister and Mareschal de
" Boufflers * before the treaty, he insisted upon the King's
" remoueal out of France, but his Most Christ: Majesty cut
" him short in that, and sayd, If the Prince of Orange stood
" upon that article, he would banish all thoughts of treating
" with him ; so nothing was sayd of that matter at Riswick :
but the P: of Orange finding his negociations so sucessfull there,
dispared of nothing, so order'd Bentinck to renew his sollicitations on that head ; the guilty consciences of his master and
those of his partie could not bear so near a sight of what
obraided them continually with their injustice and infidelitie,
and hover'd over their heads like a cloud that still threaten'd a
storm ; but in that his Most Christ: Majesty was immoveable,
he thought his honour too much engaged to let the Vsurper
trample upon him, he had stoop'd too low already in most
men's eyes, and the world was ashtonished to see he still stood
so much in awe of him, his not demanding the Queen's jointure
could not be presumed to proceed from any other motive, for
since the People of England had no more consideration for
their King, than to look upon him as dead to them, it was a
necessary consequence that the Queen † had a right at least
to her jointure, which by the Laws of England she had the

---

tended to make his Lordship answerable for the ill usage he received from him he
represented. At this Review King JAMES himself did all he could to engage the
Lord Cavendish and the other English Noblemen to accost him, but all imitated
the Earl of Portland." (Vol. 2. p. 797.) See also *Dalrymple*, (Vol. 3. p. 87.)
EDITOR.

* " As it has been proved, that the *Field Conferences* between Lord Portland
and M. de Boufflers gave the finishing stroke to The Peace, so it has been a
thousand times asserted, That these Conferences extinguished the last remains of
good understanding among the Confederates." *Ralph*, (Vol. 2. p. 793.) EDITOR.

† See *Ralph's* History of England. (Vol. 2. p. 776.) EDITOR.

priviledg of enjoying even dureing the King's life, there was
no reply to be made to this: so accordingly in a private article
it was agreed too, and so far confirm'd by the following Parliament, that mony was appropriated underhand for that use; but
when it came to be receiu'd, the Prince of Orange raising new
difficulties or demands and particularly this of the King's
removeall from St Germains, which Bentinck pretended the
Mareshall de Boufflers had underhand agreed too, thō he
positively denyd it, however his Most Christ: Majesty was so
little disposed to argue (the) matter with him, that he rather
chose to leave that mony in his hands as a bribe, than hazard
the exasperateing him a new by pressing too hard for a due
performance of what he had no mind to comply with; so that
the King and Queen had the mortification of liveing entirely
upon the benevolence of an other Prince and in the same subjection in all things, as if they had made the religious vows of
povertie and obedience.

The Bill of Banishment which follow'd immediately upon
the peace was a fresh subject of trouble and additional burthen
to the King, the Parliament in England passed an act to make
it high treason, not only for any to correspond with the King,
but obliged all those who had been in his service since the
Revolution, or even in France it self, except with a pass from
the government, to quit the Dominions in a day prefixed, or
be guilty of high treason *ex post facto*, without a possibility of
avoiding it, which was such a piece of cruelty and injustice as
has not been equal'd in any government; this his Majesty "
sayd afflicted him more than all the rest, he was sencible what "
he had suffer'd himself was nothing comparatively to what "
his past disorders might justly deserue, but to see his Loyal "
Subjects so used for their fidelity to him, was what made him "
stand in need of a more than ordinary grace to support. He "
had the like vexatious news from Ireland too, the Prince of "

The Bill of
Banishment
from England
and Ireland
was a new
trouble and
expence to the
King.

King Jam.
Letter to
Abbe de la
Trappe.
March 15:
1698.

Letter,
19 June 1698.

4 E 2

T O M.
IV.

1698.

" Orange notwithstanding all his fair pretences to the Confede-
" rate Princes, even during the Congress at Riswick passed a
" new Law in that Kingdom, for the rooting out of Popery,
" which amongst other articles order'd the Banishment of all
" Regular Priests, which Mons ͬ Ruvigny, who commanded
" there, fail'd not to put in execution; so that they came
" flocking over into France, and aboue four hundred arriued
" there in some months after : the relief of these distressed
persons, togather with such numbers of other Catholicks as
these bills of Banishment forced out of the Kingdoms, brought
" a new burthen as was sayd upon the King, who had the
" mortification even after haveing distributed amongst them
" what was necessary for his own support, to see great numbers
" ready to perish for want, without his being able to relieue
them.

LETTER,
29 Decem:
1698.

The P. of
Orange is ill
treated by the
Parliament.

But as it fortuned this peace was accompanyed with some
disapointments, even to those, who thought to reap nothing
by it, but glory, pleasure, and content; and had the pious
disposition the King was in, permited him to take satisfaction
in reveng, the Prince of Orange's treatment in England furnished him with a very fit occasion : it is true that Prince
had gain'd (if it may be so call'd) a great victory over his
Most Chrit: Majesty, in bringing him to own him as King
of England (whom he had formerly treated with so much
contempt) and even to make a league of friendship with
him, but when he came to moote points with his Parliament,
they tore those laurells from his brow, and placed them
on their own, they made him account like a Steward
for the mony they put into his hands, and yet gaue him
no settled revenue but from year to year, and forced him
not only to disband his Army, but to send back his own
Dutch troops, thõ he had truckled so far as to write a
letter in nature of a petition to the House of Commons,

to beg his Dutch * Guards at least, might be spared him: T O M.
but they were deaf to his sollicitations, and dispised his seruile   IV.
sute, as much as they laugh'd at the underhand threats of his   1698.
creatures ; but puting him in mind of his origin, or the hands
that made him, gaue him to understand, they call'd him to
be their servant not to domineer over them ; and that in case
they discover'd in his way of governing, the least bad aspect
towards their liberties, and properties, they knew how to make
a sacrifice of their own work manship, to a fresh establishment,
if their venerable rights seem'd to require it : This was a mighty
humiliation to a Prince whose aims and conduct smelt so rank
of conquest, that pamflets which seem'd to support that notion
had not only been common, but allow'd of by authority;
indeed the cours reception which Dr Burnet's Treaty of that
Subject met with, which by a vote of the House was burnt by
the hungman, put a check to such attempts, and tought the

---

* " But when the time approached when his Guards were to take their leave
of him, all the tenderness of mind of a Fellow-Soldier returned, and he made
another attempt to work on the feelings of the Nation ; deeming it impossible, that '
persons whose Religion and Liberties he had saved, could be so inattentive to his
honour in the eyes of Europe, and to those Guards who had so often defended his
life in battle, as to expel them from England with marks of suspicion and disgrace;
and therefore he wrote the following message with his own hand, and sent it by
Lord Ranelagh, paymaster of the forces, to the Commons : ' His Majesty is pleased
to let the House know, that the necessary preparations are made for transporting
the Guards who came with him into England ; and that he intends to send them
away immediately, unless, out of consideration to him, the House be disposed to
find a way for continuing them longer in his service, which his Majesty would take
very kindly.'—But the Commons stood firm to their purpose, and the foreign
troops were shipped off.

' " Upon this occasion, once, and but once in his life, WILLIAM lost his temper
in government. A well-vouched tradition relates, that when the account of the
refusal of the Commons, to pay respect to his last message, was brought to him, he
walked some time silent through the room, with his eyes fixed on the ground,
then stopped, threw them around with wildness, and said, *If I had a Son, by G—
these Guards should not quit me.*" (*Dalrymple*, Vol. 3. p. 129.) EDITOR.

T O M.
IV.

1698.
The King
turns himself
wholy to
Devotion.

Vsurper that as he owed his creation, so he must his support and subsistance to their almighty power.

But this was not the comforth the King thersted after in his afflictions, nor did he seek reveng against any, but himself, being never satisfyd with the peñance he practiced, nor the mortifications Providence dayly sent him; but according to the Royal Prophet haveing his sinns continually before his eyes, thought of nothing but how to appeas God's justice for them, and to giue a greater scope (if possible) to his pious inclinations, in the pursute of whatever he thought would conduce to his future happiness which he had ever look'd upon as the main concerne, but now consider'd as the sole business of his life: so that to giue an account of the remaining part of it (which was not very long) cannot be better perform'd than by a true and faithfull character of his Vertues, and some instances of his zeal and fervour, whereby he endeavour'd to turn all occurrances to his spiritual advancement, and to gain a Crown secure from usurpation.

This indeed had been (I may say) his sole imployment since his return from Ireland, for thō the correspondence he kept up, and attempts he made shew'd he did not neglect the business of his restoration, yet they proueing so many dis-apointments, and additional mortifications, as they threw him still back more and more in reference to this world, they advanced him in that happy carreet which led him to the felicity of the next; and finding so much benefit in order to this by his first journey to LA TRAPPE, he return'd thither once every year till that before he dy'd, the efect those visits had upon him cannot be better express'd than by his own

KING JAM:
SPIRITUAL
TREATISE,
WRIT IN HIS
OWN HAND.
pag: 67.

" relation: At first it was partely curiosity and a desire to " see whether the discourses I had heard and the relations I " had read whilest I was in England of that holy place, came " up to my expectation, and whether the Abbot who began

that reforme deserued all the commendations that were given
him. An old friend of mine the Mareshall de Belfond carryd
me thither, for which as long as he lived I gaue him many
thanks, and by degrees found myself (as I thought) improued;
for till I had been there some times, and had made a kind of
retreat for three or four days at a time (which I haue continued to do at least once a year since my comeing from
Ireland) I found not that chang which was necessary in
my self, it gaue me a true sence of the vanitie of all worldly
greatness, and that nothing was to be covited but the loue of
God, and to endeavour to liue up to his Law, and to mortify
ones self by all lawfull means, and to be sencible (at least
such a miserable creature as I that have liued so many
years almost in a continual cours of sin, till God out of his
infinite mercy call'd me by his chastisement to him) how
necessary it is to continue visiteing such a holy place to gain
strength, who haue so much need of it.

Thus did the King catch at all opertunities, (which Prouidence
had furnished him with, by bringing him into a Catholick
Country) to acquire a greater degree of perfection; he sought
the conversation of men eminent for their learning and piety,
and besides his yearly retreats at LA TRAPPE, went frequently
to Paris at the great solemnities of the Church, and there
sought out those Parishes and Convents where the Christian
duties were perform'd with greatest regularitie and devotion,
and as he drew hony from every flower himself, so he left a
sweet odor behind him, to the edification even of those who
had spent their liues in a perpetual study of spiritualitie; they
were ashtonished to find a Prince born to command, bred in
the nois of wars, and the distractions of a Court, should haue
higher notions of submission and resignation than they had
been acquainted with. One day being in conversation with
the Superiour of a Religious Convent of Nunns, soon after

the business of La Hogue, she took occasion to express her griefe, that it had not pleased God to hear the prayers so many persons had made for his success in that expedition ; to which the King makeing no reply, she fancyed he had not heard her, so began to repeat what she had sayd, upon which he answer'd, Madame, I heard very well what you sayd, and the reason why I made no reply, was because I was unwilling to contradict you, and be obliged to let you see I am not of your opinion, who seem to think that what you ask'd, was better than what it pleased God to doe ; whereas I think what he orders is best, and that indeed nothing is well done but what is done by him. In all the struggles therefore which he made to regain his right, his aim was principally the publick good which lay nearest his heart, and which he was obliged as much not to abandon, as to bear with patience the ill success of his endeavours for it, which made him lament the suffrings of his subjects when he rejoiced at his own ; and since he could not succour them, he made all the amends he could by relieveing the necessities of those that were with him, which considering their numbers and the little he had to doe it out of, nothing but his great art of management (which never stood him more in stead) and his generous compassion, could have extended so far ; he chose rather to want what on many occasions was necessary for himself, than not relieve those of others, who had the least clame to his benevolence.

Nor was his charity confined to his friends, his greatest enemies went sharers with them, as to that, thō in an other kind ; for looking upon them as the instruments of God's justice to exercise his patience, and make him do penance for his sins, he was so far from saying on occasions, any harsh or bitter things of those who had used him with the most indignity, that he would never suffer it in others, nor could any one make their court wors, than by reflecting, (thō on the blackest of his enemies) nor haue done it better than by finding some excuse to palliate their treachery ; nay like David, who would not suffer Semei to be reproued when he curs'd him, he did not only permit, but delighted to hear those pamflets read, which blam'd his government and censured his conduct : he consider'd all the occurrances of his life only as they led to the santification of his soul, and therefore Bless'd God for his misfortunes, which brought him into the occasion of knowing the truth in his youth and of following its prescriptions in his old age ; had it not been for his twelve years ·banishment occasion'd by the civil wars, he might haue liued, he sayd, all his life in the same ignorance and prejudice against it, with which he had been educated, but he soon perceiued he had wrong notions given him of the Catholick Religion, and that the professors of it were not guilty of such things as they were falsely accused of ; he was so sencibly touched with this happyness, that as he never ceased giveing thanks to Almighty God for ·what nature would have repinet at, so his desire ·that others might reap the like benefit from his observations, made him write a short Treatice for the instruction of new Converts, wherein his Zeal and humility went so far, as not ·only to invite people to immitate him, where he hoped he had done well, but to warn them to shun, what he own'd he had done amis in, not spareing his own reputation to contribite to the edification of others, and to induce them to liue up to the maxims of " Christianity, which to my shame, says he, I did not doe " so soon as I was convinced of the truth of the Religion I now " profess ; being desirous not to be an example, but a warning " to others as to that. "

The humiliations which Prouidence sent him, contented not the earnest desire he had of doing penance for his sins, so he added many corporal mortifications to his long and assiduous prayers, as fasting, discipline, and wearing at certain times·

Side notes:

T O M.
IV.
1699.

Vide his Treatises on Devotion, in his own hand, pag: 1.

Ibid. pag. 3.

Ibid: pag. 4.

The King's great mortification.

an Iron Chain with little sharp points which pierced his skin ;
and had not the discretion of his Confessor mitigated his zeal
in this particular, he had certainly carryd it to excess, for the
horrour he had of his past disorders made him think he could
never do enough to make a reparation for them : one day the
King being asked, why he abstained Saturdays betwixt
Christmas and Candelmas, which the custome of Paris allows
people to eat flesh upon, and being rather blamed by the
Queen for his singularity in that point, he sayd little to it, till
the Queen calling Mr Innes (the Almoner who then waited)
asked him, If he abstained? who replyd, No truly, that he made
use of that permission without scruple ; upon which the King
whispered the Queen in the ear, Had I liued in my youth as
Mr Innes has done, I would now doè as he does. But his
humility would not suffer him to rank himself amongst those,
who might seem exempt from distinguishing mortifications,
which made him so oft cry out as he does in one of his writen

Ibid. pag. 61.

" prayers, I detest and abhor myself when I reflect how oft I
" haue offended so good and mercifull a God, and for haveing
" liued so many years in almost a perpetual habit of Sin, not
" only in the days of my youth when I was carryd away with
" the heat of it, and ill example, but even after, when I was
" come to the years of discretion, and that thou O Lord had'st
" been pleas'd to call me out of the pit of heresy, to open my
" eyes to know and embrace thy true Religion, who had'st
" cover'd my head so often in the day of battle, deliver'd me
" so many times from the dangers of the Seas, the nois of its
" waues, and the madness of the people.

But thõ he made no difficulty of publishing thus his past
disorders, he did all he could to conceal the pennance he did
for them, and therefore haveing once accedentally left his
discipline where the Queen fortuned to see it, her Majesty
never perceiu'd him (she sayd) in greater confusion in her life ;

and therefore he took care, that his comportment in the eye of the world should apear as much as possible the same it had formerly been, he entertain'd his own subjects, or those of the Court of France, with the same affabilitie and chearfullness as usual, went a hunting, as formerly, he shun'd not the diver-tions of the French Court when invited to balls or the like, that he might not appear singular or affected, but was far from seeking them, or any other he could fairly avoid ; for though they pass for necessary amusements, yet he had other senti-ments of them, and was for takeing away, if possible, by publick authority all such dangerous divertions, as gameing, Operas, plays, and the like, nor is it to be conceiu'd (without reading what he has writ on those Subjects) how judiciously he declams against them : being therefore thus forearm'd and prepossed, those pleasures, which nurrish so much the spirit of vanity, and stifle in a manner all Christian sentiments in others, raised a new fervour in him, he turn'd into a sort of spiritual nurrishment what was so poisenous of itself, and like a rock was not only immoued but washed the cleaner with those waues, which tosses and disorders so grievously the generalitie of mankind. But when he was left to his own disposal, he sought what suted best with the penitential life Prouidence had led him into, and was so scrupulous of misaplying his time as he writ down certain rules for direction and distribution of it no less judicious and prudent, than they were pious and edify-ing : But it will not be necessary to take notice here, of all his divout Treatises and Letters which remain under his hand, they are sufficient to make a volume of themselves, I shall only giue some few instances, necessary for an historical account, how his thoughts were generally imployd on most occasions.

The year after the peace, his Most Christ: Majesty partely for the entertainment and instruction of his grand Children, and partly to convince the world it was more out of a Christian

T O M.
IV.
1699.

The King was a great enemie to Balls, Operas, Comedie &c.

Ibid: 135.
115.
135.

The King's reflections on the Camp at Compiegne.

T O M.
IV.

1700.

motiue, than want of mony that he appear'd so easy in concluding it, form'd a Camp at Compiegne, where never was
seen greater lux in eating, nor more gaudiness in cloaths and
equipages. The King was invited thither, who according to
custome, when he was come back, turns all to spirituality :

Ibid. p: 55.

" I come, says he, from the Campe at Compiegne, never was
" any thing of that kind better worth seeing, never was an
" Army of about 50 or 60 thousand men so well chozen, so well
" clad and so well mounted, what care and pains haue not the
" Officers taken, and monys haue they not spent to distinguish
" themselves, their Regiments or even each private troop or
" company, to gain the favour of their Prince ; it is com-
" mendable in them and no more than their duty, but at the
" same time I cannot hinder myself from makeing this
" malencolly reflection, how very few of that formidable
" Army think of their duty to the King of Kings, that does
" so much honour to their profession as to call himself the
" Lord of Hosts. And so goes on, lamenting the little
" conformity that appear'd in the liues and conversation of
" the generality of them with the maxims of the Religion
" they profess'd, what pains they took for trifles and how
unthinkingly negligent they were of what was only substantial
and lasting.

The King
never fail'd to
pray for his
greatest
enemies.

This zealous concern he had, to make men sencible of their
obligation to God and to liue conformable to reason and
Religion, extended itself even to Persons of the highest rank;
his gratitude and personal affection for his Most Christian
Majesty who he saw had a sence of his duty, forced him (as far
as decency would permit) to represent to him what he thought he

Ibid. 125.

did amis in ; he took a greater libertie with the Duke of Orleans
his Brother, and press'd him with vehemence on certain faileurs
which he earnestly wished to reforme him from ; seconding those
pious sollicitations with his dayly prayers, which his enemies also

(whom he could not exhort) had at least their share in, *of w^h*   T O M.
number were * his Subjects in the first place, the Emperour, the   IV.
King of Spain, My Lord Sunderland by name, and even the   1700.
Prince of Orange himself he beseeches Almighty God to "   *Ibid: pag. 128.*
have mercy on, to touch his heart, and bring him to a speedy "
repentance, that becomeing a true convert he may attain "
everlasting life: thus the memory of past injuries was so far "
from inspireing resentment, that his eyes were only turn'd to
the spiritual advantage he reap'd from them, which made him
so often bless God for his seeming infortunes (as he calls them)
of haveing been banished in his youth and lost his three "   *Ibid: 145.*
Kingdoms afterwards, without which he should never (he "
sayd) have known the true Religion nor liued to the prescripts "
of it; nay his fervour to satisfy God's justice for his past
disorders would not let him be content with the suffring he
underwent in this world, he was desirous to carry it into the   *Ibid. 162.*
next, and asked his Confessòr, Whether, since his age and
character did not permit him to do such penance for his sinns,
as was agreeable to the horrour and detestation he had of them,
if he ought not to be content to suffer the pains of Purgatorie
the longer, and for that end not beg the prayers of the Church
for his speedyer delivery from thence? but his Confessor and
the Abbot of LA TRAPPE (whom he consulted likewise in that
point) thō they were ashtonished and edifyd with his zeal,
tould him, That one could not desire to see God too soon, and
that it was more perfect to wish to enjoy him; than to suffer
for him.

These thoughts and meditations had so familiarized him
with those of Death, that all its terrours were not able to hinder
him from desireing it, not out of fear of suffring in this world,

---

* ,Inserted by the Son of James the Second, instead of the word *as.* EDITOR.

for that he sought, but for fear of falling back ; he knew the
weakness of men, and suspected none so much as himself.
" This made him often say He desired to dy, thō (as he ex-
" press'd it) was content'd to liue ; the words of St Paul on
that Subject, and many expressions of the Fathers to the same
effect, confirm'd him in those aprehentions of the continual
danger even the holyest men are exposed too, he often call'd
to mind that Saul and Salomon, thō so highly favour'd by
God were nevertheless terrible examples of it, that David fell
into grievious sinns, and St Petre denyd Christ ; he counted it
therefore a high presumption for a slender reed not to desire
to be shelter'd from such terrible gusts, as had overturn'd
those lofty cedars ; his gratitude also to Almighty God (who,
when he liued in defyance, as it were of his holy law, yet led
him by the hand into the way of Salvation) made him wish to
be out of the condition of offending him, and since that could
not be hoped for while he liued in this world, he wished for
that reason to be out of it : he would not allow that the terrible-
ness of God's judgments ought to hinder that disire since it
must come at last, and the sooner it comes the sooner an end
is put to our offending him ; he had some contest with his
friends about this principle, which made him write several
little Treatises to support it, but no one was more alarmed with
it than the Queen, who not being able to bear the thoughts of
that separation, was hugely afflicted at those sentiments and
dreaded the efficacy of his prayers when he turn'd them that
way ; representing to him, how necessary he was to the publick
and most especially to his Children ; but he would never be
perswaded his life was of consequence to others, he sayd It
was a high presumption for any man to think himself necessary

The Queen is
exceedingly
troubled at
the King's
desire to die.

in this world, as if God could not do his work without him ;
and when the Queen once arguing this point sayd with
tears in her eyes, Is it possible S^r, you should haue so little

consideration for me and your Children? what would become of
us if you were gon? Madame, he replyd, God will take care of
you and my Children, for what am I but a poor weak man,
uncapable of doing any thing without him, whereas he has no
need of me to execute his designs; and when one who was
present saw how afflicted the Queen was at this discours, beg'd
of him not to hould it any more before her, he answer'd, I do
it on purpose to prepare her for it, for according to all appearance and the cours of nature I shall dy first, and a stroke
which is forseen makes a slighter impression: he remain'd
therefore fixed and unalterable in this point, wherein he found
that advantage himself (which he had often used as an argument
to others) that it is a great point gain'd, if by desireing to dy,
one can look death in the face with an undisturbed countenance, and seem to be delighted with that, which according
to the cours of nature carrys the greatest terrours with it in
the world.

THUS did this pious Prince Sanctifie his suffrings and render
them fruitefull seeds of ablessed Immortallity, which now began
to draw near to him, for on the 4th of March 1701 he * fainted

1701.
The King is
seized with a
fainting fit
but soon
recovers,
4th March
1701 S.N.

. * " And now I cannot omit telling you two remarkable passages: The one is,
that when the King first fainted in the Chapel, when he first fell ill, it was on
Good-Friday, on singing the Anthem, the two first verses of the last Chapter of
the Lamentations, *Remember, O Lord, what is come upon us: consider and behold
our reproach. Our inheritance is turned to Strangers, our houses to Aliens.*
Which was so touching, and made such an impression on his Majesty, that he
never perfectly recover'd it, although he went to the waters of Bourbon. The
óther is, The King of France, upon his Majesty's sickness, called his great Council,
which consisted of 23 persons: All but seven were against proclaiming the Prince
so soon. The Dauphin being the last that was to speak, rose up in some heat,
and said, *It would be a great piece of cowardice, and unworthy the Crown of France,
to abandon a Prince of their own blood, especially one that was so dear to them as
the Son of King James: That for his part, he was resolved, not only to hazard his life,*

T O M.
IV.

1701.
it returns upon
him that day
sevenight.

away in the Chappel, but after some little time comeing to himself seem'd perfectly well again in a few houres ; but that day sevenight being seized again with a paraletick fit in the morning as he was dressing, it so affected one side that he had difficulty to walke, and lost the use of his right hand for some time, but after blistering, Emetique &c, he began to recover the use of it again, walked prety well, so that the Doctors thought the waters of Burbon would perfectly restore him, whither he went about three weeks after ; and thō he was almost perfectly well of his lameness at his return, yet a pain he complain'd of in his breast, and his spitting of blood now and then, even before he went to Burbon, gaue reason to apprehend that thō the Emetique he had taken might haue done him good perhaps, for his palsie, it had certainly prejudicied his breast : however he seem'd to recover strenght, took the air as usual,

On fryday the
2ᵈ of Sep: the
King falls ill,
and on Sunday
following
vomited blood
in a great
quantity.

and some times on hors back, but on fryday the second of September, was seized again with a fainting in the Chappel just as he had been at first, which returning upon him after he was carryed to his chamber, was a most afflicting sight to the most disconsolate Queen, in whose arms he fell the second time, however he was prety well next day, but on Sunday falling into another fit was for some time without life or motion, till his mouth being forced open, he vomited a great quantety *of* * *bloud*. This put the Queen, and all people except himself, into the last degree of trouble and aprehention, but his long desires of death had rendered the thoughts of it so familiar to him, that neither the terrours of its approach nor the torments that attend it, gaue him the least anxcietie or disquiet, there was no need

---

but all that was dear to him, for his Restoration. The King of France said, *I am of Monseigneur's opinion ;* and so said all the Princes of the Blood." (Somers' Tracts, Ed. 1814. Vol. xi. p. 341.) EDITOR.

* Interlined by his Son. EDITOR.

of exhorting him to resignation, or to a due preparation for it; that was the first and only thing he thought of, he had made a general confession just before he fell into that fit, and assoon as his vomiting ceased, he desir'd his * Confessor to send for the Blessed Sacrament, and fancying he could not last long press'd for expedition, minding him to take care he wanted none of the rights of the Church: in the mean time he.sent for the Prince his Son, who at his first entrance seeing the King with a pale and dying countenance, the bed all cover'd with blood, burst out as well as all about him into the most violent expressions of grief; assoon as he came to the bed side the King with a sort of contentedness in his looks, stretched forth his arms to embrace him, and then † speaking with a force and vehemence that better suted with his zeal than the weak condition he was in, conjured him to adhere firmly to the Catholick faith, let what will be ye consequence of it, and be faithfull in the service of God, to be respectfull and obediant to the Queen, the best of Mothers, and to be ever gratefull to the King of France to whom he had so many obligations:

---

* Mr. Sanders.

† " Then sending for the Prince, he told him, ' I am now leaving this world, which has been to me a sea of storms and tempests; it being God Almighty's will to wean me from it by many great Afflictions. Serve him with all your power and strength, and never put the Crown of England in competition with your Eternal Salvation. There is no Slavery like Sin, nor no Liberty like his Service. If his holy Providence shall think fit to set you upon the Throne of your Ancestors, govern your People with Justice and Clemency, and take pity of your misled Subjects. Remember Kings are not made for themselves, but for the good of the People. Set before their eyes, in your own actions, a pattern of all manner of virtues. Consider them as your Children, aim at nothing but their good in correcting them. You are the Child of Vows and Prayers. Behave yourself accordingly. Honour your Mother, that your days may be long, and be always a kind Brother to your dear Sister, that you may reap the blessing of concord and unity." (Somers' Tracts, Vol. xi. p. 342.) EDITOR.

T O M.
IV.

1701.

those who were present, apprehending the concerne and
fervour with which he spoke, might doe him prejudice, desired
the Prince might withdraw; which the King being troubled at,
sayd, Do not take away my Son till I haue given him my blessing
at least, which when he had done the Prince return'd to his
appartement, and the little Princess was brought to his bed side
to whom he * spoke to the same effect, whilst she with the
abundance of her inocent tears, shew'd how sencibly she was
touched with the languishing condition the King her Father
was in.

The King
exhorts every
body about
him to practice
vertue, and
Protestants to
embrace the
Cath: Faith.

He was not content with haveing spoke to his Children, he
made a sort of short Exhortation to almost every one about
him, with the greatest fervour and pietie immaginable, but
particularly to My Lord Middleton and his other Protestant
Servants, whom he perswaded to embrace the Catholick faith,
and did it with so much force and energie, as made no small
impression upon them; he tould them They might credit a
dying man, who assured them they would find the comforth
of following his example and advice, when they came to be in
the like condition themselves.

The King
receiues the
Viaticum,
Sep: 4.

Assoon as the Blessed Sacrament arriued, he cry'd out, The
happy day is come at least; and then recollecting himself to
receiue his holy Viaticum, the Curate came to his bed side
and (as customary on those occasions) asked him if he believed
the real and substantial presence of our Saviour's body in the
Sacrament? To which he answer'd, Yes, I believe it, I believe

---

* " Adieu, my dear Child! Serve your Creator in the days of your youth, and
consider Virtue as the greatest ornament of your sex. Follow close the steps of
that great pattern of it your Mother, who has been no less than myself over-
clouded with Calumnies; but time, the mother of truth, I hope, will at last make
her Virtue shine as bright as the Sun." (Ibid: Letter in the Somers' Tracts,
page 342.) EDITOR.

it with my whole heart ; after which haveing spent some time
in spiritual recollection, he disired to receiue the Sacrament of
extream unxion, accompanying those cerimonys with most
exemplar pietie and a singular presence of mind.

There could not be a properer time than this for makeing a
Publick declaration of his being in perfect charitie with all
the world, and that he pardon'd his enemies from the bottom
of his heart; and least his sinceretie might be doubted in
reference to those who had been so in a particular manner, he
named the Prince of Orange, the Princesse Anne of Denmark
his Daughter, and calling his Confessor to take particular
notice, Sayd, I forgiue with all my heart the Emperour too ;
but in realitie he had not waited to that moment to performe
that Christian duty of forgiveness of injuries, his heart had
been so far from any resentment on their account, that he
reckon'd them his best benefactors, and often declar'd he was
more beholden to the Prince of Orange than to all the world
besides.

All this while the poor Queen not able to support herself,
was shurnk down on the ground by the bed side, in much
greater anguish, and as little signs of life as he, the King
was sencibly touched to see her in such excessiue grief, and
seem'd to suffer more on that account than any other ; he sayd
what he could to comforth her, and to be as resigned in that as
she was in all other things to the will of God : but she was
inconsolable, till perceiveing by a sencible amendment, and
the King's haveing passed the night pretty well that his case
seem'd not so desperate, but that there was some hopes of his
recoverie.

The next day his Most Christ: Majesty came to see him, and
light at the Castle gate, as others did, to prevent the noise of
coaches comeing into the Court ; the King receiued him with
the same easyness and affabilitie as usual, and indeed was

He pardons all
his enemies,
the Emperour,
the P^{ce} of
Orange, the
Princesse of
Denmark, by
name.

The unspeake-
able affliction
the Queen was
in.

The King of
France goes
to visite the
King.

better that night, and thō the night following he had an ill fit,
yet on Wednesday he voided no more blood by stool, and his
fever abateing, gave great hopes of amendment: On Sunday
his Most Christ: Majesty made him a second visit, whom as
well as all the other Princes and people of distinction (who
were perpetually comeing) he receiu'd with as much presence
of mind and civilitie as if he had ail'd nothing; but on Munday
he falling into a dozedness, and his fever increasing, all those
hopes of recovery vanished away, the Queen was by his bed
side when that happen'd which put her into a sort of agonie
too; this the King perceiveing, was concern'd for, and notwithstanding his weak condition, sayd, Madame, do not afflict
yourself, I am going (I hope) to be happy ; to which the Queen
replyd, S', I doubt it not, and therefore it is not your condition
I lament, it is my own; and then her grief overpowering her,
she was ready to faint away, which he perceiveing beg'd of her
to retire, and order'd those present to lead her into her room ;
and then began the prayers for a soul departeing : he continued
however much what in the same way that night, when he
receiu'd the Blessed Sacrament again with most exemplar
pietie and devotion, and renewed likewise his former declaration
of forgiveness nameing again with a lowd voice the Prince
of Orange, the Princess Anne his Daughter, and the Emperour,
and sayd He wished they might be acquainted he forgaue them.
The Doctors had all along given him the kinkinna, which thō
the thing in the world he had the greatest aversion too, however
he never refused it, and now that they thought proper to blister
him in several places (which gaue him great torment) he
suffer'd it without ever complaining or shewing the least
uneasiness in that or any thing els they did, or order'd ; it was
neither hopes of recovery nor fear of death that made him so
complyant, he dispared of the one and desir'd the other, but
he thought it more perfect to obey, and that the patient suffring

of those remedies might benefit his soul, thō they were of no
advantage to his body.

The next day he continued in the same lethargick way, and
seem'd to take little notice of anything, except when prayers
were read, which he was always attentiue too, and by the
motion of his lips seem'd to pray continually himself. On
Tuseday the 13ᵗʰ about three a clock, his Most Christ: Majesty
came a therd time, to declare his resolution in reference to the
Prince, which in his former visits he had sayd nothing of, nor
indeed had he determin'd that matter before; but now seeing
the King at the last extremity, found it necessary to come to
some resolution therein, so had call'd a Council in order to it,
most of which were aprehensiue, that should he own the Prince
as King of England upon his Majestys death, it might embroil
the Nation in a new war, the thoughts of which were terrible
to them, and therefore were for finding expedients to waue it
for some time at least; but the Dolphin, the Duke of Burgundy, and all the Princes thought it so unjust in itself, and
so unbecomeing the dignitie of the Crown of France to abandon
a Prince of their own blood, who sought, and so justly merited
their protection, that they were of a contrary opinion; which
being his Most Christ: Majestys own judgment too, he came
accordingly to declare it. He first went to the Queen and
acquainted her with his resolution, which was some comforth
to her in the deep affliction she was in, and then sending for
the Prince tould him the same, assureing him, That if it pleased
God to call for the King his Father, he would be a Father to
him; upon which the Prince express'd his gratitude for so
signal a favour and sayd, He should find him as dutifull and
respectfull as if he realy were his Child, and so return'd to
his own apartement. Upon which, his Most Christian Majesty
went in to the King, and comeing to the bed side, sayd,
Sʳ I am come to see how your Majesty finds yourself to day; but

Septemb. 13.
The King of
France came a
therd time to
see the King,
and then de-
clar'd he
would own the
Pᵉᵉ of Wales
as King of
England.

T O M.
IV.

1701.

the King not hearing, made no reply, upon which one of his seruants telling him that the King of France was there, he roosed himself up and sayd, Where is he? Upon which the King of France sayd S^r I am here and am come to see how you doe; so then the King began to * thank him for all his favours, and particularly for the care and kindness he had shewn dureing his sickness, to which his Most Ch: Majesty replyd, S^r that is but a small matter, I haue something to acquaint you with of greater consequence; upon which the King's servants immagining he would be private (the room being full of people) began to retire, which his Most Christ. Majesty perceiveing, sayd out alowd, Let no body withdraw, and then went on: I am come S^r to acquaint you, that whenever it shall pleas God to call your Majesty out of this world, I will take your family into my protection and will treat your Son the Prince of Wales in the same manner I haue treated you, and acknowlidg him, as he then will be, King of England; upon which, all that were present as well French as English burst out into tears, not being able any other way to express that mixture of joy and grief with which they were so surprizingly seized; some indeed threw themselves at his Most Christ: Majestys feet, others by their iestures and countenances (much more expressiue on such occasions than words and speeches) declar'd their gratitude for so generous an action; with which

---

* "The French King coming to pay a visit to him, and asking him how he did, he answered, " I am going to pay that debt which must be paid by all Kings as well as their meanest subjects. I give your Majesty my dying thanks for all your kindnesses to me and my afflicted Family, and do not doubt of your continuance. I have always found you equally good and generous. I thank God I die with a perfect resignation, and forgive all the world, particularly the Emperor and the Prince of Orange."—The French King on taking this his last leave, with tears in his eyes embraced JAMES, saying, " Adieu, my dear Brother, the best of Christians, and the most abused of Monarchs." (Somers's Tracts, Vol. xi. p. 343.) EDITOR.

his Most Christ: Majesty was so much moued, that he could not refrain weeping himself: the King all this while, was endeavouring to say something to him upon it, but the confused nois being too great and he too weak to make himself be heard, his Most Christ. Majesty tooke his* leave and went away; and as he got into his coach, called the Officer of the Guard who waited upon the King, and gaue him directions to follow and attend the Prince of Wales, assoon as the King was dead, and to shew him the same respect and honours he had done to the King his Father when he was aliue.

The next day the King found himself something better, so the prince was permited to come to him, which he was not often suffer'd to doe, it being obscrved, that when he saw him, it raised such a commotion in him as was thought to do him harme; assoon therefore as he came into the room, the King stretching forth his arms to embrace him, Sayd, I haue not seen you since his Most Christian Majesty was here, and promised to own you when I was dead. I haue sent My Lord Middleton to Marly to thank him for it: Thus did this holy Prince talk of his aproaching death not only with indifference, but satisfaction, when he found his Son and Famiily would not be sufferers by it, and so composed himself to recciue it with greater cheerfullness, if possible, then before; nor was that happy houre far from him now, for the next day he grew much weaker, was taken with continual convulsions or shakeing in the hands, and the day following being Fryday the 16th of Septemb' about three in the afternoon render'd his pious soul into the hands of his redeemer; the day of the week, and hour, wherein our Saviour dy'd, and on which he always practiced a particular devotion to obtain a happy death.

TOM. IV. 1701.

The King expires at three o'clock on fryday 16 Sept: S.N.

---

* This Interview forms the subject of an admirable Painting made some time since by Richard Westall, Esq. R.A. EDITOR.

1701.
His exemplar
piety, resigna-
tion, patience,
&c. during his
sickness.

It were an endless work to giue an account of all the particular instances of his most exemplar Piety and Devotion
dureing the time of his sickness; as long as he had force to
pray he never ceased, and when he seem'd so dozed as to
attend almost to nothing els, it apear'd by his answering and
accompanying those who prayed by him, that he was never
asleep as to that, and thō his eyes were almost always shut
towards the end, yet dureing the time of mass, which was sayd
every day in his room, he was as vigilant and attentiue to that
as if he had been in perfect health, and this till the very day he
dy'd: he neuer complain'd of any remedys or operations thō
the kinkinna was exceeding disgustfull to him, and the blistering
very painfull, but submited himself entirely to the disposal of the
Doctors, only would say sometimes, That were it not for the sake
of the Queen and his Children, he would not haue suffer'd so
much pains to be taken about what he was so little sollicitous for.

In this manner therefore he lay fifteen days suspended
betwixt life and death, while the sorrowfull countenances of
those who continually surrounded his bed, would haue terrifyd
one of less Faith with the apprehentions of the fatal stroke;
but he all the while appear'd the only person unconcern'd,
any more than as he endeavour'd to manage those precious
moments with greater fervour in order to his future happiness.
So that as his strength decayd, his Faith and Pietie animated
him, to do even beyond what nature seem'd capable of, for in
spite of his mortal lethargie the name of Jesus would haue
awaked him to the last, no prayer was ever unheard by him
when he seem'd deaf for every thing els, and bore the torments
of a dying man as if his body had lost all sensation; for when
ever any one asked him how he did, he always answer'd He
was well, and by the civilitie and easiness wherewith he received
the Princes, or people of Qualitie that were hourely visiting
him, one would haue thought he had been so indeed. The day
but one before he dyd, the Dutchess of Burgundy being there,

he desired her not to come near his bed, least the smell about
it might be offensiue to her; and the day after, even when he
seem'd to be in his agony, he saluted the Duke of Burgundy
by lifting up his head, as he did to some others afterwards: in
fine, while speech remain'd he imployd his tongue in praysing
God, pardonning his Enemies, professing his Faith (which he
did in the most steddy and fervent manner immaginable three
days before he dyd when the Pope's Nuncio came to see him)
in exhorting his Subjects, and Servants, but most particularly
his Children to the service of God, and for no earthly consideration to abandon the true Religion, nor the ways of Vertue;
and when it grew troublesome to him to speak, one saw by
his jestures, looks and even silence itself, that his mind was
fixed upon God, and haveing his sences in a manner till the
last, he seem'd by the motion of his lips to pray till his soul
went out of his body.

The Queen who dureing his sickness had been in a continual
agony herself, when she heard he had expired, was ready to
do so too, for as there was never a more perfect example of
true conjugal affection than in that vertuous Princesse, so the
torment she underwent in the separation was unexpressable;
she never seem'd to be aliue almost herself but when there was
some hopes of his recovery, and when that was dispair'd of
she gaue herself over to such an excess of sorrow, that in reality
she deserved more pitie and compassion than the King, who
had by a most holy and Sanctifyd end put a happy period to
a mortifyd and Christian life; she immediately therefore went
to Challiot, a Convent of Nunns, where her Majesty was used
to make frequent retreats, there to lament her loss in the bitterness of her soul, and to seek comforth from him who had
sent her the affliction, and was only able to give her force to
support it. Assoon as the first anguish of her grief was over,
she faill'd not to obey one of the last commands of the

T O M.
IV.
1701.

The Queen
being over-
whelmed with
grief, retires
to Challiot.

T O M.
IV.

1701.
The Queen's
Letter to the
Princesse of
Denmark.
Sep. 27: S.N.

deceased King and write the following Letter to the Princesse of Denmark :

I think myself indispensably obliged to differ no longer the acquainting you with a message, which the best of men as well as the best of Fathers left with me for you ; some few days before his death, he bid me find meanes to let you know that he forgaue you all that's past from the bottom of his heart, *and pray'd to God to do so too, that he gaue you his last blessing and pray'd to God to convert your * heart* and confirm you in the resolution of repaireing to his Son the wrongs done to himself : to which I shall only ad, that I join my prayers to his herein, with all my heart, and that I shall make it my business to inspire into the young man, who is left to my care, the sentiments of his Father; for better, no man can haue. Sept 27: 1701.

There is no doubt but the Princess of Denmark was moued with this letter, she had for a long time been (or pretended to be) in a disposition of makeing some reparation for past injuries ; but the P. of Orange dying not long after, Ambition choaked the good seed which perhaps the charitable and pious admonitions of her dying Father might haue sown in her breast, and make her forget all former protestation of makeing amends for those unjustices which she was sencible of, when in affliction herself, but forgot, when it came to her turn to reape the fruite of the common disobedience.

The King's body is deposited in the Church of the English Monks in Paris.

His body lay exposed four and twenty houres in the room where he dyd, the Clergie and Religious singing the office of the dead by him all night, and all the morning masses were sayd at two alters erected on both sides the room ; and such had been his humilitie while aliue that he had resolved it

---

* Interlined by the Son of James the Second. EDITOR.

II

should follow him to his graue, and had order'd by his Will that his body should be buried in the Parish Church where he should fortune to dy, and that no more expence should be made at his funeral than at that of a private gentleman; and no other monument or inscription than that of a bare stone with these words, HER LYS KING JAMES. He had acquainted the Curate with this and order'd him to insist upon the performance; but his Most Christ: Majesty sayd, That was the only thing he could not grant him, so in the evening he was embalmed, and part of his Bowells being carryd to the Parish Church the rest were sent to the English College at St Omers, the Braines and Fleshy part of the head to the Scotch College at Paris, where at the charge of the Duke of* Perth was erected a fair monument, as a due acknow_lidgment of their sence of being honour'd with those precious Reliques.

Assoon therefore as this distribution was made and every thing prepared for carrying away his body, they set out with it about seaven o'Clock in the evening towards the Church of the English Benedictin Monks in Paris, attended by the Duke of Berwick, the Earle of Middleton, his Majestys Chaplins, and some others of his Servants. As it went along it was accompanyed with the tears and lamentations not only of his own Subjects but of the people of the Country where it passed; they left his heart at Challiot as he had order'd, and contriued to be there about midnight, that the Queen might not hear the nois nor know the time of their comeing, to spare her that additional torment which would haue made her wound bleed

---

* The Duke of Perth, as appears by the Book of Warrants, &c. had been appointed Governor to the Son of JAMES, on the 19th of August, 1696; and on Octr 30, 1701, his Queen appointed the Duchess of Perth to be one of the Ladies of the Bedchamber. EDITOR.

so freshly again; but neither the ignorance of the time, nor the Silence of the night, could prevent the Queen's haveing a sort of presentiment of what was intended, which overwhelmed her with anguish and sorrow all the while, thō she had no certain knowlidg of what was a doing: nor did this Secrecy hinder the people from flocking to meet it in the streets of Paris, who by an equall proportion of joy and grief, shew'd their great concern for his death, and no less pleasure to haue his precious reliques left amongst them. Assoon as they arriued at the Monks, D^{tr} Ingleton Almoner to the Queen deliver'd his body with an elegant latin oration to the Prior (as he had done his heart before at Challiot) to be deposited in a side Chappel, till it pleas'd God to dispose the people of England, to repair in some measure the injuries they did him in his life, by the honours they shall think fit to shew him after his death.

The King's Character.

He was something aboue the middle stature, well shaped, very nervous and strong, his face was rather long, his complexion fair and his countenance engageing, his outward cariage was a little stif and constrain'd, which made it not so gracious as it was courtious and obligeing, he was affable and easy of access for he affected not formalitie, thō no one knew the cerimonial better, nor was more exact (when necessary) in the observance of it: in his Conversation and arguing he endeavour'd rather to convince with good reason, than fine expressions, and haveing something of a hesitation in his speech, his discours was not so gracious as it was judicious and sollid; he abhor'd the duplicitie of a refined Courtier, was an assured Friend if he profess'd it, and whom he could not Serue was always sincere enough to let him know it; his Temper was naturally hot and colerick, but in his latter days his vertue got a perfect mastery over it, and in his younger it scarce ever so

overpower'd him as to force him to any action unbecomeing T O M.
his character, that fire or vivacitie appear'd more in his com- IV.
portment in the Army, than in the prosecution of his enemies, 1701.
whom he had too much courage ever to truckle too, always
generositie enough to pardon, and too much prudence to trust;
thō he er'd against this last maxim when he stood most in need
of it, by confideing in some who had formerly betrayd him,
and whom he found by experience were not to be changed
by clemency, nor gain'd by good usage; so that for the time he
was upon the Throne, he was no less unsuccessfull in detecting
his enemies, than he had been most part of his life in the choice
of his friends..

He was a great lover of exercise especially walkeing, and
hunting, but that, nor no other divertion, made him neglect his
Business, to which he had so great an application that it seem'd
to be of the number of his divertions too. He was so distin-
guishable for this, that dureing his yonger days notwithstanding
the unsettled-ness of his condition while he lived in exile, the
distractions of the wars which he was brought up in, and the
disorders he was so inevitably exposed too, he not only perform'd his duty with great exactness in the station he bore, but
kept an Account of all Occurrances, which has obliged posteritie
with better memorialls under his own hand, than perhaps any
Sovereign Prince has been known to leaue behind him
before.

This made him all his life a great enemie to drinking, gameing,
and indeed all such pleasures as were obstructiue to business,
and which commonly render men wholy incapable of it, or at
least was but loss of time, which he always counted precious,
and managed with great circonspection; and thō he was carry'd
away for a long time with those disorders which he so pas-
sionately laments afterwards, yet they never got so entire a
mastery over him, as to make him neglect his business, be

extravagant in his expence; or totally forgetfull of his duty even
at those times when he practiced it the least; which raised a
continual conflict and struggle in his mind, and mingled so
much gall with his pleasures, that (as he often confessed afterwards, and particularly in his ADVICE * TO THE PRINCE HIS
SON) those disorders had ever more of torment than content,
and that he never enjoyd himself while he gave way to that
vice, or was two days that some new anxietie or trouble did not
spring from that root ; which was a motiue to bring him sooner
off from that bewitching habit, which the generalitie of
mankind and particularly Princes are so difficultly reclamed
from.

He was a kind Husband notwithstanding his infirmities
during his youth, but especially in his latter days, when he
repair'd his former infidelities, by a most tender affection mixed
with a respect and defference to the incomparable merit and
vertues of the Queen ; wherein he found so much satisfaction
and even advantage, that he own'd he was never truly happy
till then, and like Jacob counted his suffrings for nothing,
haveing such a support and companion of them. He was the
most indulgent Father in the world and the most unfortunate in
some of his Children; The best Master and yet the worst served,
a most constant Friend yet never Prince found fewer in his
greatest necessities; he was so good a Father (I say) that he
not only loued and cherished his two Daughters beyond expression while they remain'd dutifull, but his care and concern
follow'd them in their unnatural disertion of him, for when he
return'd from Salisbury and found the Princess Anne was gon,
instead of expressing such a ressentment as the provocation
vould haue excused, he seem'd more concern'd for her health,

---

* Printed in a subsequent page, 617. EDITOR.

than the monstrous indignitie offer'd to himself; and forgeting
how ill an influence it might haue upon his own affairs, he only
express'd an apprehention least so unseasonable a journey might
occasion her miscarrying: and for instance how good a Master
he was and a Friend, he not only heaped favours upon those he
had a kindness for, but was deaf to all suggestions against
them; this gaue full scope to his favorits to betray him with
securitie, they might act any mischief against him who would
credit no ill of them, so that his clemency and goodness in that
ungratefull age, contribited more to his ruin, than the vices of
the most cruel Tyrant could haue done; and they made him
do a severer penence for his God like vertues, than others do
for their sinns, so that he might well say as dying Cæsar did,
Mene hos servasse, ut essent qui me perderent?

While the King his Brother liued he was a pattern of
Obedience*; and when he came to be King himself was a model
to other Princes for all the qualifications that could make a
nation florish and a people happy, had not the infelicitie of
y⁰ times, jealousies about Religion, and the violent temper of
angry men, made them turn into poison the most wholesome
nurrishment and ruin themselves rather than not ruin the best
of Princes. For first as to his skill in Government, his inde-
fatigable pains and observations of mismanagements in former
reigns, qualifyd him beyond exception for it, and if he fail'd
in some of those points which he had been formerly so much
aware of in others, it was because he wanted so good and
faithfull a Councellor to himself, as he had been to the King
his Brother; for it is not always as easy to take good Councel
as to giue it, especially when a Prince (which was the King's
case) has too charitable an opinion of others, and too humble

The King's
Obedience
when a
Subject.

His skill in
Governement
when King.

---

* This particularly appears in his conduct to Charles the Second before his
Restoration. EDITOR.

T O M.
IV.

His Justice.

His great loue
of his Subjects.

an opinion of himself. This made him less cautious in the choice of friends and favorits, and less upon his guard to be deluded by them; nevertheless the mistakes he made in reference to Government, was in what related more to his own wellbeing than to that of his Subjects.

His Justice was so exempt from blemish that his fiercest enemies in their innumerable calumnies and groundless aspersions, durst never lay the least failure of it to his charge, that great principle of doing to others as one would haue others do to them, (the main groundwork of humain Societie as well as of a Christian and moral life) as it was ever in his mouth, was no less conspicuous in his actions; he had such a horrour of the contrary vice, that the fear of injureing others made him never act upon suspicion only, and so oft times differ'd the remedy till the disease was incurable; and was so far from affecting an Arbitary Power (which his enemies falsely reproach'd him with) that by his too great scrupulositie in the use of that power (in reference to them) which the Law had put in his hands, he in effect deliver'd himself up into theirs.

The loue of his Subjects was so rooted in his breast that all their infidelities could never tear it from thence, their well being was his study when on the Throne, and their suffrings his greatest trouble when dispossessed of it; he was more concern'd for the hand that struck him than for the pain he suffer'd by the blow, and could not refrain takeing a complesance in their valour * when it was exercised with most violence even against himself: it was certain views of advantageing his

---

* " When he first saw the Seamen (at the battle of La Hogue) in swarms scrambling up the high sides of the French Ships from their boats, he cried out, *Ah! none, but my brave English could do so brave an action.*" (*Dalrymple*, Vol. 1. p. 508.) EDITOR.

people, that they might encreas their riches whilst others
lavished theirs and their blood away, that made him so unwilling
to concur with them in that destructiue humour of invadeing
their neibours, so turn'd the stroke upon himself, by endevouring
to ward them from it.

Trade which is so beneficial to the Nation, was so peculiarly His Skill in Trade, and desire to improve it.
his care, that never Prince understood it better, or advanced it
more, nothing scaped his advertance that had any relation to
it, it was one great motiue to his granting libertie of Conscience, which brought back accordingly so many Dissenters,
who had left England for fear of persecution, and had set up
the Woolen Manifacture at Lewardin, Lunenbourg and Freez-
land ; it was for the sake of Trade (as was obserued) that he
appear'd so avers from entring into the Confederate League
against France, that by keeping a newtralitie he might draw
greatest part of the Trade of Europe into the hands of his
Subjects ; which was one great motiue too of the Dutch jealousie, and made them in spight of their covetous humour,
contribit so largely and treacherously to the Prince of Orange's
expedition ; so that whatever others may pretend, the King
was in great measure the Martir of the tradeing part of the
Nation, who growing rich by his care were the first that grew
disafected, and others becomeing wanton by plenty, concur'd
to charge those things upon him for Crimes, which were done
with special views of makeing them opulent and happy.

His good Management was such, that he not only discharg'd His good Management,
the expence of the Civil List without haveing recours to Parliamentary supplys, but he stocked all the forts and Ports with
arms, and provisions ; the Magazins were never so well provided with naval stores, the Ships of war in so good order, and
the Seamen so well payd ; his Army thō it was an eye sore,
was no burthen to the people, he not only payd it punctually
to the middle of December, but made the extraordinary

expences of equiping the Fleet, augmenting his Troops, togather with all other incident charges upon the Prince of Orange's invasion, yet left 150000 ℔ in the Exchequer and 400000 ℔ in arrear; but the people thō they liued thus without Taxes, yet since it was without Parliaments too, they grumbled at the blessing and thought their libertie crampt, till by frequent Sessions they had the pleasure of raising four or five millions a year. So that this augmentation of libertie, they so much contended for and so much gloryd in since the revolution, has been only to haue it in their power to giue all they had away.

His Courage.

His Courage was the terrour of his enemies, the Support of his friends, and the admiration of all that knew him; his predominant passion from his infancy *was to serue in ye Warrs and from his * infancy* he began to exercise it; which as it was his pleasure, so it became his support too in great measure during his Exile: he had two great Masters in that art, the Prince of Condé and the Mareshall de Turenne, whose esteem and friendship he so entirely gain'd that the former bore this testimony of his valour, That if ever any man was entirely void of Fear it was (he Sayd) the Duke of York; and the other had contracted such an exceeding esteem and loue for his person, that upon an intended descent before the Restoration,

Vide Ld Clarendon's Hist: of the Rebellion, Vol: 3.

he was resolued to haue lent him a considerable body of troops, even without permission from Court, thō the Duke of York was then in the Spanish Service, against whom that generous Captain commanded the French Army. His courage therefore which had been So glorious to the Nation abroad, was its defence when he return'd home, and his own chief support in those innumerable contradictions he underwent afterwards, on

---

* Interlined by the Son of James the Second. EDITOR.

account of his Religion, which render'd him the object of the people's rage, who had been their darling before : it is true his enemies pretend that his not ventring a blow for it in England, and his too early quiting of Ireland, had tarnished in some measure the lustre of his Character in that point, but whoso‑ ever well weighs the circomstances of those times, will rather lament his misfortunes than blame his conduct, and be per‑ swaded that the treachery and desertion he was surprized with in England,. and the hopes of a descent from France when he quited Ireland, might well make the wisest as well as stoutest General take the wors councel, which it is not to be denyd but he did in those occasions.

But notwithstanding his propention to war his prudence made him ever prefer peace, he was sensible (thō others were not) that the less a King of England loves wars abroad, the better it is for the people at home, he consider'd that the Kingdom had reap'd no other advantage from the conquests of Edward the therd and Henry the fifth, than a continual occasion of lamenting the vast consumption of blood and treasure which ended always in loss and disgrace ; that all acquisitions upon the Continent were like to proue as little successfull or advantagious to us, as those from the Continent would infallebly proue upon England, and therefore the less to be fear'd : that the three Kingdoms was a just Empire of themselves, not to be invaded from the Continent nor to be extended upon it. The encreas of trade and riches he knew was a more durable benefit than an empty fame, which was an other motiue for his not joining in a war against France when he consider'd, that if the therd part of the charge (which he foresaw that war must amount too) had been expended in encreasing the Naval force, it would haue made the Nation impregnable not only against France, but all the world besides ; but he was disapointed in this by the reastiness of some, the

T O M.
IV.

1701.

giddyness of others, and the artefull treachery of too many, which join'd with the flattery at first of the Churchmen and after of Fanaticks, made him uncertain which way to turn, and gaue an opertunitie to those corrupted Ministers, to betray him into such measures as brought forth the revolution at last.

His great
Sincerity.
Vide Dr Sherlock'sSermon:
1685.

He was of a punctual Veracity, and had a generous disdain of all tricking and all dissembling contrivances; he abhor'd all mean artes and equivocal reserues, scorn'd either.to desemble what he believed himself and speak what he did not think, and was far from meriteing the reproach of haveing receded from his engagement in reference to Religion and ye liberties of the people; he made not one single step in that affair without being assured by men learned in Law and antiquity that he might do it, without any breach either of his word or the Laws themselves, and if they stretched his prerogatiue beyond its due (at least convenient) limits, it must be charged upon the corruption of some Courtiers and the weakness of others, too apt to flatter Princes for private ends, and must not be presumed the King did it with intent to get loos of his engagement, for he ever remember'd his promis of protecting his Protestant Subjects of the Church of England in the quiet possession of their privileges, Religion &c; which he renew'd on all occasions, but he could not, for all that, forget clemency to others, which (notwithstanding the popular prejudice. against it) he fancy'd were not irreconciliable; he had tasted of persecution for conscience sake himself, and it was natural as well as glorious for so benigne à Prince to giue eas to others, who had wanted it himself, and be touched with that suffring in so many of his Subjects, he had felt so sencibly in his own person.

His Zeal for
Religion and
his eminent
Pietie.

Such was his Zeal for Religion, that he did not only sacrifice to it the favour of the people, his imployments, and his Country,

II

but at last his Crown itself; if ever he transgressed the rules of humain prudence it was for the sake of Religion, and in the eye of the world it was (if one may so call it) his only fault, that the Service of God out ballanced in him all temporall considerations : but as it was the origin of his Suffrings, so it was his prop and comforth in the support of them, and gaue him such an equalitie of spirit in all fortunes, as neither success could elevate, nor adversitie deject, and therefore (*he*) was observed never to have wept upon a temporal account. But when three Crowns fell to him, being infinitely more touched at the loss of the King his Brother, than delighted with the Kingdoms he left him by his death, he experienced by this means both extreames of fortune, and thō he tasted but gently of the good, he drank deeply of the other, but kept the same equanimity in both ; makeing the uncertainty of humain affairs rather a subject of moral reflection than of repineing and revengfull thoughts ; and this made him humble enough to pardon those who caus'd them, and desinteressed enough to sacrifice all to providence : in his latter days he made a sort of compound betwixt the Majesty of a King and the humility of a Christian, which put such a lustre upon his Misfortunes, that those who seem'd most sencibly touch'd with his condition could not but be delighted with his manner of supporting it ; if any thing had been capable of overcomeing his patience, it was his Subjects suffrings not his own, he was touched to the last degree with the miseries of each particular person, as if that of the Nation had not already drained his compassion and concern, he gaue the utmost penny he could spare from his bare support, to relieve the crying necessities of those that followed him, and thō he had once an occasion of laying up a considerable summe of money, and was pres'd to it, as a thing which might on a critical occasion be enough to regain his crown, he rather chose to trust entirely to providence for that, than let any indigent Subject want

relief, so long as he had any means of affording it; and least
a partial or unskilfull distribution might overlook the most
deserueing or necessitous, he took the pains, in great measure, to
be his own Almoner, and by a prudent enquiry and judicious
discernment, scarce ever fail'd to place his charitie where most
needed, and by his admirable economie (which stood him no
less in steed in his Low eb of fortune than when he had the
revenue of three Kingdoms to manage) it was ashtonishing to
see, what numbers he made it extend too

Nor was his Charitié and Good Will confined to his friends
and followers, his enemies had a share, he was so far from
obrading them with their infidelitie, that he would not suffer
others to do it, he studyed to find excuses in publick for their
blackest crimes, and fail'd not to pray for them in private,
and by an ingenious and charitable turn bless'd his greatest
enemies as his chief benefactors, who had led him into the
paths of affliction, the surest way to Salvation; he knew how
to distinguish between the visible hand that struck him, and
the invisible decree that permited it, so that instead of
blameing the one, he submited too and adored the other, and
arrived to that pitch of resignation as even to delight in it:

" Til I was with you (says he in a letter to the Abbot of LA
" TRAPPE) I did not enjoy that contempt of the world which
" now I am sencible of; I make use of that expression,
" because I was never truly happy till I had gain'd a real
" conformety to the will of God, and till I was convinced that
" it is impossible to haue content in this world but by
" dispiseing of it.

He dreaded nothing so much as Flatterie, because that
follow'd him in his digrace, he always thought calumny less
dangerous than commendation, for he easily forgot an injury
but was not sure he could as easily stifle the impression which
publick esteem might make in his mind, and therefore con-

sulted the Abbot of LA TRAPPE how to comport himself on
such occasions: this made him shun as much as possebly he
could the compliments of Preachers, and commendations of
pious people, thō done with design to encourage him in the
way of Vertue, he once asked a Preacher how he could
justify commending Princes when they did not deserve it? he
answer'd, That Princes were in so high a station they could
not use the same libertie in reproueing them as other men, and
therefore by praising them for what they were not, tought
them what they ought to be; the King was pleased with the
ingenuitie of his answer, but tould him, He did not desire to
be complemented into his Duty, would suffer them to tell him
plainly of his faults, and therefore was often used to say, He
desired their praiers but not their praises. He was never weary
of hearing Sermons, spiritual discourses, and reading good
books, of which besides the relish he had in those pious
entertainments, his humilitie made him think he had more
occasion for, than other people: The continual distractions
(says he) of those who liue in the world, makes it necessary ”
to be stir'd up by frequent admonitions and remembrances of ”
their duty, which I stand more in need of than others, who ”
began so late to apply myself seriously to the work of ”
Salvation. ”

Thus infine did this pious and penitential Prince, sanctify
his Suffrings, and endeavour'd to sanctify even those who
occasion'd them ; there is not a day (says he) that I do ”
not according to my duty pray for the conversion of the ”
unfortunate Prince of Orange, and all those who have any ”
ways injured me : he had now no other enemie but Sin,
which he resisted in himself, and deplored in others ; but it
were an endless work and a great temerity to offer at a full
account of those vertues, which heaven itself has voutsafed to
be the publisher of, by the prodigious concours of people

TOM.
IV.

1701.
LETTER
30 July.

LETTER TO
THE ABBOT OF
LA TRAPPE,
Augt: 7. 1695.

LETTER eidem
28 Apr. 1700.

TOM.
IV.

1701.

(immediately after his death) to his precious reliques, and the manifould cures it has pleased Almighty God to operate in testimony of his holy life, So publick and so well attested, that we may hope ere long to see the decision of the *Apostolick See, in favour of his Sanctitie.

---

* This is given at length in The Somers' Tracts, Vol. xi. Ed. Walter Scott, (p. 343.) being *The Pope's Speech made in a Consistory which he held on the 3d of October, 1701, to notify the Death of the late King James II. to the Sacred College.* EDITOR.

HERE ENDS THE FOURTH AND LAST VOLUME OF THE
MANUSCRIPT LIFE OF JAMES.

THE ADVICE

JAMES THE SECOND BEQUEATHED TO HIS SON

JAMES,

GENERALLY KNOWN BY THE NAME OF

THE CHEVALIER DE ST. GEORGE

Who married in 1719 Maria Clementina Sobieski, eldest daughter of Prince James Sobieski of Poland the Son of John III. King of Poland; the said Princess was descended from the illustrious House of Newburgh. By this Marriage the Chevalier St. George had two Sons, CHARLES EDWARD (whose history has been so ably given by Mr. Home in his Account of the Rebellion in 1745) and HENRY, who afterwards was created CARDINAL YORK. The CHEVALIER DE ST. GEORGE died at Rome, Dec. 30, 1765.

---

* This valuable Manuscript is bound up in a small volume consisting of 138 pages, and appears to have been written by the same Secretary who had been employed on the Life of JAMES. Her present Majesty, our most gracious . Queen, has made a beautiful Copy of the Original in her own hand.

Macpherson gives the following account of this Manuscript, in his Original Papers, (Vol. 1. p. 77.) " When
James was in Ireland, in 1690, he employed some part
of his time in drawing up Instructions for His Son.
He is very particular in his Advices to him, as to his
private conduct. But he has left only general heads of
what he intended to say about the government of this
Country, and the manner of regulating the several
departments, and filling the great Offices of State. He
gives very sensible directions about the Navy, as the
bulwark and glory of the Kingdom.....The last part
contains only general heads, upon which he intended to
enlarge.....The Instructions are in a thin folio Volume;
and authenticated by an attestation in the Queen's own
hand, declaring them to be a genuine Copy of those
originally written by her husband. They were left by
himself in the Scotch College.

FOR MY SON THE PRINCE OF WALES.

1692.

KINGS being accountable for none of their actions but to God and themselves, ought to be more cautious and circomspect then those who are in lower stations, and as tis the duty of Subjects to pay true allegiance to him, and to obserue his Laws, so a King is bound by his office to haue a fatherly love and care of them ; of which number you being the first, I look on myself as obliged to give you these follow_ ing Advices, which I am the more enduced to do, considering your age, my own, and the present posture of my affairs.

In the first place serve God in all things as becomes a good Christian and a zealous Catholick of the Church of Rome, which is the only true Catholick and Apostolick Church, and let no human consideration of any kind prevaile with you to depart from her; remember always that Kings, Princes and all the great ones of the world, must one day give an account of all their actions before the great tribunal, where every one will be judged according to his doings. Consider you come into the world to serve God Almighty, and not only to please yourself, and that by him Kings reign, and that without his

particular protection nothing you undertake can prosper.
Serve the Lord in the days of thy youth, and so shall it be
well with thee in the Land of the living, begin by times to do
it, defer it not, remember more is expected from persons in
eminent stations then from others, their Example dos much
and will be followed, what so ever it be. Have a great care
of letting any losse liver, or Atheistical persons insinuat themselves into your confidence or pleasurs, none such are to be
trusted, no more then those who make their gold their God,
they will all faile you in the time of trouble, so must all such
as have no principles of Christianity; tis want of sound reason
and judgment, as well as inconsideration which makes men
bad Christians, and knaves between man and man, who so
ever is true to his God, will, nay must be so to his King.
Employ such, rely on such, and let none but such haue your
confidence and favour. And thō tis impossible for a King to
make use of none but such, lett such always have the preference,
haue a care how you trust a Latitudinarian, they are generally
Atheists in their principles and knaves in their nature, as for
Trimmers they are generally Cowards, want sound judgment,
for had they any share of it, they could not be it; in all ages,
and in all Countrys there has still been such pittifull sort (*of*)
creatures, even so long since as Don Henrique King of Castile,
brother to Don Pedro the cruel; you would do well to read
what Don Henrique sayd to his Son on his death bed, towards
good advice.

If it please God to restore me, (which I trust in his goodness
he will do) I may then hope to settle all things so as may make
it easier for you to governe all my Dominions with safty to the
Monarchy, and the satisfaction of all the Subjets, no King can
be happy without his Subject be at ease, and the people
cannot be secure of enjoying their own without the King be
at his ease also, and in a condition to protect them and secure

his own right; therfore preserue your prerogatiue, but disturbe not the Subject in their property, nor conscience, remember the great precept, Do as you would be done to, for that is the law and the Prophets. Be very carefull that none under you oppresse the people, or torment them with vexations, suts, or projects : Remember a King ought to be the Father of his people, and must haue a fatherly tendernesse for them. Live in peace and quiet with all your Neighbours, and know that Kings and Princes may be as great robbers as theeves and pirats, and will receive their punishment for taking any thing unjustly from them, at the great tribunal, and be not carried away by Ambition or thoughts of Glory in this world, to make you forgett that divin precept, and never be persuaded to go about to enlarge your teritorys by unjust acquisitions, be content with what is your own. Endeavour to settle Liberty of Conscience by a Law, t'was a great misfortune to the people as well as to the Crown the passing the habeas corpus Act, since it obliges the Crown to keep a greater force on foot then it needed otherwise to preserve the Government, and encourages disaffected, turbulent, and unquiet spirits to contrive and carry on with more security to themselves their wicked designs, t'was contrived and carried on by the Earle of Shafsbury to that intent.

Be never without a considerable body of Catholick troops without which you cannot be safe, then people will thanke you for Liberty of Conscience. Be not persuaded by any to depart from that; our blessed Saviour whipt people out of the Temple, but I never heard he commanded any should be forced into it: tis a particular grace and favour that God Almighty shews to any, who he enlightens so as to embrasse the true Religion, tis by gentlenesse, instruction, and good example, people are to be gained, and not frighted into it, and I make no doubt if once Liberty of Conscience be well fixed, many conversions will ensue, which is a truth too many of the Protestants are persuaded of, Church of England men as well as others, and so will require more care and dexterity to obtaine it.

Nothing has been more fatal to men and to great men, then the letting themselves go to the forbiden love of Women, of all the Vices it is most bewitching and harder to be master'd if it be not crushed in the very bud, tis a Vice so universall and so followed by young men, that few there are that will give themselves time to consider the danger of it, being led away by ill example, as well as other sugestions and alurements of the divel, the common enemy of mankind; none ought to be more on their gard then you, since it has pleased God to lett you be borne what you are, for the greater men are, the more they are exposed, especially if they enjoy peace, plenty and quiet, and to make one the more on one's garde we haue but to remember that terrible example of the Royal Prophet King David, who thō a man after God's own heart, was no sooner settled in his Kingdom, but he forgott the great things God had done for him, and let himself be overcome by the sight of a beautifull Woman, not only to offend God by adultery, but murther also; may all that haue the misfortune to fall into any of those enormous crimes, Remember and immitat his true and hearty repentance, and do not forgett the punishment and troubles God brought on him in this world, that he might spare him in that to come. I cannot pretend to say more to you then what those good people I haue put to you and your Confessor haue done, to persuade you to live up to the hight of perfection, then that you will remember all the good instructions they haue given you, and that you will continue reading of good books, and avoide Idlenesse as well as ill company, the first lays one open to all sorts of tentations, and for the other tis a miracle if one be not led away by them; but above all abhor and detest prophane and Atheistical talkers and laiers, who do as much as in them lys to overturne Christianity by their turning all Religious things and practices into ridicule, not only by their discourses, but by their way of living, of which last sort God knows there are but too many. What I say and am going to say, is not only grounded on Christianity and sound reason, but on experience also, and thō tis true I had always an aversion to prophane and Atheisticall men, yet I must owne with shame and confusion, I let my self go too much to the love of Women, which but for too long gott the better of me, by ill Example, and my not being enough upon my gard at the first attaques of so dangerous an enemy, and not avoiding, as one ought, the occasions which offer themselves every day, and relying too much on my own strength, having a better opinion of my self then I ought to haue had. I haue paid dear for it, and would haue you avoyd those faults I haue run into, and lett no ill example or natural inclination carry you away against sence and good reason; do but consider that you are a Christian, and the obligations you ly under for so great a blessing, and the recompense you are sure of, if you live like one, and the miserable condition you will be in, if you dy in Sin; begin early to live well, t'will be much easyer to continue in it then to repent after one has fallen, the Church declares the conversion of a Sinner is a greater miracle then the raising one from the dead; and even as to this world, none but such as led a good Christian life, can be at any ease and quiet in it, every Sin carrys its sting with it, nothing can fill the heart of man, or make him truly happy, but the love of God. Riches, honors, voluptious pleasures are but Vanity and Vexation of Spirit, tis the saying of the wisest man that ever was, and that had enjoyd it more then any one either before or after him:

do but weygh and consider well the folly of such as give themselves up to any Vice, they are always uneasy and enjoy neither rest nor quiet, and never compas what they aim at ; a covetous man never thinks he has enough, and never enjoys what he has, grudges himself the very necessarys of life, lays aside all thoughts of honour and conscience to scrape a litle richesse togather, dys as miserable as he lived, and when that fatal hour for him comes, what is he the better for all his painfull or ill gott wealth? What will be his trouble to part with what his heart was so sett upon, and what prospect can he have, when he has not time to repent, and make satisfaction, but hell and damnation?

And now as to your ambitious and proud men, they also enjoy neither rest nor quiet, what pains do they take to become great in the world, to be respected, to be admired, what hardships do not they undergo, nay many times what mean thing leave they not undone, to satisfy that airy fancy of theirs ; and when they haue gained one point, are as far as ever from being at ease, aspire yet to be greater, and at last fall headlong into a dismal Eternity for them, when too late they find their folly and madness, and curse the day they gaue themselves up to ambition.

Who can be more unhappy in this world then a proud man, he is hated and dispised by every body, people take pleasure to vex him, which is easily done by not shewing him that respect and Civility which they shew to others of his rank and quality : I have often seen it done on purpose to make them uneasy, people take pleasure in it to vex them ; Pride and Ambition are the Sins of Lucifer, Pride has been one of the cheef causes of all the heresys haue ever been, and ought to be avoided by all men, and more especially by Princes and great men : Remember one cannot see the face of God without humility. Be carefull that Anger gett not the mastery of you at any time, it offends God, displeases and disobliges men, and for the time it lasts deprives one both of reason and judgment; many great men have been lost by it, for what they Say is not so easily forgotten, and nothing but Christianity, or feare, makes men not resent it; it renders a Prince most miserable, for how can he governe others, that cannot mastere his own passions. Sett not your heart upon good cheer, and avoid all sort of excesse, they ruin one's health, make one unfitt for businesse, even in this world, and if once one accoustums ones self to drink too largely, 'tis hard to leave it off; if it meets with a hott constitution it soon kills them, if a phlegmatickall it besotts them, besides all other inconveniances, few are reclamed that once lett themselves go to it. I hope I need not enlarge on this Subject, since few Princes in these more civilised nations have been guilty of those excesses.

What you ought to arme yourself most against, are the sins of the flesh, Princes and great men being more exposed to those temtations then others, especially if they enjoy peace and quiet; this Vice carrys its sting with it, as well as all others, and with more variety it has that wch is common with the others, which is, that one is never satisfyd, and no sooner has one obtain'd one object, but that very often at the expence of ones health, estate, nay honor and reputation, one desires change, and exposes himself again to all the former inconveniances; those of the greatest quality are not excepted, for if they once let themselves go, and give themselves up to these unlawfull and dangerous affections, they are more expos'd to the sensure of the world then others of a lower sphere, and haue much more to answer for then others for the ill example they give, and are as lyable to all the chagrins of men of less figure, and none more apt to be deceived then themselves, for the most part tis not for themselves, let them realy be never so agreable in their persons or conversations, but for their quality and being in a condition to make great settlements for them, and to satisfy their vanity. I speak knowingly, and nothing but what I haue seen, and has been related to me by undeniable witnesses, and I never knew or heard of but one, who did not one way or other deceive their galant, and am persuaded that she was misled meerly by the love of the person of the Prince which she has shew'd by her quitting the world and going into a Nunnery of a Very strict rule, where she has lived ever since a great example of pennance and mortification; and to make good what I haue Sayd, all the world knows how most of those fine Ladys haue behaved themselves, not only after their galants had quited them for others, but whilst their greatest favour lasted, by having intrigues with others and giving with one hand to their true inclination, what they gott from their abused great man, who was the only person who did not perceive how he was abused, and if they did, were so bewitched and imposed on by their faire Ladys, as not to breake quite with them, nor use them as they deserved. Would but Kings, Princes, and great men, consider and take warning of these kind of dangerous women, they would sooner take a Viper into their bosome, then one of these false and flattring creatures; antient historys are full of dismal relations of what have happen'd to Kings, great men, and whole Nations, on the account of Women; wars, desolation of Countrys, besides privat murthers and blood-shed as well as ruine of privat familys, which latter we in our days have seen happen but too offten: I wish to God that all men of all sorts and conditions would but reflect on what I say on this Subject, and but consider with themselves the ruine and losse of reputation it brings on them with relation to this world, as well as to the other; no gally-slaue is half so miserable as these bewiched men are, for they know what they have to trust to, that they cannot be worse then they are, and haue some rest and quiet; but these haue

none at all, being exposed to all the inconveniences which flow
from their own jealousy, the covetous or haughty temper of their
Mistresses, who seldome or never are satisfyd till the poore man,
(I call him so lett him be never so great) has, if a privat man
ruined his Estate, as well as reputation, and then they squonder
it away, as I have already sayd, and thō Kings and Princes
have more to give, and so are not lyable to one part of it, I
mean of runing out of house and home, and leaving their
Children on the parish, yet they are exposed to all the other
misfortunes of other people, even in being uneasy in their
affairs, and laying themselves open to their privat and publick
enemys, who will not faile to make use of that their weakness;
which we have seen in our days, of which I cannot forbear
giving one instance, for when at a club of some of the mutinous
and antimonarchiccall Lords and Commons, it was proposed
by some to fall upon the Mistressis, the Lord Mordant the
father, sayd, By no means, let us rather erect Status for them,
for were it not for them the King would not run in debt, and
then would haue no need of us: you see how carefull Kings as
well as other People ought to be not to lett themselves be led
away by any Vice; the inconveniencys are great and fatal, for
had not the King your Vncle had that weakness which crept
in him insensibly and by degrees, he had been in all apearance
a great and happy King, and had done great things for the
glory of God and the good of his Subjects; for he had courage,
judgment, witt, and all qualitys fitt for a King, as did more
eminently appear in the latter end of his raigne, by his mastring
and getting the better of the factions which drove so violently
against him and the Monarchy, under the pretence of excluding
me and the fears they affected to have of being over run with
Popery: And to lett you see how litle real pleasure and satisfaction any one has that letts themselves go to unlawfull
pleasures, I do assure you, that the King my Brother was never

two days togather without having some sensible chagrin and displeasur, and, I say it knowingly, never without uneasinesse occasion'd by those Women: tis not proper for his and their sakes to enter into particulars, or els I would do it exactly, by which it would appear how little faith or sence of kindnesse they had for him, who shew'd them such marks of his concerne and of his liberality, nay profusness to them, what care they tooke to enrich themselves, to gett marks of favor, preferment, and other conveniences on their relations, or such as made their Court to them, how unfitt so ever they might be, never consindering any thing but themselves, not caring how they expos'd the King, so they gratifyd their pride, their covetous humor, or revenge on those (who) would not make their court to them, letting themselves be made use on by privat cabals and publick enemys of the Crown, to the great prejudice of the Governement, which was very apparent in the disgrace of the Lord Chancelor Hyde, and the carrying on so far and so violently the Exclusion against me; the first instance proceeded from revenge, and the latter from Love of mony, the factious party having promist the Lady then in power, one hundred thousand pounds if she could prevaile with the King to consent to it, I mean the Exclusion, and truly she did her weake endeavours, for (as she has since owned to me) she beg'd on her knees the King to consent to it; be ware of such kind of Cattel, they never consider but themselves, do not beleeve them, lett them say never so much to the contrary: can one be so weake as to beleeve, that they that have layd all conscience and shame aside, will be true to any, but will be carryd away by inclination or interest; I speake but too knowingly in these matters, having had the misfortune to haue been led away and blinded by such unlawfull pleasurs, for which I aske from the bottome of my soule God Almighty pardon; what I have sayd, and instanced as to the King my Brother, was not only his fate, but will be so to any who haue such unlawfull intrigues, especially, that of never being at ease and quiet, and any one that will be ingenuous cannot help owning it, therefore to be at ease and quiet in this world, as well as to secure a happy Eternity, lett no Vice gett the mastery of you, they carry all their stings with them, the best way to preserue ones self from them, is to keep them at arms end, not to lett ones self go to a begining inclination, and not to rely upon ones own strength, and to avoid all occasions that might by degrees and almost unperceveidly draw one into such dangerous inconviences. Princes must be more on their gard then others, there being in all Courts men that are given that way themselves, who to cover their own Vices and to keep themselves in countenance, will use all their endeavours, all their skill, to engage Princes into such dangerous and unlawfull cources; others in hopes to engraciat themselves with their Princes, or masters, especially such as know themselves so well as to be sensible they want merite to advance their fortune by any lawfull ways, will make use of such mean and pitifull ones of raising themselves, not cayring what the world thinks of them so they gaine their point. Abhor such sad wretches and never trust them, for they who have so litle Christianity and have such meane soules, will for a litle gaine sell you and betray you; do not wonder if I enlarge so much on this Subject, having been but too much led away by it myself, having found by sad experience all what I have Sayd on it to be true, and I cannot but remember and take notice of what one of our English Historians obserues and remarkes concerning Henry 2^d, That he was punished for his sin of incontinancy, to which he was much adicted, by the rebellion of all his four Sons, who in their severall turns joyned with the factions and took armes against him, thō at last returned to their duty : I cannot help observing also, that others of our Kings have been severly punished by

God Almighty for the same sins in their posterity, namely
Edward 4, and Henry 8, both the Sons of the first were mur-
thred by their Vncle Richard 3, and the Crown taken from
that branch of the Royal family and given to that of his mortal
enemy ; and for Henry. 8, who took such pains as well as
indirect and unchristian ways to have successors, even to gett
an Act of Parliam^t past, under coulour of which he declared a
Natural Son of his, his Heir, and did all that in him lay, to
exclud his Sisters, the Queen of Scots Children, from inheriting
in their turne the Crown of Eng^d ; but the divine Providence
order'd it other ways, took away his Natural Son, and thō his
three remaining Children succeeded him, yet they all dyed
without Children, and the Kingdom cam to the line of Scotland.
The same obseruation could be made of other Kingdoms, of
which I shall name only Henry the 2^d of France, who had four
Sons who grew up to men's Estate, three of which successively
had the Crowne, and all died without legitimat Children, as
did the other brother the Duke of Alenson, and with them
ended the family of Valois, and the Crown came to those of
Bourbon, in the person of my Grand Father Henry ye 4 :
and to come to what I haue seen myself, and ought to waigh
very much with you, the late King my Brother had the misfortune to be much adicted to that fatal Vice, had Children by all
his owned Mistresses and none by the Queen, besides which he
had the mortification to haue the Duke of Montmouth, who he
beleeved to be his Son (thō all the knowing world as well as
myself had many convincing reasons to thinke the contrary,
and that he was Rob: Sidneys) fly in his face and joyne with
the Earle of Shafsbury and the factious party, in the design
they had to sease his person and rise in Rebellion against him,
thō at the same time he shew'd him all the tenderness of a
Father, and the kindness of a Friend, doing things for him
which ought to haue made him make a better returne then he

did: I must now speak as to myself, as a great punishment
God inflicts on such as haue had the misfortune to be led away
by the unlawfull love of Women, even in this world, to reclame
them and serue for an example and warning to all the world;
I praise his divine goodness for all the mortifications and
punishments he has been pleased out of his infinit mearcy to
inflict on me, which had he not been pleased to repeat offten,
I haue but too much reason to apprehend I should not haue
been awaked out of the leathergy and insensibility I was in,
and that even from the very time of the Restoration, by the
losse of a Brother, and a Sister within the very first year, after
which hardly a year past without some sensible mortification
as losse of Children, Mother, Wife, Sister, or some of the best
of my friends, and last of all, the letting me be driven out of
my three Kingdoms by the means and contrivance of a Son in
law, as well as Nephew, and my two Daughters; for all which
I praise God, and look on myself as much happyer then ever
I was in all my life, having that quiet of mind and inward
peace which cannot be understood, or enjoyd, but by such
as haue an intire resignation for the will of God, Christian
humility, a hearty repentance for sins past, and such a loue
of God, as has made one resolue by the help of his grace never
to offend his divine goodness.

There is another great inconvenience (which I think I have
not yet mention'd) which attends Kings and great men having
of Mistresses, which is, the Children they haue by those faire
Ladys, who will never be at quiet till they are owned, have
great titles given them, which consequently require great
establishments, and this is prest on by their relations, friends,
and most commonly even by flattering Ministers who are at
the head of affairs, to fixe their credit, or for some by ends of
their own; for the most part, those gentlemen as well
Mistresses seldome consider the true interest of their Masters,

but sacrifise that to enrich or preserve themselves when in
danger to be fallen on by Parliament, or some great com-
petitor, of wch I could give many instances of my own knowledge; then when they (the Children) grow up to be Men and
Women, they (the Men) are never satisfyd, except they haue
the places of the greatest honor or profit, according to what
they turne themselves to, and even then, many times are not
easy, being apt to be puffed and blown up by losse livers and
needy men that make their Court to them, for their privat
ends, without considering them in the least, and all this dos
not only make the unfortunat Prince their Father uneasy on
that account, but disatisfys many great and deserving men,
since it takes almost from them the hops of being advanced,
and finding their accounts under the government; besides
this, tis very chargeable and expencive, and hard for to find
out fonds and establishments such as are fitt to be given, when
once owned, and may be not equal to what they expect: I
am sure it has been very hard, and inconvenient for a King
of England, and considering the condition of the Crown and
the Constitution of the Government must always be so; the
Women kind of them also are no less troublesome and expen-
sive, great portions must be found for them, and offten
people of no great merit are advanced to great places, or made
Peers to marry them, grow high and insolent driven on by
their own ambition or covetousness, or their wives, which
draws on many Troubles, Vexations, and Inconveniences.

And now I must give you warning not to lett yourself at
any time be carryed away by heat of youth, ambition, or
flattring interest to embarke yourself in an offensive War,
none of which can be justifyd by Christianity or Morality;
Kings and Princes can no more justify their taking from their
neighbours, but by way of reprisal, Towns or Provinces, then

theeves or highway men their unlawfull gaines. Remember that Maxime of Chris:, That one must not do ill, that good may follow, and the other, Be content with what is your own, which dos not hinder Kings and States from preserving and defending what is justly theirs by taking arms and repelling force by force, they owe that to themselves and to their Subjects, but tis a terrible thing to begin an unjust War. Consider the consequences of it, both as to this world and the next, no forgivenesse without restitution; besides what desolation dos it not bring upon whole Kingdoms and Pro_vinces, and thō Armys that are well payd, and under good discipline may be hindred from committing great disorders even in an Enemys Country, yett what devastations dos it not cause in an active War, which cannot be avoyded, to the ruine of thousands of poor people; and besides consciencious reasons in point of government, and police, a King of England ought to be more cautious then any others, I mean a Lawfull one, (for Vsurpers may well take other measures to support their tirany, minding as litle the good of the Nation, as they do Christianity) since he must haue the help of his Parliament to maintaine and carry it on, and if once he run in debt, runs great hazard of his Crown, by having things imposed on him, tending to the ruine of the Monarchy, of which there have been too many instances in all times, and fatal ones since I came into the world.

For the same reason a King of England ought to be carefull to live within his Reveneu, and not to lett himself be carryd away to exceede his income, by flatterers or ill Ministers, who designedly would run one in debt to betray him to a Parli': besides which, not to have need of a Parliam' do all things that are truly popular, lett not your Ministers or those in your pay, whether Civil or Military, opress or domineir over their fellow subjects, or make use of your authority, or the power put into their hands by you, to do it, and where you find any of them failing, lay them aside and punish them yourself, that ill men, and a republican spirit in a Parliament may not haue a pretence to teare them from you, and by that means weaken your power and discourage honest men from serving you faithfully; and that you may not be imposed on by Flatterers on the one side, nor by those who would lessen the power and authority of the Crown, make it one of your businesses to know the true Constitution of the Government, that you may keep yourself as well as the Parliament within its true bounds. In the next place study the Trade of the Nation, and encourage it by all lawfull means, tis that which will make you at ease at home and considerable abroad, and preserve the Mastery of the Sea, for without that England cannot be safe.

As to our Antient Kingdom of Scotland, take all care to let no alterations be made in the Government of that Kingdom, they will stand by the Crown, and the Crown must stand by them, for thō there has been Rebellions and Reuolutions, as well as in other Countrys, the body of the Nobility and Gentry, and the Gen: of the Commons are very Loyal and Monarkical especially the Com: be (by) North Forth and all the Highlanders, except the Cambells; the rest of Scotland being the only place where there are numbers amongst the Commons of ridged Presbyterians, and Enthusiasts and feild Conventiclers, the first of which are the most dangerous, and will be allways bitter enemys to the Monárky and so ought to be observed, and kept out of any share of the Government; the others, thō now and then troublesome, are lesse to be feared, hardly a Gentleman amongst them, and of so extravagant principles as they can never agree amongst themselves: Trust none in the Governement but those of the Antient Loyal

familys that haue had no taint of Presb: or accoustum'd to
Rebell, be Kind to the Highlanders especially to those Clans
who haue allways stuck to the Crowne, lett their Cheef dependance be on the Crown, without doing wrong to such of the
Nobility as have interest in those parts ; tis the true interest of
the Crown to keep that Kingdom seperat from England, and
to be governed by their own Laws and constitutions, look on
any who should propose thō under some spetious pretence,
the uniting of the two Kingdoms, to be weake men, bribed by
some privat concerne, or as enemys to the Monarky ; Scotland
as it is, being a great Support to it, which could be of none if
united, which is to say, swallow'd up by England, as it was
in Cromwell's time. Great care must be taken, that no one
great man or family gett the government so into their hands,
as to tiranise over the rest of their Country men, they being
naturaly inclined to it; to avoyd that, there must always be
two Secretarys of State, one to reside at Court and the other
in Scot^d, and to releve one another every six or twelve months,
and that the Secretarys may not engrose all the power into
their hand (which they have been but too apt to) to have two
or three of the Councell to reside by turns also at London, and
to haue sett Councell days for the affairs of that Kingdom,
that you may not only heare, from one hand, what passes in
that Country. The constitutions of the Parliament there are
very good, and ought not to be altred, especially that of the
Lords of the Articles, for by that means a Parliament can do
no great harme, and I haue obserued, that those who had a
mind to be troublesome and to have it in their power to be so,
endeavour'd to take that great prerogatiue from the Crown.
As to the Highlands, send and encourage Missionnairs amongst
them and establish Scholes there, that they may haue of their
Country men to be their Pasturs, and not be beholding only to

4 M 2

the Irish, for to be Supplyd with Preists, and make some settlement on the Scots College at Paris for the breeding up young men to be fittly qualifyd for that Mission, tis what you are bound to do both as a good Christian and a King.

As to Ireland, tis the interest of the Crown to improve that Kingdom as well as the rest of their Dominions, all that may be, and to order it so as their cheef dependance may be in the Crown, this will please the old natives of whom especial care must be taken, as well for justice sake, as for their Loyalty and great sufferings in the late war, and to keep up a Catholick interest there, that at least in one of the Kingdoms there may be a superiority of those of that persuasion, and to make them the more considerable, great care must be taken to civilise the antient familys, by having the Sons of the Cheef of them bred up in England, even at the charge of the Crown, when they have not where with all out of their own estates to do it, by which means they will have greater dependance on the Crown, and by degrees be weaned from their natural hatred against the English, be more civilised, and learne to improve their Estats, by making plantations and improuing their Land as the English and Scots have done wheresoever they haue settled; this with the charge the Crown should be at in setting up Scholes, to teach the Children of the old Natives English, would by degrees weare out the Irish language, which would be for the advantage of the body of the Inhabitants, whether new or old, and would contribut much to lessen the animositys that are amongst them.

As to the Catholick Clergy, great care should be taken to fill the Dignitys with able, learned, and men of exemplary lives, and to break off that evil which has been too much practised, of giving orders to young men and then sending them abroad to study; 'twould not be amisse to make some few of the English Clergy Bishops there, and to sett up Colleges that the youth might not be obliged to be sent to study beyond Sea.

As to the Civil government the old practice is very good and needs not be changed in any material point, but that of having Cath: in imployments there, being so great partiality amongst the Nations that the Government as well as people in generall should suffer by it, for the Vlster and Munster men cannot endure one another, and the Macks and O', do not love the Lenster men, they (generally speaking) being of the old English familys which first conquered that Kingdom and planted there, and have yet lesse kindnesse for such as have gone over thether since; and thō for the good of Trade and improvement of that Kingdom the English intrest must be suported, yett there must be great care taken not to trust them too far, they being generally ill principlel'd, and Republicans, and none but trusty men ought to be put into the garrisons, which need be but few, as Kingsale, Duncannon, Galloway, London Dery, Athlone, and Charlemont, which last place should be enlarged to serue for magazine for all the North.

Tis not safe to lett any of the Natives of Ireland be Governors of these aboue named places, nor to have any troops in them but English, Scots, or Strangers, not to tempt the natives to Rebelle, they being of a very uncertain temper, and easily led by their Cheefs and Clergy, and beare with great impatience the English yoak, and one cannot beat it into their heads, that Severall of the O': and Macks, who were forfited for Rebelling in King JAMES the firsts time, and before, ought to be keept out of their Estats, and will allways be ready to rise in arms against the English, and endeavour to bring in Strangers to support them; and to please the Nobility and gentry and Cheef of Clans twill be necessary to have Several Regiments of the Natives, but let them Serue in England, Scot^d: and els where: No Natiue to be Lord Lieu^t nor no

10

Englishman that has an Estate in that Kingdom, or great
relations there, to be changed every three yeares, to buy no
land there.

Be very carefull in the choice of your cheef Ministers, tis of
the last concern to you, it being impossible for a Prince to do
all himself, they must not only be men of good Sence, and
sound judgment, but of great probity and well founded as to
Christianity, and that it appear by their way of living; for a
losse liver, or one that by his actions or discourses shews himself prophane, or Atheisticaly inclin'd, never trust or rely on,
for how can you expect that those that fly in God Almighty's
face every day, can be thorowly true to their King, when what
they think thuarts their worldly interest is not consistant with
their Loyalty? I speak knowingly of this, and by experience,
and never knew but one of the late King my Brother's
Ministers, namely the Ld Clifford, that serued him throwgh-out
faithfully, and without reproche; Let them see you haue
intire trust and confidence in them, but let them not impose
upon you, the favors and graces you do, let those on whom
you bestow them, be Sensible they owe them wholy to yourself,
and not to others, or their owne importunity; Let your eares
be open to such as you know to be good men, that you may
be truly inform'd of all truths, which others might not be
willing you should be informed of; you ought to take the
same care in the choise of your domestick Servants, and such
as you employ in any place of trust, for besides the reasons
already given, twill make you beloved by all good men, and
encourage others to lead more Christian lives, or at least hinder
them from giving publick scandal, when they see prophane and
lose-livers discountenanced; and let not any ones being a
Catholick, exempt him from these rules, for I may truly say
they are more inexcusable then most Protestants, having
generally been better instructed, and it behoues you, as well as

them, (I mean Catholicks) to be more carfull and circomspect in all your actions, you being to governe, and they living amongst Protestants, who will remarke and censure the least slip you or any of our persuasion makes, and object that tis other reasons more then true conviction, that makes us stick to and support our holy Religion; and how can we convince them, that ours is the true Faith, which we have received from our blessed Savior and his Apostles, better then by taking up his Crosse and following their examples, and endeavouring to live up to the height of perfection, not to neglect any thing that may contribut to it that is consistant with one's calling. I haue given you good Governors and Preceptors, that you may be well instructed both as to Christianity and morality, which in effect agree very well together, with this diference, that whosoever is a good Christian must be a good moral man, but the same consequence dos not allways follow morality; and when it shall please God to bring you to full age of discretion, do not forget the good Instructions you haue received.

To be carefull in the choise of Officers of State and all your family, even of those whose places are not esteemed as formerly, by the abuse of putting in mean people for mony, favor, or partiality

As Esquires of the body.
Gentlemen of the privy Chamber.
Gentlemen Hushers both of the Privy Chamber and Presence and Quarter Wayters.
Gentlemen Pensionarys.
Yeamen of the Garde.

The old method was very good which was not broke till the King my Brother's Restoration.

CIVIL OFFICES

TO BE REGULATED.

Secretary of State.
Chamberland of the Household.
Groome of the Stool.
Master of the Horse.
Treasury, Atturny and Solicitor.

MILITARY EMPLOYMENTS.

Admiral.
General Officers of the Land forces.
Master of the Ordinance.
Commissary General of the Musters.

TREASURY.

Never but in Comission it being too great for any one man; it were good to haue one of the number of Commissionarys (which should be but five) to be one that has been Com: of the Custums.

Query about Fees.

The Secretary to be Still named by the King, the rest as now

SECRETARYS OF STATE.

To be four in number,
One for Forrain affairs.
One for Home affairs.
One for the War.
One for the Navy.
None to take Fees.

Each of their cheef Clarks to be named by the King to haue Warrants to be So, and Salarys, and to remain in their places thō the Secretary shall chance to dy or be removed, that books of entrys remaine in the Office, That at the end of every year, the Secretary take care that authentick copys of Treatys, publick Letters and such other papers as need to be lodged in the paper office, be Sent there. Query; whether necessary, if the former method be observed, to haue such paper Office.

Whether fees, or none at all.

What Salarys to give the Secretarys of State, their Clarks and under Clarks.

No Settled mony for intelligence.

To Settle a way how that shall be done.

No Offices to be Sowld upon Sever penaltys, but for decencys Sake to adresse to the Cheef Officer for him to propose him to the King. If such Officer do not do it, such pretender may adresse by any freind, or straight to the King by petition. The Cheef Officer upon any vacancy to advertice the King of it, and know his pleasur.

The perquisits clamed by ill coustume by the Chamberland of the Household, Master of the Horse, or other great Officers either above or below Stairs, be layd aside, and the same method used as by the Admiral, who till the late King's time enjoyd it.

The Atturny and Solicitor General not to plead for any but the King, to haue good Salarys.

Some ingenious young Lawyers to haue pensions from the Crowne to apply themselves to Study the prerogative, and such, if able, advanced to the above named places.

A Chancellor no Lawier, a Nobleman, or Bishop.

Commissioners of the Treasury five, three Church of Eng^d one Catholick, and one dissenter.

No Admiral nor Commissionary of the Admirality.

Cabinet * Councell, two Secretarys of State, Secretary of War, of Admirality, first Commissioner of Treasury, and two others.

Secretarys of State, one of them Catholick the other Protestant, Secretary War Catholick, Secretary of the Navy Protestant.

Lord Lieutenants to haue Salarys, good Dep: Lieutenants.

Army, Household, Bed Camber, most Catholicks.

Embassadors and no Envoyes, Catholicks and Protestants.

As many Catholicks as can be in the Army, some Ch: of Eng: and Dissenters.

---

* This word, by an *s* at the end, would seem to have been intended for Counsellors. EDITOR.

THE WILL

OF

JAMES THE SECOND.

1688.

(From the Stuart MSS. in Carlton House Library.)

———————

JAMES R.

IN THE NAME OF GOD AMEN WEE JAMES the Second
by the Grace of God of England Scotland France and
Ireland King Defender of the Faith &c* Seriously Considering
the great incertainty of Humaine Life & that Wee as all other
Men are subject to Mortality Being therefore Desirous to
Compose & settle the Affaires of Our State against the time
when it shall please Almighty God to call Us from this tran-
sitory Life Doe make and Ordaine Our Last Will & Testament
in Manner following (that is to say) FIRST Wee resigne Our
Soul unto Almighty God being Stedfastly assured of Eternall
Salvation through the Meritts & Intercession of Our Blessed
Saviour Jesus Christ. Our Body Wee committ to the Earth
And It is Our Will That the same be privately Interred in
Our Royall Chappell called Henry the Seaventh's Chappell
adjoyning to Our Collegiate Church of S¹ Peters Westmʳ AND
WHEREAS Wee when Duke of Yorke by Indentures of Lease

& Release the Lease bearing date on or about the six &
twentieth day of September in the one. & thirtieth yeare of the
Reigne of Our late Dearest Brother King CHARLES the Second
& the Release bearing date on or about the day next after &
afterwards Wee by Our Letters Pattents bearing date on or
about the eight & twentieth day of August in the first yeare
of Our Reigne & also by other Letters Pattents bearing
date on or about the eight & twentieth day of August aforesaid
& also by other Letters Pattents bearing date on or about the
third day of September in the Second yeare of Our Reigne
have made a Provision for Our Intirely beloved Wife &
Royall Consort QUEENE MARY for the Support & Main-
teinance of Her Royall State & Dignity as by the said
Indentures & several Letters Pattents may at large appeare
Wee doe in all things hereby Ratifye Establish & Confirme the
Same & every of them & all & every the Grants Clauses
Powers Matters & things in them or any of them contained
AND WHEREAS imediately upon Our Decease the Imperiall
Crowne of the Realmes of England Scotland & Ireland with
Our Title of France & all the Dominions Territories Dignities
Honours Preheminences Prerogatives Authorities & Juris-
dictions to the same annexed or belonging will by Inherent
Birthright & Lawfull Succession descend & come to Our Most
Deare Sonn PRINCE JAMES Wee doe therefore give & Devise
unto Him his Heires & Successors All & singular Our
Honours Seigniorys Dominions Territories Mannors Lands
Tenements Forts Castles Possessions & Hereditaments with
their & every of their appurtenances whatsoever & where-
soever SAVING the aforesaid Interests of Our said Dearest
Consort abovementioned AND Wee doe also Give & bequeath
unto Our said Deare Sonn All Our Plate Householdstuffe
Horses Armes Artillery Ordnance Ammunition Shipps & all

things & Implements to them belonging & all other Our
Furniture of Warr And also all Our Mony & Jewells of the
Crowne & all other Our Personall Estate whatsoever SAVING
such part & portions thereof as shall be otherwise disposed of
by this Our last Will & Testament Charging & Commanding
him to be ordered & ruled by Our said Dearest Consort in
manner hereafter appointed AND Wee doe Ordaine &
Constitute Our said Dearest Consort Sole Executrix of this
Our last Will & Testament AND Wee farther bequeath unto
Our said Dearest Consort for her own proper Use all such
Jewells Plate Furniture Householdstuffe Coaches Horses &
other Goods wch shall be in her Custody Use or Service as
belonging unto Her at the time of Our Decease AND Wee
Will Ordaine & Appointe that Our said Dearest Consort have
the Sole Governance Tuition & Guardianshipp of Our said
Deare Sonn till he shall have fully compleated the fourteenth
yeare of his Age Doing nevertheless all things as under Him
and in His Name Notwithstanding His Infancy or the Tuition
aforesaid AND FURTHERMORE for the especiall Trust &
Confidence w^{cb} Wee have in His Royall Higness Prince
George of Denmark George Lord Jeffreys Our Chancellor of
England Henry Lord Arundell of Wardour Lord Privy Seale
Christopher Duke of Albemarle Henry Duke of Newcastle
Henry Duke of Beaufort Wm Duke of Hamilton Wm Duke
of Queensberry Wm Lord Marquess of Powis Robert Earle
of Lindsey Lord Great Chamberlaine of England John Earle
of Mulgrave Ld Chamberlaine of Our Household Aubrey
Earle of Oxford Theophilus Earle of Huntingdon Henry
Earle of Peterborow Philip Earle of Chesterfeild Henry Earle
of Clarendon John Earle of Bathe Wm Earle of Craven George
Earle of Berkley Daniell Earle of Nottingham Laurence
Earle of Rochester Alexander Earle of Moray James Earle

of Perth Charles Earle of Middleton Our Principall Secretary
of State John Earle of Melfort Roger Earle of Castlemain
Richard Earle of Tirconnel Thomas Viscount Fauconberg
Richard Viscount Preston One of Our Principall Secretaries
of State Nathaniell' Ld Bishop of Durham John Lord
Bellasys George Lord Dartmouth Sidney Lord Godolphin
Henry Lord Dover Sr John Ernle Kn^t Chancellor of Our
Exchequer Sr John Trevor Kn^t Master of the Rolls Sr Edward
Herbert Kn^t Ld Cheife Justice of Our Court of Common Pleas
Sr Thomas Strickland Kn^t Sr Nicholas Butler Kn^t Christopher
Vane Esqr & Silus Titus Esqr Wee Will That they & every
of them shall be of Councell for the aiding of Our Dearest
Consort when they or any of them shall be thereunto by Her
called & shall continue in the severall Offices Stations &
Imployments wch they shall respectively hold or enjoy at the
time of Our Decease untill they or any of them be removed
by Our said Dearest Consort Exhorting them for the singular
Trust & especiall Confidence wch Wee have & ever had in them
to have a due & diligent Eye perfect Zeal Love & Affection
to the Hono^r Surety Estate & Dignity of Our said Sonn &
the good State & Prosperity of these Our Realmes AND Wee
doe hereby impower Our said Deare Consort to remove or
change the said Counsellors & Officers or any of them &
thereupon to place & constitute others in their Stead as to
Her shall seeme most fitt & expedient AND FINALLY Wee
doe hereby Revoke all other Wills & Testaments by Us at
any time heretofore made & doe declare & publish this
present Writing to be Our last Will & Testament WILLING
& REQUIRING that the same be observed & taken accordingly IN WITNESS Whereof Wee have signed the Same
with our own Hand in Our Palace of Whitehall this present
the seventeenth day of November In the yeare of Our

11

Lord God 1688 And of Our Reigne the fourth, The Persons being present & called to witness the same who have subscribed their Names in Testimony thereof.

* JAMES R.

Jeffreys C.

Arundell C. P. S.   Pepys.   W^m. Bridgeman.

Melfort.   William Blathwayt †.

Belasys.   Preston.

Godolphin.

---

* The King's name at the beginning, as well as at the end of this Will, is in his own hand. EDITOR.

† A gentleman of the name of Blathwait is mentioned (Vol. 2. p. 55.) in the debate which took place in the House of Commons on the King's Speech, Nov. 9, 1685.

APPENDIX.

No. I.

" ..... and by such an open act of Rebellion begun by him, he would make himself guilty of all the evills and blood-shed that might therupon insue." (*Life of James the Second, Vol.* 1. *p.* 3.)

EXTRACT

FROM THE

ΕΙΚΩΝ ΒΑΣΙΛΙΚΉ * OF CHARLES I.

" Alii diutius Imperium tenuerunt; nemo tam fortiter reliquerit."
(*Tacit. Histor.* Lib. 2. C. 47.)

UPON His MAJESTIES *repulse at* HULL, *and the fates of the* HOTHAMS.

MY repulse at *Hull* seemed at the first view an act of so rude Disloyalty, that my greatest Enemies had scarce confidence enough to abett or own it : It was the first overt Essay to be made how patiently I could bear the Loss of my Kingdoms.

---

* In the copy before me of this work my learned relation, the Rev. *William Clarke* of Chichester, had inserted the following testimony of Rapin with an additional remark : " One of the most considerable writings of those days was Εικων Βασιλικη or THE KING'S PORTRAITURE, published in 1649. It is scarce to be doubted that Charles I. was himself the Author. He undertakes in this Work

God knows, it affected Me more with shame and sorrow for others, than with Anger for My self: nor did the Affront done to Me trouble Me so much as their Sin, which admitted no colour or excuse.

I was resolved how to bear this and much more with Patience: But I foresaw they could hardly contain themselves within the compass of this one unworthy act, who had effrontery enough to commit or countenance it. This was but the hand of that Cloud which was soon after to overspread the whole Kingdom, and cast all into Disorder and darkness.

For 'tis among the wicked Maximes of bold and disloyal undertakers, That bad actions must alwaies be seconded with worse, and rather not be begun, than not carried on; for they think the retreat more dangerous than the assault, and hate Repentance more than perseverance in a Fault.

This gave Me to see clearly through all the pious disguises and soft palliations of some men; whose words were sometime smoother than oyl, but now I saw they would prove very Swords.

Against which I having (as yet) no defence but that of a good Conscience, thought it my best policy, with Patience to bear what I could not remedy. And in this (I thank God) I had the better of *Hotham*, that no disdain or emotion of Passion transported Me, by the indignity of his carriage, to do or say any thing unbeseeming My self, or unsuitable to that temper which in greatest Injuries, I think, best becomes a Christian, as coming nearest to the great example of Christ.

---

to vindicate himself upon all the Articles laid to his Charge. It is properly an Abstract of the Reasons he had before published in several Papers printed by his Order, or addressed to both Houses of Parliament." *Rapin's Hist. of England, Pref. to Lib.* xx. *Considerat. on Authors.*

" This," adds my Grandfather, " is the Testimony of a Person no way prejudiced in Favour of Charles I., and therefore the Fact (as is here said) is scarce to be doubted. — If it should happen to be reckoned doubtful, see Dr Wagstaff's Vindication of the Εικων Βασιλικη. 4to. Lond. 1711.

To this may be subjoined another Note which a friend has communicated: " There is a very strong evidence of this Book having been written by the King, in one of the Four Tracts which were published in 1702 beginning with Sir Thomas Herbert's Memoirs. The MS. was obtained from Fairfax, and the Prayers were in CHARLES'S own handwriting." EDITOR.

And indeed I desire always more to remember I am a Christian than a King: for what the Majesty of the one might justly abhor, the Charity of the other is willing to bear; what the height of a King tempteth to revenge, the humility of a Christian teacheth to forgive. Keeping in compass all those impotent Passions, whose excess injures a man more than his greatest enemies can: for these give their Malice a full impression on our Souls, which otherways cannot reach very far, nor do us much hurt.

I cannot but observe how God not long after so pleaded and avenged my Cause in the eye of the world, that the most wilfully blind cannot avoid the displeasure to see it, and with some remorse and fear to own it as a notable stroke, and prediction of Divine Vengeance.

For Sir *John Hotham*, unreproached, unthreatned, uncursed by any language or secret imprecation of Mine, only blasted with the Conscience of his own Wickedness, and falling from one Inconstancy to another, not long after pays his own and his eldest Sons heads as forfeitures of their Disloyalty, to those men from whom surely he might have expected another reward than thus to divide their Heads from their bodies, whose Hearts with them were divided from their *KING*.

Nor is it strange, that they who imployed them at first in so high a service and so successful to them, should not find mercy enough to forgive him who had so much premerited of them: For Apostasy unto Loyalty some men account the most unpardonable sin.

Nor did a solitary Vengeance serve the turn; the cutting off one Head in a Family is not enough to expiate the affront done to the Head of the Common-weal: The eldest Son must be involved in the punishment, as he was infected with the sin of the Father against the Father of his Country: Root and Branch God cuts off in one day.

These observations are obvious to every fancy. God knows, I was so far from rejoycing in the *Hothams* ruine, (though it were such as was able to give the greatest thirst for revenge a full draught, being executed by them who first employed him against Me) that I so far pitied him, as I thought he at first acted more against the light of his Conscience than I hope many other men do in the same Cause.

For he was never thought to be of that superstitious sowrness which some men pretend to in matters of Religion; which so darkens their

Judgment, that they cannot see any thing of Sin and Rebellion in those means they use, with intents to reform to their Models, of what they call Religion, who think all is gold of Piety which doth but glister with a shew of Zeal and fervency.

Sir *John Hotham* was (I think) a man of another temper, and so most liable to those down-right temptations of Ambition, which have no cloak or cheat of Religion to impose upon themselves or others.

That which makes Me more pity him is, that after he began to have some inclinations towards a repentance for his sin and reparation of his Duty to Me, he should be so unhappy as to fall into the hands of their Justice, and not My Mercy, who could as willingly have forgiven him as he could have asked that favour of Me.

For I think Clemency a debt which we ought to pay to those that crave it, when we have cause to believe they would not after abuse it; since God himself suffers us not to pay any thing for his Mercy, but only Prayers and Praises.

Poor Gentleman, he is now become a notable monument of unprosperous Disloyalty, teaching the world by so sad and unfortunate a spectacle, That the rude carriage of a Subject towards his Soveraign carries always its own Vengeance as an unseparable shadow with it; and those oft prove the most fatal and implacable Executioners of it, who were the first Imployers in the service.

After-times will dispute it, whether *Hotham* were more infamous at *Hull* or at *Tower hill*: though 'tis certain that no punishment so stains a man's Honour, as wilful perpetrations of unworthy actions; which besides the conscience of the sin, brand with most indeleble characters of infamy the name and memory to Posterity, who not engaged in the Factions of the times, have the most impartial reflections on the actions.

BUT Thou, O Lord, who hast in so remarkable a way avenged thy Servant, suffer Me not to take any secret pleasure in it; for as his death hath satisfied the Injury he did to Me, so let Me not by it gratifie any Passion in Me, lest I make thy vengeance to be mine, and consider the affront against Me more than the sin against Thee.

Thou indeed, without any desire or endeavour of Mine, hast made his mischief to return on his own head, and his violent dealing to come down on his own pate.

Thou hast pleaded my Cause, even before the sons of men, and taken the matter into thine own hands : That men may know it was thy work, and see that Thou, Lord, hast done it.

I do not, I dare not say, So let mine Enemies perish, O Lord : yea, Lord, rather give them Repentance, Pardon and impunity, if it be thy blessed will.

Let not Thy Justice prevent the objects and opportunities of My Mercy : yea, let them live and amend who have most offended Me in so high a nature ; that I may have those to forgive, who bear most proportion in their offences to those trespasses against thy Majesty, which I hope thy Mercy hath forgiven Me.

Lord, lay not their sins (who yet live) to their charge for condemnation, but to their Consciences for amendment : Let the lightning of this thunderbolt, which hath been so severe a punishment to one, be a terror to all.

Discover to them their sin, who know not they have done amiss ; and scare them from their sin, that sin of malicious wickedness.

That preventing thy Judgments by their true Repentance, they may escape the strokes of thine eternal Vengeance.

And do Thou, O Lord, establish the Throne of thy Servant in mercy and truth meeting together : let my Crown ever flourish in righteousness and peace kissing each other.

Hear my Prayer, O Lord, who hast taught us to pray for, to do good to, and to love our Enemies for thy sake, who hast prevented us with offertures of thy love even when we were thine enemies, and hast sent thy Son Jesus Christ to dye for us when we were disposed to crucifie him.

APPENDIX, No. II.

THE ADVICE

WHICH

CHARLES I. BEQUEATHED TO HIS SON CHARLES II.

BONA AGERE, ET MALA PATI, REGIUM EST.

(*From the* Ἐικων Βασιλικη. *Page* 221.)

To the PRINCE OF WALES.

SON, if these Papers, with some others, wherein I have set down
the private reflections of my Conscience, and my most impartial
thoughts touching the chief passages which have been most remarkable
or disputed in my late Troubles, come to Your hands, to whom they
are chiefly design'd, they may be so far useful to You as to state
your Judgment aright in what hath passed; whereof a Pious is the
best use can be made: and they may also give You some directions,
how to remedy the present Distempers, and prevent (if God will) the
like for time to come.

It is some kind of deceiving and lessening the injury of my long
Restraint, when I find my leisure and Solitude have produced something worthy of My self and useful to You; that neither You nor any
other may hereafter measure my Cause by the Success, nor my Judgment of things by my Misfortunes: which I count the greater by far,
because they have so far lighted upon You, and some others, whom I
have most cause to love as well as My self, and of whose unmerited
Sufferings I have a greater sense than of Mine own.

But this advantage of Wisdom You have above most Princes, that
You have begun, and now spent some years of Discretion in the

experience of Troubles and exercise of Patience; wherein Piety, and all Vertues, both Moral and Political, are commonly better planted to a thriving, as Trees set in Winter, than in the warmth and serenity of times, or amidst those Delights which usually attend Princes Courts in times of Peace and Plenty; which are prone either to root up all Plants of true Vertue and Honor, or to be contented only with some Leaves and withering Formalities of them, without any real Fruits, such as tend to the Publick good, for which Princes should always remember they are born and by Providence designed.

The evidence of which different Education the holy Writ affords us in the contemplation of *David* and *Rehoboam :* the one prepared by many Afflictions for a flourishing Kingdom; the other softned by the unparallel'd prosperity of *Solomon's* Court, and so corrupted, to the great diminution both for Peace, Honor and Kingdom, by those Flatteries which are as unseparable from prosperous Princes as Flies are from Fruit in Summer, whom Adversity, like cold weather, drives away.

I had rather You should be *Charles le Bon* than *le Grand*, Good than Great; I hope God hath designed You to be both, having so early put You into that exercise of his Graces and Gifts bestowed upon You, which may best weed out all vitious inclinations, and dispose You to those Princely Endowments and Employments which will most gain the love and intend the welfare of those over whom God shall place You.

With God I would have You begin and end, who is King of Kings, the Soveraign Disposer of the Kingdoms of the World, who pulleth down one and setteth up another.

The best Government and highest Soveraignty You can attain to is, to be subject to Him, that the Scepter of his Word and Spirit may rule in your Heart.

The true Glory of Princes consists in advancing God's Glory, in the maintenance of true Religion and the Churches good; also in the dispensation of Civil Power with Justice and Honor to the publick Peace.

Piety will make you prosperous; at least it will keep You from being miserable : nor is he much a loser that loseth all, yet saveth his own Soul at last.

To which center of true Happiness, God (I trust) hath and will graciously direct all these black lines of Affliction which he hath been pleased to draw on Me, and by which he hath (I hope) drawn Me nearer to Himself. You have already tasted of that Cup whereof I have liberally drank, which I look upon as God's Physick, having that in Healthfulness which it wants in Pleasure.

Above all, I would have You, as I hope you are already, well grounded and setled in your Religion: the best Profession of which I have ever esteemed that of *the Church of England*, in which You have been educated: Yet I would have your own Judgment and Reason now seal to that sacred Bond which Education hath written, that it may be judiciously your own Religion, and not other mens Custom or Tradition, which You profess.

In this I charge You to persevere, as coming nearest to God's Word for Doctrine, and to the Primitive examples for Government, with some little Amendment, which I have other-where expressed, and often offered, though in vain. Your fixation in matters of Religion will not be more necessary for your Souls than your Kingdoms Peace, when God shall bring You to them.

For I have observed, that the Devil of Rebellion doth commonly turn himself into an Angel of Reformation, and the old Serpent can pretend new Lights. When some mens Consciences accuse them for Sedition and Faction, they stop its mouth with the name and noise of Religion; when Piety pleads for Peace and Patience, they cry out Zeal.

So that unless in this point You be well setled, You shall never want temptations to destroy You and Yours, under pretensions of Reforming matters of Religion; for that seems, even to worst men, as the best and most auspicious beginning of their worst Designs.

Where besides the Novelty, which is taking enough with the Vulgar, every one hath an affectation, by seeming forward to an outward Reformation of Religion, to be thought Zealous; hoping to cover those Irreligious deformities whereto they are conscious, by a severity of censuring other mens opinions or actions.

Take heed of abetting any Factions, or applying to any publick Discriminations in matters of Religion, contrary to what is in your Judgment and the Church well setled. Your partial adhering, as

Head, to any one side, gains You not so great advantages in some mens hearts (who are prone to be of their King's Religion) as it loseth You in others, who think themselves and their profession first despised, then persecuted by You. Take such a course as may either with Calmness and Charity quite remove the seeming differences and offences by impartiality; or so order affairs in point of Power, that You shall not need to fear or flatter any Faction. For if ever You stand in need of them, or must stand to their courtesie, You are un-done: The Serpent will devour the Dove. You may never expect less of Loyalty, Justice, or Humanity, than from those who engage into Religious Rebellion: Their Interest is always made God's; under the colours of Piety ambitious Policies march, not only with greatest security, but applause, as to the populacy: You may hear from them *Jacob's* voice, but You shall feel they have *Esau's* hands.

Nothing seemed less considerable than the Presbyterian Faction in *England* for many years, so compliant they were to publick Order: nor indeed was their Party great either in Church or State, as to mens Judgments. But as soon as Discontents drave men into Sidings, as ill Humors fall to the disaffected part, which causeth Inflammations, so did all at first who affected any Novelties adhere to that Side, as the most remarkable and specious note of difference (then) in point of Religion.

All the lesser Factions at first were officious Servants to Presbytery, their great Master: till Time and Military success discovering to each their peculiar Advantages, invited them to part stakes, and leaving the joynt stock of Uniform Religion, pretended each to drive for their Party the trade of Profits and Preferments, to the breaking and undoing not only of the Church and State, but even of Presbytery itself, which seemed and hoped at first to have ingrossed all.

Let nothing seem little or despicable to You in matters which concern Religion and the Churches Peace; so as to neglect a speedy reforming and effectual suppressing Errors and Schisms, which seem at first but as a hand-breath, yet by Seditious Spirits, as by strong winds, are soon made to cover and darken the whole Heaven.

When You have done Justice to God, Your own Soul, and his Church, in the profession and preservation both of Truth and Unity

in Religion; the next main hinge on which your Prosperity will
depend and move is that of Civil Justice, wherein the setled Laws of
these Kingdoms, to which You are rightly Heir, are the most excellent Rules You can govern by : which by an admirable temperament,
give very much to Subjects Industry, Liberty and Happiness, and
yet reserve enough to the Majesty and Prerogative of any King, who
owns his People as Subjects, not as Slaves: whose Subjection, as it
preserves their Property, Peace and Safety, so it will never diminish
Your Rights, nor their ingenuous Liberties, which consist in the
enjoyment of the fruits of their Industry, and the benefit of those Laws
to which themselves have consented.

Never charge your head with such a Crown as shall by its heaviness
oppress the whole Body ; .the weakness of whose parts cannot return
any thing of strength, honor or safety to the Head, but a necessary
debilitation and Ruine.

Your Prerogative is best shewed and exercised in remitting, rather
than exacting the rigor of the Laws; there being nothing worse than
Legal Tyranny.

In these two points, the preservation of established Religion and
Laws, I may (without vanity) turn the reproach of my Sufferings, as
to the world's censure, into the honor of a kind of Martyrdom, as to
the testimony of my own Conscience; the Troublers of my Kingdoms
having nothing else to object against Me but this, That I prefer
Religion and Laws establisht before those Alterations they pro-
pounded.

And so indeed I do and ever shall, till I am convinced by better
Arguments than what hitherto have been chiefly used towards Me,
Tumults, Armies, and Prisons.

I cannot yet learn that Lesson, nor I hope ever will You, That it is
safe for a King to gratifie any Faction with the Perturbation of the
Laws, in which is wrap'd up the publick Interest and the good of the
Community.

How God will deal with Me as to the removal of these Pressures
and Indignities, which his Justice by the very unjust hands of some of
my Subjects hath been pleased to lay upon Me, I cannot tell : nor am
I much solicitous what Wrong I suffer from men, while I retain in my
Soul what I believe is right before God.

I have offered all for Reformation and Safety that in Reason, Honour and Conscience I can; reserving only what I cannot consent unto without an irreparable injury to my own Soul, the Church, and my People, and to You also, as the next and undoubted Heir of my Kingdoms.

To which if the Divine Providence, to whom no Difficulties are insuperable, shall in his due time after My decease bring You, as I hope he will, my Counsel and Charge to You is, that You seriously consider the former real or objected Miscarriages which might occasion My Troubles, that You may avoid them.

Never repose so much upon any mans single Counsel, Fidelity, and Discretion, in managing affairs of the first magnitude, (that is, matters of Religion and Justice) as to create in Your self or others a diffidence of Your own Judgment, which is likely to be always more constant and impartial to the interests of your Crown and Kingdom than any mans.

Next, beware of exasperating any Factions by the crosness and asperity of some mens Passions, Humours, or private Opinions, imployed by You, grounded onely upon the differences in lesser matters, which are but the skirts and suburbs of Religion.

Wherein a charitable Connivence and Christian Toleration often dissipates their strength whom rougher opposition fortifies, and puts the despised and oppressed Party into such Combinations, as may most enable them to get a full revenge on those they count their Persecutors; who are commonly assisted by that Vulgar commiseration which attends all that are said to suffer under the notion of Religion.

. Provided the Differences amount not to an insolent opposition of Laws and Government, or Religion established, as to the essentials of them : Such motions and minings are intolerable.

Always keep up solid Piety, and those Fundamental Truths which mend both hearts and lives of men, with impartial Favour and Justice.

Take heed that outward circumstances and formalities of Religion devour not all or the best incouragements of Learning, Industry and Piety; but with an equal eye and impartial hand distribute favours and rewards to all men, as You find them for their real Goodness, both in Abilities and Fidelity, worthy and capable of them.

This will be sure to gain You the hearts of the best, and the most too ; who, though they be not good themselves, yet are glad to see the severer ways of Vertue at any time sweetned by temporal rewards.

I have, You see, conflicted with different and opposite Factions; (for so I must needs call and count all those that act not in any conformity to the Laws established in Church and State :) No sooner have they by force subdued what they counted their Common Enemy, (that is, all those that adhered to the Laws and to Me) and are secured from that fear, but they are divided to so high a rivalry, as sets them more at defiance against each other than against their first Antagonists.

Time will dissipate all Factions, when once the rough horns of private men's covetous and ambitious designs shall discover themselves, which were at first wrap'd up and hidden under the soft and smooth pretensions of Religion, Reformation, and Liberty. As the Wolf is not less cruel, so he will be more justly hated, when he shall appear no better than a Wolf under Sheeps cloathing.

But as for the seduced Train of the Vulgar, who in their simplicity follow those disguises, My charge and counsel to You is, That as You need no palliations for any designs, (as other men) so that You study really to exceed (in true and constant demonstrations of Goodness, Piety and Vertue, towards the People) even all those men that make the greatest noise and ostentations of Religion : so You shall neither fear any detection, (as they do who have but the face and mask of Goodness;) nor shall You frustrate the just expectations of your People, who cannot in reason promise themselves so much good from any Subjects Novelties, as from the vertuous Constancy of their King.

When these mountains of congealed Factions shall by the Sun-shine of Gods Mercy and the splendor of Your Vertues be thawed and dissipated, and the abused Vulgar shall have learned, that none are greater Oppressors of their Estates, Liberties and Consciences, than those men that entitle themselves the Patrons and Vindicators of them, onely to usurp power over them; let then no Passion betray You to any study of Revenge upon those whose own Sin and Folly will sufficiently punish them in due time.

But as soon as the forked arrow of factious Emulations is drawn out, use all Princely arts and Clemency to heal the Wounds ; that the smart of the Cure may not equal the anguish of the Hurt.

I have offered Acts of Indemnity and Oblivion to so great a latitude, as may include all that can but suspect themselves to be any way obnoxious to the Laws; and which might serve to exclude all future Jealousies and Insecurities.

I would have You always propense to the same way; whenever it shall be desired and accepted, let it be granted, not only as an Act of State-policy and Necessity, but of Christian Charity and Choice.

It is all I have now left Me, a power to forgive those that have deprived Me of all ; and I thank God I have a heart to do it, and joy as much in this Grace which God hath given Me, as in all my former enjoyments; for this is a greater argument of God's love to Me than any Prosperity can be.

Be confident (as I am) that the most of all sides who have done amiss, have done so not out of Malice, but Misinformation, or Misapprehension of things.

None will be more loyal and faithful to Me and You than those Subjects, who sensible of their Errors and our Injuries will feel in their own Souls most vehement motives to Repentance, and earnest desires to make some reparations for their former defects.

As Your quality sets You beyond any Duel with any Subject; so the Nobleness of your Mind must rais You above the meditating any Revenge, or executing your Anger upon the many.

The more conscious You shall be to Your own Merits upon your People, the more prone You will be to expect all Love and Loyalty from them, and to inflict no Punishment upon them for former Miscarriages : You will have more inward complacency in Pardoning one than in Punishing a thousand.

This I write to You, not despairing of God's Mercy and my Subjects affections towards You; both which I hope You will study to deserve, yet we cannot merit of God but by his own Mercy.

If God shall see fit to restore Me, and You after Me, to those enjoyments which the Laws have assigned to Us, and no Subjects without an high degree of Guilt and Sin can divest Us of; then may I have better opportunity, when I shall be so happy to see you in

Peace, to let you more fully understand the things that belong to God's Glory, your own Honour, and the Kingdom's Peace.

But if you never see my face again, and God will have Me buried in such a barbarous Imprisonment and Obscurity, (which the perfecting some men's Designs requires) wherein few hearts that love Me are permitted to exchange a word or a look with Me; I do require and entreat you as your Father and your KING, that you never suffer your heart to receive the least check against or disaffection from the true Religion established in the Church of *England*.

I tell you, I have tried it, and after much search and many disputes, have concluded it to be the best in the world; not onely in the Community, as Christian, but also in the special notion, as Reformed; keeping the middle way, between the pomp of Superstitious Tyranny, and the meanness of Fantastick Anarchy.

Not but that (the draught being excellent as to the main, both for Doctrine and Government, in the Church of *England*) some lines, as in very good Figures, may haply need some sweetning or polishing; which might here have easily been done by a safe and gentle hand, if some men's Precipitancy had not violently demanded such rude Alterations as would have quite destroyed all the Beauty and Proportions of the whole.

The scandal of the late Troubles, which some may object and urge to you against the Protestant Religion established in *England*, is easily answered to them or your own thoughts in this, That scarce any one who hath been a Beginner, or an active Prosecutor of this late War against the Church, the Laws and Me, either was or is a true Lover, Embracer, or Practiser of the Protestant Religion established in England: which neither gives such Rules, nor ever before set such Examples.

'Tis true, some heretofore had the boldness to present threatning Petitions to their Princes and Parliaments, which others of the same Faction (but of worse Spirits) have now put in execution. But let not counterfeit and disorderly Zeal abate your value and esteem of true Piety: both of them are to be *known by their fruits*. The sweetness of the Vine and Fig-tree is not to be despised, though the Brambles and Thorns should pretend to bear Figs and Grapes, thereby to rule over the Trees.

Nor would I have you to entertain any aversation or dislike of Parliaments; which in their right constitution, with Freedom and Honour, will never injure or diminish your Greatness; but will rather be as interchangings of Love, Loyalty, and Confidence between a Prince and his People.

Nor would the events of this Black Parliament have been other than such (however much biassed by Factions in the Elections) if it had been preserved from the Insolencies of Popular dictates and Tumultuary impressions: The sad effects of which will, no doubt, make all Parliaments after this more cautious to preserve that Freedom and Honour which belongs to such Assemblies (when once they have fully shaken off this yoke of Vulgar encroachment,) since the Publick Interest consists in the mutual and common good both of Prince and People.

Nothing can be more happy for all, than in fair, grave, and honourable ways to contribute their Counsels in common, enacting all things by publick consent, without Tyranny or Tumults. We must not starve our selves, because some men have surfeited of wholesom food.

And if neither I nor You be ever restored to Our rights, but God in his severest Justice will punish my Subjects with continuance in their Sin, and Suffer them to be deluded with the Prosperity of their Wickedness; I hope God will give Me and You that grace, which will teach and enable Us to want as well as to wear a Crown, which is not worth taking up or enjoying upon sordid, dishonourable and irreligious terms.

Keep You to true Principles of Piety, Vertue and Honour, You shall never want a Kingdom.

A principal point of your Honour will consist in your conferring all Respect, Love and Protection on your Mother, My Wife; who hath many ways deserved well of Me, and chiefly in this, that (having been a means to bless Me with so many hopeful Children, all which, with their Mother, I recommend to your Love and Care) She hath been content, with incomparable Magnanimity and Patience, to suffer both for and with Me and You.

My Prayer to God Almighty is, (whatever becomes of Me, who am, I thank God, wrapt up and fortified in My own Innocency and his Grace) that' he would be pleased to make you an Anchor, or Harbour rather, to these tossed and weather-beaten Kingdoms; a Repairer, by your Wisdom, Justice, Piety and Valour, of what the Folly and Wickedness of some men have so far ruined, as to leave nothing intire in Church or State, to the Crown, the Nobility, the Clergie or the Commons, either as to Laws, Liberties, Estates, Order, Honour, Conscience, or Lives.

When they have destroyed Me (for I know not how far God may permit the Malice and Cruelty of my Enemies to proceed, and such apprehensions some mens words and actions have already given Me) as I doubt not but my Bloud will cry aloud for Vengeance to Heaven; so I beseech God not to pour out his Wrath upon the generality of the People, who have either deserted Me, or ingaged against Me, through the artifice and hypocrisie of their Leaders, whose inward Horror will be their first Tormentor, nor will they escape exemplary Judgments.

For those that loved Me, I pray God they may have no miss of Me when I am gone; so much I wish and hope that all good Subjects may be satisfied with the Blessings of your Presence and Vertues.

For those that repent of any defects in their Duty toward Me, as I freely forgive them in the word of a Christian King; so I believe You will find them truly zealous to repay with interest that Loyalty and Love to you which was due to Me.

In summ, what Good I intended, do you perform, when God shall give you Power. Much Good I have offered, more I purposed to Church and State, if Times had been capable of it.

The deception will soon vanish, and the Vizards will fall off apace : This mask of Religion on the face of Rebellion (for so it now plainly appears, since my Restraint and cruel usage, that they fought not for Me, as was pretended) will not long serve to hide some mens Deformities.

Happy times, I hope, attend You, wherein your Subjects (by their Miseries) will have learned, *That Religion to their God and Loyalty to their King cannot be parted without both their Sin and their Infelicity.*

I pray God bless You, and establish your Kingdoms in Righteousness, your Soul in true Religion, and your Honor in the Love of God and your People.

And if God will have Disloyalty perfected by My Destruction, let my Memory ever with my Name live in You, as of your Father that loves You, and once a KING of Three flourishing Kingdomes ; whom God thought fit to honor not only with the Scepter and Government of them, but also with the suffering many Indignities and an untimely Death for them, while I studied to preserve the rights of the Church, the power of the Laws, the honor of my Crown, the Privilege of Parliaments, the Liberties of my People, and My own Conscience ; which, I thank God, is dearer to Me than a thousand Kingdoms.

I know God can, I hope he yet will restore Me to my Rights; I cannot despair either of his Mercy, or of my People's Love and Pity.

At worst, I trust I shall but go before You to a better Kingdom, which God hath prepared for Me, and Me for it, through my Saviour Jesus Christ, to whose Mercies I commend You and all Mine.

Farewel, till We meet, if not on Earth, yet in Heaven.

APPENDIX, No. III.

———————

" There he continued for some time, receiving the sad news of the death of his Sister the Princesse Elizabeth, who dyd at Carisbrook Castle." (*Life of James the Second, p.* 49.)

From the Council of State 27th August 1650, *concerning the King's Children.* (In the possession of G. Duchets, Esq.)

To Coll. Sydenham, Governor of the Isle of Wight.

Sir,

The Parliament hath appointed the two Children of the late King, who are now at the Earl of Leicester's at Penshurst, shall be sent out of the limits of the Commonwealth ; and have referred the same to this Councill to see done accordingly ; and untill that can be done, we have thought it fit and necessary they be sent to Carresbroke Castle ; and have sent you this notice hereof before, that you might be ready for them. And for that we are informed, there are designs of mischief carrying on in severall places, we recommend that island to your more especiall care. And if there be any persons therein, whom you shall judge may bring danger thereunto, you are hereby desired and authorized to put them out of the Isle, and to seize upon and secure the Horses, Arms, and Ammunition of any, whom you shall suspect will make an ill use of them to interrupt the public peace.

Signed in the names and by order of the Council of State appointed by the authority of Parliament.

Whitehall 27th August 1650.   JO. BRADDSHAWE, presid.

(*From Thurloe's State Papers, Vol.* 1. *p.* 158.)

APPENDIX, No. IV.

An ACCOUNT of what appeared on opening the Coffin of King CHARLES THE FIRST, in the Vault of King Henry the Eighth in St. George's Chapel at Windsor, on the 1st of April 1813. By Sir HENRY HALFORD, Bart. F.R.S. and F.A.S. Physician to the King and the Prince Regent.

(Reprinted with Sir Henry's permission.)

IT is stated by * Lord Clarendon, in his History of the Rebellion, that the Body of King Charles I. though known to be interred in St. George's Chapel at Windsor, could not be found, when searched for there, some years afterwards. It seems, by the Historian's account, to have been the wish and the intention of King Charles II. after his Restoration, to take up His Father's corpse, and to re-inter it in Westminster Abbey, with those royal honours which had been denied it under the Government of the Regicides. The most careful search was made for the body by several people, amongst whom were some of those noble persons whose faithful attachment had led them to pay their last tribute of respect to their unfortunate Master by attending Him to the grave. Yet such had been the injury done to the Chapel, such were the mutilations it had undergone, during the period of the Usurpation, that no marks were left, by which the *exact* place of burial of the King could be ascertained.

---

* Vol. 3. Part. I. p. 393. Oxford 1807.

There is some difficulty in reconciling this account, with the information which has reached us, since the death of Lord Clarendon,
particularly with that of Mr. Ashmole, and more especially with that
most interesting narrative of Mr. Herbert given in the " Athenæ
Oxonienses." Mr. Herbert had been a Groom of the bed-chamber,
and a faithful companion of the King in all circumstances, from the
time He left the Isle of Wight, until His death — was employed to
convey His body to Windsor, and to fix upon a proper place for His
interment there; and was an eye-witness to that interment, in the
Vault of King Henry VIII.

Were it allowable to hazard a conjecture, after Lord Clarendon's
deprecation of all conjectures on the subject, one might suppose,
that it was deemed imprudent, by the Ministers of King Charles II.
that His Majesty should indulge His pious inclination to re-inter His
Father, at a period, when those ill-judged effusions of loyalty, which
had been manifested, by taking out of their graves, and hanging up
the bodies of some of the most active Members of the Court, which
had condemned and executed the King, might, in the event of
another triumph of the Republicans, have subjected the body of the
Monarch to similar indignity. But the fact is, King Charles I. was
buried in the Vault of King Henry VIII. situated precisely where
Mr. Herbert has described it; and an accident has served to elucidate
a point in history, which the great authority of Lord Clarendon had
involved in some obscurity.

On completing the Mausoleum which His present Majesty has built
in the Tomb-house, as it is called, it was necessary to form a passage
to it from under the choir of St. George's Chapel. In constructing
this passage, an aperture was made accidentally in one of the walls
of the Vault of King Henry VIII. through which the workmen were
enabled to see, not only the two coffins, which were supposed to
contain the bodies of King Henry VIII. and Queen Jane Seymour,
but a third also, covered with a black velvet pall, which, from
Mr. Herbert's narrative, might fairly be presumed to hold the remains
of King Charles I.

On representing the circumstance to the Prince Regent, His
Royal Highness perceived at once, that a doubtful point in History
might be cleared up by opening this Vault; and accordingly His

Royal Highness ordered an examination to be made on the first convenient opportunity. This was done on the 1st of April last, the day after the funeral of the Duchess of Brunswick, in the presence of His Royal Highness himself, who guaranteed thereby the most respectful care and attention to the remains of the dead, during the enquiry. His Royal Highness was accompanied by His Royal Highness the Duke of Cumberland, Count Munster, the Dean of Windsor, Benjamin Charles Stevenson, Esq. and Sir Henry Halford.

The Vault is covered by an arch, half a brick in thickness, is seven feet two inches in width, nine feet six inches in length, and four feet ten inches in height, and is situated in the centre of the choir, opposite the eleventh Knight's stall, on the Sovereign's side.

On removing the pall, a plain leaden coffin, with no appearance of ever having been inclosed in wood, and bearing an inscription, " King Charles, 1648," in large legible characters, on a scroll of lead encircling it, immediately presented itself to the view. A square opening was then made in the upper part of the lid, of such dimensions as to admit a clear insight into its contents. These were, an internal wooden coffin, very much decayed, and the Body, carefully wrapped up in cere-cloth, into the folds of which a quantity of unctuous or greasy matter, mixed with resin, as it seemed, had been melted, so as to exclude, as effectually as possible, the external air. The coffin was completely full; and, from the tenacity of the cere-cloth, great difficulty was experienced in detaching it successfully from the parts which it enveloped. Wherever the unctuous matter had insinuated itself, the separation of the cere-cloth was easy; and when it came off, a correct impression of the features to which it had been applied was observed in the unctuous substance. At length, the whole face was disengaged from its covering. The complexion of the skin of it was dark and discoloured. The forehead and temples had lost little or nothing of their muscular substance; the cartilage of the nose was gone; but the left eye, in the first moment of exposure, was open and full, though it vanished almost immediately: and the pointed beard, so characteristic of the period of the reign of King Charles, was perfect. The shape of the face was a long oval; many of the teeth remained; and the left ear, in consequence of the interposition of the unctuous matter between it and the cere-cloth, was found entire.

It was difficult, at this moment, to withhold a declaration, that, notwithstanding its disfigurement, the countenance did bear a strong resemblance to the coins, the busts, and especially to the pictures of King Charles I. by Vandyke, by which it had been made familiar to us. It is true, that the minds of the Spectators of this interesting sight were well prepared to receive this impression; but it is also certain, that such a facility of belief had been occasioned by the simplicity and truth of Mr. Herbert's Narrative, every part of which had been confirmed by the investigation, so far as it had advanced: and it will not be denied that the shape of the face, the forehead, an eye, and the beard, are the most important features by which resemblance is determined.

When the head had been entirely disengaged from the attachments which confined it, it was found to be loose, and, without any difficulty, was taken up and held to view. It was quite wet *, and gave a greenish red tinge to paper and to linen, which touched it. The back part of the scalp was entirely perfect, and had a remarkably fresh appearance; the pores of the skin being more distinct, as they usually are when soaked in moisture; and the tendons and ligaments of the neck were of considerable substance and firmness. The hair

---

* I have not asserted this liquid to be blood, because I had not an opportunity of being sure that it was so, and I wished to record facts only, and not opinions: I believe it, however, to have been blood, in which the head rested. It gave to writing-paper, and to a white handkerchief, such a colour as blood which has been kept for a length of time generally leaves behind it. Nobody present had a doubt of its being blood; and it appears from Mr. Herbert's narrative, that the King was embalmed immediately after decapitation. It is probable, therefore, that the large blood vessels continued to empty themselves for some time afterwards. I am aware, that some of the softer parts of the human body, and particularly the brain, undergo, in the course of time, a decomposition, and will melt. A liquid, therefore, might be found after long interment, where solids only had been buried: but the weight of the head, in this instance, gave no suspicion that the brain had lost its substance; and no moisture appeared in any other part of the coffin, as far as we could see, excepting at the back part of the head and neck.

was thick at the back part of the head, and, in appearance, nearly black. A portion of it, which has since been cleaned and dried, is of a beautiful dark brown colour. That of the beard was a redder brown. On the back part of the head, it was more than an inch in length, and had probably been cut so short for the convenience of the executioner, or perhaps by the piety of friends soon after death, in order to furnish memorials of the unhappy King.

On holding up the head, to examine the place of separation from the body, the muscles of the neck had evidently retracted themselves considerably ; and the fourth cervical vertebra was found to be cut through its substance, transversely, leaving the surfaces of the divided portions perfectly smooth and even, an appearance which could have been produced only by a heavy blow, inflicted with a very sharp instrument, and which furnished the last proof wanting to identify King Charles the First.

After this examination of the head, which served every purpose in view, and without examining the body below the neck, it was imme- diately restored to its situation, the coffin was soldered up again, and the Vault closed.

Neither of the other coffins had any inscription upon them. The larger one, supposed on good grounds to contain the remains of King Henry VIII. measured six feet ten inches in length, and had been enclosed in an elm one of two inches in thickness : but this was decayed, and lay in small fragments near it. The leaden coffin ap- peared to have been beaten in by violence about the middle, and a considerable opening in that part of it, exposed a mere skeleton of the King. Some beard remained upon the chin, but there was nothing to discriminate the personage contained in it.

The smaller coffin, understood to be that of Queen Jane Seymour, was not touched ; mere curiosity not being considered, by the Prince Regent, as a sufficient motive for disturbing these remains.

On examining the Vault with some attention, it was found that the wall, at the West end, had, at some period or other, been partly pulled down and repaired again, not by regular masonry, but by fragments of stones and bricks, put rudely and hastily together without cement.

From Lord Clarendon's account, as well as from Mr. Herbert's narrative of the interment of King Charles, it is to be inferred, that the ceremony was a very hasty one, performed in the presence of the Governor, who had refused to allow the service according to the Book of Common Prayer to be used on the occasion; and had, probably, scarcely admitted the time necessary for a decent deposit of the body. It is not unlikely, therefore, that the coffin of King Henry VIII. had been injured by a precipitate introduction of the coffin of King Charles; and that the Governor was not under the influence of feelings, in those times, which gave him any concern about Royal remains, or the Vault which contained them.

It may be right to add, that a very small mahogany coffin, covered with crimson velvet, containing the body of an infant, had been laid upon the pall which covered King Charles. This is known to have been a still-born child of the Princess George of Denmark, afterwards Queen Anne.

HENRY HALFORD.

London, April 11, 1813.

——————

*Extract from Wood's " Athenæ Oxonienses," folio edition, Vol. II.
p. 703. Printed for Knaplock, Midwinter, and Tonson,* 1721.

" THERE was a passage broke through the wall of the Banquetting-house, by which the King passed unto the scaffold: where, after his Majesty had spoken and declared publicly that he died a Christian according to the profession of the Church of England (the contents of which have been several times printed), the fatal stroke was given by a disguised person. Mr. Herbert during this time was at the door leading to the scaffold, much lamenting; *and the Bishop coming from the scaffold with the Royal Corpse, which was immediately coffined and covered with a velvet pall, he and Mr. Herbert*

went with it to the back stairs to have it embalmed. . . . .The Royal
Corpse being embalmed and well coffined, and all afterwards wrapped
up in lead, and covered with a new velvet pall, it was removed to
St. James's. . . . .Where to bury the King was the last duty remaining.
By some Historians it is said the King spoke something to the Bishop
concerning his burial. Mr. Herbert, both before and after the King's
death, was frequently in company with the Bishop, and affirmed, that
he never mentioned any thing to him of the King's naming any place
where he would be buried; nor did Mr. Herbert (who constantly attended his Majesty, and after his coming to Hurst Castle was the
only person in his bedchamber) hear him at any time declare his
mind concerning it. Nor was it in his lifetime a proper question for
either of them to ask, notwithstanding they had oftentimes the opportunity, especially when his Majesty was bequeathing to his royal
children and friends what is formerly related. Nor did the Bishop
declare any thing concerning the place to Mr. Herbert, which doubtless
he would upon Mr. Herbert's pious care about it; which being duly
considered, they thought no place more fit to inter the corpse than in
the Chapel of King Henry VII. at the end of the Church of Westminster
Abbey, out of whose loins King Charles I. was lineally extracted, &c.
Whereupon Mr. Herbert made his application to such as were then in
power for leave to bury the King's Body in the said Chapel, among
his ancestors; but his request was denied, for this reason; that *his
burying there would attract infinite numbers of all sorts thither, to see
where the King was buried; which, as the times then were, was judged
unsafe and inconvenient.* Mr. Herbert acquainting the Bishop with
this, they then resolved to bury the King's Body in the Royal Chapel
of St. George within the Castle of Windsor, both in regard that his
Majesty was Sovereign of the Most Noble Order of the Garter, and
that several Kings had been there interred; namely, King Henry VI.
King Edward IV. and King Henry VIII. &c. Upon which consideration Mr. Herbert made his second address to the Committee of
Parliament, who, after some deliberation, gave him an order, bearing
date the 6th of February 1648, authorizing him and Mr. Anthony
Mildmay to bury the King's Body there, which the Governor was to
observe.

" Accordingly the corpse was carried thither from St. James's,
Feb. 7, in a hearse covered with black velvet, drawn by six horses
covered with black cloth, in which were about a dozen gentlemen,
most of them being such that had waited upon his Majesty at Carisbrook Castle, and other places, since his Majesty's going from Newcastle. Mr. Herbert shewed the Governor, Colonel Whitchcot, the
Committee's order for permitting Mr. Herbert and Mr. Mildmay to
bury him, the late King, in any place within Windsor Castle, that
they should think fit and meet. In the first place, in order thereunto
they carried the King's Body into the Dean's house, which was hung
with black, and after to his usual bedchamber within the palace.
After which they went to St. George's Chapel to take a view thereof,
and of the most fit and honourable place for the Royal Corpse to rest
in. Having taken a view, they at first thought that the Tomb-house,
built by Cardinal Wolsey, would be a fit place for his interment; but
that place, though adjoining, yet being not within the Royal Chapel,
they waved it: for, if King Henry VIII. was buried there (albeit to
that day the particular place of his burial was unknown to any), yet,
in regard to his Majesty King Charles I. (who was a real Defender of
the Faith, and as far from censuring any that might be), would upon
occasional discourse express some dislike in King Henry's proceedings, in misemploying those vast revenues, the suppressed abbies,
monasteries, and other religious houses, were endowed with, and by
demolishing those many beautiful and stately structures, which both
expressed the greatness of their founders, and preserved the splendour
of the kingdom, which might at the Reformation have in some
measure been kept up and converted to sundry pious uses.

" Upon consideration thereof, those gentlemen declined it, and
pitched upon the vault where King Edward IV. had been interred,
being on the North side of the choir, near the altar, that King being
one his late Majesty would oftentimes make honourable mention of,
and from whom his Majesty was lineally propagated. That therefore
induced Mr. Herbert to give order to N. Harrison and Henry Jackson
to have that vault opened, partly covered with a fair large stone of
touch, raised within the arch adjoining, having a range of iron bars
gilt, curiously cut, according to church work, &c. But as they were
about this work, some noblemen came thither; namely, the Duke

of Richmond, the Marquis of Hertford, the Earl of Lindsay, and with them Dr. Juxon, Bishop of London, who had licence from the Parliament to attend the King's Body to his grave. Those gentlemen, therefore, Herbert, and Mildmay, .thinking fit to submit, and leave the choice of the place of burial to those great persons, they in like manner viewed the Tomb-house and the choir ; and one of the Lords beating gently upon the pavement with his staff, perceived a hollow sound ; and thereupon ordering the stones and earth to be removed, they discovered a descent into a vault, where two coffins were laid near one another, the one very large, of an antique form, and the other little.   These they supposed to be the bodies of King Henry VIII. and Queen Jane Seymour his third wife, as indeed they were.   The velvet palls that covered their coffins seemed fresh, though they had lain there above 100 years.

" The Lords agreeing that the King's Body should be in the same vault interred, being about the middle of the choir, over against the eleventh stall upon the Sovereign's side, they gave order to have the King's name and year he died cut in lead ; which whilst the workmen were about, the Lords went out and gave Puddifant the sexton order to lock the chapel door, and not suffer any to stay therein till farther notice.   The Sexton did his best to clear the chapel ; nevertheless, Isaac the sexton's man said that a foot-soldier had hid himself, so as he was not discerned ; and being greedy of prey, crept into the vault, and cut so much of the velvet pall that covered the great body as he judged would hardly be missed, and wimbled also a hole through the said coffin that was largest, probably fancying that there was something well worth his adventure.   The sexton at his opening the door espied the sacrilegious person ; who being searched, a bone was found about him, with which he said he would haft a knife.   The Governor being therefore informed of, he gave him his reward ; and the Lords and others present were convinced that a real body was in the said great coffin, which some before had scrupled.   The girdle or circumscription of capital letters of lead put about the King's coffin had only these words : *King Charles*, 1648.

" The King's Body was then brought from his bedchamber down into St. George's Hall, whence, after a little stay, it was with a slow and solemn pace (much sorrow in most faces being then discernible)

carried by gentlemen of quality in mourning.   The noblemen in
mourning also held up the pall; and the Governor, with several
gentlemen, officers, and attendants, came after.   It was then observed,
that at such time as the King's Body was brought out from St. George's
Hall, the sky was serene and clear; but presently it began to snow,
and the snow fell so fast, that by that time the corpse came to the
West end of the Royal Chapel, the black velvet pall was all white (the
colour of innocency), being thick covered over with snow.   The
Body being by the bearers set down near the place of burial, the
Bishop of London stood ready, with the Service book in his hands, to
have performed his last duty to the King his Master, according to the
order and form of burial of the dead set forth in the Book of Common
Prayer; which the Lords likewise desired; but it would not be suf-
fered by Col. Whitchcot, the Governor of the Castle, by reason of the
Directory, to which (said he) *he and others were to be conformable.*
Thus went the *white King* to his grave, in the 48th year of his age,
and 22d year and 10th month of his reign."

APPENDIX, No. V.

Some other Facts respecting the Funeral of CHARLES I. *are given in a Work styled* ENGLAND'S BLACK TRIBUNAL, *page 50 ; and also in the Folio Edition of that King's Works, (p.* 206. 211.*) with His Majesty's Epitaph in Latin, by Dr. T. Pierce, President of Magdalen College Oxford. From the latter work the following extract has been taken.*

THE King's body having been embalmed, was "laid in a coffin of lead, to be seen, for some days, by the people; at length, upon Wednesday the seventh of February, it was delivered to four of his servants, *Herbert, Mildmay, Preston,* and *Joyner,* who, with some others in mourning equipage, attended the Herse that night to Windsore, and placed it in the room which was formerly the King's Bed Chamber. Next day it was removed into the Deans Hall, which was hung with black and made dark, and Lights were set burning round the Herse. About three afternoon, *the Duke of Richmond, the Marquis of Hartford, the Earls of Southampton and Lindsey,* and *the Bishop of London,* (others that were sent to refusing that last Service to the best of Princes) came thither with two Votes passed that Morning, whereby the ordering of The King's Burial was committed to the Duke, provided that the Expences thereof exceeded not five hundred pounds. This Order they shewed to *Colonel Whichcot* the Governour of the Castle, desiring that the Interment might be in SAINT GEORGE's Chapel, and according to the form of the Common Prayer. The latter request the Governour denied, saying, *That it was improbable the Parliament would permit the use of what they had so solemnly abolished, and therein destroy their own Act.* The Lords replied, *That there was a difference betwixt destroying their own Act, and dispensing with it; and that no power so binds its own hands as to disable it self in some cases.* But all prevailed not.

" The Governour had caused an ordinary Grave to be digged in
the body of the Church of Windsore for the Interment of the Corps;
which the Lords disdaining, found means by the direction of an
honest man, one of the old Knights, to use an artifice to discover a
Vault in the middle of the Quire, by the hollow sound they might
perceive in knocking with a Staff on that place; that so it might seem
to be their own accidental finding out, and no person receive blame
for the discovery. This place they caused to be opened, and entering
saw one large Coffin of Lead in the middle of the Vault covered with
a Velvet Pall, and a lesser on one side (supposed to be HENRY THE
EIGHTH, and His beloved QUEEN JANE SAINT MAURE) on the other
side was room left for another (probably intended for QUEEN
KATHERINE PARRE who survived Him) where they thought fit to
lay the King.

" Hither the Herse was borne by the Officers of the Garrison, the
four Lords bearing up the Corners of the Velvet Pall, and the Bishop
of London following. And in this manner was this Great King, upon
Friday the ninth of February, about three afternoon, silently, and
without other Solemnity than of Sighs and Tears, committed to the
Earth, the Velvet Pall being thrown into the Vault over the Coffin;
to which was fastened an Inscription in Lead of these words

KING CHARLES 1648."

APPENDIX, No. VI.

** When The Life was nearly printed, the Editor met with a Copy
of the following Letter from JAMES THE SECOND, in the possession of
the Governor of the Naval Hospital at Plymouth, Richard Creyke,
Esq., whose family suffered severely for their attachment to The
Stuart Family. This Officer has also some valuable Medals of the
CHEVALIER DE ST. GEORGE, of his wife MARIA CLEMENTINA, and of
CHARLES EDWARD their son.

James the Second to the Earle of Winchelsea.

"Feversham, Dec. 12, 1688.

"I am just now come in here, having been last night seased by
some of this towne, who telling me you were to be here this day, I
would not make myself known to them, thinking to have found you
here; but that not being, I desire you would come hether to me, and
that as privatly as you could do, that I might advise with you concerning my safty, hoping you have that true Loyalty in you, as you
will do what you can to secure me from my Enemys, of which you
shall find me as sensible as you can desire.

JAMES R.

"Copied exactly from the Original lately in the possession of
Heneage the last E. of Winchelsea, this 10th day of January 172⁴/₂ by
J. Creyke. I sent the Original with several papers relating to the
Embassy of the E: of Winchelsea at the Port, to the present E:
John.   J. CREYKE."

FINIS.

Printed by A. Strahan,
Printers-Street, London.